T0190319

Lecture Notes of the Institute for Computer Sciences, Social Informatics and Telecommunications Engineering   423

More information about this series at https://link.springer.com/bookseries/8197

Wenbo Shi · Xiaofeng Chen ·
Kim-Kwang Raymond Choo (Eds.)

Security and Privacy in New Computing Environments

4th EAI International Conference, SPNCE 2021
Virtual Event, December 10–11, 2021
Proceedings

Springer

Editors
Wenbo Shi
Northeastern University
Qinhuangdao, China

Xiaofeng Chen
Xidian University
Xi'an, China

Kim-Kwang Raymond Choo
University of Texas at San Antonio
San Antonio, TX, USA

ISSN 1867-8211   ISSN 1867-822X (electronic)
Lecture Notes of the Institute for Computer Sciences, Social Informatics
and Telecommunications Engineering
ISBN 978-3-030-96790-1   ISBN 978-3-030-96791-8 (eBook)
https://doi.org/10.1007/978-3-030-96791-8

This Springer imprint is published by the registered company Springer Nature Switzerland AG
The registered company address is: Gewerbestrasse 11, 6330 Cham, Switzerland

Preface

We are delighted to introduce the proceedings of the fourth edition of the European Alliance for Innovation (EAI) International Conference on Security and Privacy in New Computing Environments SPNCE 2021. This conference brought together researchers, developers, and practitioners around the world who are leveraging and developing security and privacy in new computing environments. The theme of SPNCE 2021 was "Secure Wireless Communication Systems: Infrastructure, Algorithms, and Management".

The technical program of SPNCE 2021 consisted of 33 full papers, comprising 24 papers accepted in the main tracks and nine papers accepted in the late track. Aside from the high-quality technical paper presentations, the technical program also featured two keynote speeches and a technical workshop. The two keynote speakers were Zhiqiang Lin from Ohio State University, USA, and Xinyi Huang from Fujian Normal University, China. The workshop focused on secure wireless communication systems: infrastructure, algorithms, and management. It aimed to enhance the security of data-driven networks, and several natural and bio-inspired algorithms have been modeled to perform secure, high-performance computing in computationally intensive applications.

Coordination with the steering chairs, Imrich Chlamtac and Ding Wang, was essential for the success of the conference. We sincerely appreciate their constant support and guidance. It was also a great pleasure to work with such an excellent organizing committee team for their hard work in organizing and supporting the conference. In particular, we are grateful to the Technical Program Committee, who have completed the peer-review process for technical papers and helped to put together a high-quality technical program. We are also grateful to all the authors who submitted their papers to the SPNCE 2021 conference and workshop.

We strongly believe that the SPNCE conference provides a good forum for all researchers, developers, and practitioners to discuss all science and technology aspects that are relevant to new computing environments. We also expect that the future SPNCE conferences will be as successful and stimulating as this year's, as indicated by the contributions presented in this volume.

Wenbo Shi
Xiaofeng Chen
Kim-Kwang Raymond Choo
Debiao He
Ding Wang
Neeraj Kumar

Organization

Steering Committee

Chair

Imrich Chlamtac   University of Trento, Italy

Member

Ding Wang   Nankai University, China

Organizing Committee

General Chairs

Wenbo Shi   Northeastern University at Qinhuangdao, China
Xiaofeng Chen   Xidian University, China
Kim-Kwang Raymond   University of Texas at San Antonio, USA
  Choo

Technical Program Committee Chairs

Debiao He   Wuhan University, China
Ding Wang   Nankai University, China
Neeraj Kumar   Thapar University, India

Sponsorship and Exhibit Chairs

Xinghua Li   Xidian University, China
Jian Shen   Nanjing University of Information Science
                     and Technology, China

Local Chair

Ning Lu   Northeastern University at Qinhuangdao, China

Workshops Chairs

Hongyu Yang   Civil Aviation University of China, China
Christian Esposito   University of Salerno, Italy

Publicity and Social Media Chairs

Jong Hyouk Loo   Sejong University, China
Hao Wang   Shandong Normal University, China

Publications Chairs

Chengyu Wang   Beijing University of Posts and Telecommunications,
                      China
Xiong Li   University of Electronic Science and Technology
                      of China, China

Web Chairs

Tong Li   Nankai University, China
Kuan Fan   Northeastern University at Qinhuangdao, China

Technical Program Committee

Anca Delia Jurcut   University College Dublin, Ireland
Ashok Kumar Das   International Institute of Information Technology, India
Chun Guo   Shandong University, China
Chunfu Jia   Nankai University, China
Debiao He   Wuhan University, China
Dimitrios Papadopoulos   The Hong Kong University of Science and
                          Technology, China
Fei Gao   Beijing University of Posts and Telecommunications,
                          China
Fuchun Guo   University of Wollongong, Australia
Haipeng Cai   Washington State University, USA
Jianfeng Wang   Xidian University, China
Jianting Ning   Singapore Management University, Singapore
Jingqiang Lin   University of Science and Technology of China, China
Juanru Li   Shanghai Jiao Tong University, China
Kuo-Hui Yeh   National Dong Hwa University, Taiwan
Lei Wang   Shanghai Jiao Tong University, China
Liang Xiao   Xiamen University, China
Linzhi Jiang   University of Surrey, UK
Long Cheng   Clemson University, USA
Longjiang Qu   National University of Defense Technology, China
Marko Hölbl   University of Maribor, Slovenia
Min Luo   Wuhan University, China
Mingwu Zhang   Hubei University of Technology, China
Peng Xu   Huazhong University of Science and Technology,
                          China
Qian Wang   Wuhan University, China
Qianhong Wu   Beihang University, China
Qingni Shen   Peking University, China
Qiong Huang   South China Agricultural University, China
Shi-Feng Sun   Monash University, Australia
Shujun Li   University of Kent, UK

Contents

Blockchain-Based Outsourcing Shared Car Risk Prediction Scheme Design

Haonan Zhai, Song He, Zeyu Wei, and Yong Xie(✉)

Department of Computer Technology and Applocation,
Qinghai University, Xining 810016, China

Abstract. With the widespread use of shared cars, the security of cars and user data sharing have become increasingly important. To prevent the leakage of data and damage or non-return of shared cars, researchers have put forward many proposals of shared cars. But there are some problems in these schemes such as security, low precision. Therefore, we propose a shared car risk prediction scheme by using support vector machine (SVM) learning and blockchain, homomorphic encryption. First of all, this scheme adopts blockchain technology to ensure that the data can not be tampered with. In addition, the homomorphic encryption algorithm is used to realize the machine learning calculation in the ciphertext state. Finally, the SVM learning algorithm is used to make the risk prediction results of shared cars more accurate. Through performance analysis and comparison, the scheme is proved to have higher accuracy and security.

Keywords: Support vector machine learning · Blockchain · Homomorphic encryption · Multi-key conversion protocol

1 Introduction

In recent years, with the rise of shared bikes, more and more cities begin to use shared bikes, which means that shared cars will enter our lives right away. Car-sharing is an emerging development direction with brand-new development prospects. The function of car-sharing is to realize the reasonable and effective distribution of vehicle resources and cease the flooding and waste of vehicles. Therefore, the number of private cars and caused problems can be reduced to some extent, such as air pollution, energy shortage, traffic congestion, and parking difficulties can be alleviated. Some questions about shared cars have gradually emerged simultaneously. For example, shared cars will have problems such as not returning them in time after renting, and vehicle damage.

Designing a special scheme combined with machine learning predictive models can improve the car sharing problem. Machine learning prediction can accurately and effectively use the user and vehicle encrypted information in the car-sharing platform to predict the security risks of renting a car, so as to avoid

W. Shi et al. (Eds.): SPNCE 2021, LNICST 423, pp. 1–14, 2022.
https://doi.org/10.1007/978-3-030-96791-8_1

as much as possible the situation where the shared car is damaged or cannot be returned. At present, many machine learning training prediction models have been proposed. Among all machine learning training prediction models, the support vector machine training prediction model can effectively analyze data and make predictions. In this paper, SVM supervised learning method is used to predict the security of car-sharing platform rental by training a predictive model. SVM machine learning has a wide range of applications. In addition to predciting the security of shared cars, it can also be used in smart healthcare, smart cities, and smart grids. The training of the support vector machine learning algorithm model requires the transmission of a large amount of data information. The traditional method is to directly transmit sensitive data information of users and vehicles to a third-party computing party and use support vector machine learning algorithms for model training, which will lead to the leakage and dissemination of private data information of users and vehicles. Therefore, during the transmission process, the privacy protection of the data transmission and training calculation process needs to be improved.

In order to solve the problem of shared cars systems' data privacy protection for users and used vehicles, we urgently need to introduce a scheme that combines privacy protection and blockchain to protect our private data in the shared cars systems. In our scheme, the shared car information and the user's information are encrypted, and then the encrypted data is transmitted and stored. This method can ensure that the personal information of the user and the rented vehicle information data will not be leaked. However, there is a risk of data information leakage during the transmission process, the adversary cannot decrypt the content of the data information after receiving the encrypted data information. In our shared car risk prediction scheme, data information can be encrypted with confidential multiple keys by using the Paillier homomorphic encryption algorithm and multi-key conversion protocol. Computing service provider (CSP) and Cloud platform(CP) adopt a multi-key conversion protocol to convert ciphertext data encrypted by multiple keys into ciphertext encrypted by a unified key. The information analysis and prediction node processes the unified key ciphertext data for SVM learning and calculation.

The immutable and decentralized nature of blockchain is particularly suitable for car-sharing scenarios. We use consortium blockchain storage to ensure that metadata cannot be tampered with in our scheme. Even if the metadata representing the ciphertext data on a blockchain node is modified, the blockchain can also periodically update the synchronized data to make it invalid through the consensus protocol. Not only does the metadata representing the ciphertext data will never be revised, but it can also be traced back to the party that modified the data.

2   Relate of Work

There are many applications of blockchain and privacy protection in domestic and foreign, such as medical treatment and smart grid. Blockchain technology in these applications can solve the problem of improving entity trust and data storage security.

In the field of car-sharing, Viktor Valaštín et al. [1] have used blockchain technology to build a decentralized car-sharing scheme. A decentralized car-sharing service created by blockchain technology ensures data integrity and anonymous identity verification. In terms of the Internet of Vehicles, messages need to be distributed more widely. So the security and privacy of the messages have higher requirements. Lei Zhang et al. [2] have proposed a Blockchain-based secure data sharing scheme that solves the challenges of security and privacy on the internet of vehicles. In terms of data privacy protection based on homomorphic encryption, Parmar PV et al. [3] have published an Overview of different homomorphic encryption algorithms. In our article, we use the Paillier homomorphic encryption algorithm. Shen M et al. [4] have published a smart city based on Paillier homomorphic algorithm, support vector machine (SVM), and blockchain. Wang Ruijin et al. [5] have established a privacy protection program for the internet of vehicles based on homomorphic encryption and blockchain technology. The scheme can achieve private data is distributed, shared, and calculated in the state of ciphertext.

In terms of multi-key conversion protocols, there was the privacy-preserving outsourced support vector machine design for secure drug discovery researched by Liu et al. [9] which realizes privacy protection through the combination of SVM, multi-key conversion protocol, homomorphic encryption.

There are also much researches on data processing SVM machine learning. Among them, Byvatov et al. [6] used the support vector machine (SVM) for the classification of drug and non-drug. Secondly, Lin and Chen [7] have considered solving the privacy problem of the dataset in SVM training and the encryption problem of SVM information for classification. The contributions of this paper:

1. Use the consortium blockchain and SVM machine learning to realize a secure and reliable shared car risk prediction that can try to avoid the damage and long-term borrowing from happening in the shared car application scenario.
2. Solve the problem of privacy in shared car data protection. With the help of blockchain and homomorphic encryption, the confidentiality, immutability, and traceability of data in storage are realized. The plaintext information can not be obtained even if the ciphertext state data is leaked during transmission.
3. The privacy-protected SVM machine prediction scheme uses multi-key conversion protocol and homomorphic encryption technology to implement the SVM model training and prediction calculations while data are all in encrypted status.

This paper introduces related work in Sect. 2; introduces basic knowledge of SVM and blockchain in Sect. 3; Sect. 4 introduces the structure model of the shared car risk prediction scheme and the process of data prediction; Sect. 5 is analysis and comparison; Sect. 6 is a summary.

3　Preliminaries

In this section, we outline the definition of blockchain, Paillier Homomorphic Encryption, SVM, which are the basic in our proposed scheme. Table 1 summarizes the key notations used in this paper.

Table 1. Summary of notations

Notations	Definition
pk_a/sk_a	Party a' public key or private key
$sigk_{KGC}/verk_{KGC}$	Strong unforgeable signature/verification key
$SK^{(1)}/SK^{(2)}$	Partial Strong private key of our scheme
$[x]_{pk_a}/x$	The ciphertext $[x]_{pk_a}$ is the plaintext x encrypted by the public key of a
CET_i/REC_i	Certificate/revocation for domain i
M_{re}	car'/user' node data and authentication in encrypted state
$\vec{x}, \vec{w}$	Parameters of SVM
g, N	Group generator, plaintext domain of our scheme

3.1　Blockchain

The blockchain is essentially a distributed database, using p2p communication technology and consensus protocol to allow multiple databases to maintain the same ledger at the same time. So the blockchain data is immutable, decentralized, and secure. Blockchain can be combined with encryption algorithms to make all the nodes invisible to the content of the ledger and realize the confidentiality of the data in the ledger.

Blockchains can be divided into three types: public chains, consortium chains, and private chains.

(1) For public chains, all users can join the blockchain network at any time to maintain or update the ledger, such as Bitcoin and Ethereum.
(2) For the consortium chains, only nodes that have been authenticated can apply to update the blockchain.
(3) For private chains, they are generally used in enterprises and institutions.

The shared car risk prediction scheme designed in this paper adopts the consortium blockchain.

3.2　Paillier Homomorphic Encryption

The Paillier homomorphic encryption algorithm can ensure that the processor does not need to know its corresponding plaintext information, allowing the processor to process the ciphertext and map the processing to the corresponding plaintext processing. So the ciphertext is processed directly, and the result of the processing after the plaintext is encrypted at the same.

The encryption function defined by Paillier cipher is defined as $E_{pk}(...)$, Paillier cipher system is defined as follows:

$$E_{pk}(m, r) = g^m * r^N \bmod N^2 \tag{1}$$

The above parameter $m \epsilon Z_n$ is the homomorphically encrypted plaintext information, N is the product of two prime numbers p, q. From the above formula, the following additive homomorphic formula and multiplicative homomorphic formula can be derived:

$$E_{pk}(a + b) = E_{pk}(a) * E_{pk}(b) \bmod N^2 \tag{2}$$

$$E_{pk}(a * b) = E_{pk}(a)^b \bmod N^2 \tag{3}$$

3.3 SVM Support Vector Machine Algorithm

The support vector machine algorithm is a machine learning training model of supervised learning. The algorithm classifies data after predicted by calculating the maximum edge hyperplane of the data. The formal formula of the hyperplane: $y = w^T x + b$, and $w^T x + b > 0, y = +1; w^T x + b < 0, y = -1$, the relevant optimizations are as follows:

$$\min_{w, b} \frac{1}{2} \left\| w^2 \right\|, s.t., y_i(w^T x + b) \geq 1, i = 1, 2..., m \tag{4}$$

4   Scheme Mechanism

In this part, we introduce the model design, design goals, and critical steps of the scheme design. In detail, the scheme model in Sect. 4.1, designed goal in Sect. 4.2, the data authentication and key distribution in Sect. 4.3, smart contracts in blockchain in Sect. 4.4, secure multiple-key transform protocol in Sect. 4.5, the request query process analysis in Sect. 4.6.

4.1   Scheme Model

From Fig. 1, we can see the shared car risk prediction scheme model structure designed in this paper. This system model includes an improved IBE cryptographic system that can realize user authentication and signature. There are eight types of entity in the scheme model structure as follows:

Key Generation Center (KGC): KGC is a fully trusted authority whose job is to allocate and manage public and private key pairs and generate keys that can be signed and authenticated.

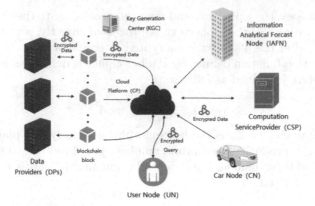

Fig. 1. The model structure of shared car risk prediction scheme

Data providers (DP): Each data provider can be an independent car-sharing platform company and each data provider can be regarded as a blockchain accounting node in the blockchain. The car rental data is encrypted and forwarded to CP is used for storage.

Data Blockchain: The blockchain stores the hash value information of the user node or vehicle node data information in multiple data providers. The data provider plays the role of the blockchain accounting node in the blockchain. Blockchain can invalidate any data provider's tampering with data. Our solution uses the alliance blockchain.

User Node (UN): The user node encrypts the relevant information data of renting a shared car and sends it to CP for storage. Once the user node receives the encrypted data, it can decrypt the result and obtain the prediction result.

Car Node (CN): After the car-sharing node is rented, it encrypts the relevant information data of its car-sharing and sends it to the CP for storage.

Cloud Platform (CP): There is almost unlimited storage space in the cloud platform which can store all the encrypted registered participants' information data in the scheme and perform partial decryption calculations on the ciphertext.

Computing Service Provider (CSP): It can partially decrypt the semi-decrypted information sent by the CP to obtain the information.

Information analytical Forecast Node (IAFN): The information-analytical forecast node is a commercial company that is used to provide security forecasts for users to rent shared cars. The Information analytical forecast node can predict the security of car rental behavior under the premise of ensuring information security.

4.2 Design Goals

Confidentiality: Homomorphic encryption ensures data is invisible. Data providers, the cloud platform, computing service provider, and information-analytical forecast node are invisible to data. The data of user nodes and shared car nodes are kept in the form of encryption during the transmission process.

Immutable: The hash value of the data of user nodes and shared car nodes will be stored on the data servers of multiple data providers through the blockchain consensus protocol PBFT. The data on blockchain will be shared in the form of blocks and synchronized. Any tampering of the data by the data provider will be invalid.

Synchronization: By using the consensus protocol PBFT of the blockchain, data providers act as blockchain accounting nodes that can update the data synchronously within a certain period of time and make the data more secure and stable on the storage side.

Anonymity: Through the light-node privacy protection identity verification scheme, data providers, cloud platforms, computing service providers, and the information-analytical forecast node can obtain encrypted data of user nodes and shared car nodes. But they cannot track and determine the identity of the user node and the car node.

Predictability: Through the support vector machine learning and prediction on the encrypted user node data and the encrypted shared car node data, the information-analytical forecast node calculate an SVM machine learning model by the encrypted data in CP. The model can predict the rental situation and return situation of the shared car by using the user node data and the shared car node data.

4.3 Certificate Authentication and Key Distribution

Certificate Assignment and Revocation
The improved IBE cryptographic system can enable KGC nodes to authenticate and sign user or car identities. If one participant P (e.g., IAFN) wants synchronously compute some encrypted data from other parties (e.g., DPs). P must get DPi's authorization time (AT) for party P from DPi, then sends the DPi's authorization time (AT) to KGC. KGC will generate

a certificate sequence (CS) for everyone certificate and uses the DPi's authorization time (AT), domain area (DA) to make a new certificate $CET_i = <cet = (CS, DA, DP_i, AT, pk_{DPi}); Sig(cet, sigk_{KGC})>$ or a revocation certificate $REC_i = <rec = (revoke, CS); Sig(cet, sigk_{KGC})>$, then send to CP and CSP for storage.

Key Distribution

To distribute keys in this shared car risk prediction scheme, the KGC generates public parameters $pp = (N, g)$, randomly select $sk_s = \Theta_x \epsilon Z_N$ (include all $x \epsilon \{DP_1, DP_2, \cdots DP_n, UN, CN, IAFN\}$), then computes $Pk_i = g^{\Theta_i}(i = 1, \cdots, n)$, on the same N and g. KGC generates CET_i for DP_i, CET_{UN} for UN, CET_{CN} for CN, CET_{IAFN} for IAFN and sends these authentications to both CP and CSP for storage. KGC also generates and sends the private keys $sk_x = \Theta_x(x = 1, \cdots, n), sk_{UN} = \Theta_{UN}, sk_{CN} = \Theta_{CN}, sk_{IAFN} = \Theta_{IANN}$ to DP_x, UN, CN, IAFN via a secure channel, respectively. KGC sends the verification key $verk_{KGC}$ to both CP and CSP. There is no one external adversary or internal party to decrypt the DP_i's ciphertexts because these parties can not get the corresponding private key sk_x by one way.

4.4   Smart Contracts in Blockchain

Smart Contract of Adding Requesting Data

All the data is divided into two sorts. One is car rental users' information, the other one is cars' information. The data is all in the ciphertext state. The blockchain will use the smart contract to detect whether the data is in requesting forecast state. When the data is sent to CP for forecasting whether the user can lend the car, CP will send hash value of these data to the main data provider node. The main data provider node will obey the adding new message of smart contract, then broadcast the hash value to all the data provider nodes in the blockchain. At last, all the data provider nodes store the hash value and add in the last blockchain's block data segment.

Smart Contract of verifying All Stored Dataset

When the IAFN needs to train the SVM model, it will send a request of needing datasets to CP. CP receives the request and sends the request of verifying all stored datasets to the main data provider node of the blockchain. The main data provider node will use the smart contract of verifying all stored datasets, then the blockchain will send all the hashes to the CP. When the CP verifies that the data corresponds to the hashes, the CP will make some processes in CP and CSP before sending encrypted data to IAFN. The process will be explained in Sect. 4.5.

Smart Contract of Adding Result Data

When the IAFN gets the processed dataset, IAFN will use the homomorphic encryption algorithm and corresponding requesting information to complete prediction result P of request lending sharing car. The prediction result will be encrypted by authorized public key pk_B, then IAFN will send the encrypted prediction result $[P]_{pk_B}$ to CP. CP will store it and send it's hash to the main data provider node of the blockchain. The main data provider node will use the smart contract of adding the hash, then the hash value of encrypted prediction result $[P]_{pk_B}$ will be broadcasted to all the data provider nodes in the blockchain and published in the blockchain. CP also uses the method (Sect. 4.5) to make the encrypted prediction result $[P]_{pk_B}$ transform to the encrypted prediction result $[P]_{pk_A}$, pk_A is the corresponding user's public key. CP will send the encrypted prediction result $[P]_{pk_A}$ to the corresponding user and the user can decrypt to know the prediction result P.

4.5 Secure Multiple-key Transform Protocol (SMT)

All the data which is about cars and users are encrypted, the ciphertext is encrypted by the unique different public key which is one of the cars' or the users' public keys. Because these data are encrypted by the different public keys, we can't use the homomorphic encryption algorithm to deal with these data directly. In this part, The method borrows the solution called Secure Domain Transformation (SDT) proposed by Liu et al. [8]. In the proposed way, we can transform ciphertexts in different public keys to one centralized key.

The goal of our method: make a ciphertext $[x]_{pk_A}$ with public key pk_A transform to $[x]_{pk_B}$ which is encrypted by an authorized public key $pk_B \epsilon CET_B$. The method is as the following steps:

Step 1 (in CP, CSP): Use $verk_{KGC}$ to verify whether both CET_A and CET_B are valid, and $[x]_{pk_A} \epsilon DA$ in CET_A. if valid, then do the following steps.

Step 2 (in CP): Select and choose a random integer number $r \epsilon Z_N$, then calculate $[x]_{pk_A} \cdot [r]_{pk_A} = [x+r]_{pk_A} \to X_1$ and use partial private key $SK^{(1)}$ decrypt X_1 to get X_1', then send X_1 and X_1' to CSP.

Step 3 (in CSP): Use partial private $SK^{(2)}$ decrypt X_1 and X_1', then obtain the data m = x + r. Then, encrypt m with an authorized public key pk_B and send $[m]_{pk_B} = [x+r]_{pk_B}$ to the CP.

Step 4 (in CP): Calculate the result that $[m]_{pk_B} \cdot ([r]_{pk_B})^{N-1} \to [m]_{pk_B}$ with authorized public key pk_B.

In a word, the method is used to transform the encrypted result $[m]_{pk_A}$ from users' or cars' public key pk_A to the encrypted result $[m]_{pk_B}$ with a domain public key pk_B. Correspondingly, It also can transform the encrypted result $[m]_{pk_B}$ from domain public key pk_B to the encrypted result $[m]_{pk_A}$ with users' or cars' public key pk_A.

4.6 Request Query Process Analysis

After the step of key distribution (Sect. 4.3), multiple data providers (DPs), user nodes (UN), shared car nodes (CN), and information-analytical forecast node (IAFN) obtain their own public-private key pair and certification signature from The Key Generation Center (KGC) by the secure channel. The IAFN information-analytical forecast node obtains data from the cloud platform (CP), and the cloud platform (CP) obtains data from data providers (DP). The mainly accounting node in the blockchain obtains all the multi-key encrypted data by using the smart contract. After the data is transmitted to the cloud platform (CP), the multi-key encrypted data is changed to unify-key encrypted data through the computing service provider (CSP) and Secure multiple-key Transform (SMT) protocol protocols. The CP sends the unify-key encrypted data to the information-analytical forecast node (IAFN), and the information-analytical forecast node (IAFN) will perform training calculations on the data and obtain the SVM classification model before accepting the car rental query data.

In the scheme, obtaining the forecast security result of car rental requires these three processes which are respectively the car rental query data are transferred to the cloud platform (CP) and uploading to the blockchain; secure data processing and predict calculation; forecast results to be uploaded on the blockchain and returned to the user. The three processes are as follows:

Step 1: The query data is transmitted to the cloud platform and uploaded on the blockchain

The platform user node (UN) uses their mobile phones to acquire shared information of car node $Data_{CN}$, the authentication information of car node CET_{CN}, the public key of the car node $PK_{CN} = g^{\Theta_{CN}}$. After confirming automotive vehicle information and authentication information is correct, the user transmits the encrypted data of authentication and information $Enc_{PK_{UN}}(CET_{UN}, Data_{UN})$, $Enc_{PK_{CN}}(CET_{CN}, Data_{CN})$, named as M_{re}. After the cloud platform (CP) receives the information M_{re}, it determines whether the information is a car rental request query information and determines whether the data is valid information. If the information is a car rental request query information and the message is valid, through the Byzantine consensus the car rental request information will be sent to the data provider which is the main accounting node in the blockchain. Then the data provider uses the smart contract (Sect. 4.4) that adds the requested information on the blockchain and store it in the databases of multiple data providers.

Step 2: Secure data processing and predictive calculation

After the cloud platform (CP) receives the information, the cloud platform (CP) uses the computing service provider (CSP) and Secure multiple-key Transform (SMT) protocols to unify the secret data and send the secret request query data to the information-analytical forecast node (IAFN). After the information-analytical forecast node (IAFN) receives the encrypted request query data, the decision function of the SVM model predicts the risk assessment result of the action of the user renting the vehicle.

$$\overrightarrow{x} = (1, [x_1], [x_2], [x_3], [x_4], [x_5], [x_6], [x_7], [x_8]) \tag{5}$$
$$\overrightarrow{w} = (b, w_1, w_2, w_3, w_4, w_5, w_6, w_7, w_8) \tag{6}$$

Step 3: Uploading and returning the prediction result

The information-analytical forecast node (IAFN) finally calculates the prediction result of the request to rent a car and sends it to the cloud platform (CP) by encrypting it with the certified public key. After receiving the data, the CP uses the Secure multiple-key Transform (SMT) protocol with the computing service provider(CSP) to transform the unify-key encrypted data into encrypted data using the public key of the user node. Then the data provider uses the smart contract (Sect. 4.4) in the blockchain to add the encrypted prediction result data $[P]_{pk_A}$ on the blockchain and store it in the databases of multiple data providers. The cloud platform (CP) will also send the encrypted prediction result data $[P]_{pk_A}$ to the user node, then the user node (UN) uses its private key sk_A to decrypt it to obtain the prediction result P.

5   Performance Analysis

5.1   Experiment Preparation

The experimental code runs on a PC. The configuration of the PC is a 6-core Intel i5-9400 processor at 2.90 GHz and 16 GB RAM. The experiment uses the real car rental information dataset CarrentalData and the real personal clothing information dataset Personal-fashion for data simulation, and simulates a dataset named SharedcarData suitable for car sharing scenarios. The CarrentalData and Personal-fashion datasets are publicly available on the Kaggle machine learning dataset resource website. The shared car dataset SharedcarData is divided into two parts proportionally, one part is the training set to train the model, and the other part is used as the test set to test the performance of the model. Table 2 is the basic situation for all the datasets.

Table 2. Basic situation of datasets Table

Dataset name	Example number	Attribute number
CarrentalData	5851	15
Personal-fashion	204	6
SharedcarData	204	9

5.2   Analysis of Experimental Results

When changing scale of the dataset to predict, the accuracy of the model is not drop significantly, indicating that the scale of the test basically has no effect on the accuracy. In order to test the impact of the scale of the test dataset on the prediction accuracy of the shared car SVM method, we set the maximum number of iterations of the SVM training parameter to 1000 and select 20, 40, and 80 samples from the SharedcarData dataset as the experimental test dataset. The experimental results are shown in Table 3.

Table 3. Accuracy statistics table

Number of test dataset samples	Training time/ms	Accuracy/%
20	63774	84.9
40	62949	83.9
80	63883	84.0

According to the accuracy in the table, the accuracy of SVM machine learning for this shared car is basically around 85%.

5.3 Time Analysis

Calculate the time from the beginning of data generation to the information-analytical forecast node receiving the data encrypted by the unified key, as shown in Table 4:

Table 4. Time calculation analysis table

Step	Step name	Homomorphic multiplication	Encryption	DSecryption
1	Data generation	0	0	1
2	SMT-step1-2	1	1	0
3	SMT-step2	0	1	1
4	SMT-step3	1	0	0

According to the data in the table, it can be seen that this section needs a total of two encryption times, two decryption times, two homomorphic multiplication times. When the prediction result is to be converted from pk_B to the personal user public key pk_A, the time required is the same as steps 2, 3, and 4 in the Table 4.

5.4 Performance Comparison

In this part, we summarize the comparison of the proposed shared car risk prediction scheme with other privacy-preserving SVM classification or blockchain schemes. All the schemes can be divided into two sorts, one is using homomorphic encryption and multi-key conversion protocol to make data more secure, the other one is the no-using privacy-preserving scheme. The no-using privacy-preserving scheme is less time consuming than the proposed privacy-preserving scheme. In order to support multiple keys situations and the strong security level, our scheme pays little time-consuming to for more security. For prediction accuracy, there is almost no dataset directly suitable for car sharing scenarios, the SharedcarData dataset generated by our simulation will reduce the accuracy of the SVM machine learning algorithm, and thus cannot reach more than 90%. We used the logistic regression algorithm and the SVM machine learning algorithm to calculate the accuracy of the SharedcarData dataset. Experiments show that the accuracy of our SVM machine algorithm (85%) is higher than that of the logistic regression algorithm (72%).

The comparison of method and Algorithm between our scheme we designed and other schemes about the secure machine learning solution is shown in Table 5.

Table 5. Time calculation analysis table

Method/Algorithm	[7]	[8]	[9]	[10]	[11]	Proposed
Support multiple keys	✗	✗	✓	✗	✓	✓
Distributed storage	✗	✗	✗	✓	✓	✓
Data synchronize	✓	✓	✓	✓	✗	✓
Support SVM training	✓	N.A.	✓	✗	✗	✓
Security Level	Weak	Strong	Strong	Weak	Weak	Strong

6   Conclusin and Future Work

In this paper, we propose a blockchain-based shared car risk prediction scheme with the following advantages: (1) Blockchain technology provides a solution for the secure and confidential storage of metadata. The blockchain realizes distributed storage, synchronization, and sharing of metadata. (2) With the use of homomorphic encryption algorithm and multi-key conversion protocol, the multiple entities' shared car, user data can be more secure and prediction can be more accurate. The scheme can provide some valuable solutions and ideas in the data privacy of SVM machine learning. In the future, we can learn and refer to more multiparty secure computing privacy protection methods to optimize the data privacy protection in SVM machine learning as much as possible. Secondly, the privacy algorithm of the shared car risk prediction platform scheme can be popularized and applied in more applications.

Acknowledgment. The work was supported in part by the National Natural Science Foundation of China (61862052), and the Science and Technology Foundation of Qinghai Province (2019-ZJ-7065).

References

1. Valaštín, V., Košt'ál, K., Bencel, R., et al.: Blockchain based car-sharing platform. In: 2019 International Symposium ELMAR, pp. 5–8. IEEE (2019)
2. Zhang, L., Luo, M., Li, J., et al.: Blockchain based secure data sharing system for internet of vehicles: a position paper. Veh. Commun. **16**, 85–93 (2019)
3. Parmar, P.V., Padhar, S.B., Patel, S.N., et al.: Survey of various homomorphic encryption algorithms and schemes. Int. J. Comput. Appl. **91**(8) (2014)
4. Shen, M., Tang, X., Zhu, L., et al.: Privacy-preserving support vector machine training over blockchain-based encrypted IoT data in smart cities. IEEE Internet Things J. **6**(5), 7702–7712 (2019)
5. Ruijin, W., Yucheng, T., Weiqi Zhang, F.Z.: Privacy protection scheme for internet of vehicles based on homomorphic encryption and block chain technology. Chin. J. Netword Inf. Secur. **6**(1), 46 (2020)
6. Byvatov, E., Fechner, U., Sadowski, J., et al.: Comparison of support vector machine and artificial neural network systems for drug/nondrug classification. J. Chem. Inf. Comput. Sci. **43**(6), 1882–1889 (2003)
7. Lin, K.P., Chen, M.S.: Privacy-preserving outsourcing support vector machines with random transformation. In: Proceedings of the 16th ACM SIGKDD International Conference on Knowledge Discovery and Data Mining, pp. 363–372 (2010)
8. Liu, X., Choo, K.K.R., Deng, R.H., et al.: Efficient and privacy-preserving outsourced calculation of rational numbers. IEEE Trans. Dependable Secure Comput. **15**(1), 27–39 (2016)
9. Liu, X., Deng, R.H., Choo, K.K.R., et al.: Privacy-preserving outsourced support vector machine design for secure drug discovery. IEEE Trans. Cloud Comput. **8**(2), 610–622 (2018)
10. Yao, Y., Chang, X., Mišić, J., et al.: BLA: blockchain-assisted lightweight anonymous authentication for distributed vehicular fog services. IEEE Internet Things J. **6**(2), 3775–3784 (2019)
11. Vaidya, J., Yu, H., Jiang, X.: Privacy-preserving SVM classification. Knowl. Inf. Syst. **14**(2), 161–178 (2008)

Fairness Protection Method of Vickery Auction Based on Smart Contract

Yuan Yu, Li Yang$^{(\boxtimes)}$, Wenjing Qin, and Yasheng Zhou

Xidian University, Xi'an 710071, Shaanxi, China
yangli@xidian.edu.cn

Abstract. In the Vickery auction rules, the highest bidder gets the goods, but deals with the second highest bid. Although Vickery auction rules can solve the problem of information asymmetry between buyers and sellers, the common fairness problems outside the bidding rules, such as buyer collusion, multi-price bidding and seller price raising, still cannot be solved. This paper proposes a new fairness protection method of Vickery auction. It builds an auction platform based on blockchain, and realizes fair bidding to prevent collusion and ensure the only bid through the automatic execution mechanism of smart contract. At the same time, this method protects bidding privacy and excludes the seller's bid based on secure multi-party computation. It improves the security of Vickery auction in practical application. This paper also builds a fairness evaluation model of bidding mechanism, and proves that the method has good performance in protecting bidding fairness.

Keywords: Vickery auction · Blockchain · Smart contract · Secure multi-party computation · Evaluation model

1 Introduction

Auction is a kind of spot trading mode in which the auction house specialized in auction business accepts the entrustment of the owner, displays the goods to be auctioned to the buyer at the specified time and place according to certain regulations and rules, so as to maximize the interests [1]. In the auction, the information asymmetry between the seller and the buyer often leads to the loss of fairness. For example, the British auction follows the principle of the one with the highest price. If the buyer collude to bid, the final price can be reduced and the fairness to the seller will be damaged.

In order to solve the problem of information asymmetry, Professor William Vickery, the Nobel Laureate in economics, proposed Vickery auction [2]. The rule of Vickery auction is: in the auction, the buyer with the highest bid is

We would like to thank the anonymous reviewers for their careful reading and useful comments. This work is supported by the National Natural Science Foundation of China (Program No. 62072352, 62072359).

W. Shi et al. (Eds.): SPNCE 2021, LNICST 423, pp. 15–34, 2022.
https://doi.org/10.1007/978-3-030-96791-8_2

qualified to buy goods, but he only needs to pay the second highest price. Vickery auction ensure the optimal Pareto efficiency, that is, after reducing the influence of the winning bidder on the final price, the buyer can eliminate the premium or decision-making error caused by guessing game to the other buyers when bidding, so as to produce a bid as close to the real value of the goods as possible, and eliminate the fairness loss caused by information asymmetry.

Vickery auction, as a representative form of sealed auction, can well solve the problem of information asymmetry in auction, and help to improve the fairness of other sealed auction. However, there are still many fairness problems caused by operation outside the mechanism. The fairness of auction will be affected by the decrease of final price caused by the collusive bidding of the buyer. As the case proposed by Athey et al. [3], in the infinitely repeated Bertrand game, collusive bidding can reduce costs for firms. The manipulation of the auction result caused by the buyer's multiple bidding prices will damage the fairness of auction. As the case proposed by Axel et al. [4], multiple bidding happens in second price Internet auctions with a fixed end time, such as those on eBay. The participation of the seller in the auction will lead to higher final price. If the seller knows the highest price and the second highest price in advance, he can bid between the two, so that the buyer has to deal at the higher price offered by seller on purpose. Therefore, a privacy protection scheme [5,6] for bidding price is very necessary.

To eliminate the privacy and security problems caused by the illegal operation of buyers and sellers in Vickery auction. From the perspective of the seller, an effective method should be proposed to prevent the buyer from colluding in bidding, so that the buyer can only bid honestly once. From the buyer's point of view, we should put forward effective method to avoid the seller's price raising, especially in shielding the buyer's bid and excluding the seller's operation. How to find an effective method to meet the above needs has become the main goal of the method proposed in this paper.

In order to solve the above problems, this paper uses blockchain, smart contract and secure multi-party computation to implement a fairness protection method of Vickery auction. The auction platform for seller and buyer to trade is built on the blockchain, and the auction process is automatically executed through the smart contract to protect the buyer's bidding privacy and ensure that the buyer has only one bid. Secure multi-party computation is used to ensure the privacy of the buyer's bid and exclude the seller's bid, which provides a fair solution for the practical application of Vickery auction. The main contributions include:

- A fairness protection method of Vickery auction based on smart contract is proposed, which realizes fair Vickery auction through invisible buyer's only bid collection and non-interference final price privacy calculation.
- A fairness evaluation model of bidding mechanism is constructed to verify the good fairness performance of our method and enrich the research perspective of bidding evaluation model.

– The fairness of our method is at least 2.5 times better than that of SAP scheme and ASAS scheme in both mean standard deviation method and Delphi method.

2   Related Work

The security of Vickery auction can be enhanced by adding privacy computing method based on cryptography. For example, in 2003, Suzuki et al. [7] used homomorphic encryption technology to strengthen the privacy security of the Vickery auction mechanism of combinatorial auctions. However, due to the addition of random mask value, the scheme will reveal some other information besides the auction results.

In 2008, Sekhavat et al. [8] proposed ASAS anonymous secure auction scheme, which has better performance than EOBA and SAP schemes. However, all participants (certification authority, seller, auctioneer, payment gateway and multiple buyers) need to hold public and private keys and certificate to verify their identities, and the communication in the bidding execution process is still complex.

In recent years, related work mainly focuses on the rational allocation of resources by using the Vickery auction principle. For example, Al-manthari et al. [9] solved the congestion pricing problem of wireless networks using the Vickery auction principle in 2011, and Zhang et al. [10] used the Vickery auction principle to select the auxiliary relay in satellite ground sensor networks in 2019. Not only in the Internet related industries, Vickery auction is also applied to the auction of animal husbandry resources [11]. When people need to choose the right supplier in the supply chain [12], Vickery auction also helps a lot. But little has been done to focus on ensuring fairness while enhancing the privacy of Vickery's auction.

To address the fairness and privacy issues of vickery auctions, and the need for invisible and anonymous buyers, unique bids, and non-interference by sellers, as a distributed shared database technology, blockchain technology has the characteristics of decentralization, transparency, fairness and openness, which coincides with the requirements of Vickery's auction.

Blockchain is widely used in different fields such as data outsourcing [13], recommendation system [14], edge computing [15] and so on because of its anonymity, de trust, point-to-point, traceability and non tamperability. At present, the idea of building an auction platform based on blockchain and smart contract has been relatively mature. For example, a transactive energy auction that operates without the need for a trusted entitys oversight is proposed by Hahn et al. [16]. However, this method does not consider the impact of the seller's operation on the fairness in the auction. Wang et al. proposed a decentralized electricity transaction mode for microgrids based on blockchain and continuous double auction (CDA) mechanism [17]. Galal et al. present a smart contract for a verifiable sealed-bid auction on the Ethereum blockchain [18]. However, they need a credible auction notary to verify the seller and the buyer's commitment, and those who participate in the auction will not get the return value of the failure bid. In reference [19], Sanchez et al. Proposed a blockchain based auction system Raziel, which combines secure multi-party computing and zero knowledge proof. The system ensures the privacy, correctness and verifiability of Auction Contracts running on the blockchain. However, because secure multi-party computing and zero knowledge proof are used to realize the complete anonymity of identity, the overall scheme is complex and difficult to popularize. At present, the challenge of Vickery auction fair protection method based on smart contract is that there is no standardization of fairness, that is, there is no quantitative method to evaluate fairness, so it is difficult to find the entry point to maintain fairness and to quantitatively evaluate the scheme.

After years of development, Vickery auction has integrated many scenes and fields, but how to improve the fairness of the operation outside the mechanism under the premise of ensuring privacy security, and how to use reasonable evaluation criteria to measure the effect of the auction mechanism still need more exploration.

In order to put forward a better fairness evaluation model of auction mechanism, we studies many evaluation mechanisms. Hobbs et al. describe a Vickrey-Clarke-Groves auction for supply and demand bidding in the face of market power and nonconcave benefits [20], which focus on its risks being revenue deficient, can be gamed by cooperating suppliers and consumers, and is subject to the information revelation and bid-taker cheating. Chen et al. focuses on mechanism design for quality assignment combinatorial procurement auctions [21]. their model focuses on how the participants maximize social surplus, the difference between gross utility and total cost in electronic procurement. The evaluation model proposed in this paper focuses more on fairness performance, and constructs a linear objective function by combining privacy evaluation and revenue evaluation.

3   Fairness Protection Method of Vickery Auction

This section introduces the fairness protection method of Vickery auction based on smart contract. The method consists of two stages: invisible buyer's only bid collection and non-interference final price privacy calculation. The fairness protection method of Vickery auction diagram is as Fig. 1.

3.1   Method

The two stages can be divided into four steps with temporal relationship, which together form the process of realizing Vickery auction. For each step, use arrows to show the data transfer relationship between them, build bidding platform on the blockchain, deploy smart contracts on the console, and return the transaction results every time the contracts are executed to collect bids. The auction parameters formed in the smart contract are automatically set into the privacy computation framework and translated into circuit files through the circuit compiler. Finally, the privacy calculation results are returned to the seller and the buyer.

The data transfer relationship also exists between the seller, the buyer and the auction platform. The seller and the buyer nodes need to submit identity authentication to join the blockchain. The blockchain network reaches a consensus on synchronization messages to the seller and the buyer nodes. Every time the buyer submits a bid by calling the smart contract, he will get the result of whether his bid is successful or not, and if it fails, the buyer can prepare for the next step in advance.

In the bidding process, the invisible buyer's only bid collection restricts the buyer's fair operation, and the non-interference transaction price privacy calculation restricts the seller's fair operation. To achieve the fairness of Vickery auction, both restrains should be met.

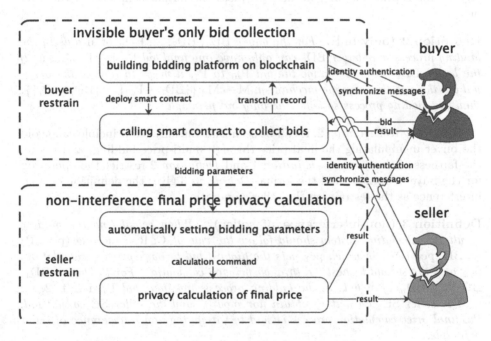

Fig. 1. Fairness protection method of Vickery auction.

3.2 Definition

In the process of online auction, in order to prevent the buyer from bidding collusion to reduce the final price and damage the fairness of the seller, it is necessary to make the buyer invisible. On the other hand, the invisibility of the bid also guarantees the fairness of the buyer and shields the seller to prevent the seller from manipulating. The following gives the basic definitions of invisible of buyer, only bid and non-interference of seller as the focus of the method proposed in this paper. The restrains of the seller and the buyer will be formalized to facilitate the quantification of the subsequent evaluation model.

Definition 1 (invisible of buyer). *For the buyer* BD_1, BD_2 ,..., BD_n *of* n *bids in the bidding process, the bid* P_i *of any buyer* BD_i *is known only by himself,* i ∈ *1, 2, ...,* n. *Because the buyer is anonymous, he can not ask other buyers for final price by means of communication, and the seller* SE *has no right to view any* P_i, *so other buyers can not obtain* P_i *by asking the seller* SE, *then the bidding process is said to be invisible to the buyer.*

According to *Definition* 1, the invisible bidding process of the buyer can avoid the buyers' collusion because they can't see other's bid. Invisible principle also benefits the buyer, shielding the seller from participating in the auction. But if we want to eliminate the manipulation of the bidding process caused by the buyer's multi-price bidding, we need to meet the formal definition of the only bid.

Definition 2 (only bid). *For the buyer* BD_1, BD_2, ..., BD_n *of* n *bids in the bidding process, any buyer* BD_i *can only have one final bid* P_i, i ∈ 1, 2, ..., n. *If the buyer* BD_i *needs to change the bid* P_{i0} *to* P_i, *it needs to replace the original bid through the mapping mechanism* $M \rightarrow M_0:\{\{BD_i \rightarrow P_{i0}\} \rightarrow \{BD_i \rightarrow P_i\}\}$, *then the bidding process satisfies the only bid principle.*

According to *Definition* 2, it can be seen that the only bid principle can avoid the buyer manipulating the final price through multi-price bidding, and realize the fairness of the auction. *Definition* 1 and *Definition* 2 restrict the operation for the buyer's fairness, and the formal *Definition* 3 gives the definition of non-interference as the restrain on the seller's operation.

Definition 3 (non-interference of seller). *When calculating the bidding result* R, *calculation system should follow the rule of* C: R = bidding (pc_1 (P) $\rightarrow$ BD, pc_2 (P)), *in which* pc_1 *gets the highest bid through privacy calculation,* pc_2 *gets the second highest bid through privacy calculation. For the buyer* BD_1, BD_2, ..., BD_n *of* n *bids in the bidding process and their bid* P_i, i ∈ 1, 2, ..., n. *The seller* SE *can neither obtain nor modify, and the seller* SE *cannot bid, the final price calculation process is said to satisfy the non-interference of seller principle.*

According to *Definition* 3, non-interference of seller principle can avoid the seller's participation in bidding, eliminate the hidden danger of the seller's price raising, and ensure the fairness of the buyer's bidding.

4   Invisible Buyer's Only Bid Collection

This section introduces the first stage of fairness protection method of Vickery auction based on smart contract - invisible buyer's only bid collection. Section 4.1 gives the model and architecture of building an auction platform on blockchain, and Sect. 4.2 gives the algorithm of calling smart contract to collect bids.

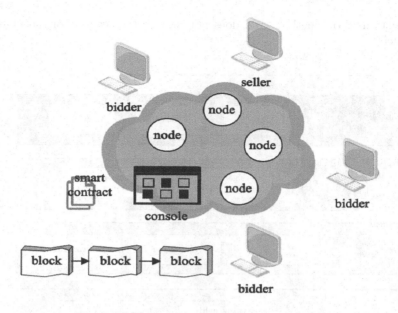

Fig. 2. Network node communication model.

4.1 Building Auction Platform on Blockchain

The blockchain auction platform is the basis for the buyer and seller to conduct node communication, data transmission, on-chain interaction and information synchronization. It can remove the dependence of bidding activities on the trusted third party, and transfer the trust of institutions to the trust of rules. The construction of blockchain auction platform can realize the network node communication model as Fig. 2.

The seller and the buyer exist in the blockchain network as indistinguishable nodes. They interact with the blockchain through the console to complete the functions of deploying contracts and querying data on blockchain. They are interconnected to form a blockchain network, jointly maintain a consensus information blockchain that follows the timing rules [22], seize the blocks according to the consensus way on blockchain, and verify and retrieve the information synchronization. As for the size of data to be stored locally, users can set their own storage policies.

The experimental platform of this paper is built by FISCO BCOS. It is an enterprise level financial permissioned blockchain platform, which was independently developed by the open source working group of Financial Blockchain Shenzhen Consortium in 2017. Because FISCO BCOS meets the national security standard, the environment and configuration are relatively lightweight, and has good scalability, this paper will use it as the technical basis for building a blockchain. Detailed technical documentation and enthusiastic community maintainers are also the reasons why we chose it. This paper focuses on the fairness construction of the method, and does not discuss the security of the platform too much.

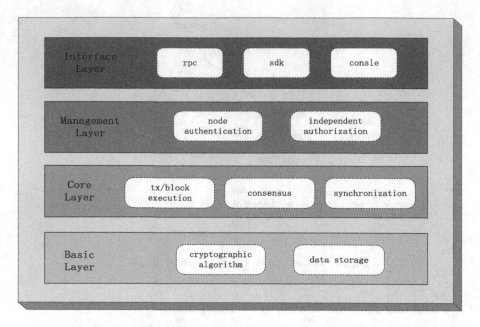

Fig. 3. Architecture of the blockchain auction platform.

Figure 3 shows the architecture of the blockchain auction platform. The blockchain auction platform is composed of interface layer, management layer, core layer and basic layer. The interface layer is responsible for controlling external access, the management layer does node authentication and independent authorization, the core layer completes the transaction and block execution and carries out consensus identity synchronization. The basic layer provides cryptographic algorithm library and local data storage.

4.2   Calling Smart Contract to Collect Bids

The key of fairness protection of Vickery auction based on smart contract is whether the mechanism of collecting buyer's bid can achieve fairness. Using the characteristics of automatic execution and non-interference of smart contract, an invisible buyer's only bid collection auction algorithm is designed as *Algorithm* 1.

According to *Algorithm* 1, the smart contract will judge the calling address. If the contract owner (i.e. the seller) offers bid, the bid will be returned to realize the fairness of excluding the seller to raise the price.

The highest price is *highest*, and the second highest bid is *secondHighest*. The buyer who bids above the *highest* gets the right to buy temporarily. *Highest* and

---

Algorithm 1. Smart Contract for Vickery Auction

Input: address, price
Output: result
initialize highest, secondHighest;
if $now <= start + time$ then
    if $address = contractOwner$ then
        $send(price, address)$;
        return $result$;
    end
    if $price > secondHighest$ then
        if $price > highest$ then
            if $address = bidder$ then
                $highest = price$;
            else
                $secondHighest = highest$;
                $highest = price$;
                $bidder = address$;
                $send(highest, bidder)$;
            end
        else
            $secondHighest = price$;
            $send(price, address)$;
        end
    end
end
if $now > start + time$ then
    $send(secondHighest, contractOwner)$;
    $send(highest - secondHighest, bidder)$;
end
return $result$;

---

secondHighest make corresponding changes. When the bid is above the second-Highest but does not exceed the highest, only the secondHighest is updated. After the bidding, the secondHighest is sent to the contract owner (i.e. the seller), and the remaining price difference between highest and secondHighest is returned to the buyer.

At the same time, Algorithm 1 can ensure the only bid. When the buyer's bid is higher than the highest he has given, it replaces the highest instead of reducing the highest to secondHighest; when the buyer's bid is between the highest and the secondHighest he given, it replaces the secondHighest.

Three bidding prices are always stored in the smart contract, and the results of Vickery auction are adjusted according to the size relationship between them. Algorithm 1 satisfies both the buyer's invisibility and the only bid. From Definition 1 and Definition 2, we can see that it satisfies the restrains on the fair operation of the buyer.

5   Non-interference Final Price Privacy Calculation

This section introduces the second stage of fairness protection method of Vickery auction based on smart contract, which is non-interference final price privacy calculation, including automatic setting of bidding parameters and privacy calculation of final price.

After the auction smart contract expires, the script will automatically set the bidding parameters to the privacy computation framework, write the circuit program in the docker container, run the multi-party computation framework, and generate the circuit file according to the program.

Firstly, we introduce the millionaires problem in two-party secure computing [23] as the basis of this paper's multi-party privacy computation. To calculate who is richer between the two millionaires without disclosing their specific property, suppose that the secret inputs of Alice and Bob are I_a and I_b respectively, the process is as follows:

- Bob generates an n-bit random integer x, encrypts it with Alice's public key to get $EnA(x)$, and sends $EnA(x) - I_b + 1$ to Alice.
- Alice calculates every $y_u = DA(k - I_b + u)$, where $u = 1, 2, ..., n$, to generate $n/2$-bit random prime p, and calculates $z_u = y_u \bmod p$.
- Each calculated z_u is used to compare with I_a. If z_u is larger, $z_u + 1$ is sent. Bob can judge the size relationship between I_a and I_b by whether it is equal to $x \bmod p$.

Process of two-party secure computing is shown in sequence diagram as Fig. 4. In addition to the data transfer between Alice and Bob, every interaction between Alice or Bob and himself is a calculation or encryption and decryption operation to change the data.

This two-party secure computing scheme is extended to three parties, which can be used as the final price privacy computing principle in this paper. Because the current highest bid and the second highest bid need to be saved in the smart contract and compared with the new bid generated by calling the contract, only three parties need to compare the size.

Process of three-party secure computing is shown in sequence diagram as Fig. 5. Suppose that the highest bid stored in the contract is Alice's bid I_a, the second highest bid is Bob's bid I_b, and the current bid generated by Charlie calling the contract is I_c. The calculation process is as follows:

- Charlie generates an n-bit random integer x, encrypts $En(x)$ with the public key of Alice and Bob, and sends $En(x) - I_c + 1$ to Alice and Bob.
- Alice and Bob compute every $y_u = D(k - I_c + u)$ and $h_u = D(k - I_c + u)$, where $u = 1, 2, ..., n$, to generate $n/2$-bit random prime p_1 and p_2, and calculate $z_u = y_u \bmod p_1$ and $l_u = h_u \bmod p_2$.
- The calculated z_u and l_u are used to compare with I_a and I_b. If z_u is larger, $z_u + 1$ will be sent. If l_u is larger, $l_u + 1$ will be sent. The size relationship of three bids can be determined respectively.

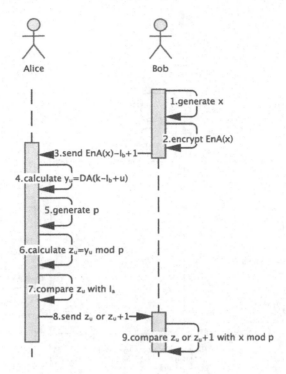

Fig. 4. Two-party secure computing.

We can get the three-party privacy calculation principle of the final price, which satisfies the non-interference of the seller. From *Definition* 3, we can see that it satisfies the restrain on the fair operation of the seller. Combined with the three-party comparison mechanism in *Algorithm* 1, the newly proposed bid only needs to compare with the current highest price and the current second highest price. Therefore, it is most appropriate to use it as Charlie in the three-party secure computation, using the common public key encryption of Alice and Bob, and comparing with the other two parties after calculations.

6 Fairness Evaluation Model of Bidding Mechanism

Bidding mechanism is a kind of market mechanism that determines the allocation of resources through a series of clear rules and the price determined by the buyer's bidding [24]. That is to say, in a certain time and place, through a certain organization, the specific goods or property rights are transferred to the highest bidder in the form of public bidding.

In the study of the evaluation index of auction mechanism, it is the cornerstone of the establishment of evaluation to formulate the measurement standard according to the actual demand. Considering the shortcomings of the related work listed in Sect. 2, this paper chooses privacy protection and bidding income

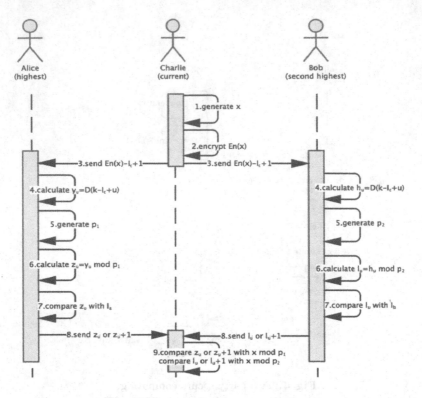

Fig. 5. Three-party secure computing.

as the evaluation content of the objective function to solve the problem of the seller and buyer's operation violation.

In the definition of fairness restrains, both invisible and non-interference need to be quantified by privacy protection in evaluation mechanism. Similar evaluation ideas are used to improve the efficiency and utility of mobile crowdsourcing systems [25] and the only bid is realized by algorithm in smart contract. In economics, revenue maximization [26] is an important index to evaluate the bidding mechanism, so the bidding income is also listed as the content of the evaluation mechanism proposed in this paper.

This section formulates the quantitative fairness evaluation model of bidding mechanism, and selects the relevant bidding mechanism to evaluate and compare with the similar method. The objective function F_A of fairness evaluation of bidding mechanism is as follows:

$$F_A = \alpha P_n + \beta B_n \tag{1}$$

P_n is the evaluation of privacy protection, which is positively related to the fairness evaluation, B_n is the evaluation of bidding income, which pursues the principle of profit maximization by bidding mechanism, B_n is positively related to the fairness evaluation, and α and β are the weight parameters.

F_A is a linear programming model, because our main goal is to select the optimal method through the quantitative calculation of the objective function. When designing the evaluation mechanism, there is often a need to transform the multi-objective programming model into the single objective programming model [27], so the linear weighted method of objective function has become the mainstream evaluation model.

For the design of evaluation mechanism in this paper, defining the proportional or inverse relationship between each part of the evaluation content and the objective function, and how to properly set the weight parameters are the key problems to be solved.

Section 6.1 gives three mechanism assumptions including consistency assumption, distribution assumption and honesty assumption. Section 6.2 introduces privacy protection evaluation P_n and Sect. 6.3 introduces bidding income evaluation B_n.

6.1 Mechanism Assumption

- Consistency assumption: the fairness evaluation of bidding mechanism has nothing to do with buyer seller node parameters and network environment. The communication ability and computing ability of the node are regarded as the same.
- Distribution assumption: buyer bids are independent of each other and subject to uniform distribution D on $[0, M]$, where M is the highest bid. This assumption is abstracted from the law of bidding price in practice, which presents a monotonic increasing law.
- Honesty Assumption: buyer offers bid v honestly. In order to eliminate the behavior deviation of bidders affected by game theory, the buyer is supposed to bid honestly on the premise that the bid is invisible.

The consistency assumption aligns the node environment, the distributed assumption abstracts the bidding into a mathematical model, and the honesty assumption eliminates the error.

6.2 Privacy Protection Evaluation

When researching the evaluation index of privacy protection, the effect of privacy protection is measured by the similarity of privacy data distribution [28]. Privacy protection evaluation P_n is calculated based on string similarity in transaction execution results after one-way function processing of buyer offer data:

$$P_n = \frac{\sum_{i=1}^{n} \sum_{j=1}^{n} Sim(s_i, s_j) - n}{2nd} \tag{2}$$

where d is the distance between similarity intervals. Privacy data should ensure that the distribution similarity among data is as average as possible to achieve the purpose of being difficult to distinguish. The string s_1, s_2 similarity formula is as follows:

$$Sim(s_1, s_2) = \frac{\sum_{i=1}^{len} u(i)}{len} \tag{3}$$

where len is the larger length of string s_1, s_2, and the formula is as follows:

$$len = max(length(s_1), length(s_2)) \tag{4}$$

For different strings s_1, s_2, the position valid value $u(i)$ is expressed as:

$$u(i) = \begin{cases} 1, & s_1(i) = s_2(i) \\ 0, & other \end{cases} \tag{5}$$

where $i = 1, ..., len$. If the characters in the corresponding positions are equal, $u(i)$ value of 1, unequal or exceed the string length, $u(i)$ value of 0.

Through the calculation of privacy protection evaluation P_n, we can quantify *Definition* 1 and *Definition* 3, and introduce fairness based on privacy security into the evaluation model of bidding mechanism.

6.3   Bidding Income Evaluation

When researching the evaluation index of bidding profit, the profit maximization effect is measured by the incentive compatible mechanism DSIC under the dominant strategy. Referring to the Bayesian model in DSIC mechanism [29], the expected revenue of the auction is designed to be calculated based on (x, p) expected E which satisfies the DSIC nature as follows:

$$B_n = \frac{nw}{\sum_{i=1}^{n} v_i E_i} \tag{6}$$

where w stands for final price, v_i stands for buyer's honest bid, and every expect E_i to be calculated as follows:

$$E = \int_0^M x f(x) dx \tag{7}$$

where M is the highest bidding price, f is the density function of distribution D, x is the buyer's bid. As (6), the income of the bidding mechanism is inversely proportional to the average value of the product of the buyer's honest bid and the best profit expectation, and is directly proportional to the final price. Because the closer the final price is to the average value, the farther away it is from the optimal value.

In the bidding, the buyer may raise his own offer in reference to another person's bid, resulting in an increase in the final price, or the seller may lower the final price without knowing the true offer v in the buyer's mind. Introducing virtual bid φ_i to measure fluctuations in final price caused by information as follows [24]:

$$\varphi_i(v_i) = v_i - \frac{1 - D(v_i)}{f(v_i)} \tag{8}$$

Through the calculation of B_n, this paper introduces fairness based on maximum profit for the evaluation model of bidding mechanism. According to the fairness method in this paper, it can eliminate the premium and price depression in the process of bidding, which is closer to the real price distribution.

As (1), we combine Sect. 6.2 and Sect. 6.3 to set appropriate weight parameters α and β. The evaluation mechanism proposed in this paper can comprehensively show the privacy performance and revenue performance, and can objectively describe the fairness of bidding mechanism. Detailed evaluation and comparison with other similar methods are shown in Sect. 7.

7 Experimental Result

According to the method and model introduced in this paper, Vickery auction based on smart contract is constructed as follows: A four node permissioned blockchain is built on the Ubuntu 16.04 system as a data communication platform for bidding. One of the nodes is used as the seller to write the bidding smart contract in *Solidity* language and deploy it to the console through *solc* compilation. The other three nodes call the contract to bid as the buyer, and the automatic execution script is written in *Linux Shell*. The secure multi-party computation framework uses *Wysteria* in docker container to convert the circuit program of three party comparison into the corresponding garbled circuit file [30].

This experiment realizes the fairness protection method of Vickery auction based on smart contract. Now we use the fairness evaluation model proposed in *Sect.* 4 to calculate the F_A of this method and the comparison method SAP and ASAS.

7.1 Data Set

Different buyer node calls the smart contract to bid on the console for five times. After each successful call of the smart contract, the corresponding transaction hash is generated, and the transaction hash field is manually extracted from the transaction return result. ASAS scheme uses RSA as public key encryption.

In order to fully consider the possible situations in the practical application, the experiment also produces failed smart contract calls. We find that when the smart contract fails to be called, the console will directly output a failure prompt without generating transaction information.

The bidding data of the buyer obeys the uniform distribution and satisfies the monotonic increasing property. Every two groups of different successful transaction hash data fields use *matlab* to calculate the string similarity, which is expressed as a matrix:

$$\begin{bmatrix} 1.0000 & 0.0150 & 0.0156 & 0.0154 & 0.0149 \\ 0.0156 & 1.0000 & 0.0159 & 0.0161 & 0.0164 \\ 0.0156 & 0.0159 & 1.0000 & 0.0167 & 0.0159 \\ 0.0154 & 0.0161 & 0.0167 & 1.0000 & 0.0163 \\ 0.0149 & 0.0164 & 0.0159 & 0.0163 & 1.0000 \end{bmatrix}$$

The results show that the model has a small range of privacy between [0.0149, 0.0167], which maintains at a stable level. The model has good privacy performance. Calculate P_n according to the similarity is 8.8222.

It is easy for us to explain some properties of matrix. The reason why the diagonal element value is unified as 1.0000 is that the distribution similarity of itself is exactly the same. Diagonal symmetric elements are equal because two identical elements get the same result no matter they are in the same calculation order.

According to the experimental data, the highest bid is 4, the final price is 3, and the buyer's bid satisfies the uniform distribution of [0, 4]. From this, for a sealed-bid auction like the Vickery auction, $B_n = 3.7500$ is calculated.

We suppose that the British auction, which is a public auction, has the same consistency assumption as Vickery auction. According to (6), $B_n = 5.0000$ is calculated. However, this method has no means of privacy protection, $P_n = 0.0000$.

7.2 Experimental Results

Calculate the privacy protection evaluation P_n and bidding income evaluation B_n of this method, SAP scheme [31] and ASAS scheme. In order to increase the richness of the experiment, we also calculate the public auction that follows the higher price. This kind of auction is also called British auction [32]. All experimental results are shown in Table 1.

The bid of SAP scheme is visible to the trusted third party, so the data similarity is 0.0000. Although the data similarity performance for ASAS is better than the method in this paper, it has a large range of variation between [0.0116, 0.0581], and the comprehensive privacy performance is poor.

Every two groups of different successful RSA encryption results data fields use *matlab* to calculate the string similarity, which is expressed as a matrix:

$$\begin{bmatrix} 1.0000 & 0.0581 & 0.0406 & 0.0116 & 0.0291 \\ 0.0581 & 1.0000 & 0.0174 & 0.0174 & 0.0174 \\ 0.0406 & 0.0174 & 1.0000 & 0.0465 & 0.0233 \\ 0.0116 & 0.0174 & 0.0465 & 1.0000 & 0.0291 \\ 0.0291 & 0.0174 & 0.0233 & 0.0291 & 1.0000 \end{bmatrix}$$

Table 1. Experimental results

Method	P_n	B_n
This paper	**8.8222**	**3.7500**
SAP	**0.0000**	**3.7500**
ASAS	**0.6250**	**3.7500**
British auction	**0.0000**	**5.0000**

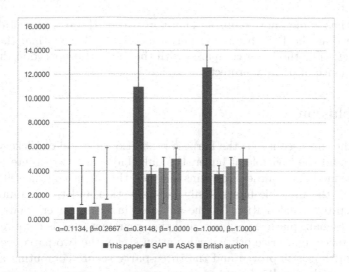

Fig. 6. Comparison of fairness evaluation of bidding methods.

Although the value of α and β can be set and adjusted subjectively by the users of the evaluation model according to the degree of attention to privacy protection and bidding income, this paper still chooses the parameters to provide general models based on several standardization and factor analysis methods to calculate F_A.

Referring to the standard deviation method [33], the value of variables is adjusted to [0, 1] interval, so that privacy protection and bidding income can play an equal role. The resulting $\alpha = 0.1134$ and $\beta = 0.2667$. However, the main purpose of this standardization method is to reduce the variable gap. Compared with the value of F_A, the parameter gap between different models should be compared.

Referring to the mean standard deviation method [34], adjust the variables evenly to the interval. The resulting $\alpha = 0.8148$ and $\beta = 1.0000$. Compared with the standard deviation method, this mean standard deviation method partially protects the scaling proportion.

Referring to the Delphi method [35], set unbalanced parameters in subjective simulation expert scoring and calculate $\alpha = 1.0000$ and $\beta = 1.0000$. The evaluation result of the three methods is as Fig. 6.

By adjusting the values of α and β, we can balance the model's emphasis on privacy protection and bidding income. Experimental results show that the proposed method has similar fairness performance with SAP scheme and ASAS scheme in standard deviation method. But in mean standard deviation method and Delphi method, the fairness performance of our method is improved by 2.9–5.7 times for SAP scheme and 2.6–4.3 times for ASAS scheme.

For the British auction, the public auction method, the best interests of the seller are better protected, but compared with the Vickery auction, the privacy protection has some shortcomings. Therefore, from the experimental results, we can see that the British auction performs slightly better than the general Vickery auction method, but compared with the method proposed in this paper, the performance of privacy protection is slightly worse.

8   Conclusion

Based on the smart contract, the fairness protection method of Vickery auction is realized, and the invisible of buyer, the only bid and the non-interference of seller are defined. The fairness restrains between the buyer and the seller is realized through the invisible buyer's only bid collection and the non-interference final price privacy calculation. In the stage of invisible buyer's only bid, the auction blockchain platform is built, and the smart contract is deployed. In the non-interference final price privacy calculation stage, the two-party secure computing algorithm is improved and the three-party secure computing algorithm is realized, which is well adapted to the comparison among the current highest price, the current second highest price and the newly proposed bid of Vickery auction.

Finally, in order to evaluate the fairness performance quantitatively, a linear evaluation model of bidding mechanism is constructed for privacy protection and bidding income, and the weight parameters of the model are adjusted according to the existing methods. Through experiments, the proposed fairness protection method of Vickery auction has good fairness compared with the existing methods.

References

1. Fang, W., Yao, X., Zhao, X., Yin, J., Xiong, N.: A stochastic control approach to maximize profit on service provisioning for mobile cloudlet platforms. IEEE Trans. Syst. Man Cybern.: Syst. **48**(4), 522–534 (2016)
2. Vickrey, W.: Counterspeculation, auctions, and competitive sealed tenders. J. Financ. **16**(1), 8–37 (1961)
3. Athey, S., Bagwell, K., Sanchirico, C.: Collusion and price rigidity. Rev. Econ. Stud. **71**, 317–349 (2004)
4. Ockenfels, A., Roth, A.E.: Late and multiple bidding in second price internet auctions: theory and evidence concerning different rules for ending an auction - sciencedirect. Games Econ. Behav. **55**(2), 297–320 (2006)
5. Yang, L., Li, C., Cheng, Y., Yu, S., Ma, J.: Achieving privacy-preserving sensitive attributes for large universe based on private set intersection. Inf. Sci. **582**, 529–546 (2022)
6. Yang, L., Li, C., Wei, T., Zhang, F., Ma, J., Xiong, N.: Vacuum: an efficient and assured deletion scheme for user sensitive data on mobile devices. IEEE Internet Things J. (2021)
7. Suzuki, K., Yokoo, M.: Secure generalized Vickrey auction using homomorphic encryption. In: Wright, R.N. (ed.) FC 2003. LNCS, vol. 2742, pp. 239–249. Springer, Heidelberg (2003). https://doi.org/10.1007/978-3-540-45126-6_17

8. Sekhavat, Y.A., Fathian, M.: Efficient anonymous secure auction schema (ASAS) without fully trustworthy auctioneer. Inf. Manage. Comput. Secur. **16**(3), 288–304 (2008)

9. Al-Manthari, B., Nasser, N., Hassanein, H.: Congestion pricing in wireless cellular networks. IEEE Commun. Surv. Tutor. **13**(3), 358–371 (2011)

10. Zhang, X., Zhang, B., An, K., Chen, Z., Guo, D.: Auction-based secondary relay selection on overlay spectrum sharing in hybrid satellite-terrestrial sensor networks. Sensors **19**(22), 5039 (2019)

11. Sitz, M.B., Calkins, R.C., Feuz, M.D., Umberger, J.W., Eskridge, M.K.: Consumer sensory acceptance and value of wet-aged and dry-aged beef steaks. J. Anim. Sci. **84**, 1221–1226 (2006)

12. Jain, V., Panchal, G.B., Kumar, S.: Universal supplier selection via multi-dimensional auction mechanisms for two-way competition in oligopoly market of supply chain. Omega **47**(sep.), 127–137 (2014)

13. Li, C., Yang, L., Ma, J.: A secure and verifiable outsourcing scheme for assisting mobile device training machine learning model. Wirel. Commun. Mob. Comput. **2020** (2020)

14. Yi, B., et al.: Deep matrix factorization with implicit feedback embedding for recommendation system. IEEE Trans. Industr. Inf. **15**(8), 4591–4601 (2019)

15. Lin, B., et al.: A time-driven data placement strategy for a scientific workflow combining edge computing and cloud computing. IEEE Trans. Industr. Inf. **15**(7), 4254–4265 (2019)

16. Hahn, A., Singh, R., Liu, C.C., Chen, S.: Smart contract-based campus demonstration of decentralized transactive energy auctions. In: Power & Energy Society Innovative Smart Grid Technologies Conference (2017)

17. Jian, W., Qianggang, W., Niancheng, Z., Yuan, C.: A novel electricity transaction mode of microgrids based on blockchain and continuous double auction. Energies **10**(12), 1971 (2017)

18. Galal, H.S., Youssef, A.M.: Verifiable sealed-bid auction on the ethereum blockchain. In: Zohar, A., et al. (eds.) FC 2018. LNCS, vol. 10958, pp. 265–278. Springer, Heidelberg (2019). https://doi.org/10.1007/978-3-662-58820-8_18

19. Raziel, S.D.: Private and verifiable smart contracts on blockchains. Raziel': chastnyye i proveryayemye smart-kontrakty na blokcheynakh (2018)

20. Hobbs, E.A., Benjamin, F.: Evaluation of a truthful revelation auction in the context of energy markets with nonconcave benefits. J. Regulatory Econ. **18**(1), 5–32 (2000)

21. Chen, J., Huang, H., Kauffman, R.J.: A public procurement combinatorial auction mechanism with quality assignment. Decis. Support Syst. **51**(3), 480–492 (2011)

22. Nakamoto, S.: Bitcoin: a peer-to-peer electronic cash system. Cryptography Mailing list (2009). https://metzdowd.com

23. Yao, A.C.: Protocols for secure computation. In: Symposium on Foundations of Computer Science (1982)

24. Myerson, R.B.: Optimal auction design. Discuss. Pap. **6**(1), 58–73 (1981)

25. Wang, Y., Cai, Z., Yin, G., Gao, Y., Tong, X.: An incentive mechanism with privacy protection in mobile crowdsourcing systems. Comput. Netw. **102**, 157–171 (2016)

26. Sandholm, T.: Algorithm for optimal winner determination in combinatorial auctions. Artif. Intell. **135**(1–2), 1–54 (2002)

27. Zimmermann, H.-J.: Fuzzy programming and linear programming with several objective functions. Fuzzy Sets Syst. **1**, 45–55 (1978)

28. Snijders, T.A.B., Dormaar, M., Schuur, W.H.V., Dijkman-Caes, C., Driessen, G.: Distribution of some similarity coefficients for dyadic binary data in the case of associated attributes. J. Classif. **7**(1), 5–31 (1990)
29. Mookherjee, D., Reichelstein, S.: Dominant strategy implementation of Bayesian incentive compatible allocation rules. J. Econ. Theory **56**, 378–399 (1992)
30. Hastings, M., Hemenway, B., Noble, D., Zdancewic, S.: SoK: general purpose compilers for secure multi-party computation. In: 2019 IEEE Symposium on Security and Privacy (SP) (2019)
31. Asgharzadeh, Y., Fathian, M.: A newly high secure auction protocol without full-trusted auctioneer. In: Proceedings of 4th Iranian Society of Cryptology Conference, pp. 39–46 (2020)
32. Shachat, J., Wei, L.: Procuring commodities: first-price sealed-bid or English auctions? Mark. Sci. **31**, 317–333 (2012)
33. Cruciani, G., Baroni, M., Clementi, S., Costantino, G., Riganelli, D., Skagerberg, B.: Predictive ability of regression models. part i: standard deviation of prediction errors (SDEP). J. Chemom. **6**(6), 335–346 (1992)
34. Eichner, T., Wagener, A.: Multiple risks and mean-variance preferences. Oper. Res. **57**(5), 1142–1154 (2009)
35. Wang, X., Gao, Z., Guo, H.: Delphi method for estimating uncertainty distributions. Int. J. Inf. **15**(2), 449–460 (2012)

An Improved Needham-Schroeder Session Key Distribution Protocol for In-Vehicle CAN Network

Yin Long, Jian Xu[✉], Chen Wang, and Zihao Wang

Software College, Northeastern University, Shenyang, China
xuj@mail.neu.edu.cn

Abstract. With the rapid development of automobile technology, the internal network of automobiles is facing more and more security problems. Many CAN-based in-vehicle applications lack security mechanisms for data confidentiality and secure session key distribution. To address the above problems, we propose an improved Needham-Schroeder session key distribution protocol suitable for in-vehicle CAN network, using message authentication code (MAC), key derivation function, digital signature, and timestamping mechanisms to resolve the defect that NSSK lacks resistance to Denning-Sacco attack. We use a random oracle model to conduct a formal security analysis of the proposed protocol, then we use Tamarin-Prover to verify the security properties of the protocol, the result indicates that the protocol is secure and applicable for in-vehicle CAN communication.

Keywords: CAN security · Security protocols · Vehicle cybersecurity · The NSSK protocol

1 Introduction

With the vigorous development of the Internet of Things, edge computing, and other contemporary technologies, more and more devices in traditional local area networks are beginning to connect to the mobile Internet. Many tasks that originally need to be performed by a single device can be deployed on the cloud now. This trend has gradually spread to the field of automobile manufacturing. The integration of technologies such as V2V and autonomous driving has driven the development of in-vehicle networks and smart car communication technologies. However, as the number of smart cars connected to the Internet increases, a series of problems related to the security of in-vehicle communication have arisen. For example, when a car system connects to the Internet via an insecure channel and communicates with other compromised cars or roadside units, a potential attacker will launch an attack on it through an exposed service of the system. If the attacker can find the vulnerabilities of the system and implant a backdoor program to monitor and analyze the data frames sent to the car's in-vehicle network (most of these data frames are non-encrypted), then he can guess the content of the protocol between the ECUs such as the engine speed or the direction of driving, then he forges

W. Shi et al. (Eds.): SPNCE 2021, LNICST 423, pp. 35–52, 2022.
https://doi.org/10.1007/978-3-030-96791-8_3

the malicious control messages and executes the attack by sending these messages to the in-vehicle network, which may lead to very dangerous driving behavior and even threaten the personal safety of passengers.

The data transmission protocols used for the in-vehicle network such as CAN and LIN have many security problems. Mainly include but are not limited to the following points: 1. Lack of access control. Since most ECUs use fixed keys provided by vehicle manufacturers for encryption or authentication, it is easy to be intercepted by malicious attackers, and illegal access requests are initiated to read the internal storage of the ECU, and the communication interface between the vehicle and external devices is used as a springboard to launch attacks on externally connected devices. 2. Broadcast communication mechanism. CAN bus communication is based on the broadcast mechanism, and any ECU in the vehicle network can send and receive data frames. Therefore, the attacker can analyze the data frame type and content by eavesdropping on the data frame message in the channel and achieve the purpose of the attack by sending the tampered data frames to the CAN bus network. 3. Lack of an effective authentication mechanism. There is no authentication mechanism in the CAN bus protocol data frame structure. A malicious node can pretend to be a legitimate node to send an attack message, while a node receiving a spoofed message cannot distinguish whether the message is from the legitimate node or the attacker. 4. For non-encrypted data frames, ECUs in the car communicate in plain text, which lacks information confidentiality protection, and it is difficult to avoid information leakage.

1.1 Related Works

To improve the security of the CAN network, some researchers have proposed many CAN-based secure communication schemes and key agreement protocols. Woo et al. [1] have shown that attacks may be launched externally by using a wireless channel to penetrate an IVN. Palaniswamy B et al. [2] provided a protocol suite for entity authentication, key management, a secure message flow for remote transmission request frames and session key update to be applied for vehicle connection with external devices. Wu et al. [3] proposed a key management scheme for in-vehicle multi-layer electronic control units (ECUs). Pullen D [4] uses implicit certificates to derive authenticated message-based group keys for ECUs. Pan Q [5] proposed a dynamic key generation algorithm to ensure the safety of CAN bus transmission and reduce the complexity of the system. Youn T Y [6] suggested an efficient key management scheme causing no communication overhead in a session key update process. Jain S [7] utilized the physical properties of the CAN bus to generate group keys. Lee H [8] showed the possibilities of triggering unprotected remote frames in CAN 2.0B, which results in a DoS attack. X Ying [9, 10] deployed an intrusion detection system TACAN a transmitter authentication in CAN by exploiting the covert channels in IVN and proposed a new masquerading attack called cloaking attack and formal analysis for clock skew based intrusion detection system. Wang Q [11] proposes a golden entropy model based on CAN ID entropy to detect various injection attacks on the CAN bus. King Z [12] used the HMAC algorithm and timestamp to generate digest and encrypt data, which is effective against denial of service attacks or repeated attacks. Fassak S [13] used Elliptic Curve Cryptography (ECC) to establish a session key in automotive CAN networks, which is then used to derive symmetric keys for authenticating CAN frames. S. Nürnberger [14] proposed a framework for embedded controllers connected to the CAN bus, which allows both senders and receivers to authenticate exchanged data. A. I. Radu [15] proposed Leia, a lightweight authentication protocol for the Controller Area Network (CAN), which allows critical vehicle ECUs to authenticate each other providing compartmentalization and preventing some attacks.

1.2 Our Goal and Contribution

Owing to the communication in the CAN network has the characteristic of broadcasting, and the CAN protocol pays more attention to the demand for real-time communication. Therefore, it is necessary to design a lightweight key distribution protocol. some protocols [4, 5, 13] introduced above use asymmetric cryptographic algorithms in the key generation and distribution phase. It may add to the computational overhead for many ECUs with low power consumption requirements. The NSSK protocol [16] is a classic session key distribution protocol based on symmetric encryption, but it cannot identify and resist the known session key attack. Moreover, The NSSK protocol is a simple three-party protocol, which cannot fit the key distribution of other ECUs in a group composed of more than two ECUs in the actual scenes. Therefore, we propose an improved NSSK protocol by adding MAC authentication, digital signature, and time-stamping mechanisms. And we design a two-stage key distribution protocol to ensure that all ECUs in a group composed of more than two ECUs can securely get the same session key.

Our main contributions are as follows:

(1) We propose an improved session key distribution scheme based on classic Needham-Schroeder SKDS, which solves the original scheme's lack of authentication and recognition of replay attacks such as the Denning-Sacco attack, and ensures the security and verifiability of the key distribution process.
(2) The two-stage key distribution protocol we designed is suitable for the session key distribution scenario in the CAN network. To securely distribute the session key generated within a pair of ECUs to other ECUs with the same CAN-ID, we designed the Second SKDS.
(3) We analyze the security of the new protocol suite by formal analysis performed in the random oracle model and confirm our security goals using a formal verification tool named Tamarin-Prover. We finally give a comparison of the new protocol and the original protocol on security issues.

The rest of the paper is organized as follows. Section 2 introduces the preliminaries of the CAN frames and NSSK. Section 3 introduces the new protocol suite we designed. Section 4 presents the formal security analysis in the random oracle model. Section 5 discusses the protocol formal verification by using Tamarin-Prover. Section 6 concludes the work.

2 Preliminaries

2.1 CAN Frame

CAN is one of the most representative protocols often used for in-vehicle networks. In the CAN protocol, each ECU transfers information to other ECUs using a data frame. The sender ECU sends the data frames with an ID. The receiver ECU retrieves the data frame and examines the ID to identify whether the data frame is sent by the right sender ECU. The CAN protocol has two types, CAN 2.0A and CAN 2.0B, The main difference between them is that there are more 18 bits in the ID field of CAN 2.0B than which in CAN 2.0A. The data composition of the CAN 2.0B data frame is shown in Fig. 1. we give a brief introduction for these segments in the CAN data frame. SOT is a bit that represents the beginning of the data frame. The arbitration field represents the priority of the frame. Its ID field is divided into two parts: Base Identifier (11 bits) and Extended Identifier (18bits). The IDE field determines whether the Extended Identifier is used. The Control field indicates the number of bytes of data and the segment of reserved bits. Data field is a maximum of 8 bytes of content that contains the data to be transmitted to receiver ECU. CRC field is responsible to detect the transmission error segment of the frame. ACK filed represents the segment that is confirmed to be received normally.

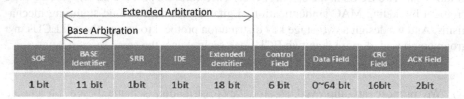

Fig. 1. The data composition of CAN 2.0B frame

2.2 System Architecture

The system architecture of the in-vehicle network is shown in Fig. 2. The ECUs are deployed in different subnets. The data bus in each subnet is indirectly connected with the central gateway. Establish communication with different subnets. The gateway can be regarded as an ECU node that provides secure communication and authentication management. We call the gateway GECU. In this scenario, GECU is responsible for session key distribution with each ECU and provides identity authentication for each ECU node.

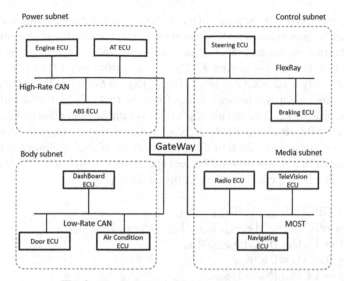

Fig. 2. The structure of the in-vehicle network

2.3 The Classic NSSK Protocol and Denning-Sacco Attack

The classic Needham-Schroeder SKDS scheme [16], which is shown in Fig. 3, GECU is responsible for generating the secret session key K_{ab}, encrypting the $K_{ab}||ID_{ECU_A}$ with the Long-term key K_{bs} of the GECU and the ECU_B to obtain the ciphertext $C_1 = \{K_{ab}, ID_{ECU_A}\}K_{bs}$, and then using the GECU and the long-term key K_{as} of ECU_A encrypts $N_a||ID_{ECU_B}||K_{ab}||C_1$ (N_a is a random number generated by ECU_A) to obtain the ciphertext $C_2 = \{N_a, ID_{ECU_B}, K_{ab}, \{K_{ab}, ID_{ECU_A}\}K_{bs}\}K_{as}$ and sends it to the sender ECU_A. After decryption by the ECU_A, the secret session key K_{ab} and C_1 are obtained. The ECU_A then sends C_1 to the ECU_B, and the ECU_B obtains the secret session key K_{ab} by decryption, and both parties use K_{ab} to encrypt communication data.

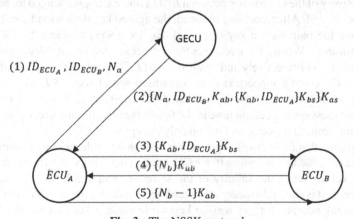

Fig. 3. The NSSK protocol

However, the classic NSSK protocol has an attack called the Denning-Sacco attack. If an adversary A records a session S between the two parties during the key distribution process of the two parties and obtains the session key K_{ab} of S. Then the adversary A initiates a new NS session S' with ECU_B, starting from step (3) of session S', and sends the previously used ticket $t = \{K_{ab}, ID_{ECU_A}\}K_{bs}$ to ECU_B. When ECU_B receives t because it cannot identify whether t comes from the real ECU_A, it will still decrypt t and accept the session key K_{ab}, and use K_{ab} to encrypt the random number N_b and send it to adversary A. After receiving N_b, the adversary A continues to forge the confirmation message $\{N_b - 1\}K_{ab}$ and send it to ECU_B. Therefore, if ECU_B continues to use K_{ab} to encrypt data, it may cause information leakage. Attack as follows, $I(ECU_A)$ denotes the adversary A who impersonates the identity of ECU_A:

1. $ECU_A \rightarrow GECU$: ID_{ECU_A}, ID_{ECU_B}, N_A
2. $GECU \rightarrow ECU_A$: $\{N_a, ID_{ECU_B}, K_{ab}, \{K_{ab}, ID_{ECU_A}\}K_{bs}\}K_{as}$
3. $I(ECU_A) \rightarrow ECU_B$: $\{K_{ab}, ID_{ECU_A}\}K_{bs}$
4. $ECU_B \rightarrow I(ECU_A)$: $\{N_b\}K_{ab}$
5. $I(ECU_A) \rightarrow ECU_B$: $\{N_b - 1\}K_{ab}$

There is a defect in classic NSSK protocol that receiver ECU_B is unable to recognize the replay message is sent by a legitimate sender ECU_A or an impersonation attacker. The protocol lacks identity verification for the sender ECU_A and time deviations as well.

3   New Protocol Suite

To solve the defects of the original NSSK, we make several modifications to the original NSSK protocol to resist the Denning-Sacco attack:

(1) Each ECU participating in key distribution is required to provide MAC verification to ensure message integrity and ensure that the message is generated by the legitimate ECU.
(2) The delivery of the session key between ECU_A and ECU_B is changed to the delivery of a secret seed. After receiving the seed, the agreed key derivation function is used to derive the pair session key (E_K, A_K). E_K for encryption and A_K for message authentication. When ECU_B receives the correct session key, it calculates the MAC and cipher-text respectively and sends them to ECU_A for session key confirmation.
(3) When ECU_A sends ciphertext data containing secret seed to ECU_B, it requires ECU_A to provide the current timestamp. To prevent ECU_B from receiving a replayed message at a certain time in the future because it cannot recognize whether it is a transmitted message and mistakenly accept it.
(4) It is required that ECU_A use the private key to sign the ciphertext containing the seed and the timestamp, and only after ECU_B can successfully use the corresponding public key to verify the validity of the signature and check the freshness of the timestamp, it is allowed to accept the secret seed to derive the session key. Otherwise ECU_B may accept a forgery session key while the attacker executes the Denning-Sacco attack by replaying the transmitted data in the past executed protocol.

The key distribution protocol in the initial session abbreviated as Initial SKDP is shown in Fig. 4. The declaration we used in the protocol is shown in Table 1.

Table 1. Notations of some Cryptography terms.

Notation	Description
ECU_i	i^{th} electronic control unit
ID_i	Identity of ECU_i
GECU	Gateway ECU
CTR_{ECU_i}	ECU_i data frame counter
$Seed_k$	Seed value of kth session
Ek_k	Encryption key of kth session
Ak_k	Authentication key of kth session
C	Ciphertext
M	Plaintext
$K_{A,i}$	Long-term symmetric key:GECU and ECU_A, i = 1 for encryption and i = 2 for authentication
$KDF_x()$	Keyed one-way function used for key derivation
H(.)	Keyed-hash Message Authentication Code (HMAC)

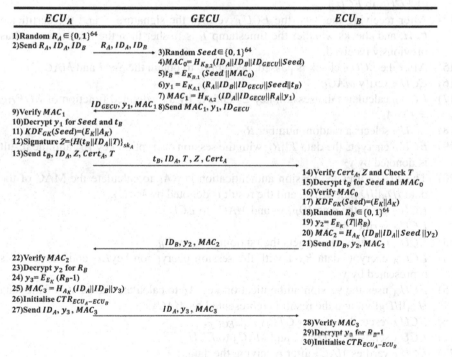

Fig. 4. The initial SKDP

The steps in the Initial SKDP are listed as follows.

(1) ECU_A selects a random number R_A.

(2) ECU_A sends the random number R_A, and its identification ID_A, and ECU_B's identification ID_B to $GECU$.

(3) $GECU$ chooses a random number as the secret seed which is denoted by $Seed$.

(4) $GECU$ calculates the MAC of data $ID_A\|ID_B\|ID_{GECU}\|Seed$ with the authentication key $K_{B,2}$ of ECU_B, and the result is denoted by MAC_0.

(5) $GECU$ uses the encryption key $K_{B,1}$ of ECU_B to encrypt the data $Seed\|MAC_0$, and the result is represented by t_B.

(6) $GECU$ uses the encryption key $K_{A,1}$ of ECU_A to encrypt the data $R_A\|ID_B\|ID_{GECU}\|Seed\|t_B$, and the result is denoted by y_1.

(7) $GECU$ uses the authentication key $K_{A,2}$ of ECU_A to calculate the MAC of the data $ID_A\|ID_{GECU}\|R_A\|y_1$, and the result is represented by MAC_1.

(8) $GECU$ sends MAC_1, y_1 and identification ID_{GECU} to ECU_A.

(9) ECU_A verifies MAC_1 after receiving the data.

(10) ECU_A decrypts y_1 to obtain the $Seed$ and t_B.

(11) ECU_A calculates the session key E_k and A_k by a predefined key derivation function of $KDF_{GK} = E_k\|A_k$.

(12) ECU_A uses the private key sk_A to calculate the digital signature $Z = \{H(t_B\|ID_A\|T)\}sk_A$, where T is the current timestamp.

(13) ECU_A sends data t_B, ID_A, Z, T and certificate $Cert$ containing the public key Pk_A of ECU_A to ECU_B.

(14) After receiving the data, the ECU_B verifies the signature Z and the certificate $Cert$, and checks whether the timestamp T is fresher than the timestamps it has previously received.

(15) After the ECU_B check is passed, decrypt t_B to obtain the $Seed$ and MAC_0.

(16) ECU_B verify MAC_0.

(17) ECU_B calculates the session key E_k and A_k by a predefined function of $KDF_{GK} = E_k\|A_k$.

(18) ECU_B selects a random number R_B.

(19) ECU_B encrypts the data $T\|R_B$ with the session encryption key E_k, and the result is denoted by y_2.

(20) The ECU_B uses the session authentication key A_k to calculate the MAC of the data $ID_B\|ID_A\|Seed\|y_2$, and the result is denoted by MAC_2.

(21) ECU_B sends the data ID_B, y_2 and MAC_2 to ECU_A.

(22) ECU_A verifies MAC_2.

(23) ECU_A decrypts y_2 and gets the random number R_B.

(24) ECU_A encrypts data R_B-1 with the session encryption keyE_k, and the result is represented by y_3.

(25) ECU_A uses the session authentication key A_k to calculate the MAC of the data $ID_A\|ID_B\|y_3$, and the result is represented by MAC_3.

(26) ECU_A resets the counter $CTR_{ECU_A-ECU_B}$.

(27) ECU_A sends data ID_A, y_3 and MAC_3 to ECU_B.

(28) ECU_B verifies MAC_3 after receiving the data.

(29) ECU_B decrypts y_3 to obtain $R_B - 1$, confirming that R_B is received correctly by ECU_A.

(30) ECU_B resets the counter $CTR_{ECU_A-ECU_B}$.

When there are more receiver ECUs, the sender ECU needs to negotiate with the GECU to obtain the seed and continue to send it to other ECUs. The protocol in the subsequent session abbreviated as Second SKDP is shown in Fig. 5.

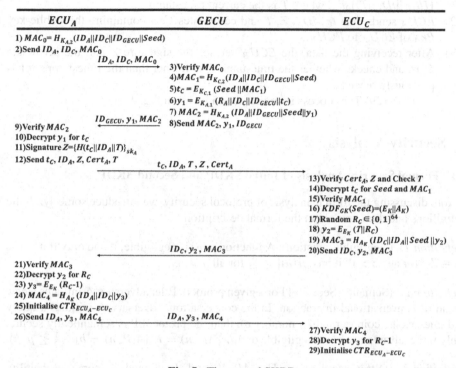

Fig. 5. The second SKDP

The steps in the Second SKDP are listed as follows.

(1) ECU_A uses its authentication key $K_{A,2}$ to calculate the MAC of the data $ID_A \| ID_C \| ID_{GECU} \| Seed$ and the result is represented by MAC_0.

(2) ECU_A sends ID_A, ID_C, MAC_0 to $GECU$.

(3) $GECU$ verifies MAC_0.

(4) $GECU$ uses the authentication key $K_{C,2}$ of ECU_C to calculate the MAC of the data $ID_A \| ID_C \| ID_{GECU} \| Seed$ and the result is represented by MAC_1.

(5) $GECU$ encrypts the data $Seed \| MAC_1$ with the encryption key $K_{C,1}$ of ECU_C, and the result is represented by t_C.

(6) $GECU$ uses the encryption key $K_{A,1}$ of ECU_A to encrypt data $R_A \| ID_C \| ID_{GECU} \| t_C$, and the result is denoted by y_1.

(7) $GECU$ uses ECU_A's authentication key $K_{A,2}$ to calculate the MAC of the data $ID_A \| ID_{GECU} \| Seed \| y_1$, and the result is represented by MAC_2.

(8) $GECU$ sends data MAC_2, y_1, ID_{GECU} to ECU_A.
(9) ECU_A receives data to verify MAC_2.
(10) ECU_A decrypts the data y_1 to obtain t_C.
(11) ECU_A uses the private key sk_A to calculate the digital signature $Z = \{H(t_C\|ID_A\|T)\}sk_A$, where T is the current timestamp.
(12) ECU_A sends data t_C, ID_A, Z, T and certificates $Cert$ containing the public key Pk_A of ECU_A to ECU_B.
(13) After receiving the data, the ECU_B verifies the signature Z and the certificate $Cert$, and checks whether the timestamp T is fresher than the timestamps it has previously received.

      (14)–(29) The process is similar to (15)–(30) in Fig. 4.

4   Security Analysis

4.1   Formal Security Analysis of Initial SKDP and Second SKDP

Before discussing the formal analysis of protocol security, we introduce some symbolic definitions and theorems about the formal description.

Definition 1: (Negligible function): A function $\mu(n)$ is negligible, if and only if it exists $n_0 \in Z^+$ for any c > 0, it has $|\mu(n)| \leq \frac{1}{n^c}$ for all $n > n_0$.

Definition 2: (Semantic Security) For a given protocol P, let adversary A initiates a new round of conversational interaction. In the conversation, adversary A initiates a query and guesses the coin (a random number b), then the protocol P is semantically secure. Only if the advantage of A is negligible or $Adv_A^{SS}(P, n) = Pr[A(P, n) = b] - \frac{1}{2} \leq \mu(n)$.

Definition 3: (Difference lemma) Use M, N, and F defined in some probability distribution. If $M \wedge \neg F \equiv N \wedge \neg F$, then $Pr[M] - Pr[N] \leq Pr[F]$.

Theorem: For a given protocol Initial SKDP or Second SKDP, there are the following assumptions: a long-term key can be guessed with the advantage Adv_P^{SS}, the length of the MAC value generated by the hash function is l bits, and the signature generated by the digital signature function is m bits, The encryption function can ensure k bits security. Then the semantic security of the protocol can be broken by adversary A with the advantage $Adv_P^{SS} \leq \frac{q_{hash}^2}{2^l} + Adv_{sk} + \frac{q_{sig}^2}{2^m} + \frac{q_{Enc}^2}{2^k}$, whose q_{hash} represents the number of times the hash function oracle is queried, q_{sig} and q_{Enc} also represent the number of times that the signature function oracle is queried and the encryption function oracle, respectively.

    Before starting to prove the theorem, we define three random oracle model query operations: $Hash(\cdot)$, $Sig(\cdot)$, $Enc(\cdot)$.

Hash(·): The adversary A initiates a hash query corresponding to the plain text M or the ciphertext C. If the corresponding record has been stored in the oracle's hash table H. according to the format (M, f) or (C, g), the hash oracle will The records f and g stored in the hash table H will be returned to the adversary A. Otherwise, the oracle returns the generated random numbers f' or g' to the adversary A, and stores (M, f') and (C, g') in the hash table H.

Enc(·): The adversary A initiates a query for the encryption result corresponding to the plain text M. If the corresponding record has been stored in the ciphertext table E of the oracle according to the format (M, C), the ciphertext oracle will store it in the ciphertext table E The record C is returned to the adversary A. Otherwise, the oracle returns the generated random number C' to the adversary A, and stores (M, C') in the ciphertext table E.

Sig(·): The adversary A initiates a query for the signature result corresponding to message M. If the corresponding record should be stored in the signature table S of the oracle according to the format (M, S), the signature oracle will return the record S stored in the signature table S To the adversary A. Otherwise, the oracle returns the generated random number S' to the adversary, and stores (M, S') in the signature table S.

In addition to the above-defined oracle model query operations, we also define the following query operations:

Send(·): Simulate the query sent by the adversary A.

Execute(·): Query that simulates an adversary's passive attack.

RevealSessKey(·): Simulate the query that the adversary A forces the protocol entity to reveal the session key.

Corrupt(·): Simulate the query of the adversary A to obtain the long-term key held by the protocol entity.

Test(·): Initiated by adversary A at the end of the game. The queried entity returns an unbiased coin value b. If $b = 1$, it returns the real session key, otherwise it returns a random number. If the opponent can distinguish b correctly, the game is won.

The following is the proof process of the agreement Initial SKDP and Second SKDP:

Proof: We define five games G_0, G_1, G_2, G_3, and G_4. S_i is the event when adversary A wins the game G_i, i = 0, 1, 2, 3, 4.

Game G_0: Describes a real attack on the semantic security of protocol P. Adversary A first sends the activation protocol and then uses it to monitor the protocol information. After collecting information through a probabilistic polynomial-time running and waiting for the query, adversary A initiates the query. The condition for adversary A to win the game is that it can successfully guess the bit b. According to the definition of semantic security, the advantage of adversary A for winning the game in this game is $Adv_P^{SS} = |Pr(S_0) - \frac{1}{2}|$.

Game G_1: The only difference between this game and the previous game G_0 is the addition of a collision with MACs. If a MAC collision occurs at a certain stage in the protocol, adversary A can modify the secret seed and force ECUs to accept forged data in the explicit key confirmation stage. According to the birthday paradox, the advantage of querying the hash table is at least approximately $\frac{q_{hash}^2}{2^l}$, Use the difference lemma to express the advantage $|Pr(S_1) - Pr(S_0)| \leq \frac{q_{hash}^2}{2^l}$.

Game G_2: This game is aimed at the key secrecy of the protocol. In this game, adversary A initiates a query for the expired session key by asking. But even with an expired session key, the adversary still needs a long-term key to calculate the current session key. The advantage Adv_{sk} of the adversary A to obtain the long-term key is used to indicate that the advantage of adversary A replacing the long-term key by using a random number is Adv_{sk}, so the advantage difference between the two games is $|Pr(S_2) - Pr(S_1)| \leq Adv_{sk}$.

Game G_3: This game is different from the previous game G_2 in which, adversary A tries to find the signature collision. If a signature collision occurs, adversary A can make the participants accept a forged ciphertext and timestamp. In the end, adversary A can successfully cheat the participants to confirm the wrong session key that they have received. This advantage is that $|Pr(S_3) - Pr(S_2)| \leq \frac{q_{sig}^2}{2^l}$.

Game G_4: This game is different from the previous game G_3 in which, adversary A tries to look up the hash table to find the collision of the ciphertext. If adversary A finds a collision, it can forge a fake secret seed and send it. The advantage of adversary A in this game by querying the hash table to try to collide is $\frac{q_{Enc}^2}{2^k}$, so the advantage of the game is $|Pr(S_4) - Pr(S_3)| \leq \frac{q_{Enc}^2}{2^k}$.

Based on the above proofs, the advantage that adversary A can win the game is calculated according to the triangle inequality as follows:

$$
\begin{aligned}
Adv_P^{SS} &= |Pr(S_4) - Pr(S_0)| \\
&= |Pr(S_4) - Pr(S_3) + Pr(S_3) - Pr(S_2) + Pr(S_2) - Pr(S_1) + Pr(S_1) - Pr(S_0)| \\
&\leq |Pr(S_4) - Pr(S_3)| + |Pr(S_3) - Pr(S_2)| + |Pr(S_2) - Pr(S_1)| + |Pr(S_1) - Pr(S_0)| \\
&\leq \frac{q_{hash}^2}{2^l} + Adv_{sk} + \frac{q_{sig}^2}{2^l} + \frac{q_{Enc}^2}{2^k}
\end{aligned}
$$

Since the advantage between each game is negligible. Therefore, for a probabilistic polynomial-time adversary A, the advantage of looking for an attack on the protocol model is negligible. According to the semantic security theorem, if the long-term key is not leaked, the protocol is semantic security.

4.2 Informal Security Analysis of Initial SKDP and Second SKDP

Proposition1: The protocols Initial SKDP and Second SKDP provide session key freshness. In the protocols, Initial SKDP and Second SKDP, the freshness of the session key is guaranteed by *Seed*, a fresh random number to generate the session key through the derivation function KDF.

Proposition2: For a given protocol Initial SKDP and Second SKDP, any replay of the message will be detected and rejected by the receiver. For example, in Initial SKDP, when an attacker impersonates ECU_A and replays data and signatures with timestamp T and ciphertext t_B in step 13 to ECU_B, ECU_B will detect the timestamp T contained in the data is the same as the previously received one, so the received data will be discarded. In other processes of sending and receiving data, the receiver will use the same authentication key as the sender to verify the MAC information in the message after receiving the data. If the verification fails and the received data is discarded. The ciphertext data received from step 21 is checked by ECU_A. If it does not contain the timestamp T sent in step 13, it will be rejected. If the ciphertext data which is sent from step 27 and is received by ECU_B is not $R_B - 1$ after decryption, the message will be rejected. The proof for Second SKDP is similar, so the protocol can resist replay attacks.

Proposition3: For a given protocol Initial SKDP and Second SKDP, any forgery attack will fail with an overwhelming probability. Because the adversary wants to attack (win the game) successfully, he must obtain the long-term keys on ECU_A and ECU_B to successfully solve the seed used to derive the session key. And the adversary also needs to be able to provide a valid signature that can be verified. This requires the adversary to know the private key of the signing party to successfully forge the signature. The difficulty of guessing the signature private key is a discrete logarithmic problem, which is difficult to solve in probabilistic polynomial time.

Proposition4: The given protocols Initial SKDP and Second SKDP can resist man-in-the-middle attacks. The adversary may control the communication channel and use the information exchanged between communication entities to carry out the attack. The adversary uses the existing communication records or the forged information items to communicate with the two parties respectively, that is, a combination of replay attacks and forgery attacks to carry out man-in-the-middle attacks. According to the results discussed above, these attack methods will be an overwhelming probability of failure.

5 Security Verification

In this section, We use Tamarin-prover to perform a security validation of our proposed protocol. For simplicity, we only present a partial script of Initial SKDP to introduce the lemmas of security goals.

5.1 Tamarin Overview

The Tamarin-prover is a powerful tool for symbolic modeling and analysis of security protocols. It takes a security protocol model as input, specifying the actions taken by agents running the protocol in different roles (e.g., the protocol initiator, the protocol responder, and the trusted key server), to demonstrate that even when arbitrarily many instances of the protocol's roles are interleaved in parallel, together with the actions of the adversary, the protocol fulfills its specified properties, and we can visualize the conditions under which the lemma proves successful or fails through the interactive mode.

Tamarin uses multiset rewriting to rewrite the rules of the protocol and lemmas. The description of a secure protocol consists of three parts: terms, facts, and rules.

Terms, consisting of variables, constants, and functional symbols that can represent the knowledge of the protocol participants, the adversary can acquire knowledge through the public terms of the protocol participants.

Facts represent the type of protocol variables. There are three types of special facts are built-in Tamarin-prover, In(), Out(), and Fr(). Respectively to simulate interactions with untrusted networks and simulate the generation of unique fresh values.

Rules declared as [L]-[A]->[R], represent the premises, action facts, and conclusion of the Protocol. The action facts can be used to express the interaction of the protocol, such as receiving events, and security properties for variables in subsequent lemmas such as interaction authentication and key privacy. Below are several important properties in protocol security validation.

(1) Aliveness is a basic authentication that ensures that an expected communication party performs certain events, namely that this communication object is present.
(2) Non-injective agreement requires both parties to agree on the transmission of data.
(3) Injective agreement needs to meet two conditions: a source and an intended destination agree on variables, and for every committed variable by a source, there uniquely exists an intended destination that accepts the variable.

In addition to the attributes listed above, the validation of the security protocol requires paying attention to data secrecy. That means a particular message content cannot be known by the adversary unless an honest entity exchanges confidential information with the captured entity. When verifying the above security properties, a lemma called the existence trace is often added to verify that the state in the protocol specification is accessible.

5.2 Verification of the Initial SKDP

We verify the security properties of the initial session key distribution protocol by clarifying the following lemma, involving the security attributes required to be verified: executable, the secrecy of session key, non-injective agreement, and injective consistent injective agreement.

```
lemma executability:
   exists-trace
   " Ex A B Rb kab #i #j #k.
     Commit_B(A,B,<'A', 'B', dec(Rb),kab>)@#i
   & Commit_A(A,B,<'A', 'B', Rb,kab>)@#j & #j<#i
   & Running_A(A,B,<'A', 'B', dec(Rb),kab>)@#j
   & Running_B(A,B,<'A', 'B', Rb,kab>)@#k & #k<#j
   & not(Ex #r1. Reveal(A)@#r1)
   & not(Ex #r2. Reveal(B)@#r2) "
```

The above lemma requires that when ECU_B receives the session key *kab*, at time *k* by executing Running_B to encrypt the random number *Nb* with *kab*, there is always ECU_A receiving the message at time *j* by executing Commit_A and $k < j$. Similarly, when ECU_A receives *Nb* and decrypts it, at the same time *j* runs Running_A to encrypt $Nb - 1$ with *kab* and sends it out. At this time, there must be ECU_B that receives the message by executing Commit_B at the time *i* and $j < i$. According to this lemma, the executability between states can be proved.

```
lemma Secrecy:
  " not( Ex A B m #i .
      Secret(A, B, m)@ #i
      & (Ex #r. K(m) @ #r)
      & not(Ex #r. Reveal(B) @ #r)
      & not(Ex #r. Reveal(A) @ #r)
  ) "
```

The above lemma describes the secrecy of the distributed session key between ECU_A and ECU_B, that no session key *m* between ECU_A and ECU_B is known by the adversary at time *r*, if not the long-term key used in ECU_A or ECU_B is leaked.

```
lemma agreement_ECUA:
"All A B t #i.
   Commit_A(A,B,t) @i
   ==> (Ex #j. Running_B(A,B,t) @j  & j < i)
     | (Ex #r. Reveal(A)@r)
     | (Ex #r. Reveal(B)@r)"
```

The above lemma describes the non-injective agreement of ECU_A, that is when ECU_A receives a message at the time *i*, there must be ECU_B sending the message at time *j* and both ECU_A and ECU_B are honest, Similarly, the non-injective agreement lemma agreement_ECUB on ECU_B can be listed by imitating it.

lemma injectiveagreement_ECUB:
"All A B t #i.
Commit_B(A,B,t) @i
==> (Ex #j. Running_A(A,B,t) @j
    & j < i
    & not (Ex A2 B2 #i2. Commit_B(A2,B2,t) @i2
            & not (#i2 = #i)))
    | (Ex #r. Reveal(A)@r)
    | (Ex #r. Reveal(B)@r)"

The above lemma describes the injective agreement of ECU_B, that is when ECU_B receives a message at the time i, it must be sent by ECU_A at time j, and there is no other time in the protocol execution round that ECU_B can receive the message, that is, sending and receiving is injective, and both ECU_A and ECU_B are honest. In the same way, the injective agreement lemma injectiveagreement_ECUA on ECU_A can be listed by imitating it.

5.3 Verification of Second SKDP

We verify that the Second SKDP is similar to those in Sect. 5.2, so we omit the verification details and only give a conclusion.

For each protocol, we list four lemmas for verifying security properties. They are executable, non-injective agreement, injective agreement, and session key secrecy. As stated in the lemma mentioned in the previous section. The executable lemma verifies the reachability of the protocol state. The non-injective agreement lemma verifies that there is a running entity corresponding to each commit operation. The injective agreement lemma verifies that the messaging between the two parties is sequential and injective. Session key confidentiality verifies that the adversary's knowledge does not contain the session key.

Table 2 provides the verification results for all protocols. It can be seen that all the protocols proposed in this article have passed the security verification of the protocol, that is, the key management is secure in the scenario proposed in this article.

Table 2. Verified lemma for the new protocol suite.

	Executable	Non-injective agreement	Injective agreement	Session key secrecy
Initial SKDP	√	√	√	√
Second SKDP	√	√	√	√

We compare the new protocol with the classic NSSK protocol and an improved NSSK protocol in [17] with several security attribute levels, and the results are shown in

Table 3. It can be seen that the new key distribution protocol we designed considers more security elements than others. It's more suitable for fast and efficient key distribution among ECUs that require exclusive session keys in the in-vehicle network.

Table 3. Comparison of new-protocol suite and NSSK.

	NSSK	Improved NSSK in [17]	Initial SKDP & Second SKDP
Key authentication	Implicit	Implicit	Explicit
Mutual entity authentication	No	No	Yes
Session key freshness	Yes	Yes	Yes
Resistance to Denning-Sacco attack	No	Yes	Yes
Resistance to replay attack	No	Yes	Yes
Resistance to MITM	Yes	Yes	Yes
Provable security	No	Yes	Yes
Key synchronization within the group	No	No	Yes

6 Summary

We propose an improved key update scheme based on Needham-Schroeder SKDP to distribute session keys, solve the shortcomings of the original scheme's lack of resistance to the Denning-Sacco attack, and ensure the security and verifiability of the key distribution process. It can resist known attacks such as replay attacks and man-in-the-middle attacks. Next, we execute formal analysis on the new protocol by using a random oracle model to simulate cryptographic games, the result proves the semantic security of the protocol. Finally, by using the Tamarin tool to verify the security properties of the protocol, it proves that the protocol has security objectives such as mutual entity authentication, explicit key confirmation, key authentication, and session key confidentiality. Compared with the scheme of updating the session keys of all ECU nodes as a whole, our scheme is more suitable for fast and efficient key distribution of single-point or multipoint CAN communication networks.

Acknowledgements. This work was supported in part by the National Natural Science Foundation of China under Grant 61872069, 62072090, and in part by the Fundamental Research Funds for the Central Universities under Grant N2017012.

References

1. Woo, S., Jo, H.J., Kim, I.S., et al.: A practical security architecture for in-vehicle CAN-FD. IEEE Transactions on Intelligent Transportation Systems **17**, 2248–2261 (2016)

2. Palaniswamy, B., et al.: An efficient authentication scheme for intra-vehicular controller area network. IEEE Trans. Inf. Forensics Secur. **PP**(99), 1 (2020)
3. Wu, Z., Zhao, J., Zhu, Y., et al.: Research on in-vehicle key management system under upcoming vehicle network architecture. Electronics **8**(9), 1026 (2019)
4. Pullen, D., Anagnostopoulos, N.A., Arul, T., et al.: Using implicit certification to efficiently establish authenticated group keys for in-vehicle networks. In: 2019 IEEE Vehicular Networking Conference (VNC). IEEE (2019)
5. Pan, Q., Tan, J.: A dynamic key generation scheme based on CAN bus. In: 2019 10th International Conference on Information Technology in Medicine and Education (ITME) (2019)
6. Youn, T.Y., Lee, Y., Woo, S.: Practical sender authentication scheme for in-vehicle CAN with efficient key management. IEEE Access **PP**(99), 1 (2020)
7. Jain, S., Guajardo, J.: Physical layer group key agreement for automotive controller area networks. In: Gierlichs, B., Poschmann, A. (eds.) CHES 2016. LNCS, vol. 9813, pp. 85–105. Springer, Heidelberg (2016). https://doi.org/10.1007/978-3-662-53140-2_5
8. Lee, H., Jeong, S.H., Kim, H.K.: OTIDS: a novel intrusion detection system for in-vehicle network by using remote frame. In: 2017 15th Annual Conference on Privacy, Security and Trust (PST). IEEE (2018)
9. Ying, X., Bernieri, G., Conti, M., Poovendran, R.: TACAN: transmitter authentication through covert channels in controller area networks. arXiv:1903.05231 (2019)
10. Ying, X., Sagong, S.U., Clark, A., Bushnell, L., Poovendran, R.: Shape of the cloak: formal analysis of clock skew-based intrusion detection system in controller area networks. IEEE Trans. Inf. Forensics Secur. **14**(9), 2300–2314 (2019)
11. Wang, Q., Lu, Z., Qu, G.: An entropy analysis based intrusion detection system for controller area network in vehicles. In: 2018 31st IEEE International System-on-Chip Conference (SOCC), pp. 90–95. IEEE (2018)
12. King, Z., Yu, S.: Investigating and securing communications in the controller area network (CAN). In: 2017 International Conference on Computing, Networking and Communications (ICNC), pp. 814–818. IEEE (2017)
13. Fassak, S., Idrissi, Y.E.H.E., Zahid, N., Jedra, M.: A secure protocol for session keys establishment between ECUs in the CAN bus. In: Proceedings of the International Conference on Wireless Networks and Mobile Communications (WINCOM), Rabat, Morocco, 1–4 November 2017, pp. 37–42 (2017)
14. Nürnberger, S., Rossow, C.: vatiCAN–vetted, authenticated CAN bus. In: Gierlichs, B., Poschmann, A. (eds.) CHES 2016. LNCS, vol. 9813, pp. 106–124. Springer, Heidelberg (2016). https://doi.org/10.1007/978-3-662-53140-2_6
15. Radu, A.I., Garcia, F.D.: LeiA: a lightweight authentication protocol for CAN. In: Askoxylakis, I., Ioannidis, S., Katsikas, S., Meadows, C. (eds.) ESORICS 2016. LNCS, vol. 9879, pp. 283–300. Springer, Cham (2016). https://doi.org/10.1007/978-3-319-45741-3_15
16. Needham, R., Schroeder, M.: Using encryption for authentication in large networks of computers. Commun. ACM **21**(12), 993–999 (1978)
17. Jin-Gang, Y., Zhi-Gang, Z.: An improved NSSK authentication protocol and its formal analysis. In: 2017 10th International Conference on Intelligent Computation Technology and Automation (ICICTA) (2017)

Research on Two-Party Cooperative Aigis-sig Digital Signature Protocol

Fu Yu and Zhao Xiufeng[✉]

Information Engineering University, Zhengzhou 450001, China

Abstract. The digital signature scheme is essential for electronic commerce and e-government security authentication. With the rapid advancement of mobile internet technologies, safe key storage in mobile terminals has become a new challenge. To solve the leak of the signature private key, a method for generating a two-party cooperative signature has been proposed. That is, each participant generates the signature secret key and shares it with the other after which the signature is generated interactively. The method is robust because one party cannot recover the secret key, which not only guarantees the correctness of the signature but can resist the security implications caused by the corruption of a single mobile terminal. Considering the threat from quantum computing technology to conventional public-key cryptographic algorithms, in this paper, the lattice-based post-quantum digital signature algorithm, Aigis-sig, published in the international conference on public-key cryptography is discussed. Furthermore, the two-party Aigis-sig signature protocol is proposed. The protocol contains two sub-protocols: distributed secret key generation and collaborative signing protocol. In addition, the homomorphic encryption scheme is introduced in the protocol to ensure that the intermediate of the protocol does not reveal the private key information. The evaluation demonstrates that the protocol has correctness and feasibility. In the case that both parties are honest, the cooperative signature is existential unforgeability against the chosen-message attack.

Keywords: Post-quantum algorithm · Digital signature · Homomorphic encryption · Aigis-sig · Cooperative signature

1 Introduction

The digital signature is applied in identity authentication, data integrity, nonrepudiation, and anonymity. The signer uses the private key to generates the message's signature, and the verifier uses the public key to verify the signature's validity. However, some mobile terminals' security in the mobile internet application is poor, and the storage security of the private key is difficult to guarantee. Therefore, this paper introduces a two-party cooperative digital signature generation method. Two-party collaborate to generate a digital signature, namely, the generation of the private key and signature is distributed. The signing procedure is realized by the interaction of the two-party, and any participant cannot recover the integrated private key, which ensures both the

W. Shi et al. (Eds.): SPNCE 2021, LNICST 423, pp. 53–63, 2022.
https://doi.org/10.1007/978-3-030-96791-8_4

correctness of the signature and the security of the signature private key. The verification process can be performed by a user using the authentication public key. The two-party cooperative generation of the digital signature can achieve better robustness and resist the weakness brought by one-party corruption. Even if one party's share of the signature key of one party is leaked, the private key of the signature will remain secure. Currently, some two-party and multiparty schemes based on the elliptic curve signature algorithm (ECDSA) have been proposed in [1, 2], and [3]. However, for post-quantum digital signature schemes, such as the CRYSTALS-Dilithium [4] and its improved algorithm Aigis-sig [5], no researchers have proposed two-party or multiparty signing schemes.

In this paper, we consider a two-party digital signature protocol based on Aigis-sig. We describe how one can build a distributed key generation and collaborative signing protocol for Aigis-sig. Our protocol achieves coordinative generating Aigis-sig signature resorts to homomorphic encryption [6] by two-party. In Sect. 2, the specific interaction process of the protocol is given and the correctness of the signature protocol is proved. In Sect. 3, the efficiency of the protocol is analyzed and the unforgeability of the cooperative signature is proved.

2 Preliminaries

2.1 Aigis-sig

Aigis-sig is a lattice-based signature scheme [5], constructed using the Fiat-Shamir heuristic [7, 8], whose security is based on the hardness of the asymmetric module learning with errors (AMLWE) problem and the asymmetric module small integer solutions (AMSIS) problem [5]. Compared with the Dilithium scheme [4], the Aigis-sig scheme can achieve better comprehensive efficiency without changing the security, and the lengths of the public key, private key, and signature are smaller. Considering both security and efficiency, the template version of the scheme without compressing the public verify key has been chosen in our protocol. The scheme includes three algorithms: Key generation, signing procedure, and verification, described as follows:

Key Generation Algorithm. $Aigis.sig - KeyGen(1^\kappa)$: At first, the κ is defined as the secure parameter. The key generation algorithm randomly chooses a seed $\rho \xleftarrow{\$} \{0, 1\}^{256}$ and generates a matrix $A = Expand(\rho) \in R_q^{k \times l}$, each of whose entries is a polynomial belong to the ring $R_q = \mathbb{Z}_q[X]/(X^N + 1)$. Afterward, the algorithm samples random secret key vectors $(s_1, s_2) \xleftarrow{\$} S_{\eta_1}^k \times S_{\eta_2}^l$. S_η denotes a polynomial set in $R = \mathbb{Z}[X]/(X^N + 1)$, each polynomial's coefficient belongs to a finite set $\{-\eta, \ldots, \eta\}$ in S_η. Finally, the public key is computed as $t = As_1 + s_2 \in R_q^k$, and the digest of the public key $tr = CRH(pk) \in \{0, 1\}^{384}$ is produced through a collection-resistant hash function $CRH: \{0, 1\}^* \rightarrow \{0, 1\}^{384}$. The key generation algorithm returns $pk = (\rho, t)$ and $sk = (\rho, tr, s_1, s_2)$. All algebraic operations in this scheme are assumed to be over the polynomial ring R_q.

Signing Algorithm. $Aigis.sig - Sign(sk, M)$: Given the secret key $sk = (\rho, tr, s_1, s_2)$ and message M, the signing algorithm computes the digest $\mu = CRH(tr||M)$ of the message, and performs the following steps:

- Sample random vector $y \overset{\$}{\leftarrow} S^l_{\gamma_1-1}$;
- Compute $w = Ay \in R^k_q$ and $w_1 = HighBits_q(w, 2\gamma_2)$;
- Compute the challenge $c = H(\mu, w_1)$, $z = y + cs_1$, and $u = w - cs_2$. Denote B_τ as the set element of R that have τ coefficients are either -1 or 1 and the rest are 0, and the hash function is defined as $H : \{0, 1\}^* \rightarrow B_\tau$.
- Compute $(r_1, r_0) = Decompose_q(u, 2\gamma_2)$;
- The potential signature is then computed as $\sigma = (z, c)$, if the rejection sampling condition $\|z\|_\infty < \gamma_1 - \beta_1$, $\|r_0\|_\infty < \gamma_2 - \beta_2$, and $r_1 = w_1$ is satisfied. If not, restart the procedure from the sampling random vector $y \overset{\$}{\leftarrow} S^l_{\gamma_1-1}$.

The signing algorithm returns the signature $\sigma = (z, c)$.

Verification. $Aigis.sig - Verify(pk, M, \sigma)$. Given the public key (ρ, t), message M, and signature $\sigma = (z, c)$, the verifying algorithm computes $A = Expand(\rho)$, $\mu = CRH(CRH(pk)\|M)$, $w'_1 = HighBits_q(Az - ct, 2\gamma_2)$. Later, the hash value $c' = H(\mu, w'_1)$ is computed. Then algorithm returns 1 if $\|z\|_\infty < \gamma_1 - \beta_1$ and $c' = c$, otherwise returns 0 (Table 1).

Table 1. Decompose algorithm in Aigis-sig scheme

$Decompose_q(r, \alpha)$:
- $r = r \, mod^+ q$
- $r_0 = r \, mod^\pm \alpha$
- if $r - r_0 = q - 1$
- then $r_1 = 0$; $r_0 = r_0 - 1$
- else $r_1 = (r - r_0)/\alpha$
- return (r_1, r_0)

According to $(r_1, r_0) = Decompose_q(r, \alpha)$, the $r_1 = HighBits_q(r, \alpha)$ and $r_0 = LowBits_q(r, \alpha)$ have been defined to extract the "higher-order" bits and "lower-order" bits from the element r in $\mathbb{Z}_q$.

For an even positive integer α, the Aigis-sig scheme defines $r' = r \, mod^\pm \alpha$ as the unique element in the range $(-\frac{\alpha}{2}, \frac{\alpha}{2}]$ such that $r' = r \, mod \, \alpha$. For an odd positive integer α, the scheme defines $r' = r \, mod^\pm \alpha$ as the unique element in the range $[-\frac{\alpha-1}{2}, \frac{\alpha-1}{2}]$ such that $r' = r \, mod \, \alpha$. For any positive integer α, the scheme defines $r' = r \, mod^+ \alpha$ as the unique element in the range $[0, \alpha)$ such that $r' = r \, mod \, \alpha$, When the above algorithm is applied to a polynomial, the implication is that the corresponding operation is applied independently to each coefficient of the polynomial. The following lemma claims a crucial property of the above supporting algorithm, which is necessary for the correctness and security of the Aigis-sig scheme.

Lemma 1 [4] . if $\|s\|_\infty \leq \beta$ and $\|LowBits_q(r, \gamma)\|_\infty \leq \frac{\gamma}{2} - \beta$, we have:

$$HighBits_q(r, \gamma) = HighBits_q(r + s, \gamma)$$

2.2 Homomorphic Encryption Scheme

Homomorphic encryption is a cryptographic primitive that allows users to perform arithmetic operations on encrypted data without decrypting it. if it allows arbitrary boolean or arithmetic circuits to be homomorphically evaluated, it is called fully homomorphic encryption. The first fully homomorphic encryption scheme was invented by Gentry in 2009 [9], and since then many efficient results have been introduced, such as Bra12 [10], BGV [11], GSW [12], FHEW [13], and CKKS [6].

In general, a homomorphic encryption scheme is a group of probabilistic polynomial-time (PPT) algorithms as follows (is the security parameter):

Key Generation. $KeyGen(\kappa, L)$: The inputs are the security parameter κ and the level parameter L, and it outputs an public encrypted key pk, a public evaluation key evk, and a secret decrypted key sk.

Encryption Algorithm. $Enc_{pk}(m)$: The input is public key pk and plaintext m, it outputs the ciphertext ct.

Decryption Algorithm. $Dec_{sk}(ct)$: The input is the secret key sk and ciphertext ct, it outputs the plaintext m.

Ciphertext Homomorphic Addition Evaluation. $Add_{evk}(ct_1, ct_2)$: The input is the ciphertext ct_1 and ct_2 of the plaintext m_1 and m_2. It outputs the ciphertext ct_{add} of the $m_1 + m_2$.

Ciphertext Homomorphic Multiply Evaluation. $Mult_{evk}(ct_1, ct_2)$: The input is the ciphertext ct_1 and ct_2 of the plaintext m_1 and m_2. It outputs the ciphertext $m_1 \cdot m_2$ of the ct_{mult}.

Homomorphic Evaluation. $HomEval_{HE}(evk_{HE}, f, ct_1, \ldots, ct_g)$: Using the evaluation key evk_{HE} applies a function f to ciphertexts $ct_i(i = 1, \ldots, g)$ and outputs a ciphertext ct_f, where f is an arithmetic circuit with addition and multiplication. We denote $ct_1 \oplus ct_2$ as the homomorphic addition of the ciphertexts ct_1 and ct_2, and the homomorphic multiplication is denoted as $ct_1 \otimes ct_2$.

2.3 Definition of Security

Assume that a standard digital signature scheme is denoted as $\pi = $ (KeyGen, Sign, Verify). The security of standard digital signatures is defined as follows [5]:

EXPERIMENT 1.3.1. ($Expt - Sign_{S,\pi}(1^\kappa)$)

1. $(pk, sk) \leftarrow KeyGen(1^\kappa)$

2. $(M^*, \sigma^*) \leftarrow S^{Sign_{sk}(\cdot)}(pk)$

3. Let Q be the set of all (M, σ) queried by S to its oracle. Then, the output of the experiment equals 1 if and only if $(M^*, \sigma^*) \notin Q$ and $Verify_{pk}(M^*, \sigma^*) = 1$

Definition 1.3.1. If for every PPT adversary S, there exists a negligible function λ such that for every κ,

$$Pr[Expt - Sign_{S,\pi}(1^\kappa) = 1] \leq \lambda(\kappa)$$

We announce that the digital signature scheme π satisfies the strongly existential unforgeability against adaptive chosen-message attack (SUF-CMA).

Next, we define the security of a distributed signing protocol.

EXPERIMENT 1.3.2. ($Expt - DistSign_{A,\Pi}(1^\kappa)$)

$\pi = (KeyGen, Sign, Verify)$ is a standard digital signature scheme.

1. $(M^*, \sigma^*) \leftarrow A^{\Pi(\cdot, \cdot)}(pk)$

2. Let Q be the set of all M queried by A to its oracle. Then, the output of the experiment equals 1 if and only if $M^* \notin Q$ and $Verify_{pk}(M^*, \sigma^*) = 1$.

If the adversary A conducts adaptive chosen-message cooperative signature queries with polynomial times and can forge the cooperative signature of the message that has not been inquired, the experiment returns 1, that is, the adversary wins the experiment and corrupts the scheme.

Definition 1.3.2. If for every PPT adversary A, there exists a negligible function λ' such that for every κ,

$$Pr[Expt - DistSign_{A,\Pi}(1^\kappa) = 1] \leq \lambda'(\kappa)$$

Then, we state that the two-party signing protocol Π that based on the signature scheme π is security.

3   Two-Party Aigis-sig Signing Protocol

In this section, based on the Aigis-sig scheme [5], we present our two-party Aigis-sig signing protocol resort to homomorphic encryption [6]. The protocol includes two sub-protocols: the distributed key generation protocol and the collaborative signing protocol. Without loss of generality, we mark the two participants as P_1 and P_2, respectively. Before proceeding with the two protocols, P_1 and P_2 conduct the homomorphic key generation algorithm and distributed the key. That is, P_1 performs the key generation algorithm of a homomorphic encryption scheme to obtain the key (pk_{HE}, evk_{HE}, sk_{HE}), and sends (pk_{HE}, evk_{HE}) it to P_2.

3.1 The Distributed Key Generation Protocol

P_1 samples random seed $\rho \xleftarrow{\$} \{0, 1\}^{256}$, vectors $(s_{11}, s_{12}) \xleftarrow{\$} S_{\eta_1}^k \times S_{\eta_2}^l$, computes $A = Expand(\rho) \in R_q^{k \times l}$, $t_1 = As_{11} + s_{12}$, and sends (t_1, ρ) to P_2.

P_2 samples random vectors $(s_{21}, s_{22}) \xleftarrow{\$} S_{\eta_1}^k \times S_{\eta_2}^l$, compute $A = Expand(\rho)$, $t_2 = As_{21} + s_{22}$, and send t_2 to P_1.

P_1 and P_2 computes $t_{pk} = t_1 + t_2$, respectively. Finally, P_1 stores $((s_{11}, s_{12}), t_{pk}, sk_{HE})$, and P_2 stores $((s_{21}, s_{22}), t_{pk}, pk_{HE}, evk_{HE})$ (Fig. 1).

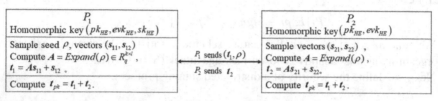

Fig. 1. Distributed secret key generation protocol

3.2 Collaborative Signing Protocol

First, P_1 samples random vector $y_1 \xleftarrow{\$} S_{\frac{\gamma_1}{2}-1}^l$, computes $W_1 = Ay_1$, $c_1 = Enc_{pk_{HE}}(W_1)$, and sends c_1 to P_2. P_2 samples random vector $y_2 \xleftarrow{\$} S_{\frac{\gamma_1}{2}-1}^l$, computes $W_2 = Ay_2$, $c_2 = c_1 \oplus Enc_{pk_{HE}}(W_2)$, $c_3 = HomEval(evk_{HE}, F_{HighBits_q()}(*, 2\gamma_2), c_2)$, and sends c_3 to P_1.

Second, P_1 decrypts the ciphertext $w_1 = Dec_{sk_{HE}}(c_3) = HighBit_q(W_1 + W_2, 2\gamma_2)$, computes the challenge $c = H(\mu, w_1)$ in which $\mu = CRH(CRH(pk)||M)$, and M is the message to be signed. Then P_1 computes $z_1 = y_1 + cs_{11}$, and verifies whether the following condition is satisfied or not [5]:

$$\|z_1\|_\infty < \frac{\gamma_1}{2} - \beta_1 \tag{1}$$

If the condition is held, P_1 computes $u_1 = Ay_1 - cs_{12}$, $c_4 = Enc_{pk_{HE}}(u_1)$, and sends z_1, c, c_4 to P_2 If not, P_1 restarts the procedure from sampling random vector $y_1 \xleftarrow{\$} S_{\frac{\gamma_1}{2}-1}^l$.

Similarly, P_2 uses the challenge c to compute $z_2 = y_2 + cs_{21}$, and conducts the verification of the rejection sampling conditions [5]:

$$\|z_2\|_\infty < \frac{\gamma_1}{2} - \beta_1 \tag{2}$$

If the condition is held, P_2 computes $u_2 = Ay_2 - cs_{22}$, $c_5 = c_4 \oplus Enc_{pk_{HE}}(u_2)$, $c_6 = HomEval\left(evk_{HE}, F_{\|LowBits_q()\|_\infty}(*, 2\gamma_2), c_5\right)$, and sends z_2, c_5 to P_1 If not, P_2 restarts the procedure from sampling random vector $y_2 \xleftarrow{\$} S_{\frac{\gamma_1}{2}-1}^l$.

P_1 utilizes the secret key to decrypt c_6, $\|r_0\|_\infty = \|LowBits_q(u_1 + u_2, 2\gamma_2)\|_\infty = Dec_{sk_{HE}}(c_6)$. Next, P_1 computes $z = z_1 + z_2 = y_1 + y_2 + c(s_{11} + s_{21})$. The two-party can generate a collaborative signature if and only if the following conditions are held [5] (Fig. 2):

$$\|z\|_\infty < \gamma_1 - \beta_1 \tag{3}$$

$$\|r_0\|_\infty = \|LowBits_q(Ay - c(s_{12} + s_{22}), 2\gamma_2)\|_\infty < \gamma_2 - 2\beta_2 \tag{4}$$

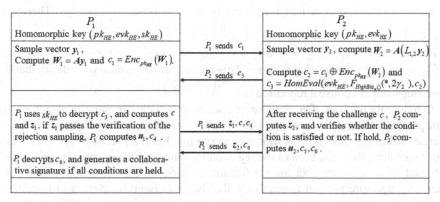

Fig. 2. Collaborative signing protocol

3.3 Correctness

The verifier uses the public key (t_{pk}, ρ) to verify the correctness of the signature (z, c).

There is $Az - ct_{pk} = u_1 + u_2 = Ay - c(s_{12} + s_{22})$, based on Lemma 1, from $\|cs_2\|_\infty = \|c(s_{12} + s_{22})\|_\infty \leq \|cs_{12}\|_\infty + \|cs_{22}\|_\infty < 2\beta_2$ and $\|r_0\|_\infty < \gamma_2 - 2\beta_2$, we conclude that:

$HighBits_q(Az - ct_{pk}, 2\gamma_2) = HighBits_q(W - c(s_{12} + s_{22}), 2\gamma_2) = HighBits_q(W, 2\gamma_2)$.

The two-party signing protocol and the verifier obtain the same w_1, therefore, the verification algorithm always accepts the signature generated by the protocol.

4 Analysis of the Two-Party Aigis-sig Signing Protocol

4.1 Collaborative Signature Generation Probability

To ensure that the output value does not reveal the private key information, the Aigis-sig scheme uses the rejection sampling technology [8]. Therefore, the signing algorithm's efficiency is determined by the number of repetitions caused by steps (1), (2), (3), and (4) of the signing protocol.

Assuming that $\|cs_{11}\|_\infty < \beta_1$ holds, then we always have $\|z_1\|_\infty \le \frac{\gamma_1}{2} - \beta_1 - 1$ whenever $\|y_1\|_\infty \le \frac{\gamma_1}{2} - 2\beta_1 - 1$. The size of this range is $\gamma_1 - 2\beta_1 - 1$. Note that each coefficient y_1 is chosen randomly from $\gamma_1 - 1$ possible values. That is, for a fixed cs_{11}, each coefficient of vector $z_1 = y_1 + cs_{11}$ has $\gamma_1 - 1$ possibilities. Thus, the probability that $\|z_1\|_\infty \le \frac{\gamma_1}{2} - \beta_1 - 1$ is $\left(\frac{\gamma_1 - 2\beta_1 - 1}{\gamma_1 - 1}\right)^{nl} \approx e^{-\frac{2nl\beta_1}{\gamma_1}}$.

Similarly, the probability that $\|z_2\|_\infty \le \frac{\gamma_1}{2} - \beta_1 - 1$ is $e^{-\frac{2nl\beta_1}{\gamma_1}}$.

If $\|z_1\|_\infty \le \frac{\gamma_1}{2} - \beta_1 - 1$ and $\|z_2\|_\infty \le \frac{\gamma_1}{2} - \beta_1 - 1$ hold, that is, $\|z\|_\infty = \|z_1 + z_2\|_\infty \le \|z_1\|_\infty + \|z_2\|_\infty < \gamma_1 - 2\beta_1 < \gamma_1 - \beta_1$ holds, which implies that if (1) and (2) both hold, then (3) holds.

Assuming that each coefficient r_0 is uniformly distributed modulo $2\gamma_2$. Therefore, the probability that $\|r_0\|_\infty < \gamma_2 - 2\beta_2$ is $\left(\frac{2(\gamma_2 - \beta_2) - 1}{2\gamma_2}\right)^{nk} \approx e^{-\frac{2nk\beta_2}{\gamma_2}}$.

By Lemma 1, if $\|cs_2\|_\infty = \|c(s_{12} + s_{22})\|_\infty \le \|cs_{12}\|_\infty + \|cs_{22}\|_\infty < 2\beta_2$, then $\|r_0\|_\infty < \gamma_2 - 2\beta_2$ implies that $r_1 = w_1$. This means that the overall probability that the above steps will not cause a repetition is $e^{-2n\left(\frac{2l\beta_1}{\gamma_1} + \frac{k\beta_2}{\gamma_2}\right)}$.

To reduce the number of homomorphic operations and the computational complexity of the protocol, the upper bound of rejection sampling P_1 and P_2 is modified accordingly because of the high cost of homomorphic encryption. First, P_1 receives c_6, to generate a valid signature, the validation of the rejection sampling condition must be performed. If P_1 and P_2 do not carry out the verification of rejection sampling conditions when generating signature portion respectively, that is, there is no restriction of conditions (1) and (2), although the probability of (3) changes from $e^{-\frac{4nl\beta_1}{\gamma_1}}$ to $e^{-\frac{2nl\beta_1}{\gamma_1}}$, homomorphic operations will be performed in the subsequent process. Second, even if P_1 and P_2 perform the verification of condition (4) respectively, although $u = u_1 + u_2$ holds, $\|LowBits_q(u, 2\gamma_2)\|_\infty = \|LowBits_q(u_1, 2\gamma_2)\|_\infty + \|LowBits_q(u_2, 2\gamma_2)\|_\infty$ maybe not hold.

4.2 Feasibility Analysis

The Cheon, Kim, Kim, and Song (CKKS) homomorphic encryption scheme is introduced into the collaborative signing protocol [6]. First, to ensure the security of transmission share; second, compared with other homomorphic encryption schemes, the CKKS scheme allows approximate encryption calculation for real or complex numbers, and supports homomorphic ciphertext comparison algorithm [14].

This section mainly analyzes whether the homomorphic operations can be realized through several homomorphic addition operations, homomorphic multiplication operations, and homomorphic ciphertext comparison operations.

$c_2 = c_1 \oplus Enc_{pk_1}(W_2)$ can be achieved by a ciphertext homomorphic addition operation. As for $c_3 = HomEval(evk_{HE}, F_{HighBits_q}(*, 2\gamma_2), c_2)$, when calculating $HighBits_q(c_2, 2\gamma_2)$ in ciphertext state, we need to invoke the $Decompose_q()$ algorithm on each coefficient of the polynomial vector. Specifically, for each coefficient, seven additions, two multiplications, and five comparison operations are required. Correspondingly, we transform these operations into the corresponding homomorphic ciphertext operations, namely, the corresponding number of ciphertext homomorphic addition, ciphertext homomorphic multiplication, and ciphertext comparison operations.

$c_5 = c_4 \oplus Enc_{pk_{HE}}(u_2)$ can be achieved by a ciphertext homomorphic addition operation as well. In the process of calculating $c_6 = HomEval(evk_{HE}, F_{\|LowBits_q()\|_\infty}(*, 2\gamma_2), c_5)$, we divide it into two steps. We compute $LowBits_q(c_5, 2\gamma_2)$ at first. when calculating it in ciphertext state, we need to invoke the $Decompose_q()$ algorithm on each coefficient of the polynomial vector as well. When it comes to computing $\|LowBits_q(c_5, 2\gamma_2)\|_\infty$ in ciphertext state, we introduce the method of calculating the maximum value of homomorphic ciphertext proposed by Cheon et al. [14]. We define a set $\Omega = \{a_1, a_2, \ldots, a_e\}$, α is precision bits, and d its iterations. The parameter d can be calculated by e and α. The time complexity of the algorithm is $\Theta(ed)$. The experimental results in reference [14] show that the maximum value of 2^{16} 32-bit integers can be solved out within 75 s. It is estimated that in our protocol, it takes about 29 s to obtain the decryption state function $\|\ \|_\infty$ when the parameter is set as parameter II of the Aigis-sig scheme.

4.3 Security Analysis

In this section, based on the security of the Aigis-sig scheme and CKKS scheme, we prove that Π is a secure two-party signing protocol.

Theorem 3.3.1. Assumeing that the CKKS homomorphic encryption scheme is indistinguishable against chosen-plaintext attacks [6] and Aigis-sig is SUF-CMA [5]. Then, in the random oracle model, the two-party Aigis-sig signing protocol is existentially unforgeable against a chosen-message attack (Fig. 3).

Fig. 3. The security reduction from Π to π

Proof. Because we define that both participants are honest, the adversary A cannot corrupt either party or participate in the protocol interaction. However, the adversary A can obtain the public key (t_{pk}, ρ) and signature (z, c) and have a view of the protocol interaction. As a result, if an adversary A attacks the protocol, and forges a cooperative signature with nonnegligible probability in experiment 3.2 by using public key, signature and the middle value of the protocol, we can construct a simulator S that forges an Aigis sig signature with nonnegligible probability in experiment 3.1. Formally, for any PPT adversary A, there exists a PPT adversary S and a negligible function λ'' such that, for any κ, it holds that:

$$\left| Pr[Expt - Sign_{S,\pi}(1^\kappa) = 1] - Pr[Expt - DistSign_{A,\Pi}(1^\kappa) = 1] \right| \le \lambda''(\kappa)$$

In combination with the Definition 1.3.1, it holds that $\left|Pr[Expt - Sign_{S,\pi}(1^\kappa) = 1]\right| \leq \lambda(\kappa)$, we conclude that:

$$\left|Pr[Expt - DistSign_{A,\Pi}(1^\kappa) = 1]\right| \leq \lambda(\kappa) + \lambda''(\kappa),$$

According to Definition 1.3.2, Π is a secure two-party Aigis-sig signing protocol.

5 Conclusion

In this paper, a new postquantum two-party cooperative digital signature protocol based on the Aigis-sig scheme is presented, which is composed of distributed key generation and collaborative signing protocol. CKKS homomorphic encryption is used in the protocol to provide a secure cooperative signature. However, under the condition of the current parameter setting, the probability of passing rejection sampling in the signature generation is relatively small, resulting in a large number of running times. The focus of our future work will be on how to improve the efficiency of the two-party cooperative signature generation scheme.

References

1. Lindell, Y.: Fast secure two-party ECDSA signing. In: Katz, J., Shacham, H. (eds.) CRYPTO 2017. LNCS, vol. 10402, pp. 613–644. Springer, Cham (2017). https://doi.org/10.1007/978-3-319-63715-0_21
2. Wang, J., Wu, L., Luo, M., et al.: Secure and efficient two-party ECDSA signature scheme. J. Commun. 42(2), 12–25 (2021)
3. Lindell, Y., Ariel, N.: Fast secure multiparty ECDSA with practical distributed key generation and applications to cryptocurrency custody. In: Proceedings of the 2018 ACM SIGSAC Conference on Computer and Communications Security, pp. 1837–1854. ACM, New York (2018)
4. Ducas, L., Kiltz, E., Lepoint, T., Lyubashevsky, V., et al.: CRYSTALS-dilithium: a lattice-based digital signature scheme. IACR Trans. Cryptogr. Hardw. Embed. Syst. 1, 238–268 (2018)
5. Zhang, J., Yu, Y., Fan, S., Zhang, Z., Yang, K.: Tweaking the asymmetry of asymmetric-key cryptography on lattices: KEMs and signatures of smaller sizes. In: Kiayias, A., Kohlweiss, M., Wallden, P., Zikas, V. (eds.) PKC 2020. LNCS, vol. 12111, pp. 37–65. Springer, Cham (2020). https://doi.org/10.1007/978-3-030-45388-6_2
6. Cheon, J.H., Kim, A., Kim, M., Song, Y.: Homomorphic encryption for arithmetic of approximate numbers. In: Takagi, T., Peyrin, T. (eds.) ASIACRYPT 2017. LNCS, vol. 10624, pp. 409–437. Springer, Cham (2017). https://doi.org/10.1007/978-3-319-70694-8_15
7. Lyubashevsky, V.: Fiat-Shamir with aborts: applications to lattice and factoring-based signatures. In: Matsui, M. (ed.) ASIACRYPT 2009. LNCS, vol. 5912, pp. 598–616. Springer, Heidelberg (2009). https://doi.org/10.1007/978-3-642-10366-7_35
8. Lyubashevsky, V.: Lattice signatures without trapdoors. In: Pointcheval, D., Johansson, T. (eds.) EUROCRYPT 2012. LNCS, vol. 7237, pp. 738–755. Springer, Heidelberg (2012). https://doi.org/10.1007/978-3-642-29011-4_43
9. Gentry, C.: Fully homomorphic encryption using ideal lattices. In: Proceedings of the Annual ACM Symposium on Theory of Computing, pp. 169–178. ACM, MD (2009)

10. Brakerski, Z.: Fully homomorphic encryption without modulus switching from classical GapSVP. In: Safavi-Naini, R., Canetti, R. (eds.) CRYPTO 2012. LNCS, vol. 7417, pp. 868–886. Springer, Heidelberg (2012). https://doi.org/10.1007/978-3-642-32009-5_50
11. Brakerski, Z., Gentry, C., Vaikuntanathan, V., et al.: (Leveled) fully homomorphic encryption without bootstrapping. ACM Trans. Comput. Theory (TOCT) 6(3), 1–36 (2014)
12. Gentry, C., Sahai, A., Waters, B.: Homomorphic encryption from learning with errors: conceptually-simpler, asymptotically-faster, attribute-based. In: Canetti, R., Garay, J.A. (eds.) CRYPTO 2013. LNCS, vol. 8042, pp. 75–92. Springer, Heidelberg (2013). https://doi.org/10.1007/978-3-642-40041-4_5
13. Ducas, L., Micciancio, D.: FHEW: bootstrapping homomorphic encryption in less than a second. In: Oswald, E., Fischlin, M. (eds.) EUROCRYPT 2015. LNCS, vol. 9056, pp. 617–640. Springer, Heidelberg (2015). https://doi.org/10.1007/978-3-662-46800-5_24
14. Cheon, J.H., Kim, D., Kim, D., Lee, H.H., Lee, K.: Numerical method for comparison on homomorphically encrypted numbers. In: Galbraith, S.D., Moriai, S. (eds.) ASIACRYPT 2019. LNCS, vol. 11922, pp. 415–445. Springer, Cham (2019). https://doi.org/10.1007/978-3-030-34621-8_15

An Efficient Unsupervised Domain Adaptation Deep Learning Model for Unknown Malware Detection

Fangwei Wang[1,2] , Guofang Chai[2] , Qingru Li[1,2] ,
and Changguang Wang[1,2(✉)]

[1] Key Lab of Network and Information Security of Hebei Province, Hebei Normal University,
Shijiazhuang 050024, China
{fw_wang,wangcg}@hebtu.edu.cn
[2] College of Computer and Cyberspace Security, Hebei Normal University,
Shijiazhuang 050024, China

Abstract. Emerging malware and zero-day vulnerabilities present new challenges to malware detection. Currently, numerous proposed malware detection approaches are based on supervised learning. However, these methods rely on a large amount of labeled data, which is usually difficult to obtain. Moreover, since the newly emerging malware has a different data distribution from the original training samples, the detection performance of the model will degrade when facing new malware. To solve the problems mentioned above, this paper proposes an unsupervised domain adaptation-based malware detection method to align the joint distribution of known malware and unknown malware. First, the distribution divergence between the source and target domain is minimized by adversarial learning to learn shared feature representations. Second, to further obtain semantic information of unlabeled target domain data, this paper reduces the class-level distribution divergence by aligning the class centers of labeled source data and pseudo-labeled target data. To improve the ability of the model for extracting feature information, this paper mainly uses a residual network with a self-attention mechanism as a pre-trained model. Extensive experiments are conducted on two datasets. The experimental results illustrate that the proposed method outperforms the state-of-art detection methods with an accuracy of 95.63% and a recall of 95.30% in detecting unknown malware.

Keywords: Deep transfer learning · Malware detection · Domain adaptation · Self-attention module

1 Introduction

With the development of 5G technology and big data, IoT is changing every aspect of our daily lives. However, while IoT brings convenience to our lives, it is also facing many malware attacks [1]. Zscaler reported that more than 575 million device transactions and 300,000 IoT-specific malware attacks were blocked during two weeks in December

W. Shi et al. (Eds.): SPNCE 2021, LNICST 423, pp. 64–76, 2022.
https://doi.org/10.1007/978-3-030-96791-8_5

2020, a 700% increase by the pre-epidemic. These attacks targeted 553 different types of devices, including printers, digital signage, and smart TVs.

Malware is one of the most common security risks to the Internet. They are massive and have complex polymorphisms. According to the AV-TEST organization, thousands of malware are born every day. Up to 2021, the total of malware has increased to more than 1.2 billion, which is an increase of 1800% compared to that of 2011. So the complexity of the IoT hardware and software environment provides more attack opportunities for attackers. Moreover, malware poses a huge threat to all our industries. Therefore, how to detect malware quickly and accurately has become one of the most important topics of current research.

Recently, machine learning is being used to improve the accuracy of detecting malware. Supervised malware detection [2] requires a large amount of labeled data to train the model. Moreover, when that model encounters a new unknown sample, the detection performance will decline. Transfer learning [3] applies the knowledge gained from solving one problem to another different but related problem. Fine-tuning [4], a branch of transfer learning, focuses on how to finely tune the model by labeled data. However, fine-tuning does not take into account the discrepancy of data distribution among different datasets. So it still does not achieve excellent results for detecting unknown malware.

All of the aforementioned methods have obvious disadvantages when detecting unknown malware. To improve the detection performance of unknown malware, this paper proposes a detection method based on unsupervised domain adaptation. The unsupervised domain adaptation uses the labeled source domain data to predict the label of target domain data under the condition that the source and target domains have different distribution [5]. Therefore, we use the malware dataset with labels as the source domain and the malware without labels as the target domain. We then transfer the knowledge learned from the source domain to the target domain through domain adaptation to detect unknown malware. The main contributions of this paper are summarized as follows:

1) We use a deep residual network with a self-attention mechanism and a discriminator network to extract features from multi-channels.
2) We adopt the joint distribution alignment approach to reduce the distribution discrepancy. Firstly, inter-domain distribution discrepancy is reduced by adversarial learning. Then, class-level alignment can be achieved by optimizing the semantic alignment loss functions. Eventually, we can achieve intra-class sample compactness and inter-class sample separation.
3) By our proposed method, we perform massive experiments on two datasets. The results show that the method can correctly classify unknown malware and outperforms the state-of-the-art detection methods.

The remainder of this paper is organized as follows: Sect. 2 describes the related work. Section 3 presents the background knowledge and the proposed method. Section 4 describes the experimental details and the related results. Finally, Sect. 5 concludes this paper.

2 Related Work

2.1 Machine Learning-Based Malware Detection

Machine learning has been widely used in the field of malware detection and is divided into two major categories: supervised learning and unsupervised learning. Supervised malware detection methods depend on large amounts of labeled data to train the model. The most common method is to convert malware raw files into grayscale images and train convolutional neural network models to detect the malware. Nataraj et al. firstly transformed malware into images to extract their GIST features and used K-nearest neighbor classification [6]. Jinpei et al. used deep neural networks to automatically extract features to reduce the expense of feature engineering [7]. Unsupervised malware classification, on the contrary, clusters samples based on their similarity [8]. Pitolli et al. proposed an online clustering algorithm to identify malware families [9]. The algorithm classified malware among existing families when running and can identify new families. However, all of these supervised learning methods rely on labeled data to train the model. When facing unknown samples, the detection capability of the model will drop. All these unsupervised detection methods must depend on a large amount of data to reach high accuracy.

2.2 Transfer Learning-Based Malware Detection

Currently, transfer learning has been extensively applied to various fields [10–15]. For example, image classification [10], semantic segmentation [12], robot recognition [15], and medical areas [13]. Transfer learning has also been utilized to detect malware. Vasan et al. proposed an image-based malware classification [16]. They improved the classification accuracy by fine-tuning the neural network as well as data augmentation. Besides fine-tuning, domain adaptation is also a branch of transfer learning. Bartos et al. proposed a new method that computed domain-invariant feature representations from network traffic and learned to identify malicious behavior [17]. Li et al. proposed a method of aligning the feature distributions of different domains [18]. This method can reduce the discrepancy of marginal distribution between the source domain and target domain. However, it does not consider the difference in class-level distribution in the source domain and target domain. Rong et al. used deep transfer learning to detect unknown malware variants [3]. The author transformed malware traffic data into RGB images and proposed a TransNet framework to solve the problem of data distribution discrepancy among different datasets. They replaced the batch normalization layer with a transfer batch normalization layer in the deep neural network to achieve data distribution alignment. However, they did not consider the class-level alignment of different domains.

In the area of computer vision, there are two main approaches to achieve global domain alignment: non-adversarial domain alignment and adversarial domain alignment. Non-adversarial domain alignment minimizes the global distribution discrepancy of domains by different metrics such as Maximum Mean Discrepancy (MMD) [19], KL [20], CORAL [21], etc. In contrast, adversarial domain adaptation methods use the adversarial learning idea from Generative Adversarial Networks (GAN) to learn domain invariant features. Currently, domain adaptation methods used for malware classification have two main disadvantages: some do not consider the joint distribution alignment between different domains, and some use raw PE files to extract features increasing feature engineering cost and domain expert knowledge. Inspired by the application of domain adaptation in computer vision, we convert malware files into gray images and narrow down the distribution discrepancy between source and target domains by domain adaption.

3 Proposed Methodology

3.1 Overview

The unsupervised domain adaptation aims to improve the model generalization ability in the target domain by minimizing the distribution discrepancy between the source and target domains. In this paper, we use $D_s = \{(x_i^s, y_i^s)\}_{i=1}^{n_s}$, $D_t = \{(x_j^t)\}_{j=1}^{n_t}$ to denote the source with labels and target domains without labels, respectively, where n_s is the number of samples in the source domain; y_i^s is the label corresponding to the source domain sample x_i^s. D_s and D_t have a different distribution. In this paper, our goal is to transfer knowledge from a labeled source domain to an unlabeled target domain and train a transferable target classifier to predict the labels of the target domain samples.

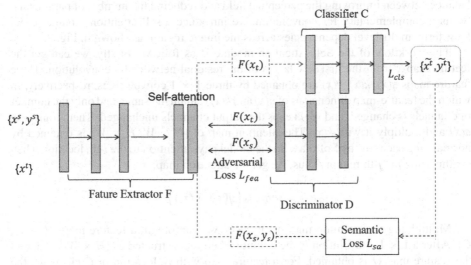

Fig. 1. Overview of the model structure.

The overall framework of the approach in this paper is shown in Fig. 1. It mainly consists of three components: feature extractor F_φ, classifier C_ϕ, and domain discriminators

D_ω, where φ, ϕ, ω are learnable parameters. The feature extractor and domain discriminator achieve global alignment by adversarial learning using labeled source domain, unlabeled target domain. To make the intra-class data more compact and inter-class data more separated, class-center alignment is achieved by source domain labeled data and target domain data with pseudo-labels. Therefore, the model needs to jointly optimize supervised classification loss L_{cls} and global domain adversarial loss L_{fea} as well as class-level semantic alignment loss functions L_{sa}. The overall optimization objectives are as follows:

$$L = L_{cls} + \alpha L_{fea} + \beta L_{sa}, \tag{1}$$

where the hyperparameters α, β are the influence factors of global alignment and semantic alignment, respectively. The supervised classification uses the Cross Entropy loss function to measure the classification error:

$$L_{cls} = E_{(x^s, y^s) \sim D_s}\left(C_\phi\left(F_\varphi(x)\right), y^s\right). \tag{2}$$

3.2 Self-attention Module

We insert a self-attention module [22] in the feature extractor. This module enables each pixel to associate with other pixels. As a result, it can solve the long-distance dependence problem in common convolutional structures. Moreover, this module achieves a better balance between improving the perceptual field and reducing the number of parameters. So as a complementary for convolution, we introduce a self-attention module to get long-term, multi-level dependencies across the image region, as shown in Fig. 2.

The workflow of the Self-Attention module is as follows. Firstly, we can get the feature map x from the first few layers of the residual network by convolution. Three feature maps $q(x)$, $k(x)$, $v(x)$ are obtained by three 1×1 convolutions, respectively. In which the feature-map dimensions of $q(x)$ and $k(x)$ remain the same, and only the number of channels is changed, and $v(x)$ keeps the output channels unchanged. Then, transpose $q(x)$ and multiply it with $k(x)$. The attention map of $[H \times W, H \times W]$ is obtained by normalizing each row by Softmax. So the model pays attention to the i-th, location when synthesizing the j-th region. Thus, we get the attention map:

$$\rho_{j,i} = softmax\left(q(x_i)^T k(x_j)\right). \tag{3}$$

Multiplying the attention map $\rho_{j,i}$ by $v(x)$, we can obtain a feature map $[H \times W, C]$. After a 1×1 convolution h, the output is then reconstructed as $[H \times W \times C]$, and the feature map O is obtained. For a feature map with N location in C channels, the output of the attention layer is $O = (o_1, o_2, \ldots, o_N) \in \mathbb{R}^{C \times N}$, and o is calculated by the following:

$$o = v \otimes \left(\sum_{i=1}^{N} \rho_{j,i} h(x)\right). \tag{4}$$

In addition, we further multiply the output of the attention layer by a parameter θ which is learned in the self-attention layer and initialize it to 0, indicating that the self-attention module has not worked yet. As training proceeds, the network slowly begins to learn more features by the residual network with the self-attention module. Thus, the final output is:

$$f = \theta o_i + x_i. \tag{5}$$

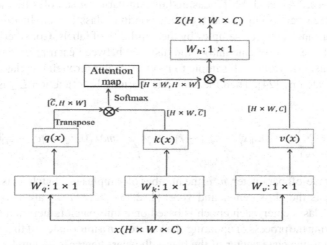

Fig. 2. The workflow of the self-attention module.

We place the self-attentive mechanism at the fourth block of the residual network due to two reasons. Firstly, we extract effectively local features and reduce the resolution by convolution. Secondly, the self-attention module is used to aggregate the global information of the feature. Therefore, the model ability to extract features is improved.

3.3 Global Domain Alignment

The global domain alignment aims to reduce the discrepancy in cross-domain feature distribution. In this paper, we align the feature distributions of two domains by minimizing the global domain adversarial loss function L_{fea} in an adversarial learning manner. The method employs the idea of generative adversarial networks, in which the feature extractor F_φ plays with the domain discriminator D_ω during the training process. The domain discriminator D_ω is trained to minimize the domain loss L_{fea} to distinguish between source and target domain features while the feature extractor F_φ obfuscates the domain discriminator D_ω by maximizing the domain loss to learn a domain-variant feature representation. When the training ends, the network can obtain domain-variant feature representation. The global domain-aligned adversarial training loss can be expressed as follows:

$$L_{fea}(F_\varphi, D_\omega) = -E_{x \sim D_t} log[1 - D_\omega(F_\varphi(x_s))] - E_{x \sim D_s}[D_\omega(F_\varphi(x_t))]. \tag{6}$$

3.4 Semantic Alignment

Global alignment alone does not achieve precise alignment. To make the model have higher classification ability and learn more differentiated depth features, we propose class-center discriminable feature learning. By this way, we can make similar data more compact and dissimilar data more discriminable in the feature space. Weston et al. [23] proposed that similar samples should be closer to each other and different samples should be further away from each other by judging the manifolds of the samples in the feature space. Wen et al. [24] measured the similarity of samples by the minimum distance between each sample and its corresponding class center. In this paper, we measure the distance between samples by the similarity of labels. Considering the high computational overhead of calculating the distance between each pair of samples, we calculate the distance from each sample to its class center through the class center loss function motivated by [24]. Then the semantic learning loss function L_{sa} is defined as follows:

$$L_{sa} = \sum_{i=1}^{n_s} max\left(0, \|x_i^s - c_{y_i}\| - r_1\right) + \gamma \sum_{i,j=1}^{m} max\left(0, r_2 - \|c_i - c_j\|\right), \qquad (7)$$

where γ is a trade-off parameter, n_s is the number of samples in a batch. m is the number of classes. c_{y_i} is the class center and $y_i \in \{1, 2, \cdots, m\}$. r_1, r_2 are two thresholds. To update the class center, each epoch is based on a min-batch rather than all samples. Therefore, during the process of updating class centers in a mini-batch, if there is a sample corresponding to the class center of the batch, the class center is updated. otherwise, it is not updated. In each iteration, the class center is updated according to the following way:

$$\Delta c_j = \begin{cases} \frac{\sum_{i=1}^{n} c_j - x_i}{1+n}, & y_i = j, \\ 0, & y_i \neq j, \end{cases} \qquad (8)$$

$$c_j^{t+1} = c_j^t - \Delta c_j^t, \qquad (9)$$

where n is the number of samples in each batch and ε is the learning rate. In class-center alignment, we need to get the labels of the target domain data, so we use the pseudo-labels. We get the pseudo labels by the following steps. Firstly, we train the model with the labeled source domain data. Then, the trained model is used to predict the labels of the target domain. The detailed process is: 1) Define $\{p_c(x_i^t)|_{c=1}^m\}$ as the output probability of the classifier. $p_c(x_i^t)$ indicates the probability that x_i^t belongs to the c-th class. m is the number of samples. 2) The pseudo-label corresponding to sample x_i^t is calculated according to $\tilde{y}_i^t = argmax_c p_c(x_i^t)$. 3) The label of the class with the highest probability is selected as the class label of x_i^t. We achieve intra-class compactness and inter-class separation by minimizing the distance between the samples and the corresponding class centers.

3.5 Model Training

The whole training process of the proposed method is listed in Algorithm1. Firstly, we minimize the classification loss by standard supervised learning using labeled source domain samples, so we get a pre-trained feature extractor F_{φ} and classifier C_{ϕ}. Second, the pre-trained model is used to assign pseudo-labels to the unlabeled target domain data according to $\tilde{y}_i^t = argmax_c p_c(x_i^t)$. Then, we use the pre-trained model to initialize the feature extractor and classifier of the target model. The global domain adversarial loss L_{fea} is minimized by domain adversarial learning with labeled source data and unlabeled target domain data. Thus, we can achieve a global alignment of the source and target domains. Meanwhile, class-center alignment is implemented by minimizing the semantic alignment loss function L_{sa} using source domain samples and pseudo-label target domain samples. Therefore, we need jointly optimize supervised classification loss L_{cls}, global domain adversarial loss L_{fea}, and semantic alignment loss L_{sa}. Then the overall training loss is as follows:

$$\min_{\varphi,\omega,\varnothing} L_{total}\left(X^S, Y^S, X^T, \widetilde{X^T}\right) = L_{cls}\left(X^S, Y^S; \varphi, \varnothing\right) + \alpha A + \beta B, \quad (10)$$

where $A = L_{fea}(X^S, X^T; \varphi, \omega)$, $B = L_{sa}(X^S, \widetilde{X^T})$.

Algorithm1 Training of our model

Input: Source domain: $D_s = \{(x_i^s, y_i^s)\}_{i=1}^{n_s}$, Target domain: $D_t = \{x_j^t\}_{j=1}^{n_t}$

      Pseudo-label: $\tilde{y}_i^t = argmax_c p_c(x_i^t)$

Initialize: parameter of target model $\Omega = \{\varphi, \phi, \omega, \alpha, \beta, \varepsilon\}$

 1: **While** not done **do**

 2:    Sample mini batch d_s ,d_t data in D_S, D_t do

 3:    **for** t=1 to batchsize **do**

 4:        Use d_s compute source domain class Center c_s and $c_t \leftarrow c_s$.

 5:        Compute Δc_j by Eq. (8) and update class $c_j^{t+1} = c_j^t - \varepsilon \Delta c_j^t$

 6:        Compute semantic alignment loss L_{sa} by Eq. (7).

 7:        Compute jointly loss function $L_{total}(X^S, Y^S, X^T, \widetilde{X^T}; \varphi, \phi, \omega)$

 8:        Back propagation L_{total} to get the gradient value of each parameter

 9:        Parameter Ω is updated by gradient descent with *Adam* optimizer

10:    **end for**

11:    Calculate mean loss and mean accuracy

12: **end while**

13: **Output:** $F_{\varphi}, C_{\phi}, D_{\omega}$

---

4 Experiment and Result Analysis

4.1 Experimental Settings

1) *Dataset*: We evaluate the proposed approach on two windows malware datasets and a benign dataset selected from the Playdrone dataset [29]. BIG-2015 is a publicly

available dataset from Microsoft on the Kaggle platform, which includes 10,868 training samples and 10,873 test samples from 9 malware families. In this experiment, we only use the training samples. The Mailing dataset includes 9339 malicious samples from 25 malware families. The BIG-2015 malware family samples are converted to grayscale images as network input, and images are normalized to a fixed size of 196 * 196 pixels. The original sample of the Malimg dataset is the grayscale image, so we only transform it to a fixed size of 196 * 196 pixels. Additionally, we use 2280 benign samples in our experiment, where 1140 benign samples are included in the source and target domains, respectively. According to the experimental setup, we use one of the families of the malware dataset as the target domain and the remaining as the source domain, and both source domain and target domain includes benign software. For example, in the BIG-2015 dataset, the Ramnit family is selected as the unlabeled target domain data and the remaining families as the source domain data. The benign data samples are different in the source and target domains. The purpose of this setting is to simulate the ability of the model to detect unknown malware.

2) *Implementation details:* In this paper, we use a residual network as the feature extractor and classifier. To extract the precise feature information of the image, the self-attention module is introduced to associate each pixel with other pixels. For the discriminator, which has the same structure as the classifier, the convolution outputs are x-2048-4096-1. Moreover, we use dropout to reduce overfitting by ignoring several neurons with some probability in each training batch. The entire training process uses the Adam optimizer. The pre-training source domain classification loss uses a cross-entropy loss function. During the training of the target model, we simultaneously optimize the cross-entropy loss function, the domain adversarial loss function, and the semantic alignment loss function. The learning rate is set to 1e-4 and the parameters $\alpha = 0.1$ and $\beta = 0.1$, respectively. The learning rate at the local class center update is set to 0.5. The two thresholds r_1, r_2 used in the semantic alignment loss function are set to 0 and 100 respectively. The batch size is set to 32. All experiments are performed in the PyTorch framework. The experimental equipment is as follows: CPU: Intel(R) Core(TM) i5-4590 CPU @ 3.30 GHz 3.30 GH; RAM: 4 GB; OS: Windows 7.

3) *Evaluation metrics:* We evaluate the detection performance of our method by four metrics: accuracy, precision, recall, and F1-score. These evaluation metrics have been extensively applied to various research areas, such as machine learning, natural language processing.

4.2   Performance Comparison of Different Models

In this paper, we have run extensive experiments and calculated the detection accuracy and recall when each class acts as unknown malware (target domain) on the two datasets. We also take into consideration that one dataset (e.g. BIG-2015) acts as the source domain and the other (e.g., Malimg) acts as the target domain for malware detection. In the experiments, the benign software used in the source domain and target domain are also different. The experimental results are shown in Fig. 3 and Fig. 4. We can see from the figures that the average accuracy and recall on the BIG-2015 dataset are 95.04% and 94.25%, respectively. Moreover, the average accuracy and recall on the Malimg dataset are 95.63% and 95.30%, respectively. In addition, this paper compares our work with traditional machine learning and the state-of-the-art malware detection method, as shown in Table 1.

From Table 1, it can be seen that our method outperforms the other methods. The first two rows are traditional machine learning methods for unknown malware detection. We can see that their accuracy and recall are generally poor. Traditional machine learning is based on feature extraction of known malware to detect unknown malware. Moreover, features are extracted based on feature engineering. Therefore, the unknown malware causes the distribution of training and test samples different. So it decreases the accuracy of model classification. To verify the effectivity of our method, we compare it with the state-of-the-art malware detection methods such as GAA-ADS [27], DART [18], BIRCH [9], and RCNN + transfer learning [28]. From Table 1, it can be seen that our method achieves higher accuracy and recall than the GAA-ADS, which used the clustering method, and RCNN + transfer learning. Moreover, it is also higher than the DART which uses the distribution alignments. DART mitigates the domain discrepancy by jointly optimizing the marginal and manifold distributions of the source and target domains. However, they process the raw data to extract the artificially designed features by traditional machine learning techniques. In this paper, we transform the raw files into grayscale images before feeding them into the neural network. Moreover, our method achieves a higher accuracy and recall by jointly aligning the global and class distributions. It shows that the approach considering class information and semantic alignment has a better performance than the previous approach only considering global domain adaptation. Moreover, it also confirms that class information helps to capture more structural information of the data.

Table 1. Comparison of the detection performance of different methods

Method	Accuracy	Recall	Precision	F1-score
SVM [25]	74.6%	84%	–	75%
SSL [26]	88.54%	90.96%	–	–
GAA-ADS [27]	92.8%	91.3%	–	–
DART [18]	93.9%	91.2%	–	90%
BIRCH [9]	95.02%	90.2%	95.2%	92.3%
RCNN + Transfer Learning [28]	92.8%	–	95.6%	–
OURS	95.63	95.30%	95.34%	93.65%

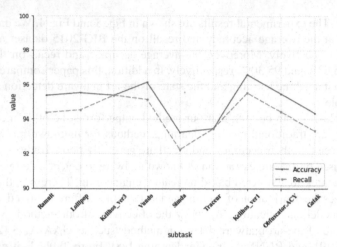

Fig. 3. Detection performance of unknown malware on the BIG-2015 dataset.

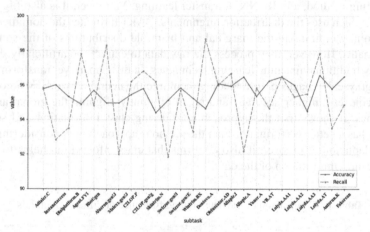

Fig. 4. Detection performance of unknown malware on the Malimg dataset.

5   Conclusion and Future Work

In this paper, we propose an unsupervised domain adaptation approach to detect unknown malware by aligning the joint distribution (global distribution and semantic distribution) of known malware and unknown malware. First, we minimize the discrepancy of the distribution between the source and target domains and learn shared feature representation by adversarial learning. Then, to further obtain the semantic information of unlabeled data, we minimize the distance from the labeled source and pseudo-labeled target domain samples to the class center. Finally, to improve the extraction capability of the model, this paper uses a residual network with a self-attention mechanism as pre-trained model. Extensive experiments are conducted on two datasets, and the results illustrate that the proposed method outperforms the state-of-art detection methods in detecting unknown malware. In the future, we will work on a more fine-grained domain adaptation approach to the classification of malware families.

Acknowledgement. This work was supported by the National Natural Science Foundation of China under Grants No. 61572170, Natural Science Foundation of Hebei Province of China under Grant No.F2019205163 and No. F2021205004, Science and Technology Foundation Project of Hebei Normal University under Grant No. L2021K06, Science Foundation of Returned Overseas of Hebei Province of China Under Grant No. C2020342, Science Foundation of Department of Human Resources and Social Security of Hebei Province under Grant No. 201901028 and No. ZD2021062, and Natural Science Foundation of Hebei Normal University under Grant No. L072018Z10.

References

1. Li, Z., Wang, D., Morais, E.: Quantum-safe round-optimal password authentication for mobile devices. IEEE Trans. Dependable Secure Comput. (2020). https://doi.org/10.1109/TDSC.2020.3040776
2. Vasan, D., Alazab, M., Wassan, S., et al.: IMCFN: image-based malware classification using fine-tuned convolutional neural network architecture. Comput. Netw. **171**(4), 107–138 (2020)
3. Rong, C., Gou, G., Cui, M., Xiong, G., Li, Z., Guo, L.: TransNet: unseen malware variants detection using deep transfer learning. In: Park, N., Sun, K., Foresti, S., Butler, K., Saxena, N. (eds.) SecureComm 2020. LNICSSITE, vol. 336, pp. 84–101. Springer, Cham (2020). https://doi.org/10.1007/978-3-030-63095-9_5
4. Kumar, S.: MCFT-CNN: malware classification with fine-tune convolution neural networks using traditional and transfer learning in internet of things. Futur. Gener. Comput. Syst. **125**(12), 334–351 (2021)
5. Wilson, G., Cook, D.J.: A survey of unsupervised deep domain adaptation. ACM Trans. Intell. Syst. Technol. **11**(5), 1–46 (2020)
6. Nataraj, L., Yegneswaran, V., Porras, P., et al.: A comparative assessment of malware classification using binary texture analysis and dynamic analysis. In: Proceedings of the ACM Conference on Computer and Communications Security, pp. 21–30. Association for Computing Machinery, New York (2011)
7. Yan, J., Qi, Y., Rao, Q.: Detecting malware with an ensemble method based on deep neural network. Secur. Commun. Netw. **2018**(7247095), 1–16 (2018)
8. Alom, M.Z., Taha, T.M.: Network intrusion detection for cyber security using unsupervised deep learning approaches. In: 2017 IEEE National Aerospace and Electronics Conference (NAECON), pp. 63–69. IEEE, Dayton (2017)
9. Pitolli, G., Laurenza, G., Aniello, L., Querzoni, L., Baldoni, R.: MalFamAware: automatic family identification and malware classification through online clustering. Int. J. Inf. Secur. **20**(3), 371–386 (2020). https://doi.org/10.1007/s10207-020-00509-4
10. Rezende, E., Ruppert, G., Carvalho, T., Theophilo, A., Ramos, F., Geus, P.: Malicious software classification using VGG16 deep neural network's bottleneck features. In: Latifi, S. (ed.) Information Technology New Generations 2018. Advances in Intelligent Systems and Computing, vol. 738, pp. 51–59. Springer, Cham (2018). https://doi.org/10.1007/978-3-319-77028-4_9
11. Qiu, S., Wang, D., Xu, G., Kumari, S.: Practical and provably secure three-factor authentication protocol based on extended chaotic-maps for mobile lightweight devices. IEEE Trans. Dependable Secure Comput. (2020). https://doi.org/10.1109/TDSC.2020.3022797

12. Cui, B., Chen, X., Lu, Y.: Semantic segmentation of remote sensing images using transfer learning and deep convolutional neural network with dense connection. IEEE Access **8**(8), 116744–116755 (2020)
13. Pathak, Y., Shukla, P.K., Tiwari, A., et al.: Deep transfer learning based classification model for COVID-19 disease. Innov. Res. BioMed. Eng. (2020). https://doi.org/10.1016/j.irbm.2020.05.003
14. Wang, C., Wang, D., Xu, G., He, D.: Efficient privacy-preserving user authentication scheme with forward secrecy for industry 4.0. Sci. China Inf. Sci. **65**(1), 1–15 (2021). https://doi.org/10.1007/s11432-020-2975-6
15. Sorocky, M.J., Zhou, S., Schoellig, A.P.: Experience selection using dynamics similarity for efficient multi-source transfer learning between robots. In: 2020 IEEE International Conference on Robotics and Automation (ICRA), pp. 2739–2745. IEEE, Paris (2020)
16. Vasan, D., Alazab, M., Wassan, S., et al.: Image-based malware classification using ensemble of CNN architectures (IMCEC). Comput. Secur. **92**(5), Article ID: 101748 (2020). https://doi.org/10.1016/j.cose.2020.101748
17. Bartos, K., Sofka, M., Franc, V.: Optimized invariant representation of network traffic for detecting unseen malware variants. In: 25th USENIX Security Symposium, pp. 807–822. USENIX, Austin (2016)
18. Li, H., Chen, Z., Spolaor, R.: DART: detecting unseen malware variants using adaptation regularization transfer learning. In: ICC 2019–2019 IEEE International Conference on Communications (ICC), pp. 1–6. IEEE, Shanghai (2019)
19. Zhu, Y., Zhuang, F., Wang, J., et al.: Multi-representation adaptation network for cross-domain image classification. Neural Netw. **119**(8), 214–221 (2019)
20. Zhuang, F., Cheng, X., Luo, P., et al.: Supervised representation learning: Transfer learning with deep autoencoders. In: Twenty-Fourth International Joint Conference on Artificial Intelligence, pp. 4119–4125. AAAI, Palo Alto (2015)
21. Sun, B., Feng, J., Saenko, K.: Return of frustratingly easy domain adaptation. In: Proceedings of the Thirtieth Conference on Artificial Intelligence, pp. 2058–2065. AAAI, Phoenix (2016)
22. Zhang, H., Goodfellow, I., Metaxas, D., et al.: Self-attention generative adversarial networks. In: International Conference on Machine Learning, pp. 7354–7363. PMLR (2019)
23. Weston, J., Ratle, F., Mobahi, H., Collobert, R.: Deep learning via semi-supervised embedding. In: Montavon, G., Orr, G.B., Müller, K.R. (eds.) Neural Networks: Tricks of the Trade 2012. Lecture Notes in Computer Science, vol. 7700, pp. 639–655. Springer, Heidelberg (2012). https://doi.org/10.1007/978-3-642-35289-8_34
24. Wen, Y., Zhang, K., Li, Z., Qiao, Y.: A discriminative feature learning approach for deep face recognition. In: Leibe, B., Matas, J., Sebe, N., Welling, M. (eds.) ECCV 2016. LNCS, vol. 9911, pp. 499–515. Springer, Cham (2016). https://doi.org/10.1007/978-3-319-46478-7_31
25. Sanjaa, B., Chuluun, E.: Malware detection using linear SVM. In: The 8th International Forum on Strategic Technology (IFOST), pp. 136–138. IEEE, Ulaanbaatar (2013)
26. Comar, P. M., Liu, L., Saha, S., et al.: Combining supervised and unsupervised learning for zero-day malware detection. In: 2013 Proceedings IEEE INFOCOM, pp. 2022–2030. IEEE, Turin (2013)
27. Moustafa, N., Slay, J., Creech, G.: Novel geometric area analysis technique for anomaly detection using trapezoidal area estimation on large-scale networks. IEEE Trans. Big Data **5**(4), 481–494 (2017)
28. Zhao, Y., Cui, W., Geng, S., et al.: A malware detection method of code texture visualization based on an improved faster RCNN combining transfer learning. IEEE Access **8**(1), 166630–166641 (2020)
29. Tzeng, E., Hoffman, J., Saenko, K., Darrell, T.: Adversarial discriminative domain adaptation. In: Proceedings of Conference on Computer Vision and Pattern Recognition, pp. 2962–2971. IEEE, Honolulu (2017)

A Lightweight PSIS Scheme Based on Multi-node Collaboration in the IoT

Lina Zhang[1,2] , Bo Yang[1(✉)] , Tao Wang[1] , and Tong Wang[2]

[1] Shaanxi Normal University, Xi'an 710119, Shaanxi, China
zhangln@xust.edu.cn, {byang,water}@snnu.edu.cn
[2] Xi'an University of Science and Technology, Xi'an, Shaanxi, China

Abstract. Traditional threshold-based SIS schemes can no longer meet some application scenarios. In contrast, Progressive Secret Image Sharing (PSIS) schemes have been continuously studied. In order to meet the different data storage methods in the nodes in the IoT, as well as the small size and limited energy of the nodes, a lightweight PSIS scheme based on multi-node collaboration in the IoT is proposed. This solution gradually recovers the secret image through the collaboration of multiple nodes in the IoT, which overcomes the drawbacks of the traditional threshold schemes and also brings convenience to the secure transmission of secret images in the IoT. Experiments have proved that the scheme has certain practicability.

Keywords: IoT · PSIS · Multi-node · Modulo operations · Interpolated polynomial

1 Introduction

IoT is a network based on information carriers such as the Internet and traditional telecommunications networks, allowing all ordinary physical objects that can be independently addressed to achieve interconnection [1]. As information carrier, images are widely used in various fields. Especially in the related applications of IoT, image security issues are particularly important.

The perception nodes are important part of IoT [2–4]. It is mainly responsible for information collection, data fusion and data transmission. As a result, it has attracted much attention of the criminals and are extremely vulnerable to physical capture and brute force cracking. Once a node in the IoT is cracked, the attacker has the legal identity to use the network and launches an internal attack, pouring massive amounts of redundant data into the network, causing network congestion. From this point of view, malicious nodes within the network pose agreat threat. Therefore, it is extremely urgent to focus on a secure transmission algorithm of IoT node information with low complexity and high compatibility [5]. Low complexity mainly includes three aspects: (1) the verification method is simple, the verifier can complete the verification of nodes data only through the exclusive OR operation. (2) the space complexity is low, the local data of nodes will be uploaded to the cloud before being used, and the verifier uses corresponding shares to check, so the space complexity is 0(1). Compatibility is reflected in the nodes that store different data. Before the result is reconstructed, the nodes are independent of each other, but when the result is reconstructed, the nodes cooperate to provide effective data and complete the result aggregation. To sum up, a lightweight PSIS scheme based on multi-node collaboration in the IoT is proposed, which is designed to protect image content, reduce energy consumption of nodes, and perform lightweight authentication between nodes.

Shamir was the first to propose (k, n) threshold secret sharing [6]. With the continuous development of research, the research trend of SIS schemes is divided into two branches: the traditional (k, n) threshold SIS schemes [7–9] and PSIS schemes [10–12]. The traditional schemes provides an all-or-nothing recovery mode, and PSIS can gradually recover the secret image. Actually, The former needs to meet two characteristics: (1) no image information can be obtained with less than k shadows, (2) the entire secret can be gained with any k shadows. For PSIS schemes, in addition to satisfying the above two characteristics, another feature must be satisfied: after obtaining any k shadows, each additional shadow will restore a new part of the image content.

The perception nodes in the IoT are deployed in any possible position. In addition, these nodes have limited energy and volume, thus, they are prone to damage and malicious attacks. Once the node holding the secret share is destroyed or its energy is completely lost, the traditional (k, n) SIS scheme will not be able to recover the original image. On the contrary, for PSIS scheme, the loss of part of the secret shares will not affect the restoration of the original image content.

Recently, researchers have proposed various PSIS schemes [10,12–16]. The work in [10] proposes a new scalable (t, s, k, n) SIS scheme with essential shadows, where k or more shadows which include at least t essential shadows can gradually reconstruct secret image. Entire secret image can be reconstructed when all s essential shadows are involved. This scheme combines the features of SIS and PSIS. The approach in [12] develops a new (k, n) PSIS based on polynomial with smaller shadow size. This method has good smoothness during recovery, however, it is not fine-grained enough. The study in [13] proposes a general (k, n) Scalable SIS (SSIS) scheme with the smooth scalability. However, its smoothness is still not good enough.

In this paper, we propose a lightweight PSIS scheme based on multi-node collaboration in the IoT. The main contributions of this paper are as follows:

1) Combined with modulo operation, a multi-interlaced spiral matrix is designed.
2) A fine-grained PSIS scheme is proposed.
3) The scheme is designed based on the multi-node collaboration in the IoT. It can transmit image data securely while also performing mutual authentication between nodes.

4) Performance with fault tolerance. The reason is that the (k, n) threshold design scheme is used in the scheme, which allows the falsified data submitted by $n - k$ nodes out of n nodes to be tolerant of $\dfrac{n - k}{k}$.

The rest of this paper is organized as follows: In next section, we prepare some preliminaries, which include basic theory of secret sharing, Thien-Lin SIS scheme [17], scalable SIS (SSIS) scheme [13], and the design of multi-interleaved spiral matrix based on modular arithmetic. In Sect. 3, we propose a lightweight PSIS scheme based on multi-node collaboration in the IoT. In Sect. 4, experimental results and analyses are used to show the performance and superiority of the proposed scheme. Comparisons with related works are given in Sect. 5. The conclusion is included in Sect. 5.

2   Preliminaries

In this section, basic theory of secret sharing, two representative SIS schemes that are Thien-Lin SIS scheme [15] and PSIS scheme [26], and the design of multi-interleaved spiral matrix based on modular arithmetic are introduced.

2.1   Basic Theory of Secret Sharing

The basic theory of secret sharing was first proposed by Shamir [14]. Let $GF(q)$ be a finite field, where q is a large prime number that satisfies $q \geq n+1$. The secret S is a random number uniformly selected on $GF(q) \backslash \{0\}$ $(i = 1, 2, 3, \cdots, k)$, denoted as $S \leftarrow {}_R GF(q) \backslash \{0\}$ $(i = 1, 2, 3, \cdots, k)$. Construct a $k - 1$-degree polynomial on $GF(q)$ as $f(x) = a_0 + a_1 x + a_2 x^2 + a_3 x^3 + \cdots + a_{k-1} x^{k-1}$.

The n participants are denoted as $P_1, P_2, P_3, \cdots, P_n$. Their assigned secret share is $f(i)(i = 1, 2, 3, \cdots, n)$. For any k participants $P_{i_1}, P_{i_2}, \cdots, P_{i_k}, i_j \in [1, n], j = 1, 2, \cdots, k$, when they want to obtain the secret s, they can utilize $f(i_j)$ to construct a linear equation system as Eq. (1).

$$
\begin{aligned}
a_0 + a_1 i_1 + \cdots + a_{k-1} i_1^{k-1} &= f(i_1) \\
a_0 + a_1 i_2 + \cdots + a_{k-1} i_2^{k-1} &= f(i_2) \\
&\;\;\vdots \\
a_0 + a_1 i_k + \cdots + a_{k-1} i_k^{k-1} &= f(i_k)
\end{aligned}
\tag{1}
$$

Since the value of i_j is different, Eq. (2) can be constructed according to the Lagrange interpolation formula:

$$
f(x) = \sum_{j=1}^{k} f(i_j) \prod_{\substack{l=1 \\ l \neq j}}^{k} \frac{(x - i_l)}{(i_j - i_l)} \quad (\bmod\ q)
\tag{2}
$$

Therefore, the secret $S = f(0)$ can be obtained from Eq. (3).

$$S = (-1)^{k-1} \sum_{j=1}^{k} f(i_j) \prod_{\substack{l=1 \\ l \neq j}}^{k} \frac{i_l}{i_j - i_l} \pmod{q} \tag{3}$$

2.2 Thien-Lin SIS Scheme

Thien and Lin propose an SIS scheme in [15]. By dividing the image pixels into non-overlapping sections and each section has k pixels. Then, the Lagrangian interpolation polynomial is constructed. The pixels of each section are used as the coefficients of the Lagrangian interpolation polynomial to generate multiple shares.

2.3 The Spiral Matrix

In order to recover the secret image in a fine-grained manner during the recovery phase, we combine modular arithmetic to design a multi-interlaced spiral matrix, see Fig. 1(c). The matrix can perform fine-grained block division of the image to be processed. The most obvious advantage is that the image blocks restored each time look uniform and random. Figure 1 shows three special matrices, where the numbering of (a) is sequential, and the numbering of (b) and (c) is spiral. Bessides, they are divided into clockwise and counterclockwise spiral matrices according to the direction of rotation. According to the starting position of the number, they are divided into spiral matrices from outside to inside and from inside to outside. Except for the different order of numbers, the basic rules of these spiral matrices are similar.

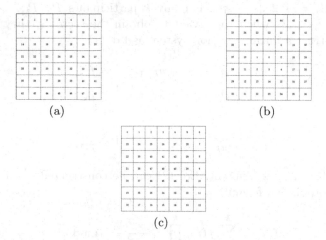

(a)   (b)

(c)

Fig. 1. Three types of matrices

In this paper, we will use the method shown in Fig. 1(c) to segment and number the image. Then, the restoration of secret image can achieve a more fine-grained progressive method. Besides, the recovered content looks very random. In fact, the matrix shown in Fig. 1(a) can also achieve fine-grained recovery, however, its recovery results do not seem to be random enough.

3 The Proposed Scheme

With the rapid development of the Internet, IoT and cloud computing have also emerged. Therefore, information security has become particularly important. How to ensure the security of image information in the IoT is one of the problems to be solved in this paper. As shown in Fig. 2, cloud computing layer: high-speed computing equipment with large-scale, distributed, high-availability, scalability and security; Edge computing layer: computing terminal equipment with light weight, high performance, low power consumption, flexible configuration of computing power, convenient access, etc.; IoT device layer: basic devices with computing and perception characteristics. The data collected at the IoT device layer need to be calculated and processed. Then, they will be uploaded to the cloud server. The safe transmission and storage of data during the whole process is very important.

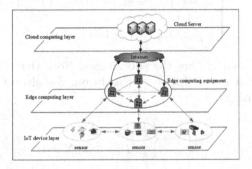

Fig. 2. The spiral matrix

Therefore, a lightweight PSIS scheme based on multi-node collaboration in the IoT is proposed in this paper. This scheme divides the secret image into multiple shares and stores them in different nodes. Our proposed scheme can not only perform mutual authentication between nodes, but also ensure the safe transmission and storage of images.

The proposed scheme is divided into two phases: the sharing phase and recovery phase, the implementation details are as follows.

Sharing Phase

1. Divide the secret image(note: IoT device completed).
   Divide the secret image I with size $a \times b$ into m non-overlapping blocks equally. Then, use the method shown in Fig. 1 to number these blocks, marked as

$I_1, I_2, I_3, \cdots, I_m$. Besides, all of these blocks should meet two conditions as Eq. (5)

$$\begin{cases} I = \bigcup_i I_i & ,i = 1, 2, 3, \cdots, m. \\ I_i \bigcap I_j = \varnothing & ,1 \leq i \neq j \leq m. \end{cases} \tag{4}$$

2. Generate the sub-images(note: Edge layer device implementation).

Perform modular operation on the numbers corresponding to these m sub-images. According to the related knowledge of number theory, $a \pmod{b} = c$, where $0 \leq c < b$ and a, b, c are all positive integers. Therefore, we perform modular operations on m numbers respectively in this paper. Then, $q \pmod{M}$ and $q \pmod{N}$ two operations shoule be performed, where $q = 1, 2, 3, \cdots, m$ and $M = k, N = k^2$. Specifically as shown in Eq. 6.

$$\begin{cases} I_1' = \bigcup_t I_t, t \in [1, m], t(modM) = 0 \\ I_2' = \bigcup_t I_t, t \in [1, m], t(modN) = 1 \\ \vdots \\ I_j' = \bigcup_t I_t, t \in [1, m], t(modN) = q \\ q \neq k \times i, q \leq N - 1, n \in [1, n] \end{cases} \tag{5}$$

In Eq. (6), $I_1', I_2', \cdots, I_j'$ are the sub-images. Note that the value q should satisfy $q \neq pi$ and $i = 1, 2, 3, \cdots$. In addition, the size of these sub-images should satisfy Eq. (7).

$$size(I_j') = \begin{cases} \frac{1}{k}|I|, j = 1 \\ \frac{1}{k^2}|I|, j \in [2, N - 1] \end{cases} \tag{6}$$

3. Generate n sub-shadows for each sub-image(note: Cloud computing layer equipment completed).

For I_1', we use Thien-Lin (k, n) SIS to generate n sub-shadows $s_{1,1}, s_{1,2}, s_{1,3}, \cdots, s_{1,n}$.

For $I_j', (j \geq 2)$, we use Thien-Lin $(k + j - 1, n)$ SIS to generate n sub-shadows $s_{j,1}, s_{j,2}, s_{j,3}, \cdots, s_{j,n}$.

4. Generate n shadow images. Besides, our standard parameter for setting the module is 257 in Thien-Lin $(k + j - 1, n)$ SIS.

The final n shadow images $S_i = s_{1,i} \cup s_{2,i} \cup s_{3,i} \cup \cdots \cup s_{n,i}, i = 1, 2, 3, \cdots, n$.

Note that the shadow size is $|S_i| = \frac{|I|}{n}(1 + \sum_{l=k+1}^{n} \frac{1}{l}), i = 1, 2, 3, \cdots, n$. Finally, we store n shadow images in different nodes and perform authentication between nodes if necessary, or upload them to the cloud server for analysis and processing.

Recovery Phase

In the recovery phase, there need at least k shadow images to recover the secret image. As the share increases, more content can be recovered. Until all shadow images participate in the restoration, the secret image can be completely restored. The difference in the number of shares leads to different recovery results. There are $n - k + 1$ cases of recovery results. Suppose there are currently s shadow images involved in the reconstruction. The specific process is as follows.

1. $s = k$. A $k - 1$-degree polynomial is constructed. Next, a linear equation system like Eq. (1) is constructed. Then, the sub-image I_1' can be obtained by solving the k coefficients of the equation system. Finaly, we put the blocks that make up I_1' back to the original positions to recover part of the original image. Note that only sub-image I_1' can be recovered from these k shadow images.

2. $s = k + j - 1, j \geq 2$. Similarly, we should construct several polynomials:

$$f(x) = a_0 + a_1 x + a_2 x^2 + a_3 x^3 + \cdots + a_{k-1} x^{k-1}.$$
$$f(x) = a_0 + a_1 x + a_2 x^2 + a_3 x^3 + \cdots + a_k x^k.$$

$$\vdots$$

$$f(x) = a_0 + a_1 x + a_2 x^2 + a_3 x^3 + \cdots + a_{k+j-2} x^{k+j-2}.$$

Then, we construct the corresponding linear equations according to these polynomials. The sub-image $I_1', I_2', \cdots, I_j'$ can be obtained by solving the coefficients of the equation system respectively. Similarly, the corresponding image content can be restored by placing these blocks of these sub-images in their original positions.

Theorem 1. *Each shadow image gives no clue about the secret image.*

Proof. We construct several Langerange interpolation polynomials in the sharing phase, namely the shadow image generation process, and the pixels of the secret image are taken as the coefficients of the polynomials.

Theorem 2. *Any set of less than k shadow images cannot obtain any information about the secret image.*

Proof. In short, any set of less than k shadow images cannot obtain any information about the secret image.

Theorem 3. *Any set of t ($k \leq t < n$) shadow images can decode the secret image in a degree.*

Proof. In short, any set of t ($k \leq t < n$) shadow images can decode the secret image in a degree.

Theorem 4. *Only when all the shadow images are involved in the reconstruction can the secret image be completely recovered*

Proof. According to **Theorem** 3, each sub-image along with the entire secret image can be recovered if all shadow images are involved in the reconstruction.

4   Experimental Results and Example

4.1   Experimental Results

In the section, we take "Lena" as an example to analyze the performance of the proposed method, the size of "Lena" is 372×372, which is shown in Fig. 3. This example is done with $k = 3$, $n = 9$. First, we should divide "Lena" into no overlapping blocks of equal size, which is shown in Fig. 4. Here, the block size is 12×12, we mark the blocks in Fig. 4 in a spiral manner, denoted as M. When $(M \bmod 3) = 0$, sub-image Q_1 is generated. Then, when $(M \bmod 9) = 1$, $(M \bmod 9) = 2$, $(M \bmod 9) = 4$, $(M \bmod 9) = 5$, $(M \bmod 9) = 7$ and $(M \bmod 9) = 8$, sub-image Q_2, Q_3, Q_4, Q_5, Q_6, Q_7 are generate shown in Fig. 5. Next, encrypt each subgraph Q_j, $j \in [1, 7]$.

Fig. 3. Secret S_1

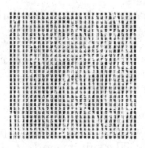

Fig. 4. Segment image

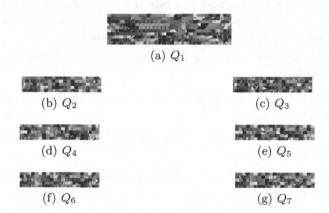

(a) Q_1

(b) Q_2

(c) Q_3

(d) Q_4

(e) Q_5

(f) Q_6

(g) Q_7

Fig. 5. Seven sub-images

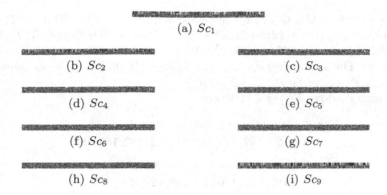

(a) Sc_1

(b) Sc_2 (c) Sc_3

(d) Sc_4 (e) Sc_5

(f) Sc_6 (g) Sc_7

(h) Sc_8 (i) Sc_9

Fig. 6. Nine shadow images

In the encryption phase, we encrypt the subgraph Q_j according to different thresholds. The encryption threshold of each sub-image is expressed as Q_j^{k+j-1}, $j \in [1, 7]$ (note: the subgraph Q_j is encrypted with $(k+j-1, n)$ threshold). Assign the shadows Sc_1, Sc_2, Sc_3, Sc_4, Sc_5, Sc_6, Sc_7, Sc_8, Sc_9 to 9 participants. The result is shown in Fig. 6.

The process and effects of the recovery phase are consistent with the schemes described.

4.2 Example

We use scalable ($k = 3$, $n = 9$) threshold to encode secret image S_2. Through our scheme processing, the secret image c generates 7 subgraphs Q_j, $j \in [1, 7]$.

Assume that Q_1 consists of three 3 pixels blocks $B_{1,1} = (210, 211, 213)$, $B_{1,2} = (215, 215, 216)$, $B_{1,3} = (231, 217, 185)$. Q_2 is one 4-pixels block, $B_{2,1} = (233, 207, 211, 212)$. Q_3 is one 5-pixels block, $B_{3,1} = (215, 211, 196, 193, 199,)$. Q_4 is one 6-pixels block, $B_{4,1} = (249, 168, 128, 84, 89, 105)$. Q_5 consists of one 7-pixels block, $B_{5,1} = (102, 105, 108, 222, 223, 224, 226)$. Q_6 is one 8-pixels block, $B_{6,1} = (176, 179, 180, 181, 183, 186, 190, 195)$. Q_7 consists of one 9-pixels block, $B_{7,1} = (159, 162, 164, 167, 168, 166, 166, 165, 165)$.

Encoding Phase

for sub-image Q_1 generate three 2 degree polynomials:

$$f_{1,1}(x) = (210 + 211x^1 + 213x^2) mod 257$$
$$f_{1,2}(x) = (215 + 215x^1 + 216x^2) mod 257 \tag{7}$$
$$f_{1,3}(x) - (231 + 217x^1 + 185x^2) mod 257$$

for each block $B_{1,1}$, $B_{1,2}$, $B_{1,3}$ respectively, and then compute the values $f_{1,i}(j)$, $i \in [1, 3]$, $j \in [1, 9]$. Thus the sub-shadow $s_{1,j}$, $j \in [1, 9]$, for each participant P_j is $s_{1,j} = (f_{1,1}(j), f_{1,2}(j), f_{1,3}(j))$.

For sub-images Q_2, Q_3,..., Q_7 generate $f_{2,1}(x) = (223 + 207x^1 + 211x^2 + 212x^3)mod257$, $f_{3,1}(x) = (215+211x^1+196x^2+193x^3+199x^4)mod257$, $f_{7,1}(x) = (159 + 162x^1 + 164x^2 + 167x^3 + 168x^4 + 166x^5 + 166x^6 + 165x^7 + 165x^8)mod257$, respectively. The subshadow $s_{2,j}$, $s_{3,j}$, ..., $s_{7,j}$, $j \in [1,9]$. For each participant P_j is $s_{2,j} = f_2(j)$, $s_{3,j} = f_3(j)$,..., $s_{7,j} = f_7(j)$.

The nine shadows $SC_j, j \in [1,9]$ are:

$$SC_1 = (s_{1,1}, s_{2,1}, s_{3,1}, s_{4,1}, s_{5,1}, s_{6,1}, s_{7,1})$$
$$= ([120, 132, 119], 82, 243, 52, 182, 185, 189)$$
$$SC_2 = (s_{1,2}, s_{2,2}, s_{3,2}, s_{4,2}, s_{5,2}, s_{6,2}, s_{7,2})$$
$$= ([199, 224, 120], 93, 238, 128, 221, 129, 35)$$
$$\cdots \tag{8}$$
$$SC_9 = (s_{1,9}, s_{2,9}, s_{3,9}, s_{4,9}, s_{5,9}, s_{6,9}, s_{7,9})$$
$$= ([87, 114, 207], 250, 197, 165, 230, 235, 251)$$

Decoding Phase

The secret image S_2 can be reconstructed from 3 to 9 shadows under progress model. Any 3 shadows can reconstruct sub-image Q_1, any 4 shadows can reconstruct the 4-pixels block, then sub-image Q_2 can be extracted together with Q_1, any 5 shadows can reconstruct Q_1, Q_2 and Q_3, any 6 shadows can reconstruct Q_1, Q_2, Q_3, Q_4. As the number of shadows increases, all subimages Q_1, Q_2, Q_3, Q_4, Q_5, Q_6, Q_7 are restored losslessly. So, all seven shadows can reconstruct the entire secret image $S_2 = Q_1||Q_2||Q_3||Q_4||Q_5||Q_6||Q_7$.

5   Conclusion

With the rapid development of the Internet, people's lives are increasingly dependent on it. For example, IoT based on the Internet has been widely applied to many aspects of life, such as transportation, security, medical care, manufacturing, agriculture, and so on. However, in the related applications of the IoT, security issues have become a focus of attention. A lightweight PSIS scheme based on multi-node collaboration in the IoT is proposed. Generally speaking, the proposed scheme can recover the entire secret image in a fine-grained manner. The difference from the existing schemes is that it is global progressive. Actually, the recovery process can also be used as a batch authentication of nodes. In addition, the size of the secret share generated by the secret image is smaller than that of the original image. Therefore, the energy of the nodes can be saved during storage or transmission. In summary, our proposed method is suitable for related applications of the IoT.

References

1. Ammar, M., Russello, G., Crispo, B.: Internet of things: a survey on the security of IoT frameworks. J. Inf. Secur. Appl. **38**, 8–27 (2018)

2. Christin, D., Reinhardt, A., Mogre, P., Steinmetz, R.: Wireless sensor networks and the internet of things: selected challenges (2009)
3. Kocakulak, M., Butun, I.: An overview of wireless sensor networks towards internet of things. In: 2017 IEEE 7th Annual Computing and Communication Workshop and Conference (CCWC), pp. 1–6 (2017)
4. Raj, A., Steingart, D.: Review-power sources for the internet of things. J. Electrochem. Soc. **165** (2018)
5. Li, F., Xiong, P.: Practical secure communication for integrating wireless sensor networks into the internet of things. IEEE Sens. J. **13**, 3677–3684 (2013)
6. Shamir, A.: How to share a secret. Commun. ACM **22**, 612–613 (1979)
7. Kanso, A., Ghebleh, M.: An efficient (t, n)-threshold secret image sharing scheme. Multimed. Tools Appl. **76**, 16369–16388 (2016)
8. Bao, L., Yi, S., Zhou, Y.: Combination of sharing matrix and image encryption for lossless (k, n) -secret image sharing. IEEE Trans. Image Process. **26**, 5618–5631 (2017)
9. Liu, Y.-X., Sun, Q.-D., Yang, C.-N.: (k, n) secret image sharing scheme capable of cheating detection. EURASIP J. Wirel. Commun. Netw. **2018**, 1–6 (2018)
10. Liu, Y.-X., Yang, C.-N.: Scalable secret image sharing scheme with essential shadows. Signal Process. Image Commun. **58**, 49–55 (2017)
11. Yan, X., Lu, Y., Liu, L.: A general progressive secret image sharing construction method. Signal Process. Image Commun. **71**, 66–75 (2019)
12. Guo, Y., Ma, Z., Zhao, M.-D.: Polynomial based progressive secret image sharing scheme with smaller shadow size. IEEE Access **7**, 73782–73789 (2019)
13. Yang, C.-N., Chu, Y.-Y.: A general (k, n) scalable secret image sharing scheme with the smooth scalability. J. Syst. Softw. **84**, 1726–1733 (2011)
14. Liu, Y., Yang, C.-N., Chou, Y.-S., Wu, S.-Y., Sun, Q.-D.: Progressive (k, n) secret image sharing scheme with meaningful shadow images by GEMD and RGEMD. J. Vis. Commun. Image Represent. **55**, 766–777 (2018)
15. Zhang, L., Zheng, X., Liu, Y.: Progressive secret image sharing scheme based on semantic segmentation. IEEE Access **8**, 173289–173297 (2020)
16. Zhang, L., et al.: Modular-based secret image sharing in internet of things: a global progressive-enabled approach. Concurrency and Computation: Practice and Experience (2020)
17. Thien, C.-C., Lin, J.-C.: Secret image sharing. Comput. Graph. **26**(5), 765–770 (2002)

SAD: Website Fingerprinting Defense Based on Adversarial Examples

Renzhi Tang[1,2], Guowei Shen[1,2(✉)], Chun Guo[1,2], and Yunhe Cui[1,2]

[1] College of Computer Science and Technology, Guizhou University,
Guiyang 550025, China
gwshen@gzu.edu.cn

[2] Guizhou Provincial Key Laboratory of Public Big Data, Guiyang 550025, China

Abstract. Website Fingerprinting (WF) attacks can infer website names from encrypted network traffic when the victim is browsing the website. Inherent defenses of anonymous communication systems such as The Onion Router (Tor) cannot compete with current WF attacks. The state-of-the-art attack based on deep learning can gain over 98% accuracy in Tor. However, the existing defense will bring high bandwidth overhead, affect the user's network experience or cannot be used in actual scenarios. Some researchers found that deep learning models are vulnerable to adversarial examples. In this paper, based on adversarial examples we propose Segmented Adversary Defense (SAD) for deep learning-based WF attacks. Network traffic is divided into multiple segments. Then, the adversarial examples for each segment of traffic can be generated by SAD. Finally, dummy packets from adversarial examples are inserted after each segment traffic. Experimentally, our results show that SAD can effectively reduce the accuracy of WF attacks. The technique drops the accuracy of the state-of-the-art attack hardened from 96% to 3% while incurring only 40% bandwidth overhead. Compared with the existing proposed defense named Deep Fingerprinting Defender (DFD), the defense effect of SAD is better under the same bandwidth overhead.

Keywords: Website fingerprinting attack · Website fingerprinting defense · Tor · Adversarial examples

1 Introduction

Anonymous communication system can protect the users' information through data encryption and multi-hop proxy. The Onion Router (Tor) [6], a kind of anonymous communication software, is widely used worldwide. However, inherent defense of Tor is difficult to against WF attacks. In WF attack, encrypted traffic is collected by WF attacker between client and guard node of Tor. Then, the website name can be infer from the traffic obtained by attackers.

© ICST Institute for Computer Sciences, Social Informatics and Telecommunications Engineering 2022
Published by Springer Nature Switzerland AG 2022. All Rights Reserved
W. Shi et al. (Eds.): SPNCE 2021, LNICST 423, pp. 88–102, 2022.
https://doi.org/10.1007/978-3-030-96791-8_7

In the past, the attacker extracts a variety of packets level features from encrypted traffic, such as number, order, direction and unique length, then use machine learning for classification [8,16,22]. In recent years, deep learning has been recognized in various fields such as image classification [15] and speech recognition [11]. Different from traditional machine learning, automatic extraction of features from original data is one of the advantages of deep learning. WF attacks based on deep learning have been proposed such as Automated Website Fingerprinting (AWF) [19], Var-CNN [2] and Deep Fingerprinting (DF) [20]. DF can gain more 98% accuracy only using direction sequence of traffic.

With the attacks are constantly updated, some WF defenses have been proposed such as WTF-PAD [14], Walkie-Talkie (WT) [23] and Deep Fingerprinting Defender(DFD) [1]. In addition, researchers have found that deep learning models are vulnerable to adversarial examples [7]. It can make a classifier based on deep learning misclassify [5]. Therefore, some WF defenses based on adversarial examples is proposed such as WF-GAN [12] and Mockingbird [18]. But, WTF-PAD, WT and DFD have expired defense capability and suboptimal bandwidth overhead. WF-GAN and Mockingbird are difficult to apply to live traffic. The reason is that they need adversarial examples based on an integral traffic flow. The situation is unrealistic.

In response to the above problems, we propose a defense SAD based on adversarial examples. SAD consists of two components: an adversarial examples generation model and a WF attack model. The former can generate adversarial examples according to direction sequence of traffic flow. The WF attack model provides an optimization scheme for SAD during training. Experiments show that SAD effectively reduces the attack success accuracy of DF, Var-CNN and AWF attack models with slight bandwidth overhead. SAD have excellent defense capabilities whether facing unknown attack or new adversarial training. The main contributions of this paper are as follow:

1) This paper proposes a WF defense, named SAD, using segmented processing and adversarial examples. Compared with some previous studies, SAD does not require global traffic sequence information when generating adversarial examples. Therefor, It can apply in live traffic.
2) SAD can be easily generated adversarial examples for different attack models based on deep learning. The input and output of SAD are the original direction sequence data rather than burst-based data. This is same data format required by the attack model.
3) SAD can effectively reduce the attack success rate, even facing adversarial training or unknown attack. For the three existing WF attack models, DF, Var-CNN and AWF, SAD can reduce these attack success rate from 96% to 1%. Compare with DFD, we have better defense whether in open-world or close-world.

2   Related Work

2.1   Website Fingerprinting Attack

Herrmann et al. [10] first applied the WF attack on Tor in 2009, but the accuracy was only 3% in close-world. In 2011, Panchenko et al. [17] proposed a WF attack based on Support Vector Machines (SVM). It improves the accuracy of WF attacks. But, the computational cost of these WF attack classifiers is too high and not practical. With the development of computers, researchers have proposed more effective attacks. In 2014, the K-Nearest Neighbors classifier proposed by Wang et al. [22]. The attack achieved higher accuracy with shorter training time and test time. In addition, Panchenko et al. [16] used the cumulative sum of packet lengths as features and SVM as a classifier, which achieved good results in close-world.

In order to overcome the shortcomings of WF attack methods based on traditional machine learning, researchers have leveraged deep learning. To skip the process that manually extracting features, Rimmer et al. [19] proposed a deep learning-based WF attack AWF. They collected a lot of training data and tried to use three different neural network structure, Stacked Denoising Autoencoder (SDAE), Convolutional Neural Network (CNN) and Long Short-Term Memory (LSTM). The action make accuracy achieve 96%. Sanjit [2] proposed Var-CNN based on ResNets [9] deep learning. It has a better recognition effect when the amount of training data is small, especially in close-world. Sirinam et al. [20] proposed a CNN-based WF attack model DF. The model has reached a high level of attack ability in both close-world and open-world.

2.2   Website Fingerprinting Defense

WF defense against WF attacks by inserting dummy packets. The defense will bring extra bandwidth overhead that affects the user's experience. All defenses aim at high misclassification rate and low bandwidth overhead. BuFLO [6] sends packets at the same constant rate in both directions of the network traffic, and ends the defense of packets within a short period of time after the page is loaded. But, it brings unreasonable bandwidth overhead. Tamaraw [4] and CS-BuFLO [3] extend BuFLO. The difference is that the download and upload rates can be set to different rates. But their bandwidth overhead exceeds 100%. The WTF-PAD proposed by Juarez et al. [22]. The defense attempts to fill a large time gap between two data packets. Whenever the gap is large, WTF-PAD will send a series of dummy packets. It reduce the accuracy of K-NN attacks. However, WTF-PAD was defeated by the WF attack DF. Walkie-Talkie (WT) [23], makes the attack success rate of DF only 49.7% with 31% bandwidth overhead. WT changed the communication mode of both parties from full-duplex to half-duplex. The change affects the user's network experience. For WF attack based on deep learning, some researchers proposed WF defense based on adversarial examples, WF-GAN [12] and Mockingbird [18]. They have excellent performance, but they difficult to be applied in live traffic due to the requirements of model input data.

The latest defense method DFD [1] injects a dummy burst sequence according to the previous burst sequence in the real-time traffic. When the injection method is the server-side injection method, the attack success rate using the convolutional neural network (CNN) as the attack model is reduced from 99.93% to 5% with 85.56% bandwidth overhead. However, he did not test the existing WF attacks. In addition, the DFD cannot stably insert dummy packets. In some cases, the number of inserted dummy packets is small. When bandwidth overhead is small, the expected defense effect cannot be achieved.

3   Preliminary

3.1   Threat Model

Tor protects browsing website information of user through data encryption and multi-hop proxy. Its working principle is shown in Fig. 1. In general, User randomly select three relay nodes from global active relay nodes. These selected nodes will form a communication link. All traffic will be encrypted when through the link. The purpose of WF attacker is to obtain the website name visited by users from encrypted traffic. To be specific, the attacker monitors and saves traffic between the guard node and user. Then, the attacker uses the traffic to infer the website name using deep learning. The attacker generally need direction sequence of traffic packet. The outgoing (client to server) and incoming (server to client) packets are represented as $+1$ and -1, respectively.

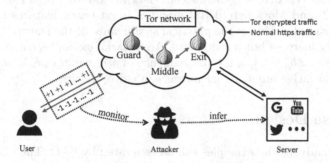

Fig. 1. WF attack mode.

However, the attacker did not own all the data of the website. We mark target websites as monitored sites, and other sites as unmonitored sites. To this end, WF attack and WF defense are evaluated in two different experimental environments: close-world and open-world. Close-world means that users can only access monitored websites. The open-world is closer to the real scene than the close-world. It allow user to access any website.

3.2   Defense Model

The goal of the defender is to reduce the accuracy of WF attacks. One of the best ways to reduce the accuracy is to change the features the traffic. For this, there are two operation: inserting dummy packets and delay packets. Considering the user's network experience, inserting dummy packets usually is adopted by WF defense. The user or the guard node only decide to send packets in a single direction, dummy packets senders are deployed at both ends. In addition, there are two scenarios for WF defense: black-box or white-box. Black-box means that the structure and parameters of the WF attack model are unknown. We only know the correspondence between the input and output of the model; white-box means that the structure and parameter information of the attack model can be obtained. We can interact deeply with the attack model.

3.3   Adversarial Examples

Adversarial examples is a carefully designed input data for deep learning model, which will cause the model to output incorrect prediction results. It was first discovered by the research in the field of image classification [21]. Fast Gradient Sign Method (FGSM) [7] is a classic adversarial examples generation method based on gradient. It can be expressed as $x' = x + \alpha Sign(\nabla_x J(\theta, x, y))$, x' is adversarial examples, θ is the parameter of deep learning model, x is the input of the model, y is the correct category for x, $J(\theta, x, y)$ is loss function, $\nabla_x J(\theta, x, y)$ is the gradient of the loss function with respect to x, α is super parameter. The WF defense generates adversarial examples is similar to FGSM. WF-GAN [12] and Mockingbird [18] modifies burst-based features to generate adversarial examples. Due to the practical significance of the feature, the feature value can only increase but not decrease. Adversarial examples can expressed as $[b_1 + \delta_1, b_2 + \delta_2, ..., b_n + \delta_n]$, b_i is burst sequence of original flow, δ_i is perturbation size and nonnegative number that means can't drop packet.

4   Defense Design

In this paper, adversarial examples will be generated by SAD. The role of adversarial examples is to mislead the attack model. The purpose for protecting user's privacy information is achieved by using adversarial examples. Misleading attack models are an intuitive way of defending. Figure 2 represents the overall flow of SAD. x_i is direction sequence that is input data of SAD. y_i is the dummy packets being inserted. Adversarial examples $x' = [x_1, y_1, x_2, y_2, ..., ..., x_i, y_i]$ is output of SAD. We assume C is attack model, L is predict label of the attack model. In that way, SAD makes $C(x') \neq C(x) = L_x$, where $x' = x \oplus y$, y is dummy packets in x', $\oplus$ indicates how to insert the dummy packets. The number of packets inserted is proportional to the increased bandwidth overhead. So, we want to minimize the number of dummy packets when the defense effect remains unchanged.

4.1   SAD Model Design

This paper uses the solution for injecting dummy packets at both ends. At the same time, SAD has the characteristics of low bandwidth overhead and diversified adversarial examples. The generating of adversarial examples is shown in Fig. 3.

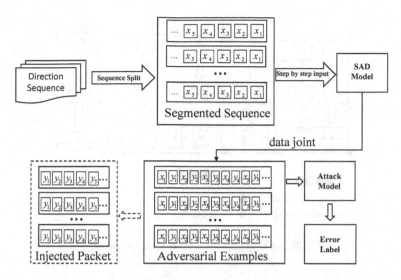

Fig. 2. SAD defense process

Packets Direction Sequence Segmentation. The segmentation refers to cutting the sequence into different lengths according to different segmented packet number (SPN). SPN set $(SPNS)$ consists of several different SPN. To public data set, each piece of data is a packets directions sequence generated during the complete access process of a certain website. The purpose of segmentation is to simulate the transmission process of packets. The segmented adversarial examples y_i is inserted after each segment of original packets until the remaining length of sequence is less than $min(SPNS)$. Finally, the segmented sequence and the segmented adversarial examples are sequentially connected to form a complete adversarial examples.

Generating Adversarial Examples. SAD contains multiple sub-models with similar structures. The number of sub-models is equal to the number of pre-set $SPNS$ elements. The sub-model structure is a simple multi-layer fully connected neural network. Its activation function is $Relu$, as in Formula 1. In order to shorten the model training time and improve the robustness of the model, $Dropout$ and $Batch\ Normalization$ are used. The input of the sub-model is direction sequence, specifically $+1$ or -1. The features dimension of the sub-model output is $\lfloor SPN*BO \rfloor$ for strictly control the bandwidth overhead, where BO is bandwidth overhead. Significantly, output of sub-model only contain -1 or $+1$, We applied $Tanh$ and $Sign$ to the model output. $Tanh$ and $Sign$ as in Formula 2 and Formula 3. Finally, output of sub-model represent the direction of dummy packets. The main function of the sub-model is to generate adversarial examples corresponding to the segmented sequence. The output of multiple sub-models is spliced with segmented sequence to generate complete adversarial examples, the process is shown in Algorithm 1.

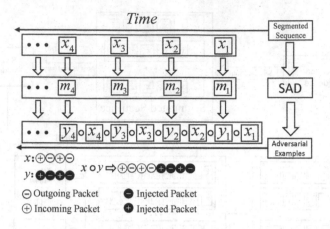

Fig. 3. SAD generates adversarial examples

$$Relu(x) = max(0, x) \tag{1}$$

$$Tanh(x) = \frac{e^x - e^{-x}}{e^x + e^{-x}} \tag{2}$$

$$Sign(x) = \begin{cases} -1, x < 0 \\ 1, x \geq 0 \end{cases} \tag{3}$$

In Algorithm 1, The input dimensions of sub-model in the SMS correspond to the $SPNS$ elements one-to-one. First, we randomly select SPN from $SPNS$. Second, we choose the corresponding sub-model m_i that input dimension is SPN. Finally, the sub-sequence $x_i(length = SPN)$ is selected from f and input into the selected sub-model to obtain the output y_i. In other words, the first segmented sequence x_1 is put into the sub-model m_1 to get output y_1. The input of the sub-model m_2 selected for the second time is x_2, and the corresponding output is y_2. By analogy, the input of the sub-model m_i is x_i, and the output is y_i. Finally, the adversarial examples generated by all sub-models are spliced with the segmented sequence to generate adversarial examples y, in the form of $[x_1, y_1, x_2, y_2, ..., x_{i-1}, y_{i-1}, x_i, y_i]$.

SAD Model Training. First, SAD outputs the adversarial examples according to the original data. Then, $loss$ will be generated when the adversarial examples are fed to the attack model, loss function is $CrossEntropyLoss$. The difference is that our goal is to make the loss larger. Moreover, we only update the parameters of SAD. In this way, the accuracy of the attack model will decrease with adversarial sample generated by SAD. The attack model can be any WF attack model based on deep learning. Significantly, we use $Sign$ to map the SAD output

---

Algorithm 1: SAD generate adversarial examples

Input: Packets direction sequence: f; Sub-model set: SMS; Segment packet
      number set: $SPNS$

Output: Adversarial examples: AE

Define: ODL : sequence f length; SI : split index of f; RL : remaining length of
   f; Res : a list; CSS : current segment sequence; CSM : current sub-model;
   SAE : segment adversarial examples; LSS: last segment sequence

while $RL \geq min(SPNS)$ **do** // RL initial value is ODL
    Initialize CandidateSPN to an empty set
    for spn in $SPNS$ **do**
        if $spn \leq RL$ **then**
            CandiiateSPN.addElement(spn)
        end
    end
    SPN $\leftarrow$ random choice a element from CandidateSPN
    CS $\leftarrow$ split f index from SI to SI + SPN
    SI $\leftarrow$ SI + SPN, RL $\leftarrow$ RL - SPN
    CSM $\leftarrow$ choice a sub-model from SMS according to SPN
    SAE $\leftarrow$ CSM(CSS) // CSM compute SAEusing CSS
    Res.addElement(CSS, SAE)// Res initial value is empty array
end
if $RL > 0$ **then**
    LSS $\leftarrow$ split f index from ODL-RL to end
    Res.addElement(LSS)
end
AE $\leftarrow$ joint Res elements in order

---

to -1 or $+1$. But this function is not diversified, the input gradient of $Sign$ as
the output gradient.

5 Experiment and Analysis

5.1 Dataset

In this paper, the experimental data set is collected by Sirinam et al. [20], which
uses tor-browser-crawler [13] to simulate the process of users visiting the website.
They visited Alexa 100 sites in the close-world, each website was visited 1250
times. In this process, tcpdump stores traffic as file in each browse. Next, they
only store the data for at least 1000 valid visits after filtering out the invalid
data. In the final result, 95 websites are stored. In the open-world, they visited
50000 Alexa websites, excluding the 100 websites in the close-world data set.
Finally, they got 40716 unmonitored website traffic data after filtering invalid
data.

    These traffic can be expressed as a sequence of (*timestamp, packet_size,
direction*), where *direction*:$+1(-1)$ means outgoing (incoming) packet. Wang et

al. [22] ignored timestamps and packet size and only remain packet direction. On this foundation, Sirinam et al. [20] verification showed that using packet length does not get a attractive improvement in the accuracy of the attack. Therefore, all data is represented by a sequence of packet directions. The sequence contains only −1 and +1.

In order to evaluate the defense performance of DFD and compare it with SAD, the data is used to generate defense data using server-side injection according to the algorithm in DFD. The average bandwidth overhead range of these defense data is $0 < BO \le 1$.

5.2   Performance Index

In this paper, we define three performance index: Attack Success Rate (ASR), Defense Success Rate (DSR) and Bandwidth Overhead (BO), as shown in Formula (4)–(6):

$$ASR = \frac{N_1}{N} \tag{4}$$

$$DSR = \frac{N_2}{N} \tag{5}$$

$$BO = \frac{I_{total}}{OV_{total}} \tag{6}$$

In Formula 4 to 6, N is the number of browsing records contained in the data set, N_1 is the number of data correctly identified by the WF attack model, N_2 is the number of error identification of the WF attack model, I_{total} is the number of inserted dummy packets, OV_{total} is the number of valid packets of the source data.

5.3   Result and Discussion

(1) WF Attack Model Evaluation in Different Sequence Length. Deep learning-based WF attacks use the direction sequence of packets as input data. The strategy adopted by WF defense is to insert dummy packets into normal traffic. The most obvious change brought by this strategy is that the length of the direction sequence becomes longer. In previous WF attacks based on deep learning, the sequence length was usually set to 5000. If the sequence length is less than 5000, fill it with 0, if it exceeds, it will be truncated directly. When the sequence length increases, the truncation length of the direction sequence is increased to obtain a credible result. Considering the range of bandwidth overhead $0 < BO \le 1$, the sequence length is set $5000 \le SecquenceLength \le 10000$, the stride is 500. In this experiment, three WF attack models, DF, Var-CNN and AWF, are used in both close-world and open-world. The result is shown in Fig. 4.

It can be seen from Fig. 4 in close-world, different sequence length have stable ASR. When the sequence length is 7500, ASR of DF reaches the highest, 98.14%.

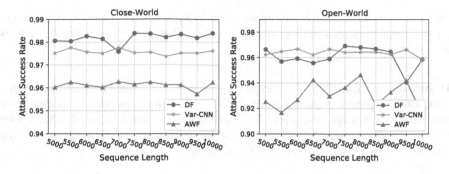

Fig. 4. Evaluation of website fingerprint attack model based on deep learning

When the sequence length is 7000, ASR of Var-CNN reaches the highest, 97.56%, which is in line with the ability performance in its original paper. In open-world, ASR of Var-CNN, AWF and DF reaches the highest, 96.39%, 91.28%, 96.04% respectively. In comparison, DF and Var-CNN are relatively stable. Therefore, in subsequent experiments related to AWF, ASR except AWF in open-world is between 96% and 97%. Finally, we can consider that the performance of the three attack models is stable in the current sequence length range.

(2) Defense Model Evaluation in Different BO. This experiment $spn \in \{10, 20, 30, 45, 40, 60, 100\}$. In different environments, the relationship between BO and DSR is shown in Fig. 5. It can be seen from Fig. 5 that DSR has been significantly improved with the increase of BO. In close-world, DSR for three attack models is above 90% when BO is 30%. DSR is close to saturation when BO is 40%. Although ASR of the three attack models in this experiment is 96%, there are differences in the defense capabilities of SAD for the three. When BO is 10%, DSR against Var-CNN is only 16.77%. With the same BO, DSR in open-world is higher. It can be seen that it is more beneficial to the attacker in close-world. It is more beneficial to the defender in open-world. In addition,

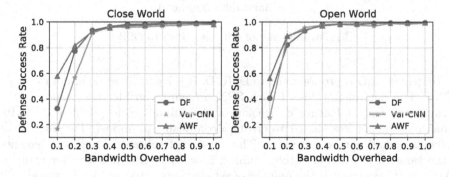

Fig. 5. SAD defense effect

DSR cannot be significantly increased when BO reaches a threshold. In practice, we can ignore unmonitored website and only confuse monitoring websites. This can save computing costs.

(3) Influence of SPNS. In the process of segmentation, the segment length is randomly selected from a certain SPNS, which increase the randomness of generating adversarial examples. To explore defense capabilities of SAD under different SPNS, we considered different SPNS on the DF attack model, as shown in Table 1. DSR under different SPNS is shown in Fig. 6.

Table 1. SPN set

$SPNS$ number	$SPNS$
1	{10, 20, 30, 45, 40, 60, 100}
2	{12, 16, 20, 35, 50, 75, 96}
3	{10, 20, 30, 45}
4	{40, 60, 100}
5	{100, 110, 130, 135, 150, 160}
6	{190, 200, 210, 215, 230, 250}

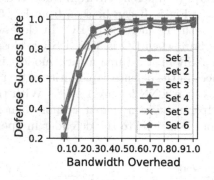

Fig. 6. Influence of different SPNS to DSR

In general, BO is proportional to DSR. DSR is basically same under different SPNS. The minimum value of each SPN set must consider the value of BO, because the output feature dimension of the sub-model is $\lfloor SPN * BO \rfloor$. Its value must be not less than 1 to create a compliant sub-model. The number of elements should not be too much. The number of sub-model and set elements is the same. If the model is too complex, it will increase difficulty for training SAD. On the contrary, if the number of set elements is too small, the model will not achieve a good defense effect because the model is not complex enough. We deliberately provide set 5 and 6, which contain larger element values than other sets. This means that the length of segment sequence is longer, which leads to a certain degree of decline to DSR. We can obtain a conclusion that defense capability is related to segment length. From the experimental results, small segments are more favorable for defense.

(4) Compared with DFD. We use the algorithm that injecting dummy packets proposed by DFD to generate defense data. Then, we calculate the average of BO based on the defense data. DF is selected as the attack model. The purpose is that compared SDA and DFD on same original data. The results are shown in Fig. 7. In different experimental environments, DFD has a higher DSR in a close-world than in open-world, which is the opposite of SAD. To our minds, a large amount of website data only appears once in open-world, even if it is confused by DFD. DSR will drop if the website will be predicted as other unmonitored website. Compared with SAD, DFD's defensive ability is not as good as SAD in open-world or close-world. When the BO increases, the gap between the DSR of the two gradually decreases.

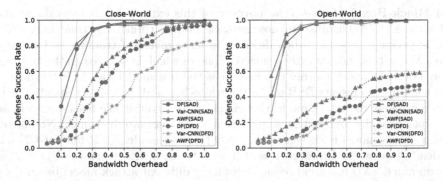

Fig. 7. Comparison of SAD and DFD in same attack model

(5) Adversary Training. Attackers can obtain defense data when the defense is public. In response to this situation, SAD can adjust BO to slow down the decline of DSR. We simulate the situation in this experiment. First, we train the DF attack model on the defense data set until ASR reaches 90%. Then, the attack model is evaluated under different BO. When the defense data sequence and the input feature dimension of the attack model are not the same, if it is not enough, it is filled with 0, and if it is too long, it will be directly truncated. The experimental results are shown in Fig. 8.

When DF uses the adversarial examples generated by SAD for training, its ASR can still reach more than 90% with the same BO. The greater the gap between BO setting of defender and attacker, the higher DSR. Therefore, SAD has excellent defense ability against WF attack model after adversary training.

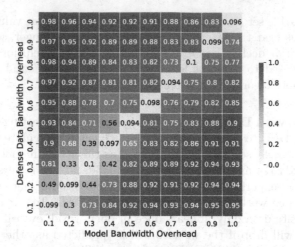

Fig. 8. Adversarial training attack models face defense data with different bandwidth overhead

(6) Black-Box Defense. The purpose of this experiment is to evaluate the robustness of SAD against unknown attack models. Unlike experiments (2)–(5), this experiment is a black-box defense. In the process of training and testing, three WF attack models can be selected, one of which is selected as the training model of SAD, and the other two is used as the test model. In Fig. 9, the dotted and solid line represents DSR under the white-box and black-box respectively. It also represents the attack model that SAD knows. Overall, the black-box defense did not cause the SAD's defense performance to fluctuate too much. No matter which attack model is chosen as the SAD training model, DSR for Var-CNN is basically the lowest. However, it is still close to saturation when the BO is 30%. In summary, SAD has good robustness facing different attack model based deep learning.

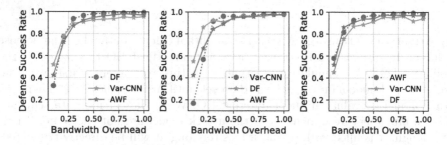

Fig. 9. SAD defense success rate in black-box defense mode

6 Conclusion

In this paper, we proposed a novel Website Fingerprinting defense, called Segment Adversarial Defense, to against deep learning-based WF attacks. SAD performs segmentation processing on live traffic, and injects dummy packets after each segment to complete the defense. SAD benefited from segmented processing can flexibly tune the bandwidth overhead. The operation effectively balance the defense success rate and bandwidth overhead. In addition, SAD can deal with adversarial training and black-box defense. Experimental results show that in a close-world and open-world, the SAD defense success rate can reach up to 99%. It only needs 30% bandwidth overhead to achieve 90% defensive success rate. In summary, SAD can effectively against WF attacks based on deep learning.

References

1. Abusnaina, A., Jang, R., Khormali, A., Nyang, D., Mohaisen, D.: DFD: adversarial learning-based approach to defend against website fingerprinting. In: IEEE INFOCOM 2020-IEEE Conference on Computer Communications, pp. 2459–2468. IEEE (2020)
2. Bhat, S., Lu, D., Kwon, A., Devadas, S.: VAR-CNN: a data-efficient website fingerprinting attack based on deep learning. arXiv preprint arXiv:1802.10215 (2018)
3. Cai, X., Nithyanand, R., Johnson, R.: CS-BuFLO: a congestion sensitive website fingerprinting defense. In: Proceedings of the 13th Workshop on Privacy in the Electronic Society, pp. 121–130 (2014)
4. Cai, X., Nithyanand, R., Wang, T., Johnson, R., Goldberg, I.: A systematic approach to developing and evaluating website fingerprinting defenses. In: Proceedings of the 2014 ACM SIGSAC Conference on Computer and Communications Security, pp. 227–238 (2014)
5. Carlini, N., Wagner, D.: Adversarial examples are not easily detected: bypassing ten detection methods. In: Proceedings of the 10th ACM Workshop on Artificial Intelligence and Security, pp. 3–14 (2017)
6. Dyer, K.P., Coull, S.E., Ristenpart, T., Shrimpton, T.: Peek-a-Boo, I still see you: why efficient traffic analysis countermeasures fail. In: 2012 IEEE Symposium on Security and Privacy, pp. 332–346. IEEE (2012)
7. Goodfellow, I.J., Shlens, J., Szegedy, C.: Explaining and harnessing adversarial examples. arXiv preprint arXiv:1412.6572 (2014)
8. Hayes, J., Danezis, G.: k-fingerprinting: a robust scalable website fingerprinting technique. In: 25th USENIX Security Symposium (USENIX Security 2016), pp. 1187–1203 (2016)
9. He, K., Zhang, X., Ren, S., Sun, J.: Deep residual learning for image recognition. In: Proceedings of the IEEE Conference on Computer Vision and Pattern Recognition, pp. 770–778 (2016)
10. Herrmann, D., Wendolsky, R., Federrath, H.: Website fingerprinting: attacking popular privacy enhancing technologies with the multinomial Naïve-Bayes classifier. In: Proceedings of the 2009 ACM Workshop on Cloud Computing Security, pp. 31–42 (2009)
11. Hinton, G., et al.: Deep neural networks for acoustic modeling in speech recognition: the shared views of four research groups. IEEE Signal Process. Mag. **29**(6), 82–97 (2012)

12. Hou, C., Gou, G., Shi, J., Fu, P., Xiong, G.: WF-GAN: fighting back against website fingerprinting attack using adversarial learning. In: 2020 IEEE Symposium on Computers and Communications (ISCC), pp. 1–7. IEEE (2020)

13. Juarez, M., Afroz, S., Acar, G., Diaz, C., Greenstadt, R.: A critical evaluation of website fingerprinting attacks. In: Proceedings of the 2014 ACM SIGSAC Conference on Computer and Communications Security, pp. 263–274 (2014)

14. Juarez, M., Imani, M., Perry, M., Diaz, C., Wright, M.: Toward an efficient website fingerprinting defense. In: Askoxylakis, I., Ioannidis, S., Katsikas, S., Meadows, C. (eds.) ESORICS 2016. LNCS, vol. 9878, pp. 27–46. Springer, Cham (2016). https://doi.org/10.1007/978-3-319-45744-4_2

15. Krizhevsky, A., Sutskever, I., Hinton, G.E.: ImageNet classification with deep convolutional neural networks. In: Advance Neural Information Processing Systems, vol. 25, pp. 1097–1105 (2012)

16. Panchenko, A., et al.: Website fingerprinting at internet scale. In: NDSS (2016)

17. Panchenko, A., Niessen, L., Zinnen, A., Engel, T.: Website fingerprinting in onion routing based anonymization networks. In: Proceedings of the 10th Annual ACM Workshop on Privacy in the Electronic Society, pp. 103–114 (2011)

18. Rahman, M.S., Imani, M., Mathews, N., Wright, M.: Mockingbird: defending against deep-learning-based website fingerprinting attacks with adversarial traces. IEEE Trans. Inf. Forensics Secur. **16**, 1594–1609 (2020)

19. Rimmer, V., Preuveneers, D., Juarez, M., Van Goethem, T., Joosen, W.: Automated website fingerprinting through deep learning. arXiv preprint arXiv:1708.06376 (2017)

20. Sirinam, P., Imani, M., Juarez, M., Wright, M.: Deep fingerprinting: undermining website fingerprinting defenses with deep learning. In: Proceedings of the 2018 ACM SIGSAC Conference on Computer and Communications Security, pp. 1928–1943 (2018)

21. Szegedy, C., et al.: Intriguing properties of neural networks. arXiv preprint arXiv:1312.6199 (2013)

22. Wang, T., Cai, X., Nithyanand, R., Johnson, R., Goldberg, I.: Effective attacks and provable defenses for website fingerprinting. In: 23rd USENIX Security Symposium (USENIX Security 2014), pp. 143–157 (2014)

23. Wang, T., Goldberg, I.: Walkie-talkie: an efficient defense against passive website fingerprinting attacks. In: 26th USENIX Security Symposium (USENIX Security 2017), pp. 1375–1390 (2017)

A Privacy-Aware and Time-Limited Data Access Control Scheme with Large Universe and Public Traceability for Cloud-Based IoD

Jiawei Zhang[1], Yanbo Yang[2(✉)], Ning Lu[3], Zhiwei Liu[4], and Jianfeng Ma[1]

[1] School of Cyber Engineering, Xidian University, Xi'an, China
jfma@mail.xidian.edu.cn
[2] School of Information Engineering,
Inner Mongolia University of Science and Technology, Baotou, China
yangyanbo@imust.edu.cn
[3] College of Computer Science and Engineering, Northeastern University,
Shenyang, China
luning@neuq.edu.cn
[4] The 27th Research Institute of China Electronics Technology Group Corporation,
Beijing, China

Abstract. Recently, the rapid development of Internet of things (IoT) and 5G techniques has greatly facilitated the emerging applications of Unmanned Aerial Vehicles (UAVs) and the Internet of Drones (IoD). Moreover, Cloud-based IoD supplies an ideal platform for UAV data outsourcing and sharing services to lower their heavy burden. As UAV data are of high sensitivity, the convincing Ciphertext-Policy Attribute-Based Encryption (CP-ABE) can be employed to provide confidentiality and fine-grained access control for UAV data shared in cloud. However, the access policies related to encrypted UAV data usually consist of much sensitive and private information. Meanwhile, there exist misbehaving insiders of UAV data consumers that conduct unlimited access to disable UAV data sharing services, which is disastrous. Besides, the high computation overhead also extremely hinders resource-limited users in IoD. To seek a solution, we propose a privacy-aware and time-limited data access control (PATLDAC) scheme for secure UAV data sharing in Cloud-based IoD. Specifically, PATLDAC achieves user privacy preserving through partially hidden access policy which conceals the values of attributes while leaves their names with no sensitive information. Moreover, PATLDAC provide public user tracing to prevent user key abuse and limits the access time for each data user to guarantee service provision. In addition, PATLDAC realizes high efficiency in both encryption and decryption. Finally, the performance complexity evaluation indicate that PATLDAC is suitable and feasible for IoD systems.

Keywords: Internet of Drone · Cloud computing · CP-ABE · Hidden access policy · Limited access times

© ICST Institute for Computer Sciences, Social Informatics and Telecommunications Engineering 2022
Published by Springer Nature Switzerland AG 2022. All Rights Reserved
W. Shi et al. (Eds.): SPNCE 2021, LNICST 423, pp. 103–116, 2022.
https://doi.org/10.1007/978-3-030-96791-8_8

1 Introduction

With the rapid development of Internet of Things (IoT) [15] and 5G communication [21] techniques, the application of Unmanned Aerial Vehicles (UAVs)
encounters its vigorous advancement. Assisted by massive mobile access of 5G
ground stations (GS) [12] and the strong connection ability among everything
of IoT [2], UAVs can be deployed in various fields for task execution, and these
interconnected UAVs facilitates the emerging Internet of Drone (IoD) [1] that
enables service provision involving traffic supervision, disastrous rescue, good
delivery and so on. In these attractive and practical applications supported by
IoD, the kernel is the massive UAV data that are collected and utilized for
analysis and predication [24]. Nevertheless, most of these applications need a
huge volume of UAV data which exceed the computing and storage capability of
resource-limited UAVs. To be a fortune, the cloud computing supplies an ideal
platform to supply the massive UAV data with sufficient resources for outsourcing and processing and raises the CLoud-based IoD systems. However, due to
most of the confidential tasks that UAVs are employed for, the huge amount
of UAV data usually contains much sensitive and private information, including
location-aware information, traffic related information, or even military-aware
data. In the meantime, the outsourced UAV data in cloud makes its control
out of the data producer, i.e., UAVs in IoV systems and vulnerable to various
attacks. Therefore, how to guarantee the security of outsourced UAV data in
cloud is a urgent requirement.

As a convincing solution for data security, Ciphertext-Policy Attribute-Based
Encryption (CP-ABE) [28–30] enables the data producer to specify an access policy over a universe of attribute and enforce this access policy on encrypted outsourced data. Thus, it can be leveraged to guarantee the confidentiality and fine-
grained access control for the massive UAV data outsourced in cloud. However,
direct deployment of conventional CP-ABE schemes still faces several serous
challenges to be addressed. The first challenge is the probable user privacy leakage in access policy. In conventional CP-ABE schemes, the access policy used to
indicate the fine-grained access control for authorized data consumers is mostly
in plaintext form. For example, an access policy "(SSN:1234 AND Role: Major
General) OR (Department: Air Force AND State: Illinois)" will reflect that the
consumer of the shared UAV data is a major general of air force office in Illinois
state and that the UAV data may contains the information about Illinois. Thus,
if these schemes are directly deployed in Cloud-based IoD systems for UAV data
access control, any users that can approach the access policy can infer extra
information of user privacy and sensitive information of UAV data, which will
cause horrubke consequences, especially in military field. Although the schemes
in [11, 26, 32] have been proposed to deal with the user privacy leakage in access
policy by providing hidden access policy for CP-ABE schemes with fully security in standard model, they still lacks high efficiency in both encryption and
decryption.

The second challenge is a long-lasting and intractable user key abuse problem
in CP-ABE schemes, which is particularly significant when used in Cloud-based

IoD systems for UAV data access control. In most user key abuse attacks, authorized insiders prefer to leak their decryption keys to outsiders for extra profits gain. Especially, in military fields, the UAV data is of high value and cannot be shared with any other party. Thus, these miliary secret will bring huge profit if illegally shared with outsiders, which will give an inside traitor enough motivation to leak his decryption key. Nevertheless, in CP-ABE schemes, user decryption keys are related with their attribute set, which bring great difficulty to reveal the real identity of its owner. Hence, many traceable CP-ABE schemes are studied and designed to effectively disclose the traitors that leak their decryption keys by combining white-box mechanism with CP-ABE, that is, embedding the identity of data users to their decryption keys. Any time a leaked decryption key is captured, the identity of the owner will be disclosed with white-box approach [13,14,19]. However, these schemes either suffer from high computation cost for user tracing or high storage overhead with a centralized user tracing authority. Therefore, to provide a public and efficient user traceable CP-ABE is a must for UAV data sharing in Cloud-based IoD systems.

The third challenge is the most common attack of Denial of Service in many service-oriented systems. As the Cloud-based IoD systems provides data sharing and outsourcing services to resource-limited UAVs and data consumers, if these services are disabled by attackers, the users will incur huge loss for it. Unfortunately, the prevention of this kind of attacks is out of consideration in most of CP-ABE schemes. For instance, an authorized but malicious user will launch DoS attack to the UAV dta sharing service by conducing continuous access which will cause great resource consumption of the services and eventually disable the service. Consequently, all other data consumers cannot access the UAV data sharing service, which is severe especially in military field and disastrous rescue applications. Thus, direct utilization of conventional CP-ABE scheme will make IoD systems vulnerable to DoS attacks by unlimited accessing to shared UAV data and disable the data sharing service to other valid users. Currently, there exist some related studies [7,25,34] that aims to limit the access time of data users for CP-ABE schemes, but they suffer from low efficiency in access verification, which are not suitable for time-sensitive applications of IoD. Thus, it is of great importance to provide efficient access time limitation method for CP-ABE schemes to adapt to UAV data sharing in Cloud-based IoD systems.

1.1 Current Research States

In UAV applications [10,18,22,27], data is a valuable resource that can be used for analysis and prediction [5,20]. Thus, the security of UAV data is most important. Ye et al. [24] designed a secure UAV system to protect the message transformed between UAVs. Then, Alladi [1] proposed an authentication scheme for UAV systems to guarantee the communication between UAVs and ground stations and Mehta et al. [16] integrated blockchain to 5G-enabled UAV to secure the UAV networks.

Ciphertext-Policy ABE (CP-ABE) [13,14,19,28–30] has been very popular in cloud data sharing for fine-grained access control. However, the traditional CP-

ABE schemes suffer from privacy leakage in access policy which is in plaintext and shared with ciphertext, which means they cannot be used in sensitive data sharing field. To address the problem, Zhang et al. [32] proposed a full secure partial hidden policy CP-ABE with large universe based on [9] with small attribute universe. However, these schemes fail to deal with user key abuse problem which may cause severe privacy and data disclosure. Thus, the scheme proposed in [11] introduced white-box user tracing mechanism into the scheme in [32] to realize user tracing, but it is a centralized tracing approach. Inspired by [31,33], the scheme in [26] proposed a partial hidden policy and public traceable CP-ABE, but it still incur high computation cost to be used in resource-limited devices.

Although CP-ABE is a promising and strong cyptographic tool, it also incurs heavy computation overhead in encryption and decryption which hinders its adoption. To solve these problem, the work in [6] introduces online/offline technique into ABE. Further, the authors in [23] integrates the idea to multi-authority CP-ABE schemes. Recently, many researches, i.e., [17] also combines online/offline into various ABE schemes. Meanwhile, to reduce the computation cost in decryption, the paradigm of outsourced decryption was introduced in [4]. Inspired by this, the scheme in [8] designed the verifiable outsourced decryption to resist malicious cloud and check if the messages are correctly decrypted. Recently, the literature [3] combines online/offline encryption and outsourced decryption for cost saving (Table 1).

Table 1. Function comparison in various schemes

Scheme	PH	LU	TLDAC	FS	SM	OOE	DT	VR	PT
Scheme [8]	✓	×	×	✓	✓	×	×	×	×
Scheme [17]	×	×	×	✓		✓	×	×	×
Scheme [6]	×	×	×	×	×	✓	×	×	×
Scheme [7]	×	✓	✓	×	×	×	×	×	×
Scheme [33]	×	✓	×	×	×	×	×	×	✓
Scheme [31]	×	✓	×	×	×	×	×	×	✓
Scheme [9]	✓	×	×	✓	✓	×	×	×	×
Scheme [32]	✓	✓	×	✓	✓	×	✓	×	×
Scheme [11]	✓	✓	×	×	×	✓	×	×	×
Scheme [26]	✓	✓	×	✓	✓	×	✓	×	✓
PATLDAC	✓	✓	✓	✓	✓	✓	✓	✓	✓

Note. PH: policy hiding; LU: large universe; TLDAC: time-limited data access; FS: full security; SM: standard model; OOE: online/offline encryption; DT: decryption test; VR: verifiability; PT: public traceability.

1.2 Motivation and Contributions

To address these challenges discussed above, in this paper, we propose a privacy-aware and time-limited data access control (PATLDAC) scheme for secure UAV data sharing in Cloud-based IoD to achieve both user privacy protection and limited access time along with efficient user tracing. To be specific, the main contributions are listed as follows:

- **Limited access time.** To counter the DoS attacks which conducts unlimited access to outsourced UAV data and guarantee the UAV data sharing service provision, PATLDAC can limits the access times for each valid user by impose a maximum access restriction to these users.
- **Partial hidden policy.** Our proposed PATLDAC achieves user privacy protection in access policy by separating each attribute in access policy into attribute name and attribute value while conceling the attribute values which may contain sensitive and private information.
- **Public user tracing.** To resist user key abuse problem, we introduce the public white-box tracing mechanism into our proposed PATLDAC scheme to guarantee that any traitor that intends to leak their decryption key for illegal profit will be efficiently revealed by anyone of the system in a public mode.

2 Preliminaries

2.1 Notations

In our work, $[l1, l2]$ is used to denote the set $\{l1, l1 + 1, \cdots, l2\}$ and $[n]$ is the set $1, 2, \cdots, n$, where $n \in Z_p^*$, while $|S|$ denotes the length of a string S.

2.2 Access Structure

Definition 1 *(Access Structures [28]). Let $E = E_1, \cdots, E_n$ be a entity collection. Given a set $C \subseteq 2^E \setminus \varnothing$, it is monotonic if $\forall D, F : D \subseteq F \bigcap D \in C \to F \in C$. Then, the set C is also a monotonic access structure and the subsets in C are called the authorized sets, otherwise, the unauthorized sets.*

2.3 Linear Secret Sharing Schemes (LSSS)

Definition 2 *(LSSS [30]). Let U be the attribute universe, where each attribute includes two parts: attribute name and its values. Each attribute has multiple values. An LSSS involves (A, ρ) on U, where A is an $l \times n$ matrix over Z_p which is called the share-generating matrix and ρ maps a row of A into an attribute name index. An LSSS consists of two algorithms.*

- *Share$((A, \rho), s)$: This algorithm is used to share a secret value s based on A. Considering a vector $v = (s, y_2, \ldots, y_n)^T$, where $s \in Z_p$ is the secret to be shared and $y_2, \cdots, y_n \in_R Z_p$, then $\lambda_x = A_x \cdot v$ is a share of the secret s corresponding to the attribute name indexed by $\rho(x)$.*

- $Reconstruction(\lambda_1, \cdots, \lambda_l, (A, \rho))$: *This algorithm is used to reconstruct* s *from secret shares. Let* P *be any authorized set and* $I = \{i | \rho(i) \in P\} \subseteq \{1, 2, \cdots, l\}$, *Then there exists coefficients* $\{w_i \in Z_p\}_{i \in I}$ *such that* $\sum_{i \in I} w_i A_i = (1, 0, \cdots, 0)$. *A subset* I *of* $\{1, 2, \cdots, l\}$ *is said to be a minimum authorized set of* (A, ρ) *if* I *satisfies* (A, ρ) *and any* $I' \subset I$ *does not satisfy* (A, ρ). *We define* $\mathbf{I}_{A, \rho}$ *as the set of subsets of* $\{1, 2, \cdots, l\}$ *that are minimum authorized sets of* (A, ρ).

2.4   Composite Bilinear Map

Definition 3 *(Composite Bilinear Maps [29]): Composite order bilinear groups are widely used in IBE and ABE systems. We denote by* $\mathcal{G}$ *a group generator, which takes a security parameter* λ *as inputs and outputs a description of a bilinear group* G. *We define the output of* $\mathcal{G}$ *as* $(N, p_1, p_2, p_3, p_4, G, G_T, \hat{e})$ *with* $G = G_{p_1} \times G_{p_2} \times G_{p_3} \times G_{p_4}$, *where* p_1, p_2, p_3, p_4 *are distinct primes,* G *and* G_T *are cyclic groups of order* $N = p_1 p_2 p_3 p_4$, *and* $\hat{e} : G \times G \to G_T$ *is a bilinear map satisfy the following properties:*

- *Bilinear:* $\hat{e}(g^a, h^b) = \hat{e}(g, h)^{ab}$, $\forall a, b \in Z_N, g, h \in G$.
- *Non-Degenerate: There exists* $g \in G$ *such that* $\hat{e}(g, g)$ *has order* N *in* G_T.
- *Computability: Assume group operations in* G *and* G_T *as well as the bilinear map* $\hat{e}$ *are computable in polynomial time with respect to the security parameter* λ

Let G_{p_i} *be the subgroup of big prime order* p_i, *where* $1 \leq i \leq 4$. *Note that for any* $X_i \in G_{p_i}, X_j \in G_{p_j}$, $\hat{e}(X_i, X_j) = 1$ *holds* $\forall i \neq j$. *The subgroups are said to be "orthogonal" to each other.*

3   The Proposed PATLDAC Scheme for UAV Data Sharing in Cloud-Based IoD

3.1   System Model

In this section, we give the description of the system model and design goals of our data access control scheme.

As shown in Fig. 1, our scheme involves four generic entities, Trusted Authority (TA), UAV Cloud Provider (UCP), Data Producer (DP) and Data Consumer (DC) which are described as follows.

(1) TA initializes the system and takes charge of the user registration and authorization. After receiving the attributes of users, TA generates secret key for users to empower their corresponding privileges.

(2) UCP is the UAV cloud provider that provides unlimited computation and storage resources together with data outsourcing services to UAVs. Moreover, UCP also supply data sharing services to authorized data consumers for their academic or industrial applications.

(3) DP is on behalf of UAVs that generate large number of spatiotemporal data that contain confidential information and have too large volume to be maintained in resource-limited UAVs. Thus, DP needs to encrypt these data for confidentiality and upload them to UCP for cost saving.

(4) DC is the consumer of UAV data for analysis and mining with machine learning related algorithms. Moreover, only authorized DCs have privileges to access the shared UAV data in UCP.

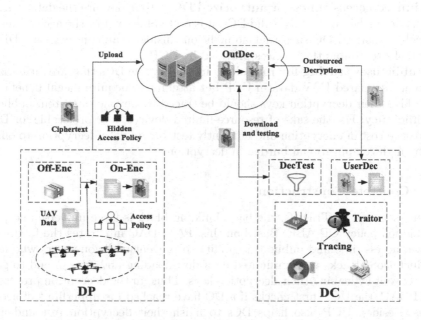

Fig. 1. The system model of our PATLDAC

We assume that the TA is a fully trusted entitiy while UCP is considered to be semi-honest which performs the pre-defined protocol honestly but is curious about the confidential information of UAV data. DP is regardes as trusted as it generates their own UAV data and uploads them to UCP for outsourcing. DC is considered to be malicious because part of them without enough privileges may intend to conduct unauthorized access and some of them may even perform unlimited access to disable the services. Moreover, there exists authorized but malicious insiders that prefer to leak their decryption keys for extra profits.

3.2   Design Goals

To confront these threats in system model, our proposal should satisfy following requirements:

- **Data confidentiality and fine-grained access control:** Due to the high level of confidentiality, the UAV data should be protected during communication among UAV, UCP and DCs, and their sharing in UCP. Moreover, only authorized DCs can obtain the content of the shared UAV data.
- **Privacy protection in access policy:** As the access policy may reveal the content of encrypted UAV data, it should be well protected in order to prevent sensitive information disclosure from being inferred by anyone accessible to shared UAV data.
- **Limited access times for authorized DCs:** To make sure the data sharing service can be available to valid DCs, it is preferable to limit the access time of each authorized DC such that no malicious insiders can conduct DoS/DDoS attacks to disable the services provided by UCP.
- **Public user tracing for malicious insiders:** The DCs that are authorized to access shared UAV data in UCP but attempt to acquire illegal benefit by leaking their decryption keys should be traced by anyone in system publicly.
- **Efficiency:** For the sake of resource-limited devices, it is preferable for DCs to save cost in encryption and efficiently test before data decryption to offset the high computational burden in decryption.

3.3   Concrete Construction

In our proposed PATLDAC, the basic building block is large universe and partial hidden policy CP-ABE. Based on this, PATLDAC integrates the feature of limited access time and public traceability to prevent malicious users who may conduct DoS attacks with unlimited data downloading and who intend to gain illegal profit by leaking their decryption keys. Thus, in the decryption process of PATLDAC, the UCP first checks if a DC have reached his upperlimit of access times. Besides, UCP also helps DCs to finish their decryption test and user decryption, which greatly save computation cost for decryption. Moreover, the user tracing mechanism is publicly executed by any entity of the system without a centralized authority.

- $Setup(\lambda) \rightarrow (PK, MSK)$: After TA receiving the security parameter λ, it invokes the bilinear group generator algorithm $\mathcal{G}(\lambda)$ to obtain a bilinear group $(N = p_1 p_2 p_3 p_4, G, G_T, \hat{e})$, where $\{p_i\}_{i \in [4]}$ are different big primes and G, G_T are two cyclic groups of composite order N with a bilinear map $\hat{e} : G \times G \rightarrow G_T$ and a generator $g \in G$. Then, TA sets the attribute universe $U = Z_N$ and chooses $\alpha, a \in_R Z_N$, $f, h \in_R G_{(p_1)}$, $A_3 \in_R G_{p_3}$, $O, A_4 \in_R G_{p_4}$ and computes $B = \hat{e}(g,g)^\alpha, F = fO$. Besides, TA picks a collision resistant hash function $H_m : \{0,1\}^* \rightarrow Z_N$. Finally, TA publishes the system public key as $PK = (N, g, g^a, h, B, F, A_4, H_m)$ and the master key is $MSK = (\alpha, f)$.
- $Setup_C(PK) \rightarrow (ctr, L, ST)$: Given the system public key PK, the UCP generates an initial counter $ctr = 0$ for data sharing service and an empty state set ST for each DC in user universe. The UCP also initiates a list L to maintain the ctr and ST for each DC.

- $Setup_U(PK) \rightarrow (pk_u, sk_u)$: On inputting the system public key PK, each DC chooses a random number $z_u \in_R Z_N$ as secret key $SK_u = z_u$ and publishes the user public key as $PK_u = h^{z_u}$.

- $KeyGen(PK, MK, PK_u, ID_u, S) \rightarrow DK_u$: After receiving the system public key PK, the decryption key request from DC with his identity ID_u and attribute set $S = (I_s, S)$, where $I_s \subset Z_N$ is the index of each attribute in S and $S = \{s_i\}_{i \in I_s}$ is the attribute value of the DC, TA randomly chooses $t \in Z_N$ and $R, R', R_i \in G_{p3}$ for $i \in I_s$. TA finally outputs the decryption key of DC $DK_u = \{S, K, K', K'', \{K_i\}_{i \in I_s}\}$, where

$$K = g^\alpha g^{atH_m(K', K'')} R, K' = g^t R', K'' = ID_u, K_i = (g^{s_i} f)^t R_i$$

- $KeyGen_{OUT}(PK, DK_u, SK_u, csi) \rightarrow TK_u$: DC takes the system public key PK, his decryption key DK_u and secret key SK_u with current state information csi as input, then he computes $TK_u^1 = \{I_s, K^1 = g^{z_u} \cdot K = g^{z_u} g^\alpha g^{atH_m(K', K')}, K', K'', \{K_i\}_{i \in I_s}\}$. Then, the DC calculates the rest components $K_c = B^{1/(z_u + H_m(csi))}, K_p = g^{1/(z_u + H_m(csi))}$. Finally, the DC gets his transformation key $TK_u = (TK_u^1, K_c, K_p, csi)$.

- $Encrypt_{off}(PK) \rightarrow IT_t$: Given the system public key PK, each DP prepares the encryption process in advance. DP selects random values $s, s' \in Z_N$ as secret value for sharing to compute $\widetilde{C}'_\delta = B^s, \widetilde{C}'_1 = B^s, \widehat{C}'_\delta = g^s, \widehat{C}'_1 = g^s$ and constructs a intermediary pool $IT_1 = \{(s, s', \widetilde{C}'_\delta, \widetilde{C}'_1, \widehat{C}'_\delta, \widehat{C}'_1)\}$. Then, DP chooses $\lambda', t', r' \in_R Z_N$ and calculates $C'_{\delta,x} = g^{a\lambda'}, C'_{1,x} = g^{a\lambda'}(g^{t'} F)^{r'}, C'_{2,x} = g^{r'}$ to construct another intermediary pool $IT_2 = \{(\lambda', t', r', C'_{\delta,x}, C'_{1,x}, C'_{2,x})\}$. Finally, DP outputs an intermediate ciphertext $IT_t = \{IT_1, IT_2\}$.

- $Encrypt_{on}(PK, IT_t, M, \mathcal{A}) \rightarrow CT$: On inputting the system public key PK, the intermediate cihertext IT_t, the UAV data M with designated access policy $\mathcal{A} = \{A, \rho, \mathcal{T}\}$, where A is a $l \times n$ share-generating matrix and $\mathcal{T} = \{t_{\rho(1)}, \cdots, t_{\rho(l)}\}$ is the value set of the access policy $\mathcal{A}$, DP chooses a random tuple $(s, s', \widetilde{C}'_\delta, \widetilde{C}'_1, \widehat{C}'_\delta, \widehat{C}'_1)$ from IT_1 and two random vectors $v = (s, v_2, \cdots, v_n), v' = (s', v'_2, \cdots, v'_n)$ of n dimentions over Z_N, where $s, s' \in_R Z_N^n$ are the shared secret value. DP also picks l different random tuples $\{(\lambda'_x, t'_x, r'_x, C'_{\delta,x}, C'_{1,x}, C'_{2,x})\}_{x \in [l]}$ from IT_2. Besides, DP chooses $O_\delta \in_R G_{p4}$ and $O_{\delta,x}, O_{c,x}, O_{d,x} \in_R G_{p4}$, where $1 \leq x \leq l$. Then, DP can calculate the ciphertext $CT = \{(A, \rho), \widetilde{C}_\delta, \widehat{C}_\delta, \{C_{\delta,x}\}_{1 \leq x \leq l}, \widetilde{C}_1, \widehat{C}_1, \{C_{1,x}, C_{2,x}, C_{3,x}, C_{4,x}, C_{5,x}\}_{1 \leq x \leq l}\}$, where

$$\widetilde{C}_\delta = \widetilde{C}'_\delta, \widehat{C}_\delta = \widehat{C}'_\delta \cdot O_\delta, C_{\delta,x} = C'_{\delta,x} \cdot (g^{t_{\rho(x)}} F)^{-s'} O_{c,x},$$

$$\widetilde{C}_1 = M \cdot \widetilde{C}'_1, \widehat{C}_1 = \widehat{C}'_1, C_{1,x} = C'_{1,x} \cdot O_{c,x}, C_{2,x} = C'_{2,x} \cdot O_{d,x},$$

$$C_{3,x} = A_x \cdot v - \lambda'_x, C_{4,x} = A_x \cdot v' - \lambda'_x, C_{5,x} = r'_x(t_{\rho(x)} - t'_x)$$

Finally, DP uploads the ciphertext CT to UCP for data outsourcing and sharing.

- $DecryptTest(PK, CT, TK_u, SK_u) \to True/False$: The algorithm is an interaction between UCP and DC as below.
  - After receiving the system public key PK and the UAV data access request from DC with his transformation key TK_u, UCP first checks if the access time of the DC reach the maximum as follows:
    1) $\hat{e}(g^{H_m(csi)} \cdot Z_u, K_p) = E$ and $K_c = \hat{e}(g \cdot Z_u, K_p)$;
    2) $ctr + 1 \leq \varepsilon$, where ε is the maximum access time of the outsourced decryption service request for UAV data sharing;
    3) $K_c \notin ST$.

    If the above equations do not hold, UCP prohibit the further data access for the DC. Otherwise, UCP updates $ctr = ctr + 1$ and stores K_c in ST for future use.
  - UCP calculates $I_{A,\rho} \subset \{1, 2, \cdots, l\}$ that satisfies the partial hidden access policy (A, ρ) of CT and the following equation:

$$P_0 = \hat{e}(\prod_{i \in I} C_{\delta,i}^{w_i}, (K')^{H_m(K',K'')}) \cdot \hat{e}(\widehat{C_\delta}, K^{-1} \prod_{i \in I} K_{\rho(i)}^{w_i}),$$

$$P_1 = \frac{\hat{e}(\widehat{C_1}, K)}{\prod_{i \in I}(\hat{e}(C_{1,i}, K')\hat{e}(C_{2,i}, K_{\rho(i)}))^{w_i}} = \hat{e}(g, g)^{\alpha s}\hat{e}(g, g)^{z_u s}$$

    Then, UCP allows the DC to download the ciphertext CT and returns P_0, P_1 to DC.

- $UserDec(PK, CT, P_0, P_1, SK_u)$: With the system public key PK and secret key SK_u, DC computes following to check if there exists a subset $I \in I_{A,\rho}$ that satisfies $\{\rho(i)|i \in I\} \subseteq I_s$ and checks the following equation

$$\widetilde{C_\delta}^{-1} \stackrel{?}{=} P_0 \cdot \hat{e}(g^{SK_u}, \widehat{C_\delta})$$

where $\sum_{i \in I} w_i A_i = (1, 0, \cdots, 0)$ for some constants $w_{i i \in I}$. If no such I exists, it outputs $\perp$ to indicate that attribute set S of the DC does not satisfy the partially hidden access policy (A, ρ). Otherwise, the ciphertext is valid and authorized and the DC can calculate the following equation:

$$M = \widetilde{C_1} \cdot \hat{e}(g^{SK_u}, \widehat{C_1})/P_1$$

Finally, DC gets the plaintext M of the shared UAV data.

- $UTrace(PK, DK_u) \to ID$ or $null$: Given the system public key PK and the leaked decryption key DK_u, anyone of the system can execute the algorithm. First, it checks if $DK_u = \{S, K, K', K'', \{K_i\}_{i \in I_s}\}$ and its components satisfies $K, K', K_i \in G, K'' \in Z_N$. Then, the algorithm executes **Key Sanity Check:**

$$\hat{e}(g, K) = B \cdot \hat{e}(g^a, (K')^{H_m(K',K'')}) \tag{1}$$

If the decryption key DK_u does not satisfy **Key Sanity Check**, the algorithm abort and outputs $null$. Otherwise, we consider it as a well-formed decryption key. Then, the algorithm outputs the real identity of the owner as $ID_u = K''$.

4 Analysis of Our PATLDAC Scheme

This section demonstrates the theoretical analysis of our proposed PATLDAC scheme in Table 2 and Table 3.

We analyze the complexity of our scheme and three related schemes in [11, 26,32]. Here, we let E and E_T denote exponentiation in group G and G_T, P denote pairing operation in $\hat{e}$, $|S|$ denotes the number of access attribute set S, $|G_{p_i}|$, $|G_{p_i p_j}|$, $|G_T|$ and $|Z_N|$ denote the length of element of G_{p_i}, $G_{p_i} \cdot G_{p_j}$, G_T and Z_N.

Table 2. Computation comparison in various schemes

Schemes	KeyGen	UserEnc
[32]	$(2|S|+3)E$	$(7l+4)E+2E_T$
[11]	$(2|S|+4)E$	$(7l+5)E+2E_T$
[26]	$(2|S|+3)E$	$(6l+2)E+2E_T$
PATLDAC	$(2|S|+3)E$	$2|S|E$

Schemes	UserDec	UserTrace
[32]	$2|I|E+(|I|+1)E_T+(2|I|+3)P$	–
[11]	$(3|I|+4)E+(|I|+1)E_T+(2|I|+4)P$	$(2|S|+2)E+(2|S|+5)P$
[26]	$(4|I|+4)E+E_T+4P$	$E+2P$
PATLDAC	$2E$	$E+2P$

Note. "l" is the row number in access policy, "$|I|$" is the complexity of access policy in decryption.

From the view of computation complexity, we emphases on the aspects of the time cost in $KeyGen, UserEnc, UserDec, UserTrace$. To demonstrate the advantage of our proposal, we compare the computation complexity between PATLDAC and [11,26,32] summarized in Table 2. Specifically, the time cost in $KeyGen$ algorithm in PATLDAC is just the same as that of [26,32] while less than that of [11] which needs centralized traceability. Moreover, the time cost in $UserEnc$ of PATLDAC is much less than that of other three schemes as it utilizes online/offline encryption to offload the complex attribute-related computations to offline phase. More important, the time cost in $UserDec$ algorithm is only $2E$ which is also significantly less than others. In addition, the time cost in $UserTrace$ of PATLDAC is the same as that of [26] and much less than that of [11] which incurs extra cost for attribute-related operations in key sanity check.

From the view of storage complexity, we emphases on the aspects of the storage cost in $Setup, KeyGen, UserEnc, UserTrace$. To demonstrate the advantage of our proposal, we compare the storage complexity between PATLDAC and [11,26,32] summarized in Table 3. It is obvious that the size of system public key of PATLDAC is the same as that of [11] while more than the other two as it introduces another one element in G for user public key generation to realize outsourced decryption in standard model. In the storage cost of user decryption

Table 3. Storage comparison in various schemes

Schemesl	PPSize	DKSize	CTSize	TraceSize
[32]	$4|G_{p_i}| + |G_T|$	$(|S| + 2)|G_{p_ip_j}|$	$(2l + 3)|G_{p_ip_j}| + 2|G_T|$	–
[11]	$5|G_{p_i}| + |G_T|$	$(|S| + 3)|G_{p_ip_j}| + |Z_N|$	$(3l + 4)|G_{p_ip_j}| + 2|G_T|$	$|L||Z_N|$
[26]	$4|G_{p_i}| + |G_T|$	$(|S| + 2)|G_{p_ip_j}| + |Z_N|$	$(2l + 2)|G_{p_ip_j}| + 2|G_T|$	$\odot$
PATLDAC	$5|G_{p_i}| + |G_T|$	$(|S| + 2)|G_{p_ip_j}| + |Z_N|$	$(2l + 3)|G_{p_ip_j}| + 2|G_T| + 3l|Z_N|$	$\odot$

Note. "$|L|$" is the size of user table for tracing, "$\odot$" is the efficient symbol.

key, PATLDAC is the same as [26] and less than that of [11] for centralized user tracing. The ciphertext size in PATLDAC is somewhat more than the other schemes as it introduces extra three elements in Z_N for online/offline encryption to achieve cost saving. Most important, PATLDAC and the scheme in [26] realize high efficiency in user tracing, which is much less than that of [11].

5 Conclusion

In this paper, we proposed a privacy-aware and time-limited data access control (PATLDAC) scheme for secure UAV data sharing in Cloud-based IoD system. The proposed PATLDAC can achieve user privacy preserving in access policy through partially hidden access policy to conceal the values of attributes while leaves their names with no sensitive information. To resist user key abuse efficiently, PATLDAC provided public user tracing. In the meantime, for the security of data sharing security to guarantee service provision, PATLDAC supports data access time limitation that each data consumer can only perform a maximum times of access to shared UAV data. In addition, PATLDAC realize high efficiency in both encryption and decryption. The complexity analysis and comparison show that PATLDAC is suitable for IoD systems.

Acknowledgment. This work is supported by Natural Science Foundation of Inner Mongolia, China, 2020 (No. 2020LH06007), Innovation Fund of Inner Mongolia University of Science and Technology, China (No. 2019QDL-B51) and Inner Mongolia Major science and technology projects: artificial intelligence application technology and product research, development Application Research and demonstration in modern pastures (2019ZD025).

References

1. Alladi, T., Bansal, G., Chamola, V., Guizani, M., et al.: SecAuthUAV: a novel authentication scheme for UAV-ground station and UAV-UAV communication. IEEE Trans. Veh. Technol. **69**(12), 15068–15077 (2020)
2. Boursianis, A.D., et al.: Internet of Things (IoT) and agricultural unmanned aerial vehicles (UAVs) in smart farming: a comprehensive review. Internet of Things, p. 100187 (2020)
3. De, S.J., Ruj, S.: Efficient decentralized attribute based access control for mobile clouds. IEEE Trans. Cloud Comput. **8**(01), 124–137 (2020)

4. Green, M., Hohenberger, S., Waters, B., et al.: Outsourcing the decryption of ABE ciphertexts. In: USENIX Security Symposium, vol. 2011 (2011)
5. Gupta, L., Jain, R., Vaszkun, G.: Survey of important issues in UAV communication networks. IEEE Commun. Surv. Tutor. **18**(2), 1123–1152 (2015)
6. Hohenberger, S., Waters, B.: Online/offline attribute-based encryption. In: Krawczyk, H. (ed.) PKC 2014. LNCS, vol. 8383, pp. 293–310. Springer, Heidelberg (2014). https://doi.org/10.1007/978-3-642-54631-0_17
7. Hong, J., Xue, K., Gai, N., Wei, D.S., Hong, P.: Service outsourcing in F2C architecture with attribute-based anonymous access control and bounded service number. IEEE Trans. Dependable Secure Comput. **17**(5), 1051–1062 (2018)
8. Lai, J., Deng, R.H., Guan, C., Weng, J.: Attribute-based encryption with verifiable outsourced decryption. IEEE Trans. Inf. Forensics Secur. **8**(8), 1343–1354 (2013)
9. Lai, J., Deng, R.H., Li, Y.: Expressive CP-ABE with partially hidden access structures. In: Proceedings of the 7th ACM Symposium on Information, Computer and Communications Security, pp. 18–19 (2012)
10. Li, M., Cheng, N., Gao, J., Wang, Y., Zhao, L., Shen, X.: Energy-efficient UAV-assisted mobile edge computing: resource allocation and trajectory optimization. IEEE Trans. Veh. Technol. **69**(3), 3424–3438 (2020)
11. Li, Q., Zhang, Y., Zhang, T., Huang, H., Xiong, J.: HTAC: fine-grained policy-hiding and traceable access control in mhealth. IEEE Access **PP**(99), 1 (2020)
12. Li, X., Zhou, R., Zhang, Y.J.A., Jiao, L., Li, Z.: Smart vehicular communication via 5G mmWaves. Comput. Netw. **172**, 107173 (2020)
13. Liu, Z., Duan, S., Zhou, P., Wang, B.: Traceable-then-revocable ciphertext-policy attribute-based encryption scheme. Futur. Gener. Comput. Syst. **93**, 903–913 (2019)
14. Liu, Z., Xu, J., Liu, Y., Wang, B.: Updatable ciphertext-policy attribute-based encryption scheme with traceability and revocability. IEEE Access **7**, 66832–66844 (2019)
15. Lv, Z., Qiao, L., Li, J., Song, H.: Deep-learning-enabled security issues in the internet of things. IEEE Internet Things J. **8**(12), 9531–9538 (2020)
16. Mehta, P., Gupta, R., Tanwar, S.: Blockchain envisioned UAV networks: challenges, solutions, and comparisons. Comput. Commun. **151**, 518–538 (2020)
17. Miao, Y., Tong, Q., Choo, K.K.R., Liu, X., Deng, R.H., Li, H.: Secure online/offline data sharing framework for cloud-assisted industrial internet of things. IEEE Internet Things J. **6**(5), 8681–8691 (2019)
18. Mukherjee, A., Misra, S., Chandra, V.S.P., Obaidat, M.S.: Resource-optimized multiarmed bandit-based offload path selection in edge UAV swarms. IEEE Internet Things J. **6**(3), 4889–4896 (2018)
19. Ning, J., Dong, X., Cao, Z., Wei, L.: Accountable authority ciphertext-policy attribute-based encryption with white-box traceability and public auditing in the cloud. In: Pernul, G., Ryan, P.Y.A., Weippl, E. (eds.) ESORICS 2015. LNCS, vol. 9327, pp. 270–289. Springer, Cham (2015). https://doi.org/10.1007/978-3-319-24177-7_14
20. Pathak, N., Misra, S., Mukherjee, A., Roy, A., Zomaya, A.Y.: UAV virtualization for enabling heterogeneous and persistent UAV-as-a-service. IEEE Trans. Veh. Technol. **69**(6), 6731–6738 (2020)
21. Wazid, M., Das, A.K., Shetty, S., Gope, P., Rodrigues, J.J.: Security in 5G-enabled internet of things communication: issues, challenges, and future research roadmap. IEEE Access **9**, 4466–4489 (2020)

22. Wu, Q., Zeng, Y., Zhang, R.: Joint trajectory and communication design for multi-UAV enabled wireless networks. IEEE Trans. Wirel. Commun. **17**(3), 2109–2121 (2018)
23. Xue, K., et al.: RAAC: robust and auditable access control with multiple attribute authorities for public cloud storage. IEEE Trans. Inf. Forensics Secur. **12**(4), 953–967 (2017)
24. Ye, J., Zhang, C., Lei, H., Pan, G., Ding, Z.: Secure UAV-to-UAV systems with spatially random UAVs. IEEE Wirel. Commun. Lett. **8**(2), 564–567 (2018)
25. Yuen, T.H., Liu, J.K., Au, M.H., Huang, X., Susilo, W., Zhou, J.: k-times attribute-based anonymous access control for cloud computing. IEEE Trans. Comput. **9**(64), 2595–2608 (2015)
26. Zeng, P., Zhang, Z., Lu, R., Choo, K.K.R.: Efficient policy-hiding and large universe attribute-based encryption with public traceability for internet of medical things. IEEE Internet of Things J. (2021)
27. Zeng, Y., Zhang, R.: Energy-efficient UAV communication with trajectory optimization. IEEE Trans. Wirel. Commun. **16**(6), 3747–3760 (2017)
28. Zhang, J., Li, T., Obaidat, M.S., Lin, C., Ma, J.: Enabling efficient data sharing with auditable user revocation for IoV systems. IEEE Syst. J. (2021)
29. Zhang, J., Ma, J., Li, T., Jiang, Q.: Efficient hierarchical and time-sensitive data sharing with user revocation in mobile crowdsensing. Secur. Commun. Netw. **2021** (2021)
30. Zhang, J., et al.: Efficient hierarchical data access control for resource-limited users in cloud-based e-health. In: 2019 International Conference on Networking and Network Applications (NaNA), pp. 319–324. IEEE (2019)
31. Zhang, K., Li, H., Ma, J., Liu, X.: Efficient large-universe multi-authority ciphertext-policy attribute-based encryption with white-box traceability. Sci. China Inf. Sci. **61**(3), 1–13 (2017). https://doi.org/10.1007/s11432-016-9019-8
32. Zhang, Y., Zheng, D., Deng, R.H.: Security and privacy in smart health: efficient policy-hiding attribute-based access control. IEEE Internet Things J. **5**(3), 2130–2145 (2018)
33. Zhang, Z., Zeng, P., Pan, B., Choo, K.K.R.: Large-universe attribute-based encryption with public traceability for cloud storage. IEEE Internet Things J. **7**(10), 10314–10323 (2020)
34. Zhou, J., Cao, Z., Qin, Z., Dong, X., Ren, K.: LPPA: lightweight privacy-preserving authentication from efficient multi-key secure outsourced computation for location-based services in VANETs. IEEE Trans. Inf. Forensics Secur. **15**, 420–434 (2019)

Multi-party High-Dimensional Related Data Publishing via Probabilistic Principal Component Analysis and Differential Privacy

Zhen Gu[1,2]($\boxtimes$) (iD), Guoyin Zhang[1] (iD), and Chen Yang[1] (iD)

[1] College of Computer Science and Technology, Harbin Engineering University,
Harbin 150001, China
{guzhen,zhangguoyin}@hrbeu.edu.cn
[2] The Department of Basic Education, East University of Heilongjiang,
Harbin 150066, China

Abstract. In this paper, we study the problem of multi-party horizontal split high-dimensional related data publishing that satisfies differential privacy. The dataset held by each party contains sensitive personal information, directly aggregating and publishing the local dataset from multiple parties will leak personal privacy. Usually, high-dimensional data are correlated, adding noise directly to the data will cause repeated noise addition and reduce the utility of the released data. To solve this problem, we proposed a method that horizontally split data publishing via probabilistic principal component analysis and differential privacy, the data owners add noise to low-dimensional data to reduce noise intake, and collaborate with a semi-trusted curator to reduce the dimensionality, finally, the data owners use the generative model of probabilistic principal component analysis to generate a synthetic dataset for publishing. The experimental results show that the synthetic dataset can maintain more efficient under the guarantee of differential privacy.

Keywords: Data publishing · Differential privacy ·
High-dimensional · Multi-party · Probability model

1 Introduction

With the development of the artificial intelligence and Internet of Things (IoT), various forms of data have been increasingly collected and used. How to better share, describe, use and manage data has become the problem in the era of big

Supported by the Natural Science Foundation of Heilongjiang Province of China under Grant LH2019F011, and the Open Project of State Key Laboratory of Information Security under Grant 2019-ZD-05, and Natural Science Foundation of East University of Heilongjiang HDFKY210117.

data and Internet of Things (IoT). Analyzing and mining the information behind these data can improve the quality of various services or formulate commercial strategies. For example, in the smart grid, it is necessary to upload the data collected by the Internet of Things (IoT) devices and smart meters to the control center. However, while analyzing and using data, it also faces many challenges. For example, data contains personal privacy, and direct sharing or publishing will lead to leakage of grid data and user privacy [1], that is to say, data is facing serious privacy leakage risks in the process of data sharing, network transmission and storage [2]. Therefore, data security and privacy have become the focus of attention of users. It is very important to protect the privacy of shared data and weigh the security and availability of data [3–5]. High-dimensional and related data are usually stored by different owners, as if the dataset is split horizontally among multiple data owners. For example, in Table 1, the records 1 to 4 come from the data owner 1, the records 5 to 8 come from the data owner 2, and the records 9 to 11 come from the data owner 3. If all these records can be aggregated, data analysts will be able to better mine the information behind the data and provide people with better services and decision-making. However, the data contains sensitive personal information, simply integrating and publishing the local dataset will cause serious privacy leakage. Therefore, the data needs to be processed for privacy protection before publishing. In recent years, there have been some studies on privacy-preserving data publishing. The first type is traditional privacy models k-anonymity [6], but studies have shown that k-anonymity is vulnerable to attacks with background knowledge, and the second type is encryption technology [7–9], encryption technology can provide better privacy guarantees. However the computational performance of such encryption technology does not scale well with a large number of users. The third type is based on differential privacy, the principle of differential privacy is to add random noise to data, which makes the attacker unable to distinguish the original input data. Differential privacy can quantitatively measure the degree of privacy protection, and can resist attacks from attackers with background knowledge, so using differential privacy to protect the privacy of publishing data has become a research hotspot in recent years, such as [10–15]. However, the following two problems need to be considered, one is that a large amount of data is often stored by different data owners, directly aggregating the data and publishing it will lead to personal privacy leakage, the second is that when the data has high dimensionality and relevance, directly adding noise into the high-dimensional data will reduce the utility of the publishing data under the same degree of privacy protection, and even make the data unavailable. In view of the above two points, this paper proposes a horizontally split data publishing method based on probabilistic principal component analysis and differential privacy. The contributions of our work are as follows:

1) We propose a method of multi-party high-dimensional related data publishing based on probabilistic principal component analysis and differential private (PPCA-DP-MH). When high-dimensional related data is stored by different owners, the data owners and a semi-trusted curator collaborate to reduce

dimensionality, then the data owners use the generative model of probabilistic principal component analysis to generate a synthetic dataset for publishing.

2) We propose to add noise to low-dimensional data to reduce noise intake. Each data owner uses the Laplace mechanism to randomly perturb the local covariance matrix which will be sent to the semi-trusted curator, so the information of each dataset by different owners is fully utilized while ensuring privacy.

3) We conduct experiments on different real datasets. The experimental results show that the synthetic dataset released by the PPCA-DP-MH method proposed in this paper can maintain high utility in SVM classification.

Table 1. Aggregated dataset of each data owner.

ID	Age	Job	Gender	Hours-per-week	Income
1	39	Shopkeeper	Male	40	>50K
2	55	Lawyer	Male	13	≤50K
3	38	Dancer	Male	20	≤50K
4	30	Dancer	Male	25	≤50K
5	28	Builder	Female	40	>50K
6	37	Dancer	Female	23	≤50K
7	49	Teacher	Female	16	≤50K
8	52	Builder	Male	45	>50K
9	31	Lawyer	Female	50	>50K
10	42	Builder	Male	40	>50K
11	37	Teacher	Male	55	>50K

2 Related Work

In recent years, there has been a number of studies on data security and privacy protection. Yang et al. [16] proposed that differential privacy may not guarantee privacy against arbitrary adversaries if the data are correlated. Jiang et al. [17] proposed that due to the relevance of data, if we add noise to each dimension of high-dimensional related data, the statistics of the data will be change drastically, which will reduce the utility of the publishing data, therefore, adding noise to fewer but more important part of data will improve the utility of publishing data. There have been some related studies, one type of algorithms are to add noise to the covariance matrix of data, such as [17–22]. Jiang et al. [17] proposed adding Laplace noise to the covariance matrix and projection matrix, and then use the noisy projection matrix to get the synthetic dataset for publishing. Blum et al. [18] proposed a Sub-Linear Query(SULQ) input perturbation framework, the algorithm adds noise to the covariance matrix, but this framework can only be used for querying the projection subspace and cannot be used for data publishing. Chaudhury *et al.* [19] improved the SUQL algorithm and proposed the principal component analysis algorithm, this algorithm meet the differential privacy through the exponential mechanism, and the algorithm is suitable for data publishing. Kapralov *et al.* [20] pointed out that the principal component analysis algorithm lacks the guarantee of convergence time, which will affect the privacy guarantee, and they proposed a low-rank approximate matrix algorithm for differential privacy, however, the implementation of this algorithm is more complicated and difficult to process high-dimensional data. Dwork *et al.* [21] proposed adding Gaussian noise to the covariance matrix to obtain the optimal low-rank approximation of the covariance matrix, this algorithm satisfies (ε, δ) the differential privacy. Jiang *et al.* [22] proposed an algorithm to add a noise matrix that obeys the Wishart distribution, it can maintain the noise covariance matrix is positive semi-definite. Only the [17] and [19] algorithms can be used for data publishing. Another type of algorithms are suitable for data publishing, such as [23–27]. They built a probabilistic graphical model, such as Bayesian network, Markov network or a tree model, and added noise to the low-dimensional marginal distribution, then generate a synthetic dataset based on the probabilistic graphical model. Zhang *et al.* [23] proposed the PrivBayes method, they used the relationship between attributes to construct a Bayesian network, and added Laplace noise to the low-dimensional marginal distribution, then generated a synthetic dataset for publishing. Chen *et al.* [24] proposed the Jtree method, firstly, they studied the relationship between attributes based on sparse vector sampling technology, and then constructed a Markov network, the joint distribution of all attributes is obtained through the joint tree algorithm. Zhang *et al.* [25] proposed the PrivHD method based on the Jtree method, this method used high-pass filtering technology to accelerate the construction of Markov network, and then used the maximum spanning tree method to build a better joint tree. Xu *et al.* [26] proposed the DPPro method, they randomly projected the original high-dimensional data into a low-dimensional space, and theoretically proved that the DPPro method generated a high-dimensional vector synthetic data sets with similar squared Euclidean distances. Zhang *et al.* [27] proposed the PrivMN algorithm, they constructed a Markov model to express the relationship of attributes, and then used the constructed model to generate a synthetic dataset for publishing.

From the above, we can see the studies are all about the privacy protection of data released by a single data owner, at present, there are fewer studies on the privacy protection of multi-party horizontal split data publishing, one type is multi-party data owners collaborate to reduce dimensionality and publish statistics of the data under differential privacy, such as [28–30], Ge *et al.* [28] proposed a distributed principal component analysis (DPS-PCA) algorithm with privacy protection. In a distributed environment, data owners collaborate to analyze the principal components while restricting the disclosure of private information, this algorithm can weigh the relationship between estimation accuracy and privacy protection, but this method only outputs low-dimensional subspaces of high-dimensional sparse data. Wang *et al.* [29] designed an efficient and scalable distributed PCA protocol for privacy protection for horizontal split data, the data owner encrypts his shared data and sends them to a semi-trusted third party, the semi-trusted third party performs a private aggregation algorithm on the encrypted data, and then outputs the aggregated data to the data user, the data user calculates the principal component, the algorithm satisfies the (ε, δ) differential privacy. Imtiaz *et al.* [30] proposed a distributed principal component analysis (DPdisPCA) method that satisfies (ε, δ) differential privacy. This method used Gaussian noise to perturb the local covariance matrix, multi-party data owners collaborate to reduce dimensionality while ensuring local data privacy. The above algorithms publish statistical information of the data set, rather than publishing a data set of the same size as the original data set. Alhadidi *et al.* [31] proposed a two-party data publishing method that satisfies differential privacy, the dataset published by this method is suitable for data classification tasks. Hong *et al.* [32] proposed a collaborative sanitization framework for differential privacy search log publishing, the framework only satisfies (ε, δ) differential privacy, and their framework is not generic to handle other types of data. Cheng *et al.* [33] proposed a differential privacy sequential update of Bayesian network (DP-SUBN3) method, the parties and the semi-trusted curator collaboratively constructed the Bayesian network, the parties can treat the intermediate results as prior knowledge, and then used the constructed Bayesian network to synthesize the dataset for publishing. These algorithms are suitable for publishing a data set of the same size as the original data set, but the published data set does not support all types of data analysis.

Inspired by the above research, when the data is stored by multiple data owners, we propose a horizontally split data publishing method based on probabilistic principal component analysis and differential privacy (PPCA-DP-MH). The data owners cooperate with the semi-trusted curator to reduce dimensionality. In order to protect the local data privacy, each data owner adds Laplace noise to the local covariance matrix, and then sends it to the semi-trusted curator to perform principal component analysis, and returns the principal components to the data owner, the data owner uses principal components and probability model to generate a dataset for publishing.

3   Preliminaries

3.1   Differential Privacy

Differential privacy provides a rigorous privacy protection for sensitive information, it can be quantified by mathematical formulas. The essence of differential privacy is to randomly perturb the data. There are Laplace mechanism and exponential mechanism, the Laplace mechanism is suitable for numerical queries and the exponential mechanism is suitable for non-numerical queries.

Definition 1 *(Differential Privacy)* [10]. *A randomized algorithm M satisfies ϵ differential privacy, if for any two neighboring databases D_1, D_2 and for any $S(S \in Rang(M))$ there is:*

$$P_r\{M(D_1 = S)\} \leq e^\varepsilon P_r\{M(D_2 = S)\} \tag{1}$$

where ε is privacy budget.

Definition 2 *(Sensitivity)* [10]. *Let f be a function that maps a database into a fixed size vector of real numbers, $f : D \to R^d$, for any neighboring databases D_1 and D_2, the sensitivity of f is defined as:*

$$\Delta f = \max_{D_1, D_2} \|f(D_1) - f(D_2)\|_1 \tag{2}$$

where$\| \cdot \|_1$ *denotes the L_1 norm.*

Definition 3 *(Laplace mechanism)* [34]. *For any function $f : D \to R^d$, if the output of the algorithm M satisfies the equation:*

$$M(D) = f(D) + (Lap_1(\frac{\Delta f}{\varepsilon}), \cdots, Lap_d(\frac{\Delta f}{\varepsilon})) \tag{3}$$

then the algorithm satisfies differential privacy, where $Lap_1(\frac{\Delta f}{\varepsilon}), \cdots, Lap_d(\frac{\Delta f}{\varepsilon})$ are independent Laplace variables.

Theorem 1 *(Sequential Composition)* [34]. *Let $M_1, M_2, \cdots, M_n$ be a series of privacy algorithms, and their privacy budgets are $\varepsilon_1, \varepsilon_2, \cdots, \varepsilon_n$, for the same dataset D, the combined algorithm $M(M_1(D), M_2(D), \cdots, M_n(D))$ provides $\sum_{i=1}^{n} \varepsilon_i$ differential privacy.*

Theorem 2 *(Parallel Composition)* [34]. *Let $M_1, M_2, \cdots, M_n$ be a series of privacy algorithms, which privacy budgets are $\varepsilon_1, \varepsilon_2, \cdots, \varepsilon_n$, $D_1, D_2, \cdots, D_n$ are disjoint databases, the combined algorithm $M(M_1(D_1), M_2(D_2), \cdots, M_n(D_n))$ provides $\max_{1 \leq i \leq n} \varepsilon_i$ differential privacy.*

3.2   Probabilistic Principal Component Analysis(PPCA)

Principal component analysis (PCA) is a well technique for simplifying data in statistics, principal component analysis simplifies the original high-dimensional variables into fewer low-dimensional comprehensive hidden variables. Hidden variables are also called principal components, the principal components can retain most of the information of the original variables, and the principal components are not correlated. The covariance matrix is Σ, Eigenvalue decomposition of the matrix Σ, $\Sigma = U^T \Lambda U$, where $\Lambda = diag(\lambda_1, \lambda_2, \cdots, \lambda_p)$ is a diagonal matrix, the elements on the diagonal are the eigenvalues of the matrix Σ, $\lambda_1 \geq \lambda_2 \geq \cdots \geq \lambda_p \geq 0$, and U is an orthogonal matrix consists of the eigenvectors, the eigenvectors are the principal components, the number of principal components retained is determined by the cumulative contribution rate $c = \sum_{i=1}^{k} \lambda_i / \sum_{i=1}^{p} \lambda_i$.

However, principal component analysis (PCA) is a non-generative model, a notable feature of the definition of PCA is the absence of an associated probabilistic model for the observed data, therefor, Michael *et al.* [35] proposed the generative model called probabilistic principal component analysis (PPCA). A latent variable model can correlate high-dimensional observable variables with low-dimensional latent variables, the most common model is factor analysis where the relationship is $x = Ws + \mu + \xi$, where x is p dimensional observation vector, s is k dimensional latent variables vector, $\xi \sim N(0, \Psi)$, the matrix W relates the variables x and s, and the vector μ permits the model to have non-zero mean, the motivation is that, when $k < p$, the latent variable will provide a more parsimonious explanation of the dependence between the observed variables. Principal component analysis can be regarded as the maximum likelihood solution of a factor analysis model with an isotropic covariance matrix.

Fig. 1. Graphical model for principal component analysis

Theorem 3 [35]. *From Fig. 1 and the latent variable model $x = Ws + \mu + \xi$, when $\xi \sim N(0, \sigma^2 I)$, $s \sim N(0, I_k)$, then $x|s \sim N(Ws + \mu, \sigma^2 I_p), \sigma > 0, W \in R^{p \times k}$, where the maximum likelihood estimation of μ, σ^2, and W are:*

$$\hat{\mu} = \tilde{\mu} \tag{4}$$

$$\hat{\sigma}^2 = \frac{1}{p-k} \sum_{i=k+1}^{p} \lambda_i \tag{5}$$

$$\hat{W} = U_k (\Lambda_k - \hat{\sigma}^2 I)^{\frac{1}{2}} \tag{6}$$

where $\tilde{\mu}$ is the sample mean vector, the column vectors in U_k is the eigenvectors corresponding to the first k eigenvalues of the sample covariance matrix.

4 The PPCA-DP-MH Approach

4.1 Problem Statement

There exist $m(m \geq 2)$ local dataset owners, the i-th data owner holds a local dataset $X_{n_i \times p} = (x_1^T, \cdots, x_{n_i}^T)^T$, each row $x_i(1 \leq i \leq n_i)$ of the matrix $X_{n_i \times p}$ represents an individual, where n_i denotes the number of individuals owned by the i-th data owner, p denotes the number of attributes. All the local datasets have the same attributes, and do not intersect with each other. The datasets $X_{n_1 \times p}, X_{n_2 \times p}, \cdots, X_{n_m \times p}$ can be viewed as horizontally split the integrated dataset $X = \bigcup_{i=1}^{m} X_{n_i \times p}$ by m data owners. Our goal is that m data owners and semi-trusted curator collaborate to publish a synthetic dataset that satisfies ε differential privacy.

Algorithm 1. PPCA-DP-MH algorithm

Input: Data sets $X_{n_i \times p}(i = 1, 2, \cdots, m)$, privacy budget ε, cumulative contribution rate c

Output: Synthetic dataset $X' = \bigcup\limits_{i=1}^{m} X'_{n_i \times p}$

1: **for** $i = 1$ to m **do**
2:    generate noise matrices $L^1_{p \times 1}$ and $L^2_{p \times p}$, each element of the matrices obeys $Lap(\frac{2p}{n_i \varepsilon})$
3:    compute:
$$\hat{E}(X^T_{n_i \times p}) = E(X^T_{n_i \times p}) + L^1_{p \times 1}$$
$$\hat{E}(X^T_{n_i \times p} X_{n_i \times p}) = E(X^T_{n_i \times p} X_{n_i \times p}) + L^2_{p \times p}$$
$$\hat{\Sigma}_i = \hat{E}(X^T_{n_i \times p} X_{n_i \times p}) - \hat{E}(X^T_{n_i \times p})\hat{E}(X_{n_i \times p})$$

4: **end for**
5: compute: $\hat{\Sigma} = \dfrac{\sum\limits_{i=1}^{m} n_i \hat{\Sigma}_i}{\sum\limits_{i=1}^{m} n_i}$

6: perform eigenvalue decomposition of matrix $\hat{\Sigma}$, return eigenvalues and corresponding eigenvectors in descending order $\lambda_1 \geq \lambda_2 \geq \cdots \geq \lambda_p \geq 0$, and $U = (u_1, u_2, \cdots, u_p)$
7: **for** $k = 1$ to p **do**
8:    **if** $\sum\limits_{i=1}^{k} \lambda_i / \sum\limits_{i=1}^{p} \lambda_i \geq c$ **then**
9:        $\Lambda_k = (\lambda_1, \lambda_2, \cdots, \lambda_k)$
10:       $U_k = (u_1, u_2, \cdots, u_k)$
11:   **end if**
12: **end for**
13: **return** Λ_k, U_k
14: **for** $i = 1$ to m **do**
15:   compute $S_{n_i p} = X_{n_i p} \times U_k$
16:   use the model defined in Theorem 3 to generate a synthetic data set $X'_{n_i \times p}$
17: **end for**
18: **return** $X' = \bigcup\limits_{i=1}^{m} X'_{n_i \times p}$

4.2 Proposed Algorithm

In view of the above scenarios, we proposed a multi-party horizontal split data publishing method based on probabilistic principal component analysis and differential privacy (PPCA-DP-MH), the basic idea is that the data owners and the semi-trusted curator collaborate to reduce the dimensionality to obtain the principal components that satisfy the ε differential privacy, and then use the generative model of probabilistic principal component analysis to generate a synthetic dataset for publishing. Firstly, the data owners use the Laplace mechanism to perturb every local covariance matrix, and then send them to the semi-trusted curator, secondly, the semi-trusted curator aggregates the local noisy covariance matrices to obtain the covariance matrix of the overall data, and performs eigenvalue decomposition on the noisy covariance matrix of the overall data, then the semi-trusted curator sends the first k principal components to each data owner, lastly, the data owner uses the k principal components and Theorem 3 to generate a dataset $X'_{n_i \times p}(i = 1, 2, \cdots, m)$, and sends it to the semi-trusted curator, the semi-trusted curator obtains a synthetic dataset $X' = \bigcup_{i=1}^{m} X'_{n_i \times p}$ which satisfies ε differential privacy. Please see Algorithm 1 for details, assuming that the data has been normalized, that is, the value of the data is in the interval $[0, 1]$.

4.3 Privacy Analysis

For the PPCA-DP-MH algorithm proposed in this paper, there is a risk of privacy leakage only when the data owner sends the covariance matrix of the local data to the semi-trusted curator, therefore, the data owner uses the Laplace mechanism of differential privacy to perturb the local covariance matrix. Because the local datasets do not intersect each other, according to the parallel combination theorem of differential privacy, as long as the local covariance matrix satisfies ε differential privacy, the covariance matrix of the overall data satisfies ε differential privacy, that is, the PPCA-DP-MH algorithm satisfies ε differential privacy.

Theorem 4. *The PPCA-DP-MH algorithm satisfies ε differential privacy.*

Proof. The normalized dataset is still denoted as $X_{n_i \times p}$, since the data is normalized to $[0, 1]$, that is, each entry in $X_{n_i \times p}$ is bounded to $[0, 1]$, so the sensitivity of $E(X_{n_i \times p}^T)$ and $E(X_{n_i \times p}^T X_{n_i \times p})$ are $\frac{p}{n_i}$, because

$$\hat{E}(X_{n_i \times p}^T) = E(X_{n_i \times p}^T) + L_{p \times 1}^1$$

$$\hat{E}(X_{n_i \times p}^T X_{n_i \times p}) = E(X_{n_i \times p}^T X_{n_i \times p}) + L_{p \times p}^2$$

and each element of the matrices $L_{p \times 1}^1$ and $L_{p \times p}^2$ obeys $Lap(\frac{2p}{n_i \varepsilon})$, so the stage of calculating $\hat{E}(X_{n_i \times p}^T)$ and $\hat{E}(X_{n_i \times p}^T X_{n_i \times p})$ satisfies $\frac{\varepsilon}{2}$ differential privacy, and by the sequential composition theorem of differential privacy, the local covariance matrix $\hat{\Sigma}_i = \hat{E}(X_{n_i \times p}^T X_{n_i \times p}) - \hat{E}(X_{n_i \times p}^T)\hat{E}(X_{n_i \times p})$ satisfies ε differential privacy, due to the local datasets do not intersect each other and the parallel combination theorem of differential privacy, the covariance matrix of the overall data $\hat{\Sigma}$ satisfies ε differential privacy, so the PPCA-DP-MH algorithm satisfies ε differential privacy.

5 Experiment

In this section, we conducted simulation experiments on real datasets to demonstrate the effectiveness of our PPCA-DP-MH method, we used two datasets: NLTCS and Adult. NLTCS dataset is extracted from the National Long Term Care Survey, and recorded the daily activities of 21574 disabled persons at different time periods, each individual has 16 attributes. Adult dataset is extracted from the 1994 US Census, it contains 45222 individuals, each individual has 15 attributes. In order to compare with the DP-SUBN3 algorithm proposed in [33], we preprocessed data similar to [33]. We use SVM classification accuracy to evaluate the utility of our PPCA-DP-MH method and the DP-SUBN3 method.

We trained multiple SVM classifiers on the synthetic dataset. Each classifier predicts one attribute based on all other attributes in the dataset. Two classifiers are trained on NLTCS, one is to predict whether a person is unable to get outside, and the other is to predict whether a person is unable to manage money. Two classifiers are trained on Adult, one is to predict whether a person holds a post-secondary degree and the other is to predict whether a person earns more than 50K. For each classification task, we use 80% of the tuples in the dataset as the training set, and the remaining 20% as the testing set. We run each experiment 5 times, and the average results are reported. In order to better measure the effectiveness of our PPCA-DP-MH method, the same SVM classifier is also trained on the original data set. In the figures, we use "No Privacy" to represent the SVM classification accuracy on the original dataset.

For the parameter k which is the number of retained principal components, it is determined by the cumulative contribution rate c of the principal components, in our experiments, the cumulative contribution rate c for NLTCS and Adult are set to 0.85 and 0.9, respectively.

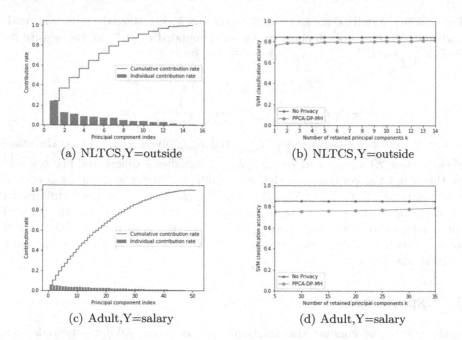

(a) NLTCS,Y=outside

(b) NLTCS,Y=outside

(c) Adult,Y=salary

(d) Adult,Y=salary

Fig. 2. Relationship between SVM classification accuracy and number of principal components

5.1   Relationship Between SVM Classification Accuracy and Number of Principal Components Retained

In order to study the relationship between the SVM classification accuracy and the number of principal components retained k, we trained two classifiers outside on NLTCS and salary on Adult separately, in this set of experiments, the number of data owners m is set to 3, the privacy budget ε is set to 0.1.

For the NLTCS dataset, Fig. 2(a) shows the cumulative contribution rate and individual contribution rate of the principal component, Fig. 2(b) shows the relationship between the SVM classification accuracy of the synthetic dataset and the number of principal components retained k. The results show that the number of principal components retained k increases (the cumulative contribution rate increases), the SVM classification accuracy also increases. It can be seen from Fig. 2(a) that the contribution rate of only the first principal component has reached more than 27%, and the cumulative contribution rate of the first 8 principal components can reach 85%, at the same time from Fig. 2(b) we can see the corresponding SVM classification accuracy can reach nearly 80%.

For the Adult dataset, Fig. 2(c) shows the cumulative contribution rate and individual contribution rate of the principal component, Fig. 2(d) shows the relationship between the SVM classification accuracy of the synthetic dataset and the number of retained principal components k. Because the Adult dataset has many attributes, we only marked the corresponding SVM classification accuracy when the number of retained principal components k is $5, 10, 15, 20, 25, 30$, and 35 in Fig. 2 (d), it can be seen that as the number of retained principal components k increases, the SVM classification accuracy also increases.

The experimental conclusions on the two datasets are similar, that is, the SVM classification accuracy increases as the number of retained principal components k increases (the cumulative contribution rate increases), this is because each principal component contains the information of the original dataset and is not related to each other, as the number of retained principal components increases, the information of the original dataset retained increases, and the synthetic dataset contains more information about the original dataset accordingly.

5.2   Relationship Between SVM Classification Accuracy and Privacy Budget

In this set of experiments, we set the number of data owners to 3, and privacy budget ε takes different values. Figure 3 shows the SVM classification accuracy of each method on NLTCS and Adult under different privacy budgets, Fig. 3(a) and Fig. 3(b) show the results of the two classifiers money and outside on the NLTCS, respectively. Figure 3(c) and Fig. 3(d) show the results of the two classifiers education and salary on the Adult, respectively. We can observe that our PPCA-DP-MH method clearly outperforms DP-SUBN3 method, only in Fig. 3(b) when the privacy budget ε is greater than 0.5, the SVM classification accuracy of the synthetic dataset released by PPCA-DP-MH method is slightly

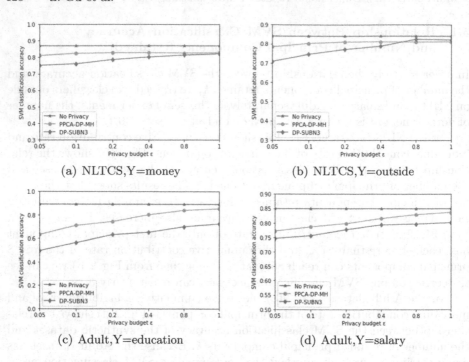

Fig. 3. Relationship between SVM classification accuracy and privacy budget

lower than DP-SUBN3 method, in other cases, the SVM classification accuracy of the synthetic dataset released by PPCA-DP-MH method is higher than DP-SUBN3 method. Especially, in Fig. 3(c), for the education classifier on the Adult, the SVM classification accuracy of the synthetic dataset released by PPCA-DP-MH method is nearly 10% higher than DP-SUBN3 method.

In Fig. 3, we can also observe a commonality, the SVM classification accuracy increases with the increase of the privacy budget ε both on the synthetic datasets released by PPCA-DP-MH method and DP-SUBN3 method, and this phenomenon is consistent with the theory that as the privacy budget ε increases, privacy protection will weaken and the availability of data will increase.

5.3 Relationship Between SVM Classification Accuracy and Number of Data Owners

In this section, the experiment studied the relationship between SVM classification accuracy and the number of data owners m. The number of data owners m is set to 2, 4, 6, 8, 10, and the privacy budget ε is set to 0.2, We trained two classifiers, education classifier and salary classifier on the Adult dataset.

The results in Fig. 4 show that the SVM classification accuracy of the synthetic dataset by PPCA-DP-MH method decreases as the number of data owners m increases, however, the SVM classification accuracy of the synthetic dataset by

DP-SUBN3 method increases as the number of data owners m increases, this is because, for DP-SUBN3 method, with the number of data owners increases, the number of update iterations increases when constructing the Bayesian network, and the Bayesian network constructed is closer to the distribution of the original data. For PPCA-DP-MH method, the number of individuals in the overall data set is fixed, generally, the more data owners, the less the number of individuals owned by each data owner, the more noise added by each data owner, so with the increase of data owners, the SVM classification accuracy of the synthetic dataset by PPCA-DP-MH method decreases. However, in Fig. 4(a), for education classifier, when there are no more than 6 data owners, the SVM classification accuracy of the synthetic data set by PPCA-DP-MH method can still be higher than DP-SUBN3 method, and in Fig. 4(b), for salary classifier, when there are no more than 10 data owners, the SVM classification accuracy of the synthetic data set released by PPCA-DP-MH method is still higher than DP-SUBN3 method.

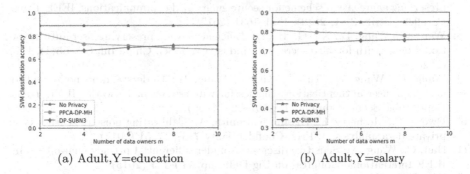

(a) Adult,Y=education   (b) Adult,Y=salary

Fig. 4. Relationship between SVM classification accuracy and number of data owners

6   Conclusion

In this paper, we proposed a method for multi-party horizontally split data publishing based on probabilistic principal component analysis and differential privacy (PPCA-DP-MH). The data owners and the semi-trusted curator cooperate with each other to reduce the dimensionality of high-dimensional related data and generate a synthetic data set for publishing. We used the Laplacian mechanism to add noise to less but more important data in order to increase the utility of the published data. The experimental results show that the synthetic data set released by our PPCA-DP-MH method can maintain high utility in SVM classification. In the future, we will study the vertically split data publishing based on differential privacy.

References

1. Kolter, J.Z., Jaakkola, T.S.: Approximate inference in additive factorial HMMs with application to energy disaggregation (2012)
2. Wang, D., Zhang, X., Zhang, Z., Wang, P.: Understanding security failures of multi-factor authentication schemes for multi-server environments. Comput. Secur. **88**, 1–13 (2020)
3. Tsou, Y.T., Lin, B.C.: PPDCA: privacy-preserving crowdsourcing data collection and analysis with randomized response. IEEE Access **6**, 76970–76983 (2018)
4. Ren, X., et al.: High-dimensional crowdsourced data publication with local differential privacy. IEEE Trans. Inf. Forensics Secur. **13**, 2151–2166 (2018)
5. Qiu, S., Wang, D., Xu, G., Kumari, S.: Practical and provably secure three-factor authentication protocol based on extended chaotic-maps for mobile lightweight devices. IEEE Trans. Dependable Secure Comput. **17**, 1–14 (2020)
6. Sweeney, L.: k-anonymity: a model for protecting privacy. Int. J. Uncertainty Fuzziness Knowl. Based Syst. **10**, 557–570 (2002)
7. Lu, R., Liang, X., Xu, L., Lin, X., Shen, X.: EPPA: an efficient and privacy-preserving aggregation scheme for secure smart grid communications. IEEE Trans. Parallel Distrib. Syst. **23**(9), 1621–1631 (2012)
8. Wang, C., Wang, D., Xu, G., He, D.: Efficient privacy-preserving user authentication scheme with forward secrecy for industry 4.0. Sci. China Inf. Sci. **65**(1), 1–15 (2020)
9. Wang, C., Wang, D., Tu, Y., Xu, G., Wang, H.: Understanding node capture attacks in user authentication schemes for wireless sensor networks. IEEE Trans. Dependable Secure Comput. **19**, 507–523 (2020)
10. Dwork, C., Mcsherry, F., Nissim, K., Smith, A.: Calibrating noise to sensitivity in private data analysis. J. Priv. Confidentiality **7**(3), 17–51 (2017)
11. Han, C., Wang, K.: Sensitive disclosures under differential privacy guarantees. In: IEEE International Congress on Big Data, pp. 110–117 (2015)
12. Wang, Q., Zhang, Y., Xiao, L., Wang, Z., Ren, K.: RescueDP: real-time spatio-temporal crowd-sourced data publishing with differential privacy. In: IEEE Infocom the IEEE International Conference on Computer Communications (2016)
13. Hao, W., Xu, Z.: CTS-DP: publishing correlated time-series data via differential privacy. Knowl.-Based Syst. **122**, 167–179 (2017)
14. Wang, H., Wang, H.: Correlated tuple data release via differential privacy. Inf. Sci. **560**, 347–369 (2021)
15. Chen, S., Fu, A., Yu, S., Ke, H., Su, M.: DP-QIC: a differential privacy scheme based on quasi-identifier classification for big data publication. Soft Comput. **25**(3), 7325–7339 (2021)
16. Yang, B., Sato, I., Nakagawa, H.: Bayesian differential privacy on correlated data. In: SIGMOD/PODS (2015)
17. Jiang, X., Ji, Z., Wang, S., Mohammed, N., Cheng, S., Ohno-Machado, L.: Differential-private data publishing through component analysis. Trans. Data Priv. **6**(1), 19 (2013)
18. Nissim, K., Mcsherry, F.D., Dwork, C., Blum, A.L.: Practical privacy: the SuLQ framework. In: Proceedings of the Twenty-Fourth ACM SIGACT-SIGMOD-SIGART Symposium on Principles of Database Systems, Baltimore, Maryland, USA, 13–15 June 2005 (2005)
19. Chaudhuri, K., Sarwate, A.D., Sinha, K.: Near-optimal differentially private principal components. In: Advances in Neural Information Processing Systems, vol. 2, pp. 989–997 (2012)

20. Kapralov, M., Talwar, K.: On differentially private low rank approximation. In: Soda, pp. 1395–1414 (2013)
21. Dwork, C., Talwar, K., Thakurta, A., Zhang, L.: Analyze gauss: optimal bounds for privacy-preserving PCA. In: Proceedings of the Annual ACM Symposium on Theory of Computing, pp. 11–20 (2014)
22. Jiang, W., Xie, C., Zhang, Z.: Wishart mechanism for differentially private principal components analysis. Comput. Sci. **9285**, 458–473 (2015)
23. Zhang, J., Cormode, G., Procopiuc, C.M., Srivastava, D., Xiao, X.: PrivBayes: private data release via Bayesian networks. ACM Trans. Database Syst. **42**(4), 1–41 (2014)
24. Rui, C., Qian, X., Yu, Z., Xu, J.: Differentially private high-dimensional data publication via sampling-based inference. In: The 21th ACM SIGKDD International Conference (2015)
25. Zhang, X., Chen, L., Jin, K., Meng, X.: Private high-dimensional data publication with junction tree. J. Comput. Res. Dev. **55**, 2794 (2018)
26. Xu, C., Ren, J., Zhang, Y., Qin, Z., Ren, K.: DPPro: differentially private high-dimensional data release via random projection. IEEE Trans. Inf. Forensics Secur. **PP**(99), 1 (2017)
27. Zhang, W., Zhao, J., Wei, F., Chen, Y.: Differentially private high-dimensional data publication via Markov network. Secur. Saf. **6**(19), 159626 (2019)
28. Ge, J., Wang, Z., Wang, M., Han, L.: Minimax-optimal privacy-preserving sparse PCA in distributed systems (2018)
29. Wang, S., Chang, J.M.: Differentially private principal component analysis over horizontally partitioned data. In: 2018 IEEE Conference on Dependable and Secure Computing (DSC) (2018)
30. Imtiaz, H., Sarwate, A.D.: Differentially private distributed principal component analysis. In: 2018 IEEE International Conference on Acoustics, Speech and Signal Processing (ICASSP), ICASSP 2018 (2018)
31. Alhadidi, D., Mohammed, N., Fung, B.C.M., Debbabi, M.: Secure distributed framework for achieving ε-differential privacy. In: Fischer-Hübner, S., Wright, M. (eds.) PETS 2012. LNCS, vol. 7384, pp. 120–139. Springer, Heidelberg (2012). https://doi.org/10.1007/978-3-642-31680-7_7
32. Hong, Y., Vaidya, J., Lu, H., Karras, P., Goel, S.: Collaborative search log sanitization: toward differential privacy and boosted utility. IEEE Trans. Dependable Secure Comput. **12**(5), 504–518 (2015)
33. Cheng, X., Tang, P., Su, S., Chen, R., Wu, Z., Zhu, B.: Multi-party high-dimensional data publishing under differential privacy. IEEE Trans. Knowl. Data Eng. **32**, 1557–1571 (2019)
34. Dwork, C., Roth, A.: The algorithmic foundations of differential privacy. Found. Trends Theor. Comput. Sci. **9**, 211–407 (2013)
35. Tipping, M.E., Bishop, C.M.: Probabilistic principal component analysis. J. Roy. Stat. Soc. **61**(3), 611–622 (2010)

Source Code Vulnerability Detection Method with Multidimensional Representation

Hongyu Yang[1,2(✉)] ⓘ, Leyi Ying[2] ⓘ, and Liang Zhang[3] ⓘ

[1] School of Safety Science and Engineering, Civil Aviation University of China,
Tianjin 300300, China
[2] School of Computer Science and Technology, Civil Aviation University of China,
Tianjin 300300, China
[3] School of Information, University of Arizona, Tucson, AZ 85721, USA

Abstract. At present, most of the source code vulnerability detection methods only rely on the source code text information for representation, and the single dimension of representation leads to low efficiency. This paper presents a source code vulnerability detection method based on multidimensional representation. Firstly, the structured text information of the source code is obtained through the abstract syntax tree of the source code; Then the source code is measured to obtain the code metrics; Finally, a deep neural network is used for feature learning to construct the source code vulnerability detection model, and the structured text features and code metrics of the source code to be detected are input into the vulnerability detection model to obtain the vulnerability detection results. The results of the comparison experiment show that the method has a good detection effect. In comparison experiments, 11 source code samples with different types of vulnerabilities were tested for vulnerability detection. The average detection accuracy of this method is 97.96%. Compared with existing vulnerability detection methods based on a single characterization, the detection accuracy of this method is improved by 4.89%–12.21%. At the same time, the miss and false-positive rates of this method are kept within 10%.

Keywords: Vulnerability detection · Structured representation · Abstract syntax tree · Code metrics · Deep neural network

1 Introduction

With the wide application of computer software in various fields, the problem of software vulnerability has become increasingly serious. Faced with a variety of software vulnerability types, how to efficiently detect vulnerabilities has become a hot issue. Vulnerability detection of source code is one of the effective means to ensure software security. At present, the methods based on code metrics and deep learning are more common source code vulnerability detection methods [1].

Code metrics [2] is a way to describe the characteristics and indicators of software code, that is, to obtain relevant defined values from software code by quantitative method.

W. Shi et al. (Eds.): SPNCE 2021, LNICST 423, pp. 132–139, 2022.
https://doi.org/10.1007/978-3-030-96791-8_10

Although code measurement is a coarse-grained representation of source code, it can represent the basic status of code to a certain extent. The vulnerability detection method based on code metrics measures the target code by using the source code metrics tool to obtain the corresponding index values and uses the machine learning algorithm to train and generate the vulnerability detector. Feren et al. [3] build a vulnerability detection model based on code metrics using machine learning algorithm and grid search algorithm and use resampling strategy to solve the imbalance of training data. Sultana [4] uses machine learning and statistical methods to track the relationship between code metrics, code patterns, and vulnerabilities, and proposes a vulnerability detection method, which is used to detect vulnerabilities in open-source software. The main drawbacks of code Metrics-based vulnerability detection methods are 1. Coarse detection granularity and poor interpretability; 2. Low precision and high false-positive rate.

With the application of deep learning technology in the field of natural language processing, researchers have focused on programming languages that share common characteristics with natural languages. Li et al. [5] introduced deep learning technology into the field of vulnerability detection for the first time and proposed a Vuldeepecker automatic vulnerability detection system, which can detect the vulnerability of source code written in C/C++ language. Nicholas et al. [6] proposed Achilles vulnerability detection method, tested on Java source code, and achieved good results, indicating that the source code vulnerability detection method based on deep learning can be applied to a variety of programming languages. The above two methods treat the source code as linear text and cannot fully represent the characteristics of the source code. To fully represent the syntax and semantics of programming language, structured representation is applied to the representation of source code. Chen Zhaoxuan et al. [7] proposed an intelligent vulnerability detection system Astor based on structural representation. The detection effect is better than the linear representation method on complex and syntax-rich data sets. The main shortcomings of the vulnerability detection method based on deep learning are as follows: 1. Need to rely on a large number of data for training; 2. The detection results of different types of vulnerabilities fluctuate greatly; 3. The precision rate and recall rate need to be improved.

To further improve the effectiveness of vulnerability detection, this paper presents a source code vulnerability detection method based on multidimensional representation to detect vulnerabilities in source code at function-level granularity. First, Structured text information is obtained by deep-first traversing the source code abstract syntax tree, then code metrics are obtained by using the source code static parsing tool. Finally, a neural network is constructed to learn the features and construct the source code vulnerability detection model.

2 Design of Source Code Vulnerability Detection Method

2.1 Method Architecture Design

The proposed source code vulnerability detection model consists of four parts: data preprocessing, data multidimensional representation, model building and training, and vulnerability detection. The core framework of the method is shown in Fig. 1. The main processes for the four parts of the vulnerability detection model are:

1. Data preprocessing: The data preprocessing phase consists of code slicing and setting supervised learning labels. This method detects vulnerabilities at the function-level granularity, so the source code data is divided into function fragments and tagged according to whether there are vulnerabilities in the function fragments.
2. Data Multidimensional Representation: To fully represent the information of function fragments, the pre-processed data is characterized from two dimensions, structured text information and code metrics. The Abstract Syntax Tree (AST) is used to characterize the text information of function fragments Define code metrics to measure function fragments.
3. Model construction and training: A neural network is constructed, and the neural network performs feature learning according to the data types of two dimensions. The neural network is trained by two kinds of representation results and preset tags to construct a vulnerability detection model.
4. Source code vulnerability detection: Use the training completed vulnerability detection model to detect vulnerabilities in the source code to be detected. The source code to be detected is pre-processed and represented in the same way as the training data, and the vulnerability detection results are obtained by entering the characterization results into the training completed vulnerability detection model.

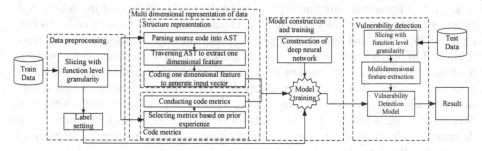

Fig. 1. Framework for vulnerability detection in this paper

3 Data Representation

To fully represent the source code characteristics, the source code is characterized from two different dimensions: code structure representation and code metrics. Code structure characterization can obtain text information of code structure, and code metrics can characterize the basic state of code.

3.1 Code Structural Representation

The programming language is a structured language, and the information in the source code has a clear structural relationship. Therefore, the method of characterizing natural language does not fully characterize the grammar and semantics in the source code.

To get more practical source code characteristics, the source code is characterized by a structured representation method. The structured representation method consists of the following three steps.

Step 1: Use the Java source code parsing tool javalang to parse the code, get the information of the node and edge of the AST, and generate the AST based on the information of the node and edge.

Step 2: depth-first traverses the abstract syntax tree to collect node information in turn. The result of depth-first traversing the abstract syntax tree transforms the tree data into one-dimensional text data.

Step 3: Transform one-dimensional text data into neural network input. Since the input of the neural network is vector data, it is necessary to further process one-dimensional text data. Firstly, the text data is segmented, and then the word in all the text is counted to generate a document dictionary. Finally, the vector representation of the text is generated based on the dictionary order.

3.2 Code Metrics

The purpose of this method is to detect the source code vulnerability at the function level, so we need to measure it at the code function level. To make the data-dependent deep learning method interact with the prior knowledge of security experts effectively and make the detection model more adaptive, it is necessary to define the code metrics manually. The code measurement processing in this method consists of two steps:

Step 1: define metrics. This paper defines the metrics of code metrics, and the main metrics used in the code metrics phase are Chidamber & Kemer metrics. Compared with the traditional McCabe metrics and Halstead metrics, chidamber & Kemer metrics are specifically proposed for an object-oriented programming language, so they are more adaptable to Java language.

Step 2: Code metrics. Code metrics using the code metrics tool yields the specific quantified value of the metrics.

4 Construction and Training of Neural Network Model

4.1 Construction of Neural Network Model

The results of multi-dimensional representation of source code are structured text information and the digital sequence generated by code measurement. Therefore, it is necessary to design a neural network for feature learning of structured text information and digital sequence and synthesize the judgment results of the two to give the final vulnerability detection results.

The neural network model constructed in this paper consists of three parts: 1. Neural network model based on self-attention (SA) mechanism [13]; 2. Deep neural networks (DNN); 3. Support vector machine (SVM). The main structure of the neural network is shown in Fig. 2.

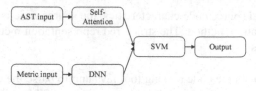

Fig. 2. The framework of neural network

4.2 Construction of Neural Network Model Based on SA

SA mechanism can reflect the direct interaction between each word and all other words in the document. Comparing long Short-Term Memory (LSTM) or Recurrent Neural Network (RNN) needs to be calculated step by step in the sequence to obtain the long-distance interdependence in the text information. The SA mechanism captures the long-distance dependencies of text information better. Therefore, SA is more suitable for structured text feature learning tasks than traditional RNN or LSTM.

The SA-based neural network constructed in this paper consists of the input layer, SA layer, full connector layer, and output layer, in which the full connector layer consists of 128 neurons. Since the calculations in SA are all linear, the function of adding a fully connected layer is to improve the fitting ability of the nonlinear characteristics of the neural network. To obtain the probability of vulnerabilities from text features, the Sigmoid activation function is applied to the output of the full connection layer.

As an activation function, the Sigmoid function maps the output of the neural network to [0, 1]. Therefore, in the text sequence feature learning phase, the learned text features are transformed into the probability of vulnerability. The SA-based neural network is trained by the results of source code structured representation and preset labels. By entering the source code structured text information into the trained neural network, the probability of vulnerabilities in the corresponding source code can be output.

4.3 Construction of DNN Model

The result of a code metrics is a sequence of numbers in which each element represents the specific value of the corresponding measure and there is no interdependence between the elements of the measure. Based on the above application scenarios, DNN can learn sequence features in a shorter time than traditional machine learning algorithms. Therefore, DNN is used to learn the characteristics of code metrics.

The DNN constructed in this paper consists of the input layer, two hidden layers, and the output layer. The number of neurons in each hidden layer is 64. For the input code metrics, after fitting the code metrics characteristics through two hidden layers, the output is mapped to [0, 1] using the Sigmoid function as the activation function. DNN is trained with code metrics and preset labels, and the probability of vulnerabilities in the corresponding source code can be output by entering code metrics into the DNN model after training.

4.4   Construction of SVM Model

To get more accurate vulnerability detection results, the output results of the two models need to be combined. Therefore, this paper takes the output of the above two models as a feature and further classifies them using Support Vector Machine (SVM) to determine whether there are any vulnerabilities in the code.

There are two main reasons for choosing SVM as the classifier in this stage: 1. SVM works well in classification tasks and its classification ideas are simple and intuitive, and it can draw its decision boundary accurately; 2. The classification method is flexible and can be used for both linear and non-linear classification by adjusting its kernel function.

Conventional SVMs are classified by drawing maximally spaced hyperplanes, but this method cannot be used for non-linear classification. Since the output of SA-based neural networks and DNNs may be linearly inseparable, the kernel function of SVM is set to classify nonlinearly. The SVM model constructed by this method uses three different kernel functions including the linear kernel, polynomial kernel, and Gaussian kernel to classify the output results of SA-based neural network and DNN respectively. In the trained SVM model, the existence probability of vulnerability based on SA neural network and DNN output is input, and the final result of vulnerability detection is output.

5   Experimental Design and Result Analysis

To test the source code vulnerability detection performance of this method, we compared the method with Astor [7], Code Metrics based vulnerability detection [3], Achilles [6], VulDeePecker [5] based on linear text representation. In the performance comparison experiment of source code vulnerability detection, the above five detection models were constructed using the TensorFlow framework. The performance indicators of the five models are shown in Table 1.

Table 1. Performance comparison of detection methods

Detection methods	A	P	R	F1	FPR
Code Metrics-based	0.8575	0.8574	0.5637	0.6668	0.0332
Astor	0.9218	0.9392	0.7776	0.8382	0.0242
Achilles	0.9307	0.8901	0.6986	0.7446	0.0463
VulDeePecker	0.9390	0.9190	0.9590	0.9290	0.0490
Method of this article	0.9796	0.9728	0.9464	0.9585	0.0092

As can be seen from Table 1, the accuracy of vulnerability detection in this method is better than that in the other 4 methods, with a lower rate of miss and false positives. The average accuracy of code Metrics-based methods, Astor, Achilles, and VulDeePecker for detecting different vulnerabilities is 85.75%, 92.18%, 93.07%, and respectively. The average accuracy of this method for detecting different vulnerabilities is 97.96%, which is superior to the other four methods. The recall rate of this method is 94.64%, which is higher than the other four methods, indicating that the miss rate of this method is the lowest. The false-positive rate of this method is 0.92%, which is lower than that of the other four methods.

This method can achieve good results in vulnerability detection for two reasons: 1. This method characterizes the source code from two dimensions: source code structure text information and code metrics. This method is more comprehensive than the single representation method. 2. Text information feature is an important feature in vulnerability detection. The SA-based neural network built in this paper can better capture the long-term dependencies in text information.

6 Conclusion

In order to further improve the accuracy of source code vulnerability detection and reduce the false alarm rate, this paper proposes a source code vulnerability detection method based on multi-dimensional representation. The source code is characterized by code measurement and structured text, and the neural network model is used for feature learning to construct a vulnerability detection model for source code vulnerability detection. The experimental results show that the proposed vulnerability detection method has higher accuracy, lower false positive rate, and false-negative rate.

This method only characterizes the source code from two dimensions, which are not comprehensive enough. The focus of future work is to explore more suitable source code representation methods for vulnerability detection and improve the representation methods to obtain better detection performance.

References

1. Li, Z., Shao, Y.: A survey of feature selection for vulnerability prediction using feature-based machine learning. In: Proceedings of the 2019 11th International Conference on Machine Learning and Computing, pp. 36–42. Association for Computing Machinery, New York (2019)
2. Kan, S.H.: Metrics and models in software quality engineering. Softw. Guide 4(9), 1333–1334 (2009)
3. Feren, R., Péter, H.: Challenging machine learning algorithms in predicting vulnerable JavaScript functions. In: 2019 IEEE/ACM 7th International Workshop on Realizing Artificial Intelligence Synergies in Software Engineering. ACM (2019)
4. Sultana, K.Z.: Towards a software vulnerability prediction model using traceable code patterns and software metrics. In: IEEE/ACM International Conference on Automated Software Engineering, pp. 1022–1025. IEEE Computer Society (2017)
5. Li, Z., Zou, D.Q.: VulPecker: an automated vulnerability detection system based on code similarity analysis. In: Proceedings of the 32nd Annual Conference on Computer Security Applications, pp. 201–213. Association for Computing Machinery, New York (2016)
6. Saccente, N., Dehlinger, J.: Project achilles: a prototype tool for static method-level vulnerability detection of java source code using a recurrent neural network. In: 2019 34th IEEE/ACM International Conference on Automated Software Engineering Workshop. ACM (2019)
7. Chen, Z., Zou, D.: Intelligent vulnerability detection system based on abstract syntax tree. J. Cyber Secur. 2020(4), 1–13 (2020)
8. Common Weakness Enumeration. https://cwe.mitre.org/. Accessed 6 May 2019

9. Liu, Y.: Research and Application of Code Vulnerability Detection Mechanism Based on Machine Learning, University of Electronic Science and Technology (2018)
10. Vaswani, A., Shazeer, N.: Attention is all you need. In: Advances in Neural Information Processing Systems, pp. 5998–6008 (2017)

A Security Enhanced Verification Framework Based on Device Fingerprint in Internet of Things

Shichen Fu[1], Liuping Huang[1], and Guangyan Zhang[2(✉)]

[1] State Grid Zhangzhou Electric Power Supply Company, Zhangzhou, China
[2] Northeastern University, Shenyang, China

Abstract. IoT device fingerprint is a critical technology for device identification and access control. It is also the first step to test the protection ability of IoT devices. Existing schemes tend to deploy the verification server in the cloud, which leads to problems such as high bandwidth pressure, failure to update the device fingerprint normally, slow verification speed and others leading to security risks. To solve the problems, this paper presents a security enhanced verification framework based on device fingerprint in IoT to reduce the bandwidth pressure, computational overhead. A device fingerprint updating mechanism is proposed to distinguish normal devices from abnormal devices. Meanwhile, this paper proposes an efficient device fingerprint matching algorithm, which realizes the compressed storage and fast matching of massive device fingerprints.

Keywords: IoT · Device fingerprint · Security · Identity authentication

1 Introduction

With the development of industrial intelligence, the number and types of Internet of Things (IoT) devices are increasing rapidly. These IoT devices with weak security protection provide a huge and extensive network attack entrance for attackers, leading to many problems and challenges facing the Internet of Things [1–6]. In July 2019, several employees of a nuclear power plant near the city of Yuzh-Noukrainsk in southern Ukraine experienced a serious security breach when they connected the plant's internal network to a public network for cryptocurrency mining. The incident has been classified as a breach of state secrets, and investigators have begun looking into whether internet-connected devices could be used by hackers to break into the plant's internal network and steal confidential information. How to improve the security of IoT devices is an urgent problem to be solved.

Authentication of devices is a critical step in protecting the Internet of Things [7–9]. The existing authentication methods can be divided into password-based

© ICST Institute for Computer Sciences, Social Informatics and Telecommunications Engineering 2022
Published by Springer Nature Switzerland AG 2022. All Rights Reserved
W. Shi et al. (Eds.): SPNCE 2021, LNICST 423, pp. 140–158, 2022.
https://doi.org/10.1007/978-3-030-96791-8_11

authentication [10], cryptographic protocol-based authentication [11,12], and device fingerprint-based authentication [13–16]. Since the verification technology based on device fingerprint has a small demand on the computing power and storage capacity of the device, it is more suitable for resource-constrained devices in the Internet of Things environment. In this paper, the source address verification technology based on device fingerprint is adopted. However, through the study of the existing methods, it is found that most of the device fingerprints extracted in the existing work are based on the device hardware attributes, such as the transient characteristics of the device switch and machine, the modulation signal, etc. In practical applications, these attributes are affected by noise and interference in the environment, which makes the fingerprint easy to change [17]. By observing the IoT devices, it is clear that the response headers returned by the devices often carry device information to distinguish services. Therefore, this paper establishes a numerical device fingerprint based on the response headers of the IoT devices, which has the advantages of uniqueness and stability.

Meanwhile, the existing authentication methods need to do an identity match on the authentication request sent by the device [18,19]. If the match is successful, then the authentication is passed, and after that, the device identity is no longer verified. As more and more devices are connected to the Internet of Things, there are more and more types of devices and more and more complex types. Therefore, for the network with numerous devices, complex structure and difficult management, the attacker is often easier to find the place with weak defense, and can easily forge the device identity and enter the network by pretending to be a legitimate device. Therefore, even if the device identity passes the authentication, it is not necessarily credible. As a supplement to the existing authentication methods, this paper argues that the authentication terminal should not trust the device except the authentication request proposed by the device, and the authentication server should verify the identity of the current networked device again, so as to enhance the protection of the identity security of the device.

This paper presents a security enhanced authentication method based on device fingerprint, through the fingerprints are consistent alignment device, which can validate device identity, but as a result of actual IoT environment, authentication server deployment in the cloud environment, so this method is still facing the following challenges: the bandwidth pressure, fingerprint cannot normal slow speed matching, validation.

To solve the problem of high bandwidth pressure and device fingerprint can not match properly, this chapter proposes a security enhancement verification framework based on device fingerprint. Aiming at the problem of slow verification speed, this paper designs and implements an efficient fingerprint matching algorithm for devices. Finally, the experiment proves that the scheme is efficient. The main contributions of this paper are as follows:

(1) To solve the problem of untrusted devices, a security enhanced authentication framework based on device fingerprint is proposed, which takes the

authentication server as the requester, and the gateway provides the authentication service to enhance the security.

(2) Aiming at the storage and matching problem of device fingerprint, an efficient device fingerprint matching algorithm is proposed. This algorithm is oriented to device fingerprint and improves the inherent defects in the basic bloom filter. It has the advantages of extensibility, low false positive rate and fast verification speed.

Organization. The remainder of this paper is organized as follows. Section 2 defines the problems of identity authentication for IoT devices under cloud services. Section 3 presents the proposed scheme in detail. Section 4 introduces an efficient device fingerprint matching algorithm. Section 5 presents the performance analysis of the scheme. Finally, the conclusions are drawn in Sect. 6.

2   Problem Definition

The existing Internet of Things structure uses a cloud server as the management center of the entire Internet of Things environment, and the authentication server is also included to provide identity authentication services for devices. However, if this method is deployed in a cloud environment, the following challenges are still faced:

(1) High bandwidth pressure: The cloud authentication server scans the terminal devices of the entire network, and the returned scan data is too concentrated. If a denial of service attack occurs at this time, the connection between the cloud and the underlying device will be cut off;

(2) Device fingerprints do not match properly: If there is a device in the network that requires a software or hardware upgrade, the IP address of the normal device will change. Because the device fingerprint does not match, the inherently legitimate device will be considered malicious by default and will eventually be ejected from the network. When this happens, the common solution is to bulk upgrade the underlying devices or to change the network configuration, which will result in re-initialization of the registry due to a large area of network failure. On the one hand, it causes communication burden, on the other hand, it provides opportunities for attackers.

(3) Slow verification speed: When the target network is initialized, the cloud obtains and establishes the device fingerprint of each device. Meanwhile, when providing verification service, the cloud environment needs to recalculate the fingerprint of each device and carry out extraction, comparison, retrieval and other operations with the previously stored fingerprint. This imposes a significant computational overhead.

To solve the first and second problems, this paper proposes a security-enhanced authentication framework based on device fingerprints. The authentication service is migrated to the gateway for execution. The gateway provides authentication services to store and update device fingerprints, which can improve retrieval efficiency. It reduces the bandwidth pressure of the cloud server, reduces the computational overhead, and proposes a device fingerprint update mechanism to distinguish between normal devices and abnormal devices, and solves the problem of normal devices matching device fingerprints. Aiming at the problem of slow verification speed, this paper designs and implements an efficient device fingerprint matching algorithm to realize fast matching while keeping accuracy.

3 Security Enhanced Verification Framework Based on Device Fingerprint in Internet of Things

This section proposes the design goals of a security-enhanced authentication framework based on device fingerprints under the Internet of Things, and on this basis, proposes an identity verification framework, and then introduces the basic execution process.

3.1 Design Goals

The framework proposed in this paper will be deployed in the Internet of Things environment, oriented to Internet of Things terminal device, so considering the particularity of the network environment and terminal device, in addition to the basic functions of enhancing the identity security of the device, the authentication technology should also have the following design goals:

(1) Low energy consumption: Most of IoT devices are resource-constrained, so the verification technology ought not to bring additional computing and storage overhead.
(2) Universality: One of the reasons for the poor deployment of existing identity verification methods is that the devices are highly heterogeneous, so the method proposed in this paper should be suitable for heterogeneous devices.
(3) High efficiency: Identity verification technology should start from the perspective of actual deployment, comprehensively consider the existing Internet of Things network structure, and propose a more reasonable and deployable identity verification technology.

3.2 System model

The core of the design of this model is to deploy identity verification services on smart gateways with application deployment capabilities. Such devices mostly appear in new network architectures proposed in recent years, such as edge computing and fog computing. Based on the smart gateway structure with application deployment capabilities, we proposes a security-enhanced authentication architecture based on device fingerprints, as shown in Fig. 1.

Three different entities are involved in this architecture: cloud, smart gateway, and IoT devices. Each entity is introduced as follows:

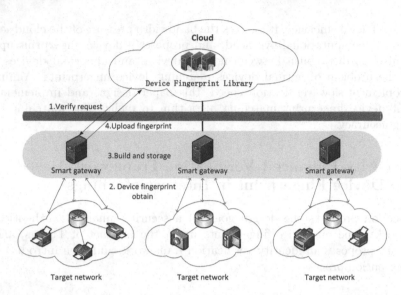

Fig. 1. Architecture diagram of identity verification system based on device fingerprint

(1) **Cloud.** Cloud is flexibility and on-demand charging. It has powerful storage and computing capabilities, but its bandwidth is limited. It cannot communicate with all sensor devices in the network environment at the same time. The cloud needs to store device fingerprints in the entire network environment and update the device fingerprint library in time.

(2) **Smart gateway.** The smart gateway is connected to the underlying sensor device and is deployed on the side of the network near the device. A smart gateway is connected to some sensor devices, and each sensor device is connected to only one smart gateway. That is, the smart gateway divides the entire terminal device set into multiple unrelated sub-sets. The gateway has certain computing and storage capabilities for device scanning, and completes the establishment and storage of device fingerprints, and provides identity verification services for its corresponding underlying devices.

(3) **IoT device.** The IoT device is an IP whose identity may be tampered with under attack. Upon receipt of an identity verification service request, data will be sent as required. Meanwhile, IoT device may be faced with software updates, hardware updates, and IP changes. At this time, the change information needs to be uploaded.

The main steps of identity verification in this framework are: identity verification request sending, device fingerprint acquisition, device fingerprint establishment, device fingerprint storage, and device fingerprint update.

(1) Identity verification request sending: the cloud server establishes the identity verification service and deploys it on the smart gateway, establishes a connection path between the cloud server and the smart gateway, and divides

the network where the underlying terminal device is located, so that the connected smart gateway can collect all The response message of the terminal device. Sending an identity verification request means that the verification server needs to verify the identity of all running devices in the network at this time, and the device responds accordingly after receiving the request.

(2) Device fingerprint acquisition: The smart gateway scans the device to the target network and receives the response information from the device. Through the incremental device scanning start-up time prediction algorithm, by sending verification requests to devices from time to time, new devices and frequently changing devices in the network can be discovered in time.

(3) Device fingerprint establishment: When scanning for the first time, the gateway uses the high-precision device fingerprint extraction algorithm to process the scanned data and establish the device fingerprint corresponding to the device, and set the device IP and device fingerprints according to a certain frequency Upload to the cloud to ensure that bandwidth fluctuations are as small as possible.

(4) Device fingerprint storage: To provide verification services faster, the gateway is responsible for storing device fingerprints of scanning devices and sending the device fingerprints to the cloud. The cloud builds a device fingerprint library for a large-scale IoT environment. When the device fingerprint database of the gateway is updated, the updated information is synchronized and uploaded to the cloud. Section 4 proposes an efficient device fingerprint matching algorithm to achieve compressed storage and fast matching of device fingerprints.

(5) Device fingerprint update: When the device is updated normally, it needs to submit a request to the gateway to update the device fingerprint. After receiving the update request, the smart gateway first retrieves the original device fingerprint in the device fingerprint database, and then calculates according to the uploaded original characteristics The fingerprint is compared with the stored fingerprint. If the match is successful, the device fingerprint will be recalculated, and the original fingerprint will be replaced in the device fingerprint library.

The process of identity verification is shown in Fig. 2. When the smart gateway reaches the scan start time and needs to verify the identity of the device, it sends a scan request to the terminal device. After receiving the scan request, the terminal device sends back corresponding response data. After the gateway receives the response data, it first uses similar devices based on hierarchical aggregation. The device fingerprint classification algorithm is used for clustering, and then the SVD-based device fingorprint dimensionality reduction algorithm is used to obtain the numerical representation of the device, and the two-tuple information of the device is obtained. Finally, an efficient device fingerprint matching algorithm is used to perform the two-tuple compressed storage and fast matching, and judge whether it is a new device or a device that is already running. If it is a new device, update the device fingerprint library and upload it to the cloud environment. If it is a running device and the device's fingerprint

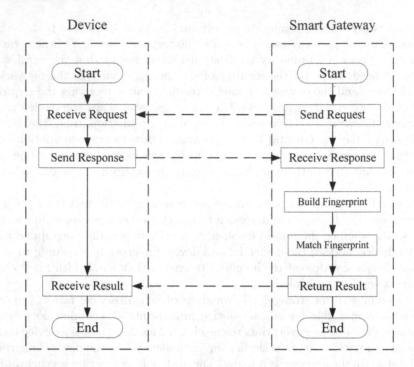

Fig. 2. Authentication flow chart

information has not changed, then the device identity is considered normal. If the device fingerprint match is unsuccessful and no fingerprint update request has been sent, the device identity is considered abnormal and its network connection is disconnected.

The framework proposed in this papermigrates the authentication service to the gateway to execute and obtains device fingerprints through network scanning. Network scanning is based on the principle of network communication. The device only needs to send corresponding response packets and does not require operations such as built-in identification or fingerprint calculation. Therefore, it does not bring additional computing overhead to the terminal, which is in line with the low energy consumption in the design goal; a unified numerical device fingerprint is established, which is in line with the versatility in the design goal. This paper proposes an incremental scanning method to meet the real-time requirement of identity verification services, and proposes a device fingerprint compression storage algorithm to improve the efficiency, so the method proposed in this paper meets the design goals.

4   Efficient Device Fingerprint Matching Algorithm

This section introduces an efficient device fingerprint matching algorithm, including a description of the research problem, an introduction to the basic principles of the algorithm, and a detailed description of the algorithm.

4.1   Problem Description

There are a large number of terminal devices in the IoT environment. This paper establishes device fingerprints for these devices on the gateway. How to store and match large amounts of data is the problem to be solved in this section.

To reduce the storage overhead and improve the verification speed, it is necessary to realize the compressed storage and fast matching of the device fingerprint library, so this paper chooses the bloom filter algorithm. Bloom filter is a kind of data structure, the realization principle of its compressed storage is: by selecting a set of hash mapping function and a bit space, using Hash function mapping, the longer elements are mapped to the bit space, which can achieve compression The purpose of the storage space.

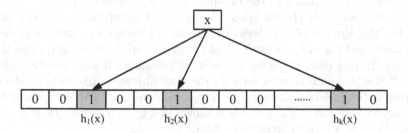

Fig. 3. Bloom filter element insertion process

The element insertion process of bloom filter is divided into two steps, as shown in Fig. 3:

(1) Calculate the k hash function values of the elements x, which are $h_1(x), h_2(x), \ldots, h_k(x)$, respectively.
(2) Search the bit space V and set the corresponding k bits of V to 1, namely

$$V[h_1(x)] = V[h_2(x)] = \ldots = V[h_k(x)] = 1$$

The element query process of bloom filter is:

(1) Calculate the k hash function value of the element y, $h_1(y), h_2(y), \ldots, h_k(y)$ respectively;
(2) Search the bit space V, if $V[h1(y)] = V[h2(y)] = \ldots = V[hk(y)] = 1$, it means that the element y to be queried already exists, if at least one of the hash function value is 0, it means that the element y does not exist.

Bloom filters have great advantages in data storage and query, but because the data is compressed and stored, it is difficult to avoid the problem of reduced accuracy. At the same time, basic bloom filters have inherent defects: (1) Weak of dynamic. This is because the number of hash functions and the length of the bit space cannot be changed after it is determined; (2) Lack of scalability. The bit space can be preset according to the size of the data, but with storage With the continuous increase of data, the size of the stored data cannot be estimated. Therefore, if the preset value of the bit space is too small, it may cause conflicts, and if it is too large, it will cause a waste of space.

Extensible Counting CBF. (1) The scalable counting CBF is designed to solve the problem that the basic bloom filter cannot dynamically add or delete elements. It draws on the idea of counting bloom filters. In counting bloom filters, it is no longer a simple setting. Operation is to set a counter in the bit space. When a conflict occurs in the bit space, it is no longer a set operation, but to count the number of times the position is set to 1. When the element is deleted, the counter corresponding to the bit space is decremented by 1.

The size setting of the bit space can be preset according to the size of the data, but the number of IoT devices in the target network cannot be predicted in advance, and the storage capacity of the extracted device fingerprints is also unknown. In this case, if the bit space is set too large, it will cause a waste of space. If the bit space is set too small, the data storage capacity is insufficient, resulting in the lack of scalability of the basic bloom filter. We design a scalable counting, and its structure diagram is shown in Fig. 4, where CBF is counting bloom filter and $Counter$ denotes counter.

The implementation method of expandable counting CBF is shown as follow. As the element stored in the bloom filter, the two-tuple $<IP, device\ fingerprint>$ is added with a mark ID, which is a monotonously increasing sequence, so that the storage element becomes a triple-tuple $<ID, IP, device\ fingerprint>$, and the stored element is sequentially stored in the bloom filter. As the stored device fingerprints continue to increase, after the current bloom filter is full, create a new CBF. The sequence ID of the new filter is the maximum ID of the current filter plus 1. When the device fingerprint is inquired, the current filter group is inquired one by one. When the device fingerprint is deleted, the filter is determined according to the filter, and then the filter is reliably deleted. An example will be given below in conjunction with Fig. 4.

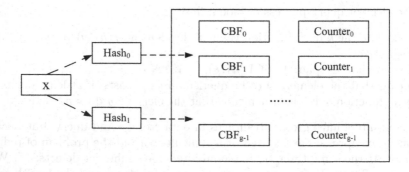

Fig. 4. Schematic diagram of bloom filter structure

Suppose the triples $<ID, IP, F>$ used for storage, where ID is a sequence of integers increasing from 0, IP denotes the IP address of the device, and F notes the device fingerprint corresponding to the address. There are 320 device fingerprints to be stored, and each CBF has a capacity of 100, which is obviously not enough.

Bloom filter initialization: only one CBF_0 is created during initialization, at this time the triplet is $<0, IP_0, F_0>$, and the ID is 0.

Device fingerprint insertion: There are 320 device fingerprints to be stored. When $ID \in [0, 99]$, the device fingerprint was inserted in the same way. When $ID = 99$, the maximum value of ID was updated to 99. Then the device fingerprints whose $ID = 100$ will continue to be inserted. At this time, the capacity of CBF_0 is full. Initialize $CBF_1 = <100, IP_0, F_0>$ and then continue to store device fingerprints in the device until all device fingerprints are stored in the bloom filter, the last established bloom filter is CBF_3, and the maximum value ID is updated to 319.

Device fingerprint deletion: Assuming that the device fingerprint is requested to be updated, the original device fingerprint needs to be deleted. First, you need to find its ID, and check in the order of CBF_3, CBF_2, CBF_1, CBF_0 in reverse order, and compare the CBF initialization ID and the device fingerprint ID. When the first initialization ID is less than or equal to the device fingerprint ID, it indicates that the device fingerprint is there, and then delete the corresponding device fingerprint according to the deletion method.

Device fingerprint query: The device fingerprint query process does not need ID. it just need to traverse the CBF. If the device fingerprint is found in any CBF, it is considered to exist; if not, it is determined that the device fingerprint does not exist.

Hash Function Split. Basic filters often use a set of hash functions and a bit space. As the number of fingerprints of storage devices increases, the conflict rate will also increase greatly, which affects the accuracy of the overall query. Therefore, this paper adopts the hash function split method. The hash functions are grouped, and the same group of hash functions are mapped to a bit space, so that the original mapping to one bit space can be changed to multiple bit spaces under the premise that the number of hash functions remains unchanged.

Assuming that the number of hash functions is h, dividing them into I groups requires I bit space. Each group has h/I hash values that is mapped to the same bit space. As shown in Fig. 5, four hash functions were selected to map the device fingerprint, which was split into two groups, and a total of two bit spaces were needed. The mapping values of $Hash_1$ and $Hash_2$ are storaged in the first bit space. The mapping values of $Hash_3$ and $Hash_4$ are storaged in the second bit space. By splitting the Hash function and adding bit space, the false positive rate will be greatly reduced. However, the increase of bit space will also increase the storage space of bloom filter. This paper analyzes the influence of the number of hash functions and the size of bit space on the false positive rate based on experiments in Sect. 5.

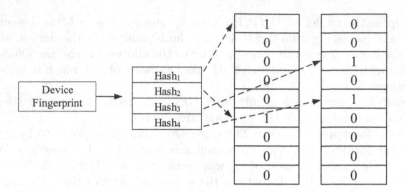

Fig. 5. Hash split mapping

Dual Feature Storage. This paper establishes the one-to-one correspondence between scanning IP and its corresponding device fingerprint. To use the device fingerprint for authentication, both the device's IP address and the device fingerprint need to be stored. If the IP is not found in the existing device fingerprint database, it is proved that the device corresponding to the IP is the new device to join the network. If the IP is found to exist and the device fingerprint is found at the same time, it is proved that the device fingerprint of the IP has not changed and the identity is credible. If the IP is searched but the corresponding fingerprint is not found, it proves that the IP's device fingerprint has changed and the identity is in doubt. To realize the simultaneous query of IP and corresponding device fingerprint, this paper chooses IP address and device fingerprint as two features to be stored simultaneously.

The efficient device fingerprint matching algorithm proposed in this paper is designed according to the above content. By designing a counting bloom filter, the scalability of the algorithm is increased to realize dynamic adding and deleting. Hash function splitting and dual feature storage are used to reduce the false positive rate. In the improved algorithm, each feature corresponds to a set of bitspaces, so the number of bitspaces is the number of hash groupings multiplied by the number of features. Of course, the device fingerprint database in this paper has two characteristics. The mapping process of the improved bloom filter algorithm is shown in Fig. 6.

4.2   Algorithm Description

This section introduces the basic operations of the device fingerprint matching algorithm, including the query, insertion, and deletion of device fingerprints, and the modification of device fingerprints. The method of deleting and inserting is used in this paper.

Device Fingerprint Query. During authentication, IP address and device fingerprint in duple $<IP, F>$ should be verified respectively. If each correspond-

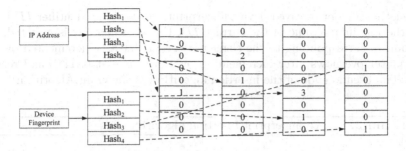

Fig. 6. Schematic diagram of the structure of the counting bloom filter based on multi-features

ing bit-space value of the IP address and device fingerprint is 1, the match is considered successful; otherwise, the match is considered unsuccessful. The main process of query algorithm is as follows: first query whether the IP address exists, if it does not, then return false, if it exists, then continue to verify its device fingerprint, if it exists, then return true, if it does not, then return false. The pseudo code of the query algorithm is shown in Algorithm 1.

Algorithm 1. Device fingerprint query algorithm

Input:
$< IP, F >$

Output:
Result

1: **for** j=0 to $l - 1$
2:    $sum \leftarrow 0$
3:    **for** i=0 to $k - 1$
4:      **if** $CBF_j [hash_i (IP)] = 0x0000$
5:        break
6:      **else if** $CBF_j [hash_i (F)] = 0x0000$
7:        break
8:      **else**
9:        $sum + +$
10:    **end for**
11:    **if** $sum == k$
12:      **return** *true*
13: **end for**
14: **return** *false*

Device Fingerprint Insertion. The insertion process of device fingerprint is as follows: find the currently active filter CBF. If the identification ID is greater than the current maximum ID and the current CBF capacity is full, a new CBF will be created. At the same time, the total number of filters will be increased by 1, and the new CBF will take the maximum ID plus 1 as its own identifier and set the number of saved device fingerprints to 0. If the identifier ID is less than the maximum value of the current ID, the identifier ID is updated, and the counter corresponding to the element after the hash is incremented by 1. If the counter overflows after incrementing by 1, it stays at $0x1111$ and returns False. The pseudo code of the insertion algorithm is shown in Algorithm 2.

Algorithm 2. Device fingerprint insertion algorithm

Input:
    $< IP, F >, elementID$
Output:
    $Result$
1: **for** $j = l - 1$ to 0
2:     $ActiveCBF \leftarrow CBF_j$
3:     **for** i=0 to $k - 1$
4:         **if** $elementID \geq ActiveCBFID$
5:             break
6: **end for**
7: **if** $elementID > maxIDandActiveCBF$ is full
8:     $ActiveCBF \leftarrow CreateCBF$
9:     $l++$
10:     $ActiveCBFID \leftarrow maxID + 1$
11:     $ActiveCBF.count \leftarrow 0$
12: **if** $elementID < maxID$
13: **for** j=0 to $k - 1$
14:     $ACtiveCBF[hash_i(IP,F)] \leftarrow ActiveCBF.array[hash_i(IP,F)] + 1$
15:     **if** 4bit counter is overflow
16:         $ACtiveCBF[hash_i(IP,F)] \leftarrow 0x1111$
17:         **return** $false$
18: **end for**
19: $ActiveCBF.count++$
20: **return** $false$

Device Fingerprint Deletion. With the dynamic changes of the scan, the IP address may apply for not using the IP address or change the IP address. Therefore, the bloom filter needs to be deleted. If the filter is not selected correctly when deleting, the counter will be decreased by 1 by mistake. Caused by accidental deletion, so reliable deletion of elements is described in the device fingerprint deletion algorithm.

When performing the delete operation, we need to correctly find the filter that holds the binary group $<IP, F>$, so we search forward from the latest CBF built, and when we find the first CBF whose ID is smaller than the identity ID, we can confirm that the element is stored in this CBF, and confirm that this CBF is an active filter. Delete the tuple $<IP, F>$. Decrease all counters at the corresponding hash position of the element by 1 to complete the deletion operation. The pseudo code of the deletion algorithm is shown in Algorithm 3. The basic operation of the bloom filter is introduced. Compared with the

---

Algorithm 3. Device fingerprint deletion algorithm

Input:
   $< IP, F >$, $elementID$
Output:
   $Result$
1: **for** $j = l$
2:    $ActiveCBF \leftarrow CBF_j$
3:    **if** $elementID \geq ActiveCBFID$
4:      **for** i=0 to $k-1$
5:        $ACtiveCBF[hash_i(IP,F)] \leftarrow ActiveCBF.array[hash_i(IP,F)] - 1$
6:        **if** 4bit counter is decrementing zero
7:          $ACtiveCBF[hash_i(IP,F)] \leftarrow 0x0000$
8:          **return** $false$
9:      **end for**
10:     $ActiveCBF.count--$
11:     **return** $true$
12: **end for**
13: **return** $false$

---

basic bloom filter, the improved bloom filter in this paper can realize dynamic additions and deletions, increase scalability, and reduce the rate of false positive.

4.3 False Positive Analysis

Suppose S is the total number of IP addresses in the test data set, R is the number of elements judged wrongly, F is the false positive rate, the number of Hash functions is h, and the bit space size is j, then the calculation formula of the false positive rate is as follows:

$$f = \frac{R}{S} \tag{1}$$

When the IP address of the first device is mapped through hash, the formula for calculating the probability that a bit in the bit space j of I is still 0 is as follows:

$$1 - \frac{1}{j} \tag{2}$$

In this paper, hash is used to split the bit space into group I. Therefore, the formula for calculating the probability that a bit in the bit space j of I is still 0 is as follows:

$$1 - \frac{1}{Ij} \tag{3}$$

Suppose there are n IP addresses to be stored, and each element needs to be hashed h times. When all n IP addresses are hashed, the probability that a bit is still 0 is

$$p = (1 - \frac{1}{Ij})^{hn} = (1 - \frac{1}{Ij})^{Ijhn/Ij} \tag{4}$$

According to the formula of Napierian e:

$$\lim_{x \to \infty} (1 - \frac{1}{x})^{-x} = e \tag{5}$$

get

$$p \approx e^{-hn/Ij} \tag{6}$$

When a new IP does not originally belong to the device fingerprint database, but the corresponding Hash value of the IP is no longer 0, it will be considered to be in the set, and false positive will occur. The calculation formula of false positive rate is as follows:

$$f = (1 - p)^k \approx (1 - e^{-hn/Ij})^k \tag{7}$$

For IP address and device fingerprint in this paper, the calculation formula of false positive rate is as follows:

$$f = (1 - p)^k \approx (1 - e^{-hn/Ij})^{2k} \tag{8}$$

As can be seen from the above formula, compared with the basic filter algorithm, the improved device fingerprint matching algorithm can effectively reduce the false positive rate by splitting and double features through the hash function.

5   Performance Evaluation

This section analyzes the false positive rate of the proposed efficient device fingerprint matching algorithm through real experiments. Fingerprint collection requires scanning Internet of things devices in cyberspace. For ethical considerations, we used the Censys dataset [20] as the experimental device fingerprint.

It can be seen from formula 8 that the three parameters that affect the false positive rate are: the number of hash functions, the size of the bit space, and the size of the device fingerprint library. First of all, this paper tests the influence of the number of hash functions and the size of the bit space on the false positive rate, and then comprehensively considers the accuracy of the query and the storage cost, selects the appropriate number of hash functions and the size of the bit space, and finally compares it with the basic layout. Long filter algorithm for experimental comparison.

This experiment randomly selected $1,117,241$ device fingerprints extracted and stored in the bloom filter to construct a device fingerprint library, and also selected $10,000$ data that were not in the device fingerprint library as the test data. Whether the statistics will cause false positive, and calculated the false positive rate.

To determine the influence of the number of hash functions and the size of the bit space on the false positive rate, the experiment tested the number of hash functions as 2, 4, 6, and 8, respectively. As the bit space continues to increase, the false positive rate changes as shown in Figs. 7 and Figs. 8.

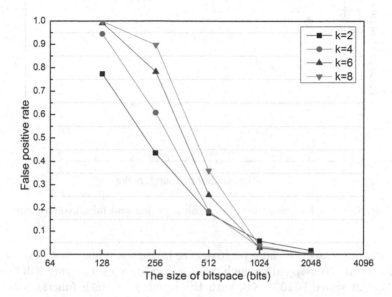

Fig. 7. The relationship between bit space and false positive rate

As shown in Fig. 7, when the number of Hash functions and the size of the device fingerprint library are determined, as the bit space increases, the false positive rate shows a downward trend. This shows that as the bit space increases, the Hash in the bit space. The probability of conflict will be greatly reduced, and the false positive rate will also decrease. As can be seen in Fig. 7, there are four Hash functions. When the bit space is 128 KB, the false positive rate is 0.775, and the bit space. When the storage space is doubled, the false positive rate becomes 0.4359. It can also be seen that the method proposed reduces the false positive rate by sacrificing a certain amount of storage space. It can be observed from Fig. 7 that when the bit space is within the interval of 1024 KB to 2048 KB, although the false positive rate is also reduced, it can also be seen from the figure that the false positive rate curve at this time has become flat, which shows the increase of the bit space. A large bit space can indeed effectively reduce the false positive rate, but too large bit space will also bring about the problem of space waste, so it is necessary to choose a suitable size bit space.

As shown in Fig. 8, when the bit space size and the device fingerprint library size are determined, as the number of Hash functions increases, the increase and decrease of the false positive rate does not show a fixed pattern. When the bit space is 256 KB, as the Hash function increases and decreases. As the number

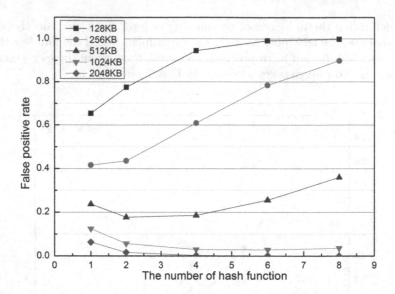

Fig. 8. The relationship between Hash function and false positive rate

of functions increases, the false positive rate increases. This is because the more Hash functions are mapped to the bit space, the false positive rate will increase. When the bit space is 1024 KB, with the number of Hash functions increase, the false positive rate decreases, so the choice of the number of Hash functions is not as much as possible, but the size of the bit space and the number of Hash functions should be considered comprehensively.

It is necessary to meet the accuracy of the device fingerprint query, but also to realize the compressed storage of the device fingerprint library to save storage overhead. This paper believes that the false positive rate of 0.03 has achieved a relatively satisfactory experimental effect, so this paper selects the number of Hash functions It is 4, and the bit space size is 1024 KB or 1 MB. After determining the number of Hash functions to be used and the size of the bit space, this paper compares the basic Bloom filter algorithm with the algorithm proposed in this paper through the size change of the device fingerprint library. The experimental results are shown in Fig. 9.

As shown in Fig. 9, when the number of Hash functions and the size of the bit space are determined, as the number of device fingerprints increases, the false positive rate is also increasing. After the number of device fingerprints exceeds 616287, the error of the basic filter algorithm The judgment rate has also exceeded 0.03, and the false positive rate of the improved algorithm proposed in this paper has been lower than that of the basic Bloom filter, which is consistent with the theoretical false positive rate analysis, and after the number of device fingerprints stored reaches 1117241, the improved algorithm The false positive rate still does not exceed 0.03. In terms of storage capacity, the original 1117241 device fingerprints occupies 25.23 MB, and the improved bit space size is 1024

KB or 1 MB. Compared with the bit space, the storage space is reduced by 96%, and the false positive rate is not higher than 0.03. When the storage capacity is greatly reduced, the experimental analysis from the two aspects of false positive rate and storage capacity proves that the device fingerprint matching algorithm proposed in this paper is efficient in both matching and storage.

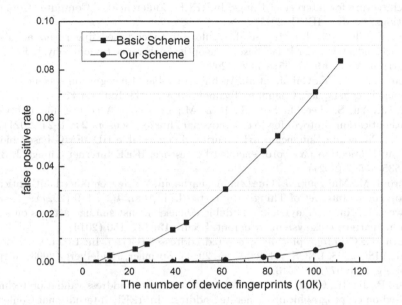

Fig. 9. The relationship between the number of device fingerprints and the false positive rate

6 Conclusion

This paper mainly introduces the IoT security enhancements based on fingerprint device under validation framework, including the architecture, design goal and the authentication service, after for device storage and fingerprint matching in framework, put forward a kind of efficient device fingerprint matching algorithm, introduces in detail the structure of the bloom filter design, the improved algorithm, the basic operation, etc. Finally, the experimental analysis proves that the algorithm has better accuracy and faster verification speed.

Acknowledgment. This work supported by science and technology project funding of State Grid Fujian Electric Power Co., Ltd (52135020002T).

References

1. Li, S., Da Xu, L., Zhao, S.: 5G internet of things: a survey. J. Ind. Inf. Integr. **10**, 1–9 (2018)

2. Luo, Y., Hu, H., Wen, Y., et al.: Transforming device fingerprinting for wireless security via online multitask metric learning. IEEE Internet Things J. **7**(1), 208–219 (2019)
3. Van Oorschot, P.C., Smith, S.W.: The internet of things: security challenges. IEEE Secur. Priv. **17**(5), 7–9 (2019)
4. Park, S.Y., Lim, S., Jeong, D., et al.: PUFSec: device fingerprint-based security architecture for internet of things. In: IEEE Conference on Computer Communications, pp. 1–9. IEEE (2017)
5. Liu, F., Shen, C., Liu, H., et al.: A flexible touch-based fingerprint acquisition device and a benchmark database using optical coherence tomography. IEEE Trans. Instrum. Meas. **69**(9), 6518–6529 (2020)
6. Ren, R.L., Gu, Y., Cui, J., et al.: Web features-based recognition specific-type IoT device in cyberspace. Commun. Technol. **50**(5), 1003–1009 (2017)
7. Oh, J., Yu, S., Lee, J., Son, S., Kim, M., Park, Y.: A secure and lightweight authentication protocol for IoT-based smart homes. Sensors **21**, 1–24 (2021)
8. Jiang, X., et al.: Enhancing IoT security via cancelable HD-sEMG-based biometric authentication password, encoded by gesture. IEEE Internet Things J. **8**(22), 16535–16547 (2021)
9. Azrour, M., Mabrouki, J., Guezzaz, A., Farhaoui, Y.: New enhanced authentication protocol for Internet of Things. Big Data Mini. Anal. **4**(1), 1–9 (2021)
10. Kwon, T., Na, S.: TinyLock: affordable defense against smudge attacks on smartphone pattern lock systems. Comput. Secur. **42**, 137–150 (2014)
11. Aura, T.: Cryptographically generated addresses (CGA). In: Boyd, C., Mao, W. (eds.) ISC 2003. LNCS, vol. 2851, pp. 29–43. Springer, Heidelberg (2003). https://doi.org/10.1007/10958513_3
12. Tan, P., Jia, H., Chen, Y., et al.: A hierarchical source address validation technique based on cryptographically generated address. In: IEEE International Conference on Computer Science and Automation Engineering, pp. 33–37 (2011)
13. Bonneau, J., Herley, C., Stajano, F.M.: Passwords and the evolution of imperfect authentication. Commun. ACM **58**(7), 78–87 (2015)
14. Uluagac, A.S., Radhakrishnan, S.V., Corbett, C., et al.: A passive technique for fingerprinting wireless devices with wired-side observations. In: IEEE Conference on Communications and network Security (CNS), pp. 305–313 (2013)
15. Kumar, K., Dalai, A.K., Panigrahy, S.K., et al.: An ANN based approach for wireless device fingerprinting. In: 2017 2nd IEEE International Conference on Recent Trends in Electronics, Information and Communication Technology (RTEICT), pp. 1302–1307 (2017)
16. Dalai, A.K., Jena, A., Sharma, S., et al.: A fingerprinting technique for identification of wireless devices. In: 2018 International Conference on Computer, Information and Telecommunication Systems (CITS), pp. 1–5. IEEE (2018)
17. Junzhou, L., Ming, Y., Zhen, L., et al.: Cyberspace security system and key technologies. Sci. China: Inf. Sci. **46**(08), 939–968 (2016)
18. Gope, P., Sikdar, B.: Lightweight and privacy-preserving two-factor authentication scheme for IoT devices. IEEE Internet Things J. **6**(1), 580–589 (2018)
19. El-hajj, M., Fadlallah, A., Chamoun, M., Serrhrouchni, A.: A survey of internet of things (IoT) authentication schemes. Sensors **19**, 1141 (2019)
20. Censys: A search engine based on Internet-wide scanning for the devices and networks (2015). https://censys.io/

RLPassGAN: Password Guessing Model Based on GAN with Policy Gradient

Deng Huang[✉], Yufei Wang, and Wen Chen

School of Cyber Science and Engineering, Sichuan University, Chengdu 610065, China
huangdeng@stu.scu.edu.cn

Abstract. The unsupervised neural network GAN can automatically generate synthetic samples conform to the distribution of learned samples. Therefore, password guessing models based on GAN, e.g. PassGAN are widely studied in recent years. However, there are two problems when dealing with discrete password data using GAN-based models. On the one hand, the non-differentiability of discrete password data may result in the failure of the backward of gradients; on the other hand, the outputs of the intermediate layers of the generator are incomplete password sequences, which cannot be directly evaluated by the discriminator until they reached the output layers, resulting in many redundant synthesized passwords. Therefore, a new password guessing method RLPassGAN based on SeqGAN with policy gradient are proposed in this paper. Policy gradient is applied to the proposed model to ensure that the model parameters can be continuously optimized. Furthermore, the incomplete password sequences of the output of the intermediate layers are evaluated by Monte Carlo search. The results show that in terms of the quality of the generated samples, the synthesized samples of RLPassGAN can cover more than 99% of the real passwords in the training set, while PassGAN and RNNPassGAN can only cover less than 30% of the real passwords in the training set; in terms of cracking on the specified site, RLPassGAN outperforms the two models by 16.4%–84.1%; in terms of cross-site cracking, RLPassGAN raised the cracking rate by 30.5%–84.9%.

Keywords: Password guessing · GAN · Gradient backhaul · Policy gradient · Monte Carlo search

1 Introduction

In recent years, a variety of new authentication methods have been proposed, such as biometric authentication [1], iris recognition [2], graphic password [3] and etc. However, password authentication is still the most widely utilized methods for authentication [4]. The main reason is that [5] the newly proposed authentication methods still faced some problems, such as high cost, difficult to use and deployment. Therefore, password will

---

Supported by: the Key Laboratory of Pattern Recognition and Intelligent Infor-mation Processing, Institutions of Higher Education of Sichuan Province (Grant: MSSB-2020-01).

W. Shi et al. (Eds.): SPNCE 2021, LNICST 423, pp. 159–174, 2022.
https://doi.org/10.1007/978-3-030-96791-8_12

remain the most important identity authentication method for a long time in the future [6].

Early password guessing relied more on "fancy" [7, 8] methods to generate password dictionaries. In 2005, Narayanan et al. [9] proposed a Markov chain-based password attacking model, which calculated the probability of password generation through the correlation relationship between characters from left to right. 2009, Weir et al. [10] proposed a password attacking model based on a probabilistic context free grammar (PCFG), in which each password is divided into letter segment L, number segment D and special character segment S. The password pattern frequency table and the character composition frequency table are counted by the model, and a set with guess frequency to simulate the probability distribution of real password is generated based on the tables. In 2016, Wang et al. [11] proposed an online targeted attacking model TarGuess based on personal information. Luo et al. [12] proposed a prediction model E-PCFG combining natural language processing (NLP) [13] and PCFG in 2017.

A series of neural network based password guessing models are proposed in recent years. In 2016, Melicher et al. [14] proposed a password guessing model based on LSTM, which predicted the next character according to the input sequence. In 2018, Xia et al. [15] proposed GenPass, which combines PCFG and LSTM to learn features from multiple password sets. The results demonstrated that it can effectively raise the cracking rate of cross-site guessing. In 2019, Hitaj B et al. [16] proposed a password generation model PassGAN,which minimizes the cross-entropy loss between generated samples and real password distribution to generate realistic guessing samples. Sungyup et al. [18] proposed RNNPassGAN in 2020. The generator and discriminator are changed from 5-layer residuals convolutional neural network in PassGAN to 1-layer RNN which is more suitable for text processing.

As it does not depend on prior knowledge, GAN-based password guessing model is considered to be a new way to replace the traditional statistical and non-parametric methods. In the GAN-based password guessing models, the parameters of generator are updated iteratively according to the backward of errors, and new candidate password samples are generated continuously through the contest between generator and discriminator. Theoretically, any differentiable function can be utilized to build generator and discriminator [17]. However, the password set contains a large number of characters and number combinations similar to "PASS +123456+@# ~", and the discrete password character data lacks continuous differentiability compared with numerical data such as pictures. Therefore, for the discrete password string data, it is difficult for the traditional GAN to effectively update the model parameters based on the discrete data through the gradient backhaul. Furthermore, it is difficult for the discriminator to evaluate the incomplete password sequence in the middle state of the generation process. These problems limit the performance improvement of GAN in the task of password guessing.

Solving the problem of GAN in gradient backhaul can effectively improve the cracking rate of relevant models in the task of password guessing. This paper makes contributions in the following aspects:

1. In this paper, a password guessing method RLPassGAN is proposed. It combines PassGAN [16] and Policy Gradient[19] in reinforcement learning. In our model,

LSTM network, which is suitable for text processing is utilized to build the generator and discriminator. In order to solve the difficult problem of gradient backhaul in traditional GAN models, both the reinforcement learning and policy gradient algorithm are utilized to update the parameters of the generated network.

2. Monte Carlo search method [20] is applied to make the password sequences in the intermediate state be complete, and thus the discriminator can generate rewards for these completed sequences. Finally, RLPassGAN is compared with two GAN-based password guessing models (PassGAN [16] and RNNPassGAN [18]).

2 Related Wrok

2.1 Password Guessing Model Based on GAN

GAN-based password guessing model, PassGAN, was applied to password security research by Hitaj B et al. [16] in 2019, which was based on IWGAN(Improved training of Wasserstein GANs) [21]. The method trains the neural network to learn the data distribution of the password, and then uses the neural network to generate a guess set with the same distribution as the training set. The generator of PassGAN imitates the distribution of the password in the training process, and the task of the discriminator is to determine whether the samples generated by the generator come from the real password sets. The process of the confrontation makes the discriminator reveal the information about the original training set, while the generator makes full use of the information to show the distribution of the original password training set, and finally optimizes the loss function through the gradient descent method. After several iterations, the discrimination ability of the discriminator is gradually improved, and the output of the generator is closer to the distribution of the original password set. 5-layer Residual Convolutional Neural Network (ResNets) is adopted in PassGAN's generator and discriminator, and its specific model structure is shown in Fig. 1.

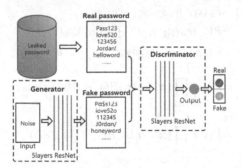

Fig. 1. The network structure of PassGAN

Sungyup et al. [18] made improvements based on PassGAN in 2020 and proposed RNNPassGAN, which utilize a 1-layer LSTM as the generator and can be more suitable for processing text. At the same time, the memory of the recurrent neural network is

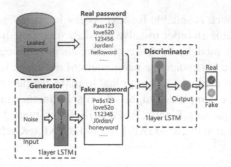

Fig. 2. The network structure of RNNPassGAN

used to improve the quality of the generated samples. The specific model structure is shown in Fig. 2.

Compared with traditional methods, GAN-based password guessing methods have the advantage that they can generate high-quality password dictionary without prior knowledge. However, they also have an obvious disadvantage that the non-differentiability of discrete password data may result in the failure of the backward of gradients, so that a good model can not be trained.

2.2 Policy Gradient

Policy gradient is an optimization algorithm in reinforcement learning, and the random strategy gradient SPG [22] is adopted in our model. In the model, the basic principle is that the agent randomly generates an action in the initial state, and a reward based on the action generated by the environment. Then the policy is dynamically adjusted by the agent based on the reward: increasing the probability of actions receiving positive rewards or decreasing the probability of actions receiving negative rewards.

$$
\begin{aligned}
P_\theta(\tau) &= P_\theta(s_1, a_1, s_2, a_2, \cdots, s_T) \\
&= P(s_1)\pi_\theta(a_1|s_1)P(s_2|s_1, a_1)\pi_\theta(a_2|s_2) \\
&\quad \ldots P(s_T|s_1, a_1, s_2, a_2 \ldots s_T - 1, a_T - 1) \\
&= P(s_1)\prod_{t=1}^{T-1}(\pi_\theta(a_t|s_t)P(s_t + 1|s_1, a_1, \ldots s_t, a_t)) \\
&= P(s_1)\prod_{t=1}^{T-1}(\pi\theta(a_t|s_t)P(s_t + 1|s_t, a_t))
\end{aligned}
\tag{1}
$$

Policy gradient [19] contains the object system, policy π_θ (a|s), trajectory τ, round, and round-reward $R(\tau)$. The object system is the learning object of policy gradient. Policy π_θ (a|s) represents the probability of producing action a under the condition of state s and parameter θ; Round represents the process of the agent interacting with the object system from the initial state based on a policy. The track τ indicates the order of state s, action a and reward r in the policy gradient during a learning round, i.e. $\tau = (s_1,$

a_1, r_1, s_2, a_2, r_2..., s_t). The probability of generating track τ with parameter θ in each round is $P_\theta(\tau)$, the specific calculation formula is as formula 1. Where $P(s_1)$ represents the probability that the initial state is s_1, $P(s_{t+1}|s_t,a_t)$ represents the probability that the environment updates status to s_{t+1} based on state s_t and action a_t. According to the markov property [23], the state S_{t+1} of the next timestamp is only related to the current state s_t and the current action a_t, so the conditional probability

$$P(s_t + 1|s_1, a_1, \ldots s_t, a_t) = P(s_t + 1|s_t, a_t) \tag{2}$$

Round-reward $R(\tau)$ stands for the sum of the rewards generated by all actions in a round:

$$R(\tau) = \sum_{t=1}^{T} r(s_t, a_t) \tag{3}$$

The learning of policy gradient is a process of strategy optimization. A policy is randomly generated at the beginning, and the same policy is used in one round of learning until the end of this round of learning. Then, a new round of learning is started by changing the policy through gradient ascent, and so on until the cumulative reward no longer increases. Since the actions generated by the policy are uncertain and the same policy can produce multiple different trajectories after multiple rounds of learning, the policy gradient [19] defines the objective function as the expected return of the reward obtained by trajectory τ under strategy π_θ:

$$J(\theta) = E[R\tau|\pi_\theta] = \sum_\tau P_\theta(\tau)R(\tau) \tag{4}$$

The goal of training is to find a set of parameters θ to maximize $J(\theta)$, so the expected return is needed to find the partial derivative of network parameter θ, which is specifically calculated as:

$$\nabla_\theta J(\theta) = \sum_\tau P_\theta(\tau)\nabla_\theta \log P_\theta(\tau)R(\tau)$$

$$= \sum_\tau P_\theta(\tau)\nabla_\theta \log\left(P(s_1)\prod_{t=1}^{T-1}(\pi_\theta(a_t|s_t)P(s_t + 1|s_t, a_t))\right)R(\tau)$$

$$= \sum_\tau P_\theta(\tau)\nabla_\theta(\log P(s_1) + \sum_{t=1}^{T-1}\log \pi_\theta(a_t|s_t) +$$

$$\ldots \sum_{t=1}^{T-1}\log P(s_t + 1|s_t, a_t))R(\tau)$$

$$= \sum_\tau P_\theta(\tau)\left(\sum_{t=1}^{T-1}\nabla_\theta \log \pi_\theta(a_t|s_t)\right)R(\tau) \tag{5}$$

Where $P_\theta(\tau)$ indicates the probability of the generated trajectories $\tau = (s_1, a_1, r_1, s_2, a_2, r_2..., s_t)$, $\log p_\theta(\tau)$ means the logarithm of the probability of trajectory τ, and $R(\tau)$ stands for the reward of producing the entire track τ. Considering that in the expression of $J(\theta)$, the action a_t with timestamp t has no effect on the trajectory $\tau_{1:\,t-1}$ before t, but just for subsequent trajectory $\tau_{t:\,T}$. So for $\pi_\theta(a_t|s_t)$, only the cumulative reward $R(\tau_{t:\,T})$ starting with the timestamp t is considered, so $J(\theta)$ transforms into:

$$\nabla_\theta J(\theta) = \sum_\tau P_\theta(\tau)\left(\sum_{t=1}^{T-1} \nabla_\theta \log \pi_\theta(a_t|s_t) R(\tau_t : T)\right)$$

$$= \sum_\tau P_\theta(\tau)\left(\sum_{t=1}^{T-1} \nabla_\theta \log \pi_\theta(a_t|s_t) Q(s_t, a_t)\right) \tag{6}$$

Where $Q(s_t, a_t)$ [19] is the action-vaue function, which represents the expected return.

Value of policy π_θ after the action based on the state a_t. In the above equation, $R(\tau_{t:\,T})$ is substituted by $Q(s_t, a_t)$. From the above derivation, it can be seen that the policy gradient eventually transforms the value function $R(\tau)$ in the expected return into the action value function $Q(s_t, a_t)$. The advantage of this method is to identify the incomplete sequence of any intermediate state that can be evaluated by the discriminator. Finally, the parameters of network are updated as follows through gradient ascent:

$$\theta_{new} \leftarrow \theta_{old} + \eta \nabla_\theta J(\theta) \tag{7}$$

Where η is the learning rate.

Policy gradient can effectively solve the difficulty of gradient return in GAN, so the password guessing model proposed in this paper, RLPassGAN, introduces the iterative training of policy gradient, and its implementation process will be introduced in the next section.

3   Reinforcement Learning PassGAN

3.1   Model Structure of RLPassGAN

Different from PassGAN [16] and RNNPassGAN [18], in our model, the proposed RLPassGAN is regarded as a reinforcement learning system, in which the generator is the agent, and each generated password sequence S_f represents a complete trajectory τ, each character comes from generating process is treated as an action, e.g. the character generated by the timestamp t is action a_t. Each action a_t is generated in the current state S_t based on a random policy, and the state S_t is determined by the generated incomplete sequence. Generator generates passwords from arbitrary characters under a set of random policy until a preset length is met. The discriminator is regarded as a reward function for the evaluation of the generated password sequences to update the neural network's parameters.

The discriminator outputs the probability of the generated password comes from the real data set as a reward, and guides the generator to adjust its policy through feedback to generate more realistic passwords. The discriminator of PassGAN only evaluates the final generated complete password. However, we want to evaluate the rewards obtained from the incomplete sequence generated in the intermediate state during the password generation process, so as to guide the generation of subsequent characters.

In order to evaluate the incomplete sequence $Y_{1:t}$ in an intermediate state, RLPass-GAN utilizes the Monte Carlo search [20] to randomly select T-t characters to padding the incomplete password sequences in the state under the guidance of the policy G_β [24]. Then, the discriminator evaluates the complete password sequence after completion, and takes the reward value as the action-value Q [19] to adjust the policy G_β. The discriminator evaluates the incomplete password sequence of all intermediate states through an iterative Monte Carlo search process until the generator produces a complete password sequence. In order to reduce deviation, the model carries out N rounds of Monte Carlo searches [20] and takes the average value of the actions returned by the discriminator. The specific search process is shown in Fig. 3, and the Monte Carlo searches are defined as:

$$\left\{ Y_{1:T}^1, \dots, Y_{1:T}^N \right\} = MC^{G\beta}(Y_{1:t}; N) \tag{8}$$

Where $Y_{1:t}$ represents the intermediate state sequence of length t, and $Y_{1:T}^N$ represents the complete sequence generated by the Nth time Monte Carlo search, which is generated by sampling under the guidance of the random policy G_β [24]. Therefore, the final action-value function of RLPassGAN is defined as:

$$Q(s = Y_{1:t-1}, a = yt) = \left\{ \begin{array}{ll} \frac{1}{N}\sum_{n=1}^{N} R\left(Y_{1:T}^n\right), Y_{1:T}^n \in MC^{G\beta}(Y1:t; N) & t < T \\ R(Y1:T) & t = T \end{array} \right\} \tag{9}$$

Where $R\left(Y_{1:T}^n\right)$ represents the reward generated by the discriminator for the Nth time Monte Carlo search, and $R(Y_{1:T})$ represents the reward generated by the discriminator for the final generation of a complete password sequence of length T.

The generator and discriminator of the RLPassGAN are changed from 5-layer residual convolutional neural network ResNets to 1-layer LSTM, which is more suitable for processing sequence data. The network structure is shown in Fig. 3.

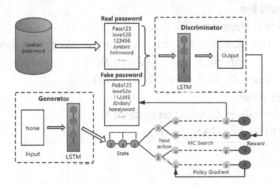

Fig. 3. The network structure of RLPassGAN

Algorithm 1 shows the steps of RLPassGAN in the training process. G_θ and G_β correspond to the random policy used in generator and Monte Carlo search. We select the same parameters when initializing the two models, thus they can adopt the same policy to generate characters at the beginning of training. D_φ denotes the discriminator. The parameters of G_θ and D_φ are initialized with random weights before training. After the training starts, the generator randomly selects characters to generate password sequence S_f, obtains the action-value Q [19] of each intermediate transition in S_f through Monte Carlo search. Then, the reward of the complete sequence are given by the discriminator. Finally, the parameter θ is updated by generator through Formula (7) mentioned in Sect. 2. The generated guessing sample S_f and the real password S_r are input into the discriminator at the same time when the model is training the discriminator, and the reward of the guessing sample S_f is calculated and returned to the generator. The discriminator is optimized continuously by minimizing the cross entropy between the real password tag and the predicted probability. G_θ and D_φ are carried out synchronously during the whole process, and the parameters of the network are updated continuously through iterative training until the generator and discriminator are stable.

Algorithm 1 Training Process of RLPassGAN

Require: generator policy G_θ ; roll-out policy G_β; discriminator D_φ;
   an input password with T length: S_{ro}

  1:   Initialize G_θ, D_φ with random weights θ, φ;
  2:   Initialize G_β with the same parameter θ
  3:   **Repeat**
  4:    **for** g-steps **do**
  5:     Use G_θ to generate a T length password S_f
  6:     **for** t in $1 : T$ **do**
  7:      Compute $Q(a_t = y_t, s_t = S_f[1: t\text{-}1])$ by Eq. (9)
  8:     **end for**
  9:     Update parameters of G_θ via policy gradient by Eq. (7)
 10:    **end for**
 11:    **for** d-steps **do**
 12:     Use current G_θ to generate fake passwords and combine
        with given real passwords S_r
 13:     Train D_φ for k epochs by Eq. (10)
 14:    **end for**
 15:   Reinitializes G_β based on updated θ
 16:   **until** RLPassGAN converges

3.2 Generator

Convolutional Neural Network takes advantage of weight sharing and the local correlation of data to reduce the complexity of the network, and it is suitable for processing continuous data such as images. Therefore, the generator of RLPassGAN is LSTM. The generator first encodes the input random strings by word embedding to obtain the word vector of the discrete data, and then passes through a masking layer to skip the filled part of the sequence when it is encoded, so that LSTM can only act on the original part of the sequence during training. Then the model is trained by 1 layer of LSTM, and finally the password guessing set is output by a layer of full connection layer. The specific structure of the generator is shown in Fig. 4.

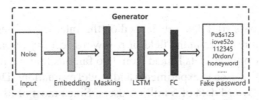

Fig. 4. The network structure of the generator of RLPassGAN

3.3 Discriminator

The discriminator of RLPassGAN is regarded as a reward function to dynamic update the parameters θ of the generator. The generator is improved by further iteration, once a more realistic set of sequences is generated, the model retrains the discriminator. Therefore, the optimization goal of the discriminator is to minimize the cross entropy between the real password tag and the predicted probability, and its specific formula is as follows:

$$\min_{\varphi}(Ey{\sim}preal[\ln D\varphi(Y)] - Ey{\sim}G\theta[\ln(1 - D\varphi(Y))]) \tag{10}$$

Where Y represents a complete password sequence, $D_{\varphi}(Y)$ represents the output of the discriminator, and the parameter φ is updated at a specified learning rate to optimize the performance of the discriminator.

The structure of the discriminator is shown in Fig. 5. First, the real password set is mixed with the password set generated by the generator, and then the word vectorization is processed by an embedding layer, followed by a LSTM layer for training. In order to improve the efficiency of the discriminator's training, a highway network [25] architecture is added to the discriminator based on feature set mapping. Finally, a fully connected sigmoid activation function is used to output the probability that the generated password is the real password as the reward value. The specific structure of the discriminator is shown in Fig. 5.

4 Experiment

4.1 Password Data Set

In 2009, the SQL injection of RockYou.com by attacker resulted in 32 million user passwords being leaked, and these passwords were all plaintexts. This is the first batch

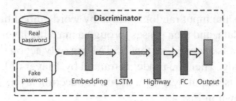

Fig. 5. The network structure of the discriminator of RLPassGAN

of ten-million-level password data sets leaked on the Internet, so these passwords have become an important resource in the field of password security research. In addition to RockYou [26], password data sets leaked from two famous Internet portals, CSDN [27] and Yahoo [28], are also used to experiments and model evaluations. Data set from CSDN [27] includes the password data of 6 million users. Since most of its users are working in the Internet industry, the password structure of the website is relatively more complex and the password security intensity is higher. Therefore, it is also more conducive for model training to improve the cracking rate and universality of the password test set. Yahoo [28] suffered a major data breach in 2012, in which 450,000 plaintext passwords of its users were stolen by hackers. The specific information of the data set is shown in Table 1.

Table 1. Password set information used in this paper.

Password set	Service type	Language	Leakage time	Original number
Rockyou	Social	English	2009	32503388
CSDN	IT BBS	Chinese	2011	6428277
Yahoo	News	English	2012	453492

4.2 Data Preprocessing

Most of the leaked password data sets are usually not stored in plaintext, but in a hash format. However, in the task of password guessing, the model needs to be trained on plaintext passwords, so the password data sets selected in this paper are all from websites that store in plaintext. Therefore, the real password sets leaked from RockYou [26], CSDN [27] and Yahoo [28] were selected as the data sets of this experiment.

Due to the large number of original data sets, it is necessary to preprocess the password sets. In the experiment, the data sets are processed by random sampling, which reduces the time cost of the experiment without affecting the experimental effect. The experiment in this paper only considers the password information in the data sets, so the irrelevant information including personal information and account number from the data sets were eliminated. At the same time, since most web sites have registration rules, users are only allowed to enter 95 printable characters (does not contain Spaces) such as

numbers, letters and symbol, and as a result of the limitation of password strength pro-
filers, users are only allowed to enter the length of the password for 6–20, and the leaked
password data sets contain many useless passwords with no reference value, Therefore,
the experiment only reserves the password with the length of 6 to 20 and composed of
95 printable characters.

In this experiment, three password data sets are divided into training set and test set
in a 4:1 ratio (80% is training set and 20% is test set). The training set is put into three
GAN-based models for training to generate guessing set, while the test set is used to
match with the guessing set and calculate its cracking rate to complete the performance
comparison of the three models.

5 Evaluation

5.1 The Quality of the Generated Samples

It is proved that the model has reached an equilibrium point in GAN when the discriminator is difficult to identify the samples generated by the generator. In order to evaluate
the quality of the generated samples of RLPassGAN, we compare the generation coverage rate of three models (RLPassGAN, PassGAN [16] and RNNPassGAN [18]) on
different password data sets (that is, the model was trained and tested on the same data
set, then calculate the ratio of the guessing samples to the repetition of the training set).
The higher the generation coverage is, the stronger the fitting ability of the generator is,
that is, it can generate more similar guessing samples to the training set.

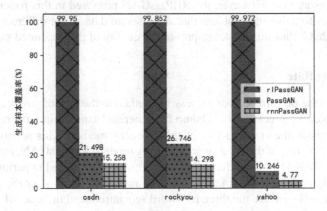

Fig. 6. Generation coverage of different models on different password sets

In order to form a comparison, we strictly controls the conditions in the experiment.
No matter the training set or the guess set, the experimental data scale of different models
are consistent. The quality of samples generated by different models was compared by
the coverage rate of samples generated on the original training set. In order to make the
experimental results more convincing, this paper conducted a comparison under different
data scales(The training set scale is 10000000, 100000000 and 1000000 respectively).

Three data sets, RockYou [26], CSDN [27] and Yahoo [28] in the experiment, are randomly sampled during the training. The generator generates 10,000,000 guess samples to match the training set. Finally, take an average of the results of different size. As shown in Fig. 6. on the data set of CSDN, the guessing samples generated by RLPassGAN training can cover 99.95% of the real passwords in the training set, and the guessing samples generated by PassGAN [16] training can cover 21.498% of the real passwords in the training set. However, the guessing samples generated by RNNPassGAN [18] can only cover 15.58% of the real passwords in the training set. On the data set RockYou, the three models also achieved similar results. The guessing samples generated by the training of RLPassGAN can cover 99.852% of the real passwords in the training set, and the guessing samples generated by the training of PassGAN [16] can cover 26.746% of the real passwords in the training set. However, the guessing samples generated by RNNPassGAN [18] can only cover 14.298% of the real passwords in the training set. On Yahoo, the guessing samples generated by RLPassGAN can cover 99.972% of the real passwords in the training set, still maintaining a high generation coverage, while the guessing samples generated by PassGAN [16] can only cover 10.246% of the real passwords in the training set. However, the guessing samples generated by the training of RNNPassGAN [18] can only cover 4.77% of the real passwords in the training set.

It can be seen from the comparison experiment that no matter which data set is tested, the guessing samples generated by RLPassGAN can cover more than 99% of the real passwords in the training set, while the guessing samples generated by models PassGAN [16] and RNNPassGAN [18] do not cover more than 30% of the training set. A very important reason for this difference is that the discrete password data in the traditional GAN lead to the failure of the gradient backhaul of the discriminator when facing the password guessing task. However, the RLPassGAN proposed in this paper applies the policy gradient to solve the problem that the discrete data is not differentiable on the gradient backhaul, thus this model improves the quality of the generated samples.

5.2   Cracking Rate

In order to test the performance of a guessing method in the task of password guessing, the most simple and direct way is to bump the generated samples into the real password data set, and check the cracking rate of this guessing method. This section also compares the cracking rate of three password guessing models, RLPassGAN, PassGAN [16] and RNNPassGAN [18], on different data sets through controlled experiments, which are specifically divided into same-site cracking rate and cross-site cracking rate. The password data sets used are the three password sets introduced in Sect. 4.1.

Same-Site Cracking Rate. It is not difficult to understand that the same password data set is used in the training and testing of the same-site cracking process. In the experiment, three kinds of models are used to test on RockYou, CSDN and Yahoo. Each password data set is divided into a training set and a test set in a 4:1 ratio (The training set accounts for 80% and the test set for 20%), and the sample sizes generated by the three models after training are 10, 10^2, 10^3, 10^4, 10^5, 10^6 and 10^7. The cracking rate of each model under each generation scale is recorded.

As can be seen from Fig. 7, no matter which data set the experiment is conducted on, the cracking rate of RLPassGAN is higher than that of PassGAN [16] and RNNPass-GAN [18] in the beginning. When the generation size reaches 104, the cracking rate of RLPassGAN is significantly higher than that of the other two models: The cracking rate of RLPassGAN on different password sets is 6.1%–15.32%, while that of PassGAN [16] is 0.65%–11.38%, and the cracking rate of RNNPassGAN [18] is only 0.43%–10.99%. Since the method RLPassGAN and the two models of the control experiment are proposed in the scenario of trawling attacking, rather than the target attacking, the cracking rate obtained from small-scale generated samples should not be used as the final evaluation criterion.

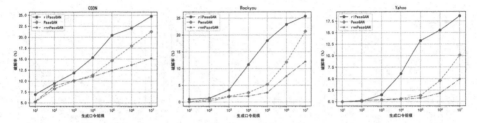

Fig. 7. The same-site cracking rate of different generation adversarial network models

With the increase of generation scale, the same-site cracking rate of the three models gradually increases, and the advantages of RLPassGAN become obvious gradually. When the generation scale is 10^5, the cracking rate of RLPassGAN on different password data sets ranges from 13.25% to 20.42%, while that of PassGAN [16] on the same-site ranges from 1.34% to 14.64%, and the cracking rate of RNNPassGAN [18] on the same-site ranges from 0.78% to 12.42%.

When the generation size reaches 10^7, each model achieves a relatively high same-site cracking rate on different password sets. The cracking rate of RLPassGAN can reach 18.6%–24.75%, and that of PassGAN [16] can reach 10.1%–21.26%, while that of RNNPassGAN [18] is only 4.91%–15.18%.

It can be seen from the experimental results that different password data sets affect the same-site cracking rate of the model, but the comprehensive performance of RLPassGAN is the best. Comparing with the cracking rate of the same-site, RLPassGAN outperform PassGAN [16] by 16.4%–84.1%. RLPassGAN can achieve a 63.1% higher cracking rate than RNNPassGAN [18]. Under the guidance of policy strategy, the RLPassGAN proposed in this paper can realize the sufficient training of GAN, which makes it better fit the distribution of real passwords, and effectively improves the cracking rate of trawling attacking.

Cross-Site Cracking Rate. In addition to compare the cracking rate of the three models on same-site attacking, we also compare that of the three models on cross-sites attacking. That is to say, the passwords of training and test come from different data sets. In practical applications, cross-site attacking is a common application scenario in the task of password guessing. Generally, it is difficult to obtain leaked plaintext passwords from websites, so the real password data sets that can be used for research are relatively limited. Therefore, a method of password guessing with better generalization ability should not only achieve better cracking rate in the same-site guesswork, but also shows good results in cross-site guessing, which indicates that the model has good generalization ability and can be applied to different data sets. In this section, three groups of guessing experiments are conducted to compare the cross-site cracking rates of three models, RLPassGAN, PassGAN [16] and RNNPassGAN [18], as follows: RockYou → Yahoo, Yahoo → CSDN and RockYou → CSDN. The sample size of the three models is consistent with that of the same-site. The cracking rate of each model under each generation scale is recorded.

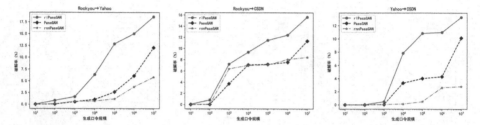

Fig. 8. The cross-site cracking rate of different generation adversarial network models

As can be seen from Fig. 8, because of the difference in the spatial distribution of the different password data sets, the cracking rate of cross-site is lower than that of same-site. However, it is found that the cross-site cracking rate of RLPassGAN is significantly better than the other two models through comparison. In the comparative experiment of cross-site guessing from RockYou to Yahoo, the cracking rate of RLPassGAN is always higher than that of the other two models, and the advantage is gradually obvious as the size of generated samples increases. When the size of generated samples exceeds 10^7, the cracking rate of RLPassGAN can reach 18.4%, while the cross-site cracking rates of PassGAN [16] and RNNPassGAN [18] are 12.04% and 5.79%, respectively. Compared with the other two models, the cross-site cracking rate of RLPassGAN is 51.2% higher than that of the better model, PassGAN [16].

In the control experiment of cross-site guessing of CSDN from Yahoo, the cracking rate of RLPassGAN reaches 13.28% after the generation scale reaches 10^7, which is 30.5% higher than that of the model with the best performance of PassGAN [16] and RNNPassGAN [18]. In the control experiment of cross-site guessing CSDN from Rock-You, the cracking rate of RLPassGAN can reach 15.63%, and that of PassGAN [16] is 11.37%, while of RNNPassGAN [18] is only 8.45% with the increase of the generation scale. The cracking rate of RLPassGAN is 37.4% higher than that of PassGAN [16] and 84.9% higher than that of RNNPassGAN [18].

To sum up, RLPassGAN performs best on different password datasets in both the same-site guessing scenario and the cross-site guessing scenario. The guessing samples generated by the same model have significantly different cracking rates on different test sets. It is not difficult to understand that the three password data sets used in this paper are from different websites, and the service types and languages of websites are not exactly the same. Therefore, the passwords constructed by each user have different characteristics, which will result in significant differences in cracking rate. The three GAN-based password guessing models involved in this paper are all studied based on trawling attacking, and the performance of RLPassGAN is better than the other two models. One of the main reasons is that RLPassGAN uses Policy gradient and Monte Carlo search to solve the difficulty of GAN when processing discrete password sequence with gradient backhaul and discriminator can not evaluate incomplete sequence.

6 Conclusion

In this paper, a new password guessing method RLPASSGAN is proposed. The policy gradient is applied to PassGAN to solve the problem of gradient backhaul caused by discrete password data. At the same time, Monte Carlo search is utilized to enable the discriminator to evaluate the incomplete password sequence at any stage. Thus, the cracking rate on the password set and the quality of generated samples are improved. In this paper, RLPassGAN is compared with two other widely utilized password guessing methods, PassGAN and RNNPassGAN. The result shows that the performance of RLPassGAN is better than the other two models in both the quality of generated samples and the cracking rate. In terms of the quality of generated samples, the guessing samples generated by RLPassGAN can cover over 99% of the real passwords in the training set. However, PassGAN and RNNPassGAN can only cover less than 30% of the real passwords in the training set. In terms of the cracking rate of the same-site, RLPassGAN is also better than the other two models. Compared with the guessing samples generated by PassGAN, the crack rate of RLPassGAN is improved by 16.4%–84.1%, and it is improved by 63.1% compared with the best performance of RNNPassGAN. In terms of cross-site cracking rate, RLPassGAN has the highest cracking rate of 30.5%–50.2% compared to PassGAN, and the best performance of RLPassGAN is 84.9% higher than that of RNNPassGAN.

For a long time in the future, password will still be one of the most important ways of identity authentication, so the study on password guessing has far-reaching significance for password security. In the future work, we will further study the characteristics of passwords, and apply the personal information and character structure in passwords to GAN, so as to improve the performance of the password guessing model.

References

1. Yang, Y., Lu, H., Liu, J.K., et al.: Credential wrapping: from anonymous password authentication to anonymous biometric authentication. In: Proceedings of ASIACCS, pp. 141–151. ACM, New York (2016)
2. Wildes, R.P.: Iris recognition: an emerging biometric technology. Proc. IEEE **85**(9), 1348–1363 (1997)
3. Biddle, R., Chiasson, S., Van Oorschot, P.C.: Graphical passwords: Learning from the first twelve years. ACM Comput. Surv. (CSUR) **44**(4), 1–41 (2012)
4. Wang, P., Wang, D., Huang, X.Y.: Advances in password security. J. Comput. Res. Dev. **53**(10), 2173–2188 (2016)

5. Bonneau, J., Herley, C., Oorschot, P., et al.: The quest to replace passwords: a framework for comparative evaluation of web authentication schemes. In: Proceedings of IEEE S&P 2012, pp. 553–567. IEEE, Piscataway (2012)
6. Herley, C., Van Oorschot, P.: A research agenda acknowledging the persistence of passwords. IEEE Secur. Priv. **10**(1), 28–36 (2012)
7. Morris, R., Thompson, K.: Password security: a case history. Commun. ACM **22**(11), 594–597 (1979)
8. Wu, T.: A real-world analysis of Kerberos password security. In: 1999 Network and Distributed System Security Symposium, San Diego, USA, pp. 13–22 (1999)
9. Narayanan, A., Shmatikov, V.: Fast dictionary attacks on passwords using time-space tradeoff. In: Proceedings of CCS 2005, pp. 364–372. ACM, New York (2005)
10. Weir, M., Aggarwal, S., De Medeiros, B., et al.: Password cracking using probabilistic context-free grammars. In: 2009 30th IEEE Symposium on Security and Privacy, 391–405. IEEE (2009)
11. Wang, D., Zhang, Z., Wang, P., et al.: Targeted online password guessing: an underestimated threat. In: Proceedings of the 2016 ACM SIGSAC Conference on Computer and Communications Security, pp. 1242–1254 (2016)
12. Min, L., Yang, Z.: A password cracking method based on name initials shorthand structure. Comput. Eng. **43**, 188–195 (2017)
13. Veras, R., Collins, C., Thorpe, J.: On semantic patterns of passwords and their security impact. In: NDSS (2014)
14. Melicher, W., Ur, B., Segreti, S.M., et al.: Fast, lean, and accurate: modeling password guess ability using neural networks. In: The 25th USENIX Security Symposium, Austin, USA, pp. 175–191 (2016)
15. Xia, Z., Yi, P., Liu, Y., et al.: GENPass: a multi-source deep learning model for password guessing. IEEE Trans. Multimedia **22**(5), 1323–1332 (2019)
16. Hitaj, B., Gasti, P., Ateniese, G., Perez-Cruz, F.: Passgan: a deep learning approach for password guessing. In: Deng, Robert H., Gauthier-Umaña, Valérie, Ochoa, Martín, Yung, Moti (eds.) Applied Cryptography and Network Security: 17th International Conference, ACNS 2019, Bogota, Colombia, June 5–7, 2019, Proceedings, pp. 217–237. Springer, Cham (2019). https://doi.org/10.1007/978-3-030-21568-2_11
17. Goodfellow, I., Pouget-Abadie, J., Mirza, M., et al.: Generative adversarial nets. In: Advances in Neural Information Processing Systems, pp. 2672–2680 (2014)
18. Nam, S., Jeon, S., Kim, H., et al.: Recurrent GANs password cracker For IoT password security enhancement. Sensors **20**(11), 3106 (2020)
19. Sutton, R.S., McAllester, D.A., Singh, S.P., Mansour, Y., et al.: Policy gradient methods for reinforcement learning with function approximation. In: NIPS, pp. 1057–1063 (1999)
20. Browne, C.B., Powley, E., Whitehouse, D., et al.: A survey of Monte Carlo tree search methods. IEEE Trans. Comput. Intell. AI Games **4**(1), 1–43 (2012)
21. Gulrajani, I., Ahmed, F., Arjovsky, M., et al.: Improved training of Wasserstein GANs. In: Advances in Neural Information Processing Systems, vol. 30, pp. 5767–5777 (2017)
22. Ng, A.Y., Jordan, M.I.: PEGASUS: a policy search method for large MDPs and POMDPs. arXiv preprint arXiv:1301.3878 (2013)
23. Frydenberg, M.: The chain graph Markov property. Scandinavian J. Stat. 333–353 (1990)
24. Yu, L., Zhang, W., Wang, J., et al.: SeqGan: sequence generative adversarial nets with policy gradient. In: Thirty-First AAAI Conference on Artificial Intelligence, vol. 31, no. 1 (2017)
25. Srivastava, R.K., Greff, K., Schmidhuber, J.: Highway networks. arXiv preprint arXiv:1505.00387 (2015)
26. Rockyou http://www.Rockyou.com
27. CSDN. http://www.CSDN.net
28. Yahoo. http://www.Yahoo.com

Linear Policy Recommender Scheme for Large-Scale Attribute-Based Access Control

Jing Wang[✉], Weijia Huang, Wenfen Liu, Lingfu Wang, and Mingwu Zhang

School of Computer Science and Information Security,
Guilin University of Electronic Technology, Guilin, China
wjing@guet.edu.cn

Abstract. In the large-scale data sharing platform, access control mechanism plays an important role in protecting data security and privacy. Significantly, Attribute-Based Access Control (ABAC) can support fine-grained access control, which would make the data sharing platform more flexible, efficient and manageable. However, in ABAC, data owner need to manually assign access policies for each data, which would incur lots of workload and limit the usability of the system. Thus, we propose a linear policy recommender scheme for ABAC in this work. Firstly, we propose a general form of access policy named linear policy, which describes the policy as a linear function. Comparing with other forms of policy, linear policy is more flexible and efficient. Secondly, we propose a matrix factorization based linear policy recommender scheme. The scheme learns a policy matrix and a security threshold vector from access logs and recommends the optimal linear policy for each data by a binary matrix factorization model. Intuitively, the policy matrix and security threshold vector can be viewed as the optimal linear policy of each data, which is helpful for ABAC to improve policy generation and management. Finally, sufficient experiments are given to present the performance of the proposed policy recommender system. The result shows that our policy recommender system is efficient and accurate in calculation.

Keywords: Data sharing · Attribute-based access control · Access policy · Matrix factorization

1 Introduction

With the development of Internet and cloud, data sharing services become more and more popular. Thus, the data security of such large-scale data sharing system arouses lots of concerns. Access control mechanism provides an efficient way to protect the data security and privacy for such systems. Different from traditional access control mechanism, Attribute-Based Access Control (ABAC) provides fine-grained access control which supports the complex access requirement of the large-scale data sharing system. In ABAC, the access privilege of each data

W. Shi et al. (Eds.): SPNCE 2021, LNICST 423, pp. 175–191, 2022.
https://doi.org/10.1007/978-3-030-96791-8_13

is described by an access policy which usually presented as a logical formula based on user attributes. A user is permitted to access a data iff the user attribute satisfies the access policy of the data. Since the flexibility of policy, ABAC is more flexible, efficient and manageable than traditional access control mechanisms.

However, in such a large-scale and complex system, the management of access policies will cost lots of workload. For instance, a data owner will cost a lot of time to deal the access policy for each data before he/she uploads the data to the center. Intuitively, such problem will seriously limit the application of ABAC. Additionally, considering of the personal security requirement, it is hard to assign an access policy with unified standards for each data, it requires the precise matching of data and policies. Thus, in this paper, we propose a policy recommender scheme for ABAC. The scheme can recommend a linear policy for each data, which considers the fine-grained data security requirement. The linear policy is a novel form of access policy, which presents as a linear function of user attributes. It is important that the linear policy can provide strong flexibility and computability.

One of the core challenges of our policy recommender scheme is presenting the formalized model to extract the access policy of each data from access logs. On the one hand, data owner is usually hard to give an accurate and comprehensive description of authorized users and unauthorized users in the large-scale system. On the other hand, it is hard to extract the differences of each data from the sparse access logs. Thus, it requires a generalized, simple, and intuitional expressing form of access policy, which presents interpretability and controllability. Next, we should give a formalized model to extract the information of access policies from access logs.

In this paper, we propose a matrix factorization based linear policy recommender scheme for the ABAC mechanism, which can extract the fine-grained data access privilege from access logs and present as the linear policy for each data. First, in the proposed recommender scheme, access logs are transformed into a user-data access matrix. Then, a matrix factorization algorithm is provided to estimate the access privilege of each data for each user. In fact, the algorithm outputs two factored matrices named policy matrix and user attribute matrix, respectively. It implies that the policy matrix is used to describe the access policy of each data and the user attribute matrix is used to describe the attribute feature of each user. Meanwhile, it is reasonable to simplify the access matrix and user attribute matrix as binary matrix in this work. In fact, there are only two case of a access matrix element: *unaccessable* denoted by 0 and *accessable* denoted by 1, respectively. Similarly, in this work, we only consider nunnumerical user attribute which can be easily translated into a binary vector by one hot encoding. Thus, the attribute threshold and security threshold are introduced to binarize the predicted access matrix and the user attribute matrix, respectively. Finally, the recommender scheme outputs a linear policy for each data. The linear policy is a novel form of policy proposed in this work, which presents the policy as a linear function of user attributes. Furthermore, each linear policy is assigned a security threshold to distinguish its security hierarchy. Thus, the linear policy is flexible and manageable cause of the efficient linear function and the intuitional security threshold. In brief, the contributions of this paper can be summarized as follows:

1. A novel kind of access policy, named linear policy, is provided to describe access privileges, which presents a linear relation between user attributes and access privileges;
2. A matrix factorization based policy recommender scheme is proposed to extract the policy of each data, which considers the fine-grained security requirement of data;
3. Lots of experiments demonstrate the proposed linear policy recommender scheme is efficient and accurate.

2 Related Work

2.1 Access Control

The access control mechanism protects and prevents data from unauthorized access. Discretionary Access Control (DAC) and Mandatory Access Control (MAC) are two early mechanisms of access control that were applied in Department of Defense applications in the 1960s and 1970s. With the growth of networks, DAC and MAC are hard to satisfy the access control with complex access requirements. Role-based Access Control (RBAC) realizes the flexible access control based on the predefined roles assigned to users by the system administrator [1]. However, RBAC only realizes the coarse-grained access control and lacks of dynamics, which is not suitable for the current dynamic and real-time network environment. ABAC permits or denies a user's access request to a specific data based on the attribute associated with the user and the data [2,3]. It is a suitable access control mechanism for the current network environment, because ABAC realizes the dynamic and fine-grained access control.

Because of the advantage of ABAC, transforming the traditional access control mechanism to the ABAC mechanism is attractive. ABAC policy mining has become an important approach for migrate from a traditional access control mechanism to an ABAC mechanism. Xu et al. [4] proposed a policy mining algorithms for different ABAC mechanisms. Their algorithms realize the policy mining with positive authorization. Iyer et al. [5] considered the importance of negative authorization and proposed a policy mining algorithm to support negative authorization. However, those algorithms are not suitable to mine policy from multiples access control mechanisms that have different policy frameworks. Thus, Karimi et al. [6] proposed an unsupervised learning based approach for mining ABAC policies which clusters the access right tuples based on the similarity and extracts policies for clusters. Additionally, Bui et al. [7] considered part of the attribute values of some entities are unknown, and proposed an ABAC policy mining algorithm with unknown values.

Except the mechanism migration, policy mining also uses to solve the inherent flaws of the ABAC mechanism in the policy assignment phase. In the ABAC mechanism, the number of user attributes and the complexity of policy definition are increasing with the size of the network. In order to reduce the number of user attributes in the large-scale system and increase the flexibility of the ABAC mechanism, Benkaouz et al. [8] proposed a policy mining algorithm based on k-nearest neighbors. In addition, over-privilege and under-privilege are two kinds of assignment errors in the access control mechanism. Over-privilege grants the privilege to the unauthorized user that increases the security risk of the access control mechanism. Under-privilege denies the access request from the authorized user that reduces the availability of the access control mechanism. Thus, Sanders et al. [9] proposed a rule mining approach to create least privilege ABAC policies which achieves a balance between minimizing over-privilege and under-privilege assignment error.

In this paper, we propose an access policy recommender scheme to extract access policies for each data which considers both the fine-grained security requirement and the user attribute. In addition, we propose a linear policy model that consists of a policy vector and a security threshold. It is easy to adjust the security level of data by the magnitude of the security threshold.

2.2 Recommender System

Recently, there are a lot of recommender systems have been proposed, which usually generate personalized recommendations for users. It has been widely used in various real scenes, such as restaurant recommendations [10], shopping recommendations [11], movie recommendations [12], and so on. The neighborhood approach is a kind of collaborative filtering technique for recommender system which focus on relationships between items or between users [13]. Su et al. [14] designed a rating prediction algorithm based on the users' historical behavior probabilities which can improve the accuracy of predictions and reduce the number of the required neighbors. Yue et al. [15] proposed a modified collaborative filtering algorithm by combining the advantages of user-based and item-based collaborative filtering methods. Furthermore, this algorithm makes full use of the positively and negatively correlated neighbors to further improve the prediction accuracy.

Matrix factorization is another kind of collaborative filtering technique which approximate the original data matrix by the product of factored matrices [16–18]. Because of the accuracy and scalability of matrix factorization, it is getting more and more attention from researchers. Funk [19] proposed the singular value decomposition (SVD) approach, it can be viewed as the first matrix factorization based recommender system. Koren [20] proposed an SVD++ approach, which consists of SVD and the neighborhood model. Significantly, the SVD++ model is better than the SVD model in prediction accuracy. Furthermore, Koren [21] proposed the timeSVD, which considered the affect of record time. In order to improve the accuracy and the interpretability of the matrix factorization model, some researchers proposed various convolutional matrix factorization methods by combining the matrix factorization and Convolutional Neural Networks (CNN) [22,23]. Additionally, many researchers considered various meanings of missing value in different applications and proposed different ways to weight the missing value [10–12]. Such recommender system models are helpful for the application of recommender system in different scenes.

Intuitively, such recommender systems are feasible to recommend a corresponding access policy for each data. Thus, in this paper, we propose a matrix factorization based linear policy recommender scheme. Different from the traditional recommender system, our linear policy recommender scheme recommends a policy vector and a security threshold for each data. It can decrease the difficulty of policy definition and greatly improve the efficiency of deploying the ABAC mechanism.

3   Linear Access Policy Recommender system

3.1   ABAC system

An ABAC system can be described by a quadruple (S, O, P, E), where S denotes a subject, O denotes a object, P denotes the permission and E denotes the environment conditions [2]. Generally, a subject can be a user who want to access a data; a object represents a data which shares by the data owner; the permission represents a operation that the subject requests to perform on the object, including read, write, modify, and so on; the environment usually includes current time, location of a user, threat level, and so on. In this work, environment conditions is only considered as user attributes.

In general, the access control system includes the Policy Enforcement Point (PEP), the Policy Decision Point (PDP), the Policy Information Point (PIP), and the Policy Administration Point (PAP). The whole ABAC system includes two operational phases: the preparation phase and the execution phase [3]. As shown in Fig. 1, our ABAC system includes the Policy Decision Point (PDP), the Policy Administration Point (PAP), and the Policy Recommendation Point (PRP). In the preparation phase, PAP collects attribute sets and access logs, and requests access policies from PRP. Then, PRP extracts the fine-grained access privilege from access logs and attribute sets and generates linear policies, that is the proposed linear policy recommender scheme for PAP to manage access policies of data. The proposed scheme extracts the relation of attributes and privileges by matrix factorization and describes the access policy by the linear policy model. It is efficient and accurate for the relationship extraction. Finally, PAP assigns and manages access policies for each data based on the recommended linear policy. In the execution phase, PDP requests the corresponding access policy from PAP when it receives an access request from a subject. If the attribute set of the subject satisfies the access policy, PDP permits the access request (i.e. queries the object and responses to the subject). Otherwise, denies the access request. In most ABAC systems, PDP decides by matching the attribute value of the access request with each corresponding attribute value in the access policy. In our work, the linear model needs only one comparison which can reduce the workload of PDP.

3.2   Matrix Factorization Based Access Privilege Recommendation

The matrix factorization model aims to learn two matrices with a product that can approximate the original data matrix [16,17], where the two matrices represent cluster centroid attributes and cluster indicator information [18]. In our

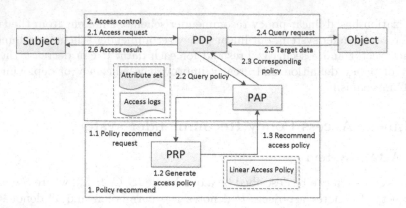

Fig. 1. The framework of ABAC system

matrix factorization based policy recommender system, it tries to learn a user attribute matrix and a policy matrix with a product that can approximate the access matrix.

Let $\mathbf{P} = (p_{u,j})_{m \times f}$ denotes the user matrix, where m denotes the number of users, f denotes the number of user attributes and each row represents a specified user. $\mathbf{Q} = (q_{j,i})_{f \times n}$ denotes the item matrix, where n denotes the number of items and each column represents a specified item. The predicted access matrix $\mathbf{R}$ is calculated as the inner product of $\mathbf{P}$ and $\mathbf{Q}$. It tries to approximate $\mathbf{R}$ as follows:

$$\min_{p,q} \sum_{(u,i) \in \kappa} \left((r_{u,i} - \sum_{j=1}^{f} p_{u,j} q_{j,i})^2 + \lambda \sum_{j=1}^{f} (p_{u,j}^2 + q_{j,i}^2) \right), \tag{1}$$

where κ is the set of the (u, i) pairs for which $r_{u,i}$ is known in rating matrix (the training set), $\lambda \in [0, 1]$ denotes the regularized coefficient. Furthermore, the Mini-Batch Gradient Descent approach is proposed to solve the solution of Eq. (1). In fact, the system predicts each $r_{u,i}$ in the training set and computes the prediction error $e_{u,i} = r_{u,i} - \sum_{j=1}^{f} p_{u,j} q_{j,i}$. Let $\gamma \in [0, 1]$ denotes the learning rate, b denotes the size of batch. Then, $p_{u,j}$ and $q_{j,i}$ are updated as follows:

$$p_{u,j} \leftarrow p_{u,j} + \sum_{i'=i}^{i+b} \gamma(e_{u,i'} q_{j,i'} - \lambda p_{u,j}), \tag{2}$$

$$q_{j,i} \leftarrow q_{j,i} + \sum_{u'=u}^{u+b} \gamma(e_{u',i} p_{u',j} - \lambda q_{j,i}), \tag{3}$$

3.3 Linear Policy Recommendation

Access policy is also known as access structure which influences the efficiency and the flexibility of the ABAC system. It is usually defined as follow:

Definition 1 (Access Policy [24]**).** *Let* $\{P_1, P_2, ..., P_n\}$ *be a set of parties. An access structure is a collection* $\mathbb{A}$ *of non-empty subsets of* $\{P_1, P_2, ..., P_n\}$, *i.e.* $\mathbb{A} \subseteq 2^{\{P_1, P_2, ..., P_n\}} \setminus \{\emptyset\}$. *Furthermore,* $\forall A \in \mathbb{A}$ *is called the authorized set, and* $\forall \bar{A} \notin \mathbb{A}$ *is called the unauthorized sets. A collection* $\mathbb{A}$ *is monotone iff* $\forall B \in \mathbb{A}, B \subset C \Leftrightarrow C \in \mathbb{A}$.

Attributes collection set $\mathbb{A}$ is a generalized form of access policy. It describes a access policy by a *minimum authorized set* or a *maximum unauthorized set*. Furthermore, the access policy is usually described by various specific forms, such as Access Tree [25], Linear Secret Sharing Scheme Matrix (LSSS) [26], AND-gates Access Structure [27], Threshold Access Structure [24], and so on.

In this paper, we proposed a form of access policy named linear policy. For each data, the access policy can be expressed as a policy vector and a security threshold. Let $\mathcal{A} = \{a_k, 1 \leq k \leq f\}$ be a set of attributes. The attribute set of a user u can be expressed as a binary vector $P_u = (p_{u,1}, ..., p_{u,f})$ where $\{p_{u,k} = 1, 1 \leq k \leq f\}$ iff the user get the kth attribute of $\mathcal{A}$. Meanwhile, a linear policy of a data i can be given as (Q_i, s_i), where $Q_i \in [0,1]^f$ denotes a policy vector and $s_i \in [0,1]$ denotes a security threshold. Thus, the data i can be accessed by user u iff $P_u \times Q_i \geq s_i$.

In the proposed policy recommender scheme, the access matrix $\mathbf{R}$ is factorized as the product of policy matrix $\mathbf{Q}$ and attribute matrix $\mathbf{P}$, where $\mathbf{Q}$ can be used to describe the linear policy of each data. In fact, the linear policy model is more flexible than Threshold Access Structure and more efficient than complex access structures, such as Access Tree and LSSS. In most cases, a complex access structure can directly transform into a linear policy. A data owner can request linear policy for a data by the proposed recommender scheme as follow. Firstly, the data owner uploads the data access logs or labels part of authorized users and unauthorized users. Then, the proposed policy recommender scheme can recommend a linear policy (i.e. a policy vector and a security threshold) for the data by the access information and some user attribute information. Finally, the data owner can assign an access policy for the data base on the recommended policy. Furthermore, the data owner can adjust the security threshold according to different security requirements.

4 Linear Policy Recommender Scheme Based on Binary Matrix Factorization

Our policy recommender scheme takes the access logs $\mathbf{A}$ and the user attribute information $\mathbf{U}$ as inputs and outputs fine-grained access policy for each shared data, the whole scheme includes four functions: data preprocessing, access matrix factorization, attribute matrix binarization, and security threshold calculation. As shown in Fig. 2. Firstly, it transforms the access logs $\mathbf{A}$ and the user attribute information into a *uniform* user-data access matrix $\mathbf{R}_{m \times n}$ and a binary known user attribute matrix $\mathbf{P}'_{m \times f}$, which can be viewed as the data preprocessing. Secondly, it gets the user attribute matrix $\mathbf{P}_{m \times f}$ and the policy matrix $\mathbf{Q}_{f \times n}$

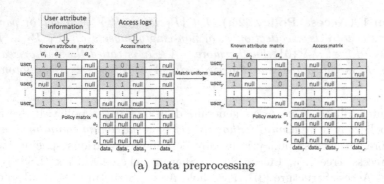

(a) Data preprocessing

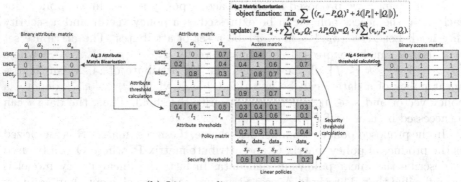

(b) Linear policy recommending

Fig. 2. The overview of the linear policy recommender scheme

from $\mathbf{R}$ and $\mathbf{P}'_{m \times f}$ by a matrix factorization algorithm. Because a part of user attributes are unknown, our policy recommender scheme also learns the unknown user attribute by the matrix factorization algorithm. Obviously, the user attribute matrix consists of the known user attribute matrix and the learned user attribute matrix. Because the attribute matrix is a binary matrix, we introduce a method to binarize $\mathbf{P}$. Finally, a security threshold is chosen for each data. The policy matrix $\mathbf{Q}$ and security threshold vector $\mathbf{s}$ are used to describe access policies.

4.1 Data Preprocessing

The policy recommender scheme needs to extract the relationship of user attributes from access logs and user attribute information, and recommend access policies for each data. In this section, we transform access logs $\mathbf{A}$ into a binary matrix $\mathbf{R}$, where each row of $\mathbf{R}$ denotes a user, each column of $\mathbf{R}$ denotes a data. We consider the following cases:

1. The uth user used to access the ith data successfully, $r_{u,i}$ is set to be 1;
2. The uth user ever failed to access the ith data, $r_{u,i}$ is set to be 0;

3. The uth user never accessed the ith data before, $r_{u,i}$ is set to be *null*.

Similarly, the user attribute information $\mathbf{U}$ is transformed into a binary matrix $\mathbf{P'}$, where each row of $\mathbf{P'}$ denotes a user, and each column of $\mathbf{P'}$ denotes an attribute. We consider the following cases:

1. The uth user gets the jth attribute, $p'_{u,j}$ is set to be 1;
2. The uth user dose not get the jth attribute, $p'_{u,j}$ is set to be 0;
3. The user attribute information dose not explicitly describe weather the uth user get the jth attribute or not, $p'_{u,j}$ is set to be *null*.

In order to make the elements (i.e. '0' or '1') are *uniform* distributed in $\mathbf{R}$, Analysis of Variance (ANOVA) [28] is introduced to determine the matrix $\mathbf{R}$. Let y_i be the total of known element in the ith row of $\mathbf{R}$ and $k = \lceil m/b \rceil$, we get

$$S_e = \sum_{j=0}^{k-1} \sum_{i=bj}^{(j+1)b-1} (y_i - \bar{y}_j)^2 + \sum_{i=kb}^{m-1} (y_i - \bar{y}_k)^2, f_e = m - (k+1), \tag{4}$$

$$S_A = b \sum_{j=0}^{k-1} (\bar{y}_j - \bar{y})^2 + b'(\bar{y}_k - \bar{y})^2, f_A = k, \tag{5}$$

where

$$\bar{y}_j = \begin{cases} \dfrac{1}{b} \sum_{i=bj}^{(j+1)b-1} y_i, & j < k, \\ \dfrac{1}{b'} \sum_{i=bk}^{m-1} y_i, & j = k, \end{cases} \tag{6}$$

$$\bar{y} = \sum_{i=0}^{m-1} y_i, \tag{7}$$

$$b' = m - kb. \tag{8}$$

In fact, S_e denotes the sum of *intraclass* variance and S_A denotes the sum of *interclass* variance, they can describe the distribution of known elements of $\mathbf{R}$. Then, we calculate F as follow:

$$F = \frac{S_A/f_A}{S_e/f_e}. \tag{9}$$

The matrix $\mathbf{R}$ can be accepted as a *row-uniform* matrix, iff $F_{1-\alpha}(f_A, f_e) < F < F_{1-\alpha}(f_e, f_A)$, where $\alpha \in [0,1]$, f_e and f_A denote the degree of freedom, $F_{1-\alpha}(f_A, f_e)$ and $F_{1-\alpha}(f_e, f_A)$ denote the upper percentage points of F-distribution. Similarly, the notion of *column-uniform* matrix can be given in the same way here. Furthermore, a matrix can be accepted as a *uniform* matrix iff it is *row-uniform* and *column-uniform*.

The data preprocessing is shown in Algorithm 1, which takes the access logs $\mathbf{A}$, user attribute information $\mathbf{U}$, batch size b, and quantile α as inputs and

---

Algorithm 1. Matrix Initialization $MI(\mathbf{A}, \mathbf{U}, b, \alpha)$

Input: Access logs $\mathbf{A}$; User attribute information $\mathbf{U}$; Size of batch b; Quantile α
Output: *Uniform* User-data access matrix $\mathbf{R}$; Known user attribute matrix $\mathbf{P}'$
1: Transform the access logs $\mathbf{A}$ and the user attribute information $\mathbf{U}$ into an access matrix $\mathbf{R}$ and a user attribute matrix $\mathbf{P}'$
2: Calculate the degree of freedom f_e and f_A of rows of $\mathbf{R}$ as shown in Eq. (4) (5)
3: Calculate the statistic parameter F of rows of $\mathbf{R}$ as shown in Eq. (9)
4: **while** $F < F_{1-\alpha}(f_A, f_e)$ or $F > F_{1-\alpha}(f_e, f_A)$ **do**
5:    $\mathbf{R} \leftarrow$ randomly permute the row of $\mathbf{R}$
6:    Calculate the statistic parameter F of rows of $\mathbf{R}$
7: **end while**
8: Calculate the degree of freedom f_e and f_A of columns of $\mathbf{R}$
9: Calculate the statistic parameter F of columns of $\mathbf{R}$
10: **while** $F < F_{1-\alpha}(f_A, f_e)$ or $F > F_{1-\alpha}(f_e, f_A)$ **do**
11:    $\mathbf{R} \leftarrow$ random permute the cloumn of $\mathbf{R}$
12:    Calculate the statistic parameter F of columns of $\mathbf{R}$.
13: **end while**
14: **return** $\mathbf{R}, \mathbf{P}'$

---

initializes the access matrix $\mathbf{R}$ and the user attribute matrix $\mathbf{P}'$. Then, the matrix $\mathbf{R}$ is randomly permuted with rows and columns until it gets *uniform*. Finally, the algorithm outputs a *uniform* access matrix $\mathbf{R}$ and a corresponding user attribute matrix $\mathbf{P}'$.

4.2 Access Matrix Factorization

In a recommender system, the *null* records always contain some information. For instance, in our policy recommender scheme, we consider two cases of *null* records:

1. The user never accesses the data because he/she knows that he/she does not get the access privilege;
2. The user never accesses the data because he/she does not need to access the data.

In brief, the *null* records actually denote 0 in the first case. Thus, we deal the *null* as 0 with a little weight $\omega \in (0, 1)$. The recommender scheme can be defined as follows:

$$L = \min_{p_{u,j}, q_{j,i}} \sum_{u,i} \omega_{u,i}((r'_{u,i} - \sum_j p_{u,j} q_{j,i})^2 + \lambda(\sum_j p_{u,j}^2 + \sum_j q_{j,i}^2)), \qquad (10)$$

$$s.t. \begin{cases} p_{u,j} \in \{0,1\}, q_{j,i} \in [0,1], \\ r'_{u,i} = \begin{cases} 1 & \text{if } r_{u,i} = 1, \\ 0 & \text{if } r_{u,i} = 0 \text{ or } null, \end{cases} \\ \omega_{u,i} = \begin{cases} 1 & \text{if } r_{u,i} \text{ is not } null, \\ \omega & \text{if } r_{u,i} \text{ is } null. \end{cases} \end{cases} \qquad (11)$$

where L denotes the objective function and λ denotes the weight of regular terms. Considering of efficiency and accuracy, Mini-Batch Gradient Descent (MBGD) is used to iteratively search for the optimal solution of the above problem. Let γ be the learning rate, in the lth round of the iteration, $p_{u,j}^{(l)}$ and $q_{j,i}^{(l)}$ is updated as follows:

$$p_{u,j}^{(l)} = p_{u,j}^{(l-1)} + \gamma \frac{1}{b} \sum_{i=kb}^{(k+1)b-1} \omega_{u,i'}((r'_{u,i'} - \sum_{j=1}^{f} p_{u,j}^{(l-1)} q_{j,i'}^{(l-1)}) q_{j,i'}^{(l-1)} - \lambda p_{u,j}^{(l-1)}), \quad (12)$$

$$q_{j,i}^{(l)} = q_{j,i}^{(l-1)} + \gamma \frac{1}{b} \sum_{u=kb}^{(k+1)b-1} \omega_{u',i}((r'_{u',i} - \sum_{j=1}^{f} p_{u',j}^{(l-1)} q_{j,i}^{(l-1)}) p_{u',j}^{(l-1)} - \lambda q_{j,i}^{(l-1)}), \quad (13)$$

where $i' = i \mod m$ and $u' = u \mod n$. The matrix factorization algorithm of our recommender scheme is shown in Algorithm 2. In particular, it firstly initializes an attribute matrix $\mathbf{P} = (p_{u,j})_{m \times f} \in \{0,1\}^{m \times f}$ with known user attribute matrix $\mathbf{P}'$ and initializes a policy matrix $\mathbf{Q} = (q_{j,i})_{f \times n} \in [0,1]^{f \times n}$ randomly. Then, $\mathbf{P}$ and $\mathbf{Q}$ are iteratively updated by Eq. (12) and Eq. (13) respectively to minimize the objective function L. The iterative algorithm would be terminated iff $|L^{(l)} - L^{(l-1)}| \leq \theta$ or $l \geq T$, where $L^{(l)}$ and $L^{(l-1)}$ denote the value of L in the lth and $(l-1)^{th}$ iteration respectively, θ denotes the convergence threshold and T denotes the maximum iterations. Furthermore, in this work, $\mathbf{P}$ and $\bar{\mathbf{R}}$ are binary matrices, the binarization mechanism should be introduced into the matrix factorization algorithm. For efficiency, our scheme binarizes $\mathbf{P}$ each k iterations and binarizes $\bar{\mathbf{R}}$ after the end of Algorithm 2.

4.3   Attribute Matrix Binarization

In this work, user attributes are given as a binary vector, in which each row of $\mathbf{P}$ represents a user attribute set. However, there are some unknown user attributes learned by Algorithm 2 which are non-binary. Thus, a binarization algorithm of $\mathbf{P}$ is proposed to deal such learned attributes. As shown in Algorithm 3 which outputs an attribute threshold t_j for each column P_j to binarize it. The algorithm includes the following four steps:

1. Pick k samples $\{a_{j,i'}, 0 \leq i' \leq k-1\}$ of each column P_j in descending order;
2. Calculate candidate threshold set $\mathbf{T}_j = \{t_{j,i'}, 1 \leq i' \leq k-1\}$ as follows:

$$t_{j,i'} = a_{j,i'} - \frac{i'(a_{j,i'} - a_{j,i'+1})}{k}; \quad (14)$$

3. Choose the optimal threshold t_j from $\mathbf{T}_j$ which minimizing the objective function L;
4. Binarize attribute matrix P_j by threshold t_j.

Algorithm 2. Matrix Factorization $MF(\mathbf{R}, \mathbf{P}')$

Input: User-data access matrix $\mathbf{R}$; Known user attribute $\mathbf{P}'$
Output: Attribute matrix $\mathbf{P}$; Policy matrix $\mathbf{Q}$
1: Initialize $\mathbf{P} \in [0,1]^{m \times f}$ with $\mathbf{P}'$ and initialize $\mathbf{Q} \in [0,1]^{f \times n}$ randomly;
2: Calculate the objective function $L^{(0)}$ as shown in Eq. (10).
3: $l = 0$, $L^{(-1)} = 0$
4: **while** $|L^{(l)} - L^{(l-1)}| > \theta$ or $l < T$ **do**
5:     $//\theta$ denotes the convergence threshold and T denotes the maximum iterations
6:     **for** t from 1 to k **do**
7:         **for** u from 1 to m **do**
8:             **for** j form 1 to f **do**
9:                 **if** $p'_{u,j} = null$ **then**
10:                     $p_{u,j} \leftarrow p_{u,j} + \gamma \frac{1}{b} \frac{\partial L^{(l-1)}}{\partial p_{u,j}}$
11:                 **end if**
12:             **end for**
13:         **end for**
14:         **for** i from 1 to n **do**
15:             **for** j form 1 to f **do**
16:                 $q_{j,i} \leftarrow q_{j,i} + \frac{1}{b} \frac{\partial L^{(l-1)}}{\partial q_{j,i}}$
17:             **end for**
18:         **end for**
19:     **end for**
20:     $\mathbf{P} \leftarrow AMB(\mathbf{P})$ //i.e. call the Algorithm 3
21:     $l \leftarrow l + 1$
22: **end while**
23: **return** $\mathbf{P}, \mathbf{Q}$

Algorithm 3. Attribute Matrix Binarization $AMB(\mathbf{P})$

Input: Attribute matrix $\mathbf{P}$
Output: Binary attribute matrix $\mathbf{P}$
1: **for** j form 1 to f **do**
2:     Choose k samples $\{a_{j,i'}, 0 \leq i' \leq k-1\}$ from P_j in descending order
3:     $L_j \leftarrow null$
4:     **for** i' from 1 to $k-1$ **do**
5:         Calculate $t_{j,i'}$ as shown in Eq. (14)
6:         Calculate $\bar{P}_j$ as binary $P_j = \{\bar{p}_{j,i}\}: \bar{p}_{j,i} = \begin{cases} 0, & p_{j,i} < t_{j,i'} \\ 1, & p_{j,i} \geq t_{j,i'} \end{cases}$
7:         Compute the objective function L with $\bar{P}_j$
8:         **if** $L_j = null$ or $L_j \geq L$ **then**
9:             $t_j \leftarrow t_{j,i'}, L_j \leftarrow L, P'_j \leftarrow \bar{P}_j$
10:         **end if**
11:     **end for**
12:     $P_j \leftarrow P'_j$
13: **end for**
14: **return** $\mathbf{P}, t_j, 1 \leq j \leq f$

Algorithm 4. Security Threshold Calculation $STC(\mathbf{R}, \mathbf{P}, \mathbf{Q})$

Input: User-data access matrix $\mathbf{R}$; Attribute matrix $\mathbf{P}$; Policy matrix $\mathbf{Q}$
Output: Policy matrix $\mathbf{Q}$; security threshold vector $\mathbf{s}$
1: $\hat{\mathbf{R}} \leftarrow \mathbf{PQ}$
2: **for** i form 1 to n **do**
3:     Get the descending sort $\mathbf{i}'$ of $\hat{R}_i$, where $\hat{R}_i$ denotes the ith column of $\hat{\mathbf{R}}$
4:     $num = 0$
5:     **for** j from 1 to $m - 1$ **do**
6:       **if** $r_{i'_j, i} \neq r_{i'_{j+1}, i}$ **then**
7:         $// r_{i'_j, i}, r_{i'_{j+1}, i}$ denotes the components of original matrix $\mathbf{R}$
8:         $\bar{s}_{i, num} \leftarrow \hat{r}_{i'_j, i}, num \leftarrow num + 1$
9:       **end if**
10:     **end for**
11:     $\bar{L}_i \leftarrow null$
12:     **for** k from 1 to $num - 1$ **do**
13:       $s_{i,k} \leftarrow \bar{s}_{i,k} - \frac{k(\bar{s}_{i,k} - \bar{s}_{i,k+1})}{num}$
14:       Calculate $\bar{R}_i$ as shown in Eq. (16)
15:       **if** $\bar{L}_i = null$ or $L_i(\bar{R}_i) < \bar{L}_i$ **then**
16:         $s_i \leftarrow s_{i,k}, \bar{L}_i \leftarrow L_i(\bar{R}_i)$
17:       **end if**
18:       $k \leftarrow k + 1$
19:     **end for**
20: **end for**
21: **return** $s_i, 1 \leq i \leq n$

4.4 Security Threshold Calculation

The predicted matrix $\bar{\mathbf{R}}$ of the original matrix $\mathbf{R}$ is also a binary matrix in this work. Thus, the security threshold vector $\mathbf{s}$ is required to binarize the matrix $\hat{\mathbf{R}} = \mathbf{P} \times \mathbf{Q}$, where $\mathbf{P}$ and $\mathbf{Q}$ denote the learned attribute matrix and policy matrix, respectively. As shown in Algorithm 4, the security threshold calculation algorithm is similar to Algorithm 3, which includes the following three steps:

1. Compute the matrix $\hat{\mathbf{R}}$ by attribute matrix $\mathbf{P} \in \{0,1\}^{m \times f}$ and policy matrix $\mathbf{Q} \in [0,1]^{f \times n}$.
2. Calculate candidate thresholds. For each column $\hat{R}_i$ of $\hat{\mathbf{R}}$, a candidate threshold set $S_i = \{s_{i,k}\}$ is chosen. Note that, $s_{i,k}$ is chosen as local optimum, the processing is similar to $t_{j,i'}$ choosing.
3. Choose the best threshold. Let the objective function be simplified as follows:

$$L_i(s_{i,k}) = \sum_{u=1}^{m} w_{u,i}(r_{u,i} - \bar{r}_{u,i,s_{i,k}})^2, \tag{15}$$

$$\bar{r}_{u,i,s_{i,k}} = \begin{cases} 0, & \hat{r}_{u,i} \leq s_{i,k} \\ 1, & otherwise \end{cases}, \tag{16}$$

where $\hat{r}_{u,i} = \sum_j p_{u,j} q_{j,i}$ and $s_{i,k}$ is k^{th} candidate threshold of R_i. The final security threshold $s_i \in S_i$ is the solution which makes L_i minimum.

5   Performance Evaluation

5.1   Data Sets and Metrics

In this paper, we use Amazon Access Samples Data Set (AAS) to evaluate the performance of our scheme[1] We extract 3 datasets from AAS by years: AAS56, AAS08, and AAS10. AAS56 contains more than 60 thousand records of the access right for 4249 users to 856 data. AAS08 contains more than 130 thousand records of the access right for 7623 users to 3017 data. AAS10 contains more than 230 thousand records of the access right for 13530 users to 6059 data. There are 12 attributes for each user, we choose 10 attributes in our experiments. Table 1 shows the detail of datasets. We randomly split each dataset into a training set (80%) and a testing set (20%), and we report the average results of five experiments.

Our scheme can be viewed as a binary classification model. Normally, *precision* and *recall* are two important evaluation metrics to measure the prediction accuracy of classification, and *F1-score* is a composite metric of *precision* and *recall*. The definition is shown as follows:

$$precision = TP/(TP + FP), \tag{17}$$

$$recall = TP/(TP + FN), \tag{18}$$

$$F1\text{-}score = \frac{2 \times precision \times recall}{precision + recall}, \tag{19}$$

where TP, FP, TN, and FN denote the number of true positive, false positive, true negative, and false negative respectively.

5.2   Experimental Evaluation

In this section, all presented experiments were conducted on a cloud server with two intel(R) Xeon(R) CPU E5-2640 v3 @ 2.60 GHz 2.60 GHz and 32 GB RAM. Let γ denotes the learning rate, λ denotes the regularization parameter, b denotes the size of batch, k denotes the frequency of binarization, $\omega_{u,i}$ denotes the weight of unknown elements, and T denotes the maximum iterations.

Firstly, we analyze the influence of the batch size b and the binarization frequency k in AAS56, where $\gamma = 0.001$, $\lambda = 0.01$, $\omega_{u,i} = 0.0001$, and $T = 300$. Fig. 3 shows that, the *F1-score* increases with the growth of the binarization frequency, but the effect of the batch size is not signification. When the binarization frequency is greater than 30, *F1-score* remains stable in the range of 0.93 to 0.94.

Then, we analyze the influence of the learning rate γ and the weight of unknown element $\omega_{u,i}$ in AAS56, AAS08, and AAS10. Figure 4 shows *F1-score* decreases with the growth of learning rate, where $\lambda = 0.01$, $\omega_{u,i} = 0.0001$, $b = 150$, $k = 50$, and $T = 300$. Because the greater learning rate can't make

---

[1] http://archive.ics.uci.edu/ml/datasets/Amazon+Access+Samples.

Table 1. The description of datasets

Dataset	Accessable	Unaccessable	Users	Items	Density
AAS56	13078	1147	4249	856	0.017648
AAS08	42759	1466	7623	3017	0.005704
AAS10	96272	2660	13530	6059	0.002865

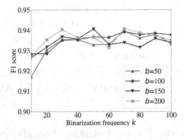

Fig. 3. The influence of the binarization frequency and the batch size for *F1-score*

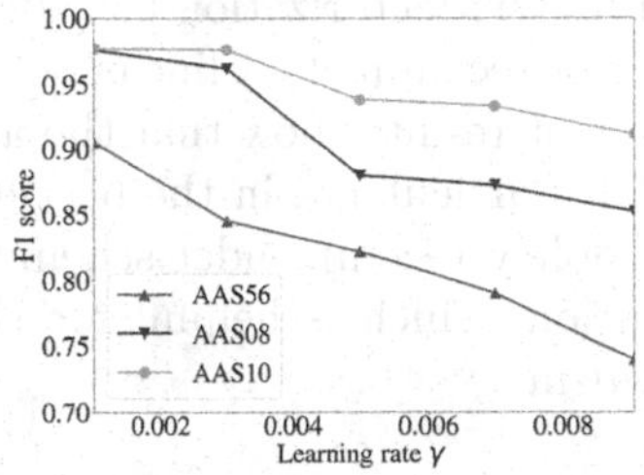

Fig. 4. Effect of learning rate in different datasets

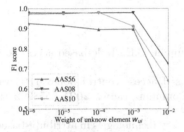

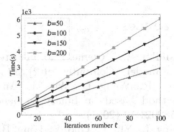

Fig. 5. Effect of the weight of unknown element in different datasets

Fig. 6. The influence of the iterations number and the batch size for running time

the prediction achieving the optimum. As Fig. 5 shows, the *F1-score* increases with the decrease of the weight of unknown element, where $\gamma = 0.001$, $\lambda = 0.01$, $b = 150$, $k = 50$, and $T = 300$. In AAS56 and AAS08, *F1-score* remains stable, when the weight of unknown element is less than 0.001. However, in AAS10, *F1-score* remains stable, when the weight of unknown element is less than 0.0001. Because the rate of unaccessable in AAS10 is less than AAS56 and AAS08. In addition, the best *F1-score* in AAS56 is less than AAS08 and AAS10. Because the size of AAS56 is smaller than AAS08 and AAS10.

Finally, We analyze some parameters that affect the running time of the access policy recommender scheme. Fig. 6 shows the influence of the number of iterations and the batch size in AAS56, where $\gamma = 0.0001$, $\lambda = 0.01$, $\omega_{u,i} = 0.0001$, $b = 150$, and $k = 50$. Obviously, the running time increases with the growth of the number of iterations and the batch size.

6 Conclusion

In an ABAC mechanism, a policy recommender scheme can provide efficient policy management for each data. In this paper, we firstly propose a novel expressing form of access policy named linear policy. It can not only directly describe the fine-grained access privilege by a linear function, but also flexibly adjust the data security level by updating the security threshold of the data. Secondly, we propose a matrix factorization based linear policy recommender scheme for ABAC, which can recommend a linear policy for each data accurately and quickly. The experiment results show that the accuracy of the recommended policy is always over 0.9. Particularly, in the best case, the accuracy achieves 0.98. In brief, our access policy recommender scheme can greatly enhance the efficiency of policy assignation, which is helpful for the promotion and application of the ABAC mechanism.

Acknowledgment. This work was supported by the National Science Foundation of China (No. 61802083, 61862011), the Natural Science Foundation of Guangxi (2018GXNSFB A281164, 2018GXNSFAA138116) and Innovation Project of GUET Graduate Education (2021YCXS074).

References

1. Sandhu, R.S., Coyne, E.J., Feinstein, H.L., Youman, C.E.: Role-based access control models. Computer **29**(2), 38–47 (1996)
2. Pan, R., Wang, G., Wu, M.: An attribute-based access control policy retrieval method based on binary sequence. Secur. Commun. Netw. **2021**, 5582921:1-5582921:12 (2021)
3. Fang, L., Yin, L., Guo, Y., Fang, B.: A survey of key technologies in attribute-based access control scheme. Chin. J. Comput. **40**(7), 1681–1698 (2017)
4. Xu, Z., Stoller, S.D.: Mining attribute-based access control policies. IEEE Trans. Dependable Secur. Comput. **12**(5), 533–545 (2015)
5. Iyer, P., Masoumzadeh, A.: Mining positive and negative attribute-based access control policy rules. In: Proceedings of the 23nd ACM on Symposium on Access Control Models and Technologies, pp. 161–172 (2018)
6. Karimi, L., Joshi, J.: An unsupervised learning based approach for mining attribute based access control policies. In: IEEE International Conference on Big Data, pp. 1427–1436 (2018)
7. Bui, T., Stoller, S.D.: Learning attribute-based and relationship-based access control policies with unknown values. In: Kanhere, S., Patil, V.T., Sural, S., Gaur, M.S. (eds.) ICISS 2020. LNCS, vol. 12553, pp. 23–44. Springer, Cham (2020). https://doi.org/10.1007/978-3-030-65610-2_2
8. Benkaouz, Y., Erradi, M., Freisleben, B.: Work in progress: K-nearest neighbors techniques for ABAC policies clustering. In: Proceedings of the 2016 ACM International Workshop on Attribute Based Access Control, pp. 72–75 (2016)
9. Sanders, M.W., Yue, C.: Mining least privilege attribute based access control policies. In: Proceedings of the 35th Annual Computer Security Applications Conference, pp. 404–416 (2019)

10. Liang, D., Charlin, L., McInerney, J., Blei, D.M.: Modeling user exposure in recommendation. In: Proceedings of the 25th International Conference on World Wide Web, pp. 951–961 (2016)
11. Ding, J., et al.: Improving implicit recommender systems with view data. In: Proceedings of the 27th International Joint Conference on Artificial Intelligence, pp. 3343–3349 (2018)
12. He, X., Tang, J., Du, X., Hong, R., Ren, T., Chua, T.: Fast matrix factorization with nonuniform weights on missing data. IEEE Trans. Neural Netw. Learn. Syst. **31**, 2791–2804 (2020)
13. Koren, Y., Bell, R.: Advances in collaborative filtering. In: Ricci, F., Rokach, L., Shapira, B. (eds.) Recommender Systems Handbook, pp. 77–118. Springer, Boston (2015). https://doi.org/10.1007/978-1-4899-7637-6_3
14. Su, Z., Lin, Z., Ai, J., Li, H.: Rating prediction in recommender systems based on user behavior probability and complex network modeling. IEEE Access **9**, 30739–30749 (2021)
15. Yue, W., Wang, Z., Liu, W., Tian, B., Lauria, S., Liu, X.: An optimally weighted user- and item-based collaborative filtering approach to predicting baseline data for Friedreich's ataxia patients. Neurocomputing **419**, 287–294 (2021)
16. Ma, J., Zhang, Y., Zhang, L.: Discriminative subspace matrix factorization for multiview data clustering. Pattern Recognit. **111**, 107676 (2021)
17. Meng, Y., Shang, R., Shang, F., Jiao, L., Yang, S., Stolkin, R.: Semi-supervised graph regularized deep NMF with bi-orthogonal constraints for data representation. IEEE Trans. Neural Networks Learn. Syst. **31**(9), 3245–3258 (2020)
18. Ding, C.H.Q., Li, T., Jordan, M.I.: Convex and semi-nonnegative matrix factorizations. IEEE Trans. Pattern Anal. Mach. Intell. **32**(1), 45–55 (2010)
19. Funk, S.: Netflix update: Try this at home (2006). http://sifter.org/simon/journal/20061211.html
20. Koren, Y.: Factorization meets the neighborhood: a multifaceted collaborative filtering model. In: Proceedings of the 14th ACM SIGKDD International Conference on Knowledge Discovery and Data Mining, pp. 426–434 (2008)
21. Koren, Y.: Collaborative filtering with temporal dynamics. Commun. ACM **53**, 89–97 (2010)
22. Zheng, L., Noroozi, V., Yu, P.S.: Joint deep modeling of users and items using reviews for recommendation. In Proceedings of the Tenth ACM International Conference on Web Search and Data Mining, pp. 425–434 (2017)
23. Chen, C., Zhang, M., Liu, Y., Ma, S.: Neural attentional rating regression with review-level explanations. In: Proceedings of the 2018 World Wide Web Conference, pp. 1583–1592 (2018)
24. Liu, Z., Cao, Z., Wong, D.S.: Efficient generation of linear secret sharing scheme matrices from threshold access trees. IACR Cryptol. ePrint Arch., 2010:374 (2010)
25. Li, J., Yao, W., Han, J., Zhang, Y., Shen, J.: User collusion avoidance CP-ABE with efficient attribute revocation for cloud storage. IEEE Syst. J. **12**, 1767–1777 (2018)
26. Li, J., Wang, Y., Zhang, Y., Han, J.: Full verifiability for outsourced decryption in attribute based encryption. IEEE Trans. Serv. Comput. **13**, 478–487 (2020)
27. Phuong, T.V.X., Yang, G., Susilo, W.: Hidden ciphertext policy attribute-based encryption under standard assumptions. IEEE Trans. Inf. Forensics Secur. **11**, 35–45 (2016)
28. Zhang, J., Cheng, M., Wu, H., Zhou, B.: A new test for functional one-way ANOVA with applications to ischemic heart screening. Comput. Stat. Data Anal. **132**, 3–17 (2019)

Non-interactive Privacy-Preserving Naïve Bayes Classifier Using Homomorphic Encryption

Jingwei Chen[1,2], Yong Feng[1,2], Yang Liu[3(✉)], Wenyuan Wu[1,2],
and Guanci Yang[4]

[1] Chongqing Key Laboratory of Automated Reasoning and Cognition, Chongqing
Institute of Green and Intelligent Technology, Chinese Academy of Sciences,
Chongqing, China
{chenjingwei,yongfeng,wuwenyuan}@cigit.ac.cn
[2] Chongqing College, University of Chinese Academy of Sciences, Chongqing, China
[3] Information Science and Engineering, Chongqing Jiaotong University,
Chongqing, China
liuyang13@cqjtu.edu.cn
[4] Key Laboratory of Advanced Manufacturing Technology of Ministry of Education,
Guizhou University, Guiyang, China
guanci_yang@163.com

Abstract. In this paper, we propose a privacy-preserving naive Bayes
classifier based on a leveled homomorphic encryption scheme due to
Brakerski-Gentry-Vaikuntanuthan (BGV). The classifier runs on a server
that is also the owner of the model, with input as BGV encrypted data
from a client. The classifier produces encrypted classification results
which can only be decrypted by the client, whereas the model is only
accessible to the server itself. This ensures that the classifier does not
leak any private information on either the model of the server or the
data and results of the client. More importantly, the classifier does not
require any interaction between the server and the client during the
classification phase. The main technical ingredient is an algorithm to
compute the index of the maximum of an encrypted array homomorphically, which does not require any interaction. The proposed classifier
is implemented using a homomorphic encryption library HElib. Preliminary experiments demonstrate the efficiency and accuracy of the proposed privacy-preserving naive Bayes classifier.

Keywords: Privacy-preserving data mining · Homomorphic
encryption · Naïve Bayes classifier

This research was supported in part by National Key R&D Program of China
(2020YFA0712303), NSFC (61903053), Guizhou Science and Technology Program
[2020]4Y056, Chongqing Science and Technology Program (cstc2021jcyj-msxmX0821,
cstc2018jcyj-yszxX0002, cstc2019yszx-jcyjX0003, cstc2020yszx-jcyjX0005, cstc2021
yszx-jcyjX0004, KJQN201900702), and Youth Innovation Promotion Association of
CAS (2018419).

1   Introduction

Over the past decade, Machine Learning as a Service (MLaaS) has been involved in various fields, from academia to industry. A typical application scenario is that the model vendor uses a large amount of user data to train the model and then uses the trained model to infer/predict some results based on data supplied by clients. However, as security incidents such as data breaches continue to occur, the demand for privacy-preserving MLaaS is rapidly increasing. On the one hand, the model owner is unwilling to leak information about the model. On the other hand, the data owner is reluctant to leak information about the data as well. To resolve this contradiction, privacy-preserving machine learning is proposed.

In this paper, we consider the framework presented in [2] for privacy-preserving classifiers. As shown in Fig. 1, each shaded box indicates private data that should be accessible to only one party: the model to the server, and the data and prediction result to the client. In particular, we present a privacy-preserving naïve Bayes classifier (Protocol 1) based on a leveled homomorphic encryption (LHE) scheme BGV [4], which is based on R-LWE [20] and hence thought to be post-quantum safe, and which allows us to evaluate functions with a bounded multiplicative depth on encrypted data.

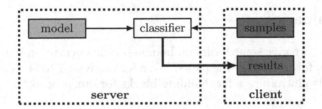

Fig. 1. Framework of privacy-preserving classifiers

In Protocol 1, the data owner (client) encrypts its data x to be predicted as a ciphertext c and sends c to the model owner (server). After receiving the ciphertext c, the server evaluates the model using the client's public key, with the input as the encrypted data c. The server sends the resulting ciphertext to the client, and the client decrypts the ciphertext using itself's secret key to specify in which class x lies. Thanks to an algorithm to compute a ciphertext of the index of the maximum of an encrypted array (Algorithm 3), no interaction between the client and the server happens during the classification phase (Step 3–6 in Protocol 1). This is one of the most important feature of our classifier.

In Sect. 2, we give a brief introduction to homomorphic encryption and present several building blocks for our classifier, including the main technical ingredient, Algorithm 3. In Sect. 3, we propose a privacy-preserving naïve Bayes classifier and prove its correctness and its security in the passive (or honest-but-curious [13]) model. In Sect. 4, we report some preliminary experimental results based on our implementation of Protocol 1.

Related Work. It seems to be impossible to list all literature on privacy-preserving protocols for classifiers. We refer to [2, Sec. II] for a good survey. Here we focus mainly on those privacy-preserving naïve Bayes classifiers based on homomorphic encryption (HE).

Naïve Bayes classifiers is a simple but powerful algorithm to predict the category label of unclassified samples; see, e.g., [7]. Bost *et al.* proposed in [2, Sec. VI] the first efficient privacy-preserving protocols for naïve Bayes classifier based on the Paillier encryption scheme [21], which would be broken by quantum attackers. Li *et al.* proposed in [18] a secure naïve Bayes classifier for four parties. Later on, Kim *et al.* [17] adapted Li *et al.*'s framework using the HE scheme BGV. Yasumura *et al.* [25] and Sun *et al.* [23] also give privacy-preserving protocols for naïve Bayes classification based on BGV. All of these privacy-preserving naïve Bayes classifiers require interaction between participants. During the classification phase, Protocol 1 presented in this paper does not require interaction at all. Furthermore, being different from those protocols based on the Paillier scheme, our protocol is post-quantum safe because of the post-quantum safe BGV.

2 Preliminaries

In this section, we give some basics on homomorphic encryption schemes, which will be helpful for the rest of the paper. We refer the reader to [4,11,14] for more details. We also introduce a few building blocks for our protocol.

2.1 Homomorphic Encryption

A *homomorphic encryption* (HE) scheme is composed of four algorithms: KeyGen, Enc, Dec and Eval. Given a security parameter λ as input, KeyGen outputs a secret key sk, a public key pk, and an evaluation key ek. The encryption algorithm encrypts a plaintext b to a ciphertext $c \leftarrow \mathsf{Enc}_{\mathsf{pk}}(b)$, and the decryption algorithm decrypts a ciphertext c to a plaintext $b := \mathsf{Dec}_{\mathsf{sk}}(c)$. The evaluation algorithm evaluates a function of f on a ciphertext $c = \mathsf{Enc}_{\mathsf{pk}}(b)$ to a new ciphertext $c' \leftarrow \mathsf{Eval}_{\mathsf{ek}}(f, c)$ satisfying $\mathsf{Dec}_{\mathsf{sk}}(c') = f(b)$. For convenience, we call f an *HE function*.

For almost all known HE schemes, every ciphertext has noise, and every operation on ciphertext introduces noise in the resulting ciphertext. A *Leveled* HE (LHE) scheme allows to evaluate any HE function f with bounded number of arithmetic/boolean operations. Beyond this bound, such an LHE scheme cannot correctly decrypt the ciphertext since the accumulated noise is too large. Contrarily, if an HE scheme supports to evaluate an arbitrary computable function, then it is called a *fully homomorphic encryption* (FHE) scheme, which depends on the so-called *bootstrapping* technique [12] to reduce noise.

Since Gentry's seminal work [12], multiple HE schemes have been designed, such as BGV [4], BFV [3,10], CKKS [5], FHEW [9], TFHE [6]. Each of them has its features. For instance, BGV and BFV are good at performing large vectorial arithmetic operations, CKKS supports floating-point computations and FHEW and TFHE run bootstrapping for one bit extremely fast but slow for arithmetic operations. Since naïve Bayes classifiers require many integer arithmetic operations, and as reported in [1,19] that BGV is faster than BFV, especially for cases with large modulus, we choose an LHE variant of the BGV scheme, which will be introduced in the next subsection.

2.2 The BGV Scheme

For completeness, we give a brief description of a variant of BGV that is implemented in HElib [15].

- Setup(1^λ). Given a security parameter λ as input, set an integer m (that defines the m-th cyclotomic polynomial $\Phi_m(x)$), a prime number p (the plaintext space is $R_p = \mathbb{Z}_p[x]/\langle\Phi_m(x)\rangle$), an odd modulus q (the ciphertext space is $R_q = \mathbb{Z}_q[x]/\langle\Phi_m(x)\rangle$), and a noise distribution χ over R_q. Output $params = (m, p, q, \chi)$.
- KeyGen($params$). Sample $s \leftarrow \chi$. Let $\boldsymbol{s} = (1, s) \in R_q^2$. Set sk $= \boldsymbol{s}$. Generate $a \leftarrow R_q$ uniformly at random and a column vector with "small" coefficients $e \leftarrow \chi$. Set $b = a \cdot s + p \cdot e$. Output sk $= \boldsymbol{s}$ and the public key $\boldsymbol{a} = (b, -a)$.
- Enc($params$, pk, b). To encrypt a message $b \in R_p$, set $\boldsymbol{m} = (b, 0) \in R_p^2$, sample a polynomimal $r \leftarrow R$ with small coefficients and output the ciphertext $\boldsymbol{c} = \boldsymbol{m} + r\boldsymbol{a} \in R_q^2$.
- Dec($params$, sk, $\boldsymbol{c}$). Output the message $b = [[\langle \boldsymbol{c}, \boldsymbol{s} \rangle]_q]_p$.

The quantity $\langle \boldsymbol{c}, \boldsymbol{s} \rangle$ is called the *noise* of the ciphertext $\boldsymbol{c}$ under the secret key $\boldsymbol{s}$. Decryption works correctly only if the noise does not wrap around modulo q. If it is the case, the correctness follows from $[[\langle \boldsymbol{c}, \boldsymbol{s} \rangle]_q]_p = [[\langle \boldsymbol{m} + r\boldsymbol{a}, \boldsymbol{s} \rangle]_q]_p = [b + p \cdot re]_p = b$. The security is based on the Ring-LWE assumption [20], which is thought to resist attacks from quantum computers.

Homomorphic Evaluation. The BGV scheme supports homomorphic addition and multiplication. Let $\boldsymbol{c}_1$ and $\boldsymbol{c}_2$ be two ciphertexts of two plaintexts b_1 and b_2 under the same secret key $\boldsymbol{s}$. Suppose that the noise of $\boldsymbol{c}_1$ and $\boldsymbol{c}_2$ is bounded from above by B. The addition (BGV.Add) of the two ciphertexts is simply $\boldsymbol{c}_+ = \boldsymbol{c}_1 + \boldsymbol{c}_2$, which is a ciphertext of $b_1 + b_2$ under the secret key $\boldsymbol{s}$. The noise of $\boldsymbol{c}_+$ is at most $2B$. For multiplication (BGV.Mul), $\boldsymbol{c}_\times = \boldsymbol{c}_1 \otimes \boldsymbol{c}_2$ is a ciphertext of $b_1 \cdot b_2$ under a new secret key $\boldsymbol{s} \otimes \boldsymbol{s}$, where $\otimes$ is the usual tensor product. The noise of $\boldsymbol{c}_\times$ can only be bounded from above by B^2. To keep the secret key with small size and to decrease the noise of evaluated ciphertext, a refresh procedure BGV.Refresh (consisting of key switching and modulus switching) follows every homomorphic addition and multiplication. Of course, one can call BGV.Refresh only if necessary for efficiency. Note that the public key pk of BGV also includes all keys for BGV.Refresh. Theoretically, the cost of each homomorphic addition or multiplication increases fast as L grows, where L is the circuit depth of the function f to be evaluated; see, e.g., [4] for more details. Besides, BGV also supports plaintext-ciphertext addition (BGV.AddConst) and plaintext-ciphertext multiplication (BGV.MulConst).

Batching. Recall the plaintext space $R_p = \mathbb{Z}_p[x]/\langle \Phi_m(X) \rangle$. Let d be the multiplicative order of p modulo m, and $\phi(m)$ be the Euler's totient function. Then d divides $\phi(m)$ and $R_p \cong \mathbb{F}_{p^d}^\ell$ with $\ell = \phi(m)/d$. Therefore each plaintext can be seen as a packed message with ℓ slots. From this view, each homomorphic operation on a ciphertext is equivalent to the same operation on all slots independently and simultaneously. This batching technique was introduced by Smart and Vercauteren in [22] and significantly decreased the amortized cost of Ring-LWE based HE schemes. For batching, BGV supports data packing (BGV.Encode), data rotating (BGV.Rotate), and data shifting (BGV.Shift). Based on these operations, one can build some advanced functions. For instance, BGV.TotalSum converts a ciphertext that encrypts $(z_1, \cdots, z_t)$ into a ciphertext that encrypts $(y, \cdots, y)$ with $y = \sum_{i=1}^t z_i$.

2.3   Building Blocks

We now describe a few necessary building blocks that will be used to build our classifier. Note that all the following algorithms will be executed on the server and that the owner of pk (the public key) in these algorithms is the client, not the server since we follow the framework given in Fig. 1.

Plaintext Matrix-Encrypted Vector Multiplication. Matrix-vector multiplication is fairly common in practice. Here we focus on plaintext matrix-encrypted vector multiplication. Given a matrix $A \in \mathbb{Z}^{s \times t}$ and an encryption of a vector $z \in \mathbb{Z}^t$, our goal is to obtain an encryption of Az. We give two methods based on different method to encrypt a vector.

Naïve Encoding. To encrypt a vector $z = (z_i)_{i \leq t} \in \mathbb{Z}^t$, one can encrypt each entry z_i of z as a ciphertext. The resulting encryption of z is a vector $c = (c_i)_{i \leq t} \in R_q^t$ of ciphertexts, whose i-th entry c_i is a ciphertext of z_i. Then we have Algorithm 1.

Input: $c' = (c'_i)_{i \leq t} \in R_q^t$ (c'_i encrypts the ith entry of $z = (z_i)_{i \leq t}$), and public key pk;
    $A = (a_{i,j}) \in \mathbb{Z}^{s \times t}$.
Output: $(c_i)_{i \leq s}$ with $c_i = \mathsf{Enc}_{\mathsf{pk}}(\sum_{j=1}^t a_{i,j} z_j)$.
1: For $i = 1, \cdots, s$ do the following:
2:    $c_i \leftarrow \mathsf{Enc}_{\mathsf{pk}}(0)$;
3:    For $j = 1, \cdots, t$, update $c_i := \mathsf{Add}_{\mathsf{pk}}(c_i, \mathsf{MulConst}_{\mathsf{pk}}(a_{i,j}, c'_j))$.
4: **return** $(c_i)_{i \leq s}$.

Algorithm 1: Naïve plaintext matrix-encrypted vector multiplication

Packed Encoding. Instead of the above elements-wise method, we can pack the vector $z \in \mathbb{Z}^t$ into t slots of one plaintext, and encrypt it to only one ciphertext $c \in R_q$, which leads to Algorithm 2.

Input: $c \in R_q$ that encrypts $u \in R_p$ with $u = \mathsf{Encode}(z)$, and public key pk; $A = (a_{i,j}) \in \mathbb{Z}^{s \times t}$.
Output: $(c_i)_{i \leq s}$ with $c_i = \mathsf{Enc}_{\mathsf{pk}}(\sum_{j=1}^{t} a_{i,j} z_j)$.
  1: For $i = 1, \cdots, s$ do the following:
  2:     Encodes the i-th row a_i of A as $v_i = \mathsf{Encode}(a_i)$;
  3:     Computes $c_i = \mathsf{TotalSum}_{\mathsf{pk}}(\mathsf{MulConst}_{\mathsf{pk}}(v_i, c)))$.
  4: **return** $(c_i)_{i \leq s}$.

Algorithm 2: Pakced plaintext matrix-encrypted vector multiplication

Comparison among Encrypted Integers. Comparison is a commonly used function in many applications. In this work, we use a very recent comparator presented by Iliashenko and Zucca in [16], which supports comparison operations for BGV (BGV.Comparator). Essentially, this method homomorphically evaluates the Lagrange interpolated polynomial of the less-than function over $S = [0, (p-1)/2]$ defined as follows:

$$\mathsf{LT}_S(x,y) = \begin{cases} 1, & \text{if } 0 \leq x < y \leq (p-1)/2, \\ 0, & \text{if } 0 \leq y \leq x \leq (p-1)/2. \end{cases}$$

Input: $c = (c_0, \cdots, c_{t-1}) \in R_q^t$ (c_i encrypts the ith entry of $z = (z_0, \cdots, z_{t-1})$) and public key pk.
Output: A ciphertext $c \in R_q$ that encrypts the index of the maximal value of z.
  1: Set $c \leftarrow \mathsf{Enc}_{\mathsf{pk}}(0)$. For $i = 0, \cdots, t-1$ do the following:
  2:     Compute $c' := \prod_{k=0, k \neq j}^{t-1} \mathsf{AddConst}_{\mathsf{pk}}(1, \mathsf{MulConst}_{\mathsf{pk}}(-1, \mathsf{Comparator}_{\mathsf{pk}}(c_j, c_k)))$.
  3:     Update $c := \mathsf{Add}_{\mathsf{pk}}(c, \mathsf{MulConst}_{\mathsf{pk}}(j, c'))$.
  4: **return** c.

Algorithm 3: Encrypted index of maximum of an encrypted array

Furthermore, one can apply the less-than function LT to compute the arg max function of an encrypted array, where the arg max function returns an encryption of the index of the maximum of an array. As a matter of fact, for a given array $z = (z_0, \cdots, z_{t-1})$, we have

$$\arg \max_i (z_i)_{0 \leq i \leq t-1} = \sum_{j=0}^{t-1} j \cdot \prod_{k=0, k \neq j}^{t-1} (1 - \mathsf{LT}(z_j, z_k)),$$

which results in Algorithm 3. Note that one would better use some recursive methods in practice to compute the encrypted product in Step 2 of Algorithm 3 for saving multiplicative depth.

3   Privacy-Preserving Naïve Bayes Classification

In this section, we first introduce the plaintext Naïve Bayes Classifier, and then adapt the classifier to the privacy-preserving setup and prove its correctness and security.

3.1   Naïve Bayes Classifier

Naïve Bayes classifier is based on the assumption that all features are conditional independent. Consider a data set with s categories $1, \cdots, s$ and n features $X_1, \cdots, X_n$, where each feature X_k has at most t different values $1, 2, \cdots, t$. Under the conditional independence assumption, the classification of a sample $\boldsymbol{x} = (x_1, \cdots, x_n)$ is

$$s^* = \arg \max_{i=1,\ldots,s} \Pr[Y = i] \prod_{k=1}^{n} \Pr[X_k = x_k | Y = i],$$

where $\Pr[Y = i]$ is the probability that each class i occurs, i.e., the *prior probability*, and $\Pr[X_k = x_k | Y = i]$ is the probability of the kth feature X_k to be $x_k \in \{1, 2, \cdots, t\}$ when $\boldsymbol{x}$ belongs to category i, i.e., the *likelihood*. As in [2], we only deal with the case that the domain of the feature values (the x_i's) is discrete and finite, so the $\Pr[X_k = x_k | Y = i]$'s are probability masses.

3.2   Preparing the Model

If the domain of the feature values is continuous, we first find a bound B on the values and then discretize them by splitting $[-B, B]$ into several equal intervals. For example, if the domain of the kth feature X_k is continuous on $[-1, 1]$, then one can discretize X_k as $X_k = 0$ if $X_k \in [-1, 0)$ and $X_k = 1$ if $X_k \in [0, 1]$. This discretization technique enables our classifier to deal with continuous features as well, possibly at the cost of decreasing the prediction accuracy.

For convenience, we can further simplify the feature values $x_1, \cdots, x_n$ to $1, \cdots, t$. Furthermore, for numerical stability, we work with the logarithm of the probability:

$$s^* = \arg \max_{i=1,\ldots,s} \left\{ \log \Pr[Y = i] + \sum_{k=1}^{n} \log \Pr[X_k = x_k | Y = i] \right\}, \qquad (1)$$

where $x_k \in \{1, \cdots, t\}$. Another convenient simplification is to take the numbering of the s classes as contiguous integers from 1 to s. Then s^* is precisely the index of the maximum over the s values in (1).

Additionally, since the BGV encryption scheme works with integers, one needs to convert each logarithm of probability in (1) to an integer by multiplying it with a certain number $K > 0$ and rounding it to the closest integer. A similar *shifting* technique is already used and analyzed in, e.g., [2,24].

In summary, for a data set with s categories and n features (each feature has at most t different values), the prior probability in the model will be converted into a vector $\boldsymbol{b} = (b_1, \cdots, b_s) \in \mathbb{Z}^s$, where b_i is obtained by rounding $K \cdot \log(\Pr[Y = i])$ for an appropriate scaling integer K. The likelihoods will be converted into n matrices $\boldsymbol{A}_k \in \mathbb{Z}^{s \times t}$ for $k = 1, \cdots, n$, where the (i, j)-entry of $\boldsymbol{A}_k$ is derived by rounding $K \cdot \log \Pr[X_k = j | Y = i]$ with the same integer K.

3.3 Privacy-Preserving Naïve Bayes Classifier

To resolve the privacy concerns, the client should only obtain the classification result s^* without learning any information about the prior probability and likelihood, and the server should learn nothing about the client's data $\boldsymbol{x}$.

The client has data $\boldsymbol{x} = (x_1, \cdots, x_n)$ with $x_k \in \{1, \cdots, t\}$ and wants the server to predict which class $\boldsymbol{x}$ is in by using a naïve Bayes classifier without leaking any information about $\boldsymbol{x}$. One choice of the client is to encrypt $\boldsymbol{x}$ using himself's public key. However, since $\boldsymbol{x}$ is encrypted, the server cannot decide which entry of $\boldsymbol{A}_k$ should be chosen. For instance, the first feature of $\boldsymbol{x}$ is x_1, i.e., $X_1 = x_1$. To access the information about $\Pr[X_1 = x_1 | Y = i]$ in $\boldsymbol{A}_1$, we need to select the (i, x_1) entry of $\boldsymbol{A}_1$. However, as the first entry of $\boldsymbol{x}$, x_1 is only available in encrypted form on the server-side. To get around this obstacle, one can encode the sample $\boldsymbol{x}$ as a 0-1 matrix

$$X = (\boldsymbol{e}_{x_1}, \cdots, \boldsymbol{e}_{x_n}) \in \{0, 1\}^{t \times n}, \tag{2}$$

where $\boldsymbol{e}_j$ is the t-dimensional vector whose jth entry is 1 and all others are 0. Now, to select the x_k-th row of a matrix $\boldsymbol{A}_k \subset \mathbb{Z}^{s \times t}$ is just to compute $\boldsymbol{A}_k \boldsymbol{e}_{x_k}$. If $\boldsymbol{e}_{x_k}$ is in encrypted form, then this is a plaintext matrix-encrypted vector multiplication discussed in Sect. 2.3.

Now we are ready to present our privacy-preserving naïve Bayes classifier as Protocol 1, which does not require any interaction between the server and the client during the classification phase (Step 3–6).

We prove the security of our protocol using the secure two-party computation framework for passive adversaries. Roughly speaking, a passive adversary tries to learn as much private information from the other party; however, this adversary follows the prescribed protocol faithfully.

Proposition 1. *Protocol 1 is correct. It is secure in the honest-but-curious model, assuming that the used LHE scheme is secure.*

Input of the client: A sample $x = (x_1, \cdots, x_n)$ to be predicted, the secret and public key sk and pk.

Input of the server: The model consisting of the likelihood information $(A_k)_{k \leq n}$ and the prior information $(b_i)_{i \leq s}$, and the client's public key pk.

1: The client encode x to a matrix X as in (2).
2: The client encrypts the column vectors e_{x_k} of X for $k = 1, \cdots, n$ and sends these ciphertexts to the server.
3: The server do the following:
4:    For $i = 1, \cdots, s$, set $c_i \leftarrow \mathsf{Enc}_{pk}(0)$ and update $c_i := \mathsf{AddConst}_{pk}(c_i, b_i)$.
5:    For $k = 1, \cdots, n$, calling Algorithm 1 or 2 with input as the ciphertexts of e_{x_k}, A_k and pk outputs $(c_i')_{i \leq s}$. Update $c_i := \mathsf{Add}_{pk}(c_i, c_i')$ for $i = 1, \cdots, s$.
6:    Calling Algorithm 3 with input as $c = (c_i)_{i \leq s}$ and pk returns c.
7: The server sends c to the client.
8: The client decrypt c to $y = \mathsf{Dec}_{sk}(c)$.

Protocol 1: Privacy-preserving naïve Bayes classifier

Proof (Sketch). The correctness follows from that what the server does is to evaluate the following procedure homomorphically:

1: Set $y := b$, the information of the prior probability.
2: For $k = 1, \cdots, n$, set $y := y + A_k \cdot e_{x_k}$.
3: **return** y as the index of the maximum of $y = (y_i)_{0 \leq i \leq s-1}$.

From the server-side, the only message received is an encryption of the client's data x , and the only message sent to the client is a ciphertext of the prediction result. From the client-side, x is encrypted, the classification result is also encrypted, and the model is not accessible. So the security of Protocol 1 follows from that of the used LHE scheme.   □

4   Experiments

We have implemented Protocol 1 in C++ using HElib (v2.1.0) [15]. In this section, we will report the prediction accuracy and calculation time of our implementation. All experiments run serially (using only one thread) on a laptop with a Ubuntu 20.04 OS as Windows Subsystem for Linux, Intel i7-10750H CPU, and 16 GB RAM.

Data Set. In this experiment, Wisconsin Breast Cancer (WBC) data set in UCI Machine Learning Repository [8] was used. The dataset has 683 effective samples, classified into two categories, i.e., $s = 2$. There are nine features for each sample, and each feature may take at most ten different values, i.e., $n = 9$ and $t = 10$. Among these 683 samples, 478 samples are used for training (70%), and the remaining 205 samples are used to test.

Parameter Setting. For WBC, the scaling factor K in Sect. 3.2 is set to 1. This leads that the entries of the rounded logarithm of likelihood A_k for $k = 1, \cdots, n$ are integers between -6 and 0, and the entries of the rounded logarithm of the prior probability b are bounded by 2. Hence the resulting integers to be compared must be at most $6n + 2 = 54$, which implies that $p = 113$ is enough for our purpose. In addition, m is fixed to 12883. In this setting, each plaintext in R_p has $\ell = 3960$ slots.

Accuracy. According to our experiments, the classification accuracy of our implementation of Protocol 1 based on HElib is about 97%. Note that this accuracy is almost the same as the plaintext (unencrypted) naïve Bayes classifier.

Timing. In Step 5 of Protocol 1, there are two choices (Algorithm 1 and Algorithm 2) for plaintext matrix-encrypted vector multiplication. We test them all and record their performance in Table 1. The row named "naïve" ("packed" resp.) is the performance of Protocol 1 based on Algorithm 1 (Algorithm 2 resp.). The columns with "Ave." is the average execution time for each sample. Table 1 shows that the naïve variant outperforms the packed variant. For comparison, Kim *et al.* [17] reported that their proposed privacy-preserving naïve Bayes classifier takes 17h40m on a single core for the Iris data set ($s = 3$, $n = 4$, $t = 5$, 30 samples to be classified) of UCI Machine Learning Repository [8].

Table 1. Performance of two variants of Protocol 1

	$\log q$	λ	Compare (s)	Total (s)	Ave. Compare (s)	Ave. Total (s)
Naïve	382	101	387.90	985.31	1.89	4.75
Packed	476	76	369.95	1931.60	1.75	9.42

5 Conclusion

In this paper, we attempt to design privacy-preserving classifier protocols in the client-server setting. The server owns the model, which should not be accessible to any other, and the client also needs to preserve the privacy of the data to be predicted. As a result, we propose a privacy-preserving naïve Bayes classifier (Protocol 1) based on the LHE scheme BGV. We show that the classifier is correct and secure in the honest-but-curious model. The main feature of our classifier is that it does not require any interaction between the client and the server during the classification phase. We are considering how to use SIMD to accelerate the classifier and experiment with more data sets. In addition, how to optimize the performance further using, e.g., parallel computing, is also an interesting problem.

References

1. Aguilar Melchor, C., Kilijian, M.-O., Lefebvre, C., Ricosset, T.: A comparison of the homomorphic encryption libraries HElib, SEAL and FV-NFLlib. In: Lanet, J.-L., Toma, C. (eds.) SECITC 2018. LNCS, vol. 11359, pp. 425–442. Springer, Cham (2019). https://doi.org/10.1007/978-3-030-12942-2_32

2. Bost, R., Popa, R.A., Tu, S., Goldwasser, S.: Machine learning classification over encrypted data. In: Proceedings of the 22nd Annual Network and Distributed System Security Symposium, San Diego USA, 8–11 February 2015. The Internet Society (2015). https://doi.org/10.14722/ndss.2015.23241

3. Brakerski, Z.: Fully homomorphic encryption without modulus switching from classical GapSVP. In: Safavi-Naini, R., Canetti, R. (eds.) CRYPTO 2012. LNCS, vol. 7417, pp. 868–886. Springer, Heidelberg (2012). https://doi.org/10.1007/978-3-642-32009-5_50

4. Brakerski, Z., Gentry, C., Vaikuntanathan, V.: (Leveled) fully homomorphic encryption without bootstrapping. ACM Trans. Comput. Theory 6(3), 13:1–13:36 (2014). https://doi.org/10.1145/2633600

5. Cheon, J.H., Kim, A., Kim, M., Song, Y.: Homomorphic encryption for arithmetic of approximate numbers. In: Takagi, T., Peyrin, T. (eds.) ASIACRYPT 2017. LNCS, vol. 10624, pp. 409–437. Springer, Cham (2017). https://doi.org/10.1007/978-3-319-70694-8_15

6. Chillotti, I., Gama, N., Georgieva, M., Izabachène, M.: TFHE: fast fully homomorphic encryption over the torus. J. Cryptol. 33(1), 34–91 (2019). https://doi.org/10.1007/s00145-019-09319-x

7. Domingos, P., Pazzani, M.: On the optimality of the simple Bayesian classifier under zero-one loss. Mach. Learn. 29(2), 103–130 (1997). https://doi.org/10.1023/A:1007413511361

8. Dua, D., Graff, C.: UCI machine learning repository (2017). http://archive.ics.uci.edu/ml

9. Ducas, L., Micciancio, D.: FHEW: bootstrapping homomorphic encryption in less than a second. In: Oswald, E., Fischlin, M. (eds.) EUROCRYPT 2015. LNCS, vol. 9056, pp. 617–640. Springer, Heidelberg (2015). https://doi.org/10.1007/978-3-662-46800-5_24

10. Fan, J., Vercauteren, F.: Somewhat practical fully homomorphic encryption. Cryptology ePrint Archive (2012). https://eprint.iacr.org/2012/144

11. Gentry, C.: A fully homomorphic encryption scheme. Ph.D. thesis, Stanford University, Stanford (2009). https://crypto.stanford.edu/craig/craig-thesis.pdf

12. Gentry, C.: Fully homomorphic encryption using ideal lattices. In: Mitzenmacher, M. (ed.) Proceedings of the Forty-First Annual ACM Symposium on Theory of Computing, Bethesda, USA, 31 May–2 June 2009, pp. 169–178. ACM, New York (2009). https://doi.org/10.1145/1536414.1536440

13. Goldreich, O.: Foundations of Cryptography - Basic Applications. Cambridge University Press, Cambridge (2004)

14. Halevi, S., Shoup, V.: Design and implementation of HElib: a homomorphic encryption library. Cryptology ePrint Archive (2020). https://eprint.iacr.org/2020/1481

15. HElib: An implementation of homomorphic encryption. https://github.com/homenc/HElib. Accessed Aug 2021

16. Iliashenko, I., Zucca, V.: Faster homomorphic comparison operations for BGV and BFV. Proc. Priv. Enhancing Technol. 2021(3), 246–264 (2021). https://doi.org/10.2478/popets-2021-0046

17. Kim, S., Omori, M., Hayashi, T., Omori, T., Wang, L., Ozawa, S.: Privacy-preserving Naive Bayes classification using fully homomorphic encryption. In: Cheng, L., Leung, A.C.S., Ozawa, S. (eds.) ICONIP 2018. LNCS, vol. 11304, pp. 349–358. Springer, Cham (2018). https://doi.org/10.1007/978-3-030-04212-7_30

18. Li, X., Zhu, Y., Wang, J.: Secure Naïve Bayesian classification over encrypted data in cloud. In: Chen, L., Han, J. (eds.) ProvSec 2016. LNCS, vol. 10005, pp. 130–150. Springer, Cham (2016). https://doi.org/10.1007/978-3-319-47422-9_8

19. Lou, Q., Feng, B., Fox, G.C., Jiang, L.: Glyph: fast and accurately training deep neural networks on encrypted data. In: Larochelle, H., Ranzato, M., Hadsell, R., Balcan, M., Lin, H. (eds.) Proceedings of NeurIPS 2020, 34th Conference on Neural Information Processing Systems, Vancouver, Canada, NeurIPS (2020). https://proceedings.neurips.cc/paper/2020/hash/685ac8cadc1be5ac98da9556bc1c8d9e-Abstract.html

20. Lyubashevsky, V., Peikert, C., Regev, O.: On ideal lattices and learning with errors over rings. J. ACM 60(6), 43:1–35 (2013). https://doi.org/10.1145/2535925

21. Paillier, P.: Public-key cryptosystems based on composite degree residuosity classes. In: Stern, J. (ed.) EUROCRYPT 1999. LNCS, vol. 1592, pp. 223–238. Springer, Heidelberg (1999). https://doi.org/10.1007/3-540-48910-X_16

22. Smart, N.P., Vercauteren, F.: Fully homomorphic SIMD operations. Des. Codes Crypt. 71(1), 57–81 (2012). https://doi.org/10.1007/s10623-012-9720-4

23. Sun, X., Zhang, P., Liu, J.K., Yu, J., Xie, W.: Private machine learning classification based on fully homomorphic encryption. IEEE Trans. Emerg. Top. Comput. 8(2), 352–364 (2020). https://doi.org/10.1109/TETC.2018.2794611

24. Tschiatschek, S., Reinprecht, P., Mücke, M., Pernkopf, F.: Bayesian network classifiers with reduced precision parameters. In: Flach, P.A., De Bie, T., Cristianini, N. (eds.) ECML PKDD 2012. LNCS (LNAI), vol. 7523, pp. 74–89. Springer, Heidelberg (2012). https://doi.org/10.1007/978-3-642-33460-3_10

25. Yasumura, Y., Ishimaki, Y., Yamana, H.: Secure naïve Bayes classification protocol over encrypted data using fully homomorphic encryption. In: Indrawan-Santiago, M., Pardede, E., Salvadori, I.L., Steinbauer, M., Khalil, I., Anderst-Kotsis, G. (eds.) Proceedings of the 21st International Conference on Information Integration and Web-Based Applications & Services, Munich, Germany, 2–4 December 2019, pp. 45–54. ACM, New York (2019). https://doi.org/10.1145/3366030.3366056

BA-Audit: Blockchain-Based Public Auditing for Aggregated Data Sharing in Edge-Assisted IoT

Mingxi Liu[1], Ning Lu[1,2], Jingli Yin[1], Qingfeng Cheng[3,4], and Wenbo Shi[1(✉)]

[1] School of Computer Science and Engineering, Northeastern University, Shenyang, China
shiwb@neuq.edu.cn
[2] School of Computer Science and Technology, Xidian University, Xi'an, China
[3] State Key Laboratory of Mathematical Engineering and Advanced Computing, Zhengzhou, China
[4] Strategic Support Force Information Engineering University, Zhengzhou, China

Abstract. With the massive placement of sensors leading to a surge in IoT data, it is wise for system administrators to use data aggregation strategies to collect and share data in edge-assisted IoT scenarios because traditional methods will exhaust bandwidth resources. Users need to verify the integrity of aggregated data to ensure security sharing. However, existing data auditing technologies are disabled because aggregate data has no metadata. This paper proposes a blockchain-based auditing scheme for aggregated data to achieve efficient and secure data sharing. First, we design a hash index balanced tree (HIBT) to reduce the computational expense of signature retrieval. Then, we propose an audit protocol to protect aggregated data immutability. Also, we provide security and performance analysis at the end of the paper.

Keywords: Data auditing · Blockchain · Data aggregation · Edge-assisted IoT

1 Introduction

The structure of Edge-assisted IoT strengthens the management capabilities for sensors by deploying edge servers close to them, which lead to explosive growth of IoT data [1]. For example, in 2025, the size of wearable devices data is up to 463 EB per day [2]. Massive sensing data is valuable for sharing. Cloud infrastructures are seem as sharing platform because hosting data to cloud is a economic option for owner application (OA). Using data aggregation technology to preprocess uploaded data can deplete the communication burden about uploading all these data to the cloud [3]. However, the absence of safety mechanisms has left

---

L. Ning—Co-first author.

W. Shi et al. (Eds.): SPNCE 2021, LNICST 423, pp. 204–218, 2022.
https://doi.org/10.1007/978-3-030-96791-8_15

such measures at the conceptual stage. Although the blockchain techniques can be used as shared data bulletin boards, [4] due to its characteristics of public and immutability [4], the security of off-chain data cannot depend on the security of bulletin boards. Therefore, only using blockchain techniques cannot directly guarantee the security of shared data. We should fundamentally restructure the aggregated data integrity validation mechanism.

The cloud may cause data loss or tampering due to equipment failure, or hacker intrusion [5]. To maintain reputation, the cloud may send fake data to user applications (UA). Existing audit proposals can efficiently verify static data and support dynamic updates [6,7]. However, due to the particularity of the Edge-assisted IoT paradigm, existing proposals cannot be directly applied. First, the total amount of aggregated data increases over time and comes from multiple Edge nodes. If the data signature cannot be quickly indexed during the audit phase, the OA will question whether the system is unresponsive. The existing audit schemes based on an index can only deal with updates of a fixed amount of data and cannot provide efficient indexing in the face of incremental data. Second, due to the semi-trusted nature of edge nodes, the audit for aggregated data should ensure the original data security. The existing audit scheme only verifies aggregated data and cannot audit original data.

In this paper, we propose a blockchain-based aggregated data sharing audit framework to realize efficient and secure aggregated sharing. The incremental data-oriented signature index structure named hash index balance tree (HIBT) is proposed to improve the efficiency of signature retrieval. Based on the HIBT, an aggregated data integrity verification protocol is proposed. The main contributions of this paper are summarized as follows:

- **Aggregated data auditing framework:** Taking advantage of Edge-Assisted IoT, we use edge servers to aggregate data collected by IoT. An OA publishes information of aggregated data to the blockchain. When a UA puts forward data requirements, the OA feeds back the results of data verification.
- **Hash index balance tree:** We use the hash value of the aggregated data as the index label to re-establish the index order. We use the tree structure to improve the retrieval efficiency and use the dynamic adjustment strategy of the balanced binary tree to make the index structure stable.
- **Auditing protocol for aggregated data sharing:** The bilinear pairing technology is used to realize batch verification of signatures. Meanwhile, our auditing protocol can auditing the original data before aggregated by searching for the user's public key.

2 Related Works

Data aggregation technology was first applied to wireless sensor networks. Fan et al. proposed a privacy-preserving data aggregation (P2DA) scheme, which used homomorphic encryption technology and combines cryptographic techniques such as bilinear pairing and curve hashing to achieve ciphertext data aggregation and data signature verification [8]. However, because signatures cannot be verified in batches, frequent bilinear pairing operations make high time overhead. In this regard, He et al. proposed a novel P2DA scheme using Boneh-Goh-Nissim public-key cryptography, which realizes batch verification of ciphertext signatures and was highly efficient [9]. The above schemes are based on honest assumptions about the aggregation nodes. In actual deployment, the aggregator may tamper or inject wrong data to illegally manipulate the data results. Lu et al. proposed a data aggregation scheme that can authenticate the legitimacy of sensor nodes using hash chain technology to achieve the correctness of the data transmitted by IoT [10]. However, it cannot resist man-in-the-middle attacks because the hash chain can be forged. Asmaa et al. proposed a data aggregation scheme based on digital signatures, which assigns a private key to each IoT node, and verifies the signature according to the respective public key to achieve data integrity protection [11]. However, this scheme causes high communication overhead because IoT nodes are elected as aggregator nodes in turn. To reduce the communication overhead, Li et al. proposed a data aggregation scheme based on homomorphic verifiable signature [12]. It can detect the wrong aggregation results produced by the semi-honest aggregator. However, this solution cannot provide a verification mechanism when the OA tampered with the stored aggregated data. Therefore, the existing data aggregation proposals have not supported any effective integrity verification strategy for aggregated data.

Data auditing technology is generally geared towards cloud-stored data. Ari Juels et al. proposed the proofs of retrievability scheme for the first time. The cloud can prove that the outsourcing data is stored instantly [13]. However, this scheme introduces a large amount of computational overhead to realize data recovery. Giuseppe Ateniese et al. proposed a provable data possession scheme, which generates auditing evidence by sampling random data blocks [14]. But only a fixed data set can be audited. Wang et al. proposed a Merkle hash tree (MHT) based data integrity audit scheme [15]. This scheme introduces an MHT dynamic data structure to store data signatures. When an update request is received, the MHT is updated at the same time to realize the new signatures are auditable. However, the MHT root needs to be recalculated while updating, which is expensive. Tian et al. proposed a scheme based on the dynamic hash table (DHT) [16]. When facing data updates, only the DHT needs to be adjusted without verifying the legitimacy. However, the complexity of DHT retrieval is $O(n)$, which cannot carry incremental data input. To this end, we design an index structure based on red-black trees to improve the retrieval efficiency of UA signatures during audits. Then we introduce an aggregated data audit protocol that enables the UA to audit the integrity of aggregated data based on IoT public keys.

3   Preliminaries

This section introduces blockchain, red-black tree, and some cryptography techniques for constructing our proposal.

3.1 Blockchain

The blockchain technology is a novel distributed database that uses an orderly chained data structure to securely store data [17]. It integrates multiple technologies such as P2P protocols, consensus mechanisms, and blockchain structures and has the characteristics of storage decentralization and low conflict rate. And it uses cryptographic technologies such as asymmetric encryption and time stamping to make stored data consistent, traceable, undeniable, and immutably.

3.2 Red-Black Tree

A red-black tree is a specific type of self-balancing binary search tree [18]. The tree nodes have the color attribute, which is red or black. For the assignment of node colors, the following properties must be observed:

1. Each root node and empty leaf node are black.
2. All paths from any node to each leaf node should have the same number of black nodes.
3. All paths from each leaf node to the root node can't contain two consecutive red nodes, i.e., two nodes for each child node should be red black.

An example of red-black is shown in Fig. 1. The retrieval complexity is $O(logn)$. When other operations (such as insertion and deletion) destroy the balance of the red-black tree, the red-black tree maintains the balance by rotating the subtrees. The rotating subtree includes two cases, left rotation and proper rotation. These operations can be completed within $O(1)$.

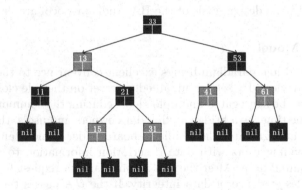

Fig. 1. Example of red-black tree

3.3 Bilinear Pairing

Let G_1, G_2 and G_T be groups of multiplicative cycles with order p, which is a prime. And the generators of G_1, G_2 are g_1 and g_2 respectively. The definition of bilinear pairing $e : G_1 \times G_2 \rightarrow G_T$ should satisfy the following three properties [19]:

1. *Bilinear:* For $\forall u \in G_1, \forall v \in G_2$ and equation $e(u^a, v^b) = e(u, v)^{a \cdot b}$ is true.
2. *Computability:* For $\lor u \in G_1$ and $\lor v \in G_2$, there exists an efficient algorithm to calculate pairing $e(u, v)$.
3. *Nondegeneracy:* With regard to the generators g_1 and g_2, $e(g_1, g_2) \neq 1$.

3.4   Boneh-Goh-Nissim (BGN) Cryptosystem

The BGN cryptosystem is divided into three algorithms: key generation, encryption, and decryption [20]. The details are introduced as follows:

1. *Key generation:* Let $\gamma \in Z_p$ as the security parameter. Given a tuple (p, q, G_1, G_T, e) and $N = p \times q$. Choose two random generators $g, x \in G_1$, and calculate $h = x^q$. Let h as a random generator of G_1. The public key of this cryptosystem is $PK = (N, G_1, G_T, e, g, h)$. And the private is $SK = p$.
2. *Encryption:* Set $[0, T]$ as plaintext space which $T < q$. Let the plaintext message is $m \in [0, T]$. Randomly select a number $r \in [0, N - 1]$. The encryption algorithm can be given as $C = g^m h^r$.
3. *Decryption:* The ciphertext C can be decrypted by using the secret key $SK = p$. First compute $C^p = (g^m h^r)^p = g^{mp} x^{pq} = (g^p)^m$. Set $\hat{g} = g^p$ so $C^p = (\hat{g})^m$. Then the message m can be deciphered by using Pollard's lambda method [21] which takes expected time $O(\sqrt{T})$.

4   The Framework of BA-Audit

In this section, firstly, we introduce the five system members involved in the BA-Audit framework. Secondly, we describe the security assumption to each member. Finally, the design goals of the BA-Audit protocol are defined.

4.1   System Model

The edge-assisted IoT paradigm brings excellent convenience to the data transmission of IoT devices. By setting up an edge server on the side close to the IoT devices, data can be aggregated and uploaded, reducing the communication burden. At the same time, as a bridge linking data owners and users, the blockchain can be used as an aggregated data bulletin board under its non-tampering characteristics, providing users with data description information to facilitate the selection of required data. After the UA submits a data request to the OA, the OA first provides evidence of data integrity. If the UA passes the verification, it then offers a data transmission request to the OA. We propose the BA-Audit system model based on the implementation process conceived above, as depicted in Fig. 2.

System members are introduced as follows:

– **IoT Devices:** It is a collective term for data collection equipment. It has limited storage capacity and regularly transmits data to data applications (Such as smart meter, which uploads data every 15 min [22]). The built-in cryptography module can encrypt data and calculate signatures.

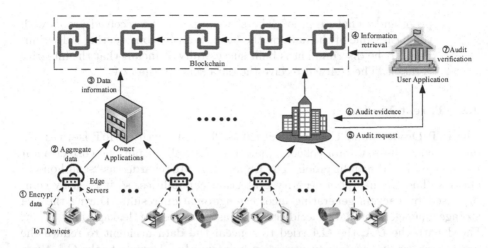

Fig. 2. BA-Audit model framework

- **Edge Server (ES):** A computing power equipment deployed in the gateway device has storage and computing capabilities. It can be regarded as an aggregator to perform data aggregation and signature aggregation tasks.
- **Owner Application (OA):** Owner of aggregated data. The OA analyzes the aggregation results to improve system stability or predict future trends, such as status evaluation [23] and failure prediction [24]. Then, this data will be shared with other applications.
- **Blockchain:** It is a bulletin board for recording data description information. Due to the high cost of storing all data on the chain, only data description information for retrieval is stored on the blockchain. Because of its immutability, data recording is effective for a long time.
- **User Application (UA):** They are applications that require aggregated data of OA. For example, by providing traffic data through a map application, business-related applications as UA can judge the commercial value of a specific location based on this.

Under the ideal conditions, BA-Audit works as follows:

Step 1: **Data Aggregation.** IoT devices periodically send the collected data to ESs. ESs will sum the collected data at regular intervals and upload the aggregation results to the OA. The OA analyzes the aggregated data.

Step 2: **Data Sharing.** The OA uploads the data description information to the blockchain. For each aggregated data m_i, the description information is defined as $\{OA_{ID}, ES_{ID}, T_j, h(m_i)\}$, where, T_j represents the timestamp when the OA received m_i, and $h(m_i)$ represents the hash value of the data. The blockchain information is disclosed to the UA, and the UA can search for the required aggregated data set $\{m_i\}$ and send the data request $\{\{OA_{ID}\}, \{ES_{ID}\}, \{T_j\}\}$ to the OA.

Step 3: **Data Auditing.** The OA first provides evidence to prove that the integrity of the data has not been compromised, which contains data proof and signature proof. The UA compares the received proofs with the hash value of the data on the blockchain by constructing a discriminant. If the discriminant is built successfully, it means that the integrity is intact. The UA will receive the data sent by the OA.

4.2   Threat Model

The **IoT Devices** and **UA** are regarded as "honest" entities. IoT Devices will only provide the real data collected, and the UA will output the correct audit results based on the audit proofs. The **ES** and **OA** are regarded as "semi-honest" entities. The ES has poor security protection capabilities, so it is easily compromised by hackers generating incorrect aggregation results. During the OA storage management data, accidents such as data loss or leakage may occur. Faced with the UA, the OA tried to conceal the data accident to reduce the loss. Moreover, in the data transmission link from IoT Devices to the OA, there are **link hackers** attempting to obtain the data information. Some hackers even tamper with data in an attempt to make the entire aggregation system invalid.

4.3   Design Goals

The design goal will be divided into two parts, namely the **functional goal** and **security goal**. The performance expectations of the framework are also included in the functional goals. Two types of goals will be introduced below:

Functional Goals

- **Data auditing for IoT devices:** For the data verification request of UA, the proofs provided by the OA need to describe the original data as correct. In addition, it is necessary to reduce the audit time overhead.
- **Sharing for aggregated data:** The UA can initiate a valid data request to OA based on the data information in the blockchain.

Security Goals

- **Detectable for data errors of shared:** The UA can detect data tampering, replacement, and replay attacks launched by OA to trick audit results.
- **Correctness of aggregated data:** The OA can check whether the aggregated data uploaded by ES is correct.
- **Data privacy-preserving:** The hackers who launched compromise attacks on ES cannot obtain the plaintext information of the data.

5   Hash Index Balance Tree

Signature retrieval is a bottleneck affecting audit time overhead. In the face of the data request made by UA, the OA needs to retrieve the signature to generate proof. The retrieval process is divided into two stages: first, find the index set corresponding to ID_{ES}; and then, find the signature of a specific timestamp in this set. The single-level index structure provided by [16] cannot be directly applied. To this end, the straightforward solution is to establish a two-level index structure. But due to the inconsistent uploading time interval of ES, the underlying data is not uniform. The actual retrieval complexity will be greater than $2O(n)$. To avoid the uneven problem caused by the secondary index, we still adopt the design of the primary index. To achieve effective retrieval under BA-Audit conditions, we use hash technology to connect ES_{ID} and T_j, and then calculate the hash value $H(ES_{ID}||T_j)$, according to The result of the hash value is sorted. Moreover, the complexity of updating the index is $O(n)$. When facing incremental data, it is impossible to achieve effective retrieval while updating [15]. We adopt a tree structure to achieve efficient indexing, and the time complexity of search and insertion are both $O(logn)$. To achieve the balance of nodes in the tree, we use the red-black tree balance strategy. Compared with the balanced binary tree, the average balance overhead of the red-black tree is lower. A simple example of HIBT is shown in Fig. 3.

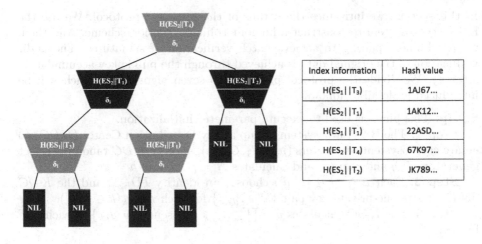

Fig. 3. Example of HIBT

In each node, three variables need to be stored, which are the index coding $h(ES_{ID}||T_j)$, the signature storage δ_{m_i}, and the Red-black Indicator $RB_I = \{0/1\}$. HIBT defines a set of atomic operations $O_x = \{create, find, insert\}$ for the data information set $N = \{\{ES_{ID}, T_j, \delta_{T_j}^{ES_{ID}}\}\}$. The specific execution steps are described as follows:

- **Create**(N). Firstly, the creator calculates each hash value and ranks it according to the hash value. Secondly, the creator initializes HIBT nodes for each element in N and generates a tree structure according to the order. Thirdly, the creator assigns a value to the RB_I of each node according to the definition of the red-black tree.

- **Find**(ES_{ID}, T_j). The index manager first calculates the hash value according to the input parameters and then finds the signature value corresponding to the node according to the red-black tree search rules.
- **Insert**(ES_{ID}, T_j). Firstly, the index manager first calculates the hash according to the input parameters and creates a HIBT node. Secondly, the index manager uses the *find* function to retrieve the insertion position and uses a pointer to connect the insertion node. Thirdly, the index manager uses the red-black tree balance strategy to determine the color of the inserted node and maintain stability.

In the BA-Audit system model, HIBT is deployed in the OA. After receiving the aggregated data from ES, OA calls the *insert* operation to insert a new node into HIBT. When faced with a data request from the UA, the OA calls the *find* operation to retrieve the signature of the data block involved and generate auditing proofs.

6   Security Protocol for BA-Audit

In this section, we introduce the details of the proposed protocol. We use the BGN cryptosystem to construct a homomorphic encryption scheme. And then, we use bilinear pairing to achieve batch verification of signatures. The audit verification of the original data is achieved through the public key accumulation strategy. We divide the protocol process into seven algorithms, which will be introduced in detail as follows:

Setup. This phase is used to execute parameter initialization.

Step 1: The BA-Audit system set up a Key Distribution Center (KDC) to create cryptosystem parameters (p, q, G_1, G_T, e), and the KDC randomly select generators f, g and x of G_1 and calculates $N = p \times q$ and $h = x^q$.

Step 2: Each $ES_j, (j \in [1, m])$ chooses an identity ID_{ES_j}, and the KDC distributes public-private key pair $\{h^{y_{j,k}}, y_{j,k}\}$ for each $IoT_{j,k}(k \in [1, n])$.

Step 3: The KDC calculates $v = \prod_{k=1}^n y_{j,k}$ and sends $\{v, y_{j,k}\}$ to each IoT by secure channel.

DataCollection. In this phase, the $IoT_{j,k}$ encrypts the data and generates signatures.

Step 1: The $IoT_{j,k}$ encrypts $m_{I_{j,k}}^{TS_{u_{ES}}} \in [0, T]$ to $C_{I_{j,k}} = g^{m_{I_{j,k}}} \times h^{r_{I_{j,k}}}$.

Step 2: The $IoT_{j,k}$ generates data signature as follows:

$$\delta_{C_{I_{j,k}}} = (g^{m_{I_{j,k}}} h^{r_{I_{j,k}}} H(ID_{I_{j,k}})^{h(m_{I_{j,k}})})^v \tag{1}$$

Step 3: The $IoT_{j,k}$ sends $\{C_{I_{j,k}}, \delta_{C_{I_{j,k}}},\}$ to ES_j.

DataAggregation. In this phase, the ES_k aggregates encrypted data and signatures and sends them to the OA.

Step 1: The ES_k calculates $C_j^{TS_u} = \prod_{k=1}^m C_{I_{j,k}}$ to get aggregated data.

Step 2: The ES_k calculates $\delta_j^{TS_u} = \prod_{k=1}^m \delta_{C_{I_{j,k}}}$ to get aggregated signatures.

Step 3: The ES_k sends $\{ID_{ES_k}, C_j^{TS_u}, \delta_j^{TS_u}\}$ to OA_i.

Datasharing. In this phase, the OA_i verifies the aggregated signature and records the data description information on the blockchain.

Step 1: The OA_i construct the discriminant as follows:

$$e(C_j^{TS_u} \times \prod_{k=1}^{m} H(ID_{I_{j,k}})^{h(m_{I_{j,k}})}, h^u) \stackrel{?}{=} e(\delta_j^{TS_u}, h) \tag{2}$$

to verify the correctness of aggregated data.

Step 2: If the output is TRUE, the OA uses the BGN decryption algorithm to obtain the plaintext $m_{I_{j,k}}$ of the aggregated data.

Step 3: The OA_i sends $\{ID_{OA_i}, ID_{ES_k}, TS_j, h(C_j^{TS_u})\}$ to the blockchain.

DataRequest. In this phase, the UA finds the required data on the blockchain and sends a set of auditing challenges. Specially, the UA sends $\{ID_{ES_k}, \{TS\}, \{c\}\}$ to the OA_i, where $\{TS\}$ indicates the timestamps range of the data required by the UA and $\{c\}$ indicates challenge random number for each aggregated data.

ProofGeneration. In this phase, the OA_i generates data proof and signature proof to the UA.

Step 1: The OA_i calculates data proof $Pd_{OA_i} = \prod_{i \in TS} m_i \times c_i$.

Step 2: The OA_i calculates signature proof $Ps_{OA_i} = \prod_{i \in TS} \delta^{c_i}$.

Step 3: The OA_i sends $\{Ps_{OA_i}, Pd_{OA_i}\}$ to the UA.

AuditingVerify. In this phase, the UA constructs verification discriminant as follows:

$$e(Pd_{OA_i} \times \prod_{k=1}^{m} H(ID_{I_{j,k}})^{h(m_{I_{j,k}}) \times c_i}, h^u) \stackrel{?}{=} e(Ps_{OA_i}, h) \tag{3}$$

If the output is TRUE, the UA will request data from OA.

7 Security Analysis

This section has proved that BA-Audit has achieved the security goals mentioned above through security analysis.

Theorem 1 (Detectable for data errors of shared). *Before UA obtains the shared data, it can detect whether OA has tampered with, replaced, or replayed the transmitted data.*

Proof. It can be seen from the formula $e(Pd_{OA_i} \times \prod_{k=1}^{m} H(ID_{I_{j,k}})^{h(m_{I_{j,k}}) \times c_i}, h^u)$ $\stackrel{?}{=} e(Ps_{OA_i}, h)$ that the verification can be completed only when the signature generated by the $IoT_{j,k}$ private key is brought in. The OA cannot tamper with the signature because it does not have the key. When the signature is replaced or replayed, the random number in the evidence cannot correspond to the random number when constructing the discriminant, and the equation will not hold. Therefore, when OA attempts to launch tampering, replacement, or replay attacks, UA can detect it.

Theorem 2 (Correctness of aggregated data). *OA can judge whether the data uploaded by ES is correct.*

Proof. According to the discriminant $e(C_j^{TS_u} \times \prod_{k=1}^{m} H(ID_{I_{j,k}})^{h(m_{I_{j,k}})}, h^u)$ $\overset{?}{=} e(\delta_j^{TS_u}, h)$ It can be seen that the discriminant will only be established when *ES* aggregates each data from IoT Devices as required. Therefore, *OA* can detect errors in the data aggregation of *ES*.

Theorem 3 (Data privacy preserving). *ES and link hackers cannot get the data plaintext.*

Proof. The data uploaded by IoT Devices is encrypted using the BGN algorithm, which can only be decrypted at *OA*. Therefore, in aggregation and transmission, the plaintext of the data will not be leaked.

8   Performance Evaluation

In this section, we carry out the efficiency evaluation of BA-Audit. To this end, we first use theoretical analysis to look at the computational and communication overhead. Then, we construct a simulation environment to verify the results in the theoretical analysis.

8.1   Theoretical Analysis

The symbol definitions required for theoretical analysis are described in Table 1. In order to realize the auditability of aggregated data sharing, we combine [12] and [15] to form a comparison scheme DAMHT. The detailed comparison of computing overhead and communication overhead is analyzed in Table 2.

Table 1. Notations used to describe the theoretical analysis.

Notation	Describe
M_G	The time of multiplication operation to the curve in G
E_G	The time of exponent operation to the curve in G
M_{Z_p}	The time of multiplication operation in Z_p
E_{Z_p}	The time of exponent operation in Z_p
H_G	The time of hashing to the curve in G
P_G	The time of bilinear pairing operation in to the curve in G
n	The number of IoT devices
c	The number of data taken by UA from M data
Ω	Auxiliary path of constructing MHT

Table 2. Comparison of calculation and communication costs

Scheme	Computational of data aggregation	Computational of shared data auditing	Communication
DAMHT	$4nE_G + 5nM_G + 2nH_G + nP_G$	$2cE_G + 3cM_G + cH_G + 2P_G + cO(n)$	$c\|Z_p\| + 2n\|G\| + \|\Omega\|$
BA-Audit	$3nE_G + 3nM_G + 2nH_G$	$2cE_G + 3cM_G + cH_G + cO(logn)$	$c\|Z_p\| + 2n\|G\|$

In the data aggregation stage, BA-Audit can verify signatures in batches at OA, and it has a significant advantage over DAMHT in terms of the number of bilinear pairings. In the data audit phase, BA-Audit calls HIBT to retrieve the signature. Due to its low complexity, it has significant advantages over DAMHT. Since DAMHT must transmit the auxiliary path simultaneously when the incremental data is updated, BA-Audit can edit the index directly. Therefore, BA-Audit has advantages in terms of communication overhead.

8.2 Experimental Evaluation

We set up a simulation environment and experiment and test. The experiment was run on a computer equipped with a 1.60 GHz Intel i5-10210U CPU and 16GB RAM. The experiment uses the pair-based cryptographic library JPBC (java encapsulation of the PBC library) [25] to implement the encryption algorithm and sets the security parameter to 256bit. Use the MHT index mentioned in [15] to compare with HIBT. One hundred thousand nodes are used to initialize MHT and HIBT, respectively. We assume that each ES is connected to 1000 IoT devices for the aggregation and audit phase parameter setting. The number of audit data blocks will be represented in the graph as an independent variable.

First, we compare the performance of MHT and HIBT. The comparison of retrieval costs is shown in Fig. 4. Since HIBT index complexity is $O(logN)$ and MHT is $O(n)$, HIBT has significant advantages. The comparison of insertion overhead is shown in Fig. 5. The insert action includes a retrieval step. On this basis, MHT needs to perform additional intermediate node updates, and the complexity is $O(logN)$. However, HIBT only needs to perform a balancing operation, and the complexity is $O(1)$. Therefore, the insertion operation HIBT still has significant advantages.

Then we compare the time overhead of DAMHT and BA-Audit in the aggregation and audit phases, as shown in Fig. 6. The picture shows that BA-Audit has significant advantages. On the one hand, the reason is that BA-Audit implements batch verification of IoT device signatures in OA, which significantly reduces the number of bilinear pairings. On the other hand, the reason is that when calculating audit evidence, using HIBT to retrieve and aggregate data signatures has significant advantages over MHT.

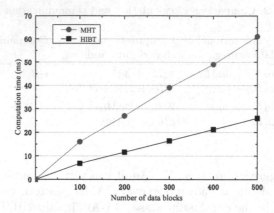

Fig. 4. Retrieval time of MHT and HIBT

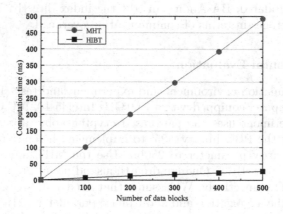

Fig. 5. Comparison of auditing time of MHT and HIBT

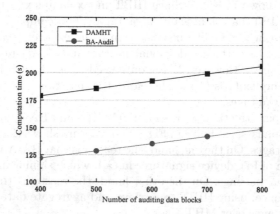

Fig. 6. Inserting time of DAHMT and BA-Audit

9 Conclusion

In this paper, we propose a blockchain-based auditing scheme for aggregated data sharing called BA-Audit. Its features will be described as follows: first, we design a blockchain-based data aggregation and sharing framework realizing that aggregated data can be disclosed and verified; second, we develop a HIBT index structure to achieve efficient indexing of signatures; third, we create an audit protocol to verify the integrity of aggregated data. Finally, the safety and efficiency of the scheme are proved through safety analysis and theoretical evaluation.

References

1. Ni, J., Lin, X., Shen, X.S.: Toward edge-assisted internet of things: from security and efficiency perspectives. IEEE Netw. **33**(2), 50–57 (2019). https://doi.org/10.1109/MNET.2019.1800229
2. A Day in Data (2021). https://www.raconteur.net/infographics/a-day-in-data/
3. Dehkordi, S.A., et al.: A survey on data aggregation techniques in IoT sensor networks. Wirel. Netw. **26**(2), 1243–1263 (2020). https://doi.org/10.1007/s11276-019-02142-z
4. Yu, K.-P., et al.: Blockchain-enhanced data sharing with traceable and direct revocation in IIoT. IEEE Trans. Ind. Inform. **17**, 7669–7678 (2021). https://doi.org/10.1016/j.cose.2019.101653
5. Yang, P., Xiong, N., Ren, J.: Data security and privacy protection for cloud storage: a survey. IEEE Access **8**, 131723–131740 (2020). https://doi.org/10.1109/ACCESS.2020.3009876
6. Yuan, H., et al.: Blockchain-based public auditing and secure deduplication with fair arbitration. Inf. Sci. **541**, 409–425 (2020). https://doi.org/10.1016/j.ins.2020.07.005
7. Zhou, L., Fu, A., Yang, G., Wang, H., Zhang, Y.: Efficient certificateless multi-copy integrity auditing scheme supporting data dynamics. IEEE Trans. Dependable Secure Comput. (2020). https://doi.org/10.1109/TDSC.2020.3013927
8. Fan, C.I., Huang, S.Y., Lai, Y.L.: Privacy-enhanced data aggregation scheme against internal attackers in smart grid. IEEE Trans. Ind. Inform. **10**(1), 666–675 (2013). https://doi.org/10.1109/TII.2013.2277938
9. He, D., et al.: Efficient and privacy-preserving data aggregation scheme for smart grid against internal adversaries. IEEE Trans. Smart Grid **8**(5), 2411–2419 (2017). https://doi.org/10.1109/TSG.2017.2720159
10. Lu, R., et al.: A lightweight privacy-preserving data aggregation scheme for fog computing-enhanced IoT. IEEE Access **5**, 3302–3312 (2017). https://doi.org/10.1109/ACCESS.2017.2677520
11. Abdallah, A., Shen, X.S.: A lightweight lattice-based homomorphic privacy-preserving data aggregation scheme for smart grid. IEEE Trans. Smart Grid **9**(1), 396–405 (2016). https://doi.org/10.1109/TSG.2016.2553647
12. Li, X., et al.: Privacy preserving data aggregation scheme for mobile edge computing assisted IoT applications. IEEE Internet Things J. **6**(3), 4755–4763 (2018). https://doi.org/10.1109/JIOT.2018.2874473

13. Ateniese, G., et al.: Provable data possession at untrusted stores. In: Proceedings of the 14th ACM Conference on Computer and Communications Security, pp. 598–609. (2007). https://doi.org/10.1145/1315245.1315318
14. Juels, A., Kaliski Jr., B.S.: PORs: proofs of retrievability for large files. In: Proceedings of the 14th ACM Conference on Computer and Communications Security, pp. 584–597. (2007). https://doi.org/10.1145/1315245.1315317
15. Wang, Q., et al.: Enabling public auditability and data dynamics for storage security in cloud computing. IEEE Trans. Parallel Distrib. Syst. **22**(5), 847–859 (2010). https://doi.org/10.1109/TPDS.2010.183
16. Tian, H., et al.: Dynamic-hash-table based public auditing for secure cloud storage. IEEE Trans. Serv. Comput. **10**(5), 701–714 (2015). https://doi.org/10.1109/TSC.2015.2512589
17. Nakamoto, S.: Bitcoin: a peer-to-peer electronic cash system. Decentralized Bus. Rev. 21260 (2008). https://doi.org/10.2139/ssrn.3440802
18. Hanke, S.: The performance of concurrent red-black tree algorithms. In: Vitter, J.S., Zaroliagis, C.D. (eds.) WAE 1999. LNCS, vol. 1668, pp. 286–300. Springer, Heidelberg (1999). https://doi.org/10.1007/3-540-48318-7_23
19. Boneh, D., Lynn, B., Shacham, H.: Short signatures from the Weil pairing. In: Boyd, C. (ed.) ASIACRYPT 2001. LNCS, vol. 2248, pp. 514–532. Springer, Heidelberg (2001). https://doi.org/10.1007/3-540-45682-1_30
20. Boneh, D., Goh, E.-J., Nissim, K.: Evaluating 2-DNF formulas on ciphertexts. In: Kilian, J. (ed.) TCC 2005. LNCS, vol. 3378, pp. 325–341. Springer, Heidelberg (2005). https://doi.org/10.1007/978-3-540-30576-7_18
21. Menezes, A.J., Van Oorschot, P.C., Vanstone, S.A.: Handbook of Applied Cryptography. CRC Press, Boco Raton (2018)
22. Jiménez-Castillo, G., et al.: Effects of smart meter time resolution when analyzing photovoltaic self-consumption system on a daily and annual basis. Renew. Energy **164**, 889–896 (2021). https://doi.org/10.1016/j.renene.2020.09.096
23. Qiu, Z., Chen, R., Yan, M.: Monitoring data analysis technology of smart grid based on cloud computing. In: IOP Conference Series: Materials Science and Engineering, vol. 750, p. 012221. IOP Publishing (2020)
24. Gao, J., Wang, H., Shen, H.: Task failure prediction in cloud data centers using deep learning. IEEE Trans. Serv. Comput. (2020). https://doi.org/10.1109/TSC.2020.2993728
25. JPBC Library (2021). http://gas.dia.unisa.it/projects/jpbc/

Predicting Congestion Attack of Variable Spoofing Frequency for Reliable Traffic Signal System

Yingxiao Xiang⬥, Tong Chen⬥, Yike Li⬥, Yunzhe Tian⬥, Wenjia Niu$^{(\boxtimes)}$⬥,
Endong Tong$^{(\boxtimes)}$⬥, Jiqiang Liu⬥, Bowei Jia⬥, Yalun Wu⬥,
and Xinyu Huang⬥

Beijing Key Laboratory of Security and Privacy in Intelligent Transportation,
Beijing Jiaotong University, Beijing 100044, China
{niuwj,edtong}@bjtu.edu.cn

Abstract. As a key component of next-generation transportation systems, the intelligent traffic signal system is designed to perform dynamic and optimal signal control. The USDOT (U.S. Department of Transportation) has sponsored a kind of such system - I-SIG based on Controlled Optimization of Phases (COP). Unfortunately, it has been revealed that a serious congestion attack can be caused just by one vehicle's data spoofing. However, the existing methods focus on detecting the congestion attack and have a certain disadvantage of delay even facing periodic attacks. Thus, how to timely detect and even predict the congestion attack has become a key issue. Considering that a practical and effective congestion attack is usually continuous and periodic, we propose a novel approach for congestion attack prediction. Firstly, we set up a spoofing attack environment and collect traffic flows of variable spoofing frequencies. Among congestion attack-caused flows, we define and extract 30 important features and implement ensemble learning to build correlations between traffic flow features and abnormal congestion and attack frequency. Through supervised learning of historical data, we can recognize the current attack frequency and further realize the prediction of the subsequent congestion attack. We also report on necessary and experienced tricks for performance improvement. Extensive experiments and analyses have been conducted to demonstrate the prediction capability of our proposed approach.

Keywords: Congestion attack · Prediction · Supervised learning · Security analysis · Traffic signal system

1 Introduction

Connected vehicle (CV) technology [1,4], empowering vehicles to communicate with the surrounding environment, such as Roadside Units (RSU) and traffic signal control infrastructure, is now transforming today's transportation systems. As a critical component, the intelligent traffic signal system is responsible

© ICST Institute for Computer Sciences, Social Informatics and Telecommunications Engineering 2022
Published by Springer Nature Switzerland AG 2022. All Rights Reserved
W. Shi et al. (Eds.): SPNCE 2021, LNICST 423, pp. 219–237, 2022.
https://doi.org/10.1007/978-3-030-96791-8_16

for performing dynamic and optimal signal control based on automatic traffic situation awareness. Since September 2016, the USDOT (U.S. Department of Transportation) has sponsored a kind of such system named I-SIG built on the classic algorithm: Controlled Optimization of Phases (COP) [14,23]. As a CV Pilot Program, I-SIG systems [5] are currently under testing in some USA states, including California, Florida, and New York, before spreading widely.

Table 1. I-SIG congestion increasing ratios under last-vehicle attacks of 5 different spoofing frequencies. A last-vehicle attack refers to the addition of an attack vehicle at the end of a queue.

Attack frequency	Sampling time (s)				
	400	800	1200	1600	1800
f_1 (Every 1 stage)	185.6%	198.4%	148.2%	292%	259.6%
f_2 (Every 2 stages)	195.8%	202.9%	128.2%	231.1%	231.2%
f_3 (Every 3 stages)	87.6%	98.5%	94.1%	188.9%	259.6%
f_4 (Every 4 stages)	46.9%	46.2%	36.4%	103.1%	140.2%
f_5 (Every 5 stages)	0	26.7%	2.1%	9.3%	11.9%

Unfortunately, there is a severe security problem with I-SIG, which is revealed by Qi Alfred Chen [10] in NDSS2018. A congestion attack can be launched via data spoofing of one attack vehicle. Due to the vulnerability of the COP algorithm, attackers can compromise the On-Board Units (OBU) on their vehicles and send malicious messages such as speed and location, which can affect the traffic control decisions at proper timing and cause unexpected heavy traffic congestion. Some data shows that one single attack vehicle can cause more than 11 times the total delay, which significantly hinders the development and future large-scale deployment. After repeated the attack scenario, we find that different spoofing frequencies can cause a similar congestion effect even for the last vehicle. The attack frequency is inversely proportional to the attack time interval. Table 1 shows I-SIG congestion increasing ratios under last-vehicle attacks of 5 different spoofing frequencies. f_1 is the highest frequency adopted in Qi Alfred Chen's work, i.e., attacking at each stage. $f_2 \sim f_5$ are low-grade attack frequencies designed in our work and denote attacking every 2, 3, 4, 5 stages, respectively. We can see that f_2, f_3 and f_4 make heavy congestion 30 min later as well, indicating that the frequency-reduced attacks exist.

Therefore, although previous work [10] reveals the congestion attack via the last vehicle, detecting it only through black-box watching of traffic flow is still an open issue. The questions are what traffic flow pattern under congestion attack is, and given a period of traffic flow, can we timely predict whether or not the system suffers a congestion attack, or even corresponding attack frequency? Ignoring such abilities will harm the security situation awareness of I-SIG. Therefore, it is significant to study the predictability of congestion attack, the timeliness of prediction, and various composed features' influence, but much remains unexplored.

In this work, we propose a prediction approach of traffic congestion attack, which can recognize the abnormal congestion and attack frequency; and timely predict the forthcoming congestion attack. This work is the first to perform a complete prediction task in supervised machine learning using historical data to demystify the predictability of the I-SIG congestion attack, from manual instance collecting, labeling, feature engineering to mainstream single learner implementation and ensemble learning. In our prediction approach, there are four singer learners, including decision tree (DT) [24], support vector machine (SVM) [8], logic regression (LR) [12], and k-nearest neighbors classifier (KNN) [16]. Compared with SVM, DT, LR, etc., Deep Neural Networks (DNN) have higher computational costs and require large-scale data for training, so they are not considered to be used here. To overcome a single learner's weakness, we employ bagging, boosting, and stacking techniques in ensemble learning, respectively. We also utilize common tricks, including rescaling, oversampling, and hyperparameter optimization for improvement. In our experiment, the dimensionality varies from 20 to 600 based on 540 traffic flow samples collected and crafted. The efficiency of the proposed approach is demonstrated through simulations, compared with a baseline approach [28]. By defining quantified traffic flow features, the influence of different feature compositions for feature selection is deeply analyzed. We eventually discover and report some distinguished patterns of traffic flow with high confidence for both general and each frequency-specified congestion attack through massive analysis efforts.

We summarize our contributions as follows:

- We are the first to study traffic congestion attack under various frequencies in the I-SIG system in order to predict the subsequent congestion attack.
- Based on solid feature engineering and special learning tricks, we propose a unified ensemble learning framework to perform supervised classification tasks.
- We evaluate our approach empirically from an actual COP algorithm through VISSIM [3]. We reveal the promising predictability of traffic congestion attack and the timeliness of congestion attack prediction, analysis the influence of different feature compositions to detection performance, and report on explainable patterns to distinguish congestion attack flows under different frequencies.

The rest of the paper is organized as follows: Sect. 2 discusses the related works. Section 3 introduces the preliminary about our research. Section 4 describes our proposed prediction framework. Section 5 demonstrates and analyses the performance of our approach by simulation, followed by a conclusion of the paper in Sect. 6.

2 Related Work

Many studies on traffic congestion problems address the optimization of the traffic signal control system to detect and reduce congestion (see, for example, the studies [6,7,11,13,17,19,26,27]). For instance, the study of [11] alleviated traffic congestion by analyzing and predicting the traffic states. Jaleel et al. [17] proposed a novel Multi-Agent RL approach to control the traffic signals phase and timing to reduce congestion. In [6], the authors proposed a rapid and reliable traffic congestion detection method based on the modeling of video dynamics using deep residual learning and motion trajectories.

The above studies focused mainly on the detection of traffic congestion, rather than the congestion attack problems. From the congestion attack aspect, Jeske [18] demonstrated how hackers can take control of navigation systems in practice, in order to trick navigation services and cause congestion. Chen et al. [10] revealed a threat of data spoofing over the intelligent traffic signal system - I-SIG. The data spoofing can cause traffic severe congestion via one single attack vehicle.

Data spoofing attack in [10] belongs to position faking attack of GPS spoofing, but is different with tunnel attack. In a tunnel attack, where each vehicle of a vehicular ad hoc network (VANET) [30,32] is equipped with a positioning system (receiver), a transmitter that generates stronger localization signals than those generated by the real satellites [9,21] are used, so that the victim could be waiting for a GPS signal after leaving a physical tunnel or a jammed-up area. In comparison, the position spoofing attack to I-SIG refers that authenticated vehicle only sends the wrong position to affect the COP algorithm, which has a lower attack cost and easier implementation. In such an attack, the spoofing is just a causing factor, while the mechanism of the COP algorithm is the key. For GPS spoofing attack, our work focuses on the revealing of algorithm-level security analysis caused by spoofing, rather than the security of GPS spoofing itself. The work in [10] lacks consideration about the potential features and the quantified correlation between the attack and congestion degree. In comparison, we develop a unified ensemble learning framework to demystify the predictability of I-SIG congestion attack based on solid feature engineering and special learning tricks.

There are only very few studies on the prediction methods of traffic congestion caused by spoofing attacks. Li et al. [20] proposed a CycleGAN-based prediction approach using traffic image feature. Their approach reflects the relation between attack and the caused congestion. They revealed the vulnerability to the spoofing attack in [10] from the perspective of image features. Unlike [20], our approach would extract traffic flow feature and find the traffic flow patterns under different attack frequencies. The authors in [28] proposed an explainable congestion attack prediction approach using a deep learning model - TGRU. They try to explain the relationship between the traffic flow feature and the lanes where the congestion attack vehicle locates. While their model uses the traffic flow of one second as a sample, our approach uses the traffic flow of 20 seconds to represent the traffic feature better.

The main difference between our work and the previous studies is that we propose an approach for detecting the congestion attack to predict the subsequent congestion attack. The main focus of our work is the extraction of traffic flow features, the recognition of the abnormal congestion and the current attack frequency, and the generation of traffic flow patterns to predict the congestion attack.

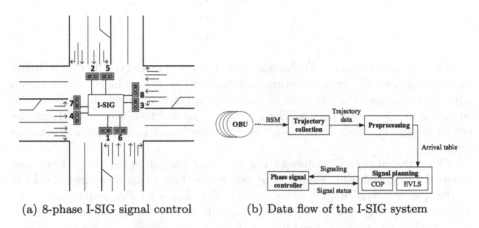

(a) 8-phase I-SIG signal control   (b) Data flow of the I-SIG system

Fig. 1. I-SIG system overview.

3 Preliminaries

3.1 I-SIG Data Flow

In I-SIG, there are 8 phases, as shown in Fig. 1(a), called phases. The data flow of the I-SIG system is revealed in Fig. 1(b). Each OBU of vehicles sends Basic Safety Messages (BSM) to the RSU for a trajectory collection in real time. Such data will then be preprocessed to form an arrival table (see Table 2) as an input to signal planning with COP and EVLS modules. If the penetration rate (PR) of OBU for vehicles is below 95%, the arrival table will be sent to the Estimation of Location and Speed (EVLS) algorithm for an update. The EVLS algorithm will estimate the trajectory data of the unequipped vehicles. Otherwise, it will be sent directly to COP for planning. According to the results of COP, a downward signaling command is transferred to the phase signal controller. After each stage of signal control, the following signal status is returned as feedback for continuous COP planning.

In Table 2, $T_i = i (0 \le i \le M)$ denotes the time to arrive at the stop bar from the current location. I-SIG sets $M = 130$ seconds, covering an over two-minute BSM statistic. $N_{ij} (i \in [0, M], j \in [1, 8])$ denotes that in phase j, there will be N_{ij} vehicles are going to reach the stop bar only within T_i seconds. Here, the stop bar is set in front of the traffic light, as what we can see at an actual road intersection.

Table 2. Arrival table.

Arrival time (T_M)	Phase			
	1	2	$\cdots$	8
T_0	N_{01}	N_{02}		N_{08}
T_1	N_{11}	N_{12}	$\cdots$	N_{18}
T_2	N_{21}	N_{22}	$\cdots$	N_{28}
$\cdots$	$\cdots$	$\cdots$	$\cdots$	$\cdots$
T_M	N_{M1}	N_{M2}	$\cdots$	N_{M8}

The EVLS is based on Wiedemann's car-following model which fills the blank monitoring area of the monitoring segment and inserts vehicle data between equipped vehicles. The key is to estimate the queued vehicles, and it is critical to estimate the queue length. The queue is assumed to always start from the stop bar, the last vehicle in queue needs to be found to determine the queue length.

First, the history distances to the stop bar and stopping time of the last stopped connected vehicle and the second to the last stopped connected vehicle in the queue are calculated, noted as L_{q1}, T_{q1}, L_{q2}, and T_{q2}, respectively. The current time is T_c, and the estimated queue length is L_{es}. Assuming the queue propagation speed v_q is constant, we have $v_q = \frac{L_{q1}-L_{q2}}{T_{q1}-T_{q2}} = \frac{L_{es}-L_{q1}}{T_c-T_{q1}}$. Then, $L_{es} = L_{q1} + v_q(T_c - T_{q1})$. If the average vehicle length is C, the number N_{0i} of vehicles in the queue is then calculated as $N_{0i} = \lceil L_{es}/C \rceil, i \in [1,8]$.

However, while this estimation supports a low penetration rate effectively, it also introduces a new threat of data spoofing attack to COP.

3.2   Congestion Attack

In our case, the main goal of the attack vehicle is to spoof the signal planning algorithm COP by incorrect traffic flow data leading to an ineffective traffic signal schedule, which sets a longer green time for the lanes with a shorter queue length. There are two attack strategies of data spoofing proposed in I-SIG (see Fig. 2). The first one is a direct attack on the arrival table without considering penetration rate; the second one is indirect attack on EVLS when penetration rate is less than 95%.

The first strategy, arrival time and phase spoofing, applies to both full deployment and transition periods. The attacker alters the arrival time of the vehicle and its requested phase by changing the location and speed information in the vehicles' BSM message, thus changing the corresponding arrival table elements in Table 2. This attack strategy can directly attack input data flow regardless of PR. As shown in Fig. 2(a), the attacker adds a spoofed vehicle into the original vehicle queue at any location as a late arrived one. The join of spoofed vehicle makes the queue of vehicles on the lane longer, and there is an increment of the duration of green light allocated by COP algorithm for the current phase, which delays the next start time of green light of all the phases, increasing the delay for vehicles to pass.

The second strategy is queue length spoofing, which only works during the transition period. The purpose of this strategy is to extend the queue length estimated by EVLS algorithm through changing the location and speed values in the BSM message. As shown in Fig. 2(b), the attacker adds a stopped vehicle that has the farthest distance to the stop bar. Since the EVLS algorithm estimates the queue length based on the location of the last stopped connected vehicle, this attack results in an increase in the estimated queue length L_{es}, and the number N_{0i} of vehicles in queue.

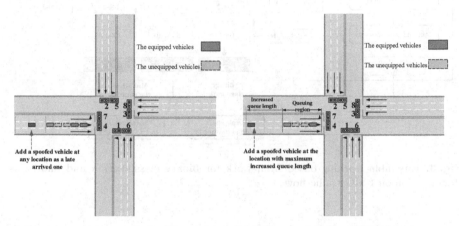

(a) Direct attack on arrival table without considering penetration rate

(b) Indirect attack on EVLS when penetration rate is less than 95%

Fig. 2. Two strategies of congest attack.

4 Congestion Attack Prediction

We propose a unified ensemble learning-based framework for binary classification and multi-class classification on I-SIG traffic flow. As Fig. 3 shows, there are three parts: preprocessing, training set, and ensemble learning. In preprocessing, we extract features from the collected traffic flow of the I-SIG system. Next, we use standardization, a kind of rescaling trick, to adjust feature values. Furthermore, through labeling, we separate two dataset D_1 and D_2 for binary classification and multi-class classification respectively. In D_1, for the traffic samples that are not attacked, we give them a label of 0, otherwise 1. While for D_2, we give labels 1, 2, 3, 4 and 5 to those samples with five attack frequencies f_1 to f_5 respectively. To ensure a balanced sample dataset, we also utilize SMOTE oversampling trick. Ensemble learning is the core component of this framework. It involves complete ensemble learning methods, including bagging, boosting and stacking, and grid search trick, an optimization of hyperparameter tuning. We chose four basic learner types: DT, SVM, LR, and KNN. For each class, we train 10 basic learners. Bagging and boosting are used for learners of the same type, while stacking is used for heterogeneous learners. The above framework is designed for comprehensive supervised learning to discover patterns of traffic flow for both general and each frequency-specified congestion attack.

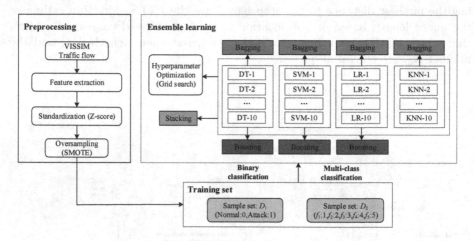

Fig. 3. Ensemble learning-based framework for binary classification and multi-class classification on I-SIG traffic flow.

4.1 Feature Definition

We have feature definition as following:

- *Vehicle capacity ratio(CR).* C_k^{max} is the maximum vehicle capacity of each phase, and the vehicle capacity of all 8 phases is computed as $C_{total}^{max} = \sum_{k=1}^{8} C_k^{max}$, then the vehicle capacity ratio can be denoted by $CR = \sum_{k=1}^{8} N_k/C_{total}^{max}$, where N_k is the vehicle number of the kth phase.
- *Congestion degree (CD).* The vehicle number of queuing of the kth phase is denoted as Q_k, and Q_{normal} is the vehicle number of normal queuing, it's a constant, then the congestion degree of the kth phase can be computed by $PCD_k = Q_k/Q_{normal}$, and the global congestion degree for an intersection is $ICD = \sum_{k=1}^{8} PCD_k$.
- *Attack acceleration.* Let t_0 be the start time of data spoofing attack, then the acceleration of CR, PCD_k and ICD at time t are respectively calculated by: $\alpha_{CR}(t) = (CR(t) - CR(t_0))/(t - t_0)$, $\alpha_{PCD}(t, k) = (PCD(t, k) - PCD(t_0, k))/(t - t_0)$ and $\alpha_{ICD}(t) = (ICD(t) - ICD(t_0))/(t - t_0)$.
- *Attack amplification ratio.* Let t_0 be the start time of data spoofing attack, then the amplification ratio of CR, PCD_k and ICD at time t are respectively computed by: $\beta_{CR}(t) = CR(t)/CR(t_0)$, $\beta_{PCD}(t, k) = PCD(t, k)/PCD(t_0, k)$ and $\beta_{ICD}(t) = ICD(t)/ICD(t_0)$.

4.2   Constructing Training Samples

According to whether it is for the whole intersection or a specific phase, features are divided into macro features and micro features, as shown in Table 3. For discussing interpretability, macro features measure the congestion characteristics of the whole intersection, and micro features measure the single signal phase. For a traffic flow of 1800 s, we only sample the first 10 time of flow head and the last 10 time of flow tail. We choose macro or micro or both features for flow head,and then we choose the same ones from flow tail. Therefore, the size of composed features varies from 20 to 600.

Table 3. Feature composition schema through selecting equal features from traffic flow head and tail.

	Flow head (10 s)	Flow tail (10 s)
Macro features	CR, α_{CR}, β_{CR}, ICD, α_{ICD}, β_{ICD}	CR, α_{CR}, β_{CR}, ICD, α_{ICD}, β_{ICD}
Micro features	PCD_1, PCD_2, $\cdots$, PCD_8, α_{PCD_1}, α_{PCD_2}, $\cdots$, α_{PCD_8}, β_{PCD_1}, β_{PCD_2}, $\cdots$, β_{PCD_8}	PCD_1, PCD_2, $\cdots$, PCD_8, α_{PCD_1}, α_{PCD_2}, $\cdots$, α_{PCD_8}, β_{PCD_1}, β_{PCD_2}, $\cdots$, β_{PCD_8}

We use Z-score as standardization, a kind of rescaling trick, to adjust feature values. For values $(x_1, x_2, ..., x_n)$ of one feature in all samples, the new value is computed by $x' = \frac{x_i - \bar{x}}{s}$, in which s is the standard deviation and $\bar{x}$ is the mean value of $(x_1, x_2, ..., x_n)$.

4.3   Ensemble Learning

Bagging and Boosting. Bagging is one of the simplest but most common techniques for constructing ensembles. Based on bootstrap sampling of dataset, bagging shapes several different training sets, with the purpose of training basic learners on different training sets. The final model will be achieved by aggregating these independent base learners. In this framework, we utilize bagging technique for homogenous base learners. For D_1 of 900 samples and D_2 of 450 samples, our bootstrap sampling selects 70% random sampling and runs 10 times to train 10 base learners for each type of classifiers like DT, SVM, KNN, and LR.

Compared with the parallel construction of base learners in bagging, boosting [22] establishes a set of base classifiers in sequence for boosting the performance of a set of weak classifiers into a robust classifier. The first one learns from the whole data set, while the following learns from training sets based on the performance of the previous one. The misclassified examples are marked, and their weights increased, so they will have a higher probability of appearing in the training set of the next learner. By repeating the process, several weak classifiers will be established to achieve better classification performance. In this work, we use AdaBoost [15] to perform boosting. Similarly, for each classifier like DT, SVM, and LR, we also set 10 base learners to boost sequentially. Since KNN does not support sample weights, we ignore the boosting of KNN.

Stacking. Stacking is used for heterogeneous learners. We implement the stacking algorithm [29] shown in Algorithm 1.

Algorithm 1. The Stacking algorithm

Require: Data set $D = (x_1,y_1),(x_2,y_2),\cdots,(x_m,y_m)$;
         First-level learning algorithms $L_1,\cdots,L_N$;
         Second-level learning algorithm L.
1: **for** $j = 1,\cdots,N$ **do**
2:     $h_j = L_j(D)$ %Train a first-level individual learner h_j
               by applying the first-level
3: **end for**   %Learning algorithm L_j to the original
               data set D
4: $D' = \varnothing$ %Generate a new data set
5: **for** $i = 1,\cdots,m$ **do**
6:     **for** $j = 1,\cdots,N$ **do**
7:        $z_{ij} = h_j(\mathbf{x_i})$ %Use h_j to classify the training
                  example $\mathbf{x_i}$
8:     **end for**
9:     $D' = D'\bigcup\{((z_{i1}, z_{i2},\cdots, z_{iN}), y_i)\}$
10: **end for**
11: $h' = L(D')$ % Train the second-level learner h' by
               applying the second-level
           % Learning algorithm L to the new data set D'
Ensure: $H(\mathbf{x}) = h'(h_1(\mathbf{x}),\cdots,h_N(\mathbf{x}))$

---

5   Experiment

5.1   Setup

Through running COP and VISSIM for real-time traffic flow signal control, the corresponding traffic simulation is carried out to collect the primary traffic flow data. The traffic flow data are collected without attack and with different attack frequencies ($f_1 \sim f_5$) and converted into the features proposed in Sect. 4. D_1 class labels are 0 (without attack) and 1 (with attack); D_2 is labeled $1 \sim 5$ ($f_1 \sim f_5$). The experimental environment and sample datasets configuration are shown in Table 4.

Table 4. Experimental environment and sample datasets configuration.

Platform	Experimental Environment	Environmental Configuration
COP & VISSIM	Operating System	Windows 10
	CPU	AMD Ryzen5 3550H with Radeon Vega Mobile Gfx 2.10 GHz
	RAM	16G
	Software	PTV Vissim 4.30, Visual Studio 2019
Dataset	Sample and feature number	Label
D_1	900, 600	Normal:0, Attack:1
D_2	450, 600	$f_1 : 1$, $f_2 : 2$, $f_3 : 3$, $f_4 : 4$, $f_5 : 5$

5.2 Experiment Process

The prediction process of our approach is described as follows.

1) Collect a period of primary traffic flow data and convert it into the form of features we defined in Sect. 4.
2) The ensemble learning model trained on dataset D_1 can distinguish whether the congestion attack is occurring or not, after inputting the converted traffic data.
3) If the prediction result of step 2) is "Attack", the attack frequency can be output by the ensemble learning model trained on dataset D_2.
4) Compare the appearing frequency f_v of vehicles at the road junction with the attack frequency f_a detected at step 3), the congestion attack vehicles are found if f_v is around to f_a.
5) The discovery of attack vehicles can help the defense of I-SIG against traffic congestion attack.

In the following evaluation, extensive experiments and analyses are conducted, including the comparison with the baseline approach to demonstrate the efficiency of our defined feature and the proposed approach, the influence analyses of various composed features to find the best feature combination for different ensemble learning, the performance comparison of different ensemble learning to obtain the best learning technic, and the patterns analyses of traffic flow to explain the importance of some features.

5.3 Performance Metrics

We adopt two widely-used evaluation protocols, accuracy (ACC) and area under the curve (AUC). For D_1 dataset, we report the ACC, ROC curve [25] with AUC value and for D_2 dataset, we only report the ACC. Also, we present decision trees for both D_1 and D_2 to show the pattern of class. Here we set tree depth = 5.

5.4   Comparison with Baseline

We compare three different approaches which detect congestion based on traffic flow feature, in term of ACC. The first approach, Seasonal Auto-Regressive Integrated Moving Average (SARIMA) method [31], is prevalent in time-series prediction problems. The second approach is based on a deep learning model - TGRU [28]. The third approach is our proposed method based on ensemble learning (EL). In this case, we choose the ensemble learning of boosting with SVM, considering that the full composed feature set has the best ACC of 0.852 in that condition.

We carry out experiments for different approaches under different traffic flow feature sets. For the SARIMA method, we choose the primary traffic flow data as the traffic flow feature FS_1. In [28], the traffic flow feature set FS_2 consists of wait, slow, free, stop bar distance of 8 lanes, 32 features in total. The feature set FS_3 of our approach is shown in Table 3. According to the three approaches, we construct the three feature sets based on the traffic flow data we collect. Here, it is predicted whether or not a congestion attack occurred.

As shown in Table 5, the ACC values of SARIMA, TGRU, and EL on the feature set FS_3 are 0.784, 0.790, and 0.852, respectively. Our approach has the best ACC value, which demonstrates that our approach is superior to others. From the perspective of the feature set, the ACC value of each approach on the feature set FS_3 is higher than on other feature sets, this indicates the effectiveness of our defined traffic flow features.

Table 5. Comparison of different prediction approaches.

Feature set	FS_1(SARIMA)	FS_2(TGRU)	FS_3(EL)
SARIMA	0.744	/	0.784
TGRU	/	0.782	0.790
EL	0.762	0.820	0.852

Table 6. Influence of different feature composition on ACC in Bagging.

Normal/Attack	DT	SVM	LR	KNN	Five attacks	DT	SVM	LR	KNN
CR	0.722	0.796	**0.833**	0.765	CR	0.874	**0.904**	0.852	**0.911**
ICD	0.728	0.772	0.815	0.704	ICD	0.763	0.837	0.83	0.748
CR, ICD	0.728	0.784	0.809	0.704	CR, ICD	0.867	0.837	0.822	0.748
$CR, \alpha_{CR}, \beta_{CR}$	0.741	0.759	0.784	0.728	$CR, \alpha_{CR}, \beta_{CR}$	0.881	0.896	0.889	**0.911**
$ICD, \alpha_{ICD}, \beta_{ICD}$	0.747	0.796	0.796	0.716	$ICD, \alpha_{ICD}, \beta_{ICD}$	0.785	0.8	0.837	0.756
$CR, \alpha_{CR}, \beta_{CR},$ $ICD, \alpha_{ICD}, \beta_{ICD}$	0.728	0.735	0.753	0.716	$CR, \alpha_{CR}, \beta_{CR},$ $ICD, \alpha_{ICD}, \beta_{ICD}$	0.889	**0.911**	**0.904**	0.874
Full composed feature set	0.747	0.735	0.728	0.722	Full composed feature set	0.867	**0.926**	**0.926**	**0.919**

5.5   Feature Influence on Accuracy

We evaluate ACC of six feature compositions and even the full composition scheme. As Table 6 shows for bagging, the maximal ACC of D_1 is 0.833 from LR's bagging for single CR feature. For D_2, the ACC of {SVM, KNN}/CR, KNN/{$CR, \alpha_{CR}, \beta_{CR}$}, {SVM, LR}/{$CR, \alpha_{CR}, \beta_{CR}, ICD, \alpha_{ICD}, \beta_{ICD}$} and {SVM, LR, KNN}/{full composed feature set} are beyond 0.9.

Table 7. Influence of different feature composition on ACC in boosting

Normal/Attack	DT	SVM	LR	Five attacks	DT	SVM	LR
CR	0.747	**0.852**	0.845	CR	0.874	0.889	0.489
ICD	0.722	0.827	0.815	ICD	0.756	0.763	0.533
CR, ICD	0.716	0.827	0.815	CR, ICD	0.896	0.815	0.541
$CR, \alpha_{CR}, \beta_{CR}$	0.741	**0.852**	0.821	$CR, \alpha_{CR}, \beta_{CR}$	**0.904**	0.844	0.585
$ICD, \alpha_{ICD}, \beta_{ICD}$	0.735	**0.852**	0.815	$ICD, \alpha_{ICD}, \beta_{ICD}$	0.793	**0.915**	0.785
$CR, \alpha_{CR}, \beta_{CR},$ $ICD, \alpha_{ICD}, \beta_{ICD}$	0.747	**0.852**	0.809	$CR, \alpha_{CR}, \beta_{CR},$ $ICD, \alpha_{ICD}, \beta_{ICD}$	**0.904**	0.852	0.689
Full composed feature set	0.735	**0.852**	0.815	Full composed feature set	**0.904**	**0.926**	0.763

Table 8. Influence of different feature composition on ACC in stacking

	Normal/Attack	Five attacks
CR	0.781	0.899
ICD	**0.794**	0.777
CR, ICD	0.786	0.879
$CR, \alpha_{CR}, \beta_{CR}$	0.781	**0.921**
$ICD, \alpha_{ICD}, \beta_{ICD}$	0.791	0.756
$CR, \alpha_{CR}, \beta_{CR}, ICD, \alpha_{ICD}, \beta_{ICD}$	0.757	**0.911**
Full composed feature set	0.754	**0.915**

As Table 7 shows for boosting, the maximal ACC of D_1 is 0.852 from SVM's boosting for most feature sets excepting {ICD} and {CR, ICD}. For D_2, the ACC of DT/{$CR, \alpha_{CR}, \beta_{CR}$}, SVM/{$ICD, \alpha_{ICD}, \beta_{ICD}$}, DT/{$CR, \alpha_{CR}, \beta_{CR}, ICD, \alpha_{ICD}, \beta_{ICD}$} and {DT, SVM}/{full composed feature set} are bigger than 0.9. Table 8 shows that the maximal ACC of D_1 is 0.794 for a single ICD feature. For D_2, the ACC of {$CR, \alpha_{CR}, \beta_{CR}$}, {$CR, \alpha_{CR}, \beta_{CR}, ICD, \alpha_{ICD}, \beta_{ICD}$} and {full composed feature set} are beyond 0.9. The ensemble classification has satisfying ACC, and in practice, we recommend CR or {$CR, \alpha_{CR}, \beta_{CR}$} for efficiency.

5.6   Comparison of Bagging, Boosting and Stacking

We choose CR as the only feature in this comparison. Table 9 and Table 10 report the ACC comparison without and with grid search, respectively. SVM's boosting has a maximum ACC of 0.852 on D_1, while KNN's bagging has a maximum ACC of 0.911 on D_2. With grid search, the ACC of LR's bagging has the greatest 7.440% improvement.

Table 9. CR-based ACC comparison without grid search.

Accuracy	Bagging				Boosting			Stacking
	DT	SVM	LR	KNN	DT	SVM	LR	
Normal/Attack	0.722	0.79	0.833	0.728	0.716	**0.852**	0.84	0.757
Five attacks	0.874	0.881	0.793	**0.911**	0.867	0.881	0.474	0.898

Table 10. Grid search-based ACC improvement.

Accuracy inc.(%)	Bagging				Boosting			Stacking
	DT	SVM	LR	KNN	DT	SVM	LR	
Normal/Attack	0	+0.759%	0	+5.082%	+4.330%	0	+0.595%	+3.170%
Five attacks	0	+2.611%	**+7.440%**	0	+0.807%	+0.908%	+3.164%	+0.111%

We also give the training time of different ensemble learning in Table 11, and we can see that bagging is more efficient. Besides, AUC is used to compare bagging with boosting. As Fig. 4 shows, SVM and LR have the best AUC values in bagging, while SVM has the best AUC value 0.89 in boosting. There is only a little difference between bagging and boosting.

Table 11. Training time across different ensemble learning.

Training time(s)	Bagging				Boosting			Stacking
	DT	SVM	LR	KNN	DT	SVM	LR	
Normal/Attack	0.819	1.959	1.742	0.698	0.968	15.105	1.276	4.620
Five attacks	1.185	1.860	4.869	0.612	1.120	16.376	1.937	9.910

5.7   Traffic Flow Patterns

For D_1 and D_2, we draw decision trees respectively to characterize explainable patterns. The decision tree generated by Graphviz [2] for D_1 is shown in Fig. 5(a) and for D_2 in Fig. 5(b). $(x_1, x_2, \cdots, x_{20})$ refers to CR features in a traffic flow of 1800 s, through sampling the first 10 time of

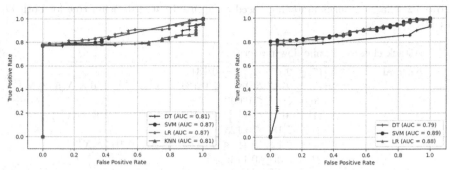

(a) ROC curve of D_1 with AUC values in bagging

(b) ROC curve of D_1 with AUC values in boosting

Fig. 4. AUC comparison between bagging and boosting.

flow head and the last 10 time of flow tail. Therefore, $(x_1, x_2, \cdots, x_{20}) = (CR(t_1), \cdots, CR(t_{10}), CR(t_{1800-9}), \cdots, CR(t_{1800}))$.

Taking Fig. 5(b) for example, the second green rectangle at the bottom level indicates that there are 57 samples as a confidence to support the classification into f_2 class, and the entropy is equal to 0.0. We can found that these patterns are relatively clear and operable. Based on our experiments, if in the first step, we have maximum probability 0.852 to identify the congest attack, and in the second step we have the maximum probability 0.926 to distinguish the five attacks, and we even have about 0.8 probability to find out a specific-frequency congestion attack from a 1800-s flow that is a valuable work as a first step for any randomly-sampled flow analysis.

According to the decision trees for D_1 and D_2, Table 12 is drawn to show traffic flow patterns of different classes, $\{Normal, Attack\}$ for D_1 and $\{f_1, f_2, f_3, f_4, f_5\}$ for D_2. The patterns of different classes are counted separately in Table 12, and we can infer the classes from the given sample data. For example, when $X[17] \leq 0.17 \wedge X[1] > 0.131$, we can infer that the sample data belongs to class "Normal", however, $X[17] > 0.17$ is one of the traffic flow patterns of class "Attack". Also, we can see that $X[17]$ is important to distinguish between "Normal" and "Attack", and $X[10]$ is the key feature to distinguish "$f_1 \sim f_5$". In the above analyses, $X[17]$ denotes the attack acceleration of the congestion degree of the 4th phase $\alpha_{PCD}(4)$, $X[1]$ is the global congestion degree for an intersection ICD, an $X[10]$ is the congestion degree of the 5th phase PCD_5. Therefore, the attack acceleration of the congestion degree of the 4th phase and the congestion degree of the 5th phase are the two most essential features for recognizing whether the traffic flow sample is "Normal" or "Attack" and which attack frequency "$f_1 \sim f_5$" the class of the sample is.

Table 12. Class patterns matching based on approximated decision tree for both D_1 and D_2.

Attack classes	Traffic flow pattern
Normal	$X[17] \leq 0.17 \wedge X[1] > 0.131$; $X[17] \leq 0.17 \wedge X[1] \leq 0.131 \wedge X[4] \leq 0.106 \wedge X[5] \leq 0.106 \wedge X[11] \leq 0.099$; $X[17] \leq 0.17 \wedge X[1] \leq 0.131 \wedge X[4] > 0.106 \wedge X[3] \leq 0.121 \wedge X[18] \leq 0.123$; $X[17] \leq 0.17 \wedge X[1] \leq 0.131 \wedge X[4] > 0.106 \wedge X[3] > 0.121 \wedge X[0] \leq 0.113$;
Attack	$X[17] > 0.17$; $X[17] \leq 0.17 \wedge X[1] \leq 0.131 \wedge X[4] \leq 0.106 \wedge X[5] > 0.106$; $X[17] \leq 0.17 \wedge X[1] \leq 0.131 \wedge X[4] \leq 0.106 \wedge X[5] \leq 0.106 \wedge X[11] > 0.099$; $X[17] \leq 0.17 \wedge X[1] \leq 0.131 \wedge X[4] > 0.106 \wedge X[3] > 0.121 \wedge X[0] > 0.113$;
f_1	$X[10] > 0.268 \wedge X[15] > 0.344 \wedge X[9] \leq 0.268 \wedge X[12] \leq 0.371 \wedge X[5] > 0.229$; $X[10] > 0.268 \wedge X[15] > 0.344 \wedge X[9] \leq 0.268 \wedge X[12] > 0.371$;
f_2	$X[10] > 0.268 \wedge X[15] \leq 0.344 \wedge X[0] \leq 0.24 \wedge X[10] \leq 0.333 \wedge X[4] > 0.064$; $X[10] > 0.268 \wedge X[15] \leq 0.344 \wedge X[0] > 0.24 \wedge X[16] \leq 0.288$; $X[10] > 0.268 \wedge X[15] > 0.344 \wedge X[9] \leq 0.268 \wedge X[18] \leq 0.382 \wedge X[19] \leq 0.349$; $X[10] > 0.268 \wedge X[15] > 0.344 \wedge X[9] \leq 0.268 \wedge X[18] > 0.382 \wedge X[13] \leq 0.394$;
f_3	$X[10] > 0.268 \wedge X[15] \leq 0.344 \wedge X[0] \leq 0.24 \wedge X[10] > 0.333$; $X[10] > 0.268 \wedge X[15] \leq 0.344 \wedge X[0] > 0.24 \wedge X[16] > 0.288 \wedge X[17] \leq 0.336$; $X[10] > 0.268 \wedge X[15] > 0.344 \wedge X[9] \leq 0.268 \wedge X[18] \leq 0.382 \wedge X[19] > 0.349$; $X[10] > 0.268 \wedge X[15] > 0.344 \wedge X[9] \leq 0.268 \wedge X[12] \leq 0.371 \wedge X[5] \leq 0.229$;
f_4	$X[10] \leq 0.268 \wedge X[13] > 0.165$; $X[10] > 0.268 \wedge X[15] \leq 0.344 \wedge X[0] \leq 0.24 \wedge X[10] \leq 0.333 \wedge X[4] \leq 0.064$;
f_5	$X[10] \leq 0.268 \wedge X[13] \leq 0.165$;

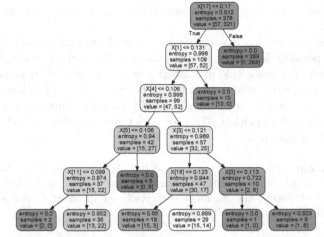

(a) Decision tree trained based on D_1 for binary classifier.

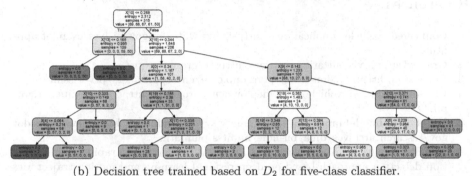

(b) Decision tree trained based on D_2 for five-class classifier.

Fig. 5. Decision tree trained based on D_1 and D_2, respectively.

6 Conclusion

In this work, we focus on the problem of detection delay and lack of prediction on the I-SIG congestion attack. There are two main challenges, one of which is how to design and extract effective features from traffic flows of variable spoofing frequencies, and the other is how to realize real effective prediction based on ensemble learning, as well as obtain the explainable pattern for detailed analyses. To address the challenges, in this article, we propose a novel approach for congestion attack prediction. We implement ensemble learning to build correlations between abnormal congestion and attack frequency. Based on supervised learning of historical data, we can recognize the current attack frequency and further realize the prediction of the subsequent congestion attack. We also report on necessary and experienced tricks, including rescaling, oversampling, and hyperparameter optimization for performance improvement. Furthermore, we have conducted extensive experiments and analyzed the experimental results in terms of accuracy and time. The experimental results have shown the superiority of our approach.

To our best knowledge, we are the first to perform and present a prediction approach for periodic I-SIG congestion attack under variable spoofing frequencies. We expect this work guidable for grounding repetition to promote the I-SIG security. This work is also expected to inspire a series of follow-up studies, including but not limited to (1) continuous prediction improvement including both framework and algorithm, (2) more concrete congestion attack prevention by leveraging our insights.

Acknowledgment. The work was supported by the National Natural Science Foundation of China under Grant Nos. 61972025, 61802389, 61672092, U1811264, and 61966009, the National Key R&D Program of China under Grant Nos. 2020YFB1005604 and 2020YFB2103802.

References

1. Connected vehicle applications. https://www.its.dot.gov/pi-lots/cv_pilot_apps.htm
2. Graphvizgraph visualization software. https://graphviz.org/
3. Ptv vissim. http://vision-traffic.ptvgroup.com/en-us/products/ptv-vissim
4. U.s.dot connected vehicle pilot deployment program. https://www.its.dot.gov/pilots/
5. Usdot: Multimodal intelligent traffic safety system (mmitss). https://www.its.dot.gov/research_archives/dma/bu-ndle/mmitss_plan.htm
6. Abdelwahab, M.A., Abdel-Nasser, M., Hori, M.: Reliable and rapid traffic congestion detection approach based on deep residual learning and motion trajectories. IEEE Access **8**, 182180–182192 (2020)
7. Anbaroglu, B., Heydecker, B., Tao, C.: Spatio-temporal clustering for non-recurrent traffic congestion detection on urban road networks. Transp. Res. Part C **48**, 47–65 (2014)
8. Angiulli, F., Astorino, A.: Scaling up support vector machines using nearest neighbor condensation. IEEE Trans. Neural Netw. **21**(2), 351–357 (2010)
9. Boualouache, A., Senouci, S., Moussaoui, S.: A survey on pseudonym changing strategies for vehicular adhoc networks. IEEE Commun. Surv. Tutor. **20**(1), 770–790 (2018)
10. Chen, Q.A., Yin, Y., Feng, Y., Mao, Z.M., Liu, H.X.: Exposing congestion attack on emerging connected vehicle based traffic signal control. In: Network and Distributed System Security Symposium, pp. 39.1–39.15 (2018)
11. Chen, Z., Jiang, Y., Sun, D.: Discrimination and prediction of traffic congestion states of urban road network based on spatio-temporal correlation. IEEE Access **8**, 3330–3342 (2020)
12. Cheng, Q., Varshney, P.K., Arora, M.K.: Logistic regression for feature selection and soft classification of remote sensing data. IEEE Geosci. Remote Sens. Lett. **3**(4), 491–494 (2006)
13. Dimri, A., Singh, H., Aggarwal, N., Raman, B., Ramakrishnan, K.K., Bansal, D.: Barosense: using barometer for road traffic congestion detection and path estimation with crowdsourcing. ACM Trans. Sens. Netw. **16**(1), 4:1–4:24 (2020)

14. Feng, Y., Head, K.L., Khoshmagham, S., Zamanipour, M.: A realtime adaptive signal control in a connected vehicle environment. Transp. Res. Part C. Emerg. Technol. **55**, 460–473 (2015)

15. Freund, Y., Schapire, R.E.: A decision-theoretic generalization of on-line learning and an application to boosting. J. Comput. Syst. Sci. **55**(1), 119–139 (1997)

16. Goin, J.E.: Classification bias of the k-nearest neighbor algorithm. IEEE Trans. Pattern Anal. Mach. Intell. **PAMI-6**(3), 379–381 (1984)

17. Jaleel, A., Hassan, M.A., Mahmood, T., Ghani, M.U., Rehman, A.U.: Reducing congestion in an intelligent traffic system with collaborative and adaptive signaling on the edge. IEEE Access **8**, 205396–205410 (2020)

18. Jeske, T.: Floating car data from smartphones: what google and waze know about you and how hackers can control traffic (2012)

19. Li, Q., Tan, H., Jiang, Z., Wu, Y., Ye, L.: Nonrecurrent traffic congestion detection with a coupled scalable bayesian robust tensor factorization model. Neurocomputing **430**, 138–149 (2021)

20. Li, Y., et al.: An empirical study on gan-based traffic congestion attack analysis: a visualized method. Wirel. Commun. Mob. Comput. **2020**, 8823300:1–8823300:14 (2020)

21. Lu, Z., Qu, G., Liu, Z.: A survey on recent advances in vehicular network security, trust, and privacy. IEEE Trans. Intell. Transp. Syst. **20**(2), 760–776 (2019)

22. Bartlett, P., Freund, Y., Lee, W.S., Schapire, R.E.: Boosting the margin: a new explanation for the effectiveness of voting methods. Ann. Stat. **26**(5), 1651–1686 (1998)

23. Sen, S., Head, K.L.: Controlled optimization of phases at an intersection. Transp. Sci. **31**(1), 5–17 (1997)

24. Suarez, A., Lutsko, J.F.: Globally optimal fuzzy decision trees for classification and regression. IEEE Trans. Pattern Anal. Mach. Intell. **21**(12), 1297–1311 (1999)

25. Sun, X., Xu, W.: Fast implementation of delong's algorithm for comparing the areas under correlated receiver operating characteristic curves. IEEE Signal Process. Lett. **21**(11), 1389–1393 (2014)

26. Ta, V., Dvir, A.: A secure road traffic congestion detection and notification concept based on V2I communications. Veh. Commun. **25**, 100283 (2020)

27. Wang, R., Xu, Z., Zhao, X., Hu, J.: V2v-based method for the detection of road traffic congestion. IET Intell. Transp. Syst. (2019)

28. Wang, X., Xiang, Y., Niu, W., Tong, E., Liu, J.: Explainable congestion attack prediction and software-level reinforcement in intelligent traffic signal system. In: 26th IEEE International Conference on Parallel and Distributed Systems, ICPADS 2020, Hong Kong, 2–4 December 2020, pp. 667–672. IEEE (2020)

29. Wolpert, D.: Stacked generalization. Neural Netw. **5**, 241–259 (1992)

30. Zeadally, S., Hunt, R., Chen, Y., Irwin, A.S.M., Hassan, A.: Vehicular ad hoc networks (vanets): status, results, and challenges. Telecommun. Syst. **50**(4), 217–241 (2012)

31. Zhang, N., Zhang, Y., Lu, H.: Seasonal autoregressive integrated moving average and support vector machine models: prediction of short-term traffic flow on freeways. Transp. Res. Rec. **2215**(1), 85–92 (2011)

32. Zhong, X., Li, L., Zhang, Y., Zhang, B., Zhang, W., Yang, T.: Oodt: obstacle aware opportunistic data transmission for cognitive radio ad hoc networks. IEEE Trans. Commun. **68**(6), 3654–3666 (2020)

Threat Detection-Oriented Network Security Situation Assessment Method

Hongyu Yang[1,2](✉) (iD), Zixin Zhang[2] (iD), and Liang Zhang[3] (iD)

[1] School of Safety Science and Engineering, Civil Aviation
University of China, Tianjin 300300, China
[2] School of Computer Science and Technology, Civil Aviation
University of China, Tianjin 300300, China
[3] School of Information, University of Arizona, Tucson, AZ 85721, USA

Abstract. To analyze the impact of network threats and accurately reflect the security situation of the network, we propose a threat detection-oriented network security situation assessment method. Firstly, a network threat detection model is designed. The model is composed of parallel feature extraction (PFE) with the sparse auto-encoder and an improved bi-directional gate recurrent (IBiGRU) with the attention mechanism. The PFE is established to extract the key information of different network threats and fuse the extracted features with the original information. Secondly, the PFE-IBiGRU is used to detect the threats in the network, and the occurrence number of each attack type and the false alarm reduction matrix are counted. Finally, according to the model detection results, combined with the proposed network security situation quantification method, the network security situation value is calculated. The experimental results show that our method is more accurate for identifying network attacks and can effectively and comprehensively evaluate the overall situation of network security.

Keywords: Parallel feature extraction · Sparse auto-encoder · Attention mechanism · False alarm reduction matrix · Network security situation assessment

1 Introduction

With the development of communication and cloud computing technology, network security is becoming increasingly important. Network security situation assessment (NSSA) can build an appropriate model according to related security incidents, and then assess the threat degree of the entire network system, and assist security managers to grasp the current network status [1].

Javaid et al. [2] used sparse auto-encoder (SAE) to extract features, the detection accuracy was significantly improved, but the model only used a single SAE to extract features, resulting in long extraction time and can not well fit the distribution of different attack types. Liu et al. [3] used a deep neural network based on the attention mechanism for real-time detection of Web attacks and proved the feasibility of this method in real

W. Shi et al. (Eds.): SPNCE 2021, LNICST 423, pp. 238–245, 2022.
https://doi.org/10.1007/978-3-030-96791-8_17

network traffic. Hu et al. [4] proposed a network security situation prediction model based on MapReduce and SVM, which solved the shortcoming of long training time of the SVM prediction model but did not conduct a comprehensive evaluation of the network situation, and the evaluation dimension was relatively single, which could not reflect the overall situation of the network. Lin et al. [5] tested the UNSW-NB15 data set based on various neural network models such as long-short term memory (LSTM) and bi-directional gate recurrent unit (BiGRU). The results show that BiGRU has the highest accuracy compared with other models.

Aiming at the difficulties in extracting feature elements and poor timeliness of available network security situation assessment methods, we propose a threat detection-oriented network security situation assessment method.

2   Threat Detection-Oriented Network Security Situation Assessment Method

The network security situation assessment framework proposed includes three parts: situation extraction, situation analysis, and situation assessment. The network security situation assessment process is designed as follows:

(1)   Situation extraction: The network traffic data is collected, and then the data is pre-processed such as feature numericalization, feature normalization, and data balance. After that, the data is input into the PFE-IBiGRU threat detection model for training.

(2)   Situation analysis: The test dataset is input into the trained threat detection model PFE-IBiGRU. Then the occurrence number of each attack type and the false alarm reduction matrix are recorded for the calculation of network security situation value in the third step.

(3)   Situation assessment: Based on the detection results of the PFE-IBiGRU network threat detection model, combined with the quantified index of the network security situation, the network security situation value is calculated and the overall situation is evaluated.

2.1   Threat Detection Model

Parallel Feature Extraction (PFE). SAE is an improvement on auto-encoder (AE). It provides an idea to avoid the auto-encoder learning to be an identity function. Firstly, the number of neurons in the hidden layer is less than that in the input layer, and it is an incomplete auto-encoder, which enables the hidden layer to learn the significant compression characteristics of the input vector. Secondly, the sparsity penalty is added to the hidden layer, which limits the activation of neurons in the hidden layer to a relatively small range and avoids the complete equivalence of x' and x. However network threats contain a variety of attack types, and the distribution of these types of information is different. Feature extraction through a single SAE takes a long time and does not fit the distribution of different attacks well. Therefore, this paper uses multiple SAEs to complete feature extraction in parallel, learn the distribution of each attack, and better express the information differences between different attack types. The parallel

240   H. Yang et al.

feature extraction is designed as follows: Firstly, according to different attack types, the preprocessed dataset is input into the SAE-based feature extractor FE_N for training. The loss function L_{SAE} is the minimum, and the FE_N training is completed. Then, the feature extraction function can be completed by taking the output of the encoder as the feature representing the original data. Finally, the extracted features are fused with the original features and input to the IBiGRU network for training.

Improved BiGRU (IBiGRU). BiGRU is an improved version of GRU. It can learn the temporal relationship between past and future states and the current state, and can effectively learn the representation relationship between network threat traffic to enhance the feature learning ability of the detection network.However, when BiGRU learns too long sequence data, it will have the problems of low efficiency and long time. The attention model [3] provides a way to solve this problem. Figure 1 shows the IBiGRU model structure designed in this paper. The specific steps of IBiGRU are as follows:

Step 1. Input data into the BiGRU network for learning and get output y_{ij}.

Step 2. Add weight to local features through the attention layer. The calculation method is as follows:

$$d_{ij} = tanh(A_w y_{ij} + C_w) \tag{1}$$

$$e_{ij} = softmax(d_{ij} + d_w) \tag{2}$$

$$z_i = \sum_j e_{ij} d_{ij} \tag{3}$$

where d_{ij} refers to the state of the hidden layer, e_{ij} refers to the weight, A_w refers to the weighting coefficient, C_w refers to the bias term, and d_w refers to the randomly initialized attention matrix.

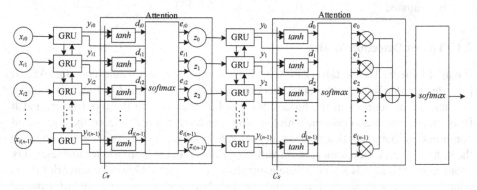

Fig. 1. IBiGRU's model structure

Step 3. Input the results obtained in Step 2 into the BiGRU network for learning. Similar to Step 2, the attention layer is used to add weight to the global features. The calculation method is as follows:

$$d_i = tanh(A_s y_i + C_s) \tag{4}$$

$$e_i = softmax(d_i, d_s) \tag{5}$$

$$z = \sum_j e_i d_i \tag{6}$$

Step 4. Input the result z of Step 3 into the classifier to complete model training.

2.2 Network Security Situation Assessment

The network security situation assessment result is determined by the threat severity and threat impact.

Threat Severity. The threat severity is obtained by the occurrence number of each attack type, the false alarm reduction matrix, and the threat severity factor of each attack type. The specific calculation process is as follows:

Step 1. Randomly select several sets of data from the test dataset, and input them into the PFE-IBiGRU model for threat detection. The occurrence number of each attack type detected by the model is N_i.

Step 2. Input the training dataset into the trained threat detection model, calculate b_{ij} based on the model test results and the actual number of attack types, then obtain the model's false alarm reduction matrix $M = [b_{ij}]_{n \times n}$.

Step 3. Use the weight coefficient generation algorithm [6] to obtain and calculate the threat severity factors F_i of each attack type.

Step 4. Use the false alarm reduction matrix to correct the occurrence number N_i of each attack type, and the corrected occurrence number is recorded as Q_i.

$$Q_i = N \cdot [b_{i1} \ b_{i2} \ ... \ b_{in}]^T \tag{7}$$

where N is a vector composed of the occurrence number of each attack type N_i.

Step 5. Calculate the threat severity S_i according to Eq. (8).

$$S_i = f(Q_i, F_i) = Q_i \times 10^{F_i} \tag{8}$$

Threat Impact. Combined with the common vulnerability scoring system (CVSS) [7] to evaluate the impact degree and scores of confidentiality (C), integrity (I), and availability (A). C, I, and A are divided into three grades according to no impact, low impact, and high impact, with values of 0, 0.22, and 0.56 respectively. Then, calculate the threat influence degree Ii of each attack type through Eq. (9).

$$I_i = Round_2(\log_2(\frac{d_1 2^{Con_i} + d_1 2^{Int_i} + d_3 2^{Ava_i}}{3})) \tag{9}$$

where Con_i, Int_i, and Ava_i represent the C, I, and A impact scores of attack type i, and d_1, d_2, and d_3 respectively correspond to the weight of threat impact degree.

Network Security Situation Quantitative Value. Calculate the network security situation value V.

$$V = \frac{1}{n} \sum_{i=1}^{n} S_i \times I_i \tag{10}$$

According to the interval of the V, refer to the "National Emergency Plan for Public Emergencies" [8], the network security situation assessment is divided into five levels: safe, low-risk, medium-risk, high-risk, and super-risk, corresponding to five intervals of 0.00–0.30, 0.31–0.60, 0.61–0.90, 0.91–1.20 and 1.21–1.50 respectively.

3 Experiments and Results

To verify the effectiveness and comprehensiveness of the method in this paper for network security situation assessment, experiments are conducted to verify the performance improvement effect of the PFE and attention mechanism on the basic model BiGRU. At the same time, through comparative experiments with typical methods, the objectivity and feasibility of the application of this method in network security situation assessment are verified.

3.1 Dataset Description and Data Preprocessing

The NSL-KDD dataset solves the problem of the KDD99 dataset [9]. And it is selected for the experiment. Data preprocessing includes feature numericalization, feature normalization, and data balance.Firstly, we apply the one-hot encoding method to convert the classification features into digital features. Secondly, the range between the maximum and the minimum value of some features in the NSL-KDD dataset is very different. To eliminate the influence of unit and scale differences between features on model training, we map the feature to the interval [0,1]. Finally, in the KDDTrain +, there are 67343 Normal data, while DoS and U2R only contain 52 and 995 data. The imbalance of data amount of different attack types will lead to the weak detection problem of the model. Therefore, we use the ADASYN algorithm to solve the problem of data imbalance to improve the detection effect.

3.2 Evaluation Metrics

To evaluate the performance of the model, we select the following metrics:

True Negatives (TN), the number of samples correctly classified as normal;

False Negatives (FN), the number of attack samples incorrectly classified as normal;

True Positives (TP), the number of samples correctly classified as attacks;

False Positives (FP), the number of normal samples incorrectly classified as attacks.

Precision (P), a percentage of the number of correctly predicted attacks and the total number of predicted samples, calculated by:

$$P = \frac{TP}{TP + FP} \times 100\% \tag{11}$$

Recall (R), a percentage of the number of correctly predicted attacks and the total number of attack samples, calculated by:

$$R = \frac{TP}{TP + FN} \times 100\% \qquad (12)$$

F1-score ($F1$), considering P and R comprehensively, is an important metric to measure the performance of model detection, calculated by:

$$F1 = \frac{2 \times P \times R}{P + R} \times 100\% \qquad (13)$$

3.3 Network Model Threat Testing Results

In the experiment, 125973 data of the KDDTrain + are selected for learning, 22543 data of the KDDTest + are selected for threat detection.To analyze the threat detection accuracy of the proposed model PFE-IBiGRU in this paper, we compare it with the original model BiGRU, the PFE-BiGRU model that only applies PFE to improve the original model, the IBiGRU model that only uses the attention mechanism to improve the original model, and the attention mechanism. The precision, recall, and $F1$ of four models are depicted in Table 1.

Table 1. Precision (%), Recall (%), $F1$ (%) of six models

Model	Precision	Recall	$F1$
BiGRU	76.85	77.71	77.28
PFE-BiGRU	79.70	80.78	80.24
IBiGRU	80.49	81.94	81.21
PFE-IBiGRU	82.13	83.36	82.74

As can be seen from Table 1, compared with the BiGRU model, the precisions of the PFE-BiGRU, and IBiGRU models are increased by 2.85%, and 3.64%. The precision of the PFE-IBiGRU is 82.13%, which is 5.28% higher than the BiGRU model. And Table 1 also shows that the recall and $F1$ of PFE-IBiGRU are better than the other three models. Compared with the BiGRU, PFE-BiGRU, and IBiGRU models, the recall rate is increased by 5.65%, 2.58%, and 1.42%; the $F1$ is increased by 5.46%, 2.5%, and 1.53% respectively. The reason is that the PFE-IBiGRU model in this paper adopts PFE to improve the characterization ability of the original data, and applies the attention mechanism for weighted feature learning, which verifies the advantages of the above two improved methods.

3.4 Network Security Situation Quantitative Assessment Results Analysis

We conduct 200 group threat tests with random data of the same size which is selected from the test dataset. SVM [4], LSTM [5], BIGRU [5], and PFE-IBIGRU carry out threat testing experiments respectively. The network security situation values based on the above four models are obtained by using the method in this paper and compared with the real network security situation. Q_i in Eq. (8) is replaced by the actual number of each attack type in the test samples, and the actual situation value is further calculated by Eqs. (9) and (10). Figure 2 shows the comparison results of the network situation values in 20 groups of experiments.

It can be seen from Fig. 2 that under the same test dataset samples, the network security situation values calculated by the PFE-IBiGRU and the real situation values are always in the same situation assessment interval, while some situation value calculated by SVM, LSTM, and BiGRU model is not in the same interval as the real situation value. This indicates that the situation assessment results of the PFE-IBiGRU are more consistent with the actual network situation.

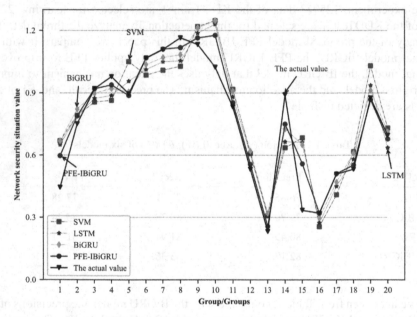

Fig. 2. Network security situation values

Besides, in some test results in Fig. 2, the situation values calculated by the four models are in the same situation assessment interval with the real situation values, but the network security situation values calculated by the PFE-IBiGRU are always closer to the real situation values. This shows that the PFE-IBiGRU model has a stronger ability to represent network threats, and the effect of this method on network security situation assessment is more intuitive and feasible.

4   Conclusion

This paper proposes a threat detection-oriented network security situation assessment method. Firstly, a threat detection model is constructed, which adopts the parallel feature extraction method to effectively improve the characterization ability of the original data. Besides, the attention mechanism is used to improve the BiGRU network to determine the best weight of different features. Then PFE-IBiGRU is applied to detect the network threat, and the network security situation is evaluated according to the detection results and the false alarm reduction matrix. Finally, by comparing with BiGRU, LSTM, SVM, and other methods, the experiment proves that the effectiveness and reliability of the network security situation assessment results obtained by the method in this paper are more advantageous.

Acknowledgements. This work was supported by the Civil Aviation Joint Research Fund Project of the National Natural Science Foundation of China under granted number U1833107.

References

1. Zhao, D.: Study on network security situation awareness based on particle swarm optimization algorithm. Comput. Ind. Eng. **125**, 764–775 (2018)
2. Javaid, A.: A deep learning approach for network intrusion detection system. In: Proceedings of the 9th EAI International Conference on Bio-inspired Information and Communications, pp. 21–26. ICST, Brussels (2016)
3. Liu, T.: Locate-then-detect: real-time web attack detection via attention-based deep neural networks. In: Proceedings of the Twenty-Eighth International Joint Conference on Artificial Intelligence (IJCAI), pp. 4725–4731. Morgan Kaufmann, San Francisco (2019)
4. Hu, J.: Network security situation prediction based on MR-SVM. IEEE Access **7**, 130937–130945 (2019)
5. Lin, Y.: Time-related network intrusion detection model: a deep learning method. In: 2019 IEEE Global Communications Conference, pp. 1–6. IEEE Press, Piscataway (2019)
6. Liu, X.W.: Fusion-based cognitive awareness-control model for network security situation. J. Softw. **27**(8), 2099–2114 (2016)
7. Common Vulnerability Scoring System v3.0: Specification Document. https://www.first.org/cvss/specification-document. Accessed 5 Feb 2020
8. Council, S.: The State Council of the People's Republic of China. Overall Emergency Plans for National Sudden Public Incidents. China Legal Press, Beijing (2006)
9. Bala, R.: A review on kdd cup99 and nsl-kdd dataset. Int. J. Adv. Res. Comput. Sci. **10**(2), 64–67 (2019)

System Business Affecting Impact Analysis Method with Crossover Probability Theory

Lixia Xie[1] , Yijia Zhang[1] , Hongyu Yang[1,2(✉)] , and Liang Zhang[3]

[1] School of Computer Science and Technology, Civil Aviation
University of China, Tianjin 300300, China
[2] School of Safety Science and Engineering, Civil Aviation
University of China, Tianjin 300300, China
[3] School of Information, University of Arizona, Tucson, AZ 85721, USA

Abstract. In view of the lack of scale calibration and the influence of expert evaluation preference on the analysis results of information system business impact analysis, an analysis method of system business affecting impact based on crossover probability theory is proposed. Firstly, the experts evaluate the relevance and influence of the business functions of the information system. Then quantify the correlation between system business functions, and generate a comprehensive cross impact matrix. Finally, the preference chain generation algorithm is used to generate the business preference chain of information system, and the interaction relationship of each business of the system is associated. The experiment shows that this method can accurately measure the extent and trend of business interruption affecting other information system businesses.

Keywords: Information system · Business affecting impact · Crossover probability theory · Preference chain

1 Introduction

Business Impact Analysis (BIA) is used to analyze the system loss caused by business interruption, which is an important link of business continuity management [1]. Cai M [2] analyzed the influence of faults through network structure entropy reflecting the characteristics of network structure. Yin R [3] evaluated node importance through node structure hole importance index and adjacent node k-core importance index. Xie L [4] proposed a business affecting impact analysis method for information system. The limitation of the above research lies in that the analysis of the business impact of information system is insufficient, and the impact and intensity of other business after the interruption of a business function of the system are not considered.

In order to solve the shortcomings of the above research, this paper proposes a method of business impact analysis based on crossover probability theory. The association between business function nodes is represented by cross impact matrix. The subjective influence of expert scoring on cross impact matrix is reduced [5], and the

W. Shi et al. (Eds.): SPNCE 2021, LNICST 423, pp. 246–253, 2022.
https://doi.org/10.1007/978-3-030-96791-8_18

business functions of information system are abstracted as nodes [6], the preference chain is generated by optimizing preference chain generation algorithm [7], the system is associated with the business function process and business function impact.

2   Analysis Method Architecture Design

The system business affecting impact analysis method based on crossover probability theory is composed of the cross impact matrix processing module and the preference chain generation and business impact analysis module.

Cross impact matrix treatment module: Firstly, the experts evaluate the relevance and influence degree between business functions. Then, the optimal weighting coefficient is obtained by subjective and objective combination weighting method to generate comprehensive weights. Finally, generate the comprehensive cross impact matrix to express the relevance and influence degree between business functions.

Preferential chain generation and business impact analysis module: Firstly, the overall impact of a business function on other business functions (Activity Sum, AS) in the cross impact matrix is used to characterize the impact of business function interruption on the information system. Then, the cross impact matrix and the AS are input to the algorithm of preference chain used to generate the system business function preference chain. Finally, according to the AS and the preference chain, the influence degree of a business function interruption and the influence trend of other business functions of the system are obtained.

3   Cross Impact Matrix

3.1   Quantification of Business Association Influence Relationship

The crossover probability theory uses the cross impact matrix to store the degree of direct influence between business functions. Business function interruption in information system will have an impact on subsequent business functions. Referring to the asset importance grade evaluation and risk grade division evaluation [8], the business importance evaluation value is 0–100, represents the business importance from low to high, and the inter business impact value is 0–5, represents the impact between businesses ranges from low to high. According to the business importance evaluation value and the inter business impact value, the business importance evaluation matrix and inter business cross impact matrix are generated by expert scoring.

3.2   Generation of Comprehensive Cross Impact Matrix

In order to reduce the subjectivity brought by experts' evaluation as much as possible, it is necessary to give reasonable weights to the inter business cross impact matrix generated by experts' evaluation. The generation process of the comprehensive cross impact matrix R is designed as follows.

Normalized the Business Importance Evaluation Matrix. M experts score the business importance according to the business importance evaluation value, and generate the business importance evaluation matrix. The ith expert denotes the importance value of the jth business as a_{ij} $(i = 1, 2,..., m; j = 1, 2,..., n)$, Normalize the business importance evaluation matrix according to formula (1).

$$b_{ij} = (a_{ij} - a_c^{min})/(a_c^{max} - a_c^{min}) \qquad (1)$$

Where a_c^{max} is the maximum value of importance of jth business function and a_c^{min} is the minimum value of importance of jth business function. The normalized decision matrix B is

$$B = \begin{pmatrix} b_{11} & \cdots & b_{1n} \\ \vdots & \ddots & \vdots \\ b_{m1} & \cdots & b_{mn} \end{pmatrix}$$

Extract Subjective and Objective Weights. The harmonic average value of the business importance evaluation matrix is calculated to obtain the subjective weight of the business function is $W_{1j} = (W_{11}, W_{12},..., W_{1n})^T$. The entropy weight method [9] is used to calculate the objective weight of experts to business is $W_{2j} = (W_{21}, W_{22}, ..., W_{2n})^T$.

Generate the Comprehensive Cross Impact Matrix. According to formula (2), the combined weight vector W_j of subjective weight W_{1j} and objective weight W_{2j} is obtained.

$$W_j = \alpha W_{1j} + \beta W_{2j} \qquad (2)$$

Where α and β are combined weighting coefficients

$$\alpha = \frac{\frac{1}{2}\sum_{i=1}^{m}\sum_{j=1}^{n} b_{ij}(W_{1j} - W_{2j}) + \sum_{j=1}^{n} W_{2j}(W_{1j} + W_{2j})}{\sum_{j=1}^{n} (W_{1j} + W_{2j})^2}, \quad \beta = \frac{\sum_{j=1}^{n} W_{1j}(W_{1j} + W_{2j}) - \frac{1}{2}\sum_{i=1}^{m}\sum_{j=1}^{n} b_{ij}(W_{1j} - W_{2j})}{\sum_{j=1}^{n} (W_{1j} + W_{2j})^2}$$

$$(3)$$

Finally, the linear weighted evaluation model is used to obtain the comprehensive evaluation value vector U.

$$U = \sum_{j=1}^{n} b_{ij} W_j \qquad (4)$$

The elements in the comprehensive evaluation value vector $U = (u_1, u_2,..., u_m)$ correspond to the weight of each expert. According to the inter business impact value, m experts score the degree of inter business impact, and generate m inter business cross impact matrix $Q = \{Q1, Q2,..., Qm\}$. According to the comprehensive evaluation value vector U, the corresponding weight of experts is multiplied by the matrix $Q1 \sim Qm$, and then the average value of the weighted m matrices is calculated to generate the comprehensive cross impact matrix R, which is the input data of the preference chain generation algorithm.

$$R = \begin{pmatrix} r_{11} & \cdots & r_{1n} \\ \vdots & \ddots & \vdots \\ r_{m1} & \cdots & r_{mn} \end{pmatrix}$$

4 Business Affecting Impact Analysis

4.1 Active Sum Calculation

In the information system, the overall impact of a business function on all other business functions is called active sum (AS), which is used to measure the impact of business function interruption on information system.

In the comprehensive cross impact matrix R, each row of the matrix shows the impact degree of the business function on others. The AS_i of business function i is

$$AS_i = \sum_{j=1}^{n} r_{ij} \tag{5}$$

r_{ij} is an element in the comprehensive cross impact matrix R.

4.2 Preference Chain Generation

The preference chain is a chain structure generated by the comprehensive cross impact matrix, which can intuitively express the relevance and priority between business functions. The steps of preference chain generation algorithm are designed as follows:

(1) Calculate the AS of each business in the system.
(2) Select the highest AS of business to insert the head of preference chain.
(3) If multiple businesses have the highest sum of AS, select the first to insert the head of preference chain.
(4) Build preference chain with selected business as root. The entry priority of the remaining business nodes is sorted by AS, the number of affected businesses and the impact value from large to small, and selected the first and the largest nodes.
(5) All nodes enter the chain according to Step (4), until all nodes enter the chain or only the nodes left cannot enter the chain due to insufficient priority.
(6) For the node that is not in the chain, select the node that has been in the chain and has the greatest impact on it as its preorder node, and this node as a branch node to enter the chain according to step (4).

4.3 Business Affecting Impact Analysis

The analysis method of business impact of information system including the measurement of the impact of business function interruption and the trend analysis of the impact of business function interruption on others. In the event of information system business interruption, by analyzing the change of information system business AS before and after the business interruption, the influence degree of the interruption on the information system can be understood.

When a business function in an information system is interrupted, the node corresponding to this business function and the edge starting from this node are deleted from the preference chain. Then, the newly added node without indegree in the preference chain is the business function that may be affected by the business function interruption. This method can reflect the influence trend of business function interruption on others of the information system.

5   Experiments and Results

5.1 Business Impact Analysis and Results

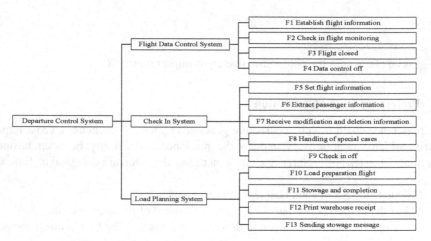

Fig. 1. Functional structure of departure control system.

In order to verify the effectiveness and accuracy of this method, the departure control system of civil aviation airport is selected as the experimental object. The functional structure of the system is shown in Fig. 1.

The experimental data comes from the system management files, business function interruption log records and expert scoring data. 20 business cross impact matrices and a business function importance evaluation matrix are generated. According to Sect. 3.2, the subjective and objective comprehensive weight vector U^T.

According to U^T, the corresponding weight of experts is multiplied by the business cross impact matrices, and then the average value of the weighted matrix is calculated

Table 1. Comprehensive cross impact matrix R and AS.

	F1	F2	F3	F4	F5	F6	F7	F8	F9	F10	F11	F12	F13	AS
F1	0	2.52	2.33	2.68	0.14	2.53	1.95	0.14	0.10	2.90	0.63	0.63	0.63	17.20
F2	0	0	0.63	0.63	0.63	0.63	0.63	0.63	0.63	0	0.29	0.29	0.29	5.30
F3	0	0	0	0	0	0	0	0	0	0	0	0	0	0
F4	0	0	2.57	0	0	0	0	0	0	0.08	2.86	2.86	2.86	11.23
F5	0	0	1.30	1.30	0	2.76	2.43	1.80	1.84	1.27	0.63	0.63	0.63	14.59
F6	0	0	1.90	1.90	0	0	3.07	2.47	1.84	0	0.63	0.63	0.63	13.07
F7	0	0	1.93	2.53	0	0	0	1.86	1.86	0	0.63	0.63	0.63	10.08
F8	0	0	0.63	0.63	0.63	0.63	0.63	0	1.93	0	0.63	0.63	0.63	6.99
F9	0	0	2.73	3.11	0	0	0	0	0	0	0.63	0.63	0.63	7.74
F10	0	0.26	0.63	0.88	0	2.43	2.46	0	1.27	0	2.85	2.53	1.90	15.21
F11	0	0	2.53	0	0	0	0	0	0	0	0	2.91	2.53	7.97
F12	0	0	2.53	0	0	0	0	0	0	0	0	0	3.17	5.69
F13	0	0	2.53	0	0	0	0	0	0	0	0	0	0	2.53

to obtain the comprehensive cross impact matrix R. The AS of each business function is calculated by formula (5) (see Table 1).

According to Table 1, the preference chain of civil aviation departure control system is generated by Sect. 4.2 preference chain generation algorithm (see Fig. 2).

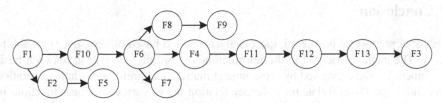

Fig. 2. System business preference chain.

5.2 Accuracy Comparison of System Influence Degree

Taking the comprehensive cross impact matrix R in Sect. 5.1 as the original data, the business function network structure entropy [2], weighted directed network structure entropy [4], structure hole importance index [3] and the AS in this method of business interruption event are calculated respectively, the change of the impact of business interruption on the information system at each time is shown in Fig. 3.

As can be seen from Fig. 3, the change of structure entropy in the event of business function interruption is similar to that of the AS. Due to the structure hole importance

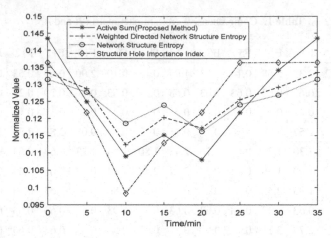

Fig. 3. Normalized data change of each method.

index can not adapt to the chain structure change, it can not accurately express the impact of business function interruption on the system; Compared with the *AS*, the network structure entropy and directed weighted network structure entropy can not accurately reflect the impact on the information system when the business function with high impact is interrupted.

To sum up, the changes of trend of the *AS* obtained by the method in this paper is more consistent with the change of business scope and influence degree in the actual situation.

6 Conclusion

This paper proposes a business impact analysis method based on crossover probability theory. The method oriented to the information system, the correlation between business functions was expressed by cross impact matrix. The preference chain generation algorithm is used to correlate the influence relationship of various business functions in the system. On this basis, the influence trend of business function interruption on other business functions is obtained by analyzing the position of business function interruption in the preference chain. Experimental results show that this method can accurately measure the impact of business function interruption on others of information system.

Acknowledgements. This work was supported by the Civil Aviation Joint Research Fund Project of the National Natural Science Foundation of China under granted number U1833107.

References

1. Al-Essa, H., Al-Sharidah, A.: An approach to automate business impact analysis. In: 2018 IEEE International Systems Engineering Symposium (ISSE), pp. 1–3. Piscataway, NJ (2018)

2. Cai, M.: A network structure entropy based on point and edge difference. Acta Phys. Sin. **60**(11), 165–173 (2011)
3. Yin, R.: Node evaluation method of scale-free network based on importance contribution. J. Softw. **30**(06), 1875–1885 (2019)
4. Xie, L.: A method of business impact analysis for information system. J. Dalian Univ. Technol. **60**(04), 420–426 (2020)
5. Ai, L., Liu, S.: A multi-attribute decision making method based on combination of subjective and objective weighting. In: IEEE 5th International Conference on Control, Automation and Robotics (ICCAR), pp. 576–580 (2019)
6. Xie, L.: A key business node identification model for internet of things security. Secur. Commun. Netw. **2020**, 6654283 (2020)
7. Thompson, R.C., Olugbara, O.O.: CIMgen method for generating cross impact matrix in impact factor analysis. In: IEEE Conference on Information Communications Technology and Society (ICTAS), pp. 1–5 (2020)
8. GB/T 20984–2007: Information security technology-Risk assessment specification for information security (2007)
9. Ou, W., Fang, X.: Evaluation of black start-up model based on entropy method and principal component analysis method. Power Syst. Prot. Control 2014 **42**(08), 22–27 (2014)

RAP: A Lightweight Application Layer Defense Against Website Fingerprinting

Yan Zhang, Li Yang$^{(\boxtimes)}$, Junbo Jia, Shirui Ying, and Yasheng Zhou

Xidian University, Xi'an 710071, China
{zhangyan_wecs,jbjia,srying,yszhou}@stu.xidian.edu.cn,
yangli@xidian.edu.cn

Abstract. Website fingerprinting (WFP) attacks threaten user privacy on anonymity networks because they can be used by network surveillants to identify webpages that are visited by users based on extracted features from the network traffic. There are currently defenses to reduce the threat of WFP, but these defense measures have some defects; some defenses are too expensive to deploy, and some have been defeated by stronger WFP attack methods. In this work, we propose a lightweight application layer defense method, *RAP*, which can resist current WFP attacks with very low data and latency overheads; more importantly, it is easy to deploy. We randomly deploy important resource files, such as JS and CSS, to multiple Tor OR servers in advance and update them regularly. By randomly scrambling the resource request order, a single request is sent and received through multiple independent paths with different Tor entry ORs. To randomize the traffic distribution, users randomly obtain the website resource files directly from the Tor node server, rather than from the original server, when browsing the website. In this way, the best attack accuracy is reduced from 98% to 53%. Additionally, to confuse the traffic, we request a small amount of additional HTML text instead of the whole website resources, which reduces the effect of state-of-the-art WFP attacks to 40% with 13% data overhead and 31% latency overhead.

Keywords: Traffic analysis · Website fingerprinting · Web privacy

1 Introduction

To conceal a user's location and usage behavior from anyone who conducts network surveillance or traffic analysis, Tor [18] provides an anonymous communication strategy through a global voluntary network that contains more than 7,000 relays. A Tor client uses an onion proxy (OP) to selects 3 onion relays (OR) in order to create a virtual encrypted data transmission tunnel called *circuit*. The three relays in the chain are called *entry*, *middle* and *exit*, respectively. Each OR

Supported by the National Natural Science Foundation of China (62072359, 62072352), the National Key Research and Development Project (2017YFB0801805).

W. Shi et al. (Eds.): SPNCE 2021, LNICST 423, pp. 254–270, 2022.
https://doi.org/10.1007/978-3-030-96791-8_19

only knows its predecessor and successor. The client separately negotiates the encryption key for communication with each OR in the chain. With the help of a key, the user's data are wrapped and encrypted like an onion, forming fixed-size chunks called *cells*.

In recent years, multiple studies [1,5,10,14–16] have shown that Tor is vulnerable to WFP attacks. A WFP attack is a special kind of traffic analysis attack that aims to identify the web content of anonymous data flow by observing traffic patterns, such as the number, direction, ordering, and timing of packets. With the development of deep learning [17,25] and computer technologytechnology [24,26], the threat of website fingerprint attacks is serious. To protect user privacy, a series of studies on defense [2–4,6,9,12] against WFP attacks have appeared. However, some defense systems add a large number of dummy packets and delay real packets, resulting in excessive latency and data overheads. Some defense systems are compromised by more advanced and effective attacks, and others cannot be deployed in the real Tor network because of the high resource costs. To counter more powerful WFP attacks, it is increasingly urgent to invent a defense.

In this paper, we propose RAP, an application layer defense that can defeat state-of-the-art WFP attacks, which not only has lower data and latency overheads, but is also easy to deploy. We find that the previous WFP attacks assume that users visit the website in the same scenario. The traffic is collected under this assumption, making the classification result very high. However, if we gather the traffic of users in different locations around the world, the accuracy will be greatly reduced. This phenomenon may be because users are located in different regions and website servers use content delivery network (CDN) technology, which leads to different load traces of the same website in different regions. Our defense uses this idea for reference and randomly distributes the static resources of the website to different Tor ORs.

Our work makes the following contributions:

(1) We design a lightweight WFP defense method, RAP, which is based on randomizing the request order and location of website resources. First, we put some unchangeable embedded resources on Tor OR nodes in advance and update them regularly so that a large number of Tor OR nodes can become our CDN servers. When a user visits a website, the HTTP request sequence of all website resources is scrambled, and the request location and sequences of website resources are scheduled. Finally, requests are sent through multiple Tor paths with different entry nodes; when the user visits the same website, the received traces are different.

(2) We explore several traffic randomization strategies that can serve as candidates for adoption in our defense. Based on four state-of-the-art WFP classifiers, we conduct real-world evaluations to analyze the efficiency of these strategies against modern WFP attacks.

(3) We conduct an extensive analysis to prove the effectiveness of our RAP defense. Our defense strategy reduces the accuracy of attacks on state-of-the-art WFP from 98% to 40%, with 13% data overhead and 31% latency overhead.

2   Related Work

2.1   WFP Attacks

In 2013, Wang and Goldberg [20] proposed replacing previous packet with Tor cells to extract fingerprints from websites. They increased the attack accuracy to more than 90%. Further works [1,5,10,14–16,19] have been proposed since then that have pushed a higher accuracy and a lower false positive rate.

In 2014, Wang et al. [19] proposed a WFP attack based on k-Nearest Neighbors (k-NN), extracting more than 3000 traffic characteristics. k-NN outperforms existing methods and reached a 91% accuracy in the closed world scenario. In 2016, Hayes and Danezis [10] proposed the k-FP classifier based on random decision forests. The K-FP classifier can correctly determine which of the 30 monitored hidden services a client is visiting with an 85% true positive rate and a false positive rate as low as 0.02%. In the same year, Panchenko et al. [14] proposed a classifier, CUMUL, which outperforms existing methods in terms of both the recognition rate and computational complexity.

Recently, several WFP classifiers based on deep learning have shown a better performance than traditional machine learning. Sirinam [16] proposed a WFP classifier, DF, with a deep convolutional neural network (CNN). DF reached an accuracy greater than 98% without defense, and it also has a very good effect on lightweight defenses, such as WTF-PAD [12] and Walkie-Talkie [22].In addition, other works [7,21–23] implement WFP attacks on multitab pages in more practical scenarios because Juarez et al. [11] criticized the assumption that the previous work is unrealistic.

2.2   WFP Defenses

To change the traffic pattern, several defenses [3,4,13,19,22] measures make use of the attacker's inability to distinguish between real and dummy data packets by adding dummy packets and delaying the real data packets to achieve the purpose of defense. Dyer et al. [8] designed Buffered Fixed Length Obfuscation (BuFLO) to achieve traffic obfuscation by sending data at a constant rate in both the sending and receiving directions. However, the huge data overhead is a flaw of this method. In 2016, Juarez et al. [12] proposed WTF-PAD, which is an implementation of adaptive padding. This defense uses a token system to generate dummy packets and fill them to the gaps of rear traces. Recently, Gong and Wang [9] proposed two zero-delay lightweight defenses, Front and Glue. Front uses WF attacks to rely on the feature-rich trace front, adding dummy packets to the trace front, while Glue uses the attacker's inability to distinguish two consecutive website split points to achieve a better effect than heavyweight defenses, such as Tamaraw. Cadena and Mitseva et al. [2] used the concept of traffic splitting to establish multiple Tor paths, send and receive packets through multiple different paths, and merge and split traffic on middle ORs.

The general defense at the application layer does not rely on adding dummy packets or delaying real packets actively. Cherubin et al. [6] proposed confusing website traffic by adding web objects and inserting additional dummy requests, but this defense only applies to onion services. Cadena et al. [2] proposed that by establishing multiple Tor paths and using the HTTP range option, the bytes of web objects are randomly requested on each path so that an attacker who controls a malicious entry node can only observe a small amount of website traffic each time. In part, the detection rate of the WFP classifier has been reduced by nearly 50%. However, this defense provides protection against malicious entry ORs only.

3   Threat Model

Based on previous WFP research work, we take a special scenario into consideration: users use network proxies. Under these circumstances, the adversary can passively collect traffic between the user and the Tor entry OR node without modifying, delaying, or intercepting the original traffic. The attacker can always observe the complete traffic generated by tor users' surfing period, regardless of what defense the Tor user uses. The attacker knows the user's identity, but does not know which website the user is visiting. We assume that the adversary can collect traffic in the user's network agent (see Fig. 1) and can deploy a local network environment similar to the user's environment. WFP attacks usually correspond to supervised machine learning classification problems. After defining a set of websites to be detected, the adversary collects the traffic traces loaded on each website in the same scenario and extracts the fingerprint features. Each webpage is a class, and a particular trace belonging to this class is called an *instance*. Adversaries can use machine learning or deep learning to train classifiers to identify website categories. Finally, the adversary uses the same method to extract the features generated by the user's visit behavior. Then, the classifier is used to identify the website corresponding to this traffic.

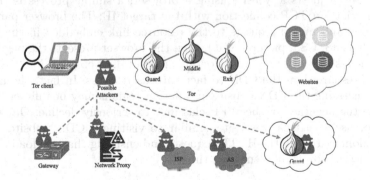

Fig. 1. The WFP threat model.

The adversary uses the same processing method to process the traffic generated by the user's visit to the website, and then uses the classifier to identify the website corresponding to this traffic. The analysis of WFP attacks generally has two scenarios: *closed world* or the *open world* [5,10,14–16,20]. In the close world scenario, we assume that the user only visits a website in a fixed website collection, and these fixed websites become monitored websites. Here, the adversary trains on a number of traces from these sites and aims to classify different traces from the training set into one of the monitored websites. Although the closed-world is less realistic-it assumes the adversary knows every site a user visits-it is a useful measure of a classifier's ability to distinguish between websites. In a more realistic open world scenario, a user can visit any website, including websites that the adversary does not know. These sites that the adversary does not know are called unmonitored sites. The attacker only has the fingerprints of the websites he is interested in, so that the adversary is in When carrying out a WFP attack, it is not only necessary to distinguish whether the website of the unknown traffic belongs to the collection of websites of interest, but also to distinguish which website is when the unknown traffic belongs to the collection of websites of interest. In addition, the adversary can bias her classifier by training on some number of unmonitored sites. Though there is no overlap between unmonitored training and testing sites, learning how to distinguish one set of unmonitored sites often helps with others. As in the previous work, we set the adversary's capabilities: (1) The adversary knows the start and end time of the victim's visit to the website, that is, the adversary's collected traffic does not include other website traffic; (2) the adversary's collected traffic sequence There is no mixed background traffic; (3) The adversary knows that the victim uses the defense system and understands its defense strategy.

4   Defense System Design

4.1   Overview

When a user requests a website using a browser, a simple process is that the browser initiates a TCP connection with the target IP; The browser parses the HTML code and makes requests to the resource link embedded in the HTML code (such as JS, CSS, pictures, etc.), then the browser presents the page to the user. Static resources occupy a considerable part of the web page. Many websites put static resources on the CDN to facilitate user access. In fact, the network traces of accessing the CDN website in different regions may be different, which will cause the accuracy of the WFP classifier to seriously decline. Our defense makes Tor users visit each website, similar to visiting a CDN website, adding other random factors to the HTTP request, and ensuring that the load tracking of the same website is different each time.

4.2   Architecture

Our defense system is composed of volunteer OR nodes, Tor directory servers (DS), and user agents. After we have determined the collection of websites to be defended by WFP, the Tor directory server will visit the websites in the collection one-by-one, recording the JS resource objects, CSS resource objects, and logo image objects. Because these resource objects are not easy to change. The Tor directory server reads the list of Tor ORs that are willing to provide defenses and builds a table of correspondence between the website resource objects and ORs (see Algorithm 1). The web object is renamed to a unique name, and then, we associate the object with multiple OR nodes to prevent some OR nodes from going offline. The directory server regularly revisits the website, updating the corresponding relationships between the website resources and OR nodes. The corresponding relationship table is called the *corTable* and is stored locally before synchronizing to other directory servers. The HTTP service is started in the selected Tor node, and the Tor node can be deemed the HTTP server. It regularly obtains the *corTable* from the directory server and finds resource objects related to itself, according to the *corTable*. The server downloads the web resource object using the resource links embedded in the original HTML code and renames the files according to the table information. Finally, resource objects are saved in the server. To reduce the storage burden, once the *corTable* is obtained from the directory server and the resource objects are downloaded the old version resource objects stored in the server can be deleted.

Algorithm 1. Generate the corresponding relationship table of web resources and OR nodes.

Input: Collection of websites that need to be defended, *webSet*;
Output: Corresponding relationship table of web resources and OR nodes, *corTable*;
1: Initialize global *corTable*;
2: **for** each $w \in webSet$ **do**
3:     DS request w to get $HTML$;
4:     $jcSet = \text{Parse}(HTML)$;
5:     **for** each $f \in jcSet$ **do**
6:         Random select ORs from $ORSet$;
7:         $newName = \text{UUID} + (.js|.css)$;
8:         $I_w = \text{combination}(w, f, newName, ORs)$;
9:         $corTable.\text{add}(I_w)$;
10:    **end for**
11: **end for**
12: **return** *corTable*;

When a user visits a website, the user usually sends a series of HTTP requests in sequence through a Tor circuit to obtain all the web objects needed to display the site. Under our defense, we first start multiple OP instances, each of which maintains a three-hop circuit, which is built using the existing Tor circuit creation concept. When a user visits a website, the original website HTML text is obtained through an HTTP request. After the HTTP request is parsed, the web object HTTP requests are not sent to the original resource server; instead, requests are sent to the RAP-local defense system (the defense system can be

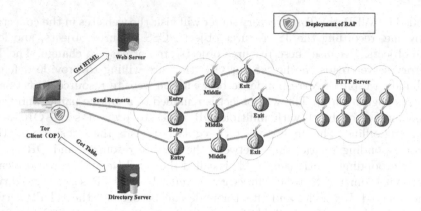

Fig. 2. Clients request websites from different servers through multiple paths.

deemed as a local proxy plug-in between the user's browser and the user's OP). As shown in Fig. 2), our defense operations are as follows:

- It completely shuffles all web HTTP requests, including requests for web embedded objects, such as JS, CSS, etc.
- It finds the relationships between resource objects and ORs according to the *corTable*. The OR node is randomly selected, which has the requested resource objects, and then a new HTTP request is constructed.
- It sends the web HTTP requests through multiple three-hop circuits established in advance according to our strategy. These requests are sent in parallel, and the web server responses are received through the request circuit.

4.3   Traffic Randomization Strategy

The main challenge of our defense strategy is to make the load traces of the same page highly different to prevent the adversary from finding fingerprint patterns. We analyze the influencing factors from three aspects: server, transmission path and client.

(1) After we determine the size of the website collection, we can obtain the website source code and obtain the number and size of all the resource files that need to be stored on the Tor OR nodes. What we need to care about is the proportion of each website's resource object to be stored on the Tor nodes, as well as how many Tor relay nodes need to be used to achieve a balance between the performance overhead and defense effects. From our preliminary cognition, using more Tor nodes can achieve better results. Therefore, we choose Tor OR nodes that are willing to provide services for us and discuss the proportion of website resource objects on Tor nodes in subsequent experiments. This means that the web resource object scheduler on the directory server selects a certain number of embedded resources to Update, according

to the given proportion. Defining the size of JS or CSS on the website as s_r, the number of stable and unchangeable resources that the website can put on the Tor OR as n_{st}, and the number of resources that are actually put on the Tor OR as n_t, we analyze the proportion P that needs to be scheduled.

$$P = \frac{\sum_{j=1}^{n_t} s_{ri}}{\sum_{i=1}^{n_{st}} s_{ri}} \tag{1}$$

(2) We analyze the traffic randomness of the number of parallel three-hop circuits used to send requests and receive responses. Although using a large number of Tor circuits with different entry ORs can reduce the amount of information available to each entry OR node and sending requests in parallel can reduce the time to receive the last HTTP request, our defense purpose is not to reduce the sequence of traffic passing on the single entry OR node. A large number of three-hop circuits will increase the local load of the client, so we set the initial number of Tor circuits to 5, according to Caneda's [2] suggestion, and then increase or decrease the number in turn to analyze the effect.

(3) We analyze the impact of different HTTP request allocation strategies on multiple circuits on the traffic randomness. Our basic scheme is round robin. We further consider a batched weighted random strategy. For all HTTP requests of a web page, we create an n-dimensional vector that is composed of the maximum number of requests sent by each circuit. We choose the probability density function of the *exponential distribution* to obtain five random numbers, and then we obtain n probabilities by weighting, the sum of which is 1. Finally, we multiply the probability according to the number of HTTP requests to obtain the random number of n-dimensional vectors and then randomly select a Tor circuit for each HTTP request. When the number of requests sent by a Tor circuit reaches the threshold set in advance, we will not use this circuit to send requests. Each time we visit the website, we will choose a new random number seed for the exponential distribution to ensure the unpredictability of the tracking of each page's loading process.

5 Experimental Setup

5.1 Dataset Description

To evaluate our WFP defense system, we deployed our defense system in the real Tor network environment. We collected a new dataset between September and November 2020 using Tor Browser 10.0 with a configured SSR proxy. A *Python* script is used to drive the Tor browser to automatically visit the website with the help of the *tcpdump* tool to record the original traffic and extract the data at the Tor cell level. The traces we collected and used for experiments were not generated by real users, so there is no moral concern. We selected 20 Tor ORs as our volunteer web resource object server, using another Tor OR node with a resource scheduling system as our directory server.

For the closed world scenario, we chose Alexa's top 100 websites to form our website collection. We first collected the dataset without applying our defenses and collected 100 rounds of the homepage of each website for 100 websites, which is called *DS-NODEF*. We deleted the trace that failed to load the page due to client or server errors, and we adopted the same solution for other subsequent datasets. For our RAP defense, we selected our traffic-randomization strategy to collect 100 traces for each website. We call this dataset *DS-DEF*. Finally, we visited each of Alexa's 10000 most popular websites once, excluding the first 100 sites used to build our closed world dataset, *DS-NODEF-BG*, without applying our defenses, and we used these websites as background for our open world evaluation. Note that all the traffic we collect has passed through the SSR network proxy. SSR can encrypt, obfuscate, and forward the original traffic. We call the dataset we collected on the Tor browser the SSR proxy *SSR-TOR-DS*. The dataset collected by Rimmer [15] is named *Rimmer-DS*, which is a comparison dataset.

5.2   Classifiers and Evaluation Setup

For our evaluation, we considered four state-of-the-art WFP attacks: k-NN [19], CUMUL [14], k-FP [10], and DF [16]. k-NN, CUMUL, and k-FP manually extract the representative features and then use machine learning methods for classification. DF directly uses the sending and receiving sequence of cells to input into the deep convolutional neural network for classification. In addition to the suggested parameters given in the original text, we also refer to the parameters given in this work [9]. We apply 10-fold cross-validation with respect to the total number of collected page loads.

We assume that the attacker can collect traffic at the user's network proxy, knows our defense strategy, and has sufficient resources to collect data and train classifiers. The higher the value of FPR is, the safer our defense system is. For our closed world analysis, we computed the accuracy, i.e., the probability of a correct prediction (either true positive or true negative). We calculated the TPR, i.e., the fraction of accesses to foreground pages that were detected, and the FPR, i.e., the probability of false alarms, for our open world experiments.

6   Evaluation and Discussion

6.1   Analysis of RAP Defense

Influence of Shuffling HTTP Requests and Multipath. First, to analyze the effect in the undefended scenario, we conducted attack experiments in the DS-NODEF dataset, adding proxy obfuscation encryption in comparison with Rimmer's dataset. With the results shown in Table 1, we found that after adding proxy obfuscation encryption, the accuracy of the four methods remained stable and did not decrease significantly; they even have a similar effect to the DF attack. This might be because the CNN model used by DF has the ability to learn the pattern of proxies, which shows that the SSR proxy cannot provide an effective defense. We compare the experimental results using our datasets and other datasets, which do not use the SSR proxy.

Table 1. Accuracy (in %) of state-of-the-art WFP attacks in scenarios without defense and against our simple traffic randomization strategies.

	Rimmer-DS undefended	SSR-TOR-DS Undefended	Multipath	Shuffle HTTP requests and multipath
k-NN	98.2	90.02	88.47	27.2
CUMUL	98.5	92.1	91.23	59.2
k-FP	98.4	94.42	90.86	71.36
DF	98.75	98.11	92.32	73.76

As shown in Table 1, we performed simple multipath defense experiments in the SSR-TOR-DS dataset, which means that we send the complete HTTP requests via five circuits based on the round robin method. Under this situation, we found that the degree of decrease for the four methods is relatively low, which verifies the conclusion of a separate study [2]. Then, we performed another experiment, which sent the HTTP requests after shuffling and analyzed the influence. The results illustrate that this strategy has more influence on the accuracy of the k-NN classifier; it decreases to 27.2%, and the accuracy of other classifiers decreases by 20%–30%, to some extent.

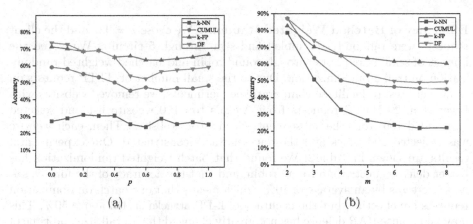

(a)   (b)

Fig. 3. Accuracy of state-of-the-art WFP attacks under different resource ratios p and circuit numbers m.

Efficiency of Resources Proportion on Tor Servers. We perform some experiments to determine the influence of resource proportion on the DS-DEF dataset. When $P = 0$, the order of HTTP requests is disrupted, and the requests are sent to the original website through multiple circuits using the round robin method. The result is shown in Fig. 3(a). We find that web object requests from different servers have little influence on the accuracy of k-NN attacks. This may be because the accuracy of k-NN attacks dropped sharply before requesting data from the Tor HTTP server. However, the accuracy of the other three attack methods has decreased significantly. When P exceeds 0.6, the drop rate decreases, or even no longer decreases, and the DF attack appears to rise. Although it cannot be stated directly that $P = 0.6$ is the optimal choice, we can almost achieve the best results when $P = 0.6$. Therefore, we set P to 0.6 in subsequent experiments.

Efficiency of the Number of Multipaths on Traffic Randomization. To analyze the impact of m (the number of multipaths) in the defense system, we set P (the resource ratio of the Tor HTTP server) to 0.6. The client's requests were randomly shuffled and then sent using the round robin method. Based on the recommendation of TrafficSliver, first the number of circuits is set to 5. To find its best range, we perform tuning on the basis of 5. Finally, we set the number of circuits $m \in [2, 8]$ to test our classification accuracy. As shown in Fig. 3(b), we found that when m is larger, the classification accuracy decrease rate is larger, and when m is greater than 5, the decrease rate of the classifier decreases. Therefore, we conclude that m = 5 is a good choice because 5 Tor paths will not significantly increase the circuit setup time; in addition, the defense effect is still acceptable.

Efficiency of Batched Weighted Random. We chose $P = 0.6$, and the client requests were randomly scrambled and sent through 5 circuits. We tested the impact of sending requests through round robin and batched weighted randomization on traffic randomization. Due to the small number of HTTP requests on some websites, to facilitate comparative experiments, we removed websites with fewer than 20 HTTP requests from Alexa's top 100 website list and selected and added 100 from the subsequent Alexa's top websites. Then, each website was collected 100 times and the dataset was reconstructed. Our experimental results are shown in Table 2. We found that batch weighted randomization has better defense effects than round robin, and that the accuracy of the four classifiers decreases by an average of 10%, which means that our batch randomization requests are effective, but the accuracy of k-FP attacks is still above 50%. This may be because RAP defense has not greatly changed the overall size and time of website traffic, resulting in k-FP finding the overall relationship of traffic packets.

Efficiency of Adding Additional Requests. In the initial stage of the traffic generating process, RAP sends HTML request to original website and *corTable*

Table 2. Accuracy (in %) of state-of-the-art WFP attacks in scenarios without defense and against our defense strategies.

	k-NN	CUMUL	k-FP	DF
Undefended	90.02	92.10	94.42	98.11
Round Robin	23.84	47.28	63.52	52.37
Batched Weighted Random	**14.25**	**38.38**	**53.54**	**42.80**

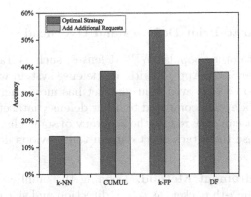

Fig. 4. Accuracy (in %) of state-of-the-art WFP attacks in different scenarios of optimal strategy and additional requests.

requests to. We think that this period is helpful for extracting the pattern of WFP attacks, so we decide to confuse the traffic at this stage. Our idea is to send a random number of HTML requests to the randomly selected websites in Alexa's top 10000 at the same time as sending original HTML requests. We set the number between 1 and 5. The results are shown in Fig. 4. We further reduce the accuracy of WFP attacks by increasing head obfuscation. Although the reduction effect is not good for k-NN and DF, the accuracy of k-FP attacks can be reduced to 40.58%. Our method is a successful defense for attackers who have sufficient traffic data. In conclusion, it is effective to add obfuscation in requests to reinforce our defense system.

Open World Evaluation. We use our optimal strategy [$P = 0.6$, $m = 5$, batch randomized requests, obfuscated headers] to evaluate the defense system in open world scenarios. As a baseline, we first used the non-defended dataset DS-NODEF as a foreground set and DS-NODEF-BG as our background set and computed TPR and FPR for each classifier. As shown in Table 3, the overall effect of our defense system in the open world scene can reach an advanced level, and our defense is effective against k-NN and CUMUL classifiers. In the face of more powerful k-FP and DF attacks, our FPR is only 61.52% and 53.42%, respectively. This may be because k-FP uses many time features, and the deep neural network structure of DF can find the defects of our defense.

Table 3. TPR and FPR (in %)of state-of-the-art WFP attacks against our defense in the open world.

	k-NN		CUMUL		k-FP		DF	
	TPR	FPR	TPR	FPR	TPR	FPR	TPR	FPR
Undefended	88.21	15.84	93.85	12.30	92.56	6.50	96.70	5.23
RAP	20.32	76.89	42.36	74.36	53.09	61.52	63.71	53.42

6.2   Comparison to Prior Defenses and Overhead

Finally, we compare other popular WFP defenses, such as Tamaraw [4], WTF-PAD [12] and TrafficSliver-App [2], with our defense system with the best strategy. It should be noted that even if our dataset has more encryption and confusion of SSR network agents compared to other defense datasets, the influence of SSR is small, and it can only reduce the accuracy of some classifiers by less than 10%. We directly use the attack effect data in the previous defense work [2].

Overhead Measurement Method. Defining the number of packets as $|P|$, the timestamp of the i-th packets as t_i, the direction and size of the i-th packets as L_i. The packet sequence generated during website loading can be expressed as:

$$P = <(t_1, L_1), (t_2, L_2), \ldots, (t_i, L_i), \ldots, (t_{|P|}, L_{|P|})> \tag{2}$$

The latency overhead $T(D)$ generated by defense system D on packet sequence P refers to the additional time generated by transmitting real packets divided by the original total transmission time. It is assumed that the time of the last real packet in defense traffic P' is t_k. Then $T(D)$ is defined as follows:

$$T(D) = \frac{t_k - t_{|P|}}{t_{|P|}} \tag{3}$$

The data overhead $O(D)$ refers to the total amount of virtual packets divided by the total amount of real data. $O(D)$ is defined as follows:

$$O(D) = \frac{\sum_{i=1}^{|P'|} |L_i| - \sum_{i=1}^{|P|} |L_i|}{\sum_{i=1}^{|P|} |L_i|} \tag{4}$$

Security Against State-of-the-Art WFP Attacks. Table 4 shows the attack effect of state-of-the-art WFP attacks in the closed world scenario. Our RAP defense effect is obviously better than that of WTF-PAD, and WTF-PAD was once considered the optimal defense strategy. Compared with Tamaraw, the effect of our defense is significantly weakened. However, the defense effect of Tamaraw depends on the data and latency overhead. Our defense system is not as good as TrafficSliver-APP in counter with CUMUL and k-FP classifiers, but we believe that the effect can meet the requirements of the Tor defense system, and the accuracy of CUMUL and kFP classifier can be reduced to 30.35% and 40.58%, respectively. It is worth noting that the accuracy of the DF classifier can be reduced by our RAP defense to 37.91%, which is better than that of TrafficSliver-App. Therefore, we conclude that our RAP defense can provide excellent defense effects.

Performance Overhead. In addition to measuring the defense effect, performance overhead is also crucial to the WFP defense system. If the website takes too much time to load, users may have bad experiences. Therefore, we measure the data and latency overhead generated by the defense, comparing it with the previous WFP defense. As shown in Table 5, compared with all previous WFP defenses, our RAP defense only has a small data overhead. This part of the overhead is generated by HTTP requests added when requesting the relationship table from the directory server, as well as obtaining the initial web HTML. In terms of latency, our defense also has a good performance, which is similar to TrafficSliver, because we do not artificially add a delay to HTTP requests. The delay comes from sending HTTP requests to our defense proxy, which influences the order of HTTP requests and selects circuits. In addition, our defense overhead is much lower than Tamaraw. Although WTF-PAD does not add any time delay, it does not provide sufficient security to defend against WFP attacks. In conclusion, our defense system only adds a small amount of overhead, and

Table 4. Accuracy (in %) of state-of-the-art WFP attacks against our RAP defense and other prior defenses.

	k-NN	CUMUL	k-FP	DF
Undefended	90.02	92.10	94.42	98.11
Tamarraw	4.86	6.86	5.50	4.11
WTF-PAD	35.23	75.73	67.50	85.62
TrafficSliver-App	14.93	24.13	28.72	57.34
RAP	13.98	30.35	40.58	37.91

Table 5. Latency and data overhead (in %) created by WFP defenses.

	Latency Overhead	Data Overhead
Undefended	0	0
Tamaraw	78.43	162.93
WTF-PAD	0	32.71
TrafficSliver-App	31.23	0
RAP(optimal)	31.75	13.60

these overheads are reasonable. We analyze the overhead of randomized HTTP requests to schedule a web object in the Tor network. We select the dataset with a web object ratio of 0.6 for analysis. Because there are very few logo images and other files that are not easy to change, we only analyze JS, CSS and file scheduling overhead. Our 100 websites have 1396 JS and CSS files, occupying 161 MB of space. On average, there are 13.96 resource files per website, 0.1153 MB per resource file, and 1.61 MB per website resource. We select P as 0.6 and back up 5 copies for each resource; that is, we select 1396*0.6*5 = 4188 files to put on 20 Tor or HTTP servers. Each relay node needs 209.4 MB of space to store our selected web resource files. If we place these resource files on 2000 Tor nodes, each Tor node only needs 2.094 MB of additional storage space. In fact, we need to use more than 200 MB of storage space to install Tor service on the host, so the space of these web resources is reasonable. As the web resource files may change when the website content is updated, the resource scheduler that we use to collect our dataset will update all the website resource files once an hour, which will have a bandwidth of 4188*0.1153/60/60 = 0.1341 MB/s. According to our observation, except for a small number of websites that often change the embedded resources, the change frequency of JS or CSS files for most websites is less than once a day; therefore, the Tor bandwidth cost of RAP may be far less than our estimation.

6.3   Discussion and Limitations

Although our defense system achieves a good defense performance with very low latency and bandwidth overhead, we may encounter the following problems: the owner of the Tor node may damage the resources maliciously or modify the resource objects. We suggest that each Tor server that stores web objects calculates the checksum for resource files, letting the client request resource files from one Tor server and obtain the checksum from another Tor server to verify the integrity of the web resource objects. One thing that may be criticized about our defense system is the inability to deploy defense to all site collections because there are a limited number of Tor nodes with an unlimited number of resource files. In fact, the arms race for fingerprint attacks and defenses on websites has never stopped. Many useful defenses in the past, such as WFP-PAD, cannot resist DF attacks anymore, and our defense can resist only existing methods of fingerprint attacks on a limited collection of websites.

7   Conclusion

We proposed a lightweight application-level RAP defense to protect against WFP performed by possible adversaries. RAP is based on the idea of CDN, where web objects are placed on the Tor node, clients obtain HTML files from the original site, all HTTP requests are obtained and sent through multiple Tor paths, some requests are sent to the TOR node instead of the original site, and additional HTTP requests are added to confuse traffic during the initial stage of visiting the site. Because RAP is a defense means acting on the application layer, it has scalability and compatibility in theory. We analyzed the traffic randomization scheme and determined the optimal system parameters. We showed that our RAP defense is able to reduce the accuracy from more than 98% to 40% for all state-of-the-art attacks, with only 31% latency and 13% data overhead. Our defense system does not need to modify the underlying Tor network. Therefore, RAP is suitable for deployment in Tor.

References

1. Bhat, S., Lu, D., Kwon, A., Devadas, S.: Var-cnn: a data-efficient website fingerprinting attack based on deep learning. Proc. Priv. Enhanc. Technol. **4**, 292–310 (2019)
2. De la Cadena, W., et al.: Trafficsliver: fighting website fingerprinting attacks with traffic splitting. In: Proceedings of the 2020 ACM SIGSAC Conference on Computer and Communications Security, pp. 1971–1985 (2020)
3. Cai, X., Nithyanand, R., Johnson, R.: Cs-buflo: a congestion sensitive website fingerprinting defense. In: Proceedings of the 13th Workshop on Privacy in the Electronic Society, pp. 121–130 (2014)
4. Cai, X., Nithyanand, R., Wang, T., Johnson, R., Goldberg, I.: A systematic approach to developing and evaluating website fingerprinting defenses. In: Proceedings of the 2014 ACM SIGSAC Conference on Computer and Communications Security, pp. 227–238 (2014)
5. Cai, X., Zhang, X.C., Joshi, B., Johnson, R.: Touching from a distance: website fingerprinting attacks and defenses. In: Proceedings of the 2012 ACM conference on Computer and communications security, pp. 605–616 (2012)
6. Cherubin, G., Hayes, J., Juarez, M.: Website fingerprinting defenses at the application layer. Proc. Priv. Enhanc. Technol. **2017**(2), 186–203 (2017)
7. Cui, W., Chen, T., Fields, C., Chen, J., Sierra, A., Chan-Tin, E.: Revisiting assumptions for website fingerprinting attacks. In: Proceedings of the 2019 ACM Asia Conference on Computer and Communications Security, pp. 328–339 (2019)
8. Dyer, K.P., Coull, S.E., Ristenpart, T., Shrimpton, T.: Peek-a-boo, i still see you: why efficient traffic analysis countermeasures fail. In: 2012 IEEE Symposium on Security and Privacy, pp. 332–346. IEEE (2012)
9. Gong, J., Wang, T.: Zero-delay lightweight defenses against website fingerprinting. In: 29th {USENIX} Security Symposium ({USENIX} Security 20), pp. 717–734 (2020)
10. Hayes, J., Danezis, G.: k-fingerprinting: a robust scalable website fingerprinting technique. In: 25th {USENIX} Security Symposium ({USENIX} Security 16), pp. 1187–1203 (2016)
11. Juarez, M., Afroz, S., Acar, G., Diaz, C., Greenstadt, R.: A critical evaluation of website fingerprinting attacks. In: Proceedings of the 2014 ACM SIGSAC Conference on Computer and Communications Security, pp. 263–274 (2014)
12. Juarez, M., Imani, M., Perry, M., Diaz, C., Wright, M.: Toward an efficient website fingerprinting defense. In: Askoxylakis, I., Ioannidis, S., Katsikas, S., Meadows, C. (eds.) ESORICS 2016. LNCS, vol. 9878, pp. 27–46. Springer, Cham (2016). https://doi.org/10.1007/978-3-319-45744-4_2

13. Nithyanand, R., Cai, X., Johnson, R.: Glove: a bespoke website fingerprinting defense. In: Proceedings of the 13th Workshop on Privacy in the Electronic Society, pp. 131–134 (2014)
14. Panchenko, A., et al.: Website fingerprinting at internet scale. In: NDSS (2016)
15. Rimmer, V., Preuveneers, D., Juarez, M., Van Goethem, T., Joosen, W.: Automated website fingerprinting through deep learning. arXiv preprint arXiv:1708.06376 (2017)
16. Sirinam, P., Imani, M., Juarez, M., Wright, M.: Deep fingerprinting: undermining website fingerprinting defenses with deep learning. In: Proceedings of the 2018 ACM SIGSAC Conference on Computer and Communications Security, pp. 1928–1943 (2018)
17. Sun, J., Wang, X., Xiong, N., Shao, J.: Learning sparse representation with variational auto-encoder for anomaly detection. IEEE Access 33353–33361 (2018)
18. Syverson, P., Dingledine, R., Mathewson, N.: Tor: the secondgeneration onion router. In: Usenix Security, pp. 303–320 (2004)
19. Wang, T., Cai, X., Nithyanand, R., Johnson, R., Goldberg, I.: Effective attacks and provable defenses for website fingerprinting. In: 23rd {USENIX} Security Symposium ({USENIX} Security 14), pp. 143–157 (2014)
20. Wang, T., Goldberg, I.: Improved website fingerprinting on tor. In: Proceedings of the 12th ACM Workshop on Workshop on Privacy in the Electronic Society, pp. 201–212 (2013)
21. Wang, T., Goldberg, I.: On realistically attacking tor with website fingerprinting. Proc. Priv. Enhanc. Technol. 4, 21–36 (2016)
22. Wang, T., Goldberg, I.: Walkie-talkie: an efficient defense against passive website fingerprinting attacks. In: 26th {USENIX} Security Symposium ({USENIX} Security 17), pp. 1375–1390 (2017)
23. Xu, Y., Wang, T., Li, Q., Gong, Q., Chen, Y., Jiang, Y.: A multi-tab website fingerprinting attack. In: Proceedings of the 34th Annual Computer Security Applications Conference, pp. 327–341 (2018)
24. Yang, L., Li, C., Wei, T., Zhang, F., Ma, J., Xiong, N.: Vacuum: an efficient and assured deletion scheme for user sensitive data on mobile devices. IEEE Internet Things J. 1 (2021)
25. Yi, B., et al.: Deep matrix factorization with implicit feedback embedding for recommendation system. IEEE Trans. Ind. Inf. 15(8), 4591–4601 (2019)
26. Zhang, J., Yang, L., Yu, S., Ma, J.: A dns tunneling detection method based on deep learning models to prevent data exfiltration. In: Liu, J.K., Huang, X. (eds.) NSS 2019. LNCS, vol. 11928, pp. 520–535. Springer, Cham (2019). https://doi.org/10.1007/978-3-030-36938-5_32

FL-DP: Differential Private Federated Neural Network

Muhammad Maaz Irfan[1,2], Lin Wang[1,2], Sheraz Ali[1,2], Shan Jing[1,2(✉)], and Chuan Zhao[1,2,3]

[1] School of Information Science and Engineering, University of Jinan,
Jinan 250022, China
jingshan@ujn.edu.cn
[2] Shandong Provincial Key Laboratory of Network-based Intelligent Computing,
University of Jinan, Jinan 250022, China
[3] Shandong Provincial Key Laboratory of Software Engineering, Jinan, China

Abstract. The rapid development of the Internet and machine learning has brought convenience and comfort to users' lives. However, due to various attacks and sensitive data leaks, the large amount of data used in machine learning training has made the issue of personal privacy a growing concern as well. In the era of big data, anyone's information can be stolen, which makes many people feel uneasy. We propose a new approach called FL-DP (Federated Learning Based on Differential Privacy). Based on differential privacy, this approach can effectively restrict the adversary's access to the client model, which has the ability to limit data leakage. In this framework, we use the DP Laplace mechanism. It is ensured that all operations (including the server-side aggregation process) are secure and do not leak any information about the training data. Also, we consider adding multiple noises to the preprocessing process so that the client-side data is secure during the training process. Our approach not only provides client-level privacy, but also balances efficiency and privacy. After evaluation, our approach is highly scalable and can be applied to most machine learning based applications.

Keywords: Federated learning · Data integrity · Privacy-preserving · Differential privacy

1 Introduction

In recent decades, machine learning-based systems have been successfully applied in various areas of social industry. From engineering solutions to advances in technology to the development of intelligent web-based systems that provide online services, machine learning plays an irreplaceable role [9]. Moreover, in order not to share data directly, the concept of federated learning has been proposed, where federated learning frameworks use distributed storage and processing of data as opposed to centralized approaches. They use sensors to collect data in

W. Shi et al. (Eds.): SPNCE 2021, LNICST 423, pp. 271–281, 2022.
https://doi.org/10.1007/978-3-030-96791-8_20

the physical environment, however, this feature poses new challenges for user privacy.

As attacks become more sophisticated over time, privacy is a huge challenge for machine learning. Powerful computer systems, such as smartphones, laptops, and desktop computers, can use sophisticated methods to observe malicious behavior and malware. However, some lightweight systems have limited computational resources, so they can only detect small attack variations, such as the Zero Day attack [8]. Joint learning (FL) algorithms can be used to enhance the IoT network and improve the efficiency of the whole system.

Research shows that the effect of deep learning model is related to model size and training data set. Deep learning is widely used in image recognition, feature extraction, classification and prediction. With the rapid growth of data and model parameters, it is often shown as a large number of model parameters, which will have high requirements for the amount of calculation. This scenario brings some challenges related to data security and privacy. These challenges come from the lack of effective tools and methods to protect large data sets. In an environment where the Internet is becoming more developed, heterogeneous data is more easily collected and the volume of data is more enormous. Data protection raises more concerns in environments where privacy protection is required.

The most advanced existing solutions consider the training of centralized ML model. But it is stored locally and preprocessed; For example, the machine learns from sensitive data such as personal images, audio, video, etc. Usually, the parameters of the training model must be transformed into secret form, not the plaintext of the training sample. In order to achieve this and provide strong privacy protection when training data sensitivity, the common practice is to use differential privacy technology. In addition, the computing and storage capacity of devices in distributed systems is growing, and powerful local computing resources can be used on each device. This has led to an increasing interest in federated learning [3], which directly explores training statistical models on remote devices. The current research results have made breakthrough progress in the fields of large-scale machine learning, privacy and distribution [1,8].

Jointly learn the general method of "bringing code into data rather than data into code", and solve the problems of data privacy, location and ownership [7]. It is far away from the use of local models, and carries out prediction on mobile devices by bringing model training to mobile devices. In this case, the key challenge is to check when training a single global model, and the data will not be distributed on the device. Overcome these problems. FedAvg [11,12] was introduced. In i.i.d, parallel SGD and related variants similar to fedavg are analyzed, which are updated locally. However, multiple attacks may occur during training and aggregation, which will lead to private data leakage [4]. In this paper, we provide a solution to this problem. Specifically, we propose a new protocol to implement secure computing.

We use differential privacy (DP) to construct an efficient federated learning framework based on Laplace noise. Our state-of-the-art FL iotdp joint learning

Internet of things protects privacy, effectively limits adversaries' access to the client model, and has the ability to limit data leakage. In this framework, we use DP Laplace mechanism. Ensure that all operations (including server-side aggregation process) are secure and will not disclose any private information about training data. At the same time, we consider adding multiple noises in the preprocessing, and each client does not need to share. It is convenient for the client to join the model update or offline at any time, which greatly improves the flexibility and scalability of the system. This is a state-of-the-art framework that provides a trade-off between privacy costs and model efficiency.

The organization of our research paper is organized as follows: we will start with the introduction, and then present related work in Sect. 2, in Sect. 3 we give an overview of technical preliminaries about federated learning and differential privacy, and then in Sect. 4 a novel protocol for FL-NNPP Federated Learning Neural Network for Privacy-Preserving. Furthermore, we give experimental results for the method of our protocol in terms of accuracy, scalability, and security trade-offs in Sect. 5. Finally in Sect. 6 we will conclude our paper with future directions.

2   Related Work

The benefits of federated learning emerge as awareness of machine learning increases, as do the number of channels for collecting personal information, and as people become more aware of information security. This is because federated learning allows users to train data locally without exchanging data, thus protecting the privacy of the data. However, as the research progressed, researchers found that the weights uploaded by users also expose some information about the user [10, 16].

The most natural way to prevent the leakage of information is to use the method of adding noise, which we know as differential privacy (DP). The existing algorithms include Local Differential Privacy (LDP). [5]adds noise to the local information to protect it from being leaked. The work in [14] proposes a solution for building LDP-compliant SGDs that support a variety of important ML tasks. The work in [15] considers the distributed estimation of client uploaded data by the server while providing protection of these data using LDP.

At present, the research on differential privacy has become mature and has mature applications [11,12]. However, it is still a difficult goal for differentiated private in-depth learning to achieve efficient use under reasonable privacy guarantee [2,4,13]. For example, some works perform well on NIST data, but it is difficult to obtain reasonable privacy parameters on cifar [2].

In 2000, Agrawal and Srikant [2] proposed two methods of privacy protection and data mining. Lindell and Pinkas built an efficient and secure function evaluation protocol for ID3 algorithm. Agrawal and srikkant [2] proposed privacy protection methods to construct a safe and effective function and evaluate the protocol of ID3 algorithm. All parties collect private data during their training and hope to jointly train the decision tree model through these data. In order to enable the parties to the agreement to calculate this tree without disclosing the personal privacy information they hold. Agrawal and Srikant demonstrated how to understand the probability distribution behind some personal data sets in the presence of interference noise (introduced to maintain privacy).

3   Preliminaries

In this section, we will briefly introduce deep learning and its possible attacks. In addition, we have defined various terms and keywords in this section. We summarize the common methods and their implementation to solve the privacy problem of deep learning (especially neural networks) [6].

3.1   Deep Learning

Neural network is a branch of artificial intelligence. CNN (convolutional neural network) is a special neural network, which is mainly used in computer vision. In CNN, it receives input in a 2D structure and has a multi-layer structure to create a feature map called sub sampling. Therefore, it has been widely used in image recognition tasks in data preprocessing and deep learning. Today, researchers [11] modify a single pixel during training, or change all pixels to a smaller number, or combine the two methods to attack the model. These attacks have a great impact on the model, and the average confidence is reduced by up to 84% [11]. After reviewing the work of other researchers, we found that they used cifar-10 [2], MNIST [13] or Imagenet datasets, just like Carlini and Wagner [4].

3.2   Adversarial Attacks in Deep Learning

This section focuses on adversarial attacks and adversarial examples, which were first proposed by szengendy et al. [2]. They discovered the process by which neural networks were attacked. In addition, they also successfully designed a network to misclassify the output images by applying a certain amount of noise. In all these programs, adding noise to the original image to increase the uncertainty of prediction is a typical attack case. In fact, if such attacks occur (for example, modifying traffic signs that may be misunderstood by autonomous vehicles and lead to accidents), it will seriously affect the application of machine learning, and even lead to serious consequences. The target of the attack is to add noise, so that the subjective model misclassifies the given output. There are three main types of adversary attacks: uncertain target attack. In this attack, it deceives the classifier by modifying the target image, makes the model unable to execute, and gives a random class output different from the real image. Target against attack: [3] in this attack, it incorrectly classifies the input image into a specific target category to modify the target image. The result of this model is only a certain class. These attacks may disguise a face as an administrator user, allowing people without permission to obtain permission.

3.3   Differential Privacy

For a randomization algorithm a (the so-called randomization algorithm means that for a specific input, the output of the algorithm is not a fixed value, but follows a certain distribution), the two output distributions obtained by acting on two adjacent data sets are difficult to distinguish. The formal definition of differential privacy is:

$$Pr[A(D) = O] \leqq e^{\epsilon} \cdot Pr[A(D') = O] \tag{1}$$

In differential privacy, researchers propose different noise distribution mechanisms to protect the privacy of data and reasoning. Next, we will introduce some of these mechanisms.

Theorem 1 (Laplace Mechanism). *For functions, the Laplace mechanism L of dataset S,*

$$L(X) = f(X) + (Lap(\Delta(f)/e))d \tag{2}$$

Theorem 2 (Exponential Mechanism).
Given data set D and an availability function $q(D,r) \to R$, Privacy protection mechanism M satisfied with ϵ-differential privacy, If and only if the following expression holds:

$$M(D, q) \propto e^{\frac{\epsilon * q(D,r)}{2\Delta q}} \tag{3}$$

This theorem implies that the Exponential mechanism can make high utility outputs exponentially more likely at a rate particularly depends on the utility score like the final outcome would be approximately optimal with respect to s, and meantime give rigorous privacy guarantee. More ever, the composition properties of differential privacy yield the privacy guarantee for a series of composition.

Theorem 3 (Sequential Composition). *Let C_1, C_2, C_r be a series of mechanisms and each C_i yields ϵ-differential privacy. Let C be some other mechanism that compute $C_1(X), \cdots, C_r(X)$ using R independent randomness for every C_i. Then C satisfies ϵ-differential privacy.*

Theorem 4 (Parallel Composition). *Let Pi that give ei-differential privacy. A series of Pi (X_i)'s over the disjoint datasets X_i yeild max ϵ-differential privacy. These mechanisms help us to distribute the privacy budget among r mechanisms to recognize ϵ-differential privacy.*

In the above paragraph, we briefly discussed differential privacy, and it's typing. As mentioned in the introduction machine learning used in various types of regression algorithms to secure users' data, one of the approach researchers used is [11]. They proposed a method using differential privacy-we [1]. The model limits how much information an adversary can gain about particular private value, by observing a function learned from a database containing values even if she knows every other value in the database. The ϵ privacy parameters in the proposed algorithm are uniform and have low margin data and inseparable data.

The strengthening of the privacy guarantee corresponds to reducing ϵ it degrades the learning performance in this case. The majority values are tested by authors in given research [11] the majority of ϵ tested. The method they introduced is superior in managing the tradeoff between privacy and learning performance. By taking care of using very small ϵ corresponding to extremely strengthen the privacy requirement. This method performs better and gives predication accuracy close to chance which is not good and useful in machine learning purposes.

4   System Architect

In this section, we describe the system architecture, objectives and possible privacy leaks in existing privacy protection technologies (such as differential Privacy), and conduct distributed training on the client. In the initial, the global model request for a parameter from clients to perform training. After receiving the K number of parameters from clients, the global model sends a signal and requests for no more parameters required to be uploaded to maintain the communication cost. After receiving a parameter from the clients it updates the gradients by using a gradient decent algorithm. Then it sends a signal to download the updated model parameters. Clients download the updated global model and train the local model using their respective dataset, during the training we insert the Laplace noise to protect user data. After updating the model the clients upload the differentially private models back to the global model. The global models combine all the updated local models and perform aggregation using the federated average theorem.

Our Differentially-Private neural network uses a Laplace mechanism [5], to guarantee a privacy for participants. It can preserve the privacy of data while building an effective model with high learning accuracy. We are proposing a novel approach known as Differentially Private Neural Network for Privacy-Preserving which can effectively restrict the adversary from accessing the clients' model, and having the ability to restrict the data leakage. In this framework, we used a DP Laplace mechanism. To ensures that all operations, including the server-side aggregation process, are secure and do not reveal any private information about the training data. At the same time, we consider adding multiple noises on preprocessing where client data will be secure during training.

Our main goal is joint learning, and the client can join and exit at any time during training. The proposed algorithm can reduce the performance loss of the model on the premise of using differential privacy, because it is completely independent of epochs. At the same time, the training process for the client also uses differential privacy, but because the training model we use on the client uses element level privacy measures, it leads to low efficiency and insufficient privacy budget. In the federated optimization framework [8], the central server aggregates the client model after each round of communication. We use a random mechanism to change and approximate this average. This is to hide the contribution of a single entity in the aggregation model, so as to hide it in the whole distributed learning process. In our proposed federated optimization framework

[17], the server aggregates the client model parameters after each round, and uses a random mechanism to approximate this aggregation. All processes are accomplished by hiding customer contributions and following the entire distributed learning process.

In our proposed framework, more noise is added to the input features with little correlation with the output, and different activation functions can be applied. It ensures that our framework can be applied to various large data sets of machine learning tasks. The problems to be solved by our proposed framework:

- To Protect user's data on distributed computation.
- To improve the efficiency of learning rate during training, methods that can provide better accuracy.
- To balance tradeoff between privacy budget and model efficiency.

First, our goal is to develop a system in which the server randomly selects updates for each customer and aggregates the updates of all customers to obtain a global model. In our federated learning system, the server aggregates the client model parameters after each round, and uses a random mechanism to approximate the aggregation. The whole process is to hide the customer's contribution and follow the whole federal learning process. Second, we send the private model to each client, where noise is immediately inserted and preprocessed.

We have completed the model training on the client, added more noise to the input features that are less related to the model output, and can apply different activation functions to our framework, which ensures that our framework can be extended to a wide range of different data sets in the deep learning model. Our solution improves the limitations of joint learning privacy problems, which usually have higher computational overhead. In addition, our solution improves privacy and protects the model from various attacks, such as reasoning attack, adversarial attack and the recently proposed back door attack in federated learning.

We train safely in a distributed environment, and our framework will automatically adjust the sensitivity analysis and noise insertion on the depth neural network. It is completely independent of the number of training rounds in the privacy budget. This makes our mechanism more practical. In addition, in distributed deep learning, our method can redistribute noise insertion to enhance the utility of the model.

In Fig. 1 we have shown our method to flow chart, the detail mechanism of our method is given below:

- The server sends the model to random IoT clients.
- Update the model parameter at the IoT client device.
- Apply Laplace noise to the updated model.
- Send the noise model back to the server, which will aggregate using fedavg.

Experiments show that differential privacy at the client level is feasible, and can still provide high accuracy when enough clients are involved.

1. By applying LRP to data d using deep neural network, the average correlation of all input features is obtained, expressed as RJ (d).

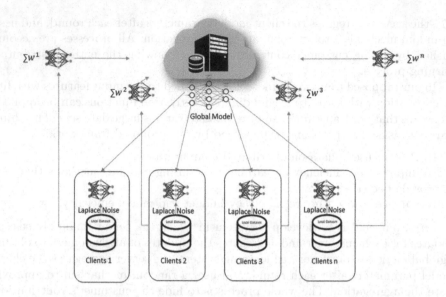

Fig. 1. Framework of differentially private federated neural network

2. Laplacian noise is injected into RJ in proportion through different correlation degrees of features
3. After local training, different IOT customers have different weights.
4. The weight of the added noise is calculated using the fedavg algorithm to generate a new weight.
5. The new weight will be transferred to the customer, and the customer will conduct a new round of training and testing.
6. The rounding value can be determined according to the values of efficiency, accuracy, etc.

5   Experiments

We have written procedures to evaluate the proposed framework. We used MNIST data sets for testing and divided the sorted MNIST sets into fragments. Each client obtains two fragments; Most customers will only have a two digit sample. Therefore, a single customer cannot train the model according to its data to obtain an available model. The following parameters are cross verified for all $K \in \{100, 200, 500, 1000\}$ scenarios: the number of batches per client. Epochs to run on each client. Number of customers participating in each round. Use Laplacian to insert noise on each client.

Digital classification accuracy of non-IIDMNIST data kept by clients during decentralized training in Fig. 2 and Fig. 3 (Figs. 4, 5, Table 1).

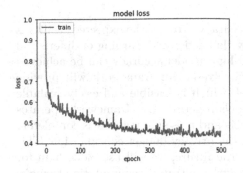

Fig. 2. Model loss during training

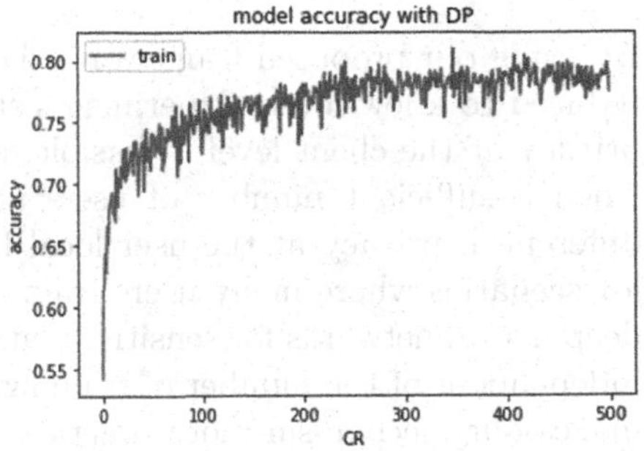

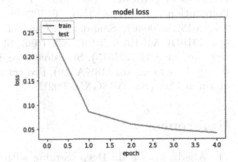

Fig. 3. Acc of clients during training

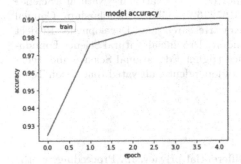

Fig. 4. Accuracy of model output with MNIST dataset without decentralization

Fig. 5. Loss of model output with MNIST dataset without decentralization

Table 1. Differentially private federated learning (DP) experimental findings and reference to non-differentially private federated learning (Non-dp).

	Clients	ACC	CR	CC
Without Noise(Non-DP)	100	98	500	35550
With Noise(DP)	200	80	500	500
//	300	81	350	1051
//	500	82	350	150
//	1000	80	350	

ACC accuracy
CR number of communication
CC communication costs
DP differential privacy

6   Conclusion

By using our proposed framework, the accuracy error of the expected results is reduced to a low level. Experiments show that federated learning of differential privacy at the client level is feasible, and high model accuracy can be achieved when a sufficient number of users are involved. Our framework will provide differential privacy at the user local level, which is feasible and easily scalable for scenarios where many users train models together. Our framework operates deep neural networks for sensitivity analysis and noise insertion. It is completely independent of the number of training in the privacy budget consumption. This makes our mechanism more practical. In the future, we will use blockchain for secure multi-party computation and use secure multi-party computation to make encrypted data more secure. Our model will be more focused on adversarial attacks.

Acknowledgement. This work is supported by National Natural Science Foundation of China (No. 61702218, 61672262), China Scholarship Council (No.201808370046), Shandong Provincial Key Research and Development Project (No.2019GGX101028, 2018CXGC0706), Shandong Provincial Natural Science Foundation(No. ZR2019LZH015), Shandong Province Higher Educational Science and Technology Program (No. J18KA349), Project of Independent Cultivated Innovation Team of Jinan City (No. 2018GXRC002).

References

1. Abadi, M., et al.: Deep learning with differential privacy. In: Proceedings of the 2016 ACM SIGSAC Conference on Computer and Communications Security, pp. 308–318 (2016)
2. Agrawal, R., Srikant, R.: Privacy-preserving data mining. In: Proceedings of the 2000 ACM SIGMOD International Conference on Management of Data (2000)
3. Bonawitz, K., et al.: Towards federated learning at scale: System design. arXiv preprint arXiv:1902.01046 (2019)
4. Li, P., et al.: Multi-key privacy-preserving deep learning in cloud computing. Futur. Gener. Comput. Syst. **74**, 76–85 (2017)
5. Dwork, C., Roth, A., et al.: The algorithmic foundations of differential privacy. Found. Trends Theor. Comput. Sci. **9**(3–4), 211–407 (2014)
6. Friedman, A., Seminar, T.: Privacy Preserving Data Mining. Springer International Publishing, Heidelberg (2014)
7. Hoekstra, M., Lal, R., Pappachan, P., Phegade, V., Del Cuvillo, J.: Using innovative instructions to create trustworthy software solutions. In: Proceedings of the 2nd International Workshop on Hardware and Architectural Support for Security and Privacy (2013)
8. Kamm, L.: Privacy-preserving statistical analysis using secure multi-party computation (2015)
9. Kuflik, T., Kay, J., Kummerfeld, B.: Challenges and solutions of ubiquitous user modeling. In: Krüger, A., Kuflik, T. (eds.) Ubiquitous Display Environments. CT, pp. 7–30. Springer, Heidelberg (2012). https://doi.org/10.1007/978-3-642-27663-7_2

10. Ma, C., et al.: On safeguarding privacy and security in the framework of federated learning. IEEE Network **34**(4), 242–248 (2020)
11. Mcmahan, H.B., Moore, E., Ramage, D., Hampson, S., Arcas, B.: Communication-efficient learning of deep networks from decentralized data (2016)
12. Nikolaenko, V., Weinsberg, U., Ioannidis, S., Joye, M., Boneh, D., Taft, N.: Privacy-preserving ridge regression on hundreds of millions of records. In: Security and Privacy (SP), 2013 IEEE Symposium on (2013)
13. Phan, N., Wu, X., Hu, H., Dou, D.: Adaptive laplace mechanism: differential privacy preservation in deep learning. arXiv (2017)
14. Wang, N., et al.: Collecting and analyzing multidimensional data with local differential privacy. In: 2019 IEEE 35th International Conference on Data Engineering (ICDE), pp. 638–649. IEEE (2019)
15. Wang, S., et al.: Local differential private data aggregation for discrete distribution estimation. IEEE Trans. Parallel Distrib. Syst. **30**(9), 2046–2059 (2019)
16. Wang, Z., Song, M., Zhang, Z., Song, Y., Wang, Q., Qi, H.: Beyond inferring class representatives: user-level privacy leakage from federated learning. In: IEEE INFOCOM 2019-IEEE Conference on Computer Communications, pp. 2512–2520. IEEE (2019)
17. Xu, J.: Edgence: a blockchain-enabled edgecomputing platform for intelligent iot-based dapps. China Commun. **17**(4), 78–87 (2020)

Analysis of Vulnerability of IPsec Protocol Implementation Based on Differential Fuzzing

Kai Tian[1], Fushan Wei[1], Chunxiang Gu[1,2(✉)], and Yanan Shi[1]

[1] Information Engineering University, Zhengzhou 450001, China
[2] Henan Key Laboratory of Network Cryptography Technology, Zhengzhou 450001, China

Abstract. Network protocol is an important means to ensure network security, but it has suffered a steady stream of attacks in recent years due to its implementation complexity and difficulty. In this paper, we present our work on using differential fuzzing to detect the behavioral divergences in multiple implementations of IPsec. The key insight behind our fuzzer is to generate various message streams compose of mutate packets and send them to the IPsec implementations to compare their different behaviors. We proposed a protocol testing framework based on differential fuzzing testing, which can be applied to test the differences and potential security issues of multiple implementations. Our case reveals the implementation differences between four protocol implementations. These differential behaviors exposed protocol implementation violations of RFC specifications and possible security vulnerabilities.

Keywords: IPsec · Protocol fuzzing · Differential fuzzing · Software security

1 Introduction

As an important guarantee for network communication, the correct implementation of network security protocols has become a key link to protect user's privacy and information transmission security. However, it's a challenge to implement the network security protocol correctly due to its complexity and diversity. With the rapid development of Internet technology, the scale of network attacks such as trojan, worm, ransomware becomes much larger and the attack means are more various, making the network's communication security face a huge test. Among them, there are many vulnerabilities caused by the implementation of network security protocols, such as the well-known Heartbleed bugs [1], a serious vulnerability in the popular OpenSSL cryptographic software library.

IPsec [2] is widely used to ensure end-to-end secure communication scenarios. It is not a separate protocol, but a complete set of architecture applied to network data security on IP layer, including AH, ESP, IKE, etc. Under reasonable configuration, IPsec protocol is considered to be secure. However, security vulnerabilities often arise not only from the protocol itself, but also from the implementation of the protocol. Among the many software vulnerability discovery techniques, fuzzing has remained highly popular.

W. Shi et al. (Eds.): SPNCE 2021, LNICST 423, pp. 282–293, 2022.
https://doi.org/10.1007/978-3-030-96791-8_21

However, it's also difficult to find vulnerabilities in protocol using fuzzing. On the one hand, the server has a large state space, and the whole state space can be traversed only by using the message sequence conforming to the protocol specification. On the other hand, strict semantic format requirements and complex cryptographic algorithms further increase the difficulty and complexity of protocol fuzzing. Existing fuzzing algorithms mostly rely on gray box testing technology guided by code coverage, and usually do not rely too much on the semantic format of the protocol, which is hard to handle complex encryption without modifying the server source code.

We propose our approach, which treats the server as a black box without code instrumentation, generates most effective messages through streams fuzzing and field mutation, and discovers the differences and bugs by observing the feedback of different server implementations.

To summary our contributions:

- We design an IPsec protocol fuzzing frame based on differential fuzzing, which can find the differences between protocol implementations naturally.
- Our test case generation method can automatically generate test cases including certificates without modifying the source code of the protocol implementation, which is more fit into the fuzzing test of the protocol.
- We have implemented our fuzzing tool and applied it to IPsec (IKEv1). Through differential fuzzing, we can find more semantic bugs in the protocol, which is also very important for protocol security analysis.

2 Background

2.1 IPsec

IPsec provides high quality, cryptographically-based security services at the IP layer including access control, connectionless integrity, data origin authentication, protection against replays and confidentiality (encryption) [2], which is widely used in various VPNs.

The protocol for key establishment is known as IKE (Internet Key Exchange), and there are two versions of IKE: IKEv1 [3] and IKEv2 [4]. IKEv1 seems to be much more complex which is split into two distinct phases. In phase 1 an ISAKMP SA is established which is used in phases 2 to set up an IPsec SA. IKEv2 provides the same level security with less interaction.

In this paper, we mainly study the implements of IPsec with IKEv1. In IKEv1, there are four authentication methods in phase 1: Pre-Shared Key based method, signature-based method, and two RSA encryption-based methods.

IKEv1 phase 1 can be divided into main mode and aggressive mode. The main mode includes six messages and aggressive mode includes three messages.

In the main mode, the first two messages are used to negotiate a proposal and provide their own *cookies*: c_I and c_R. The *cooike* value can be used to mark the conversation, which exists in the header of each message. Messages 3 and 4 are mainly used for key establishment according to the selected authentication method. The parameters passed

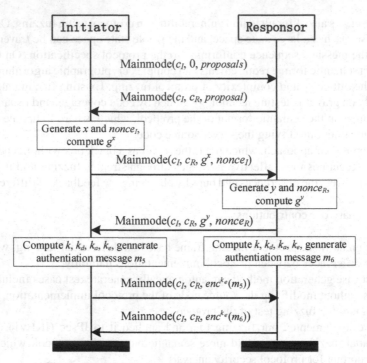

Fig. 1. Generic structure of IKEv1 Phase 1 in main mode.

in this process include DH key exchange parameters and corresponding auxiliary data according to the selected authentication method. Based on these messages and the shared DH secret, the initiator and the responder calculate the four symmetric keys (k, k_d, k_a, k_e) separately. The last two messages are used to confirm each other's keys, which are respectively encrypted with k_e, and the first phase of IKEv1 ends (Fig. 2).

The quick mode is mainly used to negotiate the security parameters used by IPsec SA, which contains three messages, and the quick mode is protected by IKE SA. The initiator will send the conversion attributes of the IPsec SA in the first message, which includes the hash value $hash_1$, the policy proposal SA, and the Nonce. The second message is similar to the first message and the third message contains a hash value, which is used to confirm the receiver's message and prove that the initiator is active. If PFS is desired, a DH Key Exchange can additionally be performed [5].

At this point, a complete connection is established between the inititor and the responsor. Our experiment mainly focuses on the signature-based method and PSK based method. Below we briefly introduce two authentication methods.

PSK-Based Authentication. PSK-based authentication requires both parties to know the same password. The two parties in communication use the shared key, the nonce during the connection, and the shared DH secret to derive the key (refer to the Fig. 1), and the calculation of the key methods is as below:

$$k = prf_{PSK}(nonce_I, nonce_R)$$

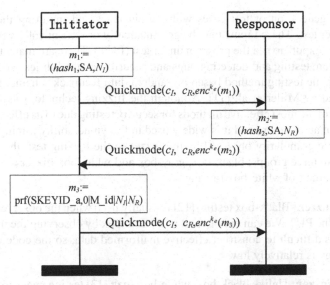

Fig. 2. Generic structure of IKEv1 Phase 1 in quick mode.

$$k_d = prf_k(g^{xy}, c_I, c_R, 0)$$

$$k_a = prf_k(k_d, g^{xy}, c_I, c_R, 1)$$

$$k_e = prf_k(k_d, g^{xy}, c_I, c_R, 2)$$

Signature-Based Authentication. Signature-based verification requires both parties to provide valid certificates for verification. Both parties' certificates and the authentication information will be sent to each other in message 5 and message 6 in the main mode. The key calculation method is as follow:

$$k = prf_{nonce_I, nonce_R}(g^{xy})$$

$$k_d = prf_k(g^{xy}, c_I, c_R, 0)$$

$$k_a = prf_k(k_d, g^{xy}, c_I, c_R, 1)$$

$$k_e = prf_k(k_d, g^{xy}, c_I, c_R, 2)$$

2.2 Fuzzing

In recent years, fuzzing has been widely used in the discovery of software vulnerabilities due to its conceptual simplicity and low deployment barrier [6]. Fuzzing test technology refers to the generation of test cases with certain rules and inputting them into the program under test. These inputs may be grammatically or semantically wrong, that is, using "fuzzing input" to run the program under test (PUT). There are many tools [7–10] used in software testing and detecting bugs and security vulnerabilities successfully.

As a dynamic testing method based on random data feedback scheme, fuzzing was first pioneered by Miller et al. [11]. Although the fuzzing technology is simple, it is currently one of the most effective methods for security testing due to its effectiveness and high degree of automation, and it is widely used in the vulnerability mining. According to the semantic granularity observed by the fuzzer in the fuzzing test, the fuzzers can be divided into three groups: black-box, gray-box and white-box fuzzers [6]. Gray-box fuzzing is a variant of white-box fuzzing.

Black-Box Fuzzer. Black-box testing [12] is usually used when the observer cannot see the inside of the PUT. We can only treat it as a black-box by observing the input/output. However, it is difficult to construct effective malformed data, so the code coverage of this technology is relatively low.

White-Box Fuzzer. Unlike black-box, white-box fuzz [13] testing needs to analyze the internal structure of the PUT and record the internal execution of the PUT at the same time.

Gray-Box Fuzzer. Gray-box [14] testing is a middle -ground approach between black box testing and white box testing. That is, part of the information of PUT execution can be obtained, however, there is no need to analyze the complete semantics of PUT.

The boundaries of the three are not very clear. In order to generate effective testcases, the black-box fuzzer will also collect some information, and the white-box fuzzer will also make some approximations to reduce complexity [6].

Differential Fuzzing. Differential fuzzing [15] is a technique that provides the same input to different but similar implementations to focus on the behavior/response of the SUT. Different from gray-box technology where code coverage is known, differential fuzzing uses the behavioral asymmetries between multiple test programs as a guide, and can find more semantic errors, which has its unique advantages in the discovery of protocol vulnerabilities.

3 Related Work

It is very important to find security vulnerabilities in protocol implementation, but there are also many challenges. In recent years, there are many learning attempts to apply fuzzing test to the discovery of network security protocol vulnerabilities.

In 2014, Sounthiraraj et al. [16] developed the SMV-HUNTER and used the idea of combining dynamic and static to detect SSL/TLS certificate verification vulnerabilities in multiple Android apps. In the same year, Brubaker et al. [17] fuzzed the SSL/TLS server certificate authentication module using forged certificates. In 2015, Gascon et al. [18] designed PULSAR system based on private protocol fuzzing, which extended the protocol reverse to the field of fuzzing, attempting to discover the hidden vulnerabilities of protocol systems. In 2016, Somorovsky [19] presented a TLS protocol analysis tool TLS-Attcker and proposed a two-stage fuzzy method to evaluate TLS server behavior.

In 2017, a domain-independent differential testing tool NEZHA was presented by Petsios [20], which uses the asymmetry of behavior between different programs to focus on triggering more semantic errors. In the same year, Walz [21] et al. proposed a new concept of Generic Message Trees to generate TLS fuzzy messages, and analyzed the implementation of TLS protocol using black-box differential fuzzing. In 2020, Reen [22] proposed the differential fuzzing tool DPIFuzz, a structure-aware and modular fuzzing framework which allows automated testing of QUIC implementations by generating and mutating communication streams and a differential analysis of the behaviour of the implementations to these communication streams. In the same year, Phamand et al. [23] designed a fuzzer called AFLNET, the first gray-box fuzzer for protocol implementation. AFLNET makes automated state model inferencing and coverage guided fuzzing work hand in hand and uses state-feedback to guide the fuzzing process. No protocol specification or message grammars are required.

According to the characteristics of the protocol, the most popular technology at present is state based black-box fuzzing, such as Sulley [24], Peach [25]. The key idea of these fuzzers is to test the target by roughly traversing the state machine model of a given system and generating effective message sequences using corresponding syntax. AFLNET was presented as the first gray-box fuzzer, which can automatically infer the state model and use code coverage to guide fuzziness. Another fuzzing method used is the protocol state fuzzing proposed by de Ruiter et al. [26], which infers the state machine of the target protocol by sending regular packets.

However, the existing fuzzing algorithms still have many challenges: Complex protocols (such as IPsec) have huge state space and complex encryption algorithms, so it is difficult to carry out fast and effective fuzzing, and the algorithm is difficult to cover the whole space; The high correlation between protocol data streams also brings challenges to fuzzing test case generation.

4   Method and System Design

4.1   Fuzzer Design Overview

To solve the above problems, we designed the fuzzer as follows (Fig. 3):

The figure above shows the architecture of our fuzzer, composed of sequence generator, packet generator, mutator, encryptor, and response analyzer.

Sequence Generator: Inspired by the protocol state fuzzing, we generate message sequences randomly. Under this module, we can generate various stream sequences and discover the security problems caused by the combination of multiple messages. Note that what is produced here is not a real packet, but an abstract representation.

Packet Generator: This module can convert the message sequence to a real packet. The subsequent packets generation will use the parameters of the previous packet. In order to ensure the correct interaction with the server, the response of the server needs

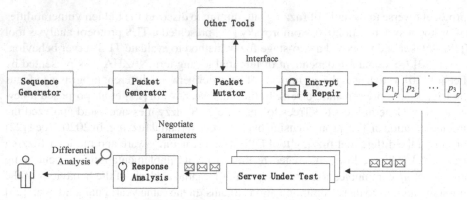

Fig. 3. The overview of our fuzzer.

to be input to the packet generator, that is, the generation of the packet is a process of continuous interaction.

Mutator: Every packet in a sequence can undergo packet mutation a certain probability. There are some fuzzing operators in our mutator. The packet-level fuzzing is mainly aimed at fields.

Encryptor: We set this module to encrypt (optional) and repair (optional) mutated packets. We assume that we are a legitimate client when performing fuzzing. The repair module is mainly to maintain the internal consistency of the packets due to the mutation, which could avoid making the packet rejected by the server. Of course, for the diversity of data packets, the repair operations are optional.

Response Analyzer: This module is mainly used to decrypt and analyze the received packets, record inconsistent replies and abnormal replies. At the same time, there is a connector between the response analyzer and the packet generator to transmit the necessary parameters.

4.2   Mutation and Encryption

4.2.1   Mutation

Different from the traditional fuzzing method, we need to use the semantics and format of IPsec. First, we select the fields to be mutated randomly, and then fuzzing them. We mainly consider the following six fuzzing operations:

Remove operator Randomly delete some bytes for the selected field.
Insert operator Insert a random payload at a random position in the field.
Duplicate operator Copy the selected field and insert it after the field.
Byte operator Randomly obfuscate some of the bytes in the selected field.
Void operator Sets the field to the string of length zero.

4.2.2   Certificate Verification

Authentication of user identity through digital certificate is a very common method, which is very important for network security. For the protocol implementation, certificate verification is a complex process. X.509 certificate has extremely complex structure and strict semantic syntax. Any direct changes to the certificate will result in validation failure, and the probability of randomly generated certificate will be directly rejected. In recent years, there have also been a lot of work related to certificate verification, such as Frankenert [17], Mucert [27] NEZHA [20] HVlearn [28], etc.

For the fuzzing test of a certificate, we mainly focus on the tbscertificate field in the certificate body, mainly including serial num, issuer, validity, subject and extension fields. Unlike frankenert, which uses a large number of seed certificates, we use the fuzzing operator to make changes on the original certificate, and use the CA's private key to sign the certificate.

4.2.3 Encryption and Repair

After a series of mutations, the frame structure of the packet will change greatly. During server authentication, some messages will be rejected prematurely. In order to avoid message inconsistency, we need to repairing the length field optionally.

Since the IPsec packet contains multiple loads, referring to Walz's [21] packet repair method, considering the trade-off between generating inconsistent packets and repairing inconsistent packets, we can selectively correct each part of the length field with a probability of correction is $\frac{1}{2}$.

IPsec enables encryption from the fifth packet in the main mode, and will provides a large number of optional encryption schemes. In order to ensure the integrity of the message, we adopt the method of mutation before encryption.

The packet processing algorithm is as follows:

Algorithm 1 The packet processing algorithm

1: **procedure** MUTATE (*pck, encrypt*)
2:      *operator* = RANDOMCHOICE ({REMOVE, INSERT, ... ,VOID, NONE})
3:      *field* = CHOICEFIELD(*pck*)
4:      *mutpck* = OPERATE(*pck, field, operator*)
5:      *need_repair* = RANDOMCHOICE ({True, False})
6:      **if** *need_repair* == True:
7:          *mutpck*=REPAIR(*mutpck*)
8:      **end if**
9:      **if** *encrypt* == True:
10:         *mutpck* = ENCRYPT(*mutpck*)
11:     **end if**
12:     **return** *mutpck*
13: **end procedure**

4.3 Sequence Generation

Traditional fuzzing method usually produces the correct stream message sequence purposefully. For example, when we are fuzzing the first packet in the quick mode, we need to provide the correct message sequence to enable the server to respond normally in the main mode. However, this method cannot reveal the relationship between different messages.

Inspired by the protocol state fuzzing, we add the sequence fuzzing at the same time. However, we have no way to perform equivalent queries, nor can we guarantee the closeness and consistency of the algorithm. Therefore, we introduce the length parameter l to control the length of the generated flow. l indicates the maximum number of repetitions of data packets. For example, if l takes 2, the frequency of all data packets in a stream shall not exceed 2. This kind of operation can not only disrupt the sequence, but also make the resulting data flow sequence do not extend indefinitely.

The sequence generation algorithm is as follows:

Algorithm 2 The sequence generation algorithm

1: **procedure** SEQGEN($\mathcal{I}$, l)
2:   $counter = \{\}$, $seq = \{\}$, $v = $ True
3:   **for** msg **in** $\mathcal{I}$ **do**
4:     $counter[msg] = 0$
5:   **end for**
6:   **while** v **do**
7:     $msg = $ RANDOMCHOICE($\mathcal{I}$)
8:     $counter[msg] = counter[msg] + l$
9:     $seq \cup = \{msg\}$
10:    **if** $counter[msg] > l$ **do**
11:      $\mathcal{I} = \mathcal{I} \setminus msg$
12:    **end if**
13:    $v = $ RANDOMCHOICE($\{$True, False$\}$)
14: **end while**
15: **return** seq
16: **end proceduce**

---

5 Result

In this section we present our experiment on IPsec implementation. We use the method above to analyze the target protocol and find the differences between the protocols. In order to ensure that our tool can communicate with the target server normally, we need to generate separate sessions for each server, record the connection parameters of each session, and ensure that only the tested field will be mutated. We implement our entire framework using python. For our experiments, we consider five open source implementations of IPsec, including strongSwan 5.3.4, strongSwan 5.9.2, Libreswan 3.0 and Libreswan 4.4.

5.1 Careless Field Checking

We found that the four similar protocol implementations have some fields that are checked carelessly, resulting in inconsistent field phasing, which shows the difficulty of protocol implementation. Although the problematic field will not have a substantial impact on the protocol security, the error handling and inconsistent resolution of the length field may lead to the server's incorrect resolution of the protocol message.

1) *Libreswan: Fields Lack of Checking*

An ISAKMP message has a fixed header format. However, some implementations lack checks on these fixed messages. For example, the Proposal Transforms field specifies the number of transforms for the Proposal, but Libreswan is lack of checking. We can pass the verification by replacing it with any octet. The default setting for the reserved field is 0. The Libreswan does not check this field, but strongSwan checks it.

2) *StrongSwan: Fields Lack of Checking*

In particular, RFC stipulates that the requests for assignment of new life types MUST be accompanied by a detailed description of the units of this type and its expiry. However, strongSwan lacks sufficient checks on IKE attribute. Life-type with unknown type and life-duration with value 0 can also pass the verification of the server.

5.2 Certificate Verification

Protocol certificate verification is a very complex process. As the key step of identity authentication, improper and lax handling of any part may lead to serious security problems. Here are strongSwan's problems in certificate processing:

1) *Host name validation is not case sensitive*

During the fuzzing, we found that strongSwan is not case sensitive in host name verification. This case insensitive verification of public name will lead to identity counterfeiting by malicious clients of the internal users.

2) *Overlong Serial number*

In RFC, the serial number can be a long integer. Certificate users must be able to handle serial number of up to 20 octets. StrongSwan allows serial number certificates greater than 20 bytes.

3) *Mishandling Certificate extension verification*

A certificate-using system MUST reject the certificate if it encounters a critical extension that it does not recognize or a critical extension that contains information that it cannot process. If there is an extended Key Usage extension, users must check the Key Usage to verify that the certificate is authorized for its purpose. strongSwan 5.3.4 does not check the use of keys and alternate names, which was fixed in 5.9.2.

A non-critical extension MAY be ignored if it is not recognized, but MUST be processed if it is recognized. Given a certificate with a known non critical extension, but not a valid value of the extension, and strongSwan chooses to accept the certificate.

6 Prospects and Future Work

In this paper, we propose a differential fuzzing framework for IPsec, which uses stream fuzzing and packet mutation to generate IPsec message streams. Compared with the previous fuzzing methods, our method can discover the difference responses between different protocols implementations effectively. The difference in the implementation of the protocol is mainly due to the large parameter space of the protocol specification and the inaccuracy of some specifications. These flexibilities will cause difficulties for experimenters. Our method can cover the main state space of the protocol implementation, which is an effective attempt to apply fuzzing to large-scale cryptographic protocols.

We also plan to further expand our work. First, we hope to add support for other cryptographic protocols, such as IKEv2, SSH, etc. In addition, our packet generation process did not use the feedback of the message. In the next step, we will enrich our mutation strategy and borrow gray box technology to optimize our packet generation process. Finally, finding multi trigger security vulnerabilities through flow ambiguity testing is another key idea. We plan to study this potential in more detail.

Acknowledgments. This work has been supported by the National Natural Science Foundation of China under Grant 61772548.

References

1. "OpenSSL 'Heartbleed' vulnerability". CVE-2014–0160 (2013)
2. Kent, S., Seo, K.: Security architecture for the internet protocol. RFC 4301 (Proposed Standard) (2005). http://www.ietf.org/rfc/rfc4301.txt
3. Harkins, D., Carrel, D.: The Internet Key Exchange (IKE). RFC 2409 (Proposed Standard) (1998). http://www.ietf.org/rfc/rfc2409.txt (obsoleted by RFC 4306. Updated by RFC 4109)
4. Kaufman, C., Hoffman, P., Nir, Y., Eronen, P.: RFC 5996: Internet Key Exchange Protocol Version 2 (IKEv2) (2010). http://www.rfc-editor.org/info/rfc5996
5. Felsch, D., Grothe, M., Schwenk, J., Czubak, A., Szymanek, M.: The dangers of key reuse: practical attacks on IPsec IKE. In: Proceedings of the 27th USENIX Conference on Security Symposium (SEC 2018), pp. 567–583. USENIX Association, USA (2018)
6. Manes, V., Han, H.S., Han, C., et al.: Fuzzing: art, science, and engineering (2018)
7. Google. Honggfuzz: security oriented software fuzzer (2015). https://github.com/google/honggfuzz
8. LLVM. libFuzzer: a library for coverage-guided fuzz testing (2015). http://llvm.org/docs/LibFuzzer.html
9. Zalewski, M.: American fuzzy lop (n. d.). http://lcamtuf.coredump.cx/afl/
10. TLS-Attacker: a Java-based framework for analyzing TLS libraries. https://github.com/RUB-NDS/TLS-Attacker
11. Miller, B.P., Fredriksen, L., So, B.: An empirical study of the reliability of UNIX utilities. Commun. ACM **33**(12), 32–44 (1990)
12. Beizer, B.: Black-box Testing: Techniques for Functional Testing of Software and Systems. Wiley, Hoboken (1995)
13. Godefroid, P., Levin, M.Y., Molnar, D.A.: Automated whitebox fuzz testing. In: Proceedings of the Network and Distributed System Security Symposium, pp. 151–166 (2008)

14. DeMott, J.D., Enbody, R.J., Punch, W.F.: Revolutionizing the field of grey-box attack surface testing with evolutionary (2007)
15. McKeeman, W.M.: Differential testing for software. Digit. Tech. J. **10**(1), 100–107 (1998)
16. Sounthiraraj, D., Sahs, J., Greenwood, G., et al.: SMV-HUNTER: large scale, automated detection of SSL/TLS man-in-the-middle vulnerabilities in android apps. In: Proceedings of the 21st Annual Network and Distributed System Security Symposium. NDSS 2014 (2014)
17. Brubaker, C., Jana, S., Ray, B., et al.: Using frankencerts for automated adversarial testing of certificate validation in SSL/TLS implementations. In: 2014 IEEE Symposium on Security and Privacy, pp. 114–129. IEEE (2014)
18. Gascon, H., Wressnegger, C., Yamaguchi, F., et al.: PULSAR: stateful black-box fuzzing of proprietary network protocols. In: Thuraisingham, B., Wang, X., Yegneswaran, V. (eds.) International Conference on Security and Privacy in Communication Systems. Springer, Cham, pp. 330–347 (2015). https://doi.org/10.1007/978-3-319-28865-9_18
19. Somorovsky, J.: Systematic fuzzing and testing of TLS libraries. In: Proceedings 2016 ACM SIGSAC Conference on Computer and Communications Security (CCS 2016), pp. 1492–1504 (2016)
20. Petsios, T., Tang, A., Stolfo, S.J., Keromytis, A.D., Jana, S.: NEZHA: efficient domain-independent differential testing. In: Proceedings of the 38th IEEE Symposium on Security & Privacy, San Jose, CA, May 2017 (2017)
21. Walz, A., Sikora, A.: Exploiting dissent: towards fuzzing-based differential black-box testing of TLS implementations. IEEE Trans. Dependable Secur. Comput. 1 (2017). https://doi.org/10.1109/TDSC.2017.2763947
22. Reen, G.S., Rossow, C.: DPIFuzz: a differential fuzzing framework to detect DPI elusion strategies for QUIC. In: Annual Computer Security Applications Conference (ACSAC 2020), pp. 332–344. Association for Computing Machinery, New York, NY, USA (2020). https://doi.org/10.1145/3427228.3427662
23. Roychoudhury, A., Pham, V.-T., Böhme, M.: AFLNET: a grey-box fuzzer for network protocols. In: IEEE International Conference on Software Testing, Verification and Validation (ICST). IEEE (2020)
24. Amini, P., Portnoy, A., Sears, R.: Sulley (n. d.). https://github.com/OpenRCE/sulley
25. Eddington, M.: Peach fuzzing platform (n. d.). http://peachfuzzer.com
26. de Ruiter, J., Poll, E.: Protocol state fuzzing of TLS implementations. In: Proceedings 24th USENIX Security Symposium (USENIX Security 15), pp. 193–206 (2015)
27. Chen, Y., Su, Z.: Guided differential testing of certificate validation in SSL/TLS implementations. In: Proceedings of the 10th Joint Meeting on Foundations of Software Engineering (FSE), pp. 793–804. ACM (2015)
28. Sivakorn, S., Argyros, G., Pei, K., Keromytis, A. D., Jana, S.: HVLearn: auto mated black-box analysis of hostname verification in SSL/TLS implementations (2017)

A Honeywords Generation Method Based on Deep Learning and Rule-Based Password Attack

Kunyu Yang[1], Xuexian Hu[1]([⊠]), Qihui Zhang[1], Jianghong Wei[1], and Wenfen Liu[2]

[1] State Key Laboratory of Mathematical Engineering and Advanced Computing, Zhengzhou, China
xuexian_hu@hotmail.com
[2] Guilin University of Electronic Technology, Guilin, China

Abstract. Honeywords is a simple and efficient method that can help the authentication server to detect password leaks. The indistinguishability between generated honeywords and real passwords is the key to the honeywords generation methods. However, the current honeywords generation methods are difficult to achieve that and are vulnerable to the Top-PW attack.

In order to improve the security of the honeywords generation method, this paper combines the deep learning and rule-based password attacks to propose a new honeywords generation method called GHDR. The method first builds a deep learning model to learn whether the rules used in the rule-based password attack are effective for different passwords. When a user sets a password, effective rules will be selected by the model according to the entered password, and then these selected rules will be used to transform the user's password to generate honeywords. Experimental results show that the proposed honeywords generation method can better resist Top-PW attacks than the state-of-the-art methods.

Keywords: Honeywords · Deep learning · Password attack · Top-PW attack

1 Introduction

Recently years, network attacks against authentication servers of many well-known websites have occurred frequently, resulting in a large number of data files storing passwords have been stolen. These network incidents pose a great threat to users' information security. Although most websites store passwords in salted-hash to improve security, this method could not prevent attackers from recovering passwords from the leaked password file [22]. With the development of password attack technologies (e.g. PCFG-based model [24], deep-learning-based model [18] and the attack model using personal information [23]) and the enhancement of computer computing power, it becomes easier for an attacker

W. Shi et al. (Eds.): SPNCE 2021, LNICST 423, pp. 294–306, 2022.
https://doi.org/10.1007/978-3-030-96791-8_22

to quickly recover most passwords from a password file. What's more serious is that the behavior of stealing password files usually does not affect the function of the server, leading to these attacks are difficult to be perceived and tracked. The website administrators do not discover the password files leak until the attackers make full use of the data and poster them online, which is usually months or even years after the passwords leak occurred.

In 2013, Juels et al. [15] proposed using honeywords to detect whether the password files in the authentication system have leaked. This method generates multiple decoy passwords called honeywords for each account, and stores them together with the real password. Assume that an attacker can still obtain the password file and recover the passwords from it. After that, the attacker still needs to identify which one is the user's real password from the password list mixed with multiple honeywords. The server can detect passwords leak if the attacker login using honeywords, and then take measures such as restricting login and requiring users to modify passwords to ensure user's information security.

According to whether the password setting interface in the client needs to be modified, the honeywords generation method can be divided into two categories, one is Legacy-UI [2,7,14] and the other is Modified-UI [3–6]. Although studies [4,6] have shown that the Legacy-UI methods are weaker than the Modified-UI methods in terms of security, the Legacy-UI methods are more feasible in practice, because no modification is required on the client without increasing users' learning costs.

In the paper [15], Jules et al. proposed several Legacy-UI methods to generate honeywords by replacing part of characters in passwords. These methods based on character replacement are highly efficient, but the generated honeywords are significantly different from the real passwords, resulting in that the honeywords can be easily identified. In order to achieve the goal of generating honeywords that are indistinguishable from real passwords, Erguler [11] proposed randomly selecting some passwords of registered users as honeywords of a new account. But for the sake of satisfying random selection, the authentication server must continuously regenerate honeywords for all users as the number of users grows, which greatly increases the computational burden of the server. Taking into account the advantages and disadvantages of the above two methods, many researchers have found that using password attack methods to generate honeywords is a feasible way. Wang et al. [22] combined the probabilistic-context-free-based method and Markov-based method to generate honeywords, Fauzi et al. [12]proposed the use of PassGAN-based method, and Dionysiou et al. [10] proposed the use of representation learning. Since the real password satisfies Zipf's distribution [21], and the distribution of honeywords generated by these methods still has a gap with the distribution of real passwords, so these methods are vulnerable to a specific attack called Top-PW attack. The Top-PW attack refers to that an attacker calculates the frequency of each sweetword (including honeywords and the real password) in the known real password dataset, and takes the sweetword with the highest frequency as the real password.

In this paper, in view of the problem that the honeywords generation method is vulnerable to Top-PW attacks, we combine deep learning and rule-based password attack methods to propose a new honeywords generation method called GHDR. To verify the security of the proposed method, we use the GHDR method to generate honeywords for the accounts in the real password dataset, and simulate the behavior of an attacker using the Top-PW attack to identify the correct password after obtaining the password file. The experimental results show that the proposed honeywords generation method can better resist Top-PW attacks than the state-of-the-art methods. We also test the time required for the GHDR method to generate honeywords, and the results indicate that the method is usable in practice.

2   Preliminaries

2.1   Authentication System with Honeywords

The symbols we used to describe the authentication system with honeywords and their corresponding meanings are given in Table 1.

Table 1. Symbols used to describe the authentication system with honeywords

Symbols	Meanings
$H()$	hash algorithm
u_i	ID of a certain user
p_i	real password of u_i
honeywords	decoy passwords generated by system for u_i
W_i	including p_i and corresponding honeywords, also called sweetwords
k	the number of elements in W_i
c_i	index of p_i in W_i

Compared with the traditional authentication system, the authentication system with honeywords adds a Honey-checker server in addition to the identity authentication server. The Honey-checker server is considered to be safe and reliable. It connects to the identity authentication server through an encrypted and trusted channel, and only allows adding, modifying, and verifying operations. The system stores the user ID and corresponding sweetwords (i.e. (u_i, W_i)) in the identity authentication server, and stores the user ID and the index of real password in the sweetwords (i.e. (u_i, c_i)) in the Honey-checker server.

Figure 1 shows how the authentication system with honeywords works. When a user registers, the identity authentication server generates multiple honeywords for the user u_i and forms W_i together with the password p_i set by the user, where the position of p_i in W_i is random. Then the identity authentication server uses the hash algorithm $H()$ to calculate the value of each element in W_i and store the tuple $(u_i, H(W_i))$. After that, the identity authentication server sends the user ID u_i and c_i (i.e. the index of p_i in W_i) to the Honey-checker, and the tuple (u_i, c_i) will be stored in the Honey-checker server.

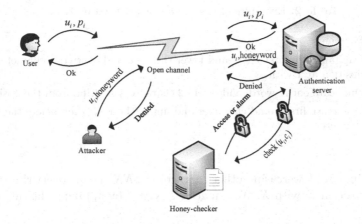

Fig. 1. Illustration of authentication system with honeywords

When a user logs in, the identity authentication server uses $H()$ to calculate the hash value $H(p_i')$ of the password p_i' entered by the user u_i and checks whether $H(p_i')$ is in $H(W_i)$. If not, it means that the user has entered the wrong password. If it is, it means that the user may have entered the correct password or an attacker has entered a honeyword, then the identity authentication server needs to use the honey-checker for further verification. The identity authentication server sends u_i and the index c_i' of $H(p_i')$ in $H(W_i)$ to the Honey-checker. Honey-checker checks whether c_i' and c_i are equal. If true, the user can log in successfully. If not, it means the login operation is using a honeyword, and the system issues an alarm.

2.2 Rule-Based Password Attack

The rule-based password attack is a kind of heuristic password attack algorithm. It can simulate the user's password generation behavior by designing various transformation rules (e.g. insertion, deletion, and reordering) to transform the strings in the carefully designed password dictionary. As early as 1979, Morris et al. [19] proposed the use of the rule-based attack to analyze the strength of passwords. Subsequent proposed password cracking tools (e.g. Hashcat, John and Ripper) are all designed with many professional rule sets and used to rule-based password guessing attacks. The methods used in papers [8,16] to implement password guessing attacks are also rule-based.

We take the rule set used in the well-known password attack tool Hashcat as an example to further illustrate how to execute a rule-based password attack. The rules in Hashcat are to express how to transform a password with custom symbols. Some examples of rules and their corresponding meanings are given in Table 2. Take *co1@* as an example, where *c* means capitalizing the first character

Table 2. Examples of rules in a rule set used by Hashcat

Rules	Meanings
co1@	Capitalize the first letter and lower the rest, and overwrite character at position at 1 with @
dO02	Duplicate entire word, and delete 2 characters starting from the position 0
C]	Lowercase first found character and upper the rest, then delete the last character

of the string and lowercasing other characters; oNX means overwrite the character at position N with X. We can get $P@ssword$ by applying the rule $co1@$ to $password$.

3   GHDR: The Proposed Method

3.1   Inspiration

On the one hand, generating honeywords that are indistinguishable from the real password is the key to a honeyword generation method [1,11,22]. On the other hand, the honeyword generation process must be time-saving, otherwise, using it will cause a poor service experience for users, which is unacceptable for service providers. In this paper, we intend to construct a method that can quickly generate honeywords similar to real passwords and can better resist Top-PW attacks.

The rule-based password attack can transform the given password to generate guessing passwords close to real passwords. Therefore, applying the rule-based password attack to honeywords generation has certain advantages. However, Pasquini et al. [20] pointed out that not all the rules are applicable to a certain password. The generated password obtained by transforming the password with an inapplicable rule is different from the real password. Inspired by the research in paper [20], a deep learning model for finding the appropriate rules for each password is built. Then we propose to use this model to generate honeywords, that is, use the model to match the password entered by a user with appropriate rules, and then take the generated passwords transformed by these rules as honeywords.

3.2   Construction of the Deep Learning Model

Denote the rule set as R, and a rule in it is denoted by r_i; denote the password dictionary as D, and a password in it is denoted by d_i. The goal of our deep learning model is to match the appropriate rules for each password d_i. This can be regarded as a multi-label classification problem, that is, each rule r_i is a label, and each d_i has multiple labels. We use 0 and 1 to indicate that a rule r_i and d_i are inappropriate and appropriate respectively.

In order to construct labeled training samples, we construct a target password set X, which consists of a large number of real passwords. If the generated password obtained by using the rule r_i to transform d_i appears in X, it means that d_i and r_i are appropriate, otherwise, it means that they are inappropriate. It can be expressed as:

$$f(d, r) = \begin{cases} 0 & r(d) \notin X \\ 1 & r(d) \in X \end{cases},$$ (1)

where $r(d)$ represents the generated password obtained by using r to transform d. Based on this, a label y_i with $|R|$ dimensions can be generated for a password d_i in D, i.e. $y_i = [f(d_i, r_1), [f(d_i, r_2), \ldots, [f(d_i, r_{|R|})]$.

In order to meet the requirement that the honeywords generation process must be time-saving, we use Gate Convolutional Neural Network (GCNN) [9] to build the model. GCNN is a type of Convolutional Neural Network and it can better exploit GPU hardware to accelerate the training process. The researches in papers [9,13] show that the effect of using the GCNN model on natural language processing exceeds that of partial recurrent neural networks. The neural network structure of the model used in GHDR is shown in Figs. 2, and 3 shows the structure of the GCNN block used in it. During the model training, passwords are divided into character sequences as input. First, the Embedding layer is used to obtain the embedding representation of the characters, and then two GCNN blocks are used to extract features. Finally, the dimensionality of the result is changed through two fully connected layers.

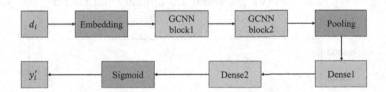

Fig. 2. The neural network structure of the model used in GHDR

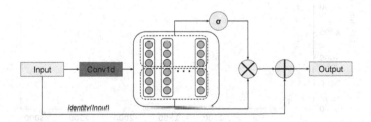

Fig. 3. The neural network structure of the GCNN blocks

3.3   Training of the Deep Learning Model

Dataset. We use the passwords leaked from *163.com* and *Twitter* as the password dictionary D, and the passwords leaked from *Mate1* and *Dodonew* as the target password set X. The above dataset information is shown in Table 3. The rule set used in this article is *generated* constructed in the Hashcat, which contains 14,728 rules in total. After removing the rules that do not have any change to passwords and some rules used to reject plains, we use 13,470 of them.

Table 3. Dataset used in model training

Dataset	Web service	Language	Password nums
163.com	Mailbox	Chinese	36,046,377
Twitter	Social forum	English	38,470,995
Mate1	Online dating	English	25,570,008
Dodonew	E-commerce	Chinese	15,578,470

Training Process. The passwords in D and X that contain non-printable ASCII characters and the password length is not between 6 and 20 are deleted, and we remove the duplicate passwords. Then all the rules in the rule set are executed for each password in D, and the labeled training samples are constructed according to Eq. 1. Finally, we get about 1.6 million valid training samples.

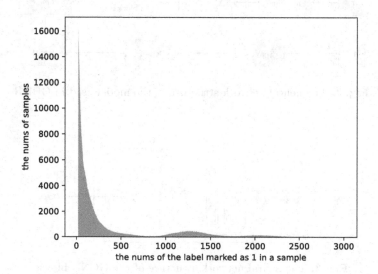

Fig. 4. The distribution of the positive instances in the training samples

Observing the training sample, we find that the positive and negative labels in the samples are seriously unbalanced. Specifically, there are far fewer labels marked as 1 in a sample than labels marked as 0. Figure 4 shows the relationship between the number of the label marked as 1 in a sample and the number of samples. Although there are 13,470 labels for a sample, less than 500 labels are marked as 1 in most samples. Aiming at this problem, Focal loss [17] is adopted as the loss function, it can be expressed as:

$$\mathcal{L} = \begin{cases} -\alpha(1 - y_i')^\gamma log y_i' & , y_i = 1 \\ -(1 - \alpha)y_i'^\gamma log(1 - y_i') & , y_i = 0 \end{cases},$$
(2)

where y_i is the ground-truth label, y_i' is the result assigned by the model, α is a parameter that can adjust the weight, and γ is an adjustable factor. According to the recommended values in the paper [17], α is set to 0.25, and γ is set to 2 in our experiment.

During training, the passwords in the training samples are input into the model, and the output result y' is obtained through the calculation of the neural network. Then use the focal loss to calculate the loss between y' and the label y of the sample. Finally, the Adam optimization algorithm is used to adjust the model parameters through backpropagation until the value of the loss function no longer decreases.

3.4   Honeywords Generation Using the Deep Learning Model

The trained model is used to generate honeywords, the specific process is shown in Algorithm 1.

Algorithm 1: Honeywords generation

Input: User's password p_u, rule set R, model M, the nums of honeywords $k - 1$
Output: Honeywords list *honeywords*
1 Initialize *honeywords* to an empty list
2 $pred \leftarrow M(p_u)$
3 $R_{sorted} \leftarrow$ sort the rules in R in descending order according to the probability in *pred*
4 **while** *honeywords*.length $< k$ **do**
5 | $r \leftarrow R_{sorted}.\text{pop}(0)$
6 | $candidate \leftarrow r(p_u)$
7 | **if** *candidate* not in *honeywords* and $candidate \neq p_u$ **then**
8 | | add *candidate* to *honeywords*
9 | **end**
10 **end**
11 **return** *seqs*

When generating honeywords for a user, the password set by the user is input into the model, and the predictions of the model are obtained firstly. The predicted values represent the probabilities that the generated passwords obtained by transforming the user's password using the corresponding rules appear in the real password dataset. Then all the rules are sorted in descending order of probabilities, and these rules are used in turn to transform the user's password to obtain generated passwords. If a generated password is different from the existing honeywords and the user's password, it can be used as a new honeyword until $k-1$ honeywords are generated. Finally, the password set by the user is randomly inserted into a random position in the honeywords list to form sweetwords. User ID and sweetwords (stored in salt-hash) are stored in the authentication server, and the honey-checker stores the user ID and the index of the user's password in the sweetwords.

4   Security Analysis and Efficiency Evaluation

4.1   Security Analysis

We use the flatness graph and success-number graph proposed by Wang et al. [22] to test the resistance against Normalized Top-PW attack ability of the proposed GHDR method, and compare with the methods Tweaking-tail and Chaffing-with-a-password-model (PCFG-based [24] model is used in this paper) proposed in the paper [15].

We use the GHDR method to generate honeywords for real passwords leaked from *Gmail* and *Mopu*, and assume that the attacker uses passwords leaked from *Rockyou* and *7k7k* as known passwords to perform the Top-PW attack. The information of these datasets is shown in Table 4. The attacker aims to distinguish the real password from k sweetwords by treating the authentication server as a querying oracle. But the number of queries that an attacker can perform is not unlimited. The honey-checker will record the number of login attempts using honeywords. When the number of such attempts against an account exceeds t_1, the attacker will be prohibited from continuing to login to this account; when the total number of such attempts exceeds t_2, the attacker will be prohibited from trying to login to any account.

Table 4. Datasets used in model security analysis

Dataset	Web service	Language	Password nums
RockYou	Social forum	English	32,368,961
7k7k	Gaming	Chinese	18,576,977
Gmail	Mailbox	English	468,992
Maopu	Entertainment forum	Chinese	294,912

In the experiment, k is set to 20, t_1 is set to 3, and t_2 is set to 10000. The results of our experiment are shown in Figs. 5 and 6. The *Random* in the Flatness graph means that an attacker cannot obtain any additional information, and can only randomly select one from sweetwords as the real password.

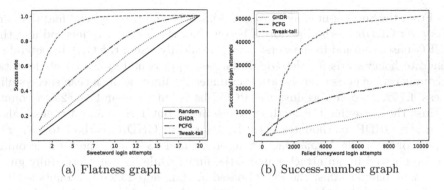

(a) Flatness graph   (b) Success-number graph

Fig. 5. Security analysis on password leaked from Gmail

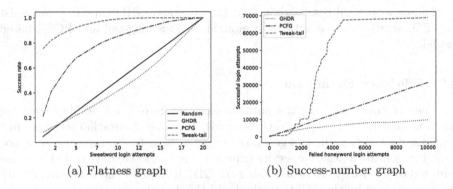

(a) Flatness graph   (b) Success-number graph

Fig. 6. Security analysis on password leaked from Maopu

From the Flatness graphs in Figs. 5(a) and 6(a), we can see that the proposed GHDR method shows higher security against Top-PW attacks on average compared with the Tweak-tail method and the PCFG-based method. Specifically, using the GHDR method to generate honeywords for the *Gmail* dataset, the probability that an attacker can successfully identify the real password with one guess is about 8.89%, while he can successfully login 16.35% accounts against the PCFG-based method and 50.16% accounts against the Tweaking-tail method, which are about 1 time and 5 times higher than the GHDR method respectively. Using the GHDR method to generate honeywords for the *Maopu* dataset, the probability that an attacker can successfully identify the real password with one guess is about 8.36%, while he can successfully login 21.17% accounts against the PCFG-based method and 75.46% accounts against the Tweaking-tail method, which are about 2 times and 8 times higher than the GHDR method respectively. What is interesting is that the number of successful attacks with more than two guesses against GHDR method is less than *Random* in Fig. 5(a), which shows that the honeywords generated by GHDR have a certain negative impact on the Top-PW attack.

From the Success-number graphs in Figs. 5(b) and 6(b), we can find that the proposed GHDR method performs better than the Tweak-tail method and the PCFG-based method in the worst case. Specifically, using the GHDR method to generate honeywords for the *Gmail* dataset, approximately 2.45% of the total accounts can be guessed by an attacker under the limit, while he can successfully guess 4.76% accounts against the PCFG-based method and 10.82% accounts against the Tweaking-tail method, which are about 1 time and 4 times higher than the GHDR method respectively. Using the GHDR method to generate honeywords for the *Maopu* dataset, approximately 3.21% of the total accounts can be guessed by an attacker under the limit, while he can successfully guess 10.56% accounts against the PCFG-based method and 23.26% accounts against the Tweaking-tail method, which are about 2 times and 6 times higher than the GHDR method respectively.

The experimental results show that the proposed GHDR method can resist Top-PW attacks more effectively compared to Tweaking-tail and PCFG-based models.

4.2   Efficiency Evaluation

The use of honeywords in the authentication system is inevitably increasing the time required for users to set passwords. Network application services must consider the time required to generate honeywords. If the consumed time is too long, it will bring a negative service experience to users. We have tested the time required to generate honeywords using the GHDR method and compared it with the time needed by the PCFG method and the Tweak-tail method.

We employ a host with a configuration of CPU Intel(R) Xeon(R) Gold 6136 CPU @ 3.00 GHz, 128 GB DDR4 DRAM, and GeForce RTX 2080 Ti GPU to evaluate the proposed method. The time needed to generate honeywords for an account is shown in Table 5.

Table 5. Dataset used in model security analysis

Honeywords generation method	Average time needed for an account
GHDR	3.06 ms
PCFG-based	0.07 ms
Tweak-tail	0.04 ms

Although the average time required for the proposed GHDR method to generate honeywords for an account is much higher than that of the PCFG-based method and the Tweak-tail method, it still only takes about 3.06 ms. Compared with the general network delay (10 ms–50 ms), it is difficult for users to perceive this time. It can be proved that the proposed GHDR method is feasible in practice.

5 Conclusion

This paper proposes a honeywords method that combines deep learning and rule-based password attacks called GHDR, which can better resist Top-PW attacks. The GHDR method first constructs a neural network model to retrieve appropriate rules from the rule set used in the rule-based password attack for the user's passwords. Then the searched rules are used to transform the user's passwords to generate honeywords. The Flatness graph and Success-number graph are used to test the security of the GHDR method. The experimental results show that the GHDR method has a higher ability to resist Top-PW attacks than the Tweak-tail method and the PCFG-based method. In addition, we analyzed the time required to generate honeywords using the GHDR method, and the results proved that it is usable in practice.

Acknowledgements. This research was supported by the National Natural Science Foundation of China (Grant Nos. 62172433, 62172434, 61862011, 61872449), and Guangxi Natural Science Foundation (Grant No. 2018GXNSFAA138116).

References

1. Camenisch, J., Lehmann, A., Neven, G.: Optimal distributed password verification. In: Proceedings of the 22nd ACM SIGSAC Conference on Computer and Communications Security, pp. 182–194 (2015)
2. Catuogno, L., Castiglione, A., Palmieri, F.: A honeypot system with honeyword-driven fake interactive sessions. In: Proceedings of the International Conference on High Performance Computing & Simulation, pp. 187–194 (2015)
3. Chakraborty, N., Mondal, S.: Few notes towards making honeyword system more secure and usable. In: Proceedings of the 8th International Conference on Security of Information and Networks, pp. 237–245 (2015)
4. Chakraborty, N., Mondal, S.: A new storage optimized honeyword generation approach for enhancing security and usability. CoRR abs/1509.06094 (2015). http://arxiv.org/abs/1509.06094
5. Chakraborty, N., Mondal, S.: On designing a modified-UI based honeyword generation approach for overcoming the existing limitations. Comput. Secur. **66**, 155–168 (2017)
6. Chakraborty, N., Singh, S., Mondal, S.: On designing a questionnaire based honeyword generation approach for achieving flatness. In: Proceedings of the 17th IEEE International Conference On Trust, Security and Privacy In Computing And Communications/12th IEEE International Conference On Big Data Science And Engineering, pp. 444–455 (2018)
7. Chang, D., Goel, A., Mishra, S., Sanadhya, S.K.: Generation of secure and reliable honeywords, preventing false detection. IEEE Trans. Dependable Secur. Comput. **16**(5), 757–769 (2019)
8. Clair, L.S., et al.: Password exhaustion: predicting the end of password usefulness. In: Bagchi, A., Atluri, V. (eds.) ICISS 2006. LNCS, vol. 4332, pp. 37–55. Springer, Heidelberg (2006). https://doi.org/10.1007/11961635_3
9. Dauphin, Y.N., Fan, A., Auli, M., Grangier, D.: Language modeling with gated convolutional networks. CoRR abs/1612.08083 (2016). http://arxiv.org/abs/1612.08083

10. Dionysiou, A., Vassiliades, V., Athanasopoulos, E.: Honeygen: generating honeywords using representation learning. In: Proceedings of the ACM Asia Conference on Computer and Communications Security, pp. 265–279 (2021)
11. Erguler, I.: Achieving flatness: selecting the honeywords from existing user passwords. IEEE Trans. Dependable Secur. Comput. **13**(2), 284–295 (2016)
12. Fauzi, M.A., Yang, B., Martiri, E.: PassGAN based honeywords system for machine-generated passwords database. In: Proceedings of the IEEE 6th International Conference on Big Data Security on Cloud, IEEE International Conference on High Performance and Smart Computing, and IEEE International Conference on Intelligent Data and Security, pp. 214–220 (2020)
13. Gehring, J., Auli, M., Grangier, D., Yarats, D., Dauphin, Y.N.: Convolutional sequence to sequence learning. CoRR abs/1705.03122 (2017). http://arxiv.org/abs/1705.03122
14. Guo, Y., Zhang, Z., Guo, Y.: Superword: a honeyword system for achieving higher security goals. Comput. Secur. **103**, 101689 (2021)
15. Juels, A., Rivest, R.L.: Honeywords: making password-cracking detectable. In: Proceedings of the 20th ACM SIGSAC Conference on Computer and Communications Security, pp. 145–160 (2013)
16. Kuo, C., Romanosky, S., Cranor, L.F.: Human selection of mnemonic phrase-based passwords. In: Proceedings of the Second Symposium on Usable Privacy and Security, pp. 67–78 (2006)
17. Lin, T.Y., Goyal, P., Girshick, R., He, K., Dollar, P.: Focal loss for dense object detection. IEEE Trans. Pattern Anal. Mach. Intell. **42**(2), 318–327 (2020)
18. Melicher, W., et al.: Fast, lean, and accurate: modeling password Guessability using neural networks. In: Proceedings of the 25th USENIX Security Symposium, pp. 175–191 (2016)
19. Morris, R., Thompson, K.: Password security: a case history. Commun. ACM **22**(11), 594–597 (1979)
20. Pasquini, D., Cianfriglia, M., Ateniese, G., Bernaschi, M.: Reducing bias in modeling real-world password strength via deep learning and dynamic dictionaries. In: Proceedings of the 30th USENIX Security Symposium, pp. 821–838 (2020)
21. Wang, D., Cheng, H., Wang, P., Huang, X., Jian, G.: Zipf's law in passwords. IEEE Trans. Inf. Forensics Secur. **12**(11), 2776–2791 (2017)
22. Wang, D., Cheng, H., Wang, P., Yan, J., Huang, X.: A security analysis of honeywords. In: Proceedings of the 2018 Network and Distributed System Security Symposium (2018)
23. Wang, D., Wang, P., He, D., Tian, Y.: Birthday, name and bifacial-security: understanding passwords of Chinese web users. In: Proceedings of the 28th USENIX Security Symposium, pp. 1537–1555 (2019)
24. Weir, M., Aggarwal, S., de Medeiros, B., Glodek, B.: Password cracking using probabilistic context-free grammars. In: Proceedings of the 30th IEEE Symposium on Security and Privacy, pp. 391–405 (2009)

Vulnerability Testing on the Key Scheduling Algorithm of PRESENT Using Deep Learning

Ming Duan[1,2], Rui Zhou[1,2]([✉]), Chaohui Fu[1], Sheng Guo[1], and Qianqiong Wu[1]

[1] Information Engineering University, Zhengzhou, China
[2] Henan Key Laboratory of Network Cryptography, Zhengzhou, China

Abstract. PRESENT is a lightweight block cipher developed for extremely constrained environment such as RFID tags and IoT (Internet of Things). In 2020, Pareek et al. suggested a neural network to retrieving the 80-bit key of block cipher PRESENT from the last round subkeys and they arrived at a conclusion that the key scheduling algorithm is strong enough against its neural aided attack. While in this paper, we get a contradict result. We present two different experiments to test the vulnerability of key scheduling algorithm using deep learning. First, we build a 3-depth Fully Connected Neural Network to retrieve the master key bit by bit. The result is that we can predict about 80% bits of a random key with very high accuracy (above 0.9). Furthermore, we train a Residual Neural Network for classification. Compared with Fully Connected Network, we need less networks and the success rate is 100%. Finally, we combine the two networks to retrieve the whole 80-bit key from the last 64-bit round subkey. We think this method can be applied to the key schedule of other block ciphers or other similar cryptographic processes.

Keywords: Key scheduling algorithm · Deep learning · PRESENT

1 Introduction

PRESENT is an ultra-lightweight block cipher. There have been several attacks conducted to test its security but few researches have been done on the key scheduling algorithm (KSA) of PRESENT. A truncated differential attack was suggested to 26 rounds in 2014 [1] and several biclique cryptanalysis were done on the full round of 80-bit PRESENT cipher in [2] and [3]. As to the KSA, [4] showcases three factors to judge its strength.

Possible connections between cryptography and machine learning have been proposed since the neural network technology started flourishing [5]. It was not until 2019, Aron Gohr proposed a neural network based differential distinguisher for round-reduced Speck in [6] that first used deep learning in black-box cryptanalysis. Speck is also a lightweight block ciphers like PRESENT. And it shows a good transformation capability in many aspects [7–9]. In 2020, it inspired Pareek, Kohli and Mishra to apply the deep learning technique to the key scheduling process of PRESENT but they failed to

W. Shi et al. (Eds.): SPNCE 2021, LNICST 423, pp. 307–318, 2022.
https://doi.org/10.1007/978-3-030-96791-8_23

learn any features [10]. The failure does not mean the KSA is absolutely secure against deep learning attack, especially when we successfully find some features.

Contribution: In this paper, we use two types of neural networks to retrieve the key of PRESENT. First, we use Fully Connected Network to fit the key schedule process. It predicts 80% of master key at the accuracy above 0.9 bit by bit. For each bit, the offline data to train the model is $2^{15.97}$. Meanwhile, the bit positions that cannot be retrieved illustrate that this neural network fails to fit the S-box function in KSA. Next, we change our goal into solving a classification problem. We use Residual Neural Networks and improve the results, that we successfully predict n bits at one time under certain conditions. And the offline data that we use is $2^{13.77}$. Finally, we use both neural networks to finish the key recovery process and the minimum online data complexity is 2^6, when $n = 2$. This can be carried out within seconds on a modern computer. For brute force attack, it needs 2^{16} data and costs 2^{16} times PRESENT inverse KSA online theoretically. As a result, the deep learning method greatly surpasses the brute force method on online computation.

It is to be pointed out that by using more training/testing data, the accuracy will be improved. As the deep learning model can be pre-trained, it will not cost more online computation time.

Organization: The rest of the paper is divided into five parts. In Sect. 2, we introduce the key scheduling algorithm of the cipher PRESENT. Followed by a brief introduction of two neural network we used in this paper: Fully Connected Neural Network (or Multi-Layer Perception) and Residual Neural Network in Sect. 3. Section 4 presents our approach to retrieve the key using Fully Connected Neural Network, while Sect. 5 uses Residual Neural Network to identify n bits at a time and proposes our key recovery method. We conclude the paper and give probable direction of further study in the future in last section.

2 PRESENT Block Cipher

2.1 Encryption Process

PRESENT is an iterated block cipher proposed by Bogdanov, Knudsen, Leander, Paar, Poschmann, Robshaw, Seurin and Vikkelsoe in 2007 [11]. It employs an S/P (substitution and permutation) structure. The block length is 64 bits. This algorithm includes 31 rounds of encryption using key of 80 and 128 bits, and we only discuss about the 80-bit key version here.

In each round, the 64-bit input state exclusive-ores (XOR) the round key and is passed through 16 parallelly applied S-boxes and one permutation layer. S-box used in this cipher is a 4-bit to 4-bit mapping as a non-linear substitution. A block diagram showing the structure of PRESENT is given in Fig. 1.

2.2 Key Scheduling Algorithm

PRESENT cipher has two versions using the key size of 80-bit and 128-bit. In this paper, the former version is considered.

First, the initial 80-bit key is loaded in the key register, which is represented as $K_{79}K_{78} \ldots K_0$. For each round (i), the key register is rotated by 61-bit positions to the left, the left-most four bits are passed through the S-box, and bits $K_{19}K_{18}K_{17}K_{16}K_{15}$ of K is XORed with the *round_counter* value i on the right. After this the left-most 64-bits of the current key register are taken as the round key for that round (i). Figure 2 shows the key updating for 80-bit PRESENT variation.

Although PRESENT has 31-round encryption, the initial key needs to update 32 iterations and produce 32 round keys in one encryption.

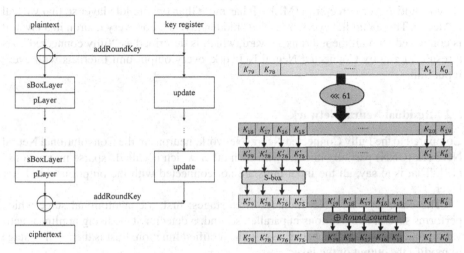

Fig. 1. Structure of PRESENT   **Fig. 2.** Key updating in PRESENT

3   Convolutional Neural Network

Deep learning can be traced back to 40s, 50s of last century, which is a comprehensive field developing from biological science. Deep Learning is a more sophisticated format of Machine Learning, using artificial neural networks. Here in this paper, we solve the problem (to retrieve the seed key) using two types of neural networks and try to find how the structure of the network impacts the result.

3.1   Deep Learning Neural Network

Deep Learning technique need to create a Deep Neural Network (DNN) and train that DNN model on the provided dataset. MP model (proposed by McCulloch and Pitts) is a basic structure of a DNN [12]. It includes an input layer, a middle layer and an output layer. The input layer has several variables and a bias. The middle layer is only one neuron to do a sum of the inputs (as a linear operation) and one non-linear function (SIGMOID, ReLU, etc.). In the end it outputs one value. The basic structure is shown in Fig. 3.

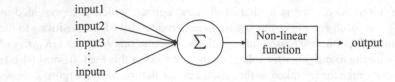

Fig. 3. MP model

The simplest and most basic DNN is "Fully Connected Neural Network", more often called Multi-Layer Perceptron (MLP). It has more than one middle layer so that we call it "deep". Those middle layers are called "hidden layers". For every neuron in a layer, it is connected with all the neurons forward, which is described as "fully connected". As a result, in a Fully Connected Neural Network, every output unit interacts with every input unit.

3.2 Residual Neural Network

Compared to the Fully Connected Neural Network, neurons in the Convolutional Neural Network (CNN) partially interact with each other which is called "sparse interactions" [12]. That is to say, all the input units are not connected with the output unit in latter layer.

The basic layer of CNN includes three stages: first, a convolutional stage which performs several convolutions in parallel; second, a detector stage using nonlinear activation function and, in this paper, we use the rectified function. Last is the pooling stage to modify the output of the layer.

Residual Neural Network (ResNet) we use in our experiment is one of the most commonly used CNNs. A basic unit in ResNet is a residual block. The output of a residual block can be described as a linear addition: $F(x) + x$, where x is input. That gives a connection between the input and output in a residual block, which is called skip connect. Figure 4 shows the structure clearly. It solves the vanishing gradients problem when a network gets deeper and deeper.

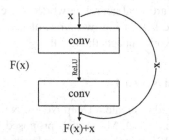

Fig. 4. Residual block

4   Key Recovery Using MLP

Pareek et al. tried to use Fully Connected Neural Network to retrieve the main key register from the final round key register of PRESENT, see [10]. That is, using 80 networks of same structure to predict each bit of the 80-bit-long master key separately. The result is that the prediction accuracy for a bit position of the master key is very close to 0.5, which means it failed to retrieve the master key. In my experiment, we first use the same type of neural network (MLP) and find that it is able to retrieve some specific bit positions of PRESENT master key. Next, we test different parameters and find that the result maintains its features.

4.1   Data Generation

We generate an 80-bit key randomly and then pass it through the key scheduling algorithm of PRESENT to obtain the final round 64-bit key as input data. The train dataset is composed of 600,00 samples and the number of samples in test data is 40,00.

4.2   Neural Network Structure

Input layer contains 64 neurons, each neuron for the individual bit of the final round key. 3 densely connected hidden layers of 32 neurons, 16 neurons, 8 neurons respectively each activated by the Rectified Linear Unit (ReLU) function. Output layer consists one neuron for the predicted bit (0 or 1), and is activated by the SIGMOID activation function. Figure 5 shows the structure of this Multi-Layer Perception.

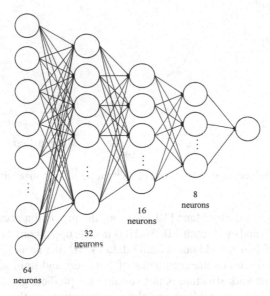

Fig. 5.   MLP structure

4.3 Results

We use the batch size of 200. Take the 38ᵗʰ bit of master key as an example in Fig. 6.

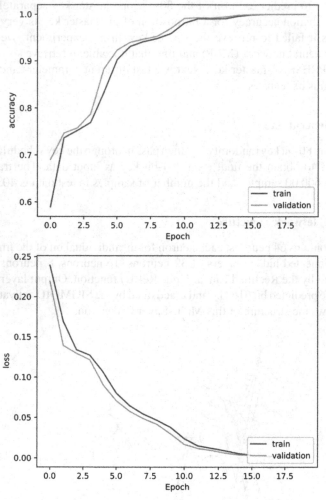

Fig. 6. The accuracy and loss rate of 38ᵗʰ bit position change with epoch

Unlike the result given by Mann [10], we find the prediction accuracies on several bits are good enough and even reach 1.0. And it is not the upper bound of the accuracy we can reach because when we add our training data to 10^5, the accuracy rises for around 0.01. However, on some bits the accuracies of both test and train set are around 0.5, which means this network structure is not suitable for predicting these bits of the key because of underfitting. Several keys are chosen randomly and the results are similar. The best validation accuracy is shown in the following Table 1.

Table 1. Test accuracy of ith bit

i^{th} bit	Accuracy	i^{th} bit	Accuracy	i^{th} bit	Accuracy	i^{th} bit	Accuracy
80	1.0000	60	0.4971	40	1.0000	20	1.0000
79	1.0000	59	0.4996	39	1.0000	19	0.9965
78	1.0000	58	0.4998	38	0.9804	18	0.9855
77	1.0000	57	0.4979	37	0.9840	17	0.9920
76	0.9805	56	0.4995	36	0.9958	16	0.9797
75	0.9843	55	0.4958	35	0.9402	15	0.9920
74	0.9657	54	0.4980	34	0.9760	14	0.9927
73	0.9803	53	0.4979	33	0.9998	13	0.9902
72	0.9860	52	0.4977	32	0.9967	12	0.9312
71	0.9908	51	0.4979	31	0.9905	11	0.9862
70	0.9955	50	0.5001	30	0.9905	10	0.9747
69	0.9910	49	0.6168	29	0.9737	9	0.9910
68	1.0000	48	0.7448	28	0.9870	8	0.9877
67	0.9768	47	0.6238	27	0.9530	7	0.9755
66	0.9902	46	0.7445	26	0.9845	6	0.9567
65	0.9912	45	0.9937	25	0.9998	5	0.9818
64	0.5046	44	1.0000	24	0.9937	4	0.9902
63	0.5005	43	0.9925	23	1.0000	3	1.0000
62	0.5045	42	0.9950	22	1.0000	2	1.0000
61	0.4981	41	1.0000	21	1.0000	1	1.0000

It does not matter when we change the one-bit output into one hot vector and the final activation function into SOFTMAX as a match. The basic neural network structure is the same with Mann but we get 80% of the master key retrievable by this fully connected network. Although we both use the same network structure, there could still exist some details that are different.

The result also shows that there are some features about the retrievable positions:

(1) The best validation accuracy of each bit is above 0.9, except (2).
(2) The 49th bit to the 64th bit can be hardly predicted (with accuracy around 0.5).

We think it results from the truncation operation in the KSA that every iteration, we truncate the 80-bit key in register to produce a 64-bit round key. If we ignore the S-box function in KSA of PRESENT, the 49th to 64th bit in master key is just the dropped-out bits from the 80-bit key register and has no relationship with the final 64-bit round key. To prove our guess, we repeat the experiment on reduced-round KSA, and the result is the same: only the dropped out 16 bits cannot be predicted by the MLP. Further, the conclusion is that the MLP cannot fit S-box function (or substitution).

5 Key Recovery Using ResNet

In order to learn the feature of S-box in the KSA, we explore a new method. As the output of the previous neural network is discrete (0 or 1), we attempt to use a classification network to replace it. Our idea is to feed the neural network with both real master keys and random data and train the network to distinguish between the two. We choose a Residual Neural Network because it has been used to build a distinguisher already [6] and its residual structure makes sure we can add more layers to the network without vanishing gradients problem.

5.1 Data Generation

Instead of predicting one bit with one network, we choose n bit from the master key to train at a time. The input data is divided into two parts: one is labeled as 1. The front of one sample is the final round key generated through key scheduling algorithm of PRESENT and the rear is n-bit data chosen from n positions of the master key. Another labeled as 0 is $(64 + n)$-bit random data. Both are stored in the form of an array. We use 10^4 training data and 4×10^3 testing data.

5.2 ResNet Structure

The input layer contains $(64 + n)$ neurons as to be consistent with the $(64 + n)$-bit input data. The hidden layers are residual network: the first layer is a convolutional layer for 1 dimension. Batch normalization is applied to its output. Following is a depth-5 residual tower with 2 layers of residual network each block. The size of the convolutional kernels is 3. Other settings are the same as above. Last two densely connected layers has 64 neurons each and output in one neuron. The activation function for the hidden layers is ReLU and the output is activated by SIGMOID (Fig. 7).

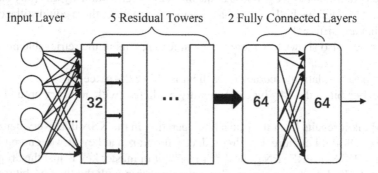

Fig. 7. Structure of Residual Neural Network

5.3 Results

We test every 16 bits ($n = 16$) in order (i.e., 8 groups). Both the accuracy of test and train set are above 0.9 for the 16 positions in sequence. That illustrates that the whole KSA of PRESENT is learnable by residual network. We can see from Fig. 8 that the neural network can reach a high accuracy at every beginning (take the last 16 bits as an example).

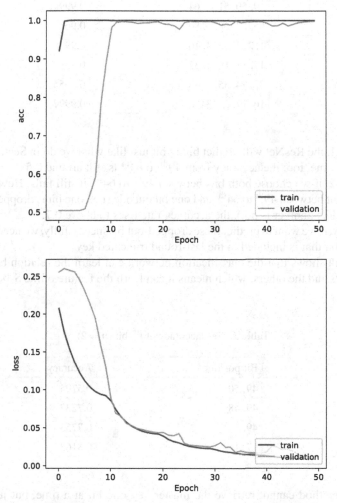

Fig. 8. The accuracy and loss rate of the last 16 bits

We specially pick those bit positions that failed to be retrieved by the previous Fully Connected Neural Network to be tested in the new network. Group A: From the 49th bit to the 64th bit position, among which only the 49th bit was successfully predicted. The Residual Neural Network works out and gets a prediction accuracy just as high as other bit positions (Table 2).

Table 2. Test accuracy of ith bit (n = 16).

Group	Bit position	Accuracy
1	1, 2, 3..., 14, 16	1.0000
2	17, 18, 19..., 32	1.0000
3	33, 34, 35..., 48	0.9998
4	49, 50, 51..., 64	0.9999
5	65, 67, 68..., 80	0.9655
6	1, 2, 3..., 14, 16	0.9998
7	17, 18, 19..., 32	0.9999
8	33, 34, 35..., 48	0.9655
A	16, 17, ..., 31	0.9997

Let $n = 1$, the ResNet will predict bit by bit just like what we do in Sect. 3. And the result is the same, too: the accuracy from 49th to 64th is still around 0.5.

Let $n = 2$, if we choose both bits between 49th to 64th, it still fails. However, if we choose one bit between 49th to 64th, and one bit outside (i.e., one bit is dropped out from last round while another is not), the accuracy rate rises to above 0.7.

Similarly, if we want to predict these dropped-out bit successfully, we need to include at least one bit that is included in the last-round truncated key.

The result shows that the classification network can learn the relation between the truncated bits and the others, which means it can learn the feature of the S-box function (Table 3).

Table 3. Test accuracy of ith bit (n = 2).

Group	Bit position	Accuracy
1	49, 50	0.5795
2	49, 48	0.7237
3	49, 1	0.7753
4	17, 1	0.8163

As this method cannot retrieve the master key one bit at a time, but just identify whether the n bits are from the real master key or not, we need one more step to search each bit.

In practical use, to retrieve the master key from the 32nd round key. We can use MLP to retrieve the 1st to 48th and 65th to 80th bits, and identify the remaining 16 bits using ResNet with n bits at a time (including 1 bit that has been retrieved by the MLP already). Then we need to go through 2^{n-1} to retrieve each bit. The search complexity is $2^n \times \frac{16}{n-1}$. To minimize the complexity, we choose $n = 2\ or\ 3$, and the search complexity is 2^6.

6 Conclusion

In summary, the Fully Connected Network can retrieve partially. The Residual Neural Network can identify the real from random. We combine the two neural networks to retrieve the total 80-bit master key with online data complexity of 2^6. Our method is also efficient that the pre-training processes can be carried out within 10 min and the online retrieving cost several seconds. But we get the online efficiency at the cost of more offline data. This drawback is also one significant feature of deep learning—relying on big data.

In terms of the vulnerability of KSA from deep learning perspective, we use Fully Connected Network to fit and Residual Neural Network to classify, and the result is that MLP fails to fit the S-box function but the classification network can identify it. We can use the features we found to dig out more in the future. And it is likely that we apply this method to similar cryptographic processes.

Acknowledgments. This work was supported by General Projects of Henan Natural Science Foundation (No. 212300410420).

References

1. Blondeau, C., Nyberg, K.: Links between truncated differential and multidimensional linear properties of block ciphers and underlying attack complexities. In: Nguyen, P.Q., Oswald, E. (eds.) EUROCRYPT 2014. LNCS, vol. 8441, pp. 165–182. Springer, Heidelberg (2014). https://doi.org/10.1007/978-3-642-55220-5_10
2. Lee, C.: Biclique cryptanalysis of PRESENT-80 and PRESENT-128. J. Supercomput. **70**(1), 95–103 (2014)
3. Sereshgi, M.H.F., Dakhilalian, M., Shakiba, M.: Biclique cryptanalysis of MIBS-80 and PRESENT-80 block ciphers. Secur. Commun. Netw. **1**(9), 27–33 (2016)
4. Hernandez-Castro, J.C., Peris-Lopez, P., Aumasson, J.-P.: On the key schedule strength of PRESENT. In: Garcia-Alfaro, J., Navarro-Arribas, G., Cuppens-Boulahia, N., de Capitani di Vimercati, S. (eds.) DPM/SETOP -2011. LNCS, vol. 7122, pp. 253–263. Springer, Heidelberg (2012). https://doi.org/10.1007/978-3-642-28879-1_17
5. Rivest, R.L.: Cryptography and machine learning. In: Imai, H., Rivest, R.L., Matsumoto, T. (eds.) ASIACRYPT 1991. LNCS, vol. 739, pp. 427–439. Springer, Heidelberg (1993). https://doi.org/10.1007/3-540-57332-1_36
6. Gohr, A.: Improving attacks on round-reduced speck32/64 using deep learning. In: Boldyreva, A., Micciancio, D. (eds.) CRYPTO 2019. LNCS, vol. 11693, pp. 150–179. Springer, Cham (2019). https://doi.org/10.1007/978-3-030-26951-7_6
7. Su, H.-C., Zhu, X.-Y., Ming, D.: Polytopic attack on round-reduced Simon32/64 using deep learning. In: Wu, Y., Yung, M. (eds.) Inscrypt 2020. LNCS, vol. 12612, pp. 3–20. Springer, Cham (2021). https://doi.org/10.1007/978-3-030-71852-7_1
8. Fu, C.H., Duan, M., Wei, Q., Wu, Q.Q., Zhou, R., Su, H.C.: Polytopic differential attack based on deep learning and its application. J. Cryptol. Res. **8**(4), 591–600 (2021)
9. Baski, A., Breier, J., Chen, Y., Dong, X.Y.: Machine learning assisted differential distinguichers for lightweight ciphers. In: 2021 Design, Automation & Test in Europe Conference & Exhibition (DATE), pp. 176–181. IEEE, Grenoble (2021)

10. Pareek, M., Kohli, V., Mishra, G.: Deep learning based analysis of the key scheduling algorithm of PRESENT cipher. https://eprint.iacr.org/2020/981. Accessed 11 May 2021
11. Bogdanov, A., et al.: PRESENT: an ultra-lightweight block cipher. In: Paillier, P., Verbauwhede, I. (eds.) CHES 2007. LNCS, vol. 4727, pp. 450–466. Springer, Heidelberg (2007). https://doi.org/10.1007/978-3-540-74735-2_31
12. McCulloch, W.S., Pitts, W.: A logical calculus of the ideas immanent in nervous activity. Bull. Math. Biophys. **5**, 115–133 (1943)
13. Goodfellow, I., Bengio, Y., Courville, A.: Deep Learning, pp. 326–352. MIT Press, Cambridge (2016)

GLV/GLS Scalar Multiplication on Twisted Edwards Curves

Chuangui Ma[1], Ruijie Zhang[2(✉)], Lei Niu[1], and Fushan Wei[2]

[1] Department of Basic, Army Aviation Institution, Beijing, China
[2] Information Engineering University, Zhengzhou, Henan, China

Abstract. At present, GLV/GLS scalar multiplication mainly focuses on finding and constructing more and more efficient computable endomorphisms. We research on the applications of GLV/GLS algorithms on twisted Edwards curves. Firstly, we present the concrete construction of efficiently computable endomorphism for this type of curves over prime field by exploiting birational equivalence between curves, and obtain 2-dimensional GLV method. Using birational equivalence and Frobenius mapping between curves, we present methods to construct efficiently computable endomorphisms of this type of curves and obtain 2-dimensional GLS method. Finally, we obtain the 4-dimensional GLV algorithm by using higher degree twists. The experimental conclusion demanstrates that the speedups of 2-dimensional and 4-dimensional GLV methods than 5-NAF method exceed 37.4% and 104.9% for twisted Edwards curves respectively.

Keywords: Elliptic curve · Twisted edwards curve · Scalar multiplication · GLV method · Computable endomorphism

1 Introduction

In the past three decades, Elliptic curve cryptography (ECC) becomes the mainstream of public key mechanism in cryptology because its high security level with small key size. Due to the advantage of storage space, processing speed and bandwidth, ECC is particularly suitable for use in wireless environments, such as the IoT and edge computing application scenarios. Since the devices in these environments are usually resource-constrained ones with limited battery, it is very important to speed up the computation of ECC in these applications. Among all the computation operations, scalar multiplication is the most computation-expensive operation in ECC. Consequently, it is of utmost importance to accelerate the computation of the scalar multiplication.

How to accelerate the scalar multiplication based on the efficiently computable endomorphism is a hot topic in ECC. Gallant et al. [1] put forward the GLV algorithm on a class of elliptic curves using endomorphism to accelerate the scalar multiplication. Their algorithm is efficient and also general. Since then, more and more researchers pay attention to the GLV method. The authors in [2, 3] have studied the decomposition of the scalar k in 2-dimensional GLV, they gives the bounds for the decomposition coefficients k_1 and k_2. The reason why the GLV algorithm is useful to accelerate the scalar

W. Shi et al. (Eds.): SPNCE 2021, LNICST 423, pp. 319–330, 2022.
https://doi.org/10.1007/978-3-030-96791-8_24

multiplication operation is that the endomorphism on the elliptic curve is effective to speed up the calculation. As a result, find out more and more efficiently computable endomorphisms are critical for the GLV algorithm. Many researchers make progress to find more endomorphism [5–7].

In recent years, a lot of effort are paid to acceralate the scalar multiplication speed of genus-2 hyperelliptic curves. In general, the Jacobian group of genus-2 curve has a wider endomorphism range than other ordinary elliptic curves, therefore the highest possible dimension of GLV decomposition on genus-2 curves is twice as large as that of the elliptic curve under the same condition. In 2013, Bos et al. [8] proposed to accelerate the scalar multiplication using 4-dimensional GLV technique, they considered the BK curves $y^2 = x^5 + b$ [9] and FKT curves $y^2 = x^5 + ax$ [10]. Guillevic and Ionica [11] proposed a 4-dimension GLV algorithm on elliptic curves. Bos et al. [12] considered the genus-2 curves over quadratic extension field F_{p^2} and studied an 8-dimensional scalar decomposition for the first time.

In recent years, different forms of elliptic curves have been proposed and widely concerned, such as twisted Edwards curve, Jacobi Quartic curve and so on. These curves have stronger resistance to side channel attacks and faster point calculation formulas, and have been considered as candidates for the next generation elliptic curve standards. At present, GLV/GLS scalar multiplication mainly focuses on the Weierstrass curves, attempting to find and construct more and higher degree efficient computable endomorphism. However, the GLV method has rarely been studied on other curve forms. In order to sovle the problem, we research on how to use the GLV/GLS algorithms in twisted Edwards curves and evaluate its efficiency. We present the concrete construction of efficiently computable endomorphism for this type of curves by exploiting birational equivalence, Frobenius mapping and twisting isomorphism between curves, and give some instances of efficiently computable endomorphism on curves. We generalize the main results of GLV/GLS method on weierstrass curve to the twisted Edwards curve, and obtain the 2-dimensional and 4-dimensional GLV method accordingly. We use experiments to evaluate the GLV method on twisted Edwards curves. The experimental results show that the speedups of 2-dimensional GLV method and 4-dimensional GLV method than 5-NAF method exceed 37.4% and 104.9% in twisted Edwards curves respectively.

2 Preliminaries

We briefly introduce some basic preliminaries for the rest of the paper, including the properties of isomorphism and GLS method. One can refer to reference [13–15] for more details. There are two special types of curves: $E_B : y^2 = x^3 + B$ and $E_A : y^2 = x^3 + Ax$, whose j invariant are 0 and 1728, respectively.

2.1 The Homomorphism

Definition 2.1. Let E_1 and E_2 be elliptic curves. An isogeny from E_1 to E_2 is a morphism $\phi : E_1 \rightarrow E_2$ satisfying $\phi(\mathcal{O}) = \mathcal{O}$. The two elliptic curves E_1 and E_2 are isogenous if there is an isogeny from E_1 to E_2 with $\phi(E_1) \neq \{\mathcal{O}\}$.

Let $\mathrm{Hom}(E_1, E_2)$ be the set of isogenies from E_1 to E_2, then $\mathrm{Hom}(E_1, E_2)$ forms a group. Let $E_1 = E_2 = E$, then $\mathrm{Hom}(E, E)$ is a ring, which is called the endomorphism ring of E, denoted as $End(E)$. Let $\phi, \varphi \in End(E)$ and $P \in E$, then $(\phi + \varphi)(P) = \phi(P) + \varphi(P)$ and $(\phi \circ \varphi)(P) = \phi(\varphi(P))$. The invertible elements of $End(E)$ form the automorphism group of E, which is denoted by $Aut(E)$. The endomorphism ring of an elliptic curve E is an important invariant of E.

Theorem 2.2. Let $\phi : E_1 \rightarrow E_2$ is an isogeny, whose dual isogeny is denoted by $\hat{\phi}$, then

(1) Let $m = \deg \phi$, then

$$\hat{\phi} \circ \phi = [m] \text{ on } E_1,$$

$$\hat{\phi} \circ \phi = [m] \text{ on } E_2.$$

(2) Let $\psi : E_2 \rightarrow E_3$ be an isogeny, then $\widehat{\psi \circ \phi} = \hat{\phi} \circ \hat{\psi}$.
(3) Let $\varphi : E_1 \rightarrow E_2$ be another isogeny, then $\widehat{\phi + \varphi} = \hat{\phi} + \hat{\varphi}$.
(4) For all integer $m \in \mathbb{Z}$, then $\widehat{[m]} = [m]$ and $\deg[m] = m^2$.

Let π be the p - Frobenius endomorphism of elliptic curve E and $(x, y) \in E$, then

$$\pi(x, y) = (x^p, y^p).$$

The quantity $t = q + 1 - \#E(F_q)$ is called the trace of Frobenius, and the Frobenius endomorphism π satisfies the characteristic equation $\pi^2 - t\pi + q = 0$ with $|t| \leq 2\sqrt{q}$.

2.2 Twisted Edwards Curves

In 2007, the twiseted Edward cureves is presented in [16]. Because of its substantial advantages [17, 18], EdDSA has been officially released in RFC 8032 [24] and deployed in many password products and libraries, such as OpenSSL [25].

Definition 2.3. Let F_q be a non-binary field, the twisted Edwards curve over F_q is a curve.

$$E_{a,d} : ax^2 + y^2 = 1 + dx^2 y^2,$$

where $a, d \in F_q$ and $ad(a - d) \neq 0$.

Let $(x_1, y_1), (x_2, y_2)$ be points on the twisted Edwards curve $E_{a,d}$. The sum of these points on $E_{a,d}$ is

$$(x_1, y_1) + (x_2, y_2) = \left(\frac{x_1 y_2 + y_1 x_2}{1 + dx_1 y_1 x_2 y_2} + \frac{y_1 y_2 - ax_1 x_2}{1 - dx_1 y_1 x_2 y_2} \right),$$

The point $(0, 1)$ is the neutral element, and the inverse of (x_1, y_1) is $(-x_1, y_1)$. The addition formula is unified, that is, it can also be applied to double a point.

In the inverted Edwards coordinates [21], we can use coordinates $(X : Y : Z)$ to represent the point $(Z/X, Z/Y)$ on an Edwards curve. Then the general form of the twisted Edwards curve is given below.

$$(X^2 + aY^2)Z^2 = X^2Y^2 + dZ^4.$$

The formulas for curve addition in inverted Edwards coordinates needs only 9M + 1S, where M and S denote the multiplication and squaring on finite field respectively.

Theorem 2.4. Let F_q be a non-binary field, every twisted Edwards curve $E_{a,d} : ax^2 + y^2 = 1 + dx^2y^2$ over F_q is birationally equivalent to a Weierstrass curve $E : v^2 = u^3 + 2(a + d)u^2 + (a - d)^2u$, the rational map is

$$\varphi : E_{a,d} \to E, (x, y) \mapsto (u, v) = \left((a - d)\frac{1+y}{1-y}, 2(a - d)x \cdot \frac{a-dy^2}{(1-y)^2}\right)$$

$$\psi : E \to E_{a,d}, (u, v) \mapsto (x, y) = \left(\frac{2v}{(u-2a)^2-4d}, \frac{u^2-4(a^2-d)}{(u-2a)^2-4d}\right)$$

2.3 GLS Method

Theorem 2.5. Let E be an elliptic curve defined over F_q such that $\#E(F_q) = q + 1 - t$. Let $\phi : E \to E'$ be a separable isogeny of degree d defined over F_{q^k} where E' is an elliptic curve defined over F_{q^m} with $m|k$. Let $r|\#E'(F_{q^m})$ be a prime such that $r > d$ and $r||\#E'(F_{q^k})$. Let π be the q-power Frobenius map on E and let $\hat{\phi} : E' \to E$ be the dual isogeny of ϕ. Define $\psi = \phi\pi\hat{\phi}$, then

1. $\psi \in End_{q^k}(E')$.
2. For every point $P \in E'(F_{q^k})$, we have $\psi^k(P) - [d^k]P = \mathcal{O}$ and $\psi^2(P) - [dt]\psi(P) + [d^2q]P = \mathcal{O}$.
3. There exists a integer $\lambda \in \mathbb{Z}/r\mathbb{Z}$ with $\lambda^k - d^k \equiv 0 \mod r$ and $\lambda^2 - dt\lambda - d^2q \equiv 0 \mod r$ such that $\psi(P) = [\lambda]P$ for all $P \in E'(F_{q^m})[r]$.

Corollary 2.6. Let $p > 3$ be a prime and let E be an elliptic curve defined over F_p with $\#E(F_p) = p + 1 - t$. Let E' over F_{p^2} be the quadratic twist of $E(F_{p^2})$. Then $\#E'(F_{p^2}) = (p - 1)^2 + t^2$. Let $\phi : E \to E'$ be the twisting isomorphism defined over F_{p^4} and let π be the p-power Frobenius map on E. Let $r|\#E'(F_{p^2})$ be a prime such that $r > 2p$. Define $\psi = \phi\pi\phi^{-1}$, then

1. For every point $P \in E'(F_{p^2})[r]$, we have $\psi^2(P) + P = \mathcal{O}$.
2. $\psi(P) = [\lambda]P$ with $\lambda = t^{-1}(p - 1) \mod r$.

Let $p \equiv 1 \mod 6$, and define elliptic curve $E : y^2 = x^3 + B$ over F_p. Choose $u \in F_{p^{12}}^*$ such that $u^6 \in F_{p^2}$ and define elliptic curve $E' : y^2 = x^3 + u^6B$ over F_{p^2}. Repeatedly choose the parameters p, B, u until $\#E'(F_{p^2})$ is prime (or almost prime). The isomorphism $\phi : E \rightarrow E'$ is given by $\phi(x, y) = (u^2x, u^3y)$ and is defined over $F_{p^{12}}$. The homomorphism $\psi = \phi\pi\phi^{-1}$ is defined over F_{p^2}, where π is the p-power Frobenius map on E. It follows that ψ satisfies the characteristic equation $\psi^4 - \psi^2 + 1 = 0$, then one obtains 4-dimensional GLV scalar multiplication.

3 Application of GLV/GLS Method on Twisted Edwards Curves

3.1 GLV Method on Twisted Edwards Curve

In this section, we consider the GLV method on the twisted Edwards curve and present the concrete construction of efficiently computable endomorphism for this type of curves over prime field. Let $p > 3$ be a prime and let $E : y^2 = x^3 + Ax + B$ be an elliptic curve defined over F_p. According to the literature [18], we know elliptic curve E is birationally equivalent over F_p to a twisted Edwards curve if and only if the group $E(F_p)$ has an element of order 4.

Theorem 3.1. Let $p > 3$ be a prime and let $E : y^2 = x^3 + Ax + B$ be an elliptic curve defined over F_p. Let $n|\#E(F_p)$ be a prime let ψ be an efficiently-computable endomorphism on E such that there exists $\lambda \in \mathbb{Z}$ satisfying $\psi(P) = \lambda P$ for every point $P \in E(F_p)[n]$. Suppose that E has a point of order 4, then there exists Edwards curve E_e and endomorphism ψ_e such that $\psi_e(P) = \lambda P$ for every point $P \in E_e(F_p)[n]$.

Proof. Let R_1 be a point of order 4 on elliptic curve E and let $2R_1 = (r_2, 0)$. Let $a_2 = 3r_2$ and $a_4 = 3r_2^2 + A$, define the elliptic curve $E_1 : y^2 = x^3 + a_2x^2 + a_4x$, then there is an isomorphism φ_1 from E to E_1 with $\varphi_1(x, y) = (x - r_2, y)$. Suppose point R_1 can be represented as $R_1 = (r_1, s_1)$, then $s_1 \neq 0$ and $r_1 \neq 0$, otherwise R_1 is a point of order 2. Below we show that coefficients a_2 and a_4 be represented by r_1 and s_1.

Due to $2R_1 = (0, 0)$, the tangent line of curve E_1 at point R_1 passes through the point $(0, 0)$, then we have

$$\frac{s_1}{r_1} = \frac{3r_1^2 + 2a_2r_1 + a_4}{2s_1},$$

Hence

$$2s_1^2 = 3r_1^3 + 2a_2r_1^2 + a_4r_1 \tag{1}$$

Since point $R_1 = (r_1, s_1)$ is on the curve E, then

$$s_1^2 = r_1^3 + a_2r_1^2 + a_4r_1 \tag{2}$$

By Eqs. (1) and (2), we have $r_1^3 - a_4r_1 = 0$. Due to $r_1 \neq 0$, then $a_4 = r_1^2$. On the other hand, substitute $a_4 = r_1^2$ into Eq. (2), we obtain $a_2 = s_1^2/r_1^2 - 2r_1$. Let $d = 1 - \frac{4r_1^3}{s_1^2}$, then $a_2 = 2r_1(1 + d)/(1 - d)$.

Define curve $E_2 : (r_1/(1-d))y^2 = x^3 + a_2x^2 + a_4x$, then there exists an isomorphism φ_2 from E_1 to E_2 with $\varphi_2(x, y) = (x, y/t)$, where $t = \pm\sqrt{\frac{r_1}{1-d}} = \pm\frac{s_1}{2r_1}$. Further, define curve $E_3 : \frac{1}{1-d}y^2 = x^3 + \frac{2(1+d)}{1-d}x^2 + x$, then there exists an isomorphism φ_3 from E_2 to E_3 with $\varphi_3(x, y) = (x/r_1, y/r_1)$. Define curve $E_e : X^2 + Y^2 = 1 + dX^2Y^2$, then E_3 is birationally equivalent over F_p to E_e according to the literature [17], and the rational map is

$$\varphi_4(x, y) = (2x/y, (x - 1)/(x + 1)).$$

By using the isomorphisms and birational maps above, we obtain a birational map from E to E_e with $\varphi = \varphi_4\varphi_3\varphi_2\varphi_1$ satisfying $\varphi(x, y) = \left(\frac{2t(x-r_2)}{y}, \frac{x-r_2-r_1}{x-r_2+r_1}\right)$.

Hence we obtain an endomorphism $\psi_e = \varphi\psi\varphi^{-1}$ of the curve E_e.

Let $P \in E_e(F_p)[n]$ and suppose the endomorphism ψ satisfies the characteristic equation $X^2 + rX + s$, then there exists $\lambda \in [0, n - 1]$ such that $\psi(P) = \lambda P$, where λ is a root of equation $X^2 + rX + s \bmod n$. Due to $\psi^2 + r\psi + s = 0$, we obtain.

$$\psi_e^2 + r\psi_e + s = \varphi\psi^2\varphi^{-1} + r\varphi\psi\varphi^{-1} + s = \varphi(-r\psi - s)\varphi^{-1} + r\varphi\psi\varphi^{-1} + s = 0.$$

That is to say, ψ_e and ψ have the same characteristic equation.

Hence, for $P \in E_e(F_p)[n]$, we have $\psi_e(P) = \lambda P$.

Theorem 3.1 extends the endomorphism on Weierstrass curve to twisted Edwards curve, so that we can obtain 2-dimensional GLV scalar multiplication algorithm on twisted Edwards curve.

Example 3.2. Let $p \equiv 1 \bmod 4$ be a prime and let $\alpha \in F_p$ be an element of order 4. We consider the elliptic curve $E_1 : y^2 = x^3 + ax$ defined over F_p, then the map $\psi(x, y) \mapsto (-x, \alpha y)$ is an endomorphism defined over F_p satisfying $\psi^2 + 1 = 0$. Suppose $R_1 = (r_1, s_1)$ is a point of order 4 on the curve E_1, then $2R_1 = (0, 0)$. According to the proof of Theorem 3.1, there exists a birational equivalence between E_1 and Edwards curve $E_e : X^2 + Y^2 = 1 + dX^2Y^2$ with $d = 1 - \frac{4r_1^3}{s_1^2}$, and the rational map is

$$\varphi : E_1 \to E_e, (x, y) \mapsto (X, Y) = \left(\frac{2tx}{y}, \frac{x - r_1}{x + r_1}\right),$$

$$\varphi^{-1} : E_e \to E_1, (X, Y) \mapsto (x, y) = \left(-\frac{r_1(Y + 1)}{Y - 1}, -\frac{2tr_1(Y + 1)}{X(Y - 1)}\right),$$

where $t = \frac{s_1}{2r_1}$. Hence we obtain the efficiently-computable endomorphism ψ_e on E_e

$$\psi_e(X, Y) = \left(-\frac{X}{\alpha}, \frac{1}{Y}\right).$$

It is easy to verify $\psi_e^2 + 1 = 0$.

Example 3.3. Let $p \equiv 1 \bmod 3$ be a prime and let $\beta \in F_p$ be an element of order 3. We consider the elliptic curve $E_2 : y^2 = x^3 + b$ defined over F_p, then the map $\psi(x, y) \mapsto (\beta x, y)$ is an endomorphism defined over F_p satisfying $\psi^2 + \psi + 1 = 0$. Suppose $R_1 = (r_1, s_1)$ is a point of order 4 on the curve E_2, then $2R_1 = (0, 0)$. According to the proof of Theorem 3.1, there exists a birational equivalence between E_2 and Edwards curve $E_e : X^2 + Y^2 = 1 + dX^2Y^2$ with $d = 1 - \frac{4r_1^3}{s_1^2}$, and the rational map is.

$$\varphi : E_2 \rightarrow E_e, (x, y) \mapsto (X, Y) = \left(\frac{2t(x - r_2)}{y}, \frac{x - m_1}{x + m_2} \right),$$

$$\varphi^{-1} : E_e \rightarrow E_2, (X, Y) \mapsto (x, y) = \left(-\frac{m_2 Y + m_1}{Y - 1}, -\frac{2tr_1(Y + 1)}{X(Y - 1)} \right).$$

where $t = \frac{s_1}{2r_1}$, $m_1 = r_1 + r_2$, $m_2 = r_1 - r_2$. Hence we obtain the efficiently-computable endomorphism ψ_e on E_e

$$\psi_e(X, Y) = \left(\frac{(\beta m_2 + r_2)Y + (\beta m_1 - r_2)}{r_1(Y + 1)} X, \frac{(\beta m_2 + m_1)Y + (\beta m_1 - m_1)}{(\beta m_2 - m_2)Y + (\beta m_1 + m_2)} \right).$$

It can be verified that $\psi_e^2 + \psi_e + 1 = 0$.

3.2 GLS Method on Twisted Edwards Curves

Let F_q be a finite field of characteristic $p > 3$ and let $E_{a,d} : ax^2 + y^2 = 1 + dx^2 y^2$ be an twisted Edwards curve defined over F_q with $a, d \in F_q$ and $ad(a - d) \neq 0$. According to the literature [18], $E_{\bar{a},\bar{d}}$ is a quadratic twist of $E_{a,d}$ if and only if $\bar{d}/\bar{a} = d/a$. Let $u = \frac{\bar{a}}{a}$ be quadratic non-residue, then there exists an isomorphism $F_{q^4}\phi : E_{a,d} \rightarrow E_{\bar{a},\bar{d}}$ defined over with $\phi(x, y) = (\sqrt{u}x, y)$.

Next, we extend the GLS method [4] to the twisted Edwards curves, and obtain the Theorem 3.4 below.

Theorem 3.4. Let $p > 3$ be a prime and let $E_{a,d}$ be an twisted Edwards curve defined over F_p with $\#E_{a,d}(F_p) = p + 1 - t$. Let $E_{\bar{a},\bar{d}}$ is a quadratic twist of $E_{a,d}(F_{p^2})$, then $\#E_{\bar{a},\bar{d}}(F_{p^2}) = (p - 1)^2 + t^2$. Let $\phi : E_{a,d} \rightarrow E_{\bar{a},\bar{d}}$ be an twisting isomorphism defined over F_{p^4} and let π be p-power Frobenius map on $E_{a,d}$. Let $r|\#E_{\bar{a},\bar{d}}(F_{p^2})$ be a prime such that $r > 2p$. Define $\psi = \phi\pi\phi^{-1}$. For $P \in E_{\bar{a},\bar{d}}(F_{p^2})[r]$, we have $\psi^2(P) + P = \mathcal{O}_{E_{\bar{a},\bar{d}}}$.

Proof. We have $\#E_{a,d}(F_{p^2}) = p^2 + 1 - (t^2 - 2p)$. Let u be a non-square in F_{p^2} and define $\bar{a} = au, \bar{d} = du$ and $E_{\bar{a},\bar{d}} : \bar{a}x^2 + y^2 = 1 + \bar{d}x^2 y^2$, then $E_{\bar{a},\bar{d}}$ is the quadratic twist of $E_{a,d}(F_{p^2})$ and $\#E_{\bar{a},\bar{d}}(F_{p^2}) = p^2 + 1 + (t^2 - 2p) = (p - 1)^2 + t^2$. The isomorphism $\phi : E_{a,d} \rightarrow E_{\bar{a},\bar{d}}$ is given by

$$\phi(x, y) = (\sqrt{u}x, y),$$

and is defined over F_{p^4}.

It is easy to know that $\psi = \phi\pi\phi^{-1}$ is a endomorphism on $E_{\bar{a},\bar{d}}$. If $r|\#E_{\bar{a},\bar{d}}(F_{p^2})$ is a prime such that $r > 2p$, then $r \nmid \#E_{a,d}(F_{p^2})$ and $\#E_{a,d}(F_{p^2}) = (p + 1 - t)(p + 1 + t)$. So $r\|\#E_{\bar{a},\bar{d}}(F_{p^4}) = \#E_{\bar{a},\bar{d}}(F_{p^2}) \cdot \#E_{a,d}(F_{p^2})$. Hence, for every point $P \in E_{\bar{a},\bar{d}}(F_{p^2})[r]$, there exists $\lambda \in \mathbb{Z}$ such that $\psi(P) = \lambda P$. Below we show that for $P \in E_{\bar{a},\bar{d}}(F_{p^2})[r]$, we have $\psi^2(P) + P = \mathcal{O}_{E_{\bar{a},\bar{d}}}$.

By definition, $\psi(x, y) = \phi\pi\phi^{-1}(x, y) = (\sqrt{u}x^p/\sqrt{u}^p, y^p)$. Since u be a non-square in F_{p^2}, then $\sqrt{u} \notin F_{p^2}$ and $\sqrt{u}^{p^2} = -\sqrt{u}$. If $P = (x, y) \in E_{\bar{a},\bar{d}}(F_{p^2})$, then $x^{p^2} = x$, $y^{p^2} = y$ and so

$$
\begin{aligned}
\psi^2(x, y) &= (\sqrt{u}x^{p^2}/\sqrt{u}^{p^2}, y^{p^2}) \\
&= (-x, y) \\
&= -(x, y)
\end{aligned}
$$

The result of Theorem 3.4 can be applied to the twisted Edwards curves defined over $F_p(p > 3)$, and 2-dimensional GLV scalar multiplication algorithm on twisted Edwards curve is obtained.

Example 3.5. Let $p = 2^{127} - 1$ and let $u = 2 + i$ be a non-square in F_{p^2}. Define the twisted Edwards curve $E : -x^2 + y^2 = 1 + 109x^2y^2$ over F_p, then $E' : -ux^2 + y^2 = 1 + 109ux^2y^2$ is the quadratic twist of $E(F_{p^2})$ and, where r is prime of 253 bits

$$
\begin{aligned}
r = &\, 72370055773322622139731865630429942407099412365 5496 \\
&\, 0197665975021634500559269
\end{aligned}
$$

The endomorphism $\psi(x, y) = (u^{(1-p)/2}x^p, y^p)$ satisfies that $\psi^2 + 1 = 0 \# E'(F_{p^2}) = 4r$.

3.3 4-Dimensional GLV Method on Twisted Edwards Curves

In order to obtain higher-dimensional GLV method on twisted Edwards curves, we usually have two methods. On the one hand, by using the idea of [7], we can combine the GLV method and GLS method and make use of two different endomorphisms at the same time. On the other hand, by using the idea of [4, 6], we can consider the curve with larger automorphism group, such as elliptic curve with j-invariants 0 or 1728.

For the first case, literature [19] has presented a 4-dimensional GLV construction for a class of curve. Consider the elliptic curve E defined over F_p with j-invariant 1728, let $E'(F_{p^2})$ be the quartic twist of $E_{a,d}(F_{p^2})$. Due to $4 \nmid \#E'(F_{p^2})$, therefore $E'(F_{p^2})$ cannot be transformed to the twisted Edwards curve form.

Below, we consider the elliptic curve with j-invariant 0. Let $p \equiv 1 \bmod 6$ be a prime and define elliptic curve $E : y^2 = x^3 + B$ over F_p. Following the Corollary 2.6 in Subsect. 2.3, choose $u \in F_{p^{12}}^*$ such that $u^6 \in F_{p^2}$ and define elliptic curve $E_1 : y^2 = x^3 + u^6B$ over F_{p^2}. Repeatedly Choose the parameters p, B, u until $\#E_1(F_{p^2})$ is almost prime and $4 | \#E_1(F_{p^2})$. The isomorphism $\phi_1 : E \to E_1$ is given by $\phi_1(x, y) = (u^2x, u^3y)$ and is defined over $F_{p^{12}}$. Let let π be p-power Frobenius map on E, then the endomorphism $\psi(x, y) = \phi_1\pi\phi_1^{-1}(x, y) = ((u/u^p)^2x^p, (u/u^p)^3y^p)$ is defined over F_{p^2} and satisfies the characteristic equation $\psi^4 - \psi^2 + 1 = 0$. Next, similar to the proof process of Theorem 3.1, we first transform the curve E_1 into the Montgomery curve form, and then transform the endomorphism ψ to the twisted Edwards curve by using birational equivalence.

Let $r_2 \in F_{p^2}$ and suppose $R_2 = (r_2, 0)$ is a point of order 2. Define curve $E_2 : Y^2 = X^3 + 3r_2X^2 + 3r_2^2X$, then $\phi_2(x, y) = (x - r_2, y)$ is an isomorphism from E_1 to E_2. Define curve $E_3 : \frac{1}{\sqrt{3}r_2}y^2 = x^3 + \sqrt{3}x^2 + x$, then $\phi_3(X, Y) = \left(\frac{X}{\sqrt{3}r_2}, \frac{Y}{\sqrt{3}r_2}\right)$ is an isomorphism from E_2 to E_3.

Let $a = (3 + 2\sqrt{3})r_2$, $d = (3 - 2\sqrt{3})r_2$ and define $E_e : aX^2 + Y^2 = 1 + dX^2Y^2$, then there exists a birational equivalence over F_{p^2} between Montgomery curve E_3 and twisted Edwards curve E_e according to [18], where the rational map from E_3 to E_e is

$$\phi_4(x, y) = (x/y, (x - 1)/(x + 1)).$$

Let $\phi = \phi_4\phi_3\phi_2\phi_1$, then it is the birational map from E to E_e and

$$\phi(x, y) = \left(\frac{u^2x - r_2}{u^3y}, \frac{u^2x - b}{u^2x - a}\right),$$

where $a = (1 - \sqrt{3})r_2$, $b = (1 + \sqrt{3})r_2$. Hence we can obtain an endomorphism $\psi_e = \phi\pi\phi^{-1}$ on elliptic curve E_e, which is given by.

$$\psi_e(X, Y) = \left(X^p \cdot \frac{a_1Y^p - a_2}{a_3(Y^p + 1)}, \frac{a_4Y^p - a_5}{a_6Y^p - a_7}\right),$$

where $a_1 = u^{p-1}(a^p - r_2u^{2(p-1)})$, $a_2 = u^{p-1}(b^p - r_2u^{2(p-1)})$, $a_3 = -3\sqrt{3}^p r_2^p$, $a_4 = a^p - bu^{2p}$, $a_5 = b^p - bu^{2p}$, $a_6 = a^p - au^{2p}$, $a_7 = b^p - au^{2p}$ are all constants.

We briefly introduce some basic preliminaries for the rest of the paper, including the properties of isomorphism and GLS method. One can refer to reference [13–15] for more details. There are two special types of curves: $E_B : y^2 = x^3 + B$ and $E_A : y^2 = x^3 + Ax$, whose j invariant are 0 and 1728, respectively.

4 Performance Comparison

We evaluate the computation complexity of the GLV/GLS scalar multiplication algorithms by experiments, and then compare performance with the algorithms on the Weierstrass curve. For the generality of comparison results, we do not give specific curve parameter selection. We suppose that the Weierstrass curve E and twisted Edwards curve E_e are selected, p_1 and p_2 are 256-bit and 128-bit prime respectively, where the parameters of curves and finite field can be flexibly selected as needed. We implement the w-NAF method, 2-dimensinal GLV method and 4-dimensional GLV scalar multiplication algorithm via Magma software on the two types of curves above, and compare the performance.

We use "M", "S" and "I" to represent an operation of multiplication, squaring and inversion on F_{p_1}, respectively. Other simple operations are ignored due to its high efficiency. Correspondingly, m, s and i denote the multiplication, squaring and inversion on F_{p_2}. According to [7], it is assumed that $1i = 66$ m, $1s = 0.76$ m, $1I = 290M$, $1S = 0.85M$ and M/m = 0.91. Table 1 presents the computation complexity of two curves.

Table 1. The comparison of computation cost of different operations

Curve	DBL	ADD	mADD
InvEdwards	3M + 4S	9M + 1S	8M + 1S
Jacobian	1M + 8S	11M + 5S	7M + 4S

The computation complexity of doubling (DBL), addition (ADD) and mixed addition (mADD) are summarized in the following.

The scalar multiplication algorithms usually include precomputation, evaluation and coordinate conversion phases. According to the analysis result of [22], we choose the optimal implementations for different scalar multiplication algorithms. For the w-NAF method, we use the 5-NAF representation. For the 2-dimensional GLV method, we use the 4-NAF-based interleaving method (denoted as 2GLV + INT(4-NAF)). For the 4-dimensional GLV method, we use the 3-NAF-based interleaving method (denoted as 4GLV + INT(3-NAF)). Using the precomputation algorithm in [23], we only nedd on inversion precomputation. In the first two stages, the cost is $1I + (15.8L + \lceil (L-2)/L \rceil + 3.4)M$ for InvEdwards curve and $1I + (9L)M + (3L+5)S$ for Jacobian curve, where L is 1/2 of precomputed points. Since the computation cost of endomorphism only occurs in precomputation stage and has little effect on the whole cost, we neglect the cost of endomorphism here. The computation cost is $1I + 2M$ for InvEdwards curve and $1I + 3M + 2S$ for Jacobian curve. Table 2 presents the costs of different algorithms on two types of curves.

Table 2. The cost of different algorithms on two curves

Curve	Implementation	Operation number	Cost	Speedup
$E_e(F_{p_1^2})$	4GLV+INT(3-NAF)	$2i + 836.8m + 320s$	$1212m$	104.9%
$E_e(F_{p_1})$	2GLV+INT(4-NAF)	$2I + 926.4M + 563.2S$	$1985.1M \approx 1806.5m$	37.4%
$E_e(F_{p_1})$	5-NAF	$2I + 1242.1M + 1066.7S$	$2728.8M \approx 2483.2m$	-
$E(F_{p_1^2})$	4GLV+INT(3-NAF)	$2i + 587m + 798s$	$1325.5m$	114.3%
$E(F_{p_1})$	2GLV+INT(4-NAF)	$2I + 561.4M + 1258.8S$	$2211.4M \approx 2012.4m$	41.1%
$E(F_{p_1})$	5-NAF	$2I + 629.7M + 2248.7S$	$3121.1M \approx 2840.2m$	-

5   Conclusion

At present, GLV/GLS scalar multiplication mainly focuses on the Weierstrass curves, and has rarely been studied on other curve forms. This paper mainly studies the applications of GLV/GLS method on twisted Edwards curves. By exploiting birational equivalence, Frobenius mapping and twisting isomorphism between curves, we present the concrete construction of efficiently computable endomorphism for Edwards curves, and also give some instances of efficiently computable endomorphism on curves. The main results of GLV/GLS method on the weierstrass curve are generalized to the twisted Edwards curve, and the 2-dimensional and 4-dimensional GLV methods are obtained accordingly.

Acknowledgment. This work is supported by the National Natural Science Foundation of China (Nos. 61772548, 61672413, 61872449) and the Foundation of Science and Technology on Information Assurance Laboratory (No. KJ-17–001).

References

1. Gallant, R.P., Lambert, R.J., Vanstone, S.A.: Faster point multiplication on elliptic curves with efficient endomorphisms. In: Kilian, J. (ed.) CRYPTO 2001. LNCS, vol. 2139, pp. 190–200. Springer, Heidelberg (2001). https://doi.org/10.1007/3-540-44647-8_11
2. Park, Y.-H., Jeong, S., Kim, C.H., Lim, J.: An alternate decomposition of an integer for faster point multiplication on certain elliptic curves. In: Naccache, D., Paillier, P. (eds.) PKC 2002. LNCS, vol. 2274, pp. 323–334. Springer, Heidelberg (2002). https://doi.org/10.1007/3-540-45664-3_23
3. Sica, F., Ciet, M., Quisquater, J.-J.: Analysis of the Gallant-Lambert-Vanstone method based on efficient endomorphisms: elliptic and hyperelliptic curves. In: Nyberg, K., Heys, H. (eds.) SAC 2002. LNCS, vol. 2595, pp. 21–36. Springer, Heidelberg (2003). https://doi.org/10.1007/3-540-36492-7_3
4. Galbraith, S.D., Lin, X., Scott, M.: Endomorphisms for faster elliptic curve cryptography on a large class of curves. J. Cryptol. **24**(3), 446–469 (2011)
5. Zhou, Z., Hu, Z., Xu, M., Song, W.: Efficient 3-dimensional GLV method for faster point multiplication on some GLS elliptic curves. Inf. Process. Lett. **110**(22), 1003–1106 (2010)
6. Hu, Z., Longa, P., Xu, M.: Implementing 4-dimensional GLV method on GLS elliptic curves with j-invariant 0. Des. Codes Crypt. **63**(3), 331–343 (2012)
7. Longa, P., Sica, F.: Four-dimensional Gallant-Lambert-Vanstone scalar multiplication. J. Cryptol. **27**(2), 248–283 (2014)
8. Bos, J.W., Costello, C., Hisil, H., Lauter, K.: Fast cryptography in genus 2. In: Johansson, T., Nguyen, P.Q. (eds.) EUROCRYPT 2013. LNCS, vol. 7881, pp. 194–210. Springer, Heidelberg (2013). https://doi.org/10.1007/978-3-642-38348-9_12
9. Buhler, J., Koblitz, N.: Lattice basis reduction, Jacobi sums and hyperelliptic cryptosystems. Bull. Aust. Math. Soc. **58**(1), 147–154 (1998)
10. Furukawa, E., Kawazoe, M., Takahashi, T.: Counting points for hyperelliptic curves of type y2 = x5 + ax over finite prime fields. In: Matsui, M., Zuccherato, R.J. (eds.) SAC 2003. LNCS, vol. 3006, pp. 26–41. Springer, Heidelberg (2004). https://doi.org/10.1007/978-3-540-24654-1_3
11. Guillevic, A., Ionica, S.: Four-dimensional GLV via the weil restriction. In: Sako, K., Sarkar, P. (eds.) ASIACRYPT 2013. LNCS, vol. 8269, pp. 79–96. Springer, Heidelberg (2013). https://doi.org/10.1007/978-3-642-42033-7_5
12. Bos, J.W., Costello, C., Hisil, H., Lauter, K.: High-performance scalar multiplication using 8-dimensional GLV/GLS decomposition. In: Bertoni, G., Coron, J.-S. (eds.) CHES 2013. LNCS, vol. 8086, pp. 331–348. Springer, Heidelberg (2013). https://doi.org/10.1007/978-3-642-40349-1_19
13. Silverman, J.H.: The Arithmetic of Elliptic Curves. Graduate Texts in Mathematics 106, 2nd edn. Springer, Berlin (2009)

14. Hankerson, D., Menezes, A.J., Vanstone, S.: Guide to Elliptic Curve Cryptography. Springer, Berlin (2004)
15. Washington, L.C.: Elliptic Curves: Number Theory and Cryptography. CRC Press, New York (2008)
16. Edwards, H.M.: A normal form for elliptic curves. Bull. Am. Math. Soc. **44**(3), 392–422 (2007)
17. Bernstein, D.J., Lange, T.: Faster addition and doubling on elliptic curves. In: Kurosawa, K. (ed.) ASIACRYPT 2007. LNCS, vol. 4833, pp. 29–50. Springer, Heidelberg (2007). https://doi.org/10.1007/978-3-540-76900-2_3
18. Bernstein, D.J., Birkner, P., Joye, M., Lange, T., Peters, C.: Twisted Edwards curves. In: Vaudenay, S. (ed.) AFRICACRYPT 2008. LNCS, vol. 5023, pp. 389–405. Springer, Heidelberg (2008). https://doi.org/10.1007/978-3-540-68164-9_26
19. Faz-Hernández, A., Longa, P., Sánchez, A.H.: Efficient and secure algorithms for GLV-based scalar multiplication and their implementation on GLV-GLS curves. J. Cryptogr. Eng. **5**(1), 31–52 (2015)
20. MAGMA Computational Algebra System. http://magma.maths.usyd.edu.au/magma/
21. Bernstein, D.J., Lange, T.: Inverted Edwards coordinates. In: Boztaş, S., Lu, H.-F. (eds.) AAECC 2007. LNCS, vol. 4851, pp. 20–27. Springer, Heidelberg (2007). https://doi.org/10.1007/978-3-540-77224-8_4
22. Dou, Y., Weng, J., Ma, C., Wei, F.: Analysis of GLV/GLS method for elliptic curve scalar multiplication. In: Hung, J.C., Yen, N.Y., Hui, L. (eds.) FC 2017. LNEE, vol. 464, pp. 210–219. Springer, Singapore (2018). https://doi.org/10.1007/978-981-10-7398-4_23
23. Longa, P., Miri, A.: New composite operations and precomputation scheme for elliptic curve cryptosystems over prime fields. In: Cramer, R. (ed.) PKC 2008. LNCS, vol. 4939, pp. 229–247. Springer, Heidelberg (2008). https://doi.org/10.1007/978-3-540-78440-1_14
24. Josefsson, S., Liusvaara, I.: Edwards-Curve Digital Signature Algorithm (EdDSA). RFC 8032, January 2017 (2017). https://rfc-editor.org/rfc/rfc8032.txt
25. Things that use Ed25519 (2019). https://ianix.com/pub/ed25519-deployment.html

Federated Learning-Based IDS Against Poisoning Attacks

Mengfan Xu[1]($\boxtimes$) and Xinghua Li[2]

[1] School of Computer Science, Shaanxi Normal University,
Xi'an 710061, Shaanxi, China
[2] School of Cyber Engineering, Xidian University, Xi'an 710071, Shaanxi, China
xhli1@mail.xidian.edu.cn

Abstract. With the implementation of the General Data Protection Regulation (GDPR), the federated learning scheme has become a hot topic in the field of private computing. However, existing federated learning scheme can only encrypt the models to ensure the privacy of the data, but can not guarantee the correctness of the uploaded models, which will lead to a significant decrease in the detection performance of the global model. In this paper, we propose a federated learning-based intrusion detection scheme (IDS) against poisoning attacks. Specifically, we first design an anti-poisoning attacks algorithm based on the encryption model. Then we define the anti-attack strategy and objective function. To achieve high detection performance for the availability and concealment of attack, we introduce the poisoning rate into the objective function. The privacy preservation for local data sources also be provided while the IDS model based on knowledge sharing among islands is constructed. We leverage the Paillier public key cryptosystem to prevent data leakage for each entity. The results of security analysis show that our scheme can meet the security requirements of local data sources. In addition, the experiment results demonstrate that the proposed scheme can significantly improve the robustness of the detection model, and its accuracy rate can reach 83.11% even after being poisoned, which means the detection performance has not significantly decreased compared with non-poisoning attacks scheme.

Keywords: Federated learning · Privacy computing · Poisoning attacks · Intrusion detection system · Homomorphic encryption

1 Introduction

With the continuous improvement of network attack methods, the traditional single-point-based detection schemes have a serious overfitting issue on the detection model [3,20,29] because data exists as islands in different local clients which resulting in a small amount of data. Therefore, an intrusion detection system based on multi-source local data came into being. Gartner, a well-known

© ICST Institute for Computer Sciences, Social Informatics and Telecommunications Engineering 2022
Published by Springer Nature Switzerland AG 2022. All Rights Reserved
W. Shi et al. (Eds.): SPNCE 2021, LNICST 423, pp. 331–345, 2022.
https://doi.org/10.1007/978-3-030-96791-8_25

international security agency, proposed the Managed Detection and Response Service (MDR) in 2016[1]. This service aims to overcome the above-mentioned overfitting issue. By integrating multiple local data sources, security experts can find potential threats, and configure a rule base and security protection strategy [11,14,16]. There are lots of machine learning-based researches have focused on above issues. However, the General Data Protection Regulation (GDPR) is introduced by the European Union and effective on May 25, 2018, clearly stipulates a total ban on the utilization of automated model decisions [9], which means that simply "**Roughly**" exchanging cross-domain data to train machine learning models will be illegal. To solve this issue, Google proposed the federated learning in 2016 [17,18,22]. The federated learning process as shown in Fig. 1, each island uploads the encrypted model to the cloud. After the cloud model aggregates the encrypted model uploaded by each island to train a more powerful detection model, the aggregation model is returned to each island to update. Because the model is transmitted and trained before encryption, no party can obtain real data information, which solves the problem of privacy disclosure. This architecture builds a global model without violating data privacy regulations.

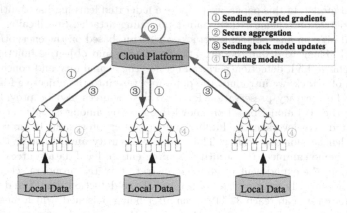

Fig. 1. Architecture for a federated learning system.

However, attackers in intrusion detection systems usually have background knowledge, including controlling models or training data and test data [7]. When the island is breached, the federated learning can only encrypt the model to ensure that the privacy of the data is not leaked. However, it cannot guarantee the correctness of the uploaded model, which makes it difficult to detect the poisoning attacks initiated during the latency phase, such as Stuxnet, OceanLotus, etc. [1,15,23]. To change the original distribution of the training data and causes the learning algorithm to change logically to threaten the target model [6,10,27], the attackers modify, delete, or inject malicious data on the training data of the target entity.

---

[1] https://www.paladion.net/buyers-guide-to-managed-detection-and-response.

To detect the above-mentioned poisoning attacks, researchers have done numerous researches. However, the existing anti-poisoning attacks schemes [21, 25, 26, 30] screen training data to improve the anti-attack capability in plaintext, which can not be used for federated learning. Specifically, if the island is breached and poisoned, as well as a large difference between the island data and the features of the verification set, the performance of the local encryption model (weak island model) will be reduced. Because the federated learning only uploads local encryption models, the cloud cannot determine whether local data has been modified, which leads the poisoning attacks cannot be detected. Furthermore, the current researches against poisoning attacks focused on reducing the availability of attacks, which is only considering the reduction of model errors, but ignoring the concealment of the attacks. It is impossible to accurately characterize actual attacks, such as Stuxnet, OceanLotus which have both availability and concealment features. Meanwhile, the local models are uploaded in federated learning further provides conditions for latency attacks. It is challenging to make the model take into account the availability and concealment of resistance to attacks.

In this paper, to address the above-mentioned issues, we propose a federal learning-based intrusion detection scheme against poisoning attacks called FLIDS, which can achieve secure data sharing between islands. In contrast, the model can effectively resist attacks. To summarize, the main contributions are as follows:

- A cryptographic model against poisoning attacks is designed. To avoid poisoning attacks in the island, the optimal local models are iteratively selected by calculating the performance residuals of the global model. Finally, a strong, robust intrusion detection model is aggregated. While ensuring the privacy-preserving for each local data source, the robustness of the global model against poisoning attacks is improved.
- An anti-poisoning attacks model is proposed based on federated learning. We first define the anti-attack strategy and the objective function. Furthermore, to detect the poisoning attacks with availability and concealment, we introduce the poisoning rate into the objective function.
- The experiments results demonstrate that the proposed scheme accuracy rate can still reach 83.11% with poisoning attacks, which is only a slight decrease compared with the detection performance without poisoning attacks.

The remaining parts of this paper are organized as follows. Section 2 shows the related work associated with our framework. Then, Sect. 3 presents some preliminary cryptographic background and Sect. 4 describes the problem formulations which include system model, threat model, and security goals. The concrete constructions of our schemes are demonstrated in Sect. 5. Later on, Sect. 6 shows the proof of security and performance analysis. Finally, the concluding remark of this whole paper is summarized in Sect. 7.

2   Related Work

2.1   Federated Learning

Nguyen et al. [13] construct federated learning on wireless networks as a convex structure optimization issue. They describe how mobile computing delay and delay affects UE energy consumption, system parameters between the learning time and learning precision balance. By all the closed forming solution of the sub-issue, the global optimal solution is achieved. Wang et al. [28] study the privacy leakage of federated learning and propose a general reconfiguration attack, which enables malicious servers not only to reconstruct actual training samples, but also to destroy the privacy of target clients. The proposed attack does not affect the standard training process and has obvious advantages over the existing attack mechanism. Brisimi et al. [2] propose a federated learning model, which can utilize the distribution between different data source of EHR data to predict future hospitalization in patients with heart disease. the proposed original dual division (cPDS) clustering algorithm can solve the issue of sparse support vector machine (SVM), which only using the small amount of features. It is beneficial to the interpretability of classification decision. Hu et al. [12] propose a new reasoning framework for urban environment perception Federated Reinforcement Learning (FRL), which inherited the basic idea of federated learning and utilized regional features in training process to improve reasoning accuracy.

However, the existing federated learning researches ensure that data privacy is not leaked through the encryption model, but can not guarantee the correctness of the upload model. Then the local data source is breached, it is difficult to detect the poisoning attacks, such as Stuxnet, OceanLotus, which is launched in the latent stage.

2.2   Poisoning Attacks

Saeed et al. [21] studied the antagonistic risk and robustness of classifiers, which are associated with metric sets in metric spaces. It is proved that any classifier with initial constant error is susceptible to antagonistic perturbation if the measurement probability space of the test instance is centralized. Suciu et al. [25] introduced a general framework for evaluating actual attacks against machine learning systems. They propose a targeted poisoning attacks which is designed to bypass existing defenses. The results show that this method is suitable for four classification tasks of three classifiers. Zhao et al. [30] transform the optimal poisoning attacks calculation issue in the multi-task relational learning model into a two-level programming which can adapt to the selection of arbitrary target task and attack task. They propose an effective algorithm for calculating the optimal attack strategy. The results show that the multi-task relational learning model is very sensitive to poisoning attacks, and the attacker can significantly degrade the performance of the target task by directly poisoning the target task. Matthew et al. [26] proposed an optimization framework specifically designed for linear regression and proved its effectiveness in a series of data sets and models.

In addition, a fast statistical attack is introduced, and a new anti-attack method is designed accordingly, which has strong flexibility against all poisoning attacks.

However, the existing researches on poisoning attacks improves the robustness of the system model by filtering plaintext data, so it is not suitable for federated learning based on encryption model. In addition, there is no research on the anti-poisoning attacks and anti-attack strategy for intrusion detection system.

3 Preliminaries

First, we introduce the cryptosystem based on additive homomorphism used in this scheme [24].

KeyGen: Given the security parameters, calculate the public key $pk = (M, g)$ and the private key sk $= \lambda$, where the private key sk can be randomly divided into $sk^{(1)}$ and $sk^{(2)}$

$Enc_{pk}(m)$: Given plaintext m, use the public key pk to compute the encrypted data $[\![m]\!]$.

$Dec_{sk}([\![m]\!])$: given the ciphertext $[\![m]\!]$, use the key sk to decrypt the plaintext m.

$SDec_{sk^{(i)}}([\![m]\!])$: given the ciphertext, the partial key sk_i is used to calculate the partially decrypted ciphertext.

$$[\![m]\!]^{(i)} = [\![m]\!]^{(sk^{(i)})} mod M^2$$

$WDec(\{[\![m]\!]^{(1)}, [\![m]\!]^{(2)}\})$: given a set of partially decrypted ciphertexts, the plaintext m is obtained.

Since this cryptosystem is based on additive homomorphism, it has the following properties:

$$[\![m_a + m_b]\!] = [\![m_a]\!] \bullet [\![m_b]\!]$$
$$[\![-m]\!] = [\![m]\!]^{M-1}$$

In addition, in order to ensure the effective operation of this scheme on ciphertext, this paper adopts the encrypted rational number comparison operation protocol proposed in reference [19]. The specific security calculation is as follows:

Here, we introduce security comparison (SCOM):

$SCOM([\![m_a]\!], [\![m_b]\!])$: Outputs a comparison result R to determine the size, if $R = 0$, $[\![m_a]\!] \geq [\![m_b]\!]$, otherwise, $[\![m_a]\!] < [\![m_b]\!]$.

4 Problem Formulation

In this section, the system model, threat model and anti-attack strategy are introduced respectively.

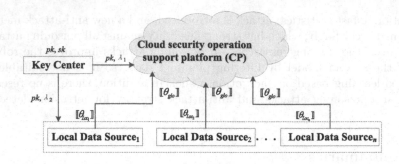

Fig. 2. System model.

4.1 System Model

As shown in Fig. 2, our system model includes n Local Data sources (LDS), Cloud platform (CP) and Key Distribution Center (KC).

KC: The trusted KC is responsible for the distribution and management of all keys in the system.

LDS: Each local data source has a local data set and is willing to contribute its detection model to build an accurate global detection model. Therefore, LDS should encrypt detection models trained on local datasets before sharing them with CP.

CP: It is a semi-honest cloud server with enough storage space to provide local data source security and can resist the global model building of poisoning attacks.

In order to initialize the password parameters in the scheme, the key of each domain is generated by a fully trusted key distribution center. The detailed process of key distribution is as follows:

- The key distribution center generates a key pair (pk, sk) and splits the key sk into λ_1 and λ_2.
- The key distribution center generates key pairs for the local data source (pk, λ_2).
- Key distribution center generates a key pair (pk, λ_1) for cloud server (CP).

If the ciphertext in this document is not specified, it indicates that the ciphertext is encrypted under the public key pk, for example: $[\![x]\!]$ represents $[\![x]\!]_{pk}$.

4.2 Threat Model

In this attack model, we assume that both CP and LDS are honest but curious entities that strictly follow predefined protocols but try to learn more data from other entities. Therefore, this paper introduces an attacker Adv with the following abilities:

- Availability attack. An attacker can generate malicious data to maximize the model's error rate or cause denial of service, making the model unavailable.
- Latency attack. In order to maintain continuous control or continuous access to useful information, attackers can conceal and steal information for a long time without being detected.

In addition, we assume that CP and any LDS are two independent semi-trusted entities that cannot collude.

5   Our Scheme

In this paper, an intrusion detection scheme against poisoning attacks based on federated learning is proposed to protect sensitive information in different networks and greatly improve the ability (robustness) of the global model against poisoning attacks. The overall process of the scheme is shown in Fig. 3. The scheme is mainly composed of attack policy and anti-attack policy. The local model of multi-source data is encrypted and uploaded to the cloud, and the global model is aggregated in ciphertext form in the cloud for local.

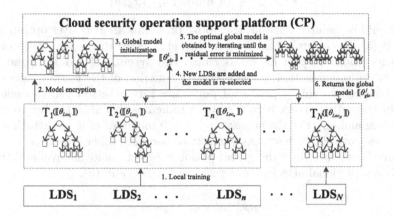

Fig. 3. The process of our scheme.

5.1   Attack Strategy

In order to fight against poisoning attacks more effectively, we first assume the attacker's ability and strategy to fit the actual attack behavior. Similar to existing studies [21,25,26,30], in this paper, we assume that the attacker has sufficient background knowledge of the attacked system, that is, the attacker can know training data D_{tr}, feature set F and model parameter θ. In addition, such as Stuxnet virus, Hailotus and other APT attacks, in the intrusion detection system, attackers need to be available and concealed at the same time in order to steal data or wait for an opportunity to damage the target network for a long time.

Firstly, the attacker hopes that the model after poisoning will be as different as possible from the original model. We define a function E to represent the available effect of local attacks, and its calculation formula is as follows:

$$E_{Loc} = ||\theta_{Loc_p} - \theta_{Loc}||_2^2 \tag{1}$$

The greater the E_{Loc}, the better the availability of local attacks.

Secondly, attackers prefer to hide attacks to avoid detection. We define a function C_{Loc} to represent the hiding effect of local attacks, and its calculation formula is as follows:

$$C_{Loc} = ||x_p - x_c||_2^2 \tag{2}$$

The smaller the C_{Loc}, the better the concealment of local attacks.

To sum up, we use W_{Loc} to represent the attacker's local objective function, whose strategy can be expressed as:

$$\arg\min_{x_p} W_{Loc} = \alpha C_{Loc}(x_p) - (1-\alpha)E_{Loc}(\theta_{Loc_p}) \tag{3}$$

$$s.t.\theta_{Loc_p} \in \arg\min_{\theta} L(D_{tr} \cup x_p, \theta) \tag{4}$$

It should be pointed out that the above problems are two-layer optimization problems [4]. The optimization of x_p in Eq. (1) is called the upper level problem, the optimization of θ_p in Eq. (3) is called the lower level problem, and L in Eq. (4) is the minimization of the objective function of the learning algorithm during training. In this paper, local poisoning rate is introduced to make the model fit the actual attack better. $\alpha = 0.5$ indicates that the attacker considers both hiding and effect of the attack, and $\alpha = 0$ indicates that the attacker only wants to execute effective attacks without considering concealment.

Similarly, we introduce the global poison rate beta, and the availability and concealment of global attacks are defined as Eqs. (5) and (6).

$$E_{glo} = ||\theta_{glo_p} - \theta_{glo}||_2^2 \tag{5}$$

$$C_{glo} = ||\theta_{Loc_p} - \theta_{Loc}||_2^2 \tag{6}$$

Combined with Eqs. (7) and (8), we use W_{glo} to represent the global objective function of the attacker, whose strategy can be expressed as:

$$\arg\min_{\theta_{Loc_p}} W_{glo} = \beta C_{glo}(\theta_{Loc_p}) - (1-\beta)E_{glo}(\theta_{glo_p}) \tag{7}$$

$$s.t.\theta_{glo_p} \in \arg\min_{\theta} L(\theta_{Loc} \cup \theta_{Loc_p}, \theta) \tag{8}$$

5.2   Anti-attack Strategy and Algorithm

In practical scenarios, it is basically safe to use original training data for intrusion detection model construction, and attackers are usually unable to manipulate it [5]. However, many intrusion detection systems require additional training data to update the model to enhance its adaptability, and this process provides an intrudable path for attackers [8]. Therefore, this paper assumes that the global model is updated every time a new data source is added. In order to secure the sharing of source data, it is necessary to build a global model by aggregating benign encryption models uploaded from local data sources. In the real world, however, it is difficult for the cloud to directly distinguish between benign and malicious models.

To solve this problem, n local models with the best performance were selected from N local data sources and aggregated to obtain the global model $[\![\theta_{glo}]\!]$ and evaluate different local data iteratively until its detection performance remained constant. Evaluate different local data in combination with Eqs. (9), (10) and (11). After that, the P_i is encrypted and uploaded to the cloud.

$$P_i = Acc_i + DR_i \tag{9}$$

$$Acc = \frac{TP + TN}{TP + TN + FP + FN} \tag{10}$$

$$DR = \frac{TP}{TP + FP} \tag{11}$$

where the larger P_i indicates, the better detection performance of the global model $[\![\theta_{glo}]\!]$ on the ith local data. $[\![RES_{P_i}]\!]$ is used to calculate the residuals of global model detection performance before and after iteration. Meanwhile, in order to deal with the attack proposed in Sect. 5.1, we define the following anti-attack target function:

$$min[\![RES_{P_i}]\!], RES_{P_i} = (\sum_{k=1}^{n} P_i - \sum_{k=1}^{n} P_{i-1})^2 \tag{12}$$

$$s.t. [\![P_i]\!] \in \{[\![P_1]\!], [\![P_2]\!], ..., [\![P_n]\!]\}, min\{[\![P_1]\!], [\![P_2]\!], ..., [\![P_n]\!]\} > max\{[\![P_{n+1}]\!], \\ [\![P_{n+2}]\!], ..., [\![P_N]\!]\} \tag{13}$$

Similar to Eqs. (3) and (4), the above problems are two-layer optimization problems. The optimization of $[\![RES_{P_i}]\!]$ in Eq. (12) is called the upper level problem, and the optimization of P in Eq. (13) is called the lower level problem.

The global model is constructed iteratively, and the local model subset with the best performance in each iteration is aggregated. Assume that the number of original local models is n, and $\alpha * n$ is the number of poisoned data sources. The total number of local data sources in federated learning is $N = n + \alpha * n$. This paper assumes that $\alpha < 1$, ensure that most local data sources are not poisoned. Ideally, we need to identify all p poisoned models and aggregate the global model from the remaining n benign models. However, it is apparently that the true distribution of local training data is unknown, making it difficult to accurately distinguish between benign and poisoned models. To address this challenge, we aggregate global models and test them locally, iteratively selecting the n submodels with the best performance (These models may also include poisoned models, but only local models that are close to benign and do not significantly affect the global model).

The iterative algorithm adopted in this paper is based on alternating minimization or expectation maximization algorithms [4]. At the beginning of the iteration, we have the encrypted local model $\{[\![\theta_{Loc_1}]\!], [\![\theta_{Loc_2}]\!]..., [\![\theta_{Loc_n}]\!]\}$ uploaded by n data sources, which is aggregated to get the global model $[\![\theta_{glo}]\!]$. When new data sources are added to the model and need to be updated, all local data sources are evaluated as the detection model by $[\![\theta_{glo}]\!]$, and n models with the highest performance are selected for reaggregation and performance residuals $[\![RES_P]\!]$ are calculated. When the residual converges to a minimum, the process terminates. At this point, it is considered that CP has aggregated the detection model with the best performance for use by local data sources.

In order to realize the safe calculation of residuals $[\![RES_P]\!]$, this paper first designs the safe maximum array operation based on SCOM security comparison, and selects the maximum n number from N numbers. The specific algorithm is as follows:

Algorithm 1: Secure Max Array

   Input: $[\![P_1]\!], [\![P_2]\!], ..., [\![P_N]\!]$
   Output: Max array $\{[\![P_1]\!], [\![P_2]\!], ..., [\![P_n]\!]\}$
1 Initialize encrypted set Set_p ;
2 for $N = n$ to $N - n$ **do**
3 $max \leftarrow [\![0]\!]$;
4   **for** $i = 1$ to N **do**
5 $s \leftarrow SCOM([\![P_i]\!], [\![P_{\max}]\!])$ **if** $s \leftarrow 0$ **then**
6 $max = [\![P_i]\!]$;
7 $Setp \leftarrow max$;
8 return Set_p /*$Set_p = \{[\![P_1]\!], [\![P_2]\!], ..., [\![P_n]\!]\}$;

Secondly, SecureRES security calculation is designed as follows:

SecureRES: LDS and CP calculate the performance of the global model on different local data sources through SCOM security operations. n data sources with maximum performance were selected by SMA security operation, and finally calculated.

6 Evaluation

This section evaluates the security and detection performance of the proposed scheme. First, we perform a security analysis of the proposed scheme to prove that the scheme can achieve the security objectives outlined in Sect. 4.2. Secondly, the experimental environment and data preprocessing process are introduced in detail. Then, the scheme is compared with the existing work. Finally, we analyze the influence of different parameters on the detection performance of the scheme.

6.1   Proof of Security

Now we present the proof of FLIDS security in the semi-honest model.

Theorem 1. *If Paillier public key cryptosystem is a semantically secure public key encryption scheme, then FLIDS is secure in the presence of a semi-honest adversary.*

Proof. We will prove the theorem by considering, in turn, the case where each of the parties has been corrupted. In each case, we invoke a simulator with the corresponding party s input and output. Our focus is in the case where party A wants to engage in the computation of the intersection. If party A does not want to proceed with the protocol, the views can be simulated in the same way up to the point where the execution stops.

Case 1. Corrupted CP. In this case, we show that we can construct a simulator Sim_{CP} that can produce a computationally indistinguishable view. In the real execution, the CP's view, $View_{CP}(\Lambda, M_N)$ is as follows:

$$\{\Lambda, r_{CP}, M_N, P_N, P_n, M_n\} \tag{14}$$

In the above view, r_{CP} is the outcome of internal random coins of the cloud. $M_N = \{m_i | i \in [1, N]\}$ is the set of N local submodels which are sent by the LDSs to the CP. $W_N = \{P_j | j \in [1, N]\}$ are calculated by formula (9), (10), (11) which are also sent to the CP. P_n is the output of Algorithm 1 and the SCOM and SMA are both proved using the ideal-real paradigm. The security proof of SCOM can be found in [19]. M_n is the first N valid set of local sub-models which is selected by index P_n.

To simulate this view, Sim_{CP} does the following: it creates an empty view and appends to it Λ and uniformly at random chosen coins r'_{CP}. N local submodels are randomly selected and encrypted by the Paillier public key cryptosystem to form the local model set M'_N of LDSs. Then, taking the M'_N as the input of Algorithm 1 to generate simulated copy P'_N, P'_n, M'_n. Finally, the simulator appends P'_N, P'_n, M'_n to the view. Therefore, $Sim_{CP}(\Lambda, M_N) = \{\Lambda, r'_{CP}, M'_N, P'_N, P'_n, M'_n\}$.

We argue that the information sequences generated by simulation is computationally indistinguishable from the real view. The input parts are identical (i.e., both are Λ), the random coins are both uniformly random, and so they are indistinguishable. The element M'_N in Sim_{CP} is randomly selected and encrypted by using the Paillier public key cryptosystem, which is consistent with the element M_N in real view. P'_N, P'_n, M'_n are similar to M'_N which are ciphertext encrypted by the Paillier public key cryptosystem. In this paper, they rely on the assumption of the existence of a semantically secure additive homomorphic encryption scheme. Therefore, we construct a simulator Sim_{CP} that can produce a computationally indistinguishable view, i.e. $Sim_{CP}(\Lambda, M_N) = View_{CP}(\Lambda, M_N)$.

Case 2. Corrupted LDS. The proof process is similar to *Case 1.*

Combining the above, we conclude the algorithms are secure and complete our proof.

6.2   Experimental Environment

The CTU-13 data set published by Technical University of Prague, Czech Republic was used to evaluate the detection performance based on temporal association analysis. CTU-13 dataset includes 14 features such as *StartTime*, *Dur* and *Proto* and 1 category *Label* in CTU-13 data set. The dataset, released in 2014, contains 13 files with consecutive 7 days of network traffic data, with an average of 2.6 million pieces of data per file. The experimental environment was PC (i5-4590 main frequency 3.3 GHz, memory 4 GB, operating system Win7 64-bit), and the experimental tools were Java and Python 3.0. In addition, real data sets are used to verify the performance of the proposed scheme. In this scheme, K = 1024 bits is selected to achieve the 80-bit security level.

6.3   Analysis of Experimental Results

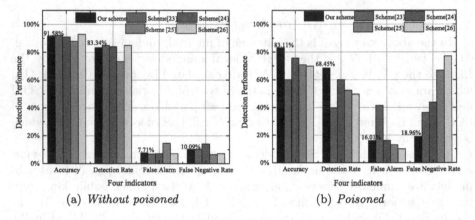

(a) *Without poisoned*   (b) *Poisoned*

Fig. 4. Comparison of the effect by using different federated learning algorithms on detection performance.

First, this scheme was compared with schemes [2, 12, 13, 28], and tested on CTU-13 data set. As shown in Fig. 4, the false alarm rate and false negative rate of this scheme are similar to those of existing algorithms when there is no poisoning attack. This is because this scheme uses integrated classifier with better detection performance to generate global model. Meanwhile, due to the limitation of training data set size, existing deep learn-based algorithms cannot achieve higher detection accuracy. When there is a poisoning attack on an existing federated learning scheme, the performance dropped substantially. This scheme can still ensure stable detection performance when being poisoned, this is because the security aggregation algorithm in this scheme design, use of multiple iterations local model to calculate the residual choose the highest performance, the greatest degree of reducing the poisoning model the impact on the global model. Among them, the detection performance of this scheme has a slight decline, mainly because the global model fails to completely eliminate the influence brought by the poisoning model, resulting in the decline of the final detection accuracy.

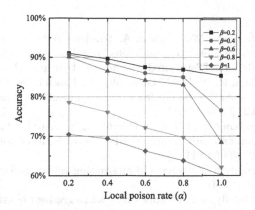

Fig. 5. The accuracy on different local poison rate and global poison rate.

With Sect. 5.1 attack strategy, can know different rate of local and global poisoning effect on the performance of the global model is different, as shown in Fig. 5, when $\alpha \leq 0.8$, $\beta \leq 0.6$, the global model testing accuracy stable at more than 83%, it shows that using this scheme the CP can iteratively select the optimal local model from LDS and aggregate it, when $\alpha = 1$, $\beta \geq 0.8$, the global model performance dropped substantially, This is because there are too many poisoned nodes at this time, and the local data is completely tampered, CP has been unable to obtain correct information from LDS. But at this time, it does not accord with the characteristics of concealment of actual attack. Therefore, $\alpha = 0.8$, $\beta = 0.6$ are selected in this paper, and it is considered that the robustness of the global model can be guaranteed when $\alpha \leq 0.8$, $\beta \leq 0.6$.

7   Conclusions

In this paper, we propose a federated learning-based intrusion detection scheme against poisoning attacks, called FLIDS, which achieves that secure data sharing between islands, ensures the privacy-preserving for each local data source, and improves the robustness of the global model against poisoning attacks. In addition, we design the resistance to poisoning attacks algorithm based on encryption model, and put forward a complete anti-attack model. The model defines the strategy and target function against the attack, while the poisoning rate is introduced to objective function. Then we make the model take into consideration with the availability and concealment in attack. The analysis showed that FLIDS is able to satisfy the proposed goals. Finally, we verify the validity and feasibility of the scheme. Experimental results show that the detection performance of this method on real data sets is significantly improved.

Acknowledgements. This work was supported by National Natural Science Foundation of China (Grant Nos. U1708262, U1736203).

References

1. Bohara, A., Noureddine, M.A., Fawaz, A., Sanders, W.H.: An unsupervised multi-detector approach for identifying malicious lateral movement. In: 2017 IEEE 36th Symposium on Reliable Distributed Systems (SRDS), pp. 224–233. IEEE (2017)
2. Brisimi, T.S., Chen, R., Mela, T., Olshevsky, A., Paschalidis, I.C., Shi, W.: Federated learning of predictive models from federated electronic health records. Int. J. Med. Inform. **112**, 59–67 (2018)
3. Caruana, R., Lawrence, S., Giles, L.: Overfitting in neural nets: backpropagation, conjugate gradient, and early stopping. Advances in Neural Information Processing Systems, pp. 402–408 (2001)
4. Csiszár, I.: Information geometry and alternating minimization procedures. Stat. Decis. **1**, 205–237 (1984)
5. Friedman, J.H.: Greedy function approximation: a gradient boosting machine. Ann. Stat. **29**, 1189–1232 (2001)
6. Fu, Z., Huang, F., Ren, K., Weng, J., Wang, C.: Privacy-preserving smart semantic search based on conceptual graphs over encrypted outsourced data. IEEE Trans. Inf. Forensics Secur. **12**(8), 1874–1884 (2017)
7. Gajewski, M., Batalla, J.M., Mastorakis, G., Mavromoustakis, C.X.: A distributed ids architecture model for smart home systems. Clust. Comput. **22**(1), 1739–1749 (2019)
8. Gozde Bakirli, D.B.: DTreeSim: a new approach to compute decision tree similarity using re-mining. Turk. J. Electr. Eng. Comput. Sci. **25**, 108–125 (2017)
9. Greengard, S.: Weighing the impact of GDPR. Commun. ACM **61**(11), 16–18 (2018)
10. Grinshpoun, T., Tassa, T., Levit, V., Zivan, R.: Privacy preserving region optimal algorithms for symmetric and asymmetric DCOPs. Artif. Intell. **266**, 27–50 (2019)
11. Hermessi, H., Mourali, O., Zagrouba, E.: Deep feature learning for soft tissue sarcoma classification in MR images via transfer learning. Expert Syst. Appl. **120**, 116–127 (2019)
12. Hu, B., Gao, Y., Liu, L., Ma, H.: Federated region-learning: an edge computing based framework for urban environment sensing. In: 2018 IEEE Global Communications Conference (GLOBECOM), pp. 1–7. IEEE (2018)
13. Jagielski, M., Oprea, A., Biggio, B., Liu, C., Nita-Rotaru, C., Li, B.: Manipulating machine learning: poisoning attacks and countermeasures for regression learning. In: 2018 IEEE Symposium on Security and Privacy (SP), pp. 19–35. IEEE (2018)
14. Jeong, G., Kim, H.Y.: Improving financial trading decisions using deep Q-learning: predicting the number of shares, action strategies, and transfer learning. Expert Syst. Appl. **117**, 125–138 (2019)
15. John, J.T.: State of the art analysis of defense techniques against advanced persistent threats. Future Internet (FI) and Innovative Internet Technologies and Mobile Communication (IITM) Focal Topic: Advanced Persistent Threats 63 (2017)
16. Joy, T.T., Rana, S., Gupta, S., Venkatesh, S.: A flexible transfer learning framework for Bayesian optimization with convergence guarantee. Expert Syst. Appl. **115**, 656–672 (2019)

17. Konečný, J., McMahan, H.B., Ramage, D., Richtárik, P.: Federated optimization: distributed machine learning for on-device intelligence. arXiv preprint arXiv:1610.02527 (2016)
18. Konečný, J., McMahan, H.B., Yu, F.X., Richtárik, P., Suresh, A.T., Bacon, D.: Federated learning: strategies for improving communication efficiency. arXiv preprint arXiv:1610.05492 (2016)
19. Liu, X., Choo, K.K.R., Deng, R.H., Lu, R., Weng, J.: Efficient and privacy-preserving outsourced calculation of rational numbers. IEEE Trans. Dependable Secur. Comput. 15(1), 27–39 (2016)
20. Luo, D., Ding, C., Huang, H.: Linear discriminant analysis: new formulations and overfit analysis. In: Proceedings of the AAAI Conference on Artificial Intelligence, vol. 25 (2011)
21. Mahloujifar, S., Diochnos, D.I., Mahmoody, M.: The curse of concentration in robust learning: evasion and poisoning attacks from concentration of measure. In: Proceedings of the AAAI Conference on Artificial Intelligence, vol. 33, pp. 4536–4543 (2019)
22. McMahan, H.B., Moore, E., Ramage, D., Arcas, B.A.: Federated learning of deep networks using model averaging. arXiv preprint arXiv:1602.05629 (2016)
23. Oprea, A., Li, Z., Yen, T.F., Chin, S.H., Alrwais, S.: Detection of early-stage enterprise infection by mining large-scale log data. In: 2015 45th Annual IEEE/IFIP International Conference on Dependable Systems and Networks, pp. 45–56. IEEE (2015)
24. Paillier, P.: Public-key cryptosystems based on composite degree residuosity classes. In: Stern, J. (ed.) EUROCRYPT 1999. LNCS, vol. 1592, pp. 223–238. Springer, Heidelberg (1999). https://doi.org/10.1007/3-540-48910-X_16
25. Suciu, O., Marginean, R., Kaya, Y., Daume III, H., Dumitras, T.: When does machine learning {FAIL}? Generalized transferability for evasion and poisoning attacks. In: 27th {USENIX} Security Symposium ({USENIX} Security 18), pp. 1299–1316 (2018)
26. Van Opbroek, A., Achterberg, H.C., Vernooij, M.W., De Bruijne, M.: Transfer learning for image segmentation by combining image weighting and kernel learning. IEEE Trans. Med. Imaging 38(1), 213–224 (2018)
27. Viejo, A., Sánchez, D.: Secure and privacy-preserving orchestration and delivery of fog-enabled IoT services. Ad Hoc Netw. 82, 113–125 (2019)
28. Wang, Z., Song, M., Zhang, Z., Song, Y., Wang, Q., Qi, H.: Beyond inferring class representatives: user-level privacy leakage from federated learning. In: IEEE INFOCOM 2019-IEEE Conference on Computer Communications, pp. 2512–2520. IEEE (2019)
29. Xie, S., Gao, J., Fan, W., Turaga, D., Yu, P.S.: Class-distribution regularized consensus maximization for alleviating overfitting in model combination. In: Proceedings of the 20th ACM SIGKDD International Conference on Knowledge Discovery and Data Mining, pp. 303–312 (2014)
30. Zhao, M., An, B., Yu, Y., Liu, S., Pan, S.J.: Data poisoning attacks on multi-task relationship learning. In: Thirty-Second AAAI Conference on Artificial Intelligence (2018)

Online Privacy of Personal Information - Perceptions v Reality

Diane Gan[⊠] and Dennis Ivory

School of Computing and Mathematical Sciences, University of Greenwich,
London, UK
{D.Gan,D.A.Ivory}@gre.ac.uk

Abstract. This empirical study investigates how (n = 252) users of online social networking sites perceived their online privacy and compares this to what can be collected by someone who has no connection to them in cyber-space. A survey was undertaken to determine each participant's perceived privacy awareness of their online personal information at different levels of distance from them, such as by a friend, friend of a friend or a complete stranger. Experiments were performed for each participant to retrieve as much personal information as possible using OSINT (open source intelligence) tools. For the majority of participants their personal information was collected in under two minutes by someone who had no connection with them in cyber-space. The results that were predicted by the participants was compared to what was actually found and are shown to support our hypothesis that the majority over-exaggerated how secure their personal information was.

Keywords: Online social networks · Online privacy · Data harvesting · Facebook · Twitter · Osint

1 Introduction

The volume of personal information published on online social networking sites (OSNs) increases each year (from 2.46 bn in 2019 to 4.2 bn in 2021 [1]) which provides an ever-growing source of information for criminals to search and abuse. Due to the huge numbers of profiles there will inevitably be many accounts with poor privacy settings from which information can be easily harvested [2]. Important personal details, publicly available online for anyone to view, can help criminals to launch successful targeted social engineering attacks [3]. The threat becomes greater the more information an individual has published about themselves on OSNs, often when they believe their information to be private.

Online privacy is defined as "he level of privacy protection an individual has while connected to the Internet. It covers the amount of online security available for personal and financial data, communications, and preferences." [4]. Personal data can include a person's full name, the names of family and friends, or more

W. Shi et al. (Eds.): SPNCE 2021, LNICST 423, pp. 346–368, 2022.
https://doi.org/10.1007/978-3-030-96791-8_26

personal data such as their date of birth or home address. Due to the fraudulent activity that is possible using this information it is vitally important that it is kept secure and that it is not viewable to anyone with a browser or at least only viewable by people with whom you choose to share this information with. Sometimes personal and sensitive information is revealed due to secondary leakage (covered in more detail in Sect. 2.2). This occurs when a person's information is leaked by a friend, a friend of a friend or a family member and often by someone who has been "riended" on the same platform who re-tweets or links a post to their own OSN [5].

Why is it important to keep your personal data private? There have been a number of celebrity users who have had their Twitter and facebook accounts hacked over the years. In 2008 during the US presidential elections Sarah Palin's private email was hacked. The email password was reset when hackers answered the three security questions, which were Mrs. Palin's date of birth, her home postal code and the location where she met her spouse. The answers to all these questions were found on her Facebook page, posted by Palin herself [6]. The founder of Facebook, Mark Zuckerburg, had his LinkedIn password stolen in 2016 and this was used to access his Pinterest and Twitter accounts as he had reused his password on these sites [7]. This demonstrates how the security settings of one user can affect the privacy settings of others when users link their OSNs together using "likes" or by sharing pictures or tweets. Users will continue to reuse their data such as name, picture, friends, etc. on multiple sites and share pictures and videos across those sites. It also demonstrates how complex it can be for a user to maintain their privacy and how aware they must be regarding their own privacy [8].

The focus of this work was to determine how individuals from a student population, perceived their own online privacy and compare this to the freely available information about them that can be found by anyone with a computer and an Internet connection. A survey was used to determine the personal information that individuals had shared knowingly and what they perceived as being private. Experiments were carried out to determine how accurate their perceptions were, by harvesting as much personal information as possible on each participant using a manual search.

An additional question posed is - can automated tools find more information than the manual search for a smaller subset of the participants? To answer this question, we carried out searches using automated tools on two smaller subsets, called the "minimal sharers" and "over sharers" (the bottom and top sharers from the survey respectively), see Table 5.

The process of harvesting each individual's information was timed and the results are compared to those obtained during the manual searches. The results of these were then compared to the individual participants' responses to the survey and also with the overall survey responses. We also compared these results to the whole survey when looking at the demographics for these subsets of participants. It was interesting to note that different information was located by the manual tools than by the automated tools.

The remainder of this paper is organised as follows. Section 2 discusses related literature. The methodology is described in Sect. 3. The results of the survey are presented in Sect. 4 and Sect. 5 analyses the experimental results. There is a discussion of the results in Sect. 6 and in Sect. 7.

2   Related Literature

2.1   Online Social Network (OSN) Investigations

People reveal information about themselves and their family through careless posts on sites such as Twitter and Instagram because they are unaware that it can be seen by anyone performing a simple search. Examples include posting pictures of new debit/credit cards on Twitter, both front and back, with the card number, security code and expiration date clearly visible [9], posting their UK driving license on Twitter [10] and birth certificates on Instagram displaying all the person's details [11]. These individuals have revealed significant personal information about themselves including their full name, place of birth, photo of the holder, signature and current address, none of which should be shared publicly for obvious reasons.

Ali et al. (2018) [12] identify Online Social Networks (OSNs) as a social graph. They also emphasise how OSNs leak a user's personal information when they publish information, upload photographs and videos which contain metadata and GPS coordinates. All this data has attracted the attention of attackers who harvest personal data during targeted attacks. They undertook a survey of undergraduate students to determine if the users were concerned about their online privacy. They found that many of the users had no idea about the privacy settings available to them. They also determined that nearly half of their participants used their real names and their pictures [12]. This differs from our research, as they have only used a survey, while our work goes on to verify the credibility of the users' perceptions of their OSN security.

Rathore and Tripathy (2020) [37] conducted a survey to determine the OSN users' awareness of their online security, which had 374 participants. The majority of these were male and aged 18–40. The survey determined that these users were worried about their privacy but did not actively modify the security available on the OSNs they used. They proposed a framework to increase security on OSNs. They found similar results to our work with their survey, except our participants were more evenly split between males and females and we had a larger age range [37].

A five year study of privacy perceptions undertaken by Tsay-Vogel, Shanahan and Signorielli (2018) [14] identified two types of users, those who were light users and those who were heavy users of social networks. At the beginning of the study the light users were more risk aware of the security issues, but as the study progressed, the heavy users became as aware as the previous group [14]. Our work also identified two similar groups of users, but our study differs in that we looked at a snap shot of the users.

Another study investigated the perceptions of over 200 non-student UK Facebook users, to measure their attitude to risk and their online behaviours though the use of an online survey. They also searched online for "16 hazards" related to the users' risk perceptions directly linked to their security and privacy settings, to determine how this modified the users' behaviour. They constructed risk profiles for each participant and concluded that the perceived risk claimed by them influenced how precautionary their online behaviour was [2]. In our study we have used a similar sized sample (n = 252) from a cross school student population and tested their security perceptions.

Wisniewski et al. (2017) [15] undertook an empirical analysis of the privacy awareness of Facebook users using an online survey based on 314 responses. This sample included a high percentage of undergraduate students, with a high proportion being female. They determined that these users had very varied perceptions of their privacy and online security. The main focus here was to determine "privacy behaviour and feature awareness" [15] by linking them using a Structural Equation Model (SEM). They determined that participants with the highest privacy settings tended to be very computer literate, while "privacy minimalists" covered the whole spectrum of users, showing that there is no simple linear relationship between these features. This paper has some similarities to our work in that we also identified different groups of users and in particular we also found a group of "privacy minimalists" that we identified as the "minimal sharers".

The majority of social network sites use an opt-out policy, which puts the onus on the user to check their own privacy settings, with many being unaware of the security implications of this [5]. Data leakage from OSNs often occurs due to the user's lack of knowledge and understanding of the privacy issues.

2.2 Secondary Leakage

Secondary leakage occurs when a user shares photos or links from friends without realising that they are actually making their friends more vulnerable to privacy breaches. Gan and Jenkins (2015) [5] identified that secondary leakage can be a serious problem which reveals a lot of information about a user to the point that their pattern of life can be determined.

Cascavilla et al. (2018) [16] demonstrated information leakage using an OSSINT (Open Source Social Network Intelligence) prototype tool that they developed, using 20 user profiles which had high privacy settings. This is an example of the use of an automated search tool which retrieves information that the user has designated as private. The tool uses the "victim's" friends list to retrieve information on all the friends, including friends of friends which are at a two hop distance. This information was then used to build a "friendship graph". They also used this to gain access to further private information such as place of work, education and their locations. A confusion matrix was used to measure the success of the OSSINT tool [16]. This work differs from our work in that we used a manual search method to retrieve personal and private information from users.

Privacy leakage was examined by looking at tweets which indicated "happy life events" [38]. They concluded that it is very easy to give away location information about yourself and the person you have tagged. They also emphasise the danger of tweeting details if the user is away from home, which can be used by burglars.

As parents become more aware of the privacy issues surrounding OSNs they also are concerned for their children's online privacy. The UK government warns about "the over-sharing of personal information" in their advice on "Child Safety Online: A practical guide for parents and carers whose children are using social media" [17].

2.3 Facebook Privacy Concerns

The Facebook and the political consultancy Cambridge Analytica incident (2017) [18] underlined how insecure our personal information can be online. Facebook estimated that approximately 305,000 people were affected because they installed the app "This is your digital life", which enabled Cambridge Analytica to harvest their personal data. What users did not realise was that Cambridge Analytica were also collecting additional information about their Facebook friends [18]. It is reported that "Facebook's 'platform policy' allowed the collection of friends' data to improve the user experience in the app but barred it being sold on or used for advertising." [19]. It was subsequently revealed that the data collected, included "emails, invoices, contracts and bank transfers" from over 50 million profiles of registered US voters, had in fact been sold on to third parties. Facebook then announced that any apps unused for three months will have their access to personal data restricted and future apps will also be restricted ("just their name, email address and profile photo") unless the user specifically grants permission by signing a contract [20].

Within Facebook, apps will no longer be able to "access certain information like religious or political views, relationship status and details, friend lists, education, and work history" [21]. These changes had a detrimental effect on some existing apps as demonstrated by the dating app Tinder, which reported that the changes that Facebook made to their policies had a knock-on effect for users of their app, as many had linked it to their Facebook profile [20].

2.4 Multimedia Privacy Concerns

The uploading and sharing of photos and videos are an integral part of OSNs. As the volume of multimedia uploaded daily to OSNs has increased, so have the risks to users, with Facebook having the most, with over 4.2 billion active users world wide, as of February 2021 [1]. Also there are approximately 995 images uploaded to Instagram per second [35], so it is not surprising that hackers utilise this huge resource for malicious purposes, such as hiding malware, spamming and identity theft.

Malware can be embedded within multimedia files and widely distributed through OSNs. GPS data, also called geotagging, can reveal the owner's location as this information is embedded in the meta-data of uploaded images, videos, posts and tweets and can be used to exploit personal information in order to determine a participant's pattern of life for the purposes of stalking [5]. This has become less effective after Twitter changed the default privacy setting for geotagging on user accounts to "off". It now requires users to actively turn this on, but many still do this. There are still some sites that have geolocation turned on by default including Flickr, which embeds the longitude and latitude of the location where an image was taken into the EXIF metadata of the image [22]. This information is easily exploited, enabling anyone to pinpoint the location where a photograph was taken or a post was uploaded.

2.5 Summary

The literature identifies that there are still security issues around OSNs, which demonstrates the importance of highlighting these issues. The main concerns are the user's lack of awareness of their privacy settings and that a great many rely on the default settings. Another concern is that many users have accounts on multiple platforms, which are often linked together for ease of use, including the same personal details (name, picture, password), which makes it easier to collect data on them in cyber space. This facilitates secondary leakage between platforms when "friends" post pictures, "likes" or messages which circumvent privacy settings, regardless of the user's intended security settings. Locations are revealed through casual multimedia uploads which have GPS coordinates embedded in them, which the user may or may not be aware of and which hackers can utilise for malicious purposes.

3 Methodology

3.1 General Methodology

A survey was used to gather data from volunteer participants (for which they gave their explicit permission and were offered feedback on their online privacy). This data was then used to determine how they perceived their online privacy and to compare this to what could actually be harvested online.

The survey was sent out to all the students studying at the University of Greenwich Maritime campus and (n = 252) individuals responded. These included a mix of participants on Computer Science, Business, Humanities, History and Law degrees (undergraduate to postgraduate). The participants were asked to provide their email address, full name, their age range, what degree they were on and what year of study they were in, to determine the demographics of the participant group. They were also asked to identify which OSNs they regularly used. The survey asked them to identify what personal information they had knowingly published online, what they thought was freely available for anyone to find and view, and what personal information they thought was private. They were also asked what information they thought could be seen by someone they were friends with on an OSN. To determine their awareness of secondary leakage, we also asked them to identify what information about themselves they thought could be found through a friend of a friend, i.e. someone that they personally had no direct connection with. There were nine options possible for each of these questions (full name, date of birth (DoB), exact home address, a picture of themselves, their email address, their phone number, names of a close family member, actual places visited in the last few days and their current (physical) location). The last two items enable anyone to determine places that they regularly visit, such as their workplace or gym and potentially where they live, if they use their OSNs from these locations [5]. There was also a free text box for anything else not covered in the list.

There are many tools available from the Internet used by companies to mine information from social networks sites for marketing purposes to identify a target audience for advertising. These applications are designed to work with Twitter as their main source of information often using the geotags present but will also search for information on a specific account from publicly visible information [5]. The functionality ranges from merely displaying someone's tweets to being able to view posted pictures from a particular locale or time period.

3.2   Manual Search Methodology

Only the participants' first and last names were used as the starting point for the searches using a search engine. In the majority of cases this returned result that included the various social networking sites that the participants were using. From these social networking accounts their personal information could be gathered, such as personal pictures and the names of family members by searching the friends lists in the accounts. Other information found was used elsewhere, such as the BT Phonebook [36](Other countries have their own equivalent resource) and FindMyPast [32]. Sites like this then enabled more personal data to be gathered, including information such as birth certificate records, current address and phone number, the manual method is about finding a piece of information from one source and then using this to narrow down a search for other information from another source.

3.3   Automated Search Methodology

The top ten "over sharers" and the bottom ten "minimal sharers" were investigated further using fully automated 'people search engine tools. These are readily available OSINT tools that automatically search through a variety of different sources (Social networking sites, Census/Birth/Marriage/Military/Death records and other online accounts) normally used for genuine purposes such as making contact with someone you didn't get contact details for or finding lost family or family from other countries amongst other uses.

The "minimal sharers" were of particular interest due to the lack of information found about these participants using the manual method (discussed in Sect. 3.2). We needed to determine if the automated tools would identify more of their personal information. Some of these searches found information which was hidden behind a 'pay wall' requiring payment to access the information. Examples of this are websites that hold the census data, birth, death and marriage records (See Table 1). The automated tools that were used to search UK sources were pipl, 192, peopletraceuk, social-searcher and findmypast [28–32]. These tools are designed to take a small piece of information (normally a persons name) and collate as much information about this person. It normally does this in such broad stroke however that you will need to sift through a large number of false entries as there is generally more that one person in the world with the same name.

4   Results of the Survey

The survey asked the participants to give details of themselves and their usage of OSNs. 252 participants completed the survey and although all were students they were representative of a quite diverse population with age ranges from 18 to 60 (See Table 1) and on a wide variety of different degrees, although the majority are in the age range 18–25.

4.1   Demographics of Survey Participants

The majority of participants (91.6%) were undergraduate students (See Table 1). The group 20 to 30 was the largest with 164 participants (65%). These have been broken into smaller ranges in Table 1 for discussion. The largest number of respondents fell within the age ranges 18 to 23 (193, 76.6%), but there were also five people in the age range 51 to 60. The reason these age brackets were chosen was that it was anticipated that there would be a much larger number of respondents between the age of 18 and 25 as the participants in this study are university students, and due to this, smaller age brackets at the lower end of the age range were used to increase fidelity. Females were the majority of respondents being 58.4% of the total and 41.2% being male with one person not specifying their gender (See Table 1).

Participants were asked to identify their year of study. The largest number (36.9%) were in their first year of study and the smallest group (8.7%) were post-graduate students ranging from masters students to PhD students. This also included a small number of post-doc researchers. There were 6 people who were working (full-time and part-time) while studying and these are included in the Master's Degree, PhD student and Postdoc category. Only 42% of survey participants were on computer orientated degrees (BSc Computer Science, BSc Computer Security and Forensics, BSc Computer Systems and Networking and BSc Business Computing). This shows that the results are not biased by "computer savvy" participants studying computer science related degrees.

Table 1. Survey participants' demographics

	Category	Number	Percentage
Gender	Male	104	41.2%
	Female	147	58.4%
	Other	1	0.4%
Current status	1st year	93	36.9%
	2nd year	57	22.6%
	3rd year	81	32.1%
	Masters, PhD, Postdoc	21	8.4%
Age range	18–19	66	26%
	20–21	70	28%
	22–23	57	23%
	24–25	20	8%
	26–30	17	7%
	31–40	14	6%
	41–50	3	1%
	51–60	5	2%

4.2 Participants' Perceptions

The participants were asked to identify which social networks they regularly used. The majority (86.5%) used Facebook, 69.4% used Instagram, 48% used Twitter, 18.7% used Tumblr and 20.2% used other social networks which were not listed in the survey. The majority also used multiple OSNs. However, eleven participants did not use any OSNs at all, although personally identifiable information was still found on six of them during the searches.

Published Online. The participants were asked to identify all information that they had voluntarily published online (See Table 2). For full name, DoB, email address and current location our results approximately matched what they believed could be found by anyone. The exception was their exact home address and the phone number. The majority (88%) had published their full name, their date of birth (68%), their email address (64%) and a picture of themselves (88%) on at least one OSN.

Information Found by a Friend. When asked what information they thought could be found in this section, the expectation was that more information could be found by someone that they were "friends" with compared to a complete stranger. The number expecting that their DoB could be found rose from 61%, to 84% their picture was up from 88% to 94%, phone number was up from 32% to 62% and family members was up from 54% to 80%. This demonstrates that

Table 2. Information voluntarily published online

Category	Number of participants	Percentage
Full name	222	88.10%
Picture of yourself	222	88.10%
Date of birth	171	67.90%
Email address	160	63.50%
Visited locations	102	40.50%
Family members	78	31.00%
Current location	70	27.80%
Phone number	47	18.70%
Exact home address	25	9.90%

they were aware that there was a greater chance of someone obtaining more of their personal information if they were friended on a OSN (See Fig. 1).

Information Found by a Stranger. Participants were asked what information they thought could be found online by someone that they had no connection with and the results are shown in Fig. 1. Almost everyone supposed that their full name (90%) and a picture of themselves (88%) could be found by a stranger. However, the majority (70%) did not think that a stranger could locate their home address, find their phone number (68%) or their current location (70%).

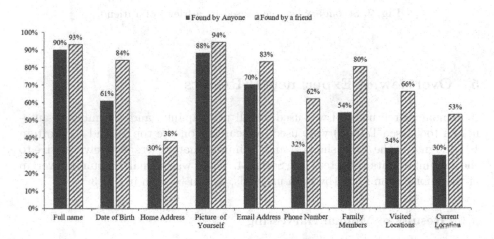

Fig. 1. Comparison of perceptions of personal information that could and could not be found by anyone and by a friend.

4.3 Secondary Leakage

The participants were asked if they thought that a friend of a friend would be able to find their personal information, to gauge their awareness of secondary leakage. The majority of participants did think that a friend of a friend could find most of their information, with the exception of where they lived, their phone number and their current location (See Fig. 2). These responses indicate that the majority had some awareness of secondary leakage. This type of secondary leakage can actually negate a person's privacy settings by leaking information which they may have set to be private.

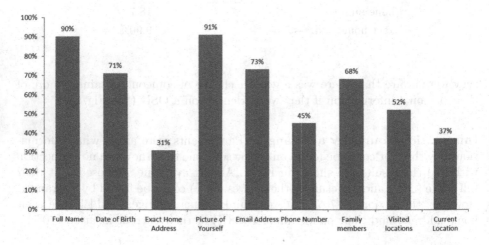

Fig. 2. Secondary leakage caused by a friend of a friend.

5 Overview of Experimental Results

A manual search method was used for all participants, and a number of auto-mated tools (see Table 4) were used for searches on the top 10 and the bottom 10 (designated the "over sharers" and "minimal sharers" respectively, relative to the amount of data collected), see Sect. 5.4. There was a small amount of overlap of the information found by both methods, as can be seen in Fig. 3.

5.1 Results of Manual Harvesting

Using simple OSINT tools, at least one piece of information was found on 79% of the participants (n = 252), see Fig. 3. As the majority did have Facebook accounts (86.5%) it was relatively easy to find their names (82.1%) and pictures (72.2%), although not everyone used their actual photograph (some used cartoons or funny pictures). Some of these people also had their birthdays listed (20%).

Some had their birthdays listed on Twitter and in Facebook on posts which were viewable by anyone, although for some only partial (incomplete) DoBs were found. For those who had weaker privacy settings the names of close family and friends were also easily found.

Recent locations were identified through posted tweets using the geotag information and for a few (11%), their current location was also identified through recent posts on Facebook. LinkedIn was useful for obtaining email addresses as these are generally not hidden by the privacy settings due to the nature of the web site. The FindMyPast web site [32] gave access to a lot of information as this was used to search public records such as the census, birth, marriages, deaths, parish records and land and survey records. These web sites revealed home addresses using only the person's name, the area where they live and their approximate age. Census records also provided the names of other family members living at the same property. The phone numbers (land lines) were harder to find using the BT Phonebook web site, as it only revealed 12 phone numbers in total, probably due to the majority of respondents being students and only having mobile phones. Phones numbers are not a requirement when registering on most OSNs [36].

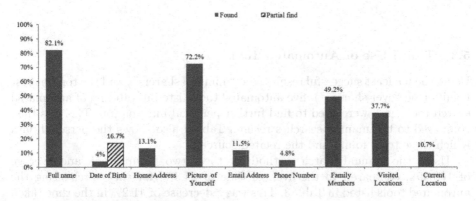

Fig. 3. Information that can be harvested by a stranger.

5.2 Timing the Manual Searches

The searches for the participants' data were undertaken in a timed experiment by someone who had no connection or link with them in cyber space. Table 3 shows the details, grouped in 1-minute time bands. It can be seen that for the majority (66%), their information was found in less than two minutes. In under three minutes 88.5% of the participants had their data exposed.

The average time taken for each search was 109 s. The fastest exploit took 14 s with the participant's full name, picture and the places that they had visited in the last few days all being identified in that time. The longest time was 460 s

(7 min 40 s) and for this participant their full name, partial DoB (month and year only), exact home address, picture and close family names were all found. This particular investigation took more time due to the participant's information being distributed across multiple web sites, which took longer to locate, see Table 3.

Table 3. Investigation in 1 min time bands

Time taken	Number of participants exploited
Less than 1 min	48
Between 1 to 2 mins	118
Between 2 to 3 mins	57
Between 3 to 4 mins	19
Between 4 to 5 mins	3
Between 5 to 6 mins	5
+7 min	2

5.3   Timed Use of Automated Tools

Using the ten least successful results (the "minimal sharers") and the top ten best results (the "over sharers"), five automated tools listed in tab:List of automated search tools used were used to find further personal information. This was then compared to the manual searches results. Table 4 also shows the personal data which these tools found and the related source.

Using the manual search method for these two groups took and average of 160.45 s, compared to the average time of 94.35 s for the search using the automated tools listed in Table 3. This was a decrease of 41.2% in the time taken for the searches. However, it was found that there was also a 37.9% decrease in the information that was found by the automated tools compared to the manual approach used, i.e. the manual searches were more successful.

5.4   Minimal Sharers vs Over Sharers

The "minimal sharers" were labelled P1 to P10 and the "over sharers" were P11 to P20. For the ten "minimal sharers", where no information at all was found using the manual method, the automated tools were more successful for 50% of them. Participants P1, P3, P4, P6 and P8 had no information found using either method. However, for participants P2, P5, P7, P9 and P10 two pieces and one partially complete piece of information was found (full name, their home address and a partial date of birth (month and year only)). So for these five people from the "minimal sharers" group the automated search was more successful.

Table 4. List of automated search tools used

Automated tools	Data found	Sources
Pipl [28]	Full name, email, current location, Recent location, photo	Online social networking sites
192 [29]	Full name, date of birth, telephone numbers, Full address, family members	Census/Birth/Marriage/ Military/Death Records
Peopletraceuk [30]	Full name, date of birth, telephone numbers, Full address, family members	Census/Birth/Marriage/ Military/Death Records
Social-searcher [31]	Full name, photo, email, family members, Current location, recent locations	Online social networking sites
Search.findmypast [32]	Full name, date of birth, telephone numbers, Full address, family members	Census/Birth/Marriage/ Military/Death records

For the ten "over sharers" some of the information from the manual searches was also found by the automated tools. However, overall the automated tools did not find as much data as the manual searches (average of 6.25 pieces of information found) compared to the automated tools average of only 2.05. Table 5 summarises the number of individual pieces of personal information found for each participant (P11 to P20) and also gives the overall average for each method. It should be noted that the 0.5.indicates a partial date of birth found. There was a 60.6% decrease in the information found by the automated tools.

The manual method found almost all of their information, except for a complete DoB, for participants P14 and P15, while the automated tools only found 3.5 and 2.5 pieces of information respectively. The least successful cases were P11 and P13 where the automated search only found 1.5 pieces of information for each. In the case of P17 and P18 the automated tools found no information at all, compared to 5.5 and 6.5 items of personal information respectively found using the manual method (See Table 5).

At this point it is worth mentioning the limitations of both the manual and automated searches that were used in this investigation. The automated tools selected for this investigation have limitations inherent within the design of the tools themselves. However, we still chose to use these automated tools as part of our methodology, as this study was carried out from the perspective of information gathering that could be conducted by someone with no prior knowledge and little to no experience in this area. In every case the manual method found more information. This demonstrates that automated tools are useful for finding information about people but are not nearly as effective as performing the searches manually, even when taking into consideration how much faster the tools are at performing the searches.

Table 5. Over sharers group data collected - manual search vs automated search

Participant #	Manual search results	Automated search results
P11	7	1.5
P12	4.5	3
P13	4.5	1.5
P14	8.5	3.5
P15	8.5	2.5
P16	6.5	3.5
P17	5.5	0
P18	6	0
P19	5.5	2.5
P20	6	2.5
Average	6.25	2.05

5.5 Participant's Perceptions Compared to Reality

Each participant in the survey had a view of their own personal privacy on the social network platforms that they used. So how did the results of the experiments, both manual and automated, compare to the participants' perceived online security?

Of the 20 participants examined in more detail only two thought that no information could be found about themselves online. One was in the "minimal sharers" group (P6) and the other, surprisingly, was in the "over sharers" group (P20). For P20 their perceptions were completely incorrect, as their full name, their picture, their email address, their phone number, a close family member and places that they had visited recently were all easily found. Only the perceptions of P6 were accurate, as no information could be found using either a manual or an automated search. Similarly, only two participants (P9 and P15), one from each group, thought that all their information could be found. P9 was incorrect, although as no information was found using the manual search, two pieces and a partial were found by the automated tools. Only P15 correctly identified that all their information could be found online and this was confirmed during the manual search. However, using the automated tools a full name, exact home address and a partial date of birth were identified for P9, P15 and P20. For P6 and P9 (minimal sharers) it can be assumed that they care about their data and keep it relatively safe. For the "over sharers" only P15 correctly identified the information that could be found. P20 was clearly naive regarding what of their personal information could be found online, with their Full Name, Photo, Email Address, Phone Number, Close Family and Recent Locations being found by the manual search. It is clear that they overestimated the privacy of their personal information and it is also important to consider how they may also be naive about the value of this personal information for impersonating or targeting an individual.

5.6   Evaluation

It was interesting to compare the results and the demographics of the "minimal sharers" and "over sharers" with the results as a whole. These two groups are a small sub-set, so no statistical analysis was undertaken, but it was interesting to compare the demographics of these two groups. The following questions were considered:- Who were these participants? Did the age range or the gender influence which group they were in? How did these participants compare to the total respondents as a whole?

For the "minimal sharers" (P1 to P10) the ratio of females to males was 50–50. This was interesting as the total number of female participants was slightly higher (58.4%). For this group 90% were aged 18 to 21 years, and only one person was in the range 51 to 60 years. These two age ranges 18–19 and 20–21 made up 54% of the total survey respondents. All were students and included one in employment. Only two of the students were studying a computer related degree. This meant that 80% of these participants were on non-computing related degrees. This is in direct contrast to the total survey where 57% were on non-computing degrees.

The "over sharers" (P11 to P20) had a majority of males (60%), which was also in direct contrast to the survey as a whole, where only 41% were male. This meant that males were over-represented in this group. The "over sharers" ages ranged from 18 to 25, which was not entirely unexpected as these three age ranges included the largest number of respondents. However, the majority (80%) fell into the range 21 to 25 and all were undergraduate students, with six on computer related degrees and only one female student included. This compares to 43% who were on computer related degrees for the total survey.

For participants P11 to P14, additional information was found as well as the nine items that had been targeted in this work. These included someone's job, their age, partner's and Mother's names, places of education and other family members' names (See Table 6). A number of these items could be useful to a hacker, for example, to reset passwords for online accounts where the answer to a secret question is required. In the case of P13 more information was found manually, although it took 7 min 40 s to retrieve this, compared to the automated search which only took 1 minute 54 s, although the automated search did not find exactly the same information (See Table 5).

A paired t-test was conducted on what was actually found by a stranger compared to the participants' perceptions for all participants. This was done to identify if there was a significant difference between our two subsets of participants and identify if this difference was due to random chance. The result is significant ($t = -10.621$, $p < .0001$, df = 251, 95% CI: -2.16, -1.49). The correlation was found to be 0.1228186, which also shows that there was very little connection between the two sample sets. The calculated effect size is therefore 0.6668677, which is reasonable. These results demonstrate that our hypothesis that the participants over-estimated the amount of information that could be found by a total stranger is correct. The p-value is significant, being less than alpha $= 0.05$, meaning there is a 95% chance that the result is not due to random

Table 6. Additional information found for the "over sharers" group

		Additional information found
P11	Manual	Birth certificate number
	Tools	Current job, places of education, current age with two-year margin, there was more data available but was locked behind a paywall
P12	Manual	
	Tools	The full names of their parents and siblings, there was more data available but was locked behind a paywall
P13	Manual	Their mothers and current partners full name, The month and year of their birth, Birth certificate number
	Tools	Mum's name, age range, there was more data available but was locked behind a paywall
P14	Manual	
	Tools	Full names of parent's siblings and other family members, Places they have been and are employed, Places of education, there was more data available but was locked behind a paywall

chance. A power analysis was calculated to be 1.000, which demonstrates that our sample size is sufficiently large. Using the same effect size, alpha, and power only a total sample size of 118 would need to be collected to achieve the same results and our sample was 252. There was no statistical analysis undertaken on the "minimal sharers" or the "over sharers" as these two samples are too small to get any meaningful results, but their demographics were examined.

6 Discussion

6.1 All Participants

The participants identified what information they had voluntarily shared online and their responses where compared to the information gathered. For the survey as a whole the majority of participants were aware that some of their personal information could be found online by a complete stranger. However, very few thought that a stranger could locate their home address (predicted 30% vs found 13%) or their current location (predicted 30% vs found 11%). Awareness amongst all participants regarding secondary leakage was high, as seen by their responses (See Fig. 2). In almost every case the information gathered was less than the participants' expectations. Only in the "visited locations" category was more information retrieved (See Table 7).

The date of birth was a very difficult piece of information to find, which the participants grossly over estimated, with 61% predicating that this could be found by anyone. In practice only 4% had their full DoB revealed and a further 16.7% had a partial DoB (month and year only) found. This was interesting as 68% claimed that they had voluntarily published this information online. An email is one piece of information that most people would willingly give if someone asked for it and 70% of the survey respondents thought that their email could be easily found by anyone. However, during the investigation only 12% of the emails were found. This is because web sites tend to obfuscate email addresses to help prevent email harvesting for phishing attacks. More than half of the respondents (54%) presumed that a complete stranger could identify the names of their close family members. Reality was that 49% were actually identified including a photograph of the family member.

Table 7. Overview of perceptions vs Information found

	Perceptions by a friend	Perceptions by a stranger	Actually found
Full name	93%	90%	82%
Picture of themselves	94%	88%	72%
Email	83%	70%	11%
DoB	84%	61%	20%
Family members	80%	54%	49%
Visited location	66%	34%	38%
Phone number	64%	32%	48%
Current location	53%	30%	11%
Home address	38%	30%	13%

Additional information collected included Blackberry messenger, Skype and Snapchat accounts. Some participants also had personal web sites and blogs, which were easily located. These can reveal a lot of information about their hobbies, interests, aspirations and even their work place. The places they had visited in the last few days were interesting, as 34% of respondents thought that this could be found. In fact 38% were actually found, see Table 7. Figure 4 shows a graphic of the comparison of results for all participants.

It was note worthy that the initial email sent out inviting people to take the survey was actually sent from the email account of a senior member of the teaching staff at the university. The email message explicitly asked people to reply directly to the second author and his email was given in the text. However, six participants responded directly to that email without noticing that the email address did not come directly from the person requesting assistance. This is exactly how phishing attacks succeed, as the attackers are hoping that the recipient will not notice that the email address does not match. This was just over 2% of the total participants, but it illustrates that if enough emails are sent out in a phishing attack, then there will always some people who will respond.

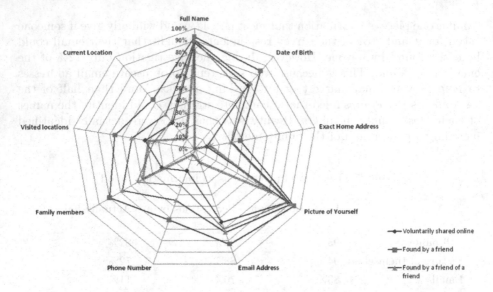

Fig. 4. Comparison of results for all participants.

6.2   Minimal Sharers vs Over Sharers

The combined average time taken to access the personal information using the manual method for the "minimal sharers" and "over sharers" was 160 s. With the automated tools this only took 94.35 s, but found 38% less information than the manual approach. Compare this to all participants, where each search took on average 109 s per person. The manual searches found more information on these participants than the automated tools. However a number of additional pieces of information were found by the automated tools which were not initially found during the manual search (See Table 6).

While statistical analysis of these two groups was not possible due to the small numbers, we did examine the demographics of each group and found significant differences and also when compared to the total population. This is highlighted in Table 8. In the "over sharers" group 60% were on computer related degrees compared to 43% of all participants, and only 20% within the "minimal sharers" group. So students studying computer related degrees are over-represented in the "over sharers" group.

The age range was split into two equal sizes (4 years each) for comparison here. The majority of the "minimal sharers" were in the younger 18 to 21 age band, with 90% in that age range, compared to the total population of 54%. The "over sharers" age range was 80% in the 22 to 25 band compared to 31% in the overall survey (see Table 8). So these two groups have different demographics to the population as a whole and between the two groups.

Gender related statistics showed that 36% of the "minimal sharers" were female and on computer related degrees, compared to only 17% in the "over sharers" group, so females were under-represented in this group. For the "mini-

Table 8. Comparison of total survey, minimal sharers and over sharers groups

		Total survey	Minimal sharers	Over sharers
Gender	Male	41%	50%	60%
	Female	59%	50%	40%
Age ranges	18–21	54%	90%	20%
	22–25	31%	10%	80%
Degree type	Non-Computing	57%	80%	40%
	Computing related	43%	20%	60%

mal sharers" only two participants (one female and one male) were on computer related degrees (one was on a BSc Computer Security and Forensics degree and the other was on BSc Business Computing degree). In total there were a higher proportion of females (50%) in the "minimal sharers" group regardless of the degree taken, compared to only 40% in the "over sharers" group. This is still lower than the total survey, in which the majority, 59% of participants were female. This implies that males are less concerned about their privacy or possibly that they are more confident in their ability to control their personal data (see Table 8).

7 Conclusion

In this work we investigated personal data leakage caused by the interaction of OSN users with friends, friends of friends and a complete stranger. We found that for the n = 252 participants, the majority of their personal information could be accessed in under two minutes by someone who had no connection with them in cyberspace. This work demonstrated that there are still people who publish too much personal information on OSNs (over sharers), either intentionally or accidentally with no regard for who can see this or appreciation of how this information may be abused. It also highlights the very real risks and threats that people can face due to their lack of awareness of online privacy. These results show that the majority of participants did not perceive their online privacy accurately, including students on computer related degrees. The paired t-test showed that the results of the survey compared to what was actually found by us to be statistically significant. Our hypothesis that the majority inaccurately predicted how secure their personal information is, was confirmed.

The manual searches were more effective at finding information than the automated tools. However, the use of automated tools for data harvesting makes it easier for someone with no computer skills to find information about a particular target. While both search methods did find some similar information, they also found different pieces of personal information for the majority, see Tables 4 and 5. It cannot be underestimated how little time it took to manually harvest the majority of the their personal data effectively - less than 2 min for two thirds of the participants. However, for these experiments it was the amount of information that was found that was more significant rather than the actual time taken, although it was not anticipated that the time taken for the majority of searches would be so low. For future work it would be interesting to see the results if this work was repeated on a more diverse survey population, i.e. non-students.

This study underlines the importance of continuing to educate users on how their existing behaviours can present a serious threat to the security of their personal information and that of their virtual "friends" on OSNs and emphasises the need for greater security awareness.

References

1. Statista Social Media Statistics. https://www.statista.com/topics/1164/social-networks/. Accessed 8 Mar 2021
2. Van Schaik, P., Jansen, J., Onibokun, J., Camp, J., Kusev, P.: Security and privacy in online social networking: risk perceptions and precautionary behaviour. Comput. Hum. Behav. **78**, 283–297 (2018)
3. Irshad, S., Soomro, T.R.: Identity theft and social media. Int. J. Comput. Sci. Netw. Secur. **18**, 43–55 (2018)
4. What is the Definition of Online Privacy?. https://www.winston.com/en/legal-glossary/online-privacy.html. Accessed 8 Mar 2021
5. Gan, D., Jenkins, L.: Social networking privacy-who's stalking you? Future Internet **7**, 67–93 (2015)
6. Palin's Email Account Hacked. https://www.huffingtonpost.co.uk/entry/palins-email-account-hack_n_127184?guccounter=1. Accessed 8 Mar 2021
7. Hacker group targets Mark Zuckerberg's online accounts - again. https://www.zdnet.com/article/hacker-group-targets-mark-zuckerberg-online-accounts-again. Accessed 8 Mar 2021
8. How to [ALMOST] keep your tinder private from your Facebook. http://www.knowyourmobile.com/apps/tinder/22254/how-keep-your-tinder-private-your-facebook. Accessed 8 Mar 2021
9. Debit card (@NeedADebitCard). https://twitter.com/needadebitcard. Accessed 8 Mar 2021
10. Driving Licence posted on Twitter. https://www.google.co.uk/search?q=twitter+picture+driving+licence+uk. Accessed 8 Mar 2021
11. Alex Jones on Instagram: Teddy Thomson is official. https://www.instagram.com/p/BRFtCCHDL_O/?hl=undefined. Accessed 8 Mar 2021
12. Ali, S., Islam, N., Rauf, A., Din, I., Guizani, M., Rodrigues, J.: Privacy and security issues in online social networks. Future Internet **10**, 114 (2018)
13. Islam, M.B., Watson, J., Iannella, R., Geva, S.: A greater understanding of social networks privacy requirements: the user perspective. J. Inf. Sec. Appl. **33**, 30–44 (2017)
14. Tsay-Vogel, M., Shanahan, J., Signorielli, N.: Social media cultivating perceptions of privacy: a 5-year analysis of privacy attitudes and self-disclosure behaviors among Facebook users. New Media Soc. **20**, 141–161 (2016)
15. Wisniewski, P.J., Knijnenburg, B.P., Lipford, H.R.: Making privacy personal: profiling social network users to inform privacy education and nudging. Int. J. Hum.-Comput. Stud. **98**, 95–108 (2017)

16. Cascavilla, G., Beato, F., Burattin, A., Conti, M., Mancini, L.V.: OSSINT - open source social network intelligence. Online Soc. Networks Media **6**, 58–68 (2018)
17. Child Safety Online: a practical guide for parents and Carers whose children are using social media. https://www.gov.uk/government/publications/child-safety-online-a-practical-guide-for-parents-and-carers. Accessed 8 Mar 2021
18. Cambridge analytica: the story so far. https://www.bbc.co.uk/news/technology-43465968. Accessed 8 Mar 2021
19. Revealed: 50 million Facebook profiles harvested for Cambridge analytica in major data breach. https://www.theguardian.com/news/2018/mar/17/cambridge-analytica-facebook-influence-us-election. Accessed 8 Mar 2021
20. The Cambridge analytica and facebook data scandal: how to tell if your data was shared. https://www.techradar.com/news/us-uk-investigating-facebooks-role-in-cambridge-analytica-data-breach. Accessed 8 Mar 2021
21. Facebook's new data-sharing policies are crashing tinder. https://www.wired.com/story/facebook-policies-tinder-crashing. Accessed 8 Mar 2021
22. Albrecht, K., Mcintyre, L.: Psst...your location is showing!: metadata in digital photos and posts could be revealing more than you realize. IEEE Consum. Electron. Mag. **4**, 94–96 (2015)
23. Pontes, H.M., Taylor, M., Stavropoulos, V.: Beyond Facebook addiction: the role of cognitive-related factors and psychiatric distress in social networking site addiction. Cyberpsychology, Behav. Soc. Netw. **21**, 240–247 (2018)
24. Pegg, K.J., O'donnell, A.W. Lala, G., Barber, B.L.: The role of online social identity in the relationship between alcohol-related content on social networking sites and adolescent alcohol use. Cyberpsychology, Behav. Soc. Netw. **21**, 50–55 (2018)
25. Hendriks, H., Den, Van, Putte, B., Gebhardt, W.A.: Alcoholposts on social networking sites: the Alcoholpost-typology. Cyberpsychology, Behav. Soc. Netw. **21**, 463–467 (2018)
26. Jensen, M., Hussong, A.M., Baik, J.: Text messaging and social network site use to facilitate alcohol involvement: a comparison of U.S. and Korean college students. Cyberpsychology. Behav. Soc. Netw. **31**, 311–317 (2018)
27. Ying, Q.F., Chiu, D.M., Venkatramanan, S., Zhang, X.: User modeling and usage profiling based on temporal posting behavior in OSNs. Online Soc. Netw. Media **8**, 32–41 (2018)
28. Pipl - identity information search and API. https://pipl.com/. Accessed 8 Mar. 2021
29. Search for people, businesses and places in the UK. http://www.192.com/. Accessed 8 Mar 2021
30. Finding people the right way. www.peopletraceuk.com/. Accessed 8 Mar 2021
31. Real-time social media monitoring. https://www.social-searcher.com/. Accessed 8 Mar 2021
32. Find my past. https://search.findmypast.co.uk/search-world-records. Accessed 8 Mar 2021
33. The top 10 worst social media cyber-attacks. https://www.infosecurity-magazine.com/blogs/top-10-worst-social-media-cyber/. Accessed 8 Mar 2021
34. Tweet location FAQs. https://help.twitter.com/en/safety-and-security/tweet-location-settings. Accessed 8 Mar 2021
35. Instagram by the numbers. https://www.omnicoreagency.com/instagram-statistics/. Accessed 8 Mar 2021
36. BT - find a person. https://www.thephonebook.bt.com/person/. Accessed 8 Mar 2021

37. Rathore, N.C., Tripathy, S.: AppMonitor: restricting information leakage to third-party applications. Soc. Netw. Anal. Min. **10**(1), 1–20 (2020). https://doi.org/10.1007/s13278-020-00662-7

38. Kekulluoglu, D, Magdy, W., Vaniea, K.: Analysing privacy leakage of life events on twitte. In: 12th ACM Conference on Web Science, 287–294 (2020)

ARTPHIL: Reversible De-identification of Free Text Using an Integrated Model

Bayan Alabdullah[1,2]($\boxtimes$) (iD), Natalia Beloff[2] (iD), and Martin White[2] (iD)

[1] Computer Science Department, Princess Nourah Bint Abdul Rahman University,
Riyadh 11543, Saudi Arabia
`b.alabdullah@sussex.ac.uk`
[2] Department of Informatics, University of Sussex, Falmar BN1 4GE, UK

Abstract. Organisations that collect and maintain individual data face the challenge of preserving privacy and security when using, archiving, or sharing these data. De-identification tools are essential for minimising the privacy risk. However, current data de-identification and anonymisation methods are widely used to alter the original data in a way that cannot be recovered. This results in data distortion and, hence, the substantial loss of knowledge within the data.

To address this issue, this paper introduces the concept of reversible data de-identification methods to de-identify unstructured health data under the Health Insurance Portability and Accountability Act (HIPAA) guidelines. The model integrates Philter [9], the state-of-the-art tool for extracting personal identifiers from free-text, to detect confidential information and encrypt them with E-ART, lightweight encryption algorithm E-ART [10]. The performance of the proposed model ARTPHIL is evaluated using i2b2 data corpus in terms of recall, precision, F-measure and execution time. The results of the experiment are consistent with the recent de-identification method with recall of 96.93%. More importantly, the original data can be recovered, if needed, and authenticated.

Keywords: Privacy · De-identification · Pseudonymisation · Reversible · Re-identification

1 Introduction

Preserving data privacy has become a significant issue, while the applications and capabilities of Big Data are expanding dramatically. There is no doubt that this expansion creates enormous opportunities and avenues to understand and solve significant problems over various domains. However, the privacy and security concerns about Big Data are also growing. Legal systems establish laws to protect the privacy of individual information. A well-known example is the General Data Protection Regulation (GDPR), which outlines a specific set of rules for sharing and storing personal data to protect individual privacy. Data minimisation is one of the fundamental principles of GDPR and has strict data retention policies. This protection means that an individual's personal data can be retained for no longer than necessary to carry out the purpose for which the data is

W. Shi et al. (Eds.): SPNCE 2021, LNICST 423, pp. 369–381, 2022.
https://doi.org/10.1007/978-3-030-96791-8_27

processed [1]. GDPR also restrict the use of personal data beyond the purpose for which the data was originally collected (purpose limitations). However, these policies could be relaxed when data is de-identified. GDPR also encourage data controllers and processors to de-identify data to reduce the liability and notification obligations for data breaches [1]. Data security and privacy issues become even more critical when the data is used in healthcare environments, which typically deal with patient-sensitive information. In the United States, standards for protecting healthcare information confidentiality were established in HIPAA's Privacy Rule [2]. HIPAA specifies 18 data elements that consider identifiable health information. Those elements must be removed or generalised from data to be considered de-identified.

Previous work on data de-identification and anonymisation techniques has been developed within the fields of statistical disclosure control [3], privacy-preserving data publishing (PPDP) [4] and privacy-preserving data mining (PPDM). In these fields, sensitive data are shared with untrusted third parties for secondary use but do not disclose information that can be linked to specific individuals. This technique primarily focuses on producing anonymised versions of data by removing, obfuscating or generalising identifiable personal data. The drawback of these methods is that they are usually irreversible; there is no mechanism by which an individual's identification can be recovered.

In many circumstances, it is essential to refer back to the original data without revealing it to the end-user. This allows it to be accessed in emergencies or by those with acceptable levels of access. For example, in the PPDM field, the knowledge obtained from mining de-identified data cannot be verified from the original data, which might cause knowledge uncertainty [5, 6]. In research platforms, where documents are shared between different specialists, including scientists, researchers, and physicians, specific cases are usually chosen for further analysis. For instance, in selected cases where specialists conduct blind diagnosis or annotation procedures, the authorised user can reverse the de-identification process and retrieve the necessary information, making a more accurate assessment [7].

Further, there are cases in clinical trials in which some of the research subjects should be approached again for further study [8]. Therefore, reversible de-identification (e.g., encryption, pseudonymisation) are often preferred. Although robust encryption solutions are available, their application in the face of ever-increasing volume, variety, and speed remains challenging. In addition, the cumbersome key management and distribution of the symmetric encryption algorithm prevent a suitable level of scalability. In addition, more lightweight and practical alternatives must be developed [30].

As a result, there is a need for a new reversible model for de-identifying unstructured data to reduce the risks for data subjects, address the requirements of preserving privacy while supporting data's use. This study addresses this need by integrating Philter [9], the information extracting tool, with the lightweight encryption algorithm E-ART [10]. This process's primary contribution is 1) a reversible, fast de-identification model ARTPHIL to de-identify unstructured textual health data cost-effectively without compromising security. And 2) implementation and evaluation of the proposed model using 2014 i2b2 testing data. The technique achieved a recall of 96.93% to detect and encrypt personal health information (PHI) specified under HIPAA guidelines [2]. However, this work does not claim to generate de-identified data to comply with HIPAA as the PHI is encrypted, not removed. The method also achieved fast execution time, making it suitable to de-identify a considerable amount of data.

2 Related Work

2.1 De-identification as Named Entity Recognition

The de-identification of structured data has been widely studied, and there are various techniques [11]–[13]. However, de-identifying unstructured data, primarily text data, is complex and requires researchers' manual intervention. The main challenge in de-identifying unstructured data is finding the sensitive attributes that spread throughout the text document.

Several techniques have been proposed to extract those sensitive attributes. Most of them can be seen in the application Named Entity Recognition (NER). NER is a technique that finds and categorises important words inside the text [14]. Many different natural language processing (NLP) applications benefit from the NER technique. Those applications include questioning-answering applications [15, 16], tweet analysis [17, 18], automatic text extraction [11, 12] and data mining applications.

In the de-identification process, NER is a useful tool for extracting identifiable and sensitive attributes from unstructured text. NER techniques can be classified into three main categories: 1) rule-based, 2) machine learning, and 3) hybrid [14]. A brief description of each method is provided below.

Rule-based: The rule-based method consists of rules, such as pattern matching, hand-crafted, heuristics, grammatical and dictionaries to recognise NER in an unstructured text [19]. This method's advantage is that it requires little or no annotated training data and is easy to implement and improve by adding additional rules. However, it is quite expensive, domain-specific and lacks robustness and portability. Examples of de-identification tools that use rule-based and pattern matching methods to detect personal health information (PHI) entities and replace them with tags indicating its category include De-ID [20], HMS Scrubber [21], and PhysioNet de-identification (deid) software [22].

Machine learning: The machine learning approach trains a statistical model to classify words into a PHI or a non-PHI group. Most recent de-identification tools use supervised learning algorithms such as support vector machines [23], conditional random fields [24], and decision trees [25]. The results obtained through supervised machine learning techniques are promising. However, these techniques require extensive, annotated data for training. Creating annotated data is an expensive task because it requires substantial time and effort with domain experts' support.

Hybrid model: The hybrid model approach combines lexicon and rule-based methods to benefit from and overcome the limitations of both [26]. For example, MITRE Identification Scrubber [27] uses pattern matching to extract all numeric data, such as phone numbers and postal codes and uses them in a conditional random fields algorithm.

An example of a recent text identification application is Philter [9]. Philter is a customisable open-source de-identification software developed and evaluated with an extensive collection of unstructured clinical notes from the University of California, San Francisco (UCSF) and 2014 i2b2. The algorithm uses rule-based and statistical NLP approaches. The algorithm uses an overlapping pipeline of methods that are state-of-the-art in each application. This combination helps classify PHI in a free-text document, including regular expressions, statistical modelling, blacklists, and whitelists, as shown in Fig. 1. The word identified as PHI is replaced with an obfuscated string of precisely the same length (for example, "David Mitchell" becomes "***** ********").

The algorithm's performance compared in [9] to the two strongest real-world competitors, PhysioNet [22] and Scrubber [27], based on recall. Philter demonstrated the highest overall recall on both corpora and the highest recall in each PHI category. A significant drawback of this approach is that it is irreversible. The removed PHI data cannot be re-generated if an authenticated user later requires full access to the data.

2.2 Reversible De-identification

To our knowledge, most of the data de-identification methods have been developed in the fields of PPDP and PPDM. These approaches protect private data from being disclosed during data mining. It often swaps, deletes or modifies the identifiable information and removes the correlation between the original and anonymised data. Consequently, it is unable to recover the original data from the de-identified data, which could create issues such as knowledge uncertainty [5, 6, 28]. For example, if original data is lost, the mined data's knowledge cannot be verified from the original data [5]. To resolve this drawback, Chen et al. [5] used the concept of reversible data hiding in the image and proposed an algorithm called privacy difference expansion (PDE). PDE perturbed and embedded private data with a customised watermark to verify the integrity of the original data. Similarly, Yamac et al. [29] proposed privacy-preserving solutions that combine a multi-level encryption scheme with compressive sensing. This approach can reverse the de-identification so that an authorised person can recover the degraded information using a key. It attempts to simplify the key management issue by watermarking the key into the sensed image. However, this computationally expensive decompression might be challenging to apply to Big Data.

Encryption is also considered an efficient method to obtain reversible de-identification [8]. For example, Landi and Rao [8] proposed a way to de-identify patient data so that only the owners of the original data or legally empowered entities can re-identify. It uses secure public-key encryption technology to generate a public key based on one or more private keys. Gulcher et al. [26] stated the need for reversible de-identification to protect genetic research data. They proposed an approach for de-identifying biological samples for genetic research based on a third-party encryption method using a 128-bit symmetric encryption algorithm-AES. This approach would allow later requested access to the research data. However, The existing encryption standards rely on increasing the key size and the number of rounds to enhance security which could negatively affect the performance [29, 30]. E-ART is a new lightweight encryption algorithm that was proposed in [10] to address the speed requirement by modern application. It uses the concept of a balanced binary tree with ASCII conversion and random key generation. The algorithm compared to existing standard encryption algorithms in terms of performance and security with promising results.

The terms anonymisation and de-identification are often used interchangeably. However, there is a significant difference between these concepts. Clete A. Kushida et al.

[35] state that de-identification of data refers to the process of deleting or obscuring any personally identifiable information from individual records in a way that reduces the risk of disclosure of the data subject identity. However, de-identified datasets are allowed to contain encrypted identifiers where only authorised users have access to the encryption key. The existence of a key makes it possible to recover the original data for the user with correct authorisation. This process is also known as pseudonymisation under GDPR privacy rules. Anonymisation, on the other hand, refers to the process of data de-identification that produces de-identified data that cannot be reversed back to the original data. Under GDPR, anonymous data is not treated as personal data. Therefore, user consent to process and share the data is not required.

Pseudonymisation is a new privacy-preserving concept introduced by the GDPR as "The processing of personal data in such a way that the data can no longer be attributed to a specific data subject without the use of additional information, as long as such additional information is kept separately and subject to technical and organisational measures to ensure non-attribution to an identified or identifiable person" [1].

Pseudonymisation is a particular type of de-identification in which the names and other information that directly identifies an individual are replaced with pseudonyms. Pseudonymisation enables linking personal data through various datasets when all identifiable information is consistently pseudonymised. Pseudonymisation can be reversed when the link between original identities and the pseudonyms is maintained or if the replacement is done with an algorithm whose parameters are known. This provides an option for the de-identification process to be reversed in the future and re-identifying the data subjects. For example, identifiable information can be encrypted with a secret key to create a pseudonym; decrypting the key reversed the pseudonymisation process, recovering the original identifier. Pseudonymised data is still personal data and cannot be equated to anonymised data. Under HIPAA, re-identifying the datasets may only be done by an organisation covered by HIPAA's rules (mostly healthcare providers), known as a covered entity.

Pseudonymisation of data is suggested by GDPR [1] as one of the protective measures that controllers can use to evaluate the feasibility of further processing of personal information for archiving purposes in the public interest, scientific or historical research purposes, or statistical purposes by processing data that do not enable or no longer enable the identification of data subjects. However, GDPR restricts a data handler's potential to benefit from pseudonymised data if re-identification processes are "reasonably likely to be employed, such as singling out, either by the controller or by another person to identify the natural person directly or indirectly" [1]. Hence, data controllers should implement several technical and organisational measures to ensure that pseudonymous data is disconnected from the key enabling re-identification. Furthermore, the risks of re-identification are dynamic and evolve over time, and this implies that data controllers should evaluate these risks on a regular basis and take necessary action when they become significant. For example, changing pseudonyms over time for each use or each type of use as a way to reduce the risk of re-identification through linkability [36].

To sum up, the GDPR provides several regulatory incentives to adopt pseudonymisation. There are, therefore, significant benefits associated with using it, which include enabling data processing for secondary purposes without the need to obtain the explicit consent of data subjects. However, for this exemption to apply, pseudonymisation should meet the GDPR standard, and the existing pseudonymisation techniques were developed long before GDPR requirements were established. Many implementations of pseudonymisation approaches use static pseudonyms for data subjects, while others may contain indirect identifiers; in both cases, these fail to protect against re-identification due to privacy breaches arising from linkage attacks.

3 Proposed Method

The proposed de-identification system ARTPHIL consists of two key components that are integrated to de-identify unstructured textual data as follow: 1) the core of the Philter package [9] for the PHI detection process onlynot for the replacement, and 2) the E-ART encryption algorithm [10] for replacement strategy. Figure 1 presents an illustration of this method. The steps and dataset details are explained in the following sections.

3.1 PHI Detection

To address the task of locating PHI, we used an overlapping pipeline of multiple state-of-the-art methods provided by Philter [9]. The pipeline includes pattern matching, statistical modelling, blacklist, and whitelist to detect PHI from free-text clinical notes. The detection process involves scanning the unstructured text line by line and dividing it into individual words. First, common words with a high probability of not being PHI are detected using pattern matching with a custom library of 133 "safe" regular expressions. Second, a customised library of 171 regular expressions is used to locate known PHI entities such as salutations, ID numbers, phone numbers, date of birth, email address and zip codes. In both scenarios, the regular expressions look for exact terms, phrases, or numbers to recognise matches using each word's immediate context. The algorithm uses statistical modelling to determine each sentence and document's structure to address the challenge of dealing with words that could be either safe or PHI, such as "white" might be a name or an adjective. To exclude names that are proper nouns, a customised blacklist is used. And the whitelist is used to preserve all the medical terms and common English words. At the end of the pipeline, a token has one of three potential labels: PHI, Non-PHI or unmarked.

3.2 Replacement Strategy

To achieve our goal of developing reversible de-identification, all tokens marked as PHI, and unmarked tokens will be replaced with generated strings that can be retrieved. For this purpose, we used E-ART, the lightweight encryption algorithm proposed in [10]. This algorithm uses the idea of the balanced binary tree along with an ASCII table for character substitution; this increases searching efficiency and reduces processing time as reported in [10]. The algorithm also uses a random key generator based on character position as a seed to generate a dynamic key for increased security. However, reverse engineering of the original values is preserved if needed.

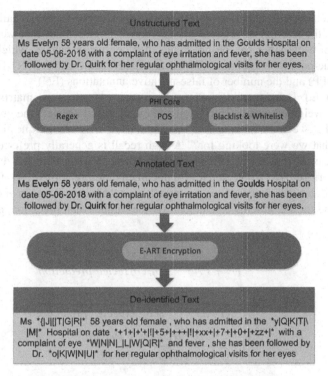

Fig. 1. A conceptual overview of the ARTPHIL process.

The system will look for PHI entities labelled in the PHI detection phase and use the E-ART algorithm to encrypt them. E-ART uses the entity's characters' index as a seed to generate a pseudo-random value. This value will be used as a key to generating an encrypted string to replace the PHI entity. The encrypted PHI entity's start and end will be marked with asterisks to be recognised if recovery of the original data is needed, as shown in the de-identified text in Fig. 1.

During the regeneration process of the original text, the de-identified text will be first scanned line by line, and all words that start and end with asterisks will be labelled as encrypted PHI. Then all encrypted PHI will be decrypted by reversing the process of E-ART encryption as described in [10].

4 Evaluation Metrics

4.1 Precision, Recall and F-measure

Because the proposed de-identification system and most existing de-identification systems treat the PHI identification as a NER task, the evaluation of the identification should use the same metrics as the NER literature [33]. Specifically, we used the 2014 i2b2 annotated data set and report performance, primarily we used three metrics: precision, recall and f-measure. Precision, also called positive predictive value, is the fraction of the relevant tokens (correctly classified) among the retrieved tokens. recall, also called sensitivity, is the fraction of relevant tokens (correctly classified) that were retrieved. The output of a classifier can be presented in a confusion matrix, which shows the number of true-positive annotations (TP), true-negative annotations (TN), false-positive annotations (FP) and the number of false-negative annotations (FN).

Precision (Eq. 1) and recall (Eq. 2) can be computed from such a matrix. F-measure (Eq. 3) is the weighted mean of precision and recall. recall answers the question, "Did we find all that we were looking for?" and precision answers the question, "Did we only label what we were looking for?" A high recall is generally preferred over high precision because it measures PHI percentage correctly identified; the data subjects' privacy is prioritised over a potential loss of document interpretability [34]. To emphasise sensitivity, we also calculate the F1 measure, which is the harmonic mean of the precision and recall, and the F2 which weighs recall (twice) higher than precision, as defined in (Eq. 4):

$$Recall = \frac{TP}{TP + FN} = \frac{\# \, of \, corrected \, entites}{\# \, of \, corrected \, prediction} \tag{1}$$

$$Precision = \frac{TP}{TP + FP} = \frac{\# \, of \, corrected \, entites}{\# \, of \, expected \, prediction} \tag{2}$$

$$F_1 = \frac{2 \times Precision \times Recall}{Precision + Recall} \tag{3}$$

$$F_2 = \frac{(\beta^2 + 1) \times Precision \times Recall}{(\beta^2 \times Precision + Recall)}, \beta = 2 \tag{4}$$

4.2 Re-identification Risk

To estimate the re-identification risk of our proposed de-identification system, we calculate the conditional probability of a leak in identifiable information [33] as follows:

$$Pr(Reidentification, leak) = Pr(Reidentification|leak) \times Pr(leak)$$

In a de-identification tool, leaks can occur if a PHI entity is not detected because it can be used to re-identify the individual whom the data describe. So, we assume that:

$$P(Reidentification|leak) = 1$$

As we described above, recall measures the percentage of PHI that is correctly identified in the detection phase. Thus, the probability of a leak in a set of documents is directly related to recall, given by:

$$Pr(leak) = 1 - Recall$$

4.3 Execution Time

We calculated the run time of the ARTPHIL model using batches of 514 notes (3.2 Mb) on a 4-core windows machine with 16 GB of RAM using the Python Time function, 'time', to estimate the feasibility of running Philter at a large scale. We conducted two experiments. In the first experiment, a single batch with 514 notes and a total size of 3.2Mb was run as a single process and timed. In the second experiment, 20 batches of the 514 notes were run as single processes and timed.

5 Results and Discussion

The ARTPHIL de-identification model is written in Python 3.7 (32 bit) using the Anaconda platform.[1] The design used the modified version of the Philter package [9] and integrated it with the E-ART encryption algorithm [10]. To evaluate the model, we used the i2b2/UTHealth 2014 de-identification corpus that was released by Stubbs et al. in [31] as part of the i2b2 National Centre for Biomedical Computing for the NLP Shared Tasks Challenges, whose de-identification guidelines reported by Stubbs and Uzuner [32] comply with the HIPAA Safe Harbor criteria.

The proposed system was evaluated using the evaluation metrics described in the previous section. We computed the overall recall and precision, as shown in Table 1 and the recall for each PHI category, as shown in Table 2, across the publicly-available 514 notes from the 2014 i2b2 test corpus.

From the six main PHI categories shown in Table 3, name, date, age, contact, and ID received a high recall of above 97%. However, location achieved a low recall of 90.92%, which was primarily affected by the tag location-other. This tag does not belong to the HIPAA PHI categories. Consequently, the i2b2 PHI categories' overall result was worse than that of the HIPAA PHI categories. However, the performance in several PHI types was excellent. For example, the recall of medical record, phone, email, fax and zip code achieved 100%, as shown in Table 2.

Table 1 shows that the de-identification method achieves generally good results, with a recall of 96.93%, precision of 79.76%, F1-score of 87.45% and F2-score of 92.92%. The recall of the method shows how likely it is for a PHI to be missed and, thus, how likely it is for re-identification to occur. Precision measures the number of false positives, thereby estimating the amount of information loss that results from applying the method. These results are consistent with recent research. More importantly, patient name achieved 99.86%, as only two names were missed out of 1,447. For contact, medical record and zip code, which most directly identify PHI, a recall of 100% was achieved, while none were missed.

In term of execution time, the time necessary to run 514 notes as a single process was 2.5147 s. The time required to run 20 batches of 514 notes, 10,240 notes total, was 54.675 s, as shown in Table 4. These results indicate the suitability of ARTPHIL for the processing of large-scale data.

In summary, the ARTPHIL system generates de-identified data that comply with the GDPR requirement for strong pseudonymisation as follows:

---

[1] https://github.com/bayan6060/phiter_eart.

Table 1. Overall model performance.

Metrics	Result (%)
Precision	79.76
Recall	96.93
F1	87.45
F2	92.92
Risk of re-identification	3.07

Table 2. Recall by tag.

Tags	Recall (%)	TPs	FNs	Risk of re-identification (%)
Medical record	100	721	0	0
Device	100	12	0	0
Username	98.91	91	1	1.09
Email	100	3	0	0
Fax	100	6	0	0
Zip code	100	143	0	0
Street	100	160	0	0
Location-Other	60	12	8	40
Patient	99.86	1445	2	0.41
Doctor	99.24	3272	25	0.76
City	98.54	338	2	1.46
Phone	100	407	0	0
State	96.10	197	8	3.9
Date	100	11880	0	0
Age	100	7	0	0
IDNUM	98.42	374	6	1.58

Table 3. Recall by PHI category.

Category	Recall (%)	TPs	FNs
Name	99.44	4718	27
Contact	99.22	416	0
ID	99.46	1113	6
Date	100	11880	0
Location	90.92	850	18
Age	100	7	0

Table 4. Runtime performance.

Experiments	Time/seconds
1- Single batch with 514 notes	2.5147
2- 20 batch with 514 notes	54.675

- Other techniques used static pseudonyms for the identifiers, which make them vulnerable to the mosaic effect[2]. ARTPHIL uses the dynamic encryption E-ART to de-identify personal data. This dynamism helps reduce the risk of re-identification via linkage attacks as it is difficult to correlate data across available datasets
- Unlike most existing pseudonymisation approaches that only remove or obscure direct identifiers, ARTPHIL de-identifies all direct and indirect identifiers with a recall of 96.93%. This decreases the possibility of retaining any personal data that could re-identify the data subject, thus decreasing the potential violation of data subject privacy.

6 Conclusion

De-identification is an essential tool that organisations can use to reduce the cost and the privacy risks associated with collecting, archiving and transferring personal information. However, current data de-identification approaches are a one-way process, and the original data cannot be recovered from the de-identified data if needed. This paper introduced a new reversible data de-identification system to preserve privacy and utility in unstructured data. ARTPHIL de-identification system combined two previously published works, Philter and E-ART, to de-identify all PHI specified under HIPAA guidelines.

However, the proposed system is highly customisable and can be easily modified to cover any domain. Experiments using 2014 i2b2 test data show that ARTPHIL achieved an overall F2 score of 92.92%, with recall of 96.93%. The average estimate of the re-identification risk was 3.07%. The proposed system ensures its suitability for the protection of individuals' privacy and reduces information loss. It helps to comply with GDPR requirements for the lawful processing of personal data.

The proposed method is useful in the data de-identification domain. Especially, when there is a need to re-identify users in the future. For example, in the research domain when the research subjects should be approached again for further study or to reduce the cost and the privacy risk associated with archiving personal data.

Further, the time required to run 20 batches of 514 notes, 10,240 notes total, was 54.675 s. This efficiency indicates the applicability of the applied ARTPHIL to large datasets or for use in delay-sensitive applications in order to reduce the privacy risk for data subject.

---

[2] The "Mosaic Effect" occurs when it is possible to determine a data subject's identity without having access to the primary identifiers (e.g., name, ID, Email address, etc.) by correlating data pertaining to the individual across multiple data sets.

References

1. European union, regulation 2016/679. Official J. Eur. Commun. **2014**, 1–88, March 2014
2. H.H.S. office for civil rights, department of health and human standards for privacy of individually. Final rule. Fed. Regist. **67**(157), 53181–53273 (2002)
3. Elliot, M.: Statistical disclosure control (2005)
4. Fung, B.C.M., Wang, K.E., Chen, R.U.I., Yu, P.S.: Privacy-preserving data publishing : a survey of recent developments see ACM for the final official version. **42**(4) (2010)
5. Chen, T.S., Lee, W.B., Chen, J., Kao, Y.H., Hou, P.W.: Reversible privacy preserving data mining: A combination of difference expansion and privacy preserving. J. Supercomput. **66**(2), 907–917 (2013)
6. Hong, T.P., Tseng, L.H., Chien, B.C.: Mining from incomplete quantitative data by fuzzy rough sets. Expert Syst. Appl. **37**(3), 2644–2653 (2010)
7. Silva, J.M., Pinho, E., Monteiro, E., Silva, J.F., Costa, C.: Controlled searching in reversibly de-identified medical imaging archives. J. Biomed. Inform. **77**(July 2017), 81–90 (2018)
8. Landi, W., Rao, R.B.: Secure De-identification and Re-identification. AMIA Annu Symp. Proce. Am. Med. Informatics Assoc. **65**(250), 905 (2003)
9. Norgeot, B., et al.: Protected health information fi lter (Philter): accurately and securely de-identifying free-text clinical notes. npj Digit. Med. 1–8 (2020)
10. Alabdullah, B., Beloff, N., White, M.: E-ART: a new encryption algorithm based on the reflection of binary search tree. Cryptography **5**(1), 4 (2021)
11. Wu, Y., Jiang, M., Lei, J., Xu, H.: Named entity recognition in Chinese clinical text using deep neural network. Stud. Health Technol. Inform. **216**, 624–628 (2015)
12. Allahyari, M., Trippe, E.D., Gutierrez, J.B.: A brief survey of text mining: classification, clustering and extraction techniques. arXiv (2017)
13. Bhasuran, B., Murugesan, G., Abdulkadhar, S., Natarajan, J.: Stacked ensemble combined with fuzzy matching for biomedical named entity recognition of diseases. J. Biomed. Inform. **64**, 1–9 (2016)
14. Keretna, S., Lim, C.P., Creighton, D.: A hybrid model for named entity recognition using unstructured medical text. In: Proceedings of the 9th International Conference System Engineering Socio-Technical Perspect. SoSE 2014, pp. 85–90 (2014)
15. Mishra, A., Jain, S.K.: A survey on question answering systems with classification. J. King Saud Univ. - Comput. Inf. Sci. 28(3), 345–361 (2016)
16. Xu, K., Reddy, S., Feng, Y., Huang, S., Zhao, D.: Question answering on freebase via relation extraction and textual evidence (2016)
17. Dugas, F., Nichols, E.: DeepNNNER : applying BLSTM-CNNs and extended lexicons to named entity recognition in tweets. In: Proceedings of the 2nd Work. Noisy User-generated Text, pp. 178–187 (2016)
18. Derczynski, L., et al.: Analysis of named entity recognition and linking for tweets. Inf. Process. Manage. **51**(2), 32–49 (2015)
19. Gkoulalas-Divanis, A., Loukides, G.: Medical data privacy handbook. Med. Data Priv. Handb. 1–832 (2015)
20. Gupta, D., Saul, M., Gilbertson, J.: Evaluation of a De-Identification (De-Id) software engine to share pathology reports and clinical documents for research. Am. J. Clin. Pathol. **121**(2), 176–186 (2004)
21. Beckwith, B.A., Mahaadevan, R., Balis, U.J., Kuo, F.: Development and evaluation of an open source software tool for de-identification of pathology reports. BMC Med. Inform. Decis. Mak. **6**, 1–10 (2006)
22. Neamatullah, I., et al.: Automated de-identification of free-text medical records. BMC Med. Inform. Decis. Mak. **8**, 1–17 (2008)

23. Steinwart, A.C.I.: Support Vector Machines. Springer Science & Business Media, London (2008).https://doi.org/10.1007/978-1-4471-5571-3_16
24. Lafferty, J., Mccallum, A.: Conditional random fields : probabilistic models for segmenting and labeling sequence data. CIS Pap. **2001**(June), 282–289 (2001)
25. Quinlan, J.R.: Induction of decision trees. Mach. Learn. **1**(1), 81–106 (1986)
26. Gulcher, J.R., Kristj, K.: Protection of privacy by third-party encryption in genetic research in Iceland. Eur. J. Hum. Genet. **8**(10), 739–742 (2000)
27. McMurry, A.J., Fitch, B., Savova, G., Kohane, I.S., Reis, B.Y.: Improved de-identification of physician notes through integrative modeling of both public and private medical text. BMC Med. Inform. Decis. Mak. **13**(1), 112 (2013). https://doi.org/10.1186/1472-6947-13-112
28. Herranz, J., Matwin, S., Nin, J., Torra, V.: Classifying data from protected statistical datasets. Comput. Secur. **29**(8), 875–890 (2010)
29. Yamac, M., Ahishali, M., Passalis, N., Raitoharju, J., Sankur, B., Gabbouj, M.: Reversible privacy preservation using multi-level encryption and compressive sensing. Eur. Signal Process. Conf. **27**, 1.5 (2019)
30. Hernández-Ramos, J.L., et al.: Protecting personal data in IoT platform scenarios through encryption-based selective disclosure. Comput. Commun. **130**(July), 20–37 (2018)
31. Stubbs, A., Kotfila, C., Uzuner, Ö.: Automated systems for the de-identification of longitudinal clinical narratives: overview of 2014 i2b2/UTHealth shared task Track 1. J. Biomed. Inform. **58**, S11–S19 (2015)
32. Stubbs, A., Uzuner, Ö.: Annotating longitudinal clinical narratives for de-identification: the 2014 i2b2/UTHealth corpus. J. Biomed. Inform. **58**, S20–S29 (2015)
33. Scaiano, M., et al.: A unified framework for evaluating the risk of re-identification of text de-identification tools. J. Biomed. Inform. **63**, 174–183 (2016)
34. Ferrández, Ó., South, B.R., Shen, S., Friedlin, F.J., Samore, M.H., Meystre, S.M.: Generalizability and comparison of automatic clinical text de-identification methods and resources. AMIA Annu. Symp. Proc. **2012**, 199–208 (2012)
35. Kushida, C.A., et al.: Strategies for de-identification and anonymisation of electronic health record data for use in multicenter research studies. Medical care 50. Suppl S82 (2012)
36. Hintze, M., LaFever, G.: Meeting upcoming GDPR requirements while maximising the full value of data analytics. SSRN 2927540 (2017)

CAFM: Precise Classification for Android Family Malware

Dan Li, Runbang Pan, Ning Lu, and Wenbo Shi(✉)

School of Computer Science and Engineering, Northeastern University,
Shenyang 110819, China
shiwb@neuq.edu.cn

Abstract. Family malware classification is becoming progressively urgent because of the increasing diversity of family malware and the different hazards it causes. There is a growing concern that classification is at a disadvantage owing to its problems. For one thing, obtaining the crucial features of innumerable families is arduous. For another, constructing a classification model that fully learns multi-class samples is intricate. To solve these problems, it proposes a precise classification for Android family malware called CAFM in this paper. It profoundly analyzes the relationship between the information implicit in features and the degree of differentiation among families. We select the features containing context information as feature representations. In addition, it employs a specially designed deep neural network model with upgraded learning capability for grasping the continuous features of family malware utterly. Experimental verification on a real-world dataset shows that the CAFM can effectively implement family classification, and the classification accuracy reaches 97.73% when the length of the opcode sequence is 700. Compared with other classifiers, the Kappa coefficient of the comprehensive evaluation indicator also reached 0.9725 and is at least 0.1225 higher than comparison classifiers.

Keywords: Android malware · Family · Classification

1 Introduction

Recent developments in the diversity of family malware have heightened the desideratum for Android mobile phone's security [1]. Users are at increased risk, which puts greater demands on anti-virus organizations and security researchers. For example, Kaspersky's mobile threat types announced in 2021, Adware, and

This work was supported by the National Natural Science Foundation of China (Nos. 62072092, 62072093 and U1708262); the China Postdoctoral Science Foundation(No. 2019M653568); the Key Research and Development Project of Hebei Province (No. 20310702D); the Natural Science Foundation of Hebei Province (No. F2020501013); the Fundamental Research Funds for the Central Universities (No. N2023020).

W. Shi et al. (Eds.): SPNCE 2021, LNICST 423, pp. 382–394, 2022.
https://doi.org/10.1007/978-3-030-96791-8_28

Risktool accounted for 57.26% and 21.34% respectively, ranking first and second [2]. Worm, which is at the end of the list, accounts for 0.01%. From a quantitative standpoint, it indicates that the Adware and Risktool types require more attention than Worm from anti-virus organizations and security researchers. Anti-virus organizations must not only implement benign and malicious classifications for malware but also further classify family malware. Research on family-level malware can concentrate more on widely spread and highly threatened families, rather than individual samples or families with less risk. Therefore, it is necessary to propose a precise classification method for family malware.

Family malware classification is to classify a group of malware with common peculiarities and behaviors together, and the members of the group share some unique peculiarities within the family [3]. It is a multi-classification problem. The central purpose is to construct a mapping model that reflects the idiosyncrasies and classes within the family. The model can predict the new sample and procure its family label. Given innumerable families and masses of software candidate features, family classification faces two technical challenges.

Challenge 1: Difficulty in obtaining features that contain enough family representative peculiarity information. Family malware is innumerable and varies in its features. It is necessary to select the feature subset that can represent innumerable families' behavior characteristics. Existing features analysis can be divided into runtime features and unpacking features in the light of different acquisition methods. Runtime features require actual or simulated running programs to obtain feature information, which consumes numerous time and computing resources [4–6]. It is inapposite for anti-virus organizations. Among the unpacking features, a single feature such as permission cannot truly represent the behavior of malware because of excessive permission requests [7]. The n-gram opcode feature will cause the feature subset to increase exponentially as the value of n increases, causing the explosion of the feature space [8]. Therefore, choosing the appropriate features is the first technical problem.

Challenge 2: Difficulty in constructing a classification model that adequately learns the peculiarities of each family. The diversity of families leads to different calling relationships to implement malicious behavior. The crucial malicious instructions or code of each family are not the same on the same feature. The signature method needs to match the signature library and cannot recognize malware that is not in the signature library [9]. Shallow machine learning methods are more suitable for processing a limited number of samples rather than large-scale datasets [10,11]. It can only learn shallow exhibitions but can not acquire high-level abstract features. Therefore, building a classification model that utterly memorizes the features of multi-class samples is the second technical challenge.

Aiming at these challenges, a precise family malware classification method is proposed in this paper. The behavioral idiosyncrasies of each family and the correlation between the features are analyzed, and the features containing as much information as possible are utilized to acquire more accurate depictions. In addition, to construct a classification model with sufficient learning samples and consider the requirements of anti-virus organizations, a one-dimensional deep neural network (1d-CNN) is adopted with automatically procuring the internal patterns of features. It can not only reduce the information loss of feature data conversion but also retain the pivotal information to the maximum extent.

The main contributions presented in this work are summarized as follows:

(1) To obtain representative features, the feature expressions in different families are analyzed, and the feature heterogeneity in diverse families is mined.
(2) A precise deep network classification model for automatic learning of internal patterns is constructed. The effective automatic extraction of the input features is realized.
(3) Experimental results show that the proposed CAFM performs well on a real-world dataset, with an accuracy of 95.45% or above when the length of opcode sequence are 700 and 5000, which is at least 5.56% higher than the comparative classifiers.

The remainder of this paper is structured as follows. Section 2 is an introduction to the feature extraction process and an explanation of the problem statement. Section 3 describes the overall framework of the proposed CAFM, the composition of each component, and the corresponding functions. Section 4 is the analysis of experimental results, which verifies the classification performance of the CAFM. Section 5 is to sort out and summarize the related literature. The conclusion is in Sect. 6.

2   Feature Extraction and Problem Statement

This section introduces the process of feature extraction, defines the family malware classification problem, and gives the formal expression of the problem.

2.1   Feature Extraction

The feature extraction is to obtain candidate features that can represent family behavior from the representable forms of a striking number of applications. It is extracted in a specific form for further processing.

The Android package is a specific packaging form of the Android application. The malicious behavior is realized by the function developed by the attacker, which needs to call the application programming interface (API). Therefore, the unpacking feature analysis can be realized by decomposing the source package to obtain specific features. The implementation of malware needs to call specific APIs to complete. For example, malicious billing software will call the API for sending SMS, and privacy stealing software will call the API for accessing the address book. Dalvik is a virtual machine designed by Google for the Android platform, and the dalvik instruction set contains operational information about the application and can be detected by analyzing dalvik opcode information.

Classes in the program code will generate smali files in the appropriate directories. Each smali file contains a format statement, and the statements in smali follow a set of grammar specifications. In the decompiled smali file is a dalvik command. In reality, the smali file is an explanation for the dalvik virtual machine. It has more than 200 dalvik instructions, each of which points to the operation of the register. The opcode feature is derived from the dalvik instruction in the smali file. The preprocessing process of acquiring APIs and opcode sequences consists of three important steps:

(1) Decompile the .apk file to get the smali file.
(2) Extract the dalvik opcodes and API from the smali file.
(3) Obtain opcode sequence according to the Android opcode constant list and API list.

2.2   Problem Statement

The opcode sequences and APIs obtained after feature extraction are the features to be analyzed. The family malware classification is represented by learning the features of the opcode sequences and APIs to obtain the predicted results. It will explain by problem definition and problem decomposition.

Problem Definition. The family malware classification is to classify the unknown attribute samples into the class of the family, that is, to give the class label of the family of the detected samples. Through the training set $\{(x_1, y_1), (x_2, y_2), \cdots, (x_n, y_n)\}$, a mapping f from the input space X to the output space Y is established, where $Y > 2$.

$$f : X \to Y \tag{1}$$

Problem Decomposition. The classification problem is to firstly build a classification model and then utilize it to make predictions. Therefore, the family malware classification can decompose into two subproblems.

Subproblem 1: Feature depiction. After feature extraction, it requires to transform into a data form that the classification model can recognize. It should not only contain as much information as possible but also facilitate model processing.

Subproblem 2: Feature memorizing and sample prediction. The classification model is constructed to obtain the internal abstract representation of features. The opcode sequences and APIs containing context and sequence information are directly input into the model for feature learning without other redundant data transformations. With the continuous iteration and parameter update of the model, new samples can be predicted after the feature learning is completed.

In summary, subproblem 1 is to process the acquired original features to get a more appropriate representation to express more information. Subproblem 2 is the construction of the classification model, which can thoroughly learn the abstract representation of multiple families and obtain the high-level expression of the features.

3   CAFM

This section describes the overall framework of CAFM, the assembly modules, and the corresponding functions of each module. It includes the method of obtaining the representation of representative features and the construction of the family classification model.

3.1   Overall Framework

Given the problems faced by the family classification, the CAFM proposes. Figure 1 illustrates its overall framework, which consists of two major modules. One is feature depiction, and the other is feature memorizing and sample prediction.

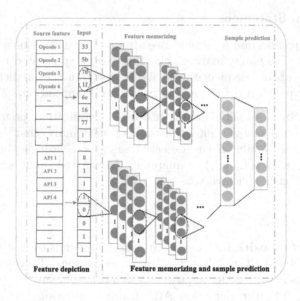

Fig. 1. The overall framework of the CAFM.

Feature Depiction. This module is to optimally represent the extracted opcode sequences and APIs features. It allows the opcode and API information to be included as much as possible while forming a corresponding data format for the input of the classification model.

Feature Memorizing and Sample Prediction. This module is utilized for training features and predicting unknown samples. Training is the stage of learning and memorizing features. The model obtains the high-level feature representation of features. The completion of training represents the formation of a classification model, which can predict the label of unknown samples.

3.2   Feature Depiction

Feature depiction is to select the pivotal elements of the extracted features and represent them in a format that can be recognized by the classification model. On one hand, it is to reduce the computation and resource consumption caused by the dimensionality of features. On the other hand, it is to reduce redundant information and obtain crucial features.

The extracted opcode sequences and APIs can not be directly sent to the model for training; consequencely, the crucial sub-features need to be represented, and the appropriate data format needs to be selected. The opcode sequences include consecutive opcode information and relative position information. API features are selected based on their frequency of occurrence in the data set, from high to low. The steps for feature depiction are as follows:

Acquire original features. The original opcode sequence is opcode 1, opcode 2, opcode 3,$\cdots$. The APIs are API 1, API 2, API 3,$\cdots$.

Coding. It will encode each opcode by that total number to get its fixed sequence number in the opcode dictionary. APIs have a fixed number in the API dictionary in descending order of frequency.

Representation. The extracted opcode sequence and the location corresponding to the API are used for data form representation. The range of each opcode is 0–256, which is a decimal number. The value of the API is 0 or 1, and the position of the API is set to 1 when this call occurs for the sample; otherwise, it is 0.

3.3   Feature Memorizing and Sample Prediction

Feature memorizing is the learning process of the classification model for feature knowledge, and sample prediction is the label prediction using the learned classification model. Both are momentous steps in the realization of classification for family malware.

To learn the internal patterns of the features more accurately, this paper chooses the 1d-CNN with two channels as the network for automatically learning the high-level abstract features [12]. This choice is based on two considerations. The first is to improve the ability of the network to obtain information. Two channels can input different features to obtain feature information from different angles in the family, providing more information. The second is to obtain the original feature information to a greater extent. The opcode sequence itself contains the sequence of the called opcodes, which includes context information and relative location characteristics. This is closer to the data format of a one-dimensional signal. The 1d-CNN is essentially the same as the convolutional neural network (CNN). It also has the advantages of CNN's translation invariance for feature recognition, and the one-dimensional large convolution kernel will not bring too many parameters and calculations. The eigenvalues of the sequence can be obtained more comprehensively while suppressing overfitting. The structure of the two-channel 1d-CNN includes two identical series of convolutional layers and pooling layers, and finally, the result is output through the fully connected layer. The main steps are as follows:

Feature Memorizing Stage. *Convolutional operation:* The convolutional layer is an important part of the CNN, which can extract highly abstract features through the convolutional operation. The equation for the convolutional operation is as follows:

$$Cov(x, y) = \sum_{a=0}^{w} F(a) \times G(x - a) \tag{2}$$

Pooling operation: The feature with spatial invariance is obtained by reducing the resolution of the feature map. When it faces the sparse feature, it can reduce the mean shift of the estimation caused by the parameter error of the convolution layer. The equation is as follows:

$$P = \max_{w}\{A^l\} \tag{3}$$

Integration: Each neuron in the fully connected layer is fully connected to all neurons in the previous layer. The goal is to integrate features from convolutional and pooling operations.

$$C = P^O \bigoplus P^A \tag{4}$$

where P^O and P^A are outputs of opcode channels and API channels, respectively. The above equation indicates that the output C of the integration layer is obtained by connecting the results of the two channels. The output C is utilized as the input of the classification layer, and the loss of this training is output through the classifier.

Sample Prediction Stage. All parameters have been obtained in the previous stage. This stage only needs to input the vectorized data from the input layer to realize predictions.

4   Experiment Studies

To verify the performance of the proposed CAFM, this section verifies it by the real-world dataset. The reliability and classification performance of the proposed CAFM is verified from different perspectives.

4.1   Experiment Setup

The experiment setup is expanded from two parts, including the description of the dataset involved in the experiment and the evaluation indicators adopted for multi-classification.

Evaluation Indicators. The evaluation indicator is a multi-classification standard, mainly including confusion matrix, F1-micro, F1-macro, Kappa, accuracy, and hamming distance.

Dataset Description. The dataset adopted in this paper includes benign software and malicious software, a total of 8791 samples from the Chinese application market and AMD datasets respectively [13]. These samples are divided into seven families, a benign comprehensive family (called pos family) and six malware families. The pos family is a collection of randomly selected benign samples, which is set as a family here regardless of type. The number of varieties contained in each family is also presented in Table 1.

Table 1. Dataset information.

Family	Varieties	Numbers
BankBot	8	637
DroidKungFu	6	546
FakeInst	5	2156
Fusob	2	1203
Kuguo	1	1189
Mecor	1	1820
Pos	–	1240

4.2   Results Analysis

To verify the classification performance of the proposed CAFM, the experimental results are presented and analyzed in this section. It is mainly developed from two aspects, one is the elaboration of the multi-classification performance of the family malware, and the other is the comparison and analysis of the classification results of CAFM and other classifiers.

Performance of Malware Familial Classification. The family classification performance of the proposed CAFM is mainly demonstrated from two perspectives: confusion matrix and the distribution of opcode sequence lengths for different malware families. In the experiment, the ratio of the training set, test set, and verification set is 8:1:1, respectively.

As shown in Fig. 2, the classification results of CAFM with an opcode length of 700 and 5000 are displayed. The correct classification samples in the confusion matrix are distributed diagonally from the top left to the bottom right. The smaller the value outside the diagonal, the better the classification result. It can be seen that the classification of most families is correct despite the uneven data sample. Only a few families with a large number of variants showed a small number of misclassified samples. When the length of the opcode sequence is 700, the classification effect is better, and only a few samples are misclassified in the face of the family with the highest similarity in the eight variants. The F1-micro and Kappa coefficients reach 0.9773 and 0.9725, respectively, which shows a favorable family classification effect.

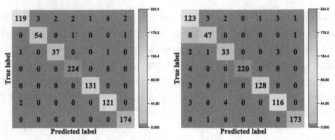

(a) The results on opcode700. (b) The results on opcode5000.

Fig. 2. The confusion matrix of CAFM on different opcode sequences length.

In addition, to further explore the relationship between opcodes and samples, the length of the opcodes sequence is statistically analyzed. The distribution of opcode length of different families is obtained. The similarity between families in the length of opcode sequences is verified. As shown in Fig. 3, the distribution of opcode sequence length is given by taking Fusob and FakeInst families as examples. The abscissa axis is the length of the opcode sequence, and the ordinate is the number of samples. It can be seen that the same family presents a certain regularity in the distribution of opcodes numbers. The length of the Fusob family opcode sequence is shorter than other families, and the basic length is less than 5000. The FakeInst family, which includes five varieties, has a wide range of length variations, with some samples appearing at 20,000. These all demonstrate similarities in the length of opcode sequences within the same family or within the same variety, reflecting similar malevolent behavior that might be possible.

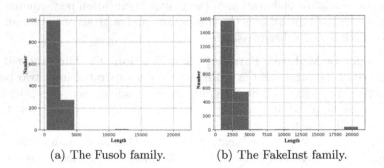

(a) The Fusob family.   (b) The FakeInst family.

Fig. 3. The opcode sequences length distribution of malware family.

Performance Comparison with Different Classifiers. To further verify the classification effect of the proposed CAFM, this paper utilizes more abundant and multi-angle classification model evaluation indicators to illustrate the experimental data. We adopt the feature of n-gram as the contrast feature and employ different classifiers to carry out a multi-indicator comparison.

Since n-gram opcode is a widely utilized analysis method based on opcode features, this paper chooses opcode analysis methods with different n values as the main comparison feature. Here we take the 2-gram opcode as an example because research shows that the increase of n may cause an explosion in the data space. Meanwhile, the classification performance does not increase with the increase of excessive n value. Many studies show that the effect is better when the value of n is 2. The classifiers are implemented by combining 2-gram opcode features with 1d-CNN, support vector machine (SVM), random forest (RF), decision tree (DT), naive Bayes (NB), and k-nearest neighbor (KNN) [14].

Figure 4 and Fig. 5 show the results of each classifier on different classification indicators. In terms of the Kappa coefficient in Fig. 4, CAFM reaches 0.9449, which is 0.0665 higher than 0.8784 of the highest RF among other classifiers. On the F1-micro, the RF reaches 0.8989 and performs well, but it is still 0.0556 lower than CAFM. On F1-macro, CAFM is 0.0615 higher than the optimal RF. Figure 5 shows the classification effect of each classifier on the hamming distance indicator. The smaller the value, the better the classification effect. Similarly, CAFM reached the smallest value of 0.0455, and the NB with the worst classification effect reached 0.4625, proving the obvious advantage of CAFM on this indicator. In short, superior results are achieved with the proposed CAFM in various indicators. The comprehensive classification indicators F1-micro, F1-macro, and Kappa have all achieved more than 0.9317, which is an ideal multi-classification effect.

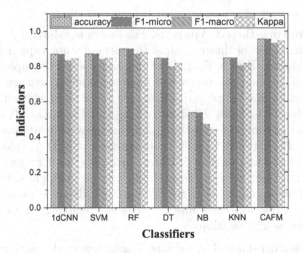

Fig. 4. The results of each classifier on different classification indicators.

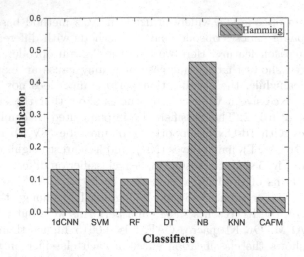

Fig. 5. The results of each classifier on hamming indicators.

5 Related Literature

Family malware classification is mainly divided into run-time feature-based and unpacking feature-based analysis methods in conformity with different feature extraction modes. This section describes the related literature from these two perspectives for illustration.

Run-Time Feature-Based Analysis. For example, Martin, A. et al. [6] proposed a classification tool that combines the form of state sequences of run-time features with Markov chains. Feng, P. et al. [5] proposed to implement malware detection based on multiple types of run-time behavior features. The feature selection algorithm was employed to remove noise or irrelevant features and extract key behavior features. Dhalaria, M. [4] and Cavli, O.F.T. et al. [15] proposed a method to combine unpacking and run-time malware analysis features. It provided an effective way to solve malware detection. D'Angelo, G. et al. [16] utilized unpacking and run-time features, including hash fingerprints, permissions, application info, network flows, and dynamic API calls, to describe the behavior peculiarities of the software. These methods are expensive in terms of computation and resource consumption. It is not befitting for the user requirements of anti-virus organizations.

Unpacking Feature-Based Analysis. For instance, the authors constructed the fingerprint of the malware families using n-grams analysis and features hashing [9]. In [17], the authors generated a fingerprint for each family. This analysis method relies on a signature library and cannot identify samples that are not in the library. Yuan, H. et al. [11] proposed an unpacking feature-based detection method based on tf-idf and machine learning, using the tf-idf algorithm to calculate the number of permissions used. Turker, S. et al. [10] proposed a framework that extracts requested permissions and API calls from Android malware samples and used them as features to train a large number of machine learning classifiers. This analysis method cannot learn deep features in view of its limitations. Alswaina, F. et al. [7] implemented a reduced permission set and fed it into a machine learning algorithm for classification. This analysis method may be subject to abuse of permission requests. Opcode feature analysis methods such as Gaviria de la Puerta, J. et al. [8] and Kang, B. et al. [18] used n-gram features combined with machine learning. This analysis method causes the data space to explode when the value of n is too large. Accordingly, these unpacking-based feature analysis methods are not considered.

Unlike the above methods, the feature representation method proposed in this paper can effectively express the diversity and behavior characteristics of software families. The two channels 1d-CNN adopted by CAFM can more fully acquire the input features and utterly learn the high-level abstract expression of the features.

6 Conclusion

This paper proposes a precise classification method for family malware. Through in-depth analysis of features, feature subsets are obtained, which can represent family diversity. The 1d-CNN with two channels is designed, which can not only utilize the original feature data format to a greater extent but also preserve the information of the source features. The design of two channels fully learns the internal abstract pattern of fusion features and provides a more accurate model for family classification.

References

1. Mercaldo, F., Santone, A.: Formal equivalence checking for mobile malware detection and family classification. IEEE Trans. Softw. Eng. (2021)
2. Kaspersky: mobile malware evolution 2020 (2021)
3. Chakraborty, T., Pierazzi, F., Subrahmanian, V.S.: Ec2: Ensemble clustering and classification for predicting android malware families. IEEE Trans. Dependable Secure Comput. 17, 262–277 (2020)
4. Dhalaria, M., Gandotra, E.: A hybrid approach for android malware detection and family classification. Int. J. Interact. Multimedia Artif. Intell. 6(6) (2021)
5. Feng, P., Ma, J., Sun, C., Xu, X., Ma, Y.: A novel dynamic android malware detection system with ensemble learning. IEEE Access 6, 30996–31011 (2018)
6. Martín, A., Rodríguez-Fernández, V., Camacho, D.: CANDYMAN: Classifying android malware families by modelling dynamic traces with Markov chains. Eng. Appl. Artif. Intell. 74, 121–133 (2018)
7. Alswaina, F., Elleithy, K.: Android malware permission-based multi-class classification using extremely randomized trees. IEEE Access 6, 76217–76227 (2018)
8. de la Puerta, J.G., Sanz, B.: Using Dalvik opcodes for malware detection on android. Logic J. IGPL 25(6), 938–948 (2017)
9. Zhang, L., Thing, V.L., Cheng, Y.: A scalable and extensible framework for android malware detection and family attribution. Comput. Secur. 80, 120–133 (2019)

10. Türker, S., Can, A.B.: Andmfc: android malware family classification framework. In: 2019 IEEE 30th International Symposium on Personal, Indoor and Mobile Radio Communications (PIMRC Workshops). pp. 1–6. IEEE (2019)
11. Yuan, H., Tang, Y., Sun, W., Liu, L.: A detection method for android application security based on TF-IDF and machine learning. PLoS ONE **15**(9), e0238694 (2020)
12. Kiranyaz, S., Avci, O., Abdeljaber, O., Ince, T., Gabbouj, M., Inman, D.J.: 1d convolutional neural networks and applications: a survey. Mech. Syst. Signal Process. **151**, 107398 (2021)
13. Wei, F., Li, Y., Roy, S., Ou, X., Zhou, W.: Deep ground truth analysis of current android malware. In: Polychronakis, M., Meier, M. (eds.) DIMVA 2017. LNCS, vol. 10327, pp. 252–276. Springer, Cham (2017). https://doi.org/10.1007/978-3-319-60876-1_12
14. Pedregosa, F., et al.: Scikit-learn: machine learning in python. J. Mach. Learn. Res. **12**, 2825–2830 (2011)
15. Cavli, O.F.T., Sen, S.: Familial classification of android malware using hybrid analysis. In: 2020 International Conference on Information Security and Cryptology (ISCTURKEY), pp. 62–67. IEEE (2020)
16. D'Angelo, G., Palmieri, F., Robustelli, A., Castiglione, A.: Effective classification of android malware families through dynamic features and neural networks. Connection Sci. 1–16 (2021)
17. Massarelli, L., Aniello, L., Ciccotelli, C., Querzoni, L., Ucci, D., Baldoni, R.: Android malware family classification based on resource consumption over time. In: 2017 12th International Conference on Malicious and Unwanted Software (MALWARE), pp. 31–38. IEEE (2017)
18. Kang, B., Yerima, S.Y., Sezer, S., McLaughlin, K.: N-gram opcode analysis for android malware detection. arXiv preprint arXiv:1612.01445 (2016)

Author Index

Printed in the United States
by Baker & Taylor Publisher Services